LUCA TURIN AND TANIA SANCHEZ

PERFUMES

THE A-Z GUIDE

'Their work is, quite simply, ravishingly entertaining, and it passes the high test that their praise is even more compelling than their criticism … its blend of technical knowledge and evocative writing is exemplary in the strict sense: people who write about smell and taste in any context should use it as an example.' John Lanchester, *New Yorker*

'Turin confirms his right to be classed alongside Proust or Patrick Süskind as a poet of smell. He promises that a colourful and sonorous world will open up, if we will only follow where he leads.' Lara Feigel, *Observer*

'What a delicious book.' Stephen Bayley

'[T]he perfect instruction manual for scent users … Turin's entries in his alphabetical guide to fine fragrances are brilliant exercises in synaesthesia' Veronica Horwell, Book of the Week, *Guardian*

'On one level this is a serious, instructive tome. On the other it is an addictive, dip-in-and-outable romp through some of the greatest and worst scents ever produced.' Caroline Jowett, *Daily Express*

'Unfailingly entertaining … their passion for a few scents and their outrage at the others' failings make for entry after entry of hilarious, catty comments interspersed with occasional erudite, eloquent disquisitions.' *Publishers Weekly* (starred review)

'Page after page of wonderful, evocative, poetic prose that will get the most diffident sniffer salivating – and often laughing.' Suzi Feay, *Independent on Sunday*

'Endlessly browsable, partly because the writing is funny, partly because it is so extraordinarily illuminating ... this book is nothing less than an essential possession.' David Sexton, Book of the Week *Evening Standard*

'*Perfumes* is a pioneering book packed with the promise of hours of pleasure. It opens the mind to the vivid intricacies of scent and is a cracking good read. Prepare to cringe and laugh out loud.' Kate Colquhoun, *Daily Telegraph*

'Compelling because it's arrestingly honest, passionately poetic.' *Grazia* (Australia)

'No one can doubt that they've written a work of the highest criticism, one which elevates writing about perfume to the best sort of writing about wine or rock music ... this is a book which knows what it's talking about.' Philip Hensher, *Independent*

'Shines a bright, revolving searchlight over an extensive, potentially limitless smellscape, and offers much to contemplate, even to regret and most importantly alerts you to the need to set aside some fairly solid prejudices ... provocative and hugely entertaining.' Angus Trumble, *TLS*

'You couldn't imagine reading about perfumes could be this entertaining.' *Pretoria News*

'Almost 1,500 alphabetically ordered perfume reviews, ranging from lyrical raves to laconic one-liners, each as deliciously descriptive and unremittingly honest as the last ... a roaringly good read.' *Zest*

'I breathed in, rather than read, in one delighted gulp; opinionated, knowledgeable, sharply written and surprisingly comprehensive, it's a purely enjoyable book.' Hilary Mantel, *Guardian*

LUCA TURIN is a scientist with a controversial theory of how we smell. He is the author of *The Secret of Scent* and the subject of the bestselling *Emperor of Scent*. **TANIA SANCHEZ** is a perfume collector and expert, and journalist. They both live in Boston, USA.

LUCA TURIN AND TANIA SANCHEZ

PERFUMES

THE A–Z GUIDE

P

PROFILE BOOKS

This revised and updated paperback edition first published in 2009

First published in Great Britain in 2008 by
Profile Books Ltd
3a Exmouth House
Pine Street
London ECIR 0JH
www.profilebooks.com

Published in the United States in 2008 by
Penguin Putnam Inc

1 3 5 7 9 10 8 6 4 2

Printed and bound in Italy by
Graphicom, Vicenza

A CIP catalogue record for this book is available from the British Library.

ISBN 978 1 86448 127 1
eISBN 978 1 84765 152 5

For the perfumers

CONTENTS

ACKNOWLEDGMENTS

I owe a heavy debt of gratitude to both Evan Izer and Victoria "Vikapedia" Frolova, whose erudition, generosity, kindness, and tiny glass vials of odorous substances have been gifts beyond value. I also thank the Makeup Alley fragrance board: we are family. I relied heavily on Robin Krug's excellent blog, Now Smell This (nowsmellthis.blogharbor.com), for dependable info on the unstoppable tide. Much of our work would have been near impossible without Michael Edwards's Fragrances of the World database. Thanks to Harvey Nichols, Liberty, Selfrides, Aedes, and LuckyScent for connecting me with elusive brands, and to Chandler Burr for telling fragrance PR people to get used to it. Heartfelt thanks to my friends Ann Gugliotti, Patti Ferrara, Laurie Harbour, Laura Ann Frankstone, and Achinta McDaniel for their steady optimism and support. A million thanks to Tom and Elaine Colchie, the best agents and friends a writer could ask for, and to all at Penguin Books and Profile Books. And thank you most of all to Luca, for the rash invitation. TS

Over the years, many kind people asked me why I didn't write a second perfume guide, this time in English. My answer was always that I would, in due course. Due course came along in the shape of Tania Sanchez, the first person I met who could halve the task and more than double the quality. It also took the form of Michael Reid Hunter, who asked his father, Alastair Reid, whether he knew an agent, which is how we met Tom and Elaine Colchie and through them Kathryn Court and her team of believers at Viking. The rest was plain sailing, helped by the tireless, generous scholarship of Michael Edwards and the patient kindness of great perfumers: my friends Calice Becker, Chris Sheldrake, and others

I only spoke to and would love to meet one day. Daniel Weber at NZZ Folio, probably the world's best editor, and Alke von Kruszynski at Park Avenue made me believe I could, with help, pull it off. To all of you, and to all the firms big and small who sent us the stuff, heartfelt thanks. LT

NOTE ON THE PAPERBACK EDITION

We have added 451 new fragrances and 16 new "frequently asked questions" and made small corrections and additions to the existing text. In particular, we have rechecked several important fragrances by Dior and the parfum concentration of Chanel No. 5, since readers expressed concern given changes in the materials available to the industry and the personnel in charge of perfumery at these firms. There is also a new index by brand. Many thanks to the readers who took the time to write to us with their suggestions, corrections, and kind encouragement. LT/TS

PERFUMES

THE A–Z GUIDE

INTRODUCTION TO PERFUME CRITICISM

How to Connect Your Nose to Your Brain
by Tania Sanchez

One late-spring afternoon, Luca and I headed to the perfume floor at Harrods, where he was leading a small group on tour—his kids' classmates' parents who had paid for the privilege as a fund-raising event for the school—no perfume fanatics, just ordinary people indulging curiosity. We guided them through Lauder, Guerlain, Hermès, Chanel, Caron, and so on; explained what they were smelling; and watched them react. Some they loved and some they hated; sometimes they strained to match words to sensation, and sometimes they snapped to attention when the ideas locked exactly into place. At one point, Luca sprayed the first fragrance from Comme des Garçons and explained it had started a trend for transparent orientals. A tall, well-dressed, intelligent man with a forecasting job in telecommunications protested, "How can a smell be in fashion?" As far as our questioner was concerned, perfume was too immaterial to fall into patterns and categories. How could something as shapeless and evanescent as a smell have a history and a culture?

The question is understandable for many reasons, not least that, until modern perfumery began at the end of the nineteenth century, advances were limited to mixtures of natural extractions of local materials, with the occasional incursion of exotic resins and plants imported from distant lands at high prices. For centuries, the greatest perfumery idea was probably the eau de cologne. Throughout the twentieth century, however, perfumery flourished as one of the great popular arts, following a flowering of ideas in the industrial age, in the same way that fashion, music, and design flourished, contributing more and more beauty to the everyday life of the everyday person. Yet perfume is probably the least understood and least appreciated of the arts. After all, it's girl stuff. Even food and wine, closely related to perfume since flavor is mostly smell, have the status of arts worth documenting, preserving, and understanding, earning whole newspaper sections and walls in the bookstore, bringing fame and TV time to their star practitioners.

Meanwhile, perfumers mostly toil in anonymous darkness, and the little writing there is on their creations falls largely into two unreadable genres: breathless purple descriptions by ad writers or poker-faced pseudoscience from aromatherapists. An example of the former, a press release quoted by the blog Now Smell This on November 17, 2007: "Humiecki and Graef asked Laudamiel to create a perfume that captures the state of 'how men cry'—eruptive and sensual. Pictures from Slavic culture, as well as how they deal with melancholia and happiness served as inspiration [sic]. The result is a perfume that combines raw eruption, sensual strength, melancholic warmth and deep mysticism." An example of the latter, from a January 2000 article in Psychology Today: "Aromatherapy seems to foster deep relaxation, which has been shown to alter perceptions of pain. Essential oils also affect the brain in the hippocampus, the seat of memory, and in the amygdala, which governs emotions; inhaling oils helps us make pleasant associations, easing tension." Neither is likely to increase the culture of perfume.

Smell psychologists and the uncritical journalists who love them get a lot of mileage out of calling smell the most primitive sense. (When I am queen of the universe, the epithets "the most primitive sense" and "the most mysterious sense" will be banned from all writing on smell.) But as with all of the work of evolutionary psychologists, the conclusions that support our desires and reinforce our prejudices are those of which we should be most wary. Skim the shelves of any bookstore nonfiction section to see a large selection of fiction: pop psychology books assuring us that, since we're no better than the average dog (never mind that dogs are much better than we think), all our behavior is nothing but the basest animal instincts in different dress, that men will always be peacocks in full strut looking to distribute their genetic material as widely as possible, and that women will always be gregarious hens pecking at each other to attract the attention of the alpha male. Psychologists seem particularly fixated on sex as the engine that secretly drives our every choice and action. This point of view never cost a psychologist his or her job or interfered with book sales, and offers the irresistible premise that biology releases us from the responsibility to make choices. Pop psychologists love smell. Smell is supposedly about sex and deeply buried memory, a sense that bypasses the rational mind, thwarts all efforts of language to describe it, and reaches sneaky neural wiring directly into regions beyond thought—for example, forcing you to be sexually attracted to or threatened by the perspiration of basketball players or generating forceful hallucinations of childhood triggered by smells of floor wax. It's the fondest hope of every perfume firm that the psychologists should be right, and that human beings should be sniffing each other to say hello and see who's been where and with whom. Psychology is supposed to be a science, and science makes profits predictable.

Unfortunately for the profits, perfume really is an art, not a science. Tocade is not a better fragrance than Dior Addict because it better approximates the mix of odors released by a fertile female. Tocade is better than Dior Addict because it's more beautiful. The varieties of beauty in art are not irreducibly animal and ineffable. Somebody puts these things together with skill and intention. Perfumes have ideas: there are surprising textures, moods, tensions, harmonies, juxtapositions. Perfumes seem to come in various weights and sizes, to have different personalities, to wear different clothes, to worship different deities. Some perfumes are facile and some are complicated; some are representative, some abstract. Above all, some are better than others.

All the same, perfume suffers several drawbacks as a subject of serious study. First, nothing can be smelled without disappearing. You don't use up a picture by looking at it, but each time you uncork a perfume, the bit that evaporates is the bit you enjoy, and after you've smelled it, there's no getting it back into the bottle. Everyone who has ever looked at the decreasing level of a beloved and discontinued perfume knows the anguish of the finiteness of resources. Therefore, preservation and appreciation can seem incompatible goals. Second, perfume changes over time in the bottle once exposed to air and light, so perfume can be a bit like those digital-rights–managed music formats that expire after you start listening to them. You can't enjoy the same bottle forever, in other words. Third, direct experience is the only experience. You can't reproduce smells in books or digitize them. Fourth, the perfume industry, in a hoary, unbroken tradition of self-defeating behavior, has done everything it can to avoid viewing its work as art. Perfume companies do not generally keep archives. They change formulas without telling customers. They discontinue their classics. They lie about contents. They hide the perfumers and art directors responsible. They shill shameless copies of great ideas and hope no one notices. They've even withdrawn advertising from magazines that criticized their work. Fifth, perfumes are lumped in with cosmetics and all the folderol that accompanies them, and therefore hidden in the veil of hope and lies that enshrouds all beauty products in jars. And sixth, we are not taught a vocabulary of perfume. Its materials are strange, save what we know from gardens and kitchen cupboards, so we find it difficult to name the different shades along a spectrum vastly more complicated and variegated than the colors in a Crayola box. As it is, the beginner struggles to pick out one or two characteristics of a perfume. For instance, if we're told two perfumes are roses, but they're clearly different, we often struggle to explain exactly how. It takes some getting used to.

In fact, until recently, talking intelligently about the art of perfume seemed impossible. Then suddenly it seemed inevitable. What changed? The obvious: the Internet. Online now you can read historical and technical information, find discontinued or otherwise elusive perfumes, order samples of raw materials to smell out of curiosity, and, most important, find communities of people clustered around this single obsession. Half of what I know I owe to the twenty-four-hour-a-day pajama party that is the fragrance board of Makeup Alley (makeupalley.com), whose members introduced me to fragrance brands I'd never heard of, fragrance categories that helped me draw connections among vastly different things, and the idea of writing about fragrance at all. Online communities can criticize perfume in a way that magazines have never dared: there's no advertising to lose. The public can say without fear that, frankly, this thing stinks, that thing was true love, this other thing is so-so. Perfume blogs now seem to outnumber the sample vials around my desk: there are men and women of intelligence sitting down every day and thinking and writing about perfume.

In time, the perfume industry is going to get used to criticism. Look at wine, movies, music, books: open and fair critical discussions keep the public interested. Would we go so often to the movies if we couldn't talk about them, if we had no clue whether a film might be good or not? Criticism makes us feel more comfortable shelling out for a ticket and also helps encourage a constant interest, leading us to check listings every week and talk about them endlessly with friends. The same goes for perfume: those who talk about it buy more of it. The trouble is that the perfume industry hasn't yet figured out the benefits of relaxing control. A prominent blogger I know once received an ominous message from the press contact for a fragrance she had panned. They wanted her address so their lawyers could get in touch. When a sleek luxury goods company unleashes its lawyers on a suburban mom for not liking their new fragrance, we know the world is changing. The age of trash perfumes, composed in a matter of months on the cheap and sold with celebrity faces and outrageous claims, must at last be nearing an end. Only quality can win out. The perfume business will certainly fare better in a world of genuine public love than it would in a world in which everyone dismisses its product as nonsense.

The fact is that this stuff is worth loving. As with the tawdriest pop melody, there is a base pleasure in perfume, in just about any perfume, even the cheapest and the most starved of ideas, that is better than no perfume at all. It decorates the day. It makes you feel as if the colors of the air have changed. It's a substitute for having an orchestra follow you about playing the theme song of your choice. Think of what the functional fragrance industry calls the magic moment, when the smell of fabric softener billows out of your dryer and you can't help but feel great. Perfume is wonderful. And it's simply not true, as some people believe, that thinking about our pleasures ruins them. For example, few things are as wonderful as having a great meal and talking about it afterward, and remembering other great meals, and planning the next one. We have found, in writing this book, that the same holds for perfume. All pleasure is connected, and the endless ride we take between disappointment and satisfaction and back again is largely what keeps us interested in life. What more is there to talk about? T S

Beauty and the Bees
by Tania Sanchez

The question that women casually shopping for perfume ask more than any other is this: "What scent drives men wild?" After years of intense research, we know the definitive answer. It is bacon. Now, on to the far more interesting subject of perfume.

It is a mistake to think that the overwhelming reason for women to wear perfume is to attract the opposite sex. But as Luca once explained to me regarding the peculiar, temperature-independent scanty dress of many young women at night, what a woman on the prowl requires is something that men will register after six beers. Thus the use of simplified sexual cues, such as short skirts and big hair, and perhaps also a loud, sweet, pervasive perfume that will cut through a fog of spilled liquor, end-of-day body odor, the occasional vomit on the bar floor, and the perfumes of the nearest five girls, dressed identically. Of course, if your mating strategy casts this wide a net, you may drag in more old boots than big tunas. But that is probably fodder for another book.

Perhaps this attention-getting olfactive strategy can also, in a way, explain the second mistake, milder than the first but still quite wrong, that women tend to make when choosing a fragrance, which is to assume that the reason to wear perfume is to impersonate a flower bed. This is a very fine strategy if your aim is to attract bees. Otherwise, you could do better. Flowers smell good, it is true. Alongside their frequently loud colors and their petal markings that in ultraviolet light flash the message "Eat at Joe's," they release a steady mixture of volatile fragrant attractants tuned to catch attention at a distance, much like the aforementioned bar beauties, and with the same hardwired goal, which is to say sexual reproduction.

Yes, everyone loves the smell of a fresh tea rose on its thorny stem, or of warm clustered jasmine blossoms like white stars against their green-ery, but truth to tell, a flower is not quite a perfume. The fragrances known as soliflores, meant to represent a single material or flower, nice as they may be, have a hard time competing with the best perfumes un-less they cheat in more interesting directions, because, unlike perfum-ers, flowers aren't interested in us. Having heard innumerable passionate panegyrics on the smell of this or that blossom—honeysuckle, mimosa, gardenia, rose, linden, lily of the valley, get out your garden catalog and fill in the rest—I have taken the time to poke my face into many flowers, after checking for biting or stinging inhabitants. They have smelled mostly pleasant, occasionally harsh or disappointingly simple, ethereal or syrupy, peppery or creamy, arresting and frequently weird, blending a sort of bad breath with almond paste, a lingering smell of feet with heavenly ambrosia, an odd smell of swimming pools behind a lemon freshness, and so on. Flowers are things I like to smell in passing, not on me. And even if I did want to smell like them, there'd be a technical problem. Flowers are more like plug-in air fresheners than like per-fumes. They emit a steady puff of stuff, which floats off and meets you at a distance and then flies away, replenished constantly. Perfumes sprayed once on the skin evaporate and—unless you're fanatical enough to keep refreshing your fragrance every hour, which will make you the least favorite co-worker on the company elevator—metamorphose and eventually fade. So let us walk away from the flower garden, as pretty as it is, and talk properly of perfume: what a woman's perfume is for, and what makes it good, great, or dismal.

Perfume is an art, and the purposes of art have been a topic of dis-cussion at least since the ancient Greeks wondered about it while flirting with each other over the cheese course; these purposes have at various times been thought to be didactic, cathartic, distracting, polluting, ele-vating, sanctifying, profaning, and for its own sake. The arts appeal in various ways to our various senses, and if you want to think long and hard about such things, I recommend reading a lot of Walter Pater. For the moment, let's just say that, like all other arts, perfume should engage our attention to a satisfying end, first creating an expectation and then satisfying it in a way different and better than you hoped.

Early in the history of an art, nobody knows what to expect, and the landscape is all frontier, with every artist a pioneer. Latecomers usually stick to the known path, with minor variations. So everyone complains that new perfumes all smell alike, but occasionally someone hits on a variation that constitutes a true advance. Great artistic advances are often spurred by technological ones: guitars go electric, Prussian blue knocks down the price barrier to painting dusky skies, and ladies casually swan about smelling like peaches. As Luca has pointed out before, Guerlain's Mitsouko was in structure basically Coty's landmark Chypre with the peach base Persicol added. However, Mitsouko didn't smell like two distinct things hashed together—far from it. Instead, it smelled like a new creature called Mitsouko: an autumnal, poignant chord, rounded and full, something that felt on first meeting as if you had known it before, the way certain people you meet seem as if they were expecting you or you them, even if you are technically strangers.

What we're really talking about is the art of abstraction in perfumery: the creation of a new smell for its own qualities, and not for any fidelity to things already known. How is it done? Magic. For example, a smart, funny, wonderful woman I know once wondered, referring to the great but long defunct Iris Gris (created by Jacques Fath), why the smells of iris and peach, in some mysterious proportion, create a third, haunting smell that is neither iris nor peach but something entirely new. She apologized for not understanding the science of it. It wasn't science but art, though both rely heavily upon a combination of inspiration and happy accident. To illustrate the elegant simplicity of this particular idea, one night, while I was doing my best to help a friend drain some bottles that might be useful if they weren't so full of wine, this friend, an amateur perfumer (toiling for love and not money), following a previous suggestion of Luca's, took some Persicol, and mixed it drop by drop into a small vial of the closest thing on hand to iris butter tincture, Serge Lutens's wonderful Iris Silver Mist. Magic is always most astonishing when done small and up close. For a while, we smelled only iris, then, for a time, both iris and peach. We were on the verge of getting bored with our game when one last drop pushed the mixture into the realm of the inexplicable. Instead of the iris and peach keeping their separate identities, we perceived billowing out of the vial a third presence, like a newborn dream object with the satin cool of its rooty father and a plummy richness inherited from its lactonic mother: it was Iris Gris in the rough. The idea itself is simple enough once you know it's there, but finding and recognizing it is not so easy. You can no more predict the next great beautiful perfumery idea than you can predict the next catchy melody before you hear it.

Now, you may think perfumery is pretty easy if so much relies on happy accidents, but three things need to be in place for a happy accident to become worthwhile: someone must be obsessed and daring enough to tinker and generate the new ideas, someone must be able to spot the one good idea among a host of useless ones, and someone needs the skill to realize the idea's full potential. The breathless claims of fragrance marketing to the contrary, it is just not true that fine ingredients guarantee a great perfume. Imagine chucking a fresh Maine lobster, a wheel of top-notch Camembert, and a pound of artisanal Venezuelan chocolate in a kettle and simmering in Chartreuse until Wednesday. Yummy? It doesn't work for perfume either. It generally takes years of training to become a perfumer, and even a talented perfumer needs to work with evaluators and clients who can recognize a good thing when they smell it.

Chacun à Son Goût

But it's all a matter of taste, you say. It's true that among the perfumes reckoned good or great, there are some that will move you more than others, and some that will leave you entirely cold or even sickened, because either they won't say what you're longing to hear or they say what you never want to hear again. All the same, when considering perfume as an art, it's possible to appreciate when something is done exceptionally well.

If you've tried several perfumes, you know things can go wrong. Many compositions smell great in the first few minutes, then fade rapidly to a murmur or an unpleasant twang you can never quite wash off. Some seem to attack with what feels like an icepick in the eye. Others smell nice for an hour in the middle but boring at start and finish. Some veer uncomfortably sweet, and some fall to pieces, with various parts hanging there in the air but not really cooperating in any useful way. Some never get around to being much of anything at all. The way you can love a person for one quality despite myriad faults, you can sometimes love a perfume for one particular moment or effect, even if the rest is trash. Yet in the thousands of perfumes that exist, some express their ideas seamlessly and eloquently from top to bottom and give a beautiful view from any angle. A rare subset of them always seem to have something new and interesting to say, even if you encounter them daily. Those are the greats. By these criteria, one can certainly admire a perfume without necessarily loving it. Love, of course, is personal (but best when deserved).

I liked to play with perfume but never thought much of it until at seventeen I found the Guerlain counter at Saks. I'd sought it out because my roommate was crazy about a forceful thing they made called Samsara, which, while something I absolutely didn't want to wear, had a worked-out quality that seemed a notch above what I was used to. The first thing I tried was the recent release Champs-Elysées, which had the starring role on the counter. I nearly ran off. It was a sharp and shallow floral to go with Lucite-heeled shoes and a ditzy high-pitched laugh that goes on so long it makes your companions gesture to the bartender to cut you off. For some reason, before heading home, I looked a little further and paused at one labeled L'Heure Bleue. The eau de toilette bottles at that time had the shape of squat lutes, a black serif typeface like a printer's error on the clear glass, and tall plastic caps imitating gilded lacquer—in a word, ugly. In this unpromising container I found the most beautiful thing I'd ever smelled. I bought it with my food budget for the month and put the silly bottle in a dark cabinet so I wouldn't have to look at it. I wore it quietly and rarely, because I couldn't afford to buy another, and I never told anyone what it was, because the name's particular combination of gargling French r's and pursed-lipped *eu* sounds was unprocessable by the American ear, most of all when pronounced correctly—all of which had the effect of giving my love for it the fraught significance of a secret affair.

The second time I fell for a perfume, things were not so complicated. I was down to the last half inch of L'Heure Bleue in the bottle, I was out of college, and I was desultorily spraying everything on the girls' side of Sephora, finding dozens of nice things but nothing that moved me much. Until I found that little black rubber puck. Look up Luca's review of Bulgari's Black farther along in the book, and then buy it and wear it and know what I mean. My first love was simply beautiful; the second was both beautiful and interesting. I began to have questions.

Since then I have met scores of fellow perfume fanatics, and I believe I can sketch out a brief trajectory of the path many of us take when we come to perfume. I admit this archetypal pattern is not, perhaps, accurate in all or even most cases, but as you may find yourself or someone you love in it, I include it here.

- ◆ Stage 1: *Mother's bathroom.*
  Early adventures splashing on Mom's Shalimar/No. 5/Miss Dior/ Tabu/Your-Memory-Here with the bathroom door shut. Belief that Old Spice/Brut/English Leather is the natural odor that God has caused fathers to emit after shaving.

- ◆ Stage 2: *Ambition and naïveté.*
  Either given a perfume by an adult or inspired to buy one at puberty: a sophisticated thing that embodies an unknown world of adult pleasures and/or a cheerful cheap spray to wear happily by the gallon.

- Stage 3: *Flowers and candy.*
  Phase of belief that feminine perfumes should smell flowery or candy-like and that everything else is an incomprehensible perversion.

- Stage 4: *First love.*
  Encounter with moving greatness. Wonder and awe. Monogamy.

- Stage 5: *Decadence.*
  An ideology of taste, either of the heavy-handed or of the barely there. The age of leathers, patchoulis, tobaccos, ambers; or, alternately, the age of pale watercolors in vegetal shades. An obsession with the hard-to-find.

- Stage 6: *Enlightenment.*
  Absence of ideology. Distrust of the overelaborate, overexpensive, and arcane. Satisfaction in things in themselves.

Choosing a Perfume

On to the more important practicalities. How is a woman to select a fragrance for herself? Let us review strategies for the two major moments of selection: in the shop and at the vanity.

First, the loved and dreaded shop, with its perky sales assistants crooning the name of the latest thing and offering to spray your arm, or hovering over you and offering unsolicited useless advice while you try to swat them away so you can think. Must you go there? Yes. There's no satisfactory substitute for smelling things in person, least of all advertising, packaging, or the descriptions put out by the firm's marketing department. While you may be able to imagine the described exotic flowers, fruits, and weather (fresh air, spring rain, and so on), these lists of notes are not a faithful list of ingredients, which, unless you're a specialist, you would find nigh incomprehensible. Still, they would like you to read the list as if it were one of those restaurant menu items that include the whole recipe, causing you to imagine an ideal mélange of delicious things and to cry out, "Oh, that sounds nice!" and buy the big bottle and the shower gel until you realize it's crap and you buy something else. The one exception to the rule of needing to go to the shop is if a sample may be acquired by mail. All the same, I hate sample vials. They're good for one or two miserly wearings, and they get lost, separated from their name cards, and crushed under bare feet. (Bigger spray samples are becoming more common; may they take over!) This book will help you find the best of the bunch, but you're going to need to do some smelling of your own. Besides, I admit, sometimes Luca is wrong.

You must be both stubborn and open-minded when you arrive at the shop. An air of feckless uncertainty will only invite aggression or condescension. The default setting for any sales assistant is to sell the latest thing, so if you want to bypass the most recent releases and get into things that came out prior to last Tuesday, you must come up with a challenge for the sales assistant: ask for the best one. If he gives you some guff about it all being a matter of taste, or comes at you with something he says is the best seller, you can ask for the one that is like nothing else. At least then you've got a conversation. Bear in mind that most sales assistants are poorly trained; frequently they understand fragrance no better than you do, and they're fed a lot of gobbledygook by the fragrance companies. Assume everything you're told is probably untrue.

You can't smell everything in one day, because eventually your sense of smell suffers fatigue. Before figuring this out, I often found that the impression I got in a department store was so incredibly wrong that the fragrance I unwrapped at home was unrecognizable. So count on smelling at most between five and ten fragrances on paper, and testing one or two of those on skin. It's chancy to spray something unknown right on yourself. It is an axiom that the more hideous you find a fragrance, the more tenacious it is. Scrub as you might, some of it will linger. Once you find something on paper that you'd really like to get to know better, you can try it on your skin. Then leave the fragrance floor. Go out for lunch.

See if it (1) vanishes, (2) bores, (3) annoys, or (4) remains wonderful. Whatever you do, remember that fragrances tend to change drastically after the first twenty minutes, except for a few clever, sneaky compositions that smell nearly the same from top to bottom. Then there are a very few fragrances, mostly older ones, that save the best for later, a few hours in, when they drop their earthly raiment to reveal angelic finery; my first bottle of Mitsouko did that, and the sudden increase in intensity and beauty was so unexpected that for a creepy moment I thought someone invisible must have entered the room.

When you love something, buy it. I say this not because I'm on the take, but because there is a very high chance that if you refuse love once, your chance will be lost forever. The fragrance will be discontinued or reformulated, and you'll find yourself scouring estate sales and eBay auctions, bidding against other fools who didn't get it while they could. Besides, one of the glories of perfume is that it is one of the most affordable luxuries in life, from the $15 eau de toilette sprays in the local pharmacy to the standard $40 to $60 eau de parfum at a beauty counter and a $300 bottle of Guerlain perfume in crystal, which lasts you years. This is one reason that it's so easy, once you get the taste for it, to amass a sizable collection.

Next: how to select a fragrance while you're standing at your dresser. If you are going to a film or a performance, during which other ticket holders will be forced to sit next to you for hours, have the decency either to wear nothing or to wear something that leaves some air in the room. Women who flounce into the cinema wearing Poison have inspired generations of people to believe they hate perfume. If you are going to dinner, wear either something that cooperates with dinner (a classic chypre or oriental worn discreetly lends a lovely background murmur) or no fragrance at all. For wine tastings and deliriously high-priced dinners, for which reservations are required months in advance, it's most sensible to go scentless, since even you should be concentrating on your $300 glass of burgundy and not your eau de toilette.

Fragrances for parties where strings of chili pepper lights throw a red glow on the proceedings should be simple declarations of happiness; such evenings are not the time for bookish, contemplative fragrances full of subtleties, or for high-priced statements of tasteful luxury, but probably the ideal moment for a delightfully trashy fruit-cocktail fragrance, or for some friendly sweet number with both softness and force like Tocade. Going to work requires another strategy entirely; it depends on your work, the mindset you need to be in, and the aura you mean to project, although generally anything you would wear to the chili pepper party is probably the wrong thing for the desk, unless you're the boss and you wear what you like.

But it is highly recommended to avoid simply wearing the thing that you believe matches your style, since it may not. If you are intellectual and wear only intellectual perfumes, or if you are flirty and wear only flirty perfumes, it is like obsessively matching your shirt and socks every day—it is timid and rule-bound and therefore must be countered once in a while with some contrariness. The world is too large and experience too vast for this kind of penned-in thinking. Some mischief and surprise are needed to keep life fresh, for you to smell your perfume anew. Therefore, I urge you, if you are a floral gal, to set aside prejudice and wear a thing without flowers. If you are a luxury goods kind of gal, with a Kelly bag on your arm and Manolos on your feet, I urge you to try on something that you believe to be beneath you. If you are ultrafeminine, wear a man's scent. And if you are butch, doll it up for once. Live a little. Try it on. It's only perfume. TS

The Classical and the Romantic
by Luca Turin

Insofar as anything meaningful can be said about masculine and feminine fragrances in general, it is probably accurate to describe them as being, respectively, classical and romantic. The litmus test lies, as always, in how a genre, school of thought, or worldview deals with the new. Masculine fragrances, masculine clothes, and film scores of the Majestic Muscle persuasion endlessly rehash Fougère Royale, Edward VIII, and Bruckner. The new is greeted with the raised eyebrows of Jeeves faced with Bertie Wooster's latest fad come up from London. Most great innovations in masculine fragrance, from Bel-Ami to Insensé, died a lingering death. When one succeeds, slavish imitation happily resumes for decades.

Feminine fragrances, by contrast, are possessed by the romantic demon of novelty. Every perfumer dreams of a tabula rasa, of tearing off a blank page and writing a formula such as no one has seen before, of the evaluator coming in and, upon smelling 3477/B, reacting the way we humans do when faced with unplanned loveliness: delighted laughter. And all perfume lovers, when tearing through the cellophane and eagerly pressing the spray button of a new fragrance, secretly hope for that rarest of things, a revelation. Conversely, the secret terror, the ghost that haunts feminine perfumery, the goad that drives so much PR drivel, is the unthinkable possibility that there may be nothing new under the sun except SPF 50. In that respect, perfumery is very much like music, painting, photography, and literature, and its professionals are constantly fretting at the notion that, like the silver of Potosí, the good stuff is going to run out any day or, worse still, has already done so without anyone noticing.

There is in fact no evidence that the new is running out in feminine perfumery, and I see three reasons for this. First, the combinatorics of perfume are so vast that it is still possible to create entirely novel fragrances within or very close to existing forms. A perfect example of this is Maurice Roucel's Tocade, which managed to sound an entirely new tune without, to my knowledge, either using a novel material or diverging far from the well-trodden path of vanillic fragrance. Second, new large-scale forms are constantly being devised (Dune, Angel, Chiffon Sorbet), and the pace of innovation, if anything, seems to be accelerating. Third, new molecules are being discovered that give not just novel smells but novel effects. So there's plenty more where that came from.

What has changed, and not for the better, is the shift from symphony to jingle. If, to pursue a musical analogy, the smell of your fabric softener is a door chime and the first Diorama a full orchestra, fine fragrance is getting dangerously close to a ringtone: inventive, often distinctive, catchy even, but with lousy sound quality. This is due to a combination of factors: (1) too many launches, more than five hundred a year, which means perfumers have no time to think, (2) the profitability of aromachemicals and the cheapening of formulas, which means the big firms tolerate expensive naturals only if nothing else will do, and (3) the necessity for a fragrance to shout ever louder to make itself heard, as happens in a restaurant until someone drops a stack of plates.

The plates did drop once, as a matter of fact, at the end of the eighties, when "quiet" (or to be exact, pale, radiant things like L'Eau d'Issey and cK One) took over. Things have got louder again since then, but a fundamental shift has taken place. I remember asking a business analyst with an interest in the perfume industry what he thought the future held, and he replied that the industry was ripe for a disruptive technology. In the event, little can be done technologically to improve perfume itself: it has no moving parts, works essentially forever, needs no batteries, uses advanced quantum technology in the nose, and so on. The breakthrough has come with the Internet. New perfume firms have found the difficulty of reaching their audience reduced by several orders of magnitude, because of the cheapness of having a presence on the Web, the cost efficiencies of selling direct online, and the way word spreads through an active community of eager, informed perfume lovers. In other words, God created niches: the small fragrance firms selling limited amounts to consumers who feel their tastes are largely ignored by the big guys.

We mammals were once niche animals before the dinosaurs died and we took over the world, so the phenomenon clearly has potential. Today, niche perfumeries have become such a major factor in the fragrance industry that even big brands are copying their style, although in the beginning, many niche firms foundered because they had good intentions but little experience. As niche business has grown, the fun of it has managed to lure away talent from mainstream houses for the unsung but hugely important task of art direction, as well as top perfumers sick of the sameness, vulgarity, and pressure usually involved in working with big-name clients. In other words, the disruptive step has been a return to quality. When Tania and I started writing this guide, I assumed that smelling all these fragrances would be like crossing the Gobi Desert with only a bottle of Allure for sustenance. I am glad to say I was wrong: both mainstream houses and, increasingly, niche firms have time and again surprised me, and I now find myself hoping, as I once did when I knew nothing about perfume, that the next feminine I open will be *the* violin concerto. LT

Masculine Elegance and What It Smells Like
by Luca Turin

B eing a guy is not always pleasant, but at least, like balding and belching, it does not require much work. True, such things as short socks, depressing underwear, elastic-waist trousers, badly cut suits, and square-toed black slip-ons can spell trouble (e.g., the girl laughs uncontrollably and is never seen again). But avoiding disaster requires a checklist as short as that for a light aircraft on final approach: flaps, gear, mixture, carb, fuel, prop. Once memorized, it can be applied widely with minimum thought. Only Tom Ford and John Edwards really need to spend as much time in front of a mirror as a woman, and that because of their lines of work. Even the most persnickety manuals of masculine elegance contain handy options for the absentminded and the short of cash. Countess Tolstoy's uncompromising book on the subject, for example, cautions against wearing new clothes too often and includes several fond references to frayed cuffs. Even such an arbiter of elegance as a writer for *Fantastic Man* magazine was prepared, when she interviewed me, to countenance my Keen fishing sandals worn over socks as a potential fashion statement. If I were a woman, I'd have to be a lot better-looking than I am to be forgiven such a lapse of judgment. In fact, in a reversal that shows how far man has diverged from birds, it is the male of our species that can afford to be as comfortingly drab as a female mallard. By the time he's thirty, a man should have figured out which of the mercifully limited fashion options available, from seersucker jacket to black roll-neck polo, is best for him, bought himself a few quality specimens, and learned to hang on to them until they fray to tatters.

Perfume is a good deal less stringent than clothes: When's the last time your mother looked up as you sat down for dinner and said,

"Sweetie, aromatic fougères are wrong for you"? The choice, however, is wide and mysterious. Finding a perfume willing to tag along with you for a stretch of your life is not easy. For a start, systematic advice is unreliable. As is true for all matters of harmony, almost every statement, rule of thumb, edict, or solemn interdiction that can be cooked up immediately invites contradiction. For instance, even the most funereally dandified of silver-haired German architects can probably add color to his aura by going for something crudely charming like Brut. Similarly, if I said that the egregiously raunchy, borderline unwashed smell of Kouros works best on a pristine young buck, an image of grinning, tousle-haired Albert Einstein with pipe and sweater, clutching a white bottle of Kouros body oil, is liable to flash before my eyes with the caption "Why not?" So abandon hope, all ye who read these words, of a Perfume Charming. Perfumes are like books and pieces of music. A fondness for, say, Barber's "Adagio for Strings" does not mean that you should rush out and buy the one-hundred-CD set of Chill Classics. There may be periods, genres, and composers that you like best, but in the end each perfume is an island. What matters is to get enough feel for the lay of the land to allow your taste GPS to lock in and lead you to the best exemplar of a particular genre. To that end I shall merely list the main styles of masculine fragrance—its continents, so to speak, each with its capital cities listed.

Eheu Fugaces

Someday a scientist, or perhaps a poet, will manage to explain why we humans are so fond of ten-carbon (terpene) alcohols and aldehydes, given that evolution designed them to lure pollinating insects to which we are not visibly related. Linalool (lavender), geraniol (rose), and citral (lemon) are the staples of "fresh" perfumery, the sort that is accompanied in ads by the noise of rushing water and freeze-flash pics of a guy pouring half a bottle on his head. They smell great, feel good, and have no pretensions other than to do just that. Sadly, they do not last long.

The best of the type are therefore those that do not needlessly complicate the formula but nevertheless manage to add sufficient fixatives (musks, usually) to delay evaporation long enough for the feel-good effect to make its way to your heart. In my search for the perfect lavender, I finally landed on the one sold by the monks on Caldey Island, Wales, which is simple and exquisite. Citrus is more difficult: too simple and it smells like stovetop cleaner, too complex and the concision is lost. A good eau de cologne, a classic eighteenth-century invention based on a mixture of citrus oils, makes a nice compromise, none better than the new Chanel Eau de Cologne. But often the style is just too hackneyed, too generic. Two beautifully done citrus fragrances are Eau de Guerlain and Jo Malone's Lime Basil & Mandarin.

Beau Brummell

Aside from the original eau de cologne, and despite protestations to the contrary by firms with prestigious and largely fake coats of arms, there are practically no fragrances extant dating to before the 1870s. There were then, roughly speaking, two schools of masculine perfumery, one English and the other French. The London firm of Floris, founded in the 1730s, was the first perfume retail firm to have standardized products and a shopfront. Until then, pharmacists and bespoke perfumers used to mix the stuff themselves, mostly on demand. Fragrances in those days were more unisex than they are now. The classic British masculine of the late Victorian period was a musky, powdery floral, typically rather sweet. Perhaps the best surviving example of the genre is Penhaligon's Hammam Bouquet (1872), still eminently wearable. The difficulty with this type of composition is that it works only if the raw materials are of exquisite quality. Nothing is harder to do on the cheap than diffuse, soft-focus luxury. Whether it is possible to achieve the proper effect without natural musks (or at any rate nitro musks), ambergris, sandalwood, and civet is questionable. Only Guerlain and Chanel still spend the money. The French equivalent of Hammam Bouquet is Guerlain's lavender-vanilla Jicky (1889), which, despite constant trimming and adjusting over the years, still contains more savoir-faire in one bottle than the complete Penhaligon's range put together. If, heaven forfend, you ever come to find Jicky too austere, there is always the more recent, but still intensely Belle Epoque, Mouchoir de Monsieur.

Ferns

The fougère (fern) genre has historically been the most fertile source of great masculine fragrances. Fougères are built on an accord between lavender and coumarin, with every conceivable variation and elaboration. Great perfumery accords are like dominoes: when juxtaposed, the materials must have a number in common. In the case of lavender and coumarin, it is a herbaceous, green, inedible, soapy character. In the other directions, lavender has a fresh, thyme-like angle and coumarin a sweet, powdery, vanilla biscuit one. Fougère thus handily spans a wide soup-to-nuts spectrum with only two cheap materials. Further, each end of the accord can be varied, on one side with other herbes de Provence or citrus, on the other with vanillic and balsamic notes, without losing balance and clarity. Sadly, in part because the idea is very old (the first, Fougère Royale, was 1881), there are very few pristine fougères around, and those that exist tend to smell cheap: Brut, Canoe. Once again, simplicity works best when the raw materials are luxurious. Ferns are usually labeled "lavender," so try a few, not necessarily expensive big names, and see which one fits you.

Aromatic Fougère

A spicy variation on the fougère theme, which frees it from the slightly one-dimensional character of the basic accord and propels it into the realm of great, abstract perfumery, is the aromatic fougère, a territory so big it seems to serve occasionally as a "none of the above." Perhaps the finest early example of this might be Paco Rabanne pour Homme, the archetypal, slightly melancholy, muted masculine aromatic that maintains a close kinship with cleansing materials (soap, shaving cream, aftershave, hair tonic, etc.) but unequivocally states its purpose: to smell good beyond the call of duty. In a duskier, more intense direction, one may list Blue Stratos, Azzaro, and Rive Gauche pour Homme in increasing order of sophistication. These are open-shirted, straightforward, virile, George Clooney fragrances, to be worn only if understated confidence comes naturally to you.

Lawrence of Arabia

The oriental genre in masculine fragrance is perhaps the hardest to pull off successfully, both as perfumer and as user. Orientals are distinguished by sweet, amber, vanillic accords enlivened with woody, animalic, or floral notes. They generally chart a surprisingly narrow route between the Charybdis of dandification (monogrammed slippers) and the Scylla of vulgarity (Tod's driving loafers). Near-perfect examples are Old Spice (or Baiser du Dragon if you want to be perverse) and Habit Rouge. My own feeling is that masculine orientals are a bit like low-calorie ice cream: no real fun is to be had without lashings of double cream. Across a thin line lies the vast territory of oriental feminines. If this is your style, why not avail yourself of Shalimar (or at any rate Shalimar Lite) or Ambre Sultan?

Affable Hybrids

In the great tradition of Jules Verne and the *voyage en chambre*, the French have over the last decade perfected a type of fragrance somewhere between fougères and orientals that is to olfaction what Gap models are to advertising: smiling, handsome, studiously multiethnic, reassuring to the point of torpor. Though the genre, like so many others, originates with Jean-François Laporte's late-seventies creations for L'Artisan Parfumeur, such as Eau du Navigateur, it properly took off only in 1995 with Kenzo Jungle and congeners. These fragrances are essentially derived from the traditional recipe of bay rum, and include spices, licorice, and maple syrup notes in their makeup. In my opinion the finest in this genre was Yohji Homme (1999), sadly discontinued at the date of writing but still widely available at discounters and online.

Gesamtkunstwerk

The chypre genre ("mossy woods" in Michael Edwards's fragrance taxonomy) is the sonata form of fragrance, a prodigiously fertile idea bestowed upon the world by the greatest perfumer of all time, François Coty. The basic accord is bergamot-labdanum-oakmoss, respectively, mouthwateringly fresh, deliciously sweet, and bracingly bitter. Good chypres are as complex as a fragrance can be without losing the plot, and their principal qualities are richness and balance. The finest masculine example of the genre is Chanel's Pour Monsieur, a fragrance whose breadth of scope and elegance of execution bring to mind an almost implausibly fine figure of a man. I have on occasion cautioned men to avoid wearing a fragrance that's seen more of the world than they have, and I believe this is the main danger of chypres. Still, the temptation is great.

Leather

I belong to those more likely to choke up with emotion while visiting Cincinnati Union Terminal than Chartres Cathedral. For me, Art Deco's combination of solid neoclassicism and steely futurism is pure, heroic magic. The perfect olfactory accompaniment to the Machine Age is the modern leather fragrance, invented in the mid-1920s. (Cyril Scott would have attributed this to the devas sending coded messages.) Leathers, via their connection with aviator jackets, interiors of luxury cars, and saddlery, have an unbroken set of associations with luxuries involving remoteness, movement, and danger. The first and still excellent masculine was Knize Ten (1924), composed by the astonishing team of François Coty, who invented chypres, among other things, and Vincent Roubert, whose Iris Gris is probably the greatest fragrance ever. Arguably the ultimate leather is Chanel's Cuir de Russie, ideal if you plan to arrive in an Isotta Fraschini 8C. Less demanding but stylish and sleekly beautiful is Lancôme's reissued Cuir.

Woods

Woody fragrances are the masculine genre least likely to offend, and have therefore been a favorite of perfumers and wearers forever. Woody notes, though often partaking of a clean, fresh character more usually associated with top notes, are nevertheless large molecules that persist well into the drydown. This allows the construction of fragrances that act coherently over a period of hours, making woods the masculine equivalent of abstract white florals. Trouble is, the first twenty woods you smell are the best, after which their salubrious chiaroscuro becomes dull. The best classical wood might be a vetiver, none better than Guerlain's weird Vetiver pour Elle (ignore the name). Contrasted, vividly synthetic woods like Chanel's Antaeus have their uses too. But to my mind the type of fragrance that has rescued woods from droning on woodenly forever are the woody florals like Timbuktu. These have a transparent, almost mystical intensity that puts them among my favorites in any category.

Sports Fragrances

The last decade has seen the unfortunate flourishing of a dismal genre, the fragrance for men and women who do not like fragrance and suspect that none of their friends do either. The result has been a slew of apologetic, bloodless, gray, whippet-like, shivering little things that are probably impossible, and certainly pointless, to tell apart. All fragrances whose name involves the words *energy, blue, sport, turbo, fresh,* or *acier* in any order or combination belong to this genre. This is stuff for the generic guy wishing to meet a generic girl to have generic offspring. It has nothing to do with any other pleasure than that of merging with the crowd. My fondest hope is everyone will stop buying them and the genre will perish. Just say no.

Lastly, and by way of contrast, remember that perfume is foremost a luxury, among the cheapest, comparable to a taxi ride or a glass of bubbly in its power to lift the mood without causing subsidence the morning after. Wear it for yourself. LT

The Wasteland
by Tania Sanchez

When pausing on C-SPAN coverage of Congress sometimes, I am seized with a passion of sadness mixed with hope for the sea of drab men, whose drabness I notice mostly when, in the landscape of gray, olive brown, and dark blue, a spot of red, yellow, purple, or sky blue blooms upon it like a lotus on a lake: a woman. Sadness arises because these men are dreary creatures working the hallways of power to mostly dreary ends, not only losing their hair and their youthful ideals but actively trying to shake them, rushing toward the total joylessness that can be called by those who love it *gravitas*. Hope arises because the spots of color are appearing more frequently on that muddy pond, which is good both because the greater presence of women in politics is generally something to cheer about and because maybe they'll inspire the men to live a little.

Men weren't always so depressing to behold. They used to take more pleasure in themselves. In 2007, the New York Public Library staged an exhilarating exhibit called "A Rakish History of Men's Wear" in which one of the juiciest shocks was an illustration of a young Venetian man of the Middle Ages wearing tight leggings under a perky green jacket cut short enough to show his shapely behind: one leg, from buttock to ankle, was all red, and the other was thickly striped vertically in black and white. Now, that's an outfit. Even older, sober men at the time had frills, peplums, ruffles, and stockings to take pleasure in. But since the famous Regency dandy Beau Brummel brought us the impeccable standard suit, it's been men's lot to worry over the inner architecture of otherwise indistinguishable gray wool sleeves, and to express themselves solely in the signaling system of cufflink and tie. Real preeners might spend a long morning worrying over the tensions between belt and shoes, but this is far from normal and worries their families and wives if they have them.

The New York Public Library exhibit optimistically championed the democratic ideals of the suit, since if men across classes and professions can share a uniform, then all men can, in principle, be seen as economic and social equals. This cheerful academic point of view is somewhat ruined by the fact that men concerned with status, power, and vanity still spend phenomenal cash on bespoke suits and shirts, and believe the shoes give you away. The vanity of ordinary grown men (I leave out rock stars and other guys with piercings) is now frittered away largely on looking nearly the same as everyone else but at different price points with subtle differences. These differences are mostly undetectable unless you are deeply steeped in the culture of minor clues. And here's where perfume comes in.

Fragrances for men are mostly identical crap, designed to trap you and give you away as a lout. Don't believe me? Smell a few dozen of them yourself and try to come to any other conclusion. Largely, they just fail the Guy Robert base criterion: a fragrance must smell good. Some of them (see Narciso Rodriguez for Him) seem to have been deliberately and carefully edited so as not to smell good. However, most of them are simply careless, condescending. They seem to say that any man vain and stupid enough to be shopping for a new, different fragrance deserves to smell like a suicide cocktail of dishwashing detergent and rubbing alcohol, and that any person fool enough to spend a lot of time near such a man deserves to breathe unwholesome air. The fragrances seem to be a punishment for trying, a prank on the guy who dares to dab on. They are also, for the most part, uniform copies of accepted forms, like varieties of suit, an array of different types of banal. You'd be forgiven for thinking this unpleasant uniformity was some kind of ideal, for suspecting that anything else was a perversion that would mark you as an eccentric or a criminal. For example, when you read the reviews in this guide or simply peruse the male fragrance counter at any perfume purveyor, you will find there are currently hundreds if not thousands of clones of Davidoff's Cool Water at widely varying price points, which have zero correlation with quality. Every year, more arrive. Furthermore, as Luca observed over the course of reviewing fragrances for this book, when feminine fragrances are reformulated and cheapened enough, they begin to smell like masculine fragrance: men have always got the short end of the stick in this realm.

My point of view on men's fragrance is simply that you should smell good or you shouldn't smell at all. Given that in this world you really can't get away with red tights but you can get away with smelling good, I say you should take your fun where you can. There's a hideous habit common to men and women alike, in which one's daily preparation for facing the world hardens into a set, unthinking ritual, the violation of which, one fears, will bring shame and misfortune. You see the effect of this ritualized toilet in women whose makeup seems to have no relation to the face beneath, whose hair is no longer recognizable as hair, who have on several pieces of jewelry that they wear habitually and that do not relate to each other or to the wearer's other clothing, and so on. You know how it works: they have put on lipstick, because getting ready involves lipstick, and they put on the necklace, because getting ready involves the necklace, the whole thing conducted in a kind of trance. With men, however, since they generally have limited choices for hair and none for makeup, most of this ritual is simply good for them. They wash, they shave, they comb, they put on deodorant. Good, all good, especially the washing. Then they slap on an aftershave. Stop.

Why are you wearing it, my friend? Are you wearing it because you think it makes you alluring to potential sexual partners? (See my essay on feminine fragrance for several arguments against this as a primary goal of perfume selection.) Are you wearing it because your dad wore it? Are you wearing it because your girlfriend or sister or mother or beloved aunt gave it to you and the bottle isn't empty yet? Are you wearing it because you think it soothes the skin after shaving? Or are you wearing it because you think it smells great?

I think you know what I'm going to tell you. You should wear it only because you like it.

Curiously, men's traditional disinterest in spending money on their grooming has worked in their favor for decades. Cheap male scents that we all take for granted—Old Spice, Brut, English Leather, Stetson—actually smell terrific. No celebrities show up on TV or in glossy double-page spreads hawking any of these scents. They are intended for the type of guy who mates with a product for life, like my father, who has for decades used the same fragrance (Old Spice), the same toothpaste (Colgate), the same toothbrush (GUM, with the gum cleaning rubber appendage stuck to one end), the same soap (Irish Spring), and the same hair gel (a tube of green slick called Score, now traumatically discontinued). When a product works for a man, he buys it until he dies or it does. In contrast, when a product works for a woman, she tends to buy it until she gets bored. This economic pressure has kept mass-market men's fragrances cheap and cheerful, since repeat business is their bread and butter, and the only reason a guy like my dad would continue to buy a fragrance is that it smells good. Crap fragrance has been mostly the realm of the luxury-branded middle range, which counts on conning aspirational men with disposable income who buy fragrances for reasons other than the smell.

Yet now that men are starting to buy fragrance more and more, according to breathless reports from the *New York Times* plus the great hope of the cosmetics industry that men are the final frontier, men are beginning to attract more of the same machinery of lies and marketing that has so long been grinding away on the endless work of parting women from their cash. So, men, let me offer you some advice, you babes in these woods I know so well. Do not be seduced by celebrities, by clever ad campaigns, by beautiful bottles and boxes, by high price tags, by exclusivity, by lush official descriptions, by exotic ingredients, by promises. Believe your nose only. Do not wear a fragrance just to wear a fragrance. Make sure it is better than nothing. And if you love something, buy two bottles, because next time the thing may be changed or gone. It's not a man's world out there anymore. TS

A Brief History of Perfume
by Luca Turin

Given the gnomes-of-Grasse picture propagated by the fragrance industry—smiling women carrying baskets of roses on their heads, worried-looking guys in lab coats staring at copper stills—anyone would be forgiven for thinking that perfumery is all about wringing fragrant oils out of live flowers. Not so: with some exceptions, all the fragrances in this guide are, to put it mildly, semisynthetic; some of their components are extracted from natural sources, while most are made by chemists. The two exceptions are perfumes that boast explicitly of being made only with natural materials and perfumes made solely with synthetics, a fact the firms keep quiet when the stuff is supposed to be "fine" fragrance. The proportion of man-made to natural varies: by weight, synthetics usually make up more than 90 percent of fragrance; by cost, the proportion is lower because naturals are expensive. A typical synthetic may cost $50 per kilogram, a typical natural at least $500 per kilo, with many naturals reaching ten or a hundred times that.

Natural materials are obtained in various ways, all of which to a greater or lesser extent damage or otherwise alter the composition of the fragrant oil. The cheapest techniques (steam distillation, hot hexane, etc.) are brutal. Delicate extraction techniques, such as supercritical CO_2, which uses high-pressure gas, and especially hydrofluorocarbon (HFC) extraction, developed by the British engineer Peter Wilde, give stunning results and leave the components largely undamaged. Whatever the method, the yield is always low, from less than 0.1 percent by weight to 1 percent at best. Collecting a ton of flowers is an awful lot of work, and floral extracts are correspondingly expensive. Extracts from dry goods such as spices are usually cheaper. (Note that the essential oil extracted does not replicate the composition of the fragrant air above the flower. In other words, rose oil does not smell like a rose. A technique called "headspace" or "living flower" attempts to remedy this discrepancy by analyzing the air above flowers and replicating the mix with synthetics, with occasionally impressive results.)

The driving force to make synthetics was, from its early days in the 1870s till now, chiefly economic, but it turned out to have artistic benefits as well. Giving perfumers pure compounds to play with changed the art entirely. The great perfumer and teacher René Laruelle has put it succinctly: synthetics are the bones of fragrance, naturals the flesh. Nobody save a few hippies wants invertebrate fragrances, but it is fair to say that many modern perfumes have gone way too far in the other direction and approximate what Tom Wolfe would have called social X-rays, all grinding, dusty bones and no juicy meat. Mercifully, niche fragrance firms, partly because they often charge the earth, partly because disintermediation puts a greater share of the cash in their pockets, seem to be going increasingly upmarket in their choice of raw materials. At the present rate of progress, five years will bring us back to circa 1965, when expensive fragrances smelled expensive and cheap ones smelled cheap.

A composed perfume, undiluted, is known as an oil. Fragrance companies (not brands, with the exception of Guerlain and Chanel) compound the oil from raw materials. Most small compounding firms use materials bought from other suppliers. The largest companies, known as the Big Five—Takasago, Firmenich, Givaudan, IFF, and Symrise—produce raw fragrance materials as well as compounding perfume oils. These firms are constantly engaged in research and development of novel materials (generally synthetics, very rarely novel naturals) because these may bring something genuinely new to fragrance, or at least make clients believe they do. Therefore, novel molecules, as well as the processes for making them, are jealously guarded, either by keeping them secret or by patenting them. Novel molecules still under exclusive use by the firm that made them first are called captives. After twenty years pass and the patents run out, unless some diabolically clever synthetic trick is involved, many firms eventually start producing generic versions, increasingly in India and China.

At bottom, and leaving cost aside, the difference between naturals and synthetics is complexity. If you smell them, pure, natural raw materials are more interesting than aromachemicals. That's because most naturals are mixtures of tens, sometimes hundreds of molecules, and our nose recognizes this as richness and depth. You might assume that because natural molecules are made of the same atoms as synthetic ones, any natural could, in principle at least, be analyzed into its components and replicated by reconstituting the whole mix from synthetics. Yet often it would be impractical and costly, and in some cases impossible: the natural sometimes contains a molecule that we can't make. Note that this works both ways: a majority of great aromachemicals, such as most musks, many ambers, several lemons, and at least two crucial lily-of-the-valley components, are not found in nature.

What are the main chemical building blocks of fragrance? There are several thousand of them, and I wager that their frequency of use, if it were made public by the fragrance firms, would follow a classic long-tailed distribution like that of words in a language. A few materials are found in almost every composition: molecules that smell of rose, violets, jasmine, wood, patchouli, sandalwood, vanilla, and musk. Some—such as vetiver, tree moss, violet-leaf compounds, isoquinolines, aldehydes, or birch tar—mostly belong to certain genres. Those in the "long tail" are rarely used.

The official birthday of fragrance chemistry is generally held to be the discovery of a synthetic route to coumarin by Perkin, as reported in volume 21 of the *Journal of the Chemical Society* as "On the artificial production of coumarin and formation of its homologues" (1868). Many pure chemicals had been isolated from natural materials before: cinnamaldehyde (cinnamon) in 1834, benzaldehyde (bitter almonds) in 1837 and even synthesized completely in 1863—but, being chiefly a flavor chemical, it doesn't count. Coumarin was a big deal. It was the main component of a popular, very expensive natural material: dried, fermented tonka beans, which have a wonderful sweet-nutty herbaceous, tobacco-like smell. When Perkin made it, he was thirty, already a fellow of the Royal Society (the United Kingdom's academy of sciences) and certainly no slouch: at eighteen he had discovered (in his top-floor home lab) how to make the first synthetic fabric dye, mauvein, which made him rich and famous. His coumarin was not much purer than the natural stuff, because the coumarin on tonka beans is crystalline and very pure already, but it was a lot cheaper.

Fourteen years later Paul Parquet used synthetic coumarin in Houbigant's Fougère Royale, which marks the true beginning of modern perfumery. By the 1870s chemists understood that something that smelled good could make money, and the pace picked up. A year after coumarin came heliotropin, a deliciously pale, refined, almost anemic note contained in small amounts in natural vanilla. Heliotropin is the main note in mimosa-type fragrances, such as Guerlain's sublime Après l'Ondée, and more generally in fresh florals. A very close relative of heliotropin called helional, which smells like a sucked silver spoon, is even more deathly pale and has a silvery sheen that made such marvels as Dazzling Silver possible.

The next blockbuster to emerge from the lab was vanillin. Vanillin had until then been made expensively from the extraction of fermented vanilla pods. Then the chemists Tiemann and Haarmann at the great German firm of Haarmann and Reimer (now Symrise) synthesized it from pinewood sap. For this reason, Haarmann and Reimer was founded in a place surrounded by forests in central Germany, appropriately called Holzminden (*holz* means "wood" in German), to be nearer the sap. Tiemann and Reimer then managed a synthesis from the much cheaper material guaiacol, and later, in the 1930s, a U.S. chemist named Howard synthesized it from even cheaper lignin, a by-product of paper manufacturing. An even better variation on vanillin was ethylvanillin, more powerful, less sweet, and more refined. There may have been perfumes that used the synthetic vanillins before Jicky (1889), but they have left no trace, and Aimé Guerlain's creation is usually listed as the first vanillic.

The Czech-Austrian chemist Zdenko Skraup discovered the sensationally bitter, leathery quinolines in 1880 and, according to some, these were used in small amounts to impart an austere bearing to fragrances such as Chypre (1917) long before they became popular as a prominent note in Bandit (1944). But the big blockbuster of the 1880s was the discovery by Baur in 1888 of nitro musks. The introduction of nitro (NO_2) groups in just about everything had been a popular pastime for chemists since time immemorial. Nitric acid was first described by Arab chemist Jabir ibn Hayyan in the ninth century, as was sulfuric acid (oil of vitriol). A mixture of the two is like a rivet gun, capable of punching an NO_2 into most things. As far back as 1759, some enterprising chemists had, for reasons that are hard to discern, first taken jewelry amber and heated it up until it became a fragrant liquid, and then treated this oil of amber with nitric acid, whereupon it smelled even better.

Nitro (NO_2), as in nitroglycerin and the N of TNT (trinitro-toluene), is great stuff if you want to blow things up because it contains oxygen and therefore allows whatever molecule it's in to burn instantaneously. Explosives were a huge business in the second half of the nineteenth century, used to blast rock for tunnels and railway lines as well as propel bullets and shells. A chemist called Baur was exploring derivatives of TNT when he discovered one that was no good as an explosive but smelled great. When he showed it to perfumers they must have smothered him in kisses. His relatively dirt-cheap Musk Baur smelled and worked not unlike a wildly expensive natural musk, extracted from the glands of the Himalayan musk deer. This was tantamount to making gold from dross, and Baur set about making money and producing many other related musks. It is difficult to overestimate the impact of these musks on perfumery, but they went out of style in the 1970s because they were photosensitizers and occasionally neurotoxic. Only musk ketone survives, and unfortunately it is not the best. They are the most lamented materials in the perfumer's palette, especially the delicious musk ambrette.

Hot on the heels of musks came the earthshaking discovery of ionones in 1893. Violet flowers smell of ionones, a scent both simple and affecting in a way that none of the great molecules described so far can attain: coumarin and vanillin are warm and food-like, while musks have an effect on perfumes far beyond their actual rather quiet smell, something akin to the transparent varnish on a painting that gives all colors depth and saturation. Ionones are another matter. They are in equal parts woody and fruity, and it is this strange contrast that makes them so interesting, as if the molecule were teaching us connections between things we thought unrelated. Ionones lowered the price of the violet smell by a factor of a million, and by the turn of the century had became the most popular smell of all. The only surviving fragrance from that period is Violettes de Toulouse, which feels wonderfully simple and old-fashioned. In my opinion, the best way to enjoy ionones untrammeled is in Choward's Violet Mints, the closest one can ever get to edible Art Nouveau.

It was another part of violets, often confused with the flower due to imprecise nomenclature, that was synthesized in 1903, when Moureau and Delange discovered the violet-leaf molecule methyl heptin carbonate. MHC contains the unusual (in perfumery) carbon-carbon triple bond, as in acetylene. The reader who has used acetylene or dropped calcium carbide in water will remember the strange, peppery smell of the gas. Heptin and octin carbonates take that gassy-peppery aspect and turn the volume up to a scream. Again, violet-leaf absolute was wildly expensive (it is still sold in small amounts as *violette pays*). Again, MHC became hugely popular to give a dry, stylish feel to otherwise soggy florals. And again, the stuff ended up all but banned because the triple bond is somewhat reactive and tends to cause allergies. The last fragrance to use the stuff in large amounts (heptins and octins are so potent that 0.1 percent is considered a lot) was the wonderful Fahrenheit by Christian Dior, now reformulated.

Next come lactones in 1906, discovered by the Russian chemists

Zhukov and Shestakov. Lactones were derived from esters, the notes that give all fresh fruit their watercolor palette of smells. But whereas esters last only minutes on the skin, some lactones, while still fruity, seemingly go on forever. Roughly speaking, every carbon atom you add to a molecule doubles its residence time on the skin or a strip. Taking four carbons as the smallest and sixteen carbons as the largest, this means the time-to-flight of perfumery materials varies by approximately a factor of four thousand, which is to say from five minutes to two weeks. The lactone that Zhukov and Shestakov discovered, gamma-undecalactone, smells intensely peachy and is capable of holding its own in any composition, basically outlasting all but the most tenacious dry-down materials. Undecalactone's summery disposition famously managed to cheer up the most determinedly glum fragrances in history. Vincent Roubert's Iris Gris used its pink powdery note to spectacular effect against the silver-gray background of iris root. And famously, Jacques Guerlain used it to put love handles on the bony, cerebral Chypre that made Coty's fortune, resulting in Mitsouko.

Determining the structure of an unknown molecule used to take months and now takes minutes. Elucidating beta-santalol, the molecule chiefly responsible for the smell of sandalwood, in 1935 was a huge achievement by Ruzicka and Thomann, the former being the only person so far to get a Nobel Prize for work in fragrance chemistry. Interestingly, minor wrinkles concerning the exact structure of santalol were not ironed out until as late as 1980. Santalol was a non-starter to replicate by chemistry (too complicated). In addition, sandalwood oil was cheap and readily available until recently. Nevertheless, a series of synthetic alternatives were discovered at the rate of roughly one every ten years. These have given us a slew of sandalwood-like materials ranging from Sandela (1960) to the fabulously powerful Javanol (2000) via Sandalore, Ebanol, Polysantol, and Osyrol. Ironically, now that natural sandalwood is (temporarily, one hopes) hard to source because of depletion and regulation, these molecules, which smell rather different from sandalwood and vastly less good, have taken over almost completely, and perfumers are hard at work making complex sandalwood "bases" to replicate the wonderfully complex sweet, powdery, milky smell of the real stuff.

Are new smells still being discovered? Certainly: the discovery of hedione in 1962, followed by the gradual fall in its price to a level where it can be used almost as a solvent in fragrance composition, has revolutionized the composition of fresh and floral fragrances. You can smell it in the groundbreaking Eau Sauvage, the first fragrance to use a lot of it, and most florals on the market today. Cheap macrocyclic musks like Velvione and cheap ambers like Cetalox are making even such humble things as laundry detergent smell great. The rosy-fruity materials known as damascones smell so good and so complex that they can be used alone to fragrance a variety of household products, and were the chief innovation allowing big rosy fragrances such as Coriandre and Estée Lauder's Knowing.

But it is becoming harder and harder to invent new synthetic materials: the testing they have to undergo before being approved for fragrance use is, understandably, stringent, far more so than anything the naturals had to endure. The fixed cost of bringing a new material to market is over a million dollars. Sales pick up only if it is responsible for at least one huge perfumery success. Time is against you: working out an industrial synthesis can take a year or two, the paperwork another two years, talking perfumers into using it another two, since their palette of available materials is already extremely broad. (However, one sort of novel material that perfumers definitely need is the kind that smells just like an old one that has been restricted as an allergen.) By the time the first big hit comes along in the shops, how many years are left on the twenty-year patent? And will you make your money back before every Chinese chemistry firm can make it for free? Remember, fragrance chemistry is not like pharmaceuticals. The entire industry is worth about $15 billion, whereas one blockbuster drug brings in that much. And unless we find out that Mitsouko cures cancer, it'll stay that way. LT

ANSWERS TO FREQUENTLY
ASKED QUESTIONS

▧ What are eau de toilette, eau de parfum, and parfum (and body spray, deodorant, eau de cologne, parfum de toilette, and so forth)?

Pure perfume is dissolved in a solution of 98 percent alcohol and 2 percent water, the preferred solvent. Different concentrations of perfume oil are sold under different names: eau de toilette (EdT) is around 10 percent perfume oil, eau de parfum (EdP) somewhere around 15–18 percent, and parfum (also known as extrait) 25 percent and higher. Occasionally, just to maintain the mystique, fragrance houses spring strange names on you: parfum de toilette is generally the same as eau de parfum, body sprays and eaux de cologne are usually lighter than eau de toilette, and for everything else you will probably have to ask and get a wrong answer. LT/TS

▧ Why don't they sell the perfume pure?

They do in some countries, but you probably wouldn't like it much. Pure oils tend to have very dense smells in which the components are hard to discern, which can make you miss most of the point of a well-crafted perfume. It's as if the story in the fragrance were written in very small print. The appropriate dilution opens up the fragrance and makes it legible to your nose. A very few fragrances are sold in wax or cream form, and usually smell rather different. These solid or semisolid fragrances are convenient if you don't mind a little grease.

Usually there is no difference in the composition of the oil used to make up EdT, EdP, and parfum. But beware: some houses, such as Hermès and Cartier, use slightly different compositions for the parfum, typically incorporating higher percentages of expensive materials. Worse still, some perfumes, including Chanel's No. 5, are completely different compositions in different dilutions. Generally speaking, one could argue that EdP is the ideal dilution, strong enough for one spritz to last all day, but not so much that small overdoses will cause the air behind you to shimmer like jet exhaust. LT

■ **How long can I keep my perfume before it goes bad?**

That depends on the perfume; a small number of perfumes seem to take a turn for the worse after a couple of years, but the majority we have collected seem to have no expiration date. If you want your perfumes to last long, protect them from light. Visible light consists of photons with energy high enough to break chemical bonds. You will notice that your perfume has a slight brown color, which means it absorbs light. A perfume kept in bright sunlight may be photochemically toasted in as little as a week. A perfume kept in dim light or darkness could last two hundred years. If you're not going to use up your fragrance quickly, save it in the box.

Keep in mind that perfumes do evolve in the bottle. Most of the evolution happens the first few days after the formula is mixed. This is known as maceration. Good houses never bottle perfumes before that process has settled down, but you may notice that things are still changing for a while after purchase. In fact, although there is no doubt that fragrance houses frequently change the formula and then swear on their grandmothers' graves that they did not, you may find that a new bottle smells somewhat different from your old bottle not because of a drastic reformulation but because the new bottle is fresh. Very old fragrances, even when well kept, tend to darken and develop a nail-varnish smell, which fortunately fades minutes after you put it on skin. If you make sure you give the perfume time to breathe before inflicting it on others, usually you can happily wear fragrances that at first sniff seem past their prime. LT/TS

What's better: splash bottles, spray atomizers, or bulb atomizers?

Bottle lovers and "juice" lovers tough it out on eBay to get their hands on a rare and precious perfume. The former pour the perfume down the drain and put the pretty glass on their vanities, while the latter decant the lovely liquid into a plain container and resell the empty bottle to crystal fanatics. If you don't care about the packaging but love fragrance, get plain glass pump atomizers, which you can buy easily online. They don't spill, and they protect the fragrance from air and give a measured dose.

Splash bottles are used usually for either parfum or eau de cologne, the former because you want a drop, not a spray, and the latter because you want to pour it on. Some people worry about contaminating the liquid with skin debris. We never fret about this, but there is a ready solution if you do: apply with cotton ball or swab.

Bulb atomizers have a certain visual appeal to the six-year-old girl within, who places them on an ideal dream vanity accompanied by pink swansdown powder puffs and silver-backed hairbrushes. This said, they are horrible. If the silly twee look of them doesn't get you after a while, bear in mind that if you keep them attached to your bottle instead of replacing them with a proper cap, the perfume sometimes evaporates through the porous balloon and you'll be really peeved when you realize it's gone after a couple of weeks. LT/TS

What are perfumes made of?

A perfume is a mixture of raw materials, usually both natural and synthetic. The latter are known as aromachemicals or, in technical parlance, odorants. They are usually pure compounds (not counting mirror-image molecules), although sometimes they are mixtures of related molecules that arise from the same synthesis. Occasionally the molecule responsible for most or all of the smell isn't even the most abundant one, as is the case for Iso E Super, a common velvety-woody material.

Aromachemicals are made from simpler building blocks in chemical factories. For example, vanillin, the main component of the vanilla bean's smell, can be synthesized from lignin, a by-product of paper manufacturing. Depending on price and usefulness, aromachemicals can be made in quantities ranging from a few hundred kilograms per year worldwide (muscone, $500 per kilogram) to thousands of tons (citral, $12 per kilogram). Price is usually related to how hard it is to make a particular chemical. Fragrance chemistry is unusual in fine chemistry in that high purity and low price are demanded by the client simultaneously, which makes manufacturing aromachemicals a highly skilled affair, incorporating many tricks of the trade and much secret knowledge to get good, distinctive, consistent quality.

Natural raw materials are naturally occurring aromachemicals, generally in mixtures. Their evolutionary purposes can be extremely diverse, ranging from antiseptic (most spicy notes) to insect attractant (most flower smells), pest repellent (some woods and herbs), or none whatsoever (aged ambergris). The compositions of the materials you can extract range from the simple (nearly pure coumarin from tonka beans) to the fiercely complex (hundreds of different chemicals in rose oil). Like any agricultural crop, these materials vary enormously in price and quality from supplier to supplier and from year to year. The great fragrance houses that use a lot of natural materials employ perfumers who trim the sails of various perfume formulas to adjust to natural variations. This is not unlike blending whiskey to achieve constant quality, and is high art.

Solvent extraction and steam distillation are the two most common ways to get the smell out of natural materials. Solvent extraction basically involves soaking the material in something like hexane (a colorless, low-boiling-point liquid) and heating, not always gently. The odorant molecules dissolve, whereupon the mixture is filtered and distilled to recover the perfume oil. Steam distillation is not really distillation but something simpler: water is added, then heated until it steams up, carrying fragrant oils on the steam droplets. Because oil and water don't mix, the steam mixture is readily separated into water and the fragrant oil.

All extraction methods involve heating to "cook" the raw material to some extent, with the attendant changes in fragrance. As Peter Wilde, inventor of a superior room-temperature extraction method, aptly puts it, "You never get oranges, always marmalade." Some expensive and sophisticated extraction methods, such as those that use carbon dioxide under pressure or HFCs, produce spectacular materials at a price. They are used only for the highest-value materials. LT

Do perfumes contain animal ingredients?

In the vast majority of cases, the answer is no. The classic animal ingredients of perfumery are musk, produced by a timid and unfortunate little ungulate called the Himalayan musk deer, in a gland known as its musk pod; civet, a powerfully fecal-smelling paste scraped from the nether regions of a presumably annoyed creature known as the civet cat; ambergris, a substance hacked up in a great big gob by sperm whales, who coat painfully sharp cuttlefish bones with the stuff in their guts, then regurgitate it into the sea, where it floats and ripens for years before washing up on a beach somewhere; and various other urines and such that you are currently begging me not to tell you about. By the time animal rights groups got around to protesting about the trade in animal ingredients, their use was on the wane, because synthetics are cheaper and more reliable. Synthetic musks changed perfumery forever; the endangerment of Himalayan musk deer these days is due not to perfumery but to traditional Chinese medicine. It is nearly impossible to find out for sure if fragrances have animal ingredients, because the public relations staff answers your question, and the average PR person has no clue what the formula is. If you're really concerned about the possibility that something might have an animal ingredient, buy something recent and cheap.

As for whether fragrances are tested on animals, the answer is that most materials in fragrances and cosmetics are required to be tested for safety so that you don't die, go blind, get burned all over, and so on. Products that boast of not being tested on animals generally use materials that have been tested already by the companies that develop and supply the ingredients; the finished product may then be tested on people. TS

Are all-natural fragrances better for you?

Some companies have trained their sales associates to tell you that their fragrances are so pricey because they use a high proportion of natural ingredients, perhaps even all natural ingredients, perhaps gathered in rustic baskets among hillsides of heather and clover by barefoot virgin tonsured monks clad in brown burlap while they pray for your soul, as they have done since the late Cretaceous. But there are really very few perfumes you could honestly call all-natural. Of those, we have yet to find any that belong aesthetically in the top tier. Most perfumers believe a judicious mixture of natural and synthetic is best; very few perfumers we've met believe in 100 percent synthetic fragrance. Furthermore, many perfumes advertised as all-natural are full of synthetic aromachemicals, either because the company is cynical or because it has been lied to by suppliers (a common problem even with big fragrance houses). But even assuming you find fragrances that are 100 percent natural, there is no guarantee that they will be healthier for you (many natural compounds are toxic), nonallergenic (the list of plant allergens is long), or even good for the environment (natural Mysore sandalwood is heavily endangered due to its use in fragrance). LT/TS

Do fragrances cause allergic reactions?

There is, particularly in Europe and the more nervous parts of Canada and California, a growing concern about the toxicity and allergenic potential of many fragrance raw materials. The issue is complex, and we can offer only one point of view. There is no question that any chemical taken in large doses will harm you. It is also true that the doses of chemicals contained in perfumes, whether natural or synthetic, can be sizable. Consider three spritzes of parfum, roughly 0.5 milliliter, sprayed on your skin. That will contain approximately 100 milligrams of perfume oil. Assume 10 percent gets absorbed by the skin: 10 milligrams. If it were Valium, that would be a good dose. If it were cyanide, you'd have trouble breathing.

But perfumery materials are neither potent drugs nor potent toxins, and 10 milligrams of a mixture thereof is dealt with by your body as part of its routine operations. There is more danger from overdosing on vitamins A or E than from applying perfume materials. Generations of Russian alcoholics drinking *odekolon* (eau de cologne) and sometimes writing novels afterward, such as Venedikt Erofeev's *Moskva-Petushki*, bear witness to the relatively low toxicity of perfume materials. Most of them have a lethal dose around 300 milligrams per kilogram of body weight, which means a medium-sized human would have to swallow a liter of perfume before feeling seriously ill.

Most everything has the potential to become an allergen. Generally you have to be exposed to high doses many times, after which there is a small probability that it will cause you to develop an allergy. Very strong-smelling molecules are used in such small doses that it's unlikely you would have the exposure needed to generate allergies. Furthermore, very rare materials are unlikely to show up frequently enough to trigger enough allergies to be noticed. You'd therefore expect allergens to be common, relatively weak materials, and most are. A few unlucky people suffer from intense respiratory allergies, which can cause airway obstruction and can be life-threatening. These people deserve to have known allergens listed on the label, much like the nut warnings on food labels. The rest of us mostly risk skin rashes. We can either insist on everything being allergen free, which means reducing the perfumer's palette and our consequent pleasure, or spray the stuff on fabric when we know we have problems.

Headaches, however, are not allergic (i.e., immune) reactions. They are more like your response to fingernails screeching on a blackboard or very bright lights shining into your eyes: a reaction to jarring or overwhelming sensory input. (However, it's known that certain medical conditions, such as autism, can make individuals extremely sensitive to smells. To such people, even a mild smell can seem like a kind of pain.) We also live in such unsmelly times, with most everyone bathing and washing clothes regularly, and public sanitation working invisibly and reliably to sweep away the foul detritus of the day, that the ordinary person may find herself sensitive to fragrance the way you might find yourself sensitive to noise after spending a week at a spiritual retreat where everyone talks in whispers and walks in cotton socks. If you'd like to overcome a general oversensitivity about perfumes, the best cure is to find perfumes you like and to let them teach you to enjoy smelling beautiful things. If instead you'd rather demand that the world be utterly scent-free, you're a drag. LT/TS

Do fragrances harm the environment?

Someone once asked where smells eventually go when they dissipate in the air. The answer is they enter the great cycle of degradation and reuse that is the work of Mother Nature. Usually, this causes no problems. But some molecules were designed to be armor-plated to survive the hostile chemical environment of laundry soap. Some of the most successful aromachemicals of all time were musks, developed for laundry in the late 1950s, that did not get chewed up by microorganisms.

Because everyone does laundry, hundreds of tons of these musks were flushed into rivers and tended to persist for long periods in the environment. In the meantime, chemists got better and better at detecting their presence and found them in tiny amounts in fish and, worst of all, in mothers' milk. Never mind that a dozen other things from the mother's diet were likely there too; this one stuck in our collective throat.

Some have argued that since perfumes do no measurable good, the level of risk that can be tolerated in their use is zero. This appears to be the puritanical subtext to some recent legislation regulating fragrance. I take the view that, much in the way that Michelangelo's *David* can topple over and kill you or your chaud-froid de grives au Gevrey-Chambertin can result in a kitchen fire, all art forms provide beauty at the expense of some risk, and the ratio of risk to pleasure afforded by perfume is as low as any. Nobody ever died from wearing Mitsouko, but lots of babies were born as a result of it. LT

Will rubbing fragrance in "bruise" it?

Vigorously rubbing fragrance into your skin, as if it were an invigorating tonic or a splash of suntan oil, is pointless and detrimental. Occasionally sales associates will warn you off from merely pressing your wrists together to distribute fragrance, or otherwise lightly spreading it, by shouting, "You will bruise the molecules!" or something colorful like that. It is no trouble to lightly spread the fragrance evenly about. What's not good is to go grinding away. What you'll do is heat up the fragrance so that much of the scent will evaporate away before its time. When you smell it, it will probably be a sad shadow of what it is supposed to be, and you certainly will be missing the top notes. I have done the experiment, by spraying my left arm and letting it air per normal and spraying my right arm and rubbing it furiously against my shin. Try it and see. TS

▓ Should I change my fragrance for the season?

I have a thing for Diorissimo when it snows. If seasons are your excuse for buying lots of fragrances, in the belief that you need a year-round wardrobe, don't let us stop you. But don't feel duty-bound to stop wearing fruity florals in December. TS

▓ Do fragrances change according to the wearer's chemistry?

For a long time, LT believed the answer to be absolutely no, and that all assertions to the contrary were marketing ploys designed to make the average person feel uniquely addressed by and bonded to the product, as if the perfume were like a mood ring or shrink-to-fit jeans, sensitive to the wearer's medical history, soul, or waistline. There's something to that; undoubtedly it makes us feel special to sigh and say, "I love this perfume because it works fantastically with my chemistry." There is also a semipolite way to tell someone you would never in a million years wear his or her perfume, which goes, "Oh, that smells lovely on you. It just doesn't work with my chemistry." (This can also mean that you find the scent pleasant on someone else but tiresome to smell all day on your own arm.) Furthermore, salespeople at fragrance counters often tell overeager shoppers to "let the fragrance meld with your chemistry" after you spray it on. That's their way of telling you to wait a few hours before you judge it. That's not chemistry making the fragrance change. That's time.

Yet perfumers do test fragrances on various people's skins as they develop them, so the variation must make some difference. Specifically, individual skins seem to affect the top notes, which are the ones you smell in the store right after you spray the tester, and are therefore the ones that most companies spend a lot of time and money getting right (sometimes forgetting to bother about much else). The relative oiliness of your skin will affect the rate at which the scent evaporates; so will your skin temperature. If you and your friend spray on a scent at the same time, it will probably smell slightly different on each of you in the minutes afterward. But after a half hour or so, when the fragrance's heart emerges, these minor differences seem to disappear. That'll teach you to be impatient.

Nevertheless, if you think we are full of it, you can easily wear fragrances that you think you can't: as long as it won't stain, spray your clothes. TS

How can we judge perfume if we all smell things differently?

Mostly, we don't smell things differently—we interpret and describe them differently. We tend to do a lot better agreeing on food smells (garlic, bread, strawberries, roast duck) that have familiar real-world referents than with fine fragrance, which is often a complex mixture of unfamiliar smells to start with.

Our disagreements on smells seem to be mostly over what we like and don't like, and what they mean to us. Then there's the fact that when smelling complex compositions, we frequently recognize one element from having met it before in something else, such that if two people encounter the same perfume, one may claim that it smells like tomatoes while the other insists it smells like something burning, simply because they've latched on to separate elements of the same mixture and have ceased to perceive it as a whole. It's a bit like going to the same movie but finding afterward that one of you considered it a meditation on landscape while the other considered it a meditation on Brad Pitt. Same data, different filters. There's also the question of burnout: you cease to register odors after prolonged exposure (which is why you don't know what your home smells like), so testing several perfumes in a row generally means your perception of them will start to suffer. Certain overexposed florals are so blinding that they burn out everything except, in my experience, a lingering aroma of dill pickles. The whole trick of smelling a jar of coffee beans in between trials seems to be sort of useless. A time in the fresh air is, in my experience, the only effective cure. As for the gloried noses you've heard of, capable of detecting and identifying a wide variety of smells, having a "nose" really means having both a nose and a mind. In the absence of interfering medical problems, the nose is a remarkably sensitive instrument, although you may not pay much attention to the copious information it delivers because these days it's usually not a matter of life and death. If you were to heed smells as if they were important, thinking about them and describing them, you probably would find after a time that you could distinguish many more smells than you thought.

However, there are a few specific anosmias scattered throughout the population. *Anosmia* means the inability to smell a specific molecule, and in drastic cases it means the inability to smell at all. A few specific aromachemicals have a different smell for a small subset of the population. But these are biological anomalies, not a retreat into pure subjectivity. For the most part, the raw data you get are mostly the same as everyone else's, but the interpretation your mind makes (would you describe it as nice? nasty? a bit like soap? lemons? candy? floor wax?) may make it seem otherwise. TS

How do you choose which perfumes to review?

We review every fragrance we can get our hands on in the given time, if we are reasonably sure that our sample is the current formula and that the fragrance is available. We try to provide comprehensive coverage of brands when possible. TS

Why do you mention a perfume in one review and then fail to review it alone?

Fallibility. Or we failed to get a fresh sample. TS

Why don't you review discontinued fragrances?

We have reviewed a small number of discontinued and largely unsung fragrances (Yohji Homme, Le Feu d'Issey) in the faint hope that the gods will bring the dead back to life, but we do not have the resources to review all the fallen. Many great fragrances of the past are not covered here but are well known. Fortunately, there are several dedicated fragrance historians documenting the genre's past. We're mostly concerned with the present. TS

Why aren't fragrances marked as feminine or masculine?

This reminds me of George Saunders's "My Amendment" in the *New Yorker* in which he denounced "Samish-Sex Marriage." You will find, when reading the guide, that we sometimes mention the relative masculinity or femininity of a fragrance but that it does not always coincide with expectations. Given that fragrances have no genitalia, we refuse to remark further. You can find lots of gender-differentiated lists of fragrances online if you're interested. TS

What is a chypre?

It is common nowadays for fragrance firms to label "chypre" (pronounced *sheep-ruh* with that French gargling *r*) any fragrance at all, as long as it contains at least one patchouli, amber, or oakmoss material. However, proper classical chypres descend from Coty's original Chypre (French for Cyprus). If you can't find a bottle, you may study it indirectly: spray and label paper blotters with pre-2008 Givenchy III, Mitsouko, and Chanel Pour Monsieur. Wait fifteen minutes. That bitter, inky green (oakmoss), sweet-amber accord they have in common is what makes them all chypres. There are floral chypres, fruity chypres, citrus chypres, leather chypres, woody chypres, and so forth, all smell-ing very different but based on this accord. Lately, due to allergen re-strictions on oakmoss, perfumers have been trying to construct a chypre accord without it. These efforts can be very good, but they don't smell much like chypres. In fact, many classic chypres have been reformulated to remove oakmoss entirely, though the industry is seeking a work-around to remove only the specific chemical responsible for irritation while preserving the inimitable smell of the natural material. Until they find it, consider stocking up against the apocalypse. TS

How are the reviews done? Which concentration? Are they blind tests?

We spray paper blotters labeled with each fragrance name and observe their evolution over a few minutes. Those that are not obviously cheap, hastily hacked together rubbish, we test on skin—sometimes on both of us—for the day. Often we spray a blotter, leave it in the room for a bit, and come back to check the radiance. These are not blind tests, except in the case that one of us shouts spontaneously across the room, "Yuck!" or "Wow!" We sometimes discuss a scent at length before one of us writes the opinion. We use the highest concentration for which we have a sample, but if significant formula differences are known to exist be-tween concentrations, we review them separately. Price indications are added at the end, though occasionally, when relevant, we mention prices in the text. To save ourselves from boredom, we usually test more than one brand at a time, which also lends perspective. We refer to agreed-upon five-, four-, three-, two-, and one-star fragrances to determine where a fragrance falls in the range. We also dip into our private collec-tion of several thousand perfumes for comparisons. TS

■ **How can you agree on so much? Why aren't there more split reviews?**

When we disagree, one of three things happens: (1) a split review, (2) proselytizing followed by conversion, or (3) the author with the most favorable or interesting opinion writes the review. Most disagreements involve a difference of one star and are resolved by these methods. In these cases, it's just not worth the trouble of writing two opinions. When a specific anosmia (inability to smell), a hyposmia or a hyperosmia (under- or oversensitivity) results in vastly different perceptions—generally in the tricky realms of musks, woody ambers, and certain nitriles—we try to note this for the reader. TS

■ **For years my favorite perfume was such and such. Now it's discontinued. What is a similar perfume?**

Michael Edwards's singular resource *Fragrances of the World* (book or Web site) is designed to point you to fragrances in a similar genre. For example, he categorizes Poison as "Floral Oriental (Rich)" and points you to others in the same classification, of whatever quality. We hope merely to point you to good fragrances; not all five- and four-star fragrances will suit your taste, but trying them should be entertaining. At any rate, a quick search on eBay often turns up a bottle of something you thought was out of reach forever. TS

■ **I bought (name of perfume), and it doesn't smell the way I remember it. Why is this?**

Choose one: (1) your memory is wrong; (2) your old bottle changed over time with exposure to air, light, or heat; (3) the fragrance uses natural materials that vary in quality from year to year; (4) your fragrance used a material that is no longer available and had to be replaced; (5)

your fragrance had to be reformulated to adhere to new industry regulations on irritants, allergens, and toxicity; (6) your fragrance was reformulated by penny-pinching scoundrels to save costs, and they were hoping you wouldn't make a fuss; or (7) your fragrance was reformulated because a junior exec hoping for promotion led a focus-group study that determined the scent was "old-fashioned" and in need of sprucing up. Honest reformulations work with the best materials available to conserve the spirit of the fragrance despite changing circumstances; dishonest reformulations are done either without fidelity to the original or absent the necessary skill. We try to credit honesty and excoriate vandalism, which is why not all reformulations receive equal treatment in the guide. TS

Why don't you include the year of release, the official list of notes, the perfumer, etc., for every fragrance?

We have no passion for data entry. TS

I love (name of perfume) and (name of perfume) and (name of perfume) but I hate (names of perfumes). Can you tell me what my taste is or recommend something else to me?

What excellent taste you have! I recommend (randomly selected five-star fragrance not mentioned by you). TS

How can some retailers offer fragrances so cheap? Are they authentic?

Authorized retailers get fragrances from authorized distributors. Authorized by whom? By the manufacturers. So their stock is guaranteed authentic because the manufacturer can tell where each bottle came from and through which hands it passed. In contrast, the gray or parallel market, which generally pays less overhead for trained staff and swank digs, sources its fragrances outside the official chain. For example, you're a buyer for a store that sells perfume cheaper than department stores or has been turned down by the manufacturer as an authorized retailer because you lack prestige. So you shop around the world and end up buying fragrances cheap from a foreign market, where local competition or currency exchange rates bring the price down; you also might buy factory overstock or clearance or discontinued goods, or the stock of retailers or distributors going out of business.

These products are often totally authentic, but because the exact provenance of each fragrance isn't verified at each step, you sometimes chance, if you're not careful, buying damaged stock or even counterfeits. (Of course, some people sell only counterfeits. I'm thinking of a cheerful New York Chinatown shop owner with a wall of designer fragrances, who told me openly, "All fake.") Many gray-market retailers guarantee freshness and authenticity and say they take returns if you get a bum bottle, though reputations vary for making good on that. Some brands almost never sell at discount unless they're fake, because stock is strictly controlled. Oddly, some brands appear to be sold only at discount, perhaps because their authorized distribution is completely outside the country. Gray-market supplies also tend to be unreliable, in that something you bought at one price three months ago may never come back at that price (or any other) again.

Naturally, fragrance manufacturers hate the gray market. They gripe that it tolerates counterfeits and interferes with brand image control. For example, how can you respect a Givenchy fragrance when you buy it for $30 in a stall with peeling paint under the freeway? (The obvious answer is: without fail, if it's real Givenchy III; impossible, if it's real Very Irrésistible, even if you pay $300 and it's wrapped in silk ribbon by four bona fide princesses with graduate degrees.) If these whingers were not the same people who rhapsodize about rare Himalayan orchids in connection with yet another Tommy Girl knockoff at four times the price, one might have sympathy. If they never flooded the markets with product when it suited their year-end numbers, one might tut-tut about all this dirty capitalism undercutting their margins. If they priced each fragrance according to actual cost of manufacture, one might be alarmed at the discount at the drugstore. But no. At least at this moment in the United States, it is still legal to buy and sell perfumes through unauthorized distributors, and free marketeers point out that parallel markets help consumers by encouraging retailers to make prices more competitive worldwide. Besides, do fragrance makers really think that in the age of Internet shopping and cheap shipping they'll be able to sell the exact same product overseas at a fraction of the price without anyone noticing? To sum up, the gray market can often give you a great deal but with a touch more risk. TS

> Why has Amarige got only one star, while it is in a top ten list in the back?

Amarige is a genius work of perfumery, utterly recognizable, memorable, technically polished, and spectacularly loud. But we hate it. In the end, we figured this was the fair thing to do. TS

> I love an expensive perfume. Can you recommend one just like it but cheaper?

Never just like it. TS

> How can I stop myself from buying so much perfume while I'm reading this book?

A worrisome number of readers have told us that they stopped buying groceries because they are buying perfume. Even if your doctor has ordered you to lose weight, you must be reasonable. You do not want to be the best-smelling resident of the area under your local bridge. Try giving yourself an allowance of $50, $75, or $100 per month, depending on circumstances, to buy perfume. If this doesn't work, fragrance junkies online have come up with solutions. There is the "split," whereby several people divide the cost by buying one big fragrance and several empty bottles and, using a little funnel, splitting the liquid up into portions. This requires several persons who all want the same perfume, which is why this solution did not arise until Internet message boards came along. There are also "decants," which operate on similar principle: a single enterprising person, anticipating demand, buys the fragrance and splits it into various little bottles for sale or trade online. Fragrance producers hate decants. Their reasons are confused. Partly, they are obsessed with brand control and despise the idea of their product being sold in unauthorized packaging, into which it is dispensed in who knows what conditions, and partly they have the curious notion that this undercuts their sales. Given that the people decanting pay for the fragrance and increase its exposure and market, this last objection makes no sense, but some brands pride themselves on being unknown and unavailable. Fortunately, an increasing number of fragrance firms have noticed the thriving business of decants and are now competing by offering smaller sizes, with lots of one-ounce bottles and more travel sprays, so again, capitalism is operating as it should. T S

▪ **A sales associate told me a perfume you reviewed either (1) was discontinued or (2) never existed. What is going on?**

Likely, you have been misinformed. Example: A reader wrote us to complain that her local Chanel beauty-counter staffer denied that the brand had ever in recorded history created a fragrance called No. 18. When our review was shown to this staffer, she reportedly snorted that she was trained to know all there was to know about the brand, and what are you going to do, trust a couple of total unknowns? Interesting point. (No. 18 is exclusive to stand-alone Chanel boutiques and certain high-end retailers, such as Bergdorf Goodman in New York and Selfridges in London.) To be fair, not every Chanel beauty-counter staffer is pompous and misinformed, but *at least one is.*

Second example: A journalist to whom we had recommended Bulgari Black phoned us in a panic to inform us that a beauty-counter staffer at a London department store had assured her the product was discontinued. We contacted Bulgari, in a panic ourselves, and received reassurance that it was still being made. (It is frequently confined to the men's section, probably because the bottle looks like a tire.) Nevertheless, we continue to receive reports of its demise, along with rumors of the death of any number of other beloved but rarely stocked fragrances.

Fragrances are in fact discontinued all the time, but sales staffers are notorious for swearing things are nonexistent simply because they don't stock them. If in doubt, search online or contact the maker. Even official press offices have been known to misinform, though, so the truth is difficult to discover. If you have been egregiously lied to, you might want to drop a line to the staffer's manager or to the manufacturer, explaining why you're buying all your stuff on the Internet from now on unless they buy a copy of this guide for every employee on their payroll pronto. If we're just plain wrong, please let us know at mail@perfumestheguide.com. TS

PERFUME REVIEWS

Ratings

★ ★ ★ ★ ★ MASTERPIECE

★ ★ ★ ★ RECOMMENDED

★ ★ ★ GOOD

★ ★ NOT RECOMMENDED

★ AVOID

Two words preceding each review describe the fragrance's main character. When the reviewers disagree, two ratings are given. Ratings represent the reviewer or reviewers' recommendation and not objective point scales: please be sure to read the full review and test the fragrance personally before buying. We try to assess the most recent formulations from samples obtained directly from firms. Bear in mind that many shops, especially if independently owned, may carry older stock, which may differ in formula or which may have changed over time, especially if bottles have been exposed to air, light, or heat.

Price

$$$$ OVER $200

$$$ FROM $101 TO $200

$$ FROM $51 to $100

$ FROM $1 to $50

Our indications are based on the standard U.S. retail price of the smallest full-size bottle of the lowest concentration in standard distribution. For example, we will take into account an individually sold one-ounce eau de toilette, but not an eighth-ounce parfum sold only as part of a gift set. We also do not count concentrations below eau de toilette or lotions, soaps, etc. Because sizes, concentrations, and cost of materials vary widely, price indications are intended to help readers shop for fragrances in a given price range and should not be interpreted as a measure of value for money.

5th Avenue (Elizabeth Arden) ★ ★ *soapy floral* $
Brings to mind the ambitiously dull suit a girl picks for her first job interview, to convince the interviewer she's a perfect fit because she's no fun. This is a variation on the aldehydic floral in nineties fashion—i.e., with a pale, sour, fruity-floral top note; a faint nondescript floral sweetness; and not much going on otherwise. TS

10 Corso Como (10 Corso Como) ★ ★ ★ *sweet woody* $$
This used to be a huge agarwood-sandalwood, and the sandalwood is now small, no doubt due to supply problems. Pleasant and well crafted nevertheless. LT

21 Costume National (Costume National) ★ ★ ★ *anisic oriental* $$
Like the rest of the Costume National range, this sheer, probably entirely synthetic composition favors radiance over anything else. Smells like Prada's first patchouli amber seen through frosted glass. TS

24, Faubourg (Hermès) ★ ★ ★ ★ *honeyed floral* $$
24, Faubourg is a set piece in the grand French manner of the nineties, a style that has not aged well. The name refers to the address of the Hermès flagship store in what was once a suburb (faux bourg) of Paris and is now the city's Fifth Avenue: rue du Faubourg St. Honoré. Like its contemporaries Samsara and Boucheron, it is the perfumery equivalent of a team of eight pulling a gilt carriage: great for a château wedding, slightly embarrassing to be seen in at a traffic light. I believe this overegged fashion was started by the great composition firm of Firmenich, who took the view that an aromachemicals manufacturer should

sell aromachemicals, not plant extracts. Taking their lead, everyone at the time strove for compositions incorporating a minimum of natural materials while remaining richly complex. This gave rise to byzantine formulas several hundred lines long, achieving density at the expense of clarity. Thanks to Maurice Roucel's brilliance, this one is probably the best of the lot. Though it is almost bewilderingly symphonic, 24 is best enjoyed, in my opinion, the way one would appreciate a great Sauternes swirling around the tongue: if you focus on the fine detail, you can identify floral, honey, iris, and woody notes amid the glorious rush of aromas, but if you step back, what strikes you is the balance between acidity and sweetness, which Roucel got perfectly right. It must have been tricky to do, and probably nothing of the sort will ever be achieved again. Note that the parfum is slightly different, lusher than the other concentrations. LT

28 La Pausa (Chanel) ★ ★ ★ ★ *woody iris* $$$
Iris root is the dominant theme of Chanel's boutique fragrances, and it's easy to see why. It smells great, at one point cost a fortune (upward of $30,000 per kilogram), and adds the surest touch of luxury to any fragrance. Cuir de Russie has a huge iris note, as do No. 18, No. 19, and 31 Rue Cambon. Until its unusual and refined vetiver drydown emerges, 28 La Pausa is almost an iris soliflore (or would that be *soliradix,* for iris root?). The richness of iris can then be enjoyed at leisure, from bread to truffle via woody violets and powdery leather. If you must have iris, the choice is between this lovely, very natural composition and Maurice Roucel's great, no-holds-barred semisynthetic Iris Silver Mist (Serge Lutens). LT

31 Rue Cambon (Chanel) ★ ★ ★ ★ ★ (★ ★ ★ ★) *floral ambery* $$$
I cannot remember the last time, if ever, a perfume gave me such an instantaneous impression of ravishing beauty at first sniff. There is an affecting softness, a gentle grace to 31 that beggars belief. Such a classical masterpiece must, by definition, be standing on the shoulders of

giants, and identifying them can be a compelling game. At times 31 brings to mind the old Chant d'Arômes, before Guerlain messed with it. There is also a touch of the first Dioressence, that overripe, blowsy milky-fruity note of lactones that Gucci Rush took to its logical extreme. But Chant d'Arômes was demure, Dioressence come-hither, and Rush a monochrome. Chanel's 31 does not play games, try to seduce, or attempt to be modern. Perhaps the real precursor of 31 is that flawed masterpiece, Yves Saint Laurent's Champagne. Champagne too was a soft, fruity chypre, but its brassy, plangent treatment of the theme suggested the decadence of a once-great lineage. By contrast, 31 shows that in the higher reaches of art, time is suspended. One of the ten greats of all time, and precious proof that perfumery is not yet dead. LT

In the press pack for 31 Rue Cambon, Chanel boasts of having composed a chypre fragrance without the sine qua non: oakmoss, a resin extracted from a lacy lichen that looks something like frisée and grows mainly on oak trees in Eastern Europe. When cooked into usable form, it becomes a thick goo with a medieval fairy-tale smell of smoke, ink, and forest mulch, which gives the rich and sweet chypre idea its bitter backbone. So what is a chypre without oakmoss? An exercise in illusion via allusion. By arranging a series of familiar cues, 31 Rue Cambon calls to mind other great fragrances, older and recent, and makes you imagine the missing element. That rich iris beginning, substituting a nose-ticklingly dry pepper for the leather, promises Chanel's own Cuir de Russie; floating in and out of focus is the jasmine heart of Diorella, fizzy and bright as cold 7UP; you find a lemon-custard moment that makes you think briefly of Shalimar Light, among others; and oh, that big, singing amber, didn't you meet it in Guerlain's Guet-Apens? This fragrance was designed to claim a great inheritance, and it fits in the family portrait perfectly. Elsewhere, LT compared its beauty to Grace Kelly lighting up the room in *Rear Window*. Yet Kelly's beauty lacked content. Compare hers to the melancholy sensuality of Rita Hayworth (or Baghari), the girlish ferocity of Bette Davis (Jolie Madame), or the carnivorous threat of Ava Gardner (Tabac Blond). I find 31 Rue Cambon lovely but not moving because not strange. But perhaps it's just not strong enough. While writing this, I've had to cram my wrist to my nose to smell it at all. Rumor has it that Chanel is hard at work formulating a parfum: let's hope they make it richer and more definite in character. I suspect this slightly inchoate thing could be coaxed into greatness. In the meantime, try on fabric to slow the slideshow. TS

100% Love (S-Perfume) ★ ★ ★ ★ ★ *chocolate rose* $$$
In case anyone still wondered, given the stellar record of great perfume impresarios like Vera Strubi (Angel) and Chantal Roos (Opium), niche firms have demonstrated beyond doubt how important art direction is to getting a perfume right. A well-funded perfume lover may be able to convince talented perfumers to compose for his firm, but mere artistic freedom and a large budget seldom give rise to great perfumes unless the composers are given an idea to work toward and are held to it through what can be a long and painful editing process. Nobi Shioya (his artistic nom de guerre is Sacré Nobi), though we have never met, strikes me from his works as a guy who desires things that are far from obvious and does not rest until he gets them. 100% Love is a case in point. It was lovely in the first version, but clearly not enough. The great, the trismegista Sophia Grojsman recomposed it after only a couple of years. Maybe my day job as a scientist has led me to put too high a value on the novel and the unexpected, but I must say that very seldom (in fact not since 1992) have I had such a feeling of surprise and delighted incomprehension when first smelling a fragrance. Oddness is easy to achieve—there are many accords nobody ever made—and coziness and comfort too, provided one sticks to the featherbed materials of perfumery: rose, vanilla, chocolate, etc. But to achieve both superlative oddness and mind-numbing comfort at the same time is pure brilliance. If there is a parallel universe in which smells are theorems, 100% Love would be something like a proof of Riemann's conjecture. LT

154 Cologne (Jo Malone) ★ ★ *dry wood* $ $
Bare-bones metallic-woody "sport" fragrance for men, not very good but not tenacious either. LT

212 (Carolina Herrera) ★ *harsh floral* $ $
Like getting lemon juice in a paper cut. TS

212 Men (Carolina Herrera) ★ ★ *woody green* $ $
An initially interesting, jarring milky-herbal note seems to presage L'Eau Bleue (Miyake) but settles for being a rather thin green-woody scent of no distinction. TS

212 Sexy Men (Carolina Herrera) ★ *musky oriental* $
Curried Gaultier2. TS

888 (Comme des Garçons) ★ ★ ★ *floral tea* $ $ $
There is about CdG in general (clothes as well as perfumes) a made-for-effect sloppiness, an inattention to detail that makes for ephemeral creations even when influential. In perfumery CdG were no doubt the first in the early nineties to see the import of Mark Buxton's brilliantly innovative ideas, and the packaging was perfect. They went on to take a scattershot approach and create far too many fragrances, launching between four and seven every year for a sum total of forty-nine to date. None that I have smelled so far are awful, many were pathbreaking, but like most trendy things they are not aging well. The recent 888 exemplifies what feels like an exhausted artistic tendency. A woody-floral tea, too little too late. LT

1000 (Jean Patou) ★ ★ ★ ★ *dry chypre* $ $ $
I have never been particularly fond of 1000. It always struck me as needlessly complex and hard to read, like an experimental novel beloved of critics that you take on holiday resolving to finish at last but swap at the airport for a Robert Ludlum thing with a cracking yarn. Upon smelling

it again for this guide, I was struck by the fact that while it is still to my mind a stylish but somewhat dowdy, deep-voiced, flat-pumps-and-string-of-pearls feminine, it would make one hell of a masculine in the Derby-Fahrenheit axis. Go, guys! LT

1270 (Frapin) ★ ★ ★ *spiced raisin* $$$
Unquestionably the most ambitious of the Frapin fragrances to date, 1270 uses to great effect a plangent, overripe raisin-persimmon note (likely a Robertet specialty) most recently found at the core of Amouage's two Lyric fragrances. This material always threatens to tip a fragrance over into the territory of wine dregs left in a glass overnight, which would be a shame for a firm like Frapin, which is chiefly known as a distiller of cognac. Nevertheless, in this skillful composition it just about works to produce an atmosphere of dusky autumnal warmth. LT

1725 (Histoires de Parfums) ★ ★ ★ ★ *anisic lavender* $$$
Anisic notes are hard to handle in perfumery: they are sweetly happy on their own (few things smell better than star anise in a bag) but usually stand out in ensemble playing as a pan flute would in a string quartet. This clever fragrance associates two such notes, licorice and star anise, to a lavender-citrus structure and somehow clips the whole thing together with a touch of heliotropin and cedarwood. Top and heart are wonderfully melodious, and the drydown comes close enough to L'Heure Bleue to feel its gravitational pull, but then escapes again. Very good. LT

1740 (Histoires de Parfums) ★ ★ ★ ★ ★ *leather immortelle* $$$
Familiarity with too many trivial perfumes can at length turn one into a libertine of smell: cynical, unmoved, cruelly practical. But every old roué hides at his core an unblemished memory of the boy he once was, ready to fall for the first creature whose intelligence revives his freeze-dried heart. I felt something give way when I smelled 1740: the shimmering classical accord of leather, immortelle, spice, rich pipe

tobacco, and a sort of lived-in buttery warmth is simply irresistible. And why resist? LT

1804 (Histoires de Parfums) ★ ★ ★ ★ *spicy floral* $$$
Histoires de Parfums demolishes a tired cliché, namely that "those who can't do, teach." Most HdP fragrances are composed by Sylvie Jourdet, professor of olfaction and perfumery accords at the ISIPCA in Versailles. She is also vice president of the French Society of Perfumers. Smelling her "date" fragrances for HdP makes me want to drop everything and go listen adoringly to her every word. Rejoice, perfume lovers, not only is perfumery not dead, but a new generation of perfumers is imbibing high art. Histoires de Parfums contrives to produce, time after time, the most beguiling top notes in contemporary perfumery, with good raw materials orchestrated to produce both a legible structure and a rich texture. Its 1804 applies this treatment to a warm floral oriental. If this fragrance fails to lift your spirits, you are in trouble. LT

1826 (Histoires de Parfums) ★ ★ ★ ★ *woody musk* $$$
In simple, familiar things, detail and quality of materials are all. It's true that 1826 is a very gentle, old-fashioned floral musk. But it's far from a crude accord: this is a white-on-white construction of tints and textures, from a sheer celadon-shaded top note as crisp as iced gin to a serene dove gray middle section of creamy musks, incense, and anise. Strangely radiant, it seems stronger at arm's length and seems to vanish up close. Several hours later, a sleek, impeccable patchouli-labdanum drydown in the classical style sneaks in. TS

1828 (Histoires de Parfums) ★ ★ ★ ★ *nutmeg wood* $$$
HdP's 1828 achieves something I never thought would happen: it retroactively makes me appreciate Cacharel pour l'Homme. I now see that the nutmeg accord that made it so memorably unpleasant was not wrong, just badly executed; 1828 sets the record straight with excellent raw materials and achieves a direct, effortless, virile elegance. LT

1872 for Men (Clive Christian) ★ ★ ★ *sweet citrus* $$$$
A pleasant but slightly phony costume-drama fragrance made up of
equal parts classic 1870s woody-resinous (say Penhaligon's Lords), 1970s
citrus, and a weird, Gucci Rush–like lactonic accord, as if the suave
character turned up on set in his green velvet dinner jacket, a little di-
sheveled after a broom-closet encounter with a lady doused in Clive
Christian's X. LT

1872 for Women (Clive Christian) ★ *green floral* $$$$
A weird, chemical thing that smells the way cheap shampoo tastes when
you inadvertently open your mouth while showering. LT

1873 (Histoires de Parfums) ★ ★ ★ ★ *grapefruit floral* $$$
Guerlain's Aqua Allegoria Pamplelune is probably the most successful
fragrance ever built around the deeply sulfurous, bitter note of grape-
fruit peel, but 1873 runs a close second. It nicks from AAP the trick of
giving the accord needed depth and persistence with sweet floral and
vanilla notes; ultimately the basic structure is a beautiful orange-blos-
som oriental that shares something with L'Heure Bleue. Excellent, clever
work. TS

1876 (Histoires de Parfums) ★ ★ ★ ★ *masculine rose* $$$
Unquestionably, and by a huge margin, the best Victorian dandy fra-
grance around: citrus, rose, benzoin, spices, and animalic notes, all of
excellent quality, soft, restful, discreet, sweetly melancholic. What Floris's and Penhaligon's dandiacal scents should have been doing all along,
had they the good fortune of an art director as imaginative and skilled
as Gérard Ghislain. LT

1969 (Histoires de Parfums) ★ ★ ★ ★ *rose peach* $$$
Contains one of the most magnificent top notes of all time: a golden late
summer landscape of every joyful childhood, with a sky painted in huge

vanilla and rose slashes, in the manner of Tocade, above shadowed woods of fruit and cedar as in Féminité du Bois. In a spirit similar to Chamade, 1969 dawdles happily for some time in a midregion of rose, fruit, and amber that feels so perfect you fear it can't go on, but unlike the spectacular Chamade it doesn't; the Chinatown-type drydown is still lovely to wear but nowhere near as grand. You'll want to keep spraying it on paper to play the first part again. TS

1 Million (Paco Rabanne) ★ ★ *sweet apple* $ $
As befits someone who claims to be the reincarnation of an Egyptian high priest and to possess visionary powers, Paco Rabanne's fragrances appear to be leading indicators of investment opportunities. Calandre (radiator grille) was released at a time when you could still buy a '67 Ferrari Berlinetta for a song, Métal heralded the rise in demand for and the price of ores, and now, three months before the turmoil on Wall Street, comes a masculine fragrance shaped like a gold ingot. I shall be watching future releases closely. A weird fragrance, 1 Million is a marriage of two distinct perfumery ideas that have never before been squished together: the tired apple tendency of Cool Water and the musky, Levantine hair-gel feel of Caron's No. 3. Trouble is, the second idea quickly vanishes, leaving the first all by itself. LT

Absinth (Nasomatto) ★ ★ *woody oakmoss* $ $
Nasomatto (crazy nose) is an Italian niche perfumery established in 2007. If the volume button on Absinth were turned way down, this fragrance would be a pleasant enough cross between joss sticks and Lutens's Chêne. At this decibel level, however, it's air care (as the room-freshener industry euphemizes it) for those past caring. LT

Absolutely Irrésistible (Givenchy) ★ ★ ★ *citrus floral* $ $
Unexpectedly, the 5,467th flanker to the horrible and horribly successful Very Irrésistible is only mostly horrible. The core orange-blossom accord is impressively good. Everything else is bad. You still should not

wear it, but if you've been following the incomprehensible decline of the once-respectable Parfums Givenchy, you may appreciate any evidence of a flattening of the curve. TS

Acaciosa (Caron) ★ *soapy floral* $ $
I am genuinely perplexed. Acaciosa was a grand jasmine, like Joy with a naughty streak, darkened with amber and an animalic honey note with all of its soiled-underwear connotations, plus a surprising tart pineapple in the top note. It was like that decades ago, if my collector friend's old bottle is accurate, and it was like that a few years ago when I bought mine. It's now a soapy-woody floral of not much character, brought into line with the rest, as if its previous distinctiveness were considered rude. TS

Acier Aluminium (Creed) ★ ★ ★ *amber banana* $ $ $
The name leads you to believe you'll get a metallic sporty fragrance. Instead you get a sort of banana-jam oriental. Very good materials, very confused composition. TS

Acqua di Giò (Armani) ★ ★ ★ ★ *melon muguet* $ $
There is a fragrance equivalent to those interiors you see in modern design magazines—vast lofts inhabited sparsely by white cubes and stainless steel tubing; layouts that contractually allow the decorator to sue you if your child jams SpongeBob figurines between the cushions. It is the clean floral of the nineties, and wearing one is like believing your lifestyle can accommodate white carpet. All descend from Diorissimo, the great lily of the valley that first perfected the ideal of lemon-scented morning sunlight without sin, and Cristalle, our lady of the green fruity-floral without mercy—both ultimately ideas of Edmond Roudnitska's. In Acqua di Giò (1995), Edouard Fléchier and Françoise Caron—two tremendous talents capable of creating rich, distinctive compositions out of inexpensive materials—engineered the hybrid hygienic floral in its present form, with the addition of a now-ubiquitous melon-aquatic fresh smell. The drydown reveals that even peach scents can be made

unfriendly. This road leads to Tommy Girl, Envy, and the entire race of American florals saving themselves for marriage. An excellent piece of perfumery. Get your feet off the furniture. TS

Acqua di Giò pour Homme (Armani) ★ ★ ★ *citrus rosemary* $ $
The team of perfumers credited with this fragrance is an all-star lineup—Morillas, Ménardo, Buzantian, Cavallier—so it's a surprise that the scent itself is so ho-hum: an aquatic citrus with woody notes and a dash of cooking herbs. TS

Acqua di Parma (Acqua di Parma) ★ ★ ★ *floral cologne* $ $
A pleasant quality cologne distinguished from the standard-issue genre by a generous floral heart accord of rose and ylang, which gives it an Edwardian feel. No great shakes, but very presentable. LT

Acqua di Parma Colonia Assoluta (Acqua di Parma) ★ ★ ★ ★
refined cologne $ $
When you know that this fragrance was composed by Bertrand Duchaufour and Jean-Claude Elléna, you wonder what such a dream team can do with a classical structure, and how it compares with the AdP Colonia. The answer is less citrus, less floral, and a far more interesting drydown in, dare I say it, a classical fougère style. LT

Acqua di Parma Profumo (Acqua di Parma) ★ ★ ★ ★
plum chypre $ $ $ $
If every fine fragrance innovation post-1980 has left you feeling as crankily abandoned as steady listeners to Roberta Flack and Al Green must feel when they hear rap on the radio, cheer up: good times are returning. Acqua di Parma is the latest brand backtracking to the point before fragrance went seriously wrong, to find an alternate way forward. Here we stand in the firmly old-fashioned realm of Rochas Femme and Diorama, in that autumnal, port-wine richness of serious fragrance

never intended to be worn while playing soccer. This is staid but solid perfumery, so convincing a period piece it seems likely this is an old formula rebottled. TS

Acqua di Sale (Profumum) ★ *helional alone* $$$$
Profumum, or as they spell it in imitation of Bulgari, Profvmvm, is the reference pretentious niche firm for those who are sure of nothing except that they do not want to wear fragrances their mothers-in-law have heard of. The Web site has a background track of bad lounge jazz and is full of pointless Flash stuff that takes ages to load. The texts scale new heights (even in Italian, never mind in translation) of remedial poetasterdom. Acqua di Sale is a gloss on Diptyque's Virgilio that substitutes cheap shampoo for the original's vetiver and misses the point by miles. LT

Adidas Moves (Adidas) ★ ★ *citrus woody* $
Claiming in its press material to contain deliriously surreal fictions such as "adrenaline accord" and "intuition accord" as well as the mind-blowing "waterfall," Adidas Moves is a dull, fresh-citrus sport fragrance with one pleasant fruity moment, quickly eclipsed. TS

Adidas Moves 0:01 (Adidas) ★ *green woody* $
Synthetic citrus, green-herbal, and woody-amber horror, like rubbing alcohol mixed with Palmolive dishwashing liquid. TS

Adidas Moves for Her (Adidas) ★ ★ *citrus woody* $
This appears to be nearly identical to the masculine Adidas Moves, only with the words *for Her* appended and the fragrance made slightly more masculine by the removal of some sweetness. TS

Adventure (Gant) ★ *watery citrus* $
Utterly nondescript herbaceous metallic "sport" fragrance. Makes you want to write a guide to sneakers. LT

Aedes de Venustas (L'Artisan Parfumeur) ★ ★ ★ ★ *incense rose* $$$
Aedes.com only
Bertrand Duchaufour's masterful incense fragrances—Timbuktu, Dzongkha, Jubilation XXV—make austerity seem rich, as it does in Rembrandt's portraits of burghers, whose penitent black and white costumes are clearly cut of luxurious cloth. These smell like ceremonial fragrances, and they decorate the wearer with a cloud of holy smoke or smear of ash. But they are also cathedral sized, using huge woody ambers to extend their reach, which can make them difficult to wear. In contrast, AdV is an incense for a domestic ceremony, scaled to a private room, and it brings to mind the generous gesture with which, when the Chinese drink excellent tea, the host passes about the dry leaves first to let you smell their unexpectedly complicated air of plum, rose, hay, and cedar, before they awake in water. TS

Affection (Mary Kay) ★ ★ ★ *spicy oriental* $
A surprisingly successful blast from the past, twenty years ago, when everyone was looking for an Opium Lite. Coco was then declared the winner, though in my opinion Krizia's Teatro alla Scala was even better and remained unknown. This one smells cheaper, more floral, and less resinous than TaS, but fine nevertheless in that spicy warm way that feels both dated and just about ready for a comeback. LT

Ageless Fantasy (Harvey Prince) ★ ★ *Tommy crone* $$$
"Inspired by recent scientific discoveries and clinical trials, we have developed a perfume called AGELESS FANTASY™. . . . Our patent-pending fragrance elixir defies your skin's natural age-revealing scent. Research has proven that men around women who use Ageless Fantasy™ believe them to be at least 8 years younger!" Pear-melon version of Tommy Girl, if you're wondering. LT

Agent Provocateur (Agent Provocateur) ★ ★ ★ *throwback rose* $$
Everything old is new again: as those with long memories have pointed

out, this is essentially a repeat of Jean Couturier's Coriandre from 1973 for the good-natured tarts too young to have worn it the first time. That said, it's fine, big, and rosy, a bit too strong (like everything in its class) with a pale woody base smelling like a fresh ream of office paper. TS

Agent Provocateur DD "Diamond Dust" (Agent Provocateur)
★ ★ ★ ★ *rose chypre* $ $ $
I know this is supposed to be the original fragrance in a limited edition bottle with diamond dust in it to sound impressive. So why is it better than the original? What kind of a crazy perfume brand improves the formula without telling anyone? Now the dark, fruity damascone aspect is turned on full blast, radiating to every corner of the party. TS

Agent Provocateur Strip (Agent Provocateur) ★ ★ ★ ★
tea chypre $ $
It seems that this stripper just performed a lapdance for a client wearing Old Spice and came away smelling great. Strip is a terrific, peppery-green tea rose with an icy angle of iris and citrus, and the sweet balsamic resin of labdanum for a friendly feeling. It smells confident and unusual, and doesn't feel embarrassingly as if you're trying too hard to make a splash. Dear Cartier, take note: this upstart panty firm just had your Baiser du Dragon for lunch. TS

Agua Verde (Salvador Dalí) ★ ★ ★ *spicy vetiver* $ $
Discreet, complex, and entirely agreeable herbaceous-spicy vetiver accord. LT

Aimez Moi (Caron) ★ ★ ★ ★ *violet vanilla* $ $
With a needier name and more relaxed requirements than N'Aimez que Moi (Love Only Me), Aimez Moi benefits from being a far simpler fragrance with modest aims. It begins with a pretty fresh violet and ends in sweet powdery vanilla, and has a humor and cheer largely missing from Caron's current lineup of feminines. TS

L'Air de Rien (Miller Harris) ★ ★ ★ ★ *Khyber Pass* $$$

The prodigiously airheaded Jane Birkin (terrible singer, lousy actress, thirty years in France and still sounding like she got off the Folkestone ferry yesterday) apparently never could find a fragrance to her taste, so Miller Harris made one. If, having lived the late sixties to the full, you cannot remember a thing about them, this will jog your memory. It smells of boozy kisses, stale joss sticks, rising damp, and soiled underwear. I love it. LT

L'Air du Désert Marocain (Tauer Perfumes) ★ ★ ★ ★ ★ *incense oriental* $$

The sweet smell of amber, the foundation of the classic perfume oriental, has long been weighed down with vanilla and sandalwood, decorated with mulling spices, bolstered with musk, made come-hither, ready for its close-up, and we are quite used to it—but this is not amber's first life. *Perfume* meant first "through smoke," named for fragrant materials burned to clean the air and therefore the spirit. If, as Carlos Santana claimed in his Grammy acceptance speech, the angel Metatron delivers messages to the world via rock guitarists, it only makes sense that the as-yet-unnamed angel of perfume speaks through an unassuming Swiss chemist from Zurich with a mustache and a buttoned shirt. L'Air du Désert Marocain is talented amateur perfumer Andy Tauer's second fragrance, after the rich oriental rose of Maroc pour Elle. One hale breath of Désert's vast spaces clears the head of all the world's nonsense. There is something about the ancient smell of these resins (styrax, frankincense) that on first inhalation strikes even this suburban American Protestant with no memories of mass as entirely holy, beautiful, purifying, lit without shadow from all sides. Even without the fragrance's name to prompt me, I would still feel the same peace when smelling it that I've felt only once before, when driving across the southwestern desert one morning: all quiet, no human habitation for miles, the upturned bowl of the heavens infinitely high above, and the sage and occasional quail clutching close to the dun earth. Each solitary object stood supersaturated with itself, full to the brim, sure to spill over if subjected to the slightest nudge. Wear this fragrance and feel the cloudless sky rush far away above you. TS

L'Air du Temps (Nina Ricci) ★ ★ *lily amber* $ $
The basic floral accord—a spicy, green, fresh, ambery bouquet—of L' Air du Temps (1948) was nothing new, but what made it and many other fifties florals great was the silken, fresh texture of benzyl salicylate, which a few people perceive as an intensely green-ambery floral note, but many people, including a number of perfumers and myself, can scarcely smell at all. Curiously, even people anosmic to the odor character of the material can smell its effect, which dresses otherwise familiar florals in satin: high gloss, weighty drape. Since benzyl salicylate was restricted as an allergen, florals haven't been the same. Today, L'Air du Temps is still, if you squint and concentrate, roughly recognizable: a lily with a salty amber background. Yet the quality has been horribly diminished over the years, worn so thin that you see its bones and nothing else. TS

L'Air du Temps parfum Anniversary Edition (Nina Ricci)
★ ★ ★ *floral chypre* $ $ $ $
This one came in a huge, black glass bottle with that most old-fashioned thing, a ground glass stopper. In times of vandalism and mediocrity, it is easy to succumb to nostalgia and to love beyond reason any relic of the past. This commendable restoration of L'Air du Temps to its 1948 glory shows it to be what it always was, an abstract floral with good bone structure, a sentimental heart, and a touch of the mean streak that was then deemed attractive in a pretty girl. LT

Aki (Tann Rokka) ★ *floral mess* $ $ $
A sweet floral disaster. LT

Alamut (Lorenzo Villoresi) ★ *hideous oriental* $ $ $
Lorenzo Villoresi is an Italian perfumer whose Web site puts forth an

idea of handmade, artisanal natural essences straight from the land, and whose perfumes put forth no ideas at all. Alamut seems to be almost a parody of a heavy-hitting oriental in that old-fashioned, dense-as-lead, potpourri, woody-powdery way, a miasma that rules of civilized warfare would forbid using on the enemy. TS

A La Nuit (Serge Lutens) ★ ★ ★ *jasmine jasmine* $$$
Death by jasmine. TS

Alba (Profumum) ★ *hazelnut coffee* $$$$
Alba means "dawn," and not since Ogni Moskvy (Fires of Moscow) was a fragrance so ineptly named. This emetically vile composition smells like a cross between Tia Maria and floor cleaner. LT

Aldehyde 44 (Le Labo) ★ ★ ★ *pale aldehydic* $$$$
From their gorgeous Web site to their Soviet sanatorium–style New York shop, Le Labo is so hip it hurts. They initially refused to send us samples, one of only two firms to do so. The reasons given? "We don't believe in critics in perfumery" and "We believe that writing about perfume is like dancing about architecture." Helpfully, though, they were also of the opinion that "if there were some more good evaluators in the press, some brands would be more afraid to launch a new crap [*sic*]." Confused? I was, but TS sorted them out. They relented when they discovered that we could smell their stuff anyway. Their philosophy appears to be that less is more, as long as it's French. I've long felt that French arrogance is fun in homeopathic doses, less so in large dollops. A sample from their Web site: "Each of the 10 Le Labo perfumes (fragrances) is built around a primary natural essence that comes directly from Grasse, France's 'perfume capital.' (Unfortunately, the Texan rose does not have the same voluptuousness and aristocratic refinement than [*sic*] its cousin from Grasse . . .)." Nonsense: the stuff you find in Grasse comes from all over the world, and aldehydes, for example, are synthetics that come from nowhere in particular. Leaving the shtick aside,

what's this fragrance like? Composed by the young and talented Yann Vasnier (perfumer for French firm Divine, and part author of Donna Karan's Gold), it is a miniature version of White Linen—snowy aldehydes refracting discreet pink fruity notes and blue woody ambers. Not enough to make you forsake Texas Rose, but not bad. By the way, Le Labo sells Aldehyde 44 only in their Dallas store. Go figure. LT

Alessandro Dell'Acqua Man (Alessandro Dell'Acqua) ★ ★ ★
waxy citrus $
Cheap-smelling but interesting citrus composition that leans toward a neglected facet of the citrus character typified by the acetal material Elintaal, a citrus that smells like hot candle wax, not snuffed candle as the odd-carbon aldehydes sometimes do. Bare but bracing. LT

Alessandro Dell'Acqua Woman (Alessandro Dell'Acqua) ★ ★ ★
floral oriental $
Sweet-creamy floral oriental in the Organza mold, perfectly presentable but not riveting. LT

Alien (Mugler) ★ ★ ★ *woody jasmine* $ $
Alien was half composed by the guy (Laurent Bruyère) who did the very first authorized clone, Angel Innocent, a good fragrance that would have been great but for the existence of the bigger archAngel. The presence of the great Ropion on the ticket is a guarantee that whatever it is, it won't be hasty or stupid. And stupid it isn't, the novelty here consisting in overlaying the brassy, synthetic core of Angel with a rich, natural, and fresh sambac jasmine note instead of the strident floral base of the original. The drydown is also better, a muted version of Bulgari's Black in place of a vanillic hangover. Not as bad as all that, but a waste of talent. Great bottle, though. LT

Alliage (Estée Lauder) ★ ★ ★ ★ *powdery green* $
In the realm of materials that smell green, galbanum resin is the odd

man out. Instead of fresh, sharp, and vegetal, it smells chalky and bit-tersweet, with a poisonous, cold, shadowed character, reminiscent sometimes of dark chocolate, sometimes of old wood. In composition, it can serve as air-conditioning: in the original Vent Vert, a March wind; in Chanel No. 19, the cold shoulder of an ice queen. In 1972, Alliage used a ton of it to make an anisic rose-and-vetiver fragrance feel dry and powdery, which is probably why Lauder marketed it as the first sports fragrance, since it smells logically inconsistent with perspiration. The fragrance today is perhaps less intensely bitter herbal, less powdery, a touch more floral, but still very good. TS

All That Matters (Anamor) ★ ★ *rubbery musk* $$$
The charming German shop owner who sent us this fragrance phoned me up at the crack of dawn and told me in great detail about the concept behind it, all of which I have forgotten. It is a light, sheer musk, faintly like the powdered inside of a latex glove, ideal if you would like to proj-ect the subliminal message that you are a trained clinician. TS

Allure (Chanel) ★ ★ *grim floral* $
In the beginning there was Must (Cartier, 1981), a very successful, nasty cheap-chocolate fragrance with a memorable drydown of vanilla, patchouli, and indole. What was remarkable about that accord, aside from its staying power, was that it achieved the exact olfactory equiva-lent of a dark shade of face powder. Ten years later Dune (Dior, 1991) brilliantly upended the original idea and created a wonderful, endlessly bleak fragrance the color of desert earth under a leaden sky. Nobody at the time saw the fun in that. Illustrating the principle that it is better to be six months late than five years early, Allure (1996) borrowed the idea of Dune and reinterpreted it in a friendlier manner, with fruity-floral top notes acting as a sweetener to the basically somber message it deliv-ers. Allure has since become the reference for women who wear fragrance

not for private pleasure or to advertise their tastes but merely to signal that their status dispenses them from being pleasant. LT

Allure Homme (Chanel) ★ *woody amber* $ $
I'm sure that when Pierre Bourdon did the beautiful and beautifully simple Cool Water he had no idea what he was starting. There have since been several hundred imitations, all trying to improve the unimprovable and ending up giving it more flab around the middle. This one is competent, utterly dull, and unworthy of Chanel. LT

Allure Homme Edition Blanche (Chanel) ★ ★ ★
sandalwood crab-apple $ $
Nondescript beige-tinted hybrid between Egoïste and Cool Water, with a good waxy citrus top note and a pleasant woody sour-apple finish. Has that Chanel touch of a cheap formula made more expensive, like a wood-veneer Ghia version of a basic Ford. Would be great in soap-on-a-rope. LT

Allure Homme Sport (Chanel) ★ *spicy citrus* $ $
A pleasant but studiedly nondescript confection of citrus-metallic notes set against a sweet-spicy background related to the drydown of Pour Monsieur. Like being stuck in an elevator for twelve hours with a tax accountant. LT

Allure Homme Sport Cologne (Chanel) ★ *woody citrus* $ $
Chanel's marketing strategy must be the envy of any politician: appeal to the masses but maintain a pristine image. This is done by having de facto two completely separate ranges: one for people who want to smell like everyone else, and one for people who want to smell like people who don't want to smell like everyone else. AHSC is one of the former, about as enticing as a lonely-hearts ad in *Railway Monthly*. It is distantly related to Cacharel pour l'Homme, a dismally dry citrus fragrance whose

success has never ceased to amaze me. Chanel, as usual, redeems itself somewhat by making sure the ingredients are of adequate quality and the bottle solid. LT

Allure Sensuelle (Chanel) ★ ★ ★ *melon balsamic* $ $
Karl Lagerfeld, clearly having a bad ponytail day, was asked at the launch of the original Allure what he thought allure was, and in his languid French-German drawl replied, "Whatever it is, it is not a fragrance." I think he would have been a little less off-message if asked for his opinion on Allure Sensuelle. As far as I know, Sensuelle signals the first appearance of an attractive idea that consists in overlaying a big, solid, complex, and unrelentingly beige woody-balsamic thing in the Lauder manner with a fresh aldehydic note, not of citrus but of melon. Tom Ford later did the same cucurbitaceous thing with Black Orchid. Beautifully crafted and utterly devoid of magic, this is for me a "date with Cindy Crawford" sort of perfume: nice idea in principle, but in practice I'd rather dine alone while reading *The New Yorker.* LT

Almost Bare (Bobbi Brown) ★ *chemical floral* $ $
Hissy bleached-bones fresh floral, likely just what the brief asked for. Smells like the latex backing on new carpet. LT

Alpona (Caron) ★ ★ ★ *lemon chypre* $ $
Another Caron that's been through several iterations, Alpona was once a resinous chypre with a singular note of candied orange peel, then became a green (neroli) chypre with lots of patchouli, and is now a patchouli chypre with a sweet lemon-drop citrus, a cross between Shalimar Light and Eau de Rochas. It works fine, though I wish they'd put years on the bottles to indicate vintage, since with all these changes it's hard to keep track. Dries down to the same dull, sour soapy-rose plus wood that all the Caron reformulations come to, instead of the candied dark carnation, heavy with the famous base of Mousse de Saxe, that Caron's original grand perfumer, Ernest Daltroff, favored. TS

Always Belong (Celine Dion) ★ ★ ★ *rose violet* $
Imitation is the highest form of flattery, and somebody really likes Sophia Grojsman's style. This is a drastically simplified rose done up in violets, pretty but no Paris. TS

Amanda (Amanda Lepore) ★ ★ ★ ★ *blinding iris* $$$$
Nine hundred fifty dollars for the 125 milliliter limited edition? As if. The little vial on my desk comes to about a hundred bucks! I feel like the lucky guy picked for a moon shot who has to tell the world what it was like. It was great, thanks. Christophe Laudamiel is a feverishly inventive perfumer who seems always to start from first principles. Those who remember his Salon Rouge for Mugler will also know that his favorite manner is the uncanny. His take on iris in Amanda, namely to bring the old vampire (iris, that is) into full sunlight and ask him to smile for the cameras, is positively scary. I have seldom smelled a perfume so tensely cheerful, so edgily toothsome. This thing feels as though it's about to explode, and yet on skin it behaves itself impeccably: the nerve-jangling top note of iris struck by lightning hardly budges for a couple of hours before drifting toward a weird suede-like drydown reminiscent of Laudamiel's S-eX. How is it done? I wish I knew. Laudamiel seems to take the gray-daylight, dusty aspect of iris and extend it with aldehydes, wood, and PEZ-candy fruit, ramping up an overcast sky into blinding brightness. The year 2008 will, in retrospect, be regarded as the second coming of iris: after ages of being used sparingly, this formerly overpriced material has been paired off with more suitors in one year than in the previous half century. Brilliant work in every sense, and a happy portent of things to come now that Laudamiel has quit his day job and started his own firm. LT

Amarige (Givenchy) ★ *killer tuberose* $$
We nearly gave it four stars: the soapy-green tobacco-tuberose accord Dominique Ropion designed for Amarige is unmissable, unmistakable, and unforgettable. However, it is also truly loathsome, perceptible even

at parts-per-billion levels, and at all times incompatible with others' enjoyment of food, music, sex, and travel. If you are reading this because it is your darling fragrance, please wear it at home exclusively, and tape the windows shut. LT

Amarige Mariage (Givenchy) ★ *prune candyfloss* $
Believe it or not, lots of people in the fragrance world were convinced that the success of the first Amarige was due in part to the subliminal bridal-shower effect of its name. Good news: this one doesn't smell at all like the original Amarige. Now the bad news: it is a sad little candied-fruit, candyfloss (cotton candy in the United States) and strawberry confection, a sort of dowager Vanilia that would have been too little too late even ten years ago. Go for the excellent Amarige d'Amour (if you can find it) instead. LT

A*Maze (People of the Labyrinths) ★ ★ ★ *rose liqueur* $$$
A*Maze delivers an excellent, bright, powerful, liqueur-like spiced rose in its top note, but as time goes on, the clove aspects of rose dominate and the woody amber gets ever louder. It feels like a halfway point between the intense, truffled woody rose of Edouard Fléchier's Une Rose and the resinous-spicy rose of Michel Roudnitska's Noir Epices (both Frédéric Malle), but not quite as good as either. TS

Amazing Grace (Philosophy) ★ *generic muguet* $
A dull, generic, cutesy-pie, pink, frilly, itsy-bitsy floral thing, mysteriously accompanied by the words "how you climb up the mountain is just as important as how you climb down the mountain." The effect of that gnomic pronouncement is somewhat blunted by the nearby list of ingredients: "benzyl salicylate, benzophenone, hydroxyisohexyl 3-cyclohexene carboxaldehyde, amyl cinnamal, benzyl alcohol, butyl phenyl methylpropional, citronellol, geraniol, hexyl cinnamal, hydroxycitronellal, hydroxymethylpentyl 3-cyclohexene 1-carboxaldehyde, limonene." In short, a muguet. LT

Amazone (Hermès) ★ ★ ★ *woody floral* $ $
A beautifully done and deeply uninteresting woody floral, notable only for the fact that the competition is so bad these days that Amazone enables you to appreciate quality in its pure state, unencumbered by any other distraction. LT

Amber (Renée) ★ ★ ★ *vetiver rose* $ $
Not particularly ambery, and certainly less so than the Musk by this Australian Jo Malone look-alike, this is a pleasant vetiver-rose accord reminiscent of Parfums de Nicolaï's wonderful candle scent Vétiver de Java. No great shakes, but well put together, creamy, and civilized. LT

Amber Absolute (Tom Ford) ★ ★ ★ *spicy amber* $ $ $
Tom Ford has time and again demonstrated his good taste and decisiveness in choosing fragrances. Nevertheless, bringing out twelve boutique fragrances in one go (six years of Lutens output, a megalomanic project) must have been daunting, even with the expert help of Lauder's Karyn Khoury. One way to do it is to corral, say, ten of the world's best perfumers and ask them to show you fragrances they've composed that they love but were deemed noncommercial by big brands. These days, that virtually guarantees you'll get great stuff to choose from. But then each fragrance must be nursed from that starting point to a finished product, preferably one that fits the rest of the lineup, and that is far from easy. I approached Amber Absolute with dread, expecting another triple-distilled extract of Moroccan souk, and was pleasantly surprised to find it spicy in a *pain d'épices* manner up top, and woody with a note of dried plums in the drydown, not overly sweet and very naturally rich throughout. AA is in some ways a subset of Youth Dew Amber Nude, but I think I prefer it to the full deck. LT

Amber and Lavender Cologne (Jo Malone) ★ ★ ★
soapy patchouli $ $
Wrong label. LT

Amber pour Homme (Prada) ★ ★ *woody amber* $ $
A studiedly dull, nondescript masculine, a medley of every drone cliché in recent years. LT

Ambra (Etro) ★ ★ *hippie amber* $ $
A very sweet, Arab-market vegetable amber. Smells curiously like ripe persimmon. Completely unoriginal, and nicely done. LT

Ambra del Nepal (I Profumi di Firenze) ★ ★ *incense amber* $ $
When LT first proposed we write this book, I moaned, "But will we have to review all five hundred fragrances named Amber, Ambra, and Ambre?" All the same, I admit there is initially something affecting about this stripped-down version in which a silken frankincense lends a cool, meditative polish to the predictable rest. TS

Ambra di Venezia (Ambra di Venezia) ★ ★ ★ ★ *Giorgio redux* $ $
Tuberose di Las Vegas is more like it: a flashing, pink and yellow, curling vision several stories high, which recalls the electric plumage that mounts the entrance to the Flamingo like the mouth of hell as decorated by Dr. Seuss. Frighteningly fruity in a Concord grape way, with muscular, powdery, woody notes broadcasting the message to the moon. Nothing ambery or Venetian in sight. Enjoy. TS

Ambre 411 (Histoires de Parfums) ★ ★ ★ ★ *benzoin rose* $ $ $
A beautiful, durable amber accord built of benzoin, patchouli, vetiver, and rose. Its transparent smoky sweetness feels weightless, as if hollowed out in the middle to make it float. TS

Ambre Cannelle (Creed) ★ ★ *light oriental* $ $ $
Strikingly devoid of either amber or cinnamon, this is a cheap, skimpy oriental, a sort of dwarf Cinnabar. Smells like a household product. LT

Ambre de Cabochard (Grès) ★ *chemical fruitcake* $$

There are so many perfectly serviceable ambers on the market (Ambre Sultan, L'Eau d'Ambre, Ambre Narguilé, Youth Dew Amber Nude, etc.) that I'd blithely assumed you couldn't screw it up. Grès has managed it with a thin, oddly waxy floral-and-spice formula so cheap Yankee Candle wouldn't stoop to it. Also, it has nothing to do with Cabochard. TS

Ambre Extrême (L'Artisan Parfumeur) ★ ★ *just amber* $$$

Extrême? Hardly—merely a concentrated version of L'Eau d'Ambre. It reminds me of a wit who described his political views as being at "extreme center." This is straight-up amber (not ambergris), a composition of various resins and perfumery oils, often including cistus and vanillin. It is the reference smell of the Maghreb and Middle East street market. Few perfumery compositions are as familiar, as immediately agreeable, as incontrovertibly right, and ultimately as boring as amber. It is the road music of perfumery: loud, simple, and great when kept where it belongs, i.e., in the souk. It became interesting one hundred years ago as the basis of what are called oriental fragrances. Every perfumer since then has done at least one oriental, most of them trying hard to get away from the basic chord. A few are masterpieces: the first, said to have been composed by Henri Alméras for Poiret's firm Rosine, is lost; the second and arguably best, Coty's Emeraude, has been ruined; the third, Jacques Guerlain's sublime Shalimar, is still extant. Why anyone would want to buy plain Ambre Extrême instead beats me. LT

Ambre Fétiche (Annick Goutal) ★ ★ *lime benzoin* $$$

What a beautiful top note, a vast smeary sunset stretching from lime-like frankincense to deep smoky balsam! And what a disappointing drydown, whittling the richness away minute by minute to a stark skeleton of synthetic woody notes plus a whiff of benzoin. TS

Ambre Gris (Balmain) ★ ★ *fake sandalwood* $$$
No resemblance to ambergris: instead, a familiar synthetic sandalwood base. Cheaters. TS

Ambre Narguilé (Hermès) ★ ★ ★ *dried fruit* $$$
Everyone is doing a Lutens these days, only some do it better than others. I take a dim view of most ambers, because while they smell good (why else would this oriental composition have been so popular for decades?), they all feel heavy, simple, and flat, and make me hanker for something less obvious. I will make an exception for Ambre Narguilé, however, because it is in no way a ditzy amber. It's hardly an amber at all, in fact, and relies on dried-plum notes and woody ambers (no relation) to give a cozy, pleasant effect. Nothing earthshaking, but fine if what you want is warmth. LT

Ambre Précieux (Maître Parfumeur et Gantier) ★ ★ ★ ★
classic amber $$$
If the history of fragrance in the last thirty years is ever written, Jean-François Laporte will have a long chapter all to himself. Laporte started out as a chemist with a passion for perfume and a vast knowledge of botany. He founded L'Artisan Parfumeur (the first niche firm) in 1976, then left in 1988 to found MPG. In 1997 he retired from MPG, but the firm is still going strong. Every niche firm has to have an amber, and Ambre Précieux is straight-up, rich, and sweet but not overly so, basically the Middle Eastern idea of an amber fragrance in full song. No surprises, and no need for any in such a classic form, but among the very best. LT

Ambre Russe (Parfum d'Empire) ★ ★ ★ ★ *huge amber* $$
Marc-Antoine Corticchiato has my respect. It takes guts to start a niche firm, and even more guts to abstain from any gimmicks, as he has done. He apparently teaches at the French perfume school ISIPCA and has collaborated with historian and author Elisabeth de Feydeau on some of

his fragrances. The plan is this: fragrances inspired by historical empires, from Roman to Russian. I find it funny that whereas everyone else does an Ambre Ottoman and a Cuir Russe, he reverses the labels and confirms my general feeling that Russia is part of the Middle East. Ambre Russe is quite simply the biggest, most over-the-top, most expansive, most nutritious amber in existence. If there was a cross between pipe tobacco and *pain d'épices,* this would be it. To call this an oriental is like saying that Nicholas II was no genius. LT

Ambre Soie (Armani Privé) ★ ★ ★ ★ *rich amber* $$$
Christine Nagel's superb Theorema (Fendi, 1998) showed how much creative room there was left in the oriental category. Nagel is probably the best in the world at this sort of fragrance, and when Theorema was discontinued she did the right thing: she reincarnated that beautiful structure as Ambre Soie, one of the best ambers around, rich but not overly opaque, lush but not too sweet, and with strange anisic notes that keep it interesting all the way through. Not cheap, but nice work. LT

Ambre Sultan (Serge Lutens) ★ ★ ★ ★ *herbal amber* $$$
The fragrant resin blend known as amber, found in Middle Eastern perfume shops and hippie stores all over, is a nearly fail-safe crowd-pleaser: sweet, rich, long-lasting, and ready-equipped with the whiff of the exotic, even if a little boring. For greatness, more is required. Lutens, who lives in Morocco, frequently looks to the Middle East for inspiration, and his influential Ambre Sultan, which dates from 1993, is a throwback oriental, a back-to-basics amber for the well-heeled perfume buyer who is too cool for the hippie shop but nevertheless prefers this kind of folk naïveté to the artfulness of a Shalimar. Every niche perfumery followed with its own high-markup amber. What distinguishes Ambre Sultan in this now-crowded arena is a high dose of fantastic dried-herb smells, which give it, in the top, a dusty, salty, outdoor air, before the more familiar vanillic balsam plot takes over. TS

Ambre Topkapi (Parfums MDCI) ★ ★ ★ *citrus spice* $$$
The only disappointment from MDCI's first five scents. Composed by
Pierre Bourdon, it makes abundant use of the molecule Bourdon made
a household smell if not name: the gray, woody-citrus note of dihydro-
myrcenol. AT has neither the depth nor the originality of the others in
the line, and feels like a rushed job by a very busy man. Too bad. LT

Ambrette 9 (Le Labo) ★ *cheap musk* $$
With only nine materials and the gorgeous smell of ambrette seed as the
main one, you'd figure they couldn't fuck this one up. Alas, the other
eight (I smell several synthetic musks in here) conspire to make this a
cheap mess. LT

L'Ame d'un Héros (Guerlain) ★ ★ ★ *herbaceous floral* $$$
Full credit to Guerlain for going against the grain: at a time when every-
one serves up different fragrances under the same name, they do just
the opposite. This was first called Coriolan, then Chamade pour Homme
(q.v.), now "A Hero's Soul." But it is the same old (and quite good) thing,
possibly slightly improved, a fresh herbaceous gray confection, slightly
nondescript but entirely pleasant, with a brief and incongruous raw-
spinach note in the heart. Vastly better than average, though still un-
memorable. LT

A*Men (Thierry Mugler) ★ ★ ★ ★ *chocolate mint* $
Angel was at once the inspiration for dozens of perfumes and a devil-
ishly hard act to follow. To this day, of all the progeny only three stand
out: Lolita Lempicka, Angel Innocent, and A*Men. The dissonance at
the heart of the original lay between the floral base and the remainder
of the fragrance, a chocolate oriental. This irreconcilable difference,
this clash at a crossroads between two marching bands playing different
tunes, was what made Angel unforgettably great. Jacques Huclier has
managed to reinterpret that effect brilliantly. Instead of flowers, he gives
one band a herbaceous lavender-mint chord brightened by aldehydes. In

the other, he reinforces the roasted section with caramel, coffee, and tar. The result, while much less radiant than Angel (thank God for that), has the same wonderful, simultaneously poisonous and delicious eat-me-and-die feel as the original. Hard to imagine on a guy, but a great feminine. LT

L'Ame Soeur (Divine) ★ ★ ★ *aldehydic woody* $$$
This combination of dry, talcum-powder wood and a slightly metallic, sweaty cast I find classical in feel and pleasingly aloof, and LT finds nerve-wracking in the extreme. Several fragrances in this vegetal, pale, unsweetened style have come down the pike in recent years, two by Pierre Bourdon (Ferré, Iris Poudre). This one from 2004 (the name means "soul mate") by young perfumer Yann Vasnier seems both steely and mild-mannered, like a sort of woman you might have known whose soft, maternal build belies an icy manner. TS

Amethyst (Lalique) ★ ★ ★ *rose blackcurrant* $$$
The combination of blackcurrant and rose had been done long before 2007 (see L'Ombre dans l'Eau), but this one is pleasantly dense, peppery, sweet, and savory like a good chutney, thanks in part to the salty green smell of tomato leaf. Beautiful bottle, as you'd expect from a company specializing in crystal. TS

Amethyst (Olivier Durbano) ★ *pepper pine* $$$
Olivier Durbano is a jeweler in semiprecious stones. His Amethyst reminds me of those photocopies of mimeographs of carbon copies of fifty-year-old arithmetic problems we used to get in elementary school, in which the numeral 2 was indistinguishable from the letter *B* or a mark made with your thumb. This was an attempt to copy something interesting, yet I have no idea what. TS

Amor Amor (Cacharel) ★ ★ *fruit salad* $
Dismal fruity floral, for the modern-day Emma Bovary. LT

Amor pour Homme (Cacharel) ★ *woody amber* $

Masculine perfumery has devolved to this point: you apparently take any old soap-fragrance formula; add a dose of the most potent, chemical-smelling woody amber on your shelf; stir; and hold your nose while you pour it in bottles. TS

Amouage Gold (Amouage) ★★★★★ *huge floral* $$$$

I love the bold, hybrid idea behind Amouage. The firm was started in 1983 by a senior member of the Omani royal family to restore the tri-millennial tradition of perfume in Oman. With the mixture of local pride and interest in faraway lands that befits an ancient seafaring nation, they called it Amouage, from the Arabic *amwaj* (waves), gallicized to make it sound more like *amour*. I have no idea what Oman perfumery is like today, though I've seen documentaries about Muscat guys spraying on clouds of bespoke mixtures in little shops with evident glee. In any event, twenty years ago Amouage hired the great Guy Robert and gave him a brief most perfumers can only dream of: "Put whatever you like in it, no matter how much it costs." Now called Amouage Gold, the fragrance comes in a solid, beautifully made black and gold cardboard display case, which snaps shut like a wolf trap. A little signed card says mine was made by one Naeema, a nice touch. Folded satin cushions hold the bottle, which is made of crystal containing 24 percent lead: holding it in your hand makes you wonder whether gravitation has suddenly quadrupled. The whole thing is put together in a happy, slightly naive, manifestly handcrafted style, which reminds me of the few really valuable things Russia used to produce, like Red October chocolates, confirming my long-held opinion that Moscow is a big Damascus with snow. No doubt a makeover is coming, and chances are some of the charm will be lost. The fragrance? Guy Robert describes it in the press pack as the crowning glory of his career, and I agree. Robert is perhaps the most symphonic of the old-school French perfumers still working today, and Gold is his Bruckner's Ninth. This perfume is about texture rather than structure, a hundred flying carpets of scent overlapping each other. It's as if Joy had eloped with Scheherazade for a thousand and one nights of illicit fun. After smelling a skimpy modern thing, Guy Robert once despairingly told me, "Un parfum doit avant tout sentir bon." (A perfume must above all smell good.) With Gold, he put the sultanate's money where his mouth was and produced the richest perfume in existence. Small wonder they used to call the region Arabia Felix. LT

Amouage Gold for Men (Amouage) ★ ★ ★ ★ *romantic floral* $$$$
Calling this a fragrance "for men" is like addressing King Solomon as Sol. This is a floral on an epic scale, starting with a blast of rose and mimosa, followed by the wonderful, dusty, lemony feel of the high-grade frankincense for which Oman is famous, and tapering off into an almost Guerlain-like (Vol de Nuit) near-edible balsamic drydown of great distinction. Very few guys I've met would dare wear this, though that says more about men than about the fragrance. If you want the panoramic lushness of Mouchoir de Monsieur without a trace of the aging-dandy feel, go for Gold. LT

Amoureuse (Parfums DelRae) ★ ★ ★ ★ *green lily* $$$
DelRae was one of the few firms to flatly refuse to send us fragrances, hence its absence from the first edition. But despite its small distribution, DelRae is by definition in the public domain, so we managed to obtain fresh samples by other means. Michel Roudnitska's creations for DelRae are well-put-together classical perfumery, with every material pulling lustily in the same direction. The downside of this vigor is that the DelRae perfumes confidently speak a little too loud, as if slightly tipsy. Amoureuse starts out with a deliciously complex and realistic floral (lily) then settles into a pleasantly old-fashioned, powdery floral heart, a sort of Ma Griffe with the claws filed down. LT

I owned a bottle of this at one point, since at the end of a long day I stumbled upon it in a shop and found it deliciously heady, dizzying, dense green—a sensation like falling asleep under a tree in summer, overwhelmed by damp heat. Sober assessment later revealed that this combination of powerful greens plus syrupy white floral and cardamom was just too much to wear at any time, anywhere. I give it its due as an impressive composition, but I confess I gave it away nearly full. TS

Anaïs Anaïs (Cacharel) ★ ★ ★ ★ *fresh floral* $
Anaïs Anaïs (1978) is credited to four perfumers (probably a record) and is the great-granddad of all florals aimed at the adolescent market, which makes it one of the most influential fragrances in history. It was also the first example of coherent top-down design in a fragrance launch. The idea was girls in quantity, a sort of harem steam bath spruced up to seventies health-and-safety standards. Hence the double name, the groups of indistinguishable pretty, pale blondes in the photos, the bathroomy porcelain bottle. Taken together, the image was designed to appeal both to a vaguely dykey camaraderie and to the voyeur instincts of the opposite sex. But most important, the girls were underage, and in 1978 that was hot news. The fragrance was devoid of all attempts at seductive warmth, and was instead bright, slightly chrysanthemum-bitter, squeaky clean, soapy, and utterly memorable. It was a cheap composition and as a result has not been messed with in the intervening years. The smell was considered mawkish in 1978, but the oceans of syrup that have flowed since make it a curiously prim, dry fragrance today, so much so that I would recommend it (in small doses) as a masculine. A monument. LT

Ananas Fizz (L'Artisan Parfumeur) ★ ★ ★ *grapefruit actually* $$
The distinctive feature of pineapple (think about it next time you bite into one) is the fact that it is a cheesy smell, because the molecule that says "pineapple" is a butyric ester and releases some butyric acid (*boutyron*, Greek for "butter") in your nose. The only true pineapple fragrance I can remember was the strange Colony (Patou). Ananas Fizz is much

more of a grapefruit (and an homage to Lubin's extinct Gin Fizz) than a pineapple, with a very interesting transition between citrus and lily of the valley halfway into the fragrance. Very fresh and skillful overall, it could be seen as a less saturated version of Guerlain's Pamplelune, if you find the latter too intense. LT

L'Anarchiste (Caron) ★ ★ ★ *apple lavender* $ $
Aimed at the edgy young man via its political-rebel name and provocative gasoline-can packaging, as if ready for use in a Molotov cocktail. I remember it as very different: a rich, spiced baked-apple oriental. Today it seems much more like every other fragrance in the Cool Water mode (apple, violet, lavender, violet leaf). TS

Andy Warhol Lexington Avenue (Bond No. 9) ★ ★
almond nail polish $ $ $
Bond continues to perfect the art of packaging—the pink and black, the drawings of shoes, adorable—while not getting the fragrance right. Lexington Avenue is reminiscent of Jour de Fête (L'Artisan Parfumeur) but never rises above a hodgepodge of milky notes (anise, almond) trying not to curdle when faced with a screechy peony. TS

Andy Warhol's Silver Factory (Bond No. 9) ★ ★ ★ *iris incense* $
Bond's late foray into the spicy incense territory populated early on by Comme des Garçons and other niche firms has resulted in a perfectly friendly if unadventurous incense, with an interesting accord of iris and waxy smoke, like Dzongkha without the genius. As it goes on, it starts to approximate the drydown of Bond's cedar-amber West Broadway, no bad thing in itself. TS

Andy Warhol Union Square (Bond No. 9) ★ *lemony floral* $ $ $
Lightweight copy of Elizabeth Arden's Sunflowers, at something like ten times the price. TS

Angel (Thierry Mugler) ★ ★ ★ ★ ★ *fruity patchouli* $

The first time I smelled Angel, a flamboyant six-foot-three salesman with the shoulders of a linebacker encased in a baby blue zoot suit leaned over the counter and sprayed me. I recoiled. "Is this a joke?" I thought of it, for years, as possibly the worst thing I had ever smelled. I suffered then from the naive belief that women should smell only like flowers or candy; yet Angel, perversely, smells of both, with the same relation to your average sweet floral as the ten-story-high demonic Stay Puft Marshmallow Man from *Ghostbusters* has to your average fireside toasted sweet.

In that sense, Angel certainly is a joke. Countless perfumes have copied parts of it (for a sample, see Euphoria, Flowerbomb, and Prada), but they mistakenly play it straight. Although Angel is sold as a gourmand for girls, spoken of as if it were a fudge-dipped berry in a confectioner's shop, it's all lies. Look for Angel's Adam's apple: a handsome, resinous, woody patchouli straight out of the pipes-and-leather-slippers realm of men's fragrance, in a head-on collision with a bold blackcurrant (Neocaspirene) and a screechy white floral. These two halves, masculine and feminine, share a camphoraceous (mothball) smell, which gives Angel a covering of unsentimental, icy brightness above its overripe (some say "rotting") rumble. The effect kills the possibility of cloying sweetness, despite megadoses of the cotton-candy smell of ethylmaltol, leaving Angel in a high-energy state of contradiction. Many perfumes are beautiful or pleasant, but how many are exciting? Like a woman in a film who seethes, "He's so annoying!" and marries him in the end, I returned to smell Angel so many times I had to buy it.

When this striking idea proved a hit, it gave perfumers hope that, as once was done with Chypre, they could mask this structure a thousand different ways to create new effects. It doesn't really work, though not for lack of trying. The fruity chypres, leather chypres, floral chypres, green chypres, and so on, smell very different. But the Angel format, combining masculine and feminine, in nearly all cases still smells like Angel no matter what you use from columns A and B. Don't fuss with pretenders. Buy the perverse, brilliant original, but wear it only if you know how to tell the joke properly. TS

Angel Innocent (Thierry Mugler) ★ ★ ★ ★ *fruity oriental* $
I've never quite understood this one: the original Angel was composed by Olivier Cresp at Quest in 1992. Six years later Mugler decided to do a tenor sax version of the original sousaphone. You'd think they would go to Quest, who, after all, had the original formula. Not a bit: Laurent Bruyère at Charabot was saddled with this one, no doubt with the help of some serious analytical chemistry. Is it good? Excellent, a lighter, more floral, less high-calorie version of the original. Is it interesting? Only insofar as Angel was. Was it necessary? No. LT

Angélique Encens (Creed) ★ ★ ★ *incense oriental* $$$
One of the better fragrances in the Creed line, a fairly conventional, straightforward amber oriental extended in the drydown by a solid, natural-smelling frankincense note. LT

Angélique Noire (Guerlain) ★ ★ *bitter floral* $$$$
One expects a high-end Guerlain to be attractive either in texture (raw materials) or structure (ideas). AN is based on a dissonant bitter top-note accord that feels like your liver wouldn't thank you if you drank it, fading into an intense, banal drydown reminiscent of the oily-soapy florals of the eighties, such as Ivoire and Madame Carven. The general impression is of something put together in a hurry. LT

Angéliques sous la Pluie (Frédéric Malle) ★ ★ ★ *bracing liqueur* $$
Jean-Claude Elléna has emerged in the last few years as one of the great creative perfumers at work today, not least for his extraordinary skill in creating subtle, natural, transparent accords, a sort of nouvelle cuisine of perfumery. Sadly, Angéliques is not his best effort, and smells much like the variety of wormwood used in the pleasant, peppery-herbaceous liqueur called Génépy in the French Alps. Angéliques, despite its lan-

guid name, is more of a masculine fragrance, but I'd frankly rather drink this kind of stuff than wear it. LT

Angel La Rose (Thierry Mugler) ★ ★ ★ ★ *Godzilla floral* $ $
Does what it says on the can. Angel was never exactly demure and always felt rather like standing next to a jet at takeoff. This one adds a fruity rose with afterburners. Put this on and tongues of pink flame with shock diamonds propel you everywhere. The air roils behind you for hours. A half ounce of ALR should, according to my calculations, last you eleven thousand years in daily use. Great. LT

Angel Lys (Thierry Mugler) ★ ★ ★ *lily Angel* $ $
Given that the original Angel was apparently composed in anger by mixing a chocolate-patchouli base with a screechy floral composition, why not regress under hypnosis and relive that primal 1992 Olivier Cresp moment, pick a different flower, and thereby alter all subsequent history? What is amusing about these parodic Angel-something versions is that everyone has been doing just that for years without acknowledgment. Smelling the Mugler "what-if" variations is like touring recent perfumery, this one being closest to Allure Sensuelle and Black Orchid. Question for home study: Who is copying whom? LT

Angelo di Fiume (Linari) ★ ★ *vanilla biscuit* $ $ $
The Italian-sounding but actually German outfit Linari (just how German can be gauged by their Web page: "the requisition and conjunction of interdisciplinary knowledge, a crossfire of different skills") is actually more Italian in spirit than is good for it. The ratio of packaging to substance is high enough for Milan, and both are intensely derivative. The bottles come from Bulgari Black via Nasomatto; the fragrances are reminiscent of countless others on the market. The dead hand at Linari's helm has even managed to throttle one of the great talents of contemporary perfumery, Mark Buxton. His Angelo di Fiume, which means "wa-

ter spirit" (great name), is a vanillic Petit Beurre affair that has little to say and takes ages saying it. LT

Angel Pivoine (Thierry Mugler) ★ ★ ★ *peony Angel* $$
The notion of doing a peony version of Angel brings to mind cheap Italian superhero films of the sixties that, having run out of straight-up plots, such as "Maciste, strongest man in the world" and "Maciste's triumph," began to generate strange hybrids such as "Maciste vs. Zorro." This together-at-last fragrance pits Giant Transvestite against Ditzy Blonde from Hell. After an hour of slugging it out on the smelling strip (fifteen minutes in the warmer climate of skin), Angel wins. LT

Angel Violet (Thierry Mugler) ★ ★ ★ *violet Angel* $$
Perfumer Françoise Caron was faced with a difficult task here, namely, to arrange the rapidly shrinking note of synthetic violets and the huge accord of Angel in such a way that both can be perceived at once, which is a bit like trying to cover an eighteen-wheeler with a purple handkerchief. Amazingly, it even works for a few minutes, after which the violets are flattened and left behind like floral roadkill. LT

Ange ou Démon (Givenchy) ★ *floral oriental* $$
In one of Boris Vian's magical novels, there is a machine called a pianocktail, a grand piano fitted with an inner mechanism that mixes a cocktail according to the notes played, and delivers it through a small side door when ready. If the ingredient bottles were instead filled with the last thirty fragrances launched, and a two-year-old let loose to bang fists on the keys for five minutes, Ange ou Démon would result. LT

Anglomania (Vivienne Westwood) ★ *dessert woody* $$
After an intense gourmand top note with too much going on, Anglomania poops out early and reveals a boring synthetic woody-amber drydown plus PVC raincoat. TS

Anice (Etro) ★ ★ ★ ★   *aniseed musk* $ $ $
Anice means "aniseed," and this one manages by several tricks to remain anisic from top to bottom. Jacques Flori has put star anise in the top note, and fennel seed and an ingredient described as jasmine (but that can only be cis-jasmone) in the heart. Cis-jasmone smells like fennel, contributes to the unique smell of jasmine, and fits here like a glove. But the best bit is the use of a macrocyclic musk with a luscious, anisic ambrette character in the drydown. Really clever work, lovely fragrance. LT

Anné Pliska (Anné Pliska) ★ ★ ★ ★   *orange oriental* $ $
Given that most niche brands insist on offering a dozen derivative fragrances with insulting prices and pretentious names, Pliska's modesty in selling but one, and cheaply, deserves laurels. Its top note is among the few good orange accords in perfume, connected at the crisp end to bergamot and at the resinous-woody end to a simple but excellent molasses-like drydown of labdanum and vanilla. The first impression is of the classic fruited tea Constant Comment, and on skin it smells powerfully of Christmas—gingerbread, oranges—without smelling strictly gourmand. Distinctive, simple, of no certain era, and beautifully made. TS

Antaeus (Chanel) ★ ★ ★ ★   *woody masculine* $ $
I have it on good authority that the fragrance was christened by the great publisher Dan Halpern, who at the time ran a literary magazine of the same name, during a conversation with Chanel's owner, Jacques Wertheimer. I confess I missed the point of Antaeus when it first came out in 1981, partly because it became the first gay masculine fragrance and several years had to pass before the guys learned to use less than half a bottle per day. In retrospect, it is the best of the cigar-box woody fragrances of the time (Krizia Uomo three years later was another). It feels a bit dated and would probably fare better on a woman than on a man today, but still smells really good. LT

Antico Caruso (Profumum) ★ ★ *cheap cologne* $$$$
Profumum does cologne. Badly. LT

Antidote (Viktor & Rolf) ★ ★ *mutant lavender* $$
There is a new chemical beast prowling the streets, a strange molecule with the feel of a light, volatile top note and the strength and tenacity of the most powerful drydown materials. Smelling it at length gives the feeling of alarm one would get from trying to pick up a two-year-old child and finding that he weighed as much as a car. This strange creature is called sclarene, an intermediate in the synthesis of Ambrox from clary sage, and has a fresh-herbaceous dry smell that simply goes on forever. It is currently being used in many masculines to endow linear lavender-like fragrances with more staying power. Unfortunately, in Antidote it doesn't work: there seems little point in having delicate, airy lavender walking around with this strange hulk in tow pretending they're friends. Ten seconds into this second fragrance from Viktor and Rolf, you can imagine yourself in a Mini Cooper with the young buck at the wheel wearing this, sixty miles of winding road in front of you, and reaching for the window switch or the barf bag. LT

Antihéros (Etat Libre d'Orange) ★ ★ ★ ★ *lavender soap* $$
A curiously affecting, poetic fragrance that fulfills a wish I didn't know I'd made: it smells just like cheap lavender soap, only strong. Wonderful. LT

L'Antimatière (LesNez) ★ ★ *woody musk* $$$
In Flann O'Brien's delirious novel *The Third Policeman,* one of the said policemen displays to the narrator a few examples of his craft hobby, including a series of nested wooden chests, each identical to the previous one down to the nails but an order of magnitude smaller. The most impressive ones are absolutely invisible. The high concept of L'Antimatière, done by the talented Isabelle Doyen, is called, in the

highly literary press kit, a "topless" fragrance—lacking top notes—and "a project in minimalism." Although I smell nothing but a nearly undetectable creamy-woody musk, and that almost immediately, I shall keep nodding reverently, "My goodness, what astonishing craft . . ." TS

Antonia's Flowers (Antonia's Flowers) ★ ★ ★ *lavender violets* $
Launched in 1984, this is supposed to be a freesia soliflore, described in the press pack as a "living freesia," meaning a reconstruction of the real thing based on sampling of the air around freesias. The latter contains upward of 90 percent linalool, the rest being mostly violet notes. It is no surprise, therefore, that AF is basically a nice lavender with a violet drydown. I love both, and I've added AF to my short list of restful masculine lavenders to be worn as needed. LT

Anvers (Ulrich Lang) ★ ★ ★ *dry woody* $$
A very comfortable, discreet, dry woody-spicy fragrance, less interesting than Anvers 2 but still head and shoulders above the average contemporary masculine. LT

Anvers 2 (Ulrich Lang) ★ ★ ★ ★ *sweet leather* $$
Why *Anvers,* French for Antwerp, in Flanders? Who's the brooding, plain bloke on the box? Who cares? But more important, who composed the fragrance? One thing's for sure: this is a light, complex, skillfully put-together leather chypre with a touch of the honeyed sweetness that made the old English Leather so appealing, only much more refined. LT

Aomassaï (Parfumerie Générale) ★ ★ ★ ★ *roasted hazelnut* $$$
I remember seeing an interesting chemistry demo in which common sugar was analyzed before and at several stages during its conversion to caramel. The number of components in the mix rapidly went from one (saccharose) to several dozen (the combinatorial products of successive heat-induced chemical reactions). Roasted flavors, from sugar to nuts

and meat, clearly have something in common that says "high heat" to our nose. At one time the fragrance industry used this effect by deliberately subjecting pure aromachemicals to "pyrogenation" to increase their complexity. Aomassaï is an object lesson in roasted aromas, from caramel to hazelnut, on a background of wood, licorice, and what feels like dried banana. Intense, appetizing, and completely distinctive. LT

Aoud Damascus (Montale) ★ ★ *metallic rose* $$$
In response to our repeated entreaties, Montale has kindly promised to send us samples. In fact, they have promised at least twice. We procured some anyway. Aoud Damascus is a helional-dominated floral made with good stuff but overall of no great interest. LT

Après l'Ondée (Guerlain) ★ ★ ★ ★ ★ *heavenly heliotrope* $$$
The advantages of working with a clean sheet of paper are priceless: see the perfection of the first Windsurfer, the first small jet airliner (the SE-210 Caravelle), and in this case (1906) the first serious heliotropin fragrance. The almond-floral note of heliotropin, so reminiscent of the spring-like powdery pallor of mimosa, demands a certain type of wan radiance, which Après l'Ondée embodies perfectly. But as usual with Guerlain, there is a lot more to it than that. The slightly one-dimensional, cheap feel of heliotropin is offset by a melancholy, powdery iris note. If you left things at this point, you'd have a first-class funeral, complete with four horses and gray ostrich feathers. But Guerlain suffuses the whole thing with optimistic sunlight by using, as in so many of their classic fragrances, a touch of what a chef would call bouquet de Provence: thyme, rosemary, sage. This discreet hint of earthly pleasures is what makes Après l'Ondée smile through its tears. Among pale, romantic fragrances, only Après l'Ondée has the unresolved but effortless feel of the watery piano chords that make Debussy's pieces (*Images* is exactly contemporary) so poignant. One of the twenty greatest perfumes of all time. LT

Après Tout (Fragonard) ★ ★ ★ *transparent rose* $ $

I have to declare an interest: the owner of Fragonard is a friend, and many years ago I helped her put together a now-discontinued line of four fragrances called Absolus. Fragonard is, from the standpoint of perfumery, a weird outfit. They own a prime location in the center of Grasse and do tours of a perfume museum there and in two other locations, Eze farther down the coast and another one in Paris. The museum visit is free, but ends in a shop full of beautifully presented products where tourists drop unconscionable amounts of cash. The Grasse museum tour amusingly used to include a station in front of the perfumer's office, which consisted of a front room with the perfumery "organ," all little bottles in neat rows, and a spartan back office with a table and a phone. Like an endangered mammal in a zoo, the perfumer usually hid in the back and was seldom visible to the crowd pressing their noses against the glass. When I worked with them twelve years ago, Fragonard's line consisted of unremarkable knockoffs, and I was urging them to do better. It's good to see that the niche market has now made this possible. Après Tout is a tea-rose fragrance of good quality and conventional structure, with woody wine-like notes typical of the genre. LT

Aqua Allegoria Angélique-Lilas (Guerlain) ★ ★ *Calone floral* $
An unnecessary footnote to L'Eau d'Issey, fifteen years later. TS

Aqua Allegoria Cherry Blossom (Guerlain) ★ *chemical floral* $ $
An indescribably awful citrus floral bearing no connection to cherry or any other kind of blossom. LT

Aqua Allegoria Figue Iris (Guerlain) ★ ★ *dusty green* $ $
I give up on the Aqua Allegorias. They started out as a nifty idea: simple bold things done with nice raw materials, a sort of Guerlain Lite. They gradually degenerated into garish accords done with blaring aromachemicals, a sort of Impulse Heavy. This thing smells neither of figs

nor iris (more like fig leaf and dust) and makes no sense except as an expensive air freshener. LT

Aqua Allegoria Grosellina (Guerlain) ★ *dire fruity* $
The recent Aquas have jettisoned everything that gave Guerlain an edge in the field of lightweight fragrances: elegance of construction and quality of materials. Grosellina, named after *groseilles* (French for "redcurrants"), is a repellent, brutal chemical composition that instantly re-creates the smell in the lobby of a fragrance firm, the tutti-frutti belch from the lab down the hall. Guerlain has so far been merciless in ditching Aquas that didn't sell, so let's hope this one is headed for the scrapyard. LT

Aqua Allegoria Herba Fresca (Guerlain) ★ ★ ★ *weird mint* $
Exercise: Use mint as a core note in a fragrance without recalling toothpaste. Most perfumers would desist, but Guerlain gives it a try. First, use the weird mint (shiso, aka *Perilla frutescens*) that the Japanese sometimes use in sushi, and that has an odd anisic feel. Second, marry it with the freshest, most deliciously soothing infusion of lime, verbena, and tea, with a floral touch to offset the almost medicinal effect. Stir well, and serve in a lovely bottle. Simple, really. LT

Aqua Allegoria Laurier Réglisse (Guerlain) ★ ★ *citrus floral* $ $
Please, guys, shape up or quit now. Whatever happened to the old Aquas where the name was apt, the fragrance fresh and humorous, and the quality adequate? This silly thing smells of neither licorice nor bay leaves (that might have been interesting) and instead is a dull, anorexic citrus floral full of cute but overly powerful aromachemicals, basically a shower gel scent with bells on. A waste of (their) time and (your) money. LT

Aqua Allegoria Lemon Fresca (Guerlain) ★ *flat lemon* $
Despite the amusing Asterix Latin name, which sounds like one of Claudius's centurions shopping at Harrods, this is a dull, short little citrus.

To be avoided particularly when you consider that the Guerlain range contains two outstanding citrus fragrances, Eau de Guerlain and Philtre d'Amour. LT

Aqua Allegoria Lilia Bella (Guerlain) ★ ★ ★ *lily lily* $
A pleasant, well-executed lily soliflore, if you like that sort of thing. LT

Aqua Allegoria Mandarine-Basilic (Guerlain) ★ ★ *mandarin base* $
Someone has come up with a delightful, fresh mandarin base. It's too bad Guerlain didn't put together a full fragrance to show it off. TS

Aqua Allegoria Pamplelune (Guerlain) ★ ★ ★ ★
glowing grapefruit $
The "Guerlain for beginners" idea of the Aqua Allegoria (surely *-ica*, but Guerlain are better perfumers than classical scholars) line was a very good one, and the first five released in 1999 were cause for celebration. Great firms like Guerlain have access, exclusive in some instances, to exceptional raw materials. These enter into masterpieces such as Mitsouko and Shalimar, but popular taste wanted them in more legible form. Until then, Guerlain, constrained by the canons of great perfumery, seemed reluctant to compose jingles when it could do symphonies. The first five Aqua Allegoria fragrances created a new category of perfume, close to what the French touchingly used to call a *sent-bon* (smells good), but stamped with greatness. The early ones were unfussy, clear compositions with enough intelligence to be called fragrances, and with all their structure explicit. They also benefited from the artistry of the brilliant Mathilde Laurent, who composed the first Shalimar Eau Légère and later left to take charge of bespoke perfumery at Cartier, the saddest waste of human talent since Rimbaud decided to study engineering. Pamplelune, the only survivor of that first batch along with Herba Fresca, became an instant best seller, and established Laurent in the business. It is without question the best grapefruit fragrance ever, and has that magical quality, typical of perfectly conceived and executed

fragrances, of being much more than the sum of its parts. Until Pample-lune, grapefruit had been used chiefly as a citrus variant in masculine top notes, followed by a predictable diminuendo toward woody notes. Laurent married grapefruit instead with an intensely pink floral accord and somehow gave it durability and that elusive quality of radiance: the ability to project an accurate image of itself at a distance. A sunny masterpiece. LT

Aqua Allegoria Pivoine Magnifica (Guerlain) ★ *nasty floral* $
The last thing on earth that needed simplifying is the kick-ass peony accord typical of contemporary ditzy florals (there you go, a new perfume category). Like chewing tinfoil while staring at a welding arc. LT

Aqua Allegoria Tiaré Mimosa (Guerlain) ★ *not either* $$
This thing smells neither of the glorious Polynesian flower nor of the lovely European one. What does it smell of? Some stupid combination of fruity, floral, and citrus. LT

Aqua Allegoria Tutti Kiwi (Guerlain) ★ *not kiwi* $
This one is done in the new "flavors from hell" style of recent Aquas, and furthermore the perfumers are getting lazy, since it bears no resemblance whatever to kiwi. I couldn't think of any use for it, but my daughter, age seven, stole it and occasionally wears it to school. I think it smells rather good on her, though not as good as nothing. LT

Aqua pour Homme (Bulgari) ★ ★ *citrus woody* $
If I were queen, one of my first acts would be to declare a moratorium on men's sport fragrances. This one keeps a low profile in an effort not to offend but can't hide its bareness. TS

Aqua pour Homme Marine (Bulgari) ★ ★ *pepper melon* $
An absolutely impeccable fragrance for the complimentary shower gel at the gym. Good for nothing else. TS

Aqua Velva Classic Ice Blue (Combe, Inc.) ★★ *minty herbaceous* $
One of the more mysterious things men used to do is abrade the top
layer of the face with blunt razor blades, stanch the bleeding with styptic
stone, and then splash 98 percent alcohol on the whole seeping mess.
This daily rite of passage ensured they were ready to go out and sell
mainframes. I was waiting for that primal-scream feeling, but none
came (no cuts, razors have moved on), and the smell is nowhere near as
good as it was. LT

Aquawoman (Rochas) ★ *watery floral* $$
As near nonexistence as it is possible to be while still remaining techni-
cally a fragrance. LT

Arabie (Serge Lutens) ★★★★ *herbal bitters* $$$
A cousin to Ambre Sultan, Arabie is slightly more daring and less com-
fortable, with fewer debts to Shalimar than to the herbal, anisic floral of
L'Heure Bleue. Playing on the plaintive interval of bitter and sweet that
makes liqueurs like Hungary's Unicum so memorable, Arabie sets a
powerful suite of herbs like basil and bay against a polished mahogany
backdrop of dried dates. The combination is dense, delectable, and uncanny, a familiar tune transcribed to a strange scale. TS

Aramis (Aramis) ★★★★ *leather chypre* $
Aramis, still touchingly encased in the same burl-walnut-veneer-effect
box I remember from my adolescence, is the Rock of Gibraltar of masculines, around since forever (1965) and, for some reason, largely un-
dented. Aramis and Brut were the first fragrances that ordinary young
men like myself actually thought about, as opposed to merely splashed
on. It had an aura of sophistication, and the girls liked it. I always loved
Aramis, and found out today who composed it: Bernard Chant, he of
Cabochard (1959). I immediately had a belated epiphany, embarrassingly obvious in hindsight: Aramis is none other than Cabochard

slimmed down for masculine use. Now that Cabochard has been damaged beyond repair, you might as well get Aramis if you want a leather chypre. LT

Aramis 900 (Aramis) ★ ★ ★ ★ *floral oriental* $
How time flies, and how it comes back eventually! In my mind, Aramis was the seventies, and Aramis 900 the eighties. Wrong again: Aramis was 1965, and thus took a mere five years to go from my nose to my brain, while 900 (1973) required fully seven. Both are by the colossally great Bernard Chant, composer of Cabochard, Cinnabar, Estée, and Beautiful. A900 feels as if it has been modernized, and I do not have at hand a sample of the old to make sure. Not that it matters: the structure is still the same outrageous thing: a resinous oriental in the manner of Youth Dew overlaid with a dry green-chypre floral. And by the way, it's for guys, smells terrific, and costs little. As W. F. Deedes would have said, "Shurely shome mishtake." LT

Arcus (Amouage) ★ ★ *short grapefruit* $$$
After a terrific, sulfuraceous grapefruit blast lasting five minutes, Arcus settles down to a dull woody-citrus (nootkatone) accord like a thousand others. Pointless. LT

Aria di Capri (Carthusia) ★ ★ ★ ★ *iced amaro* $$
The Italian perfume house of Carthusia apparently dates from 1948, beginning as a collection of fragrances said to be based on centuries-old monastery recipes. True or not, the originals have undoubtedly been reorchestrated to modern ingredients and tastes. Whoever did Aria di Capri, whether in 1948 or just a few years ago, should be proud: it is the standout of this line, a winning, multifaceted, but unfussy woody floral with the freshness and medicinal strangeness of infused botanicals. It reminds me of a delicious drink of Italian bitters called a *lavorato,* which I had over ice with a view of the Duomo in Milan: each

astringent sip shot me through with that invigorating sensation of increased clarity that only bitter food and drink will give. Original and well done. TS

Armani Attitude (Armani) ★ ★ ★ *patchouli coffee* $ $
This is one of those fragrances that work not because the structure is particularly interesting or the materials exotic or luxurious, but because the balance between known quantities in play has been adjusted until the composition feels just so—if this were recorded music, it would be more a producer's than a composer's achievement. Attitude at first has a generic, early-twenty-first-century guy feel about it, until you realize that the lemon, coffee, cardamom, and patchouli seem to get on with one another unusually well, and appear disposed to spread a little happiness. I'd prefer to smell this on a woman, but I guess a guy or a smelling strip will do. LT

Armani Code Elixir de Parfum (Armani) ★ *sugared floral* $ $
A concentrated variation of the original eau de parfum, still a syrupy concoction of achingly sweet florals and sugary notes, freshened only slightly by a better-quality citrus than in the original. I have nightmares of being the chihuahua imprisoned in the purse of the woman who wears it. She would be everyone. TS

Armani Code for Women (Armani) ★ *candy floral* $ $
When floral orientals work, you get well-rounded things that are pretty in an expected way: brushed shoulder-length hair, a strand of pearls, low navy pumps. Code seems to be aiming that way, but instead of gently sweetened woods, it throws in a massive dose of the cotton-candy note of ethylmaltol, which turns its orange blossom directly to syrup. That it takes three heavy-hitting big-name perfumers (Carlos Benaïm, Dominique Ropion, and Olivier Polge) to stir this soup is mysterious, but you can almost see the committee at work: Benaïm bringing the ethylmaltol overdose from Flowerbomb, Ropion engineering a synthetic

white floral the size of a house, and Polge sneaking in the orange-hard-candy note of Liberté. TS

Armani Code pour Homme (Armani) ★ ★ ★ *mild woody* $$
A sedate but pleasant masculine with no surprises, just a light, milky sweetness. TS

Armani Mania pour Homme (Armani) ★ ★ *metallic cedar* $$
The smell of Home Depot: hammers and lumber. TS

Armani pour Homme (Armani) ★ ★ ★ *woody citrus* $$
Armani tries to do an Eau Sauvage with bells on, and briefly succeeds. The citrus top is pretty similar, and is followed by a complex and cleverly put-together heart of spices and woods. Sadly, the cash runs out at $t=8$ minutes and ApH smells a bit naff thereafter. LT

Aromatics Elixir (Clinique) ★ ★ ★ ★ ★ *woody floral* $
Smelling Aromatics Elixir on a strip and especially in the air following a string of "modern" fragrances is like watching Lauren Bacall in *The Big Sleep* after twelve episodes of *Cheers*. The thing fills the room with such a confident presence that it is hard to countenance the fact that Bernard Chant was using the same fragrance materials as everyone else. In his hands everything becomes larger and lighter than life. His trademark structure of a bold herbaceous-patchouli-floral accord buttressed by a chiaroscuro of dozens of related balsamic notes produced very sultry, grown-up fragrances (see Cabochard and Cinnabar). It works even better when done in the bright, fresh, herbaceous, almost medicinal manner of Aromatics Elixir. AE achieves at once salubrious radiance and luxurious dusk, a balancing act to my knowledge only attained since by Patou's Sublime. A masterpiece. LT

Around Midnight (By Mark Buxton) ★ ★ ★ *incense storax* $$$
Actors want to direct, nerds want pectorals, columnists wish copy editors

would rot in hell, and perfumers want their own brand. With the possible exception of pectorals, these are all manifestations of the Peter Principle; i.e., that everything tends to rise to its level of incompetence. Of these, the frustration of perfumers is the easiest to understand: talents like Mark Buxton are capable of masterworks and probably have to answer, day in, day out, to depressingly banal briefs. Unfortunately, in achieving complete freedom they get rid of useful as well as redundant constraints and tend to submit unedited work to the scrutiny of the world. I find Around Midnight to be an unremarkable incense fragrance in a field crowded with them (incense has been popular of late). Remarkably, however, the list of materials includes no incense. If that is true, it is at the very least an interesting technical achievement. LT

Arpège (Lanvin) ★ ★ ★ ★ *unisex classic* $$
I have long held the opinion that, much as people's politics tend to drift rightward with age, perfumes become more masculine with time. This is partly due to the fact that most classic feminines undergo breast reduction at each reformulation, and partly due to the outrageous, borderline-slutty girliness of many modern feminines, which makes the ladylike masterpieces of an earlier age seem positively virile. Add to that the fact that most modern masculines are either fresh-woody nonentities or chemical foghorns, and you will see why the discerning guy raids his grandma's shelves. Arpège is a case in point. It was reformulated many times, both stealthily and openly, all the while claiming absolute fidelity to the original formula. Today it is an elegant, nutty, woody floral with an overall cashmere beige tonality that would be very dowdy on all but a guy. Recommended. LT

Arpège pour Homme (Lanvin) ★ ★ ★ *woody spicy* $
Mainstream male perfumery is so dire at the moment that one is pathetically grateful for a fragrance that, while adhering to the requisite unrelieved dullness, includes ingredients beyond the reach of a fabric

softener budget. Such is Arpège pour Homme: gray-brown, nondescript, but at least affable. LT

Artemisia (Penhaligon's) ★ ★ ★ *powdery floral* $$
Warning: despite the name, this does not smell of wormwood. It is a Climat-style bluestocking floral that smells cheap, slightly vulgar, but not bad. Overpriced. LT

Art of Perfumery 1 (Art of Perfumery) ★ *metallic citrus* $$
What on earth can be the point of a niche firm bringing out low-quality mainstream perfumes? The same, only more expensive? This is a nasty metallic masculine that could have been produced by any one of a hundred trashy brands. AoP clearly suffers from a total lack of creative direction. LT

Art of Perfumery 2 (Art of Perfumery) ★ *herbal cologne* $$
Curiously unadventurous fresh citrus herbal top note with a faded, oily-smelling, unpleasantly dense woody-floral drydown. TS

Art of Perfumery 3 (Art of Perfumery) ★ *white floral* $$
A disastrous attempt at producing a more "natural," more recognizably jasmine version of Beyond Paradise by mixing good natural materials with a brutal top note of nasty white-floral aromachemicals. As pleasant as a chronic toothache. LT

Art of Perfumery 4 (Art of Perfumery) ★ ★ *watery woody* $$
In this familiar but competent dry woody masculine, in which pepper and gin notes dominate, the once trendsetting aquatic note of Calone (Escape, L'Eau d'Issey) seems more screechy than fresh. TS

Art of Perfumery 5 (Art of Perfumery) ★ *hay rose* $$
This balsamic tobacco rose is a noisy, clumsy composition of no particular interest. LT

Art of Perfumery 6 (Art of Perfumery) ★ ★ *hickory smoke* $$
What initially seems an interesting exercise in woodsmoke notes doesn't add up well with its woody-rose setting. AoP6 quickly fades to something vague and dull, which means it must be a masculine. Might be useful if you need to claim you were at a barbecue this afternoon. TS

Art of Perfumery 7 (Art of Perfumery) ★ *woody rose* $$
A failed attempt at emulating Fléchier's Une Rose for Frédéric Malle, using a huge amount of a hideously powerful woody amber that makes this one of the most unpleasant perfumes I have ever encountered. LT

Aspen (Coty) ★ ★ ★ *crisp herbal* $
Aspen is a very good Cool Water–style green-apple fougère with a winning herbal-minty crispness up top, better than most of the luxury brand variations on the same theme. Surprising till you remember that the great secret of the nonluxury perfumes is that the only allure they have for the buyer is their smell. TS

Astor Place (Bond No. 9) ★ ★ *cucumber green* $$$
How can you make a fragrance named for an intersection with three Starbucks cafés and fail to include a coffee note? I realize this is not a legitimate complaint, so I put to you: who is responsible for shilling a base containing violet nitrile (cucumber) as swank iris? TS

Atlas Cedar (Jean-Charles Brosseau) ★ *peppery woody* $
Our masculine soup of the day is Pine-Sol with freshly ground pepper. Unconscionably hideous. TS

Atman (Phat Farm) ★ *cheap amber* $$
Depressing, poverty-stricken thing. Kimora Lee and Russell Simmons allegedly donate the profits on this fragrance to charity. The loss of earnings should be manageable. LT

A Travers le Miroir (Thierry Mugler) ★ ★ ★ ★ *bitter tuberose* $$$

The Miroir series of five fragrances is subtitled "Dare the Metamorphosis," which seems an oddly appropriate slogan considering that Thierry Mugler has left the building, is now a bodybuilder called Manfred and almost unrecognizable. ATlM (Through the Looking Glass) is a very interesting, bitter, herbaceous tuberose, a sort of Amarige without the lace and white cowboy boots, almost a masculine. I normally hate this type of fragrance, but I'll make an exception, because this one is really arresting. It was put together by a young perfumer, Alexis Dadier of the Grasse firm Mane, clearly a talent to watch. LT

Attrape-Coeurs (Guerlain) ★ ★ ★ ★ *amber violets* $$$

Composed by the brilliant Mathilde Laurent and initially released as Guet-Apens for Christmas 1999, this fragrance, renamed Attrape-Coeurs, was the centerpiece of the opening party for the new flagship store in 2005, by which time Laurent had, sadly, left Guerlain for Cartier. At least the formula hasn't been messed with. This is an essay on amber (to be exact, a De Laire base called Ambre 83) in the manner of Chanel's Bois des Iles, but with the powdery opacity typical of the Guerlain style. The rest of the accord is an intense, radiant, Wurlitzer organ blast of rose, violet, and iris notes. It smells rich and wonderful, a Christmas pudding doused in brandy flames, to be washed down with more of same. LT

L'Autre (Diptyque) ★ ★ ★ ★ *garam masala* $$

Observe two strains of gourmand orientals in fragrance: first, the Shalimar school, lush and sweet, based on amber and joined to exotic fantasies that said more about the mind of Europe than the life of Asia; second, the postmodern school of the original Comme des Garçons fragrance and other recent niche creations, based on the smell of import shops and the cuisine of actual Near Eastern friends and neighbors. While the Shalimar strain, as a perfume daydream with no debt owed to reality, has flourished, producing a long line of beautiful fragrances, the latter strain can seem hobbled by a desire for authenticity. L'Autre dates from 1973 and shows both the strengths and weaknesses of this hippie style: on the plus side, it smells both new and ancient in its combination of appealing resinous smells, emphasizing the pine-and-lime facets of coriander and cumin, and on the minus side, it does rather make you smell like a chutney. A fine but too literal-minded effort. About twenty years after L'Autre, Chris Sheldrake at Serge Lutens moved this style of oriental fragrance out of the pantry and into the realm of true invention. TS

Avatar (Coty) ★ *crap fougère* $
I used to think Houbigant's Duc de Vervins was the worst fougère of all time. Wrong: Avatar beats it hands down, with a composition that would smell cheap even if they gave it away. LT

Aveda Men Pure-Formance (Aveda) ★ ★ ★ ★ *spicy lavender* $$
Aveda's in-house perfumer, the brilliant Koichi Shiozawa, has one of the hardest jobs in the world, getting harder. I met him some years back at the World Perfumery Congress, and he explained in impeccable French that, just when he'd finally figured out how to make decent fragrances using only naturals, Aveda had moved the goalposts and now required him to use only organic materials, which of course are far rarer. Amazingly, Mr. Shiozawa seems to have succeeded: Aveda Men is a perfectly lovely lavender-vetiver overlaid with, Aveda says, a myrtle material (kunzea) and some citrus notes. It is wholesome, harmonious, surprisingly fresh for such a rich accord, and just as surprisingly durable. Beautiful work. LT

Aziyadé (Parfum d'Empire) ★ ★ ★ *Persian dessert* $$$
A fruit gourmand in the spice-shop category of Diptyque's L'Autre, Serge Lutens's Arabie, and Kenzo Jungle for Women. Aziyadé's bright magenta fruit notes of prune and pomegranate have a joyously trashy appeal, made only trashier by an exaggerated Amy Winehouse's eyeliner ap-

proach to exoticism: bit of cardamom, bit of cumin, and you're the Queen of Sheba! A crude idea done better elsewhere, but undeniably fun for attention-getting dress-up. TS

Azurée (Estée Lauder) ★ ★ ★ ★ ★ *citrus leather* $
Why is it that, in my years of collecting and talking about fragrances with other people passionate about the stuff, nobody has ever mentioned Azurée? All those connoisseurs love leather, love pre-eighties perfumery, complain that the classics have been debased by lousy substitutions with cheaper stuff. They weep that Cabochard has had its complicated, stormy bits removed; they mourn the streamlining of Jolie Madame; they cry that Caron has tampered with their Tabac Blond; they sigh that an era has passed. Meanwhile, Estée Lauder, faithful keeper of one of the most consistently high-quality lines of fragrances ever created, falls prey to the usual notion that only the new is worth mentioning, and hides the old stuff under the counter like contraband. We hope these fragrances see more of the light of day after this book comes out. Azurée is a grand, confident leather from 1969 by Bernard Chant, creator of Cabochard and Aromatics Elixir, with some of the surprisingly persistent lemony-woody sunshine of Monsieur Balmain and a soft, dusty, almost grimy leather-chypre heart as comfortable as an old work glove, a fragrance now as good as it's ever been and just about as good as it gets. TS

Azzaro Couture (Azzaro) ★ ★ ★ ★ *fruity chypre* $$$
The two recent Azzaro Now fragrances showed signs of life, and Azzaro Couture, with its neo-seventies bottle, continues the revival of this long-dormant firm. Composed by Aurélien Guichard, son of the great Jean and, one assumes, steeped in perfume from birth, this is a brilliant re-interpretation of the late-seventies chypre structure. It has something of the creamy-woody texture of Ivoire and Madame Carven, but drier, with a cedarwood side borrowed from masculines of that era (Krizia Uomo comes to mind). It also has something of the sunny Italian dispo-

sition of the original Diorama and its distant relative, the lamented Helietta (by Helietta Caracciolo). What makes it novel and effective is a
very clever accord, which while not overtly foody is reminiscent of ripe
mango and elegantly joins together the creamy, fruity, and resinous
sides of the fragrance. Recommended. LT

Azzaro Men Now (Azzaro) ★ ★ ★ ★ *woody citrus* $
Read the PR and your heart sinks: this fragrance is allegedly made of
two accords, one called Vibration Sphere, the other Cocoon Sphere. But
spray the thing in the strange bilobate bottle that looks like it's about to
reproduce by fission, and you're in for a great surprise: the reader may
choose not to believe this without verification, but this may be that rarest of things, a good modern masculine. For once all the materials familiar to the genre—wood, citrus, discreet spices, etc.—are fused in a
single smooth, transparent, buff-colored top note: spray it on fabric to
make it last. That this should exist at all is a surprise. That it should arise
at Azzaro, which had done little of note since 1979, is a miracle. LT

Azzaro pour Homme (Azzaro) ★ ★ ★ ★ ★ *anisic lavender* $
The monotheists among us believe there is only one proper genre of
masculine fragrance, the fougère, and that its apex was reached with the
aromatic fougères of the late 1970s. Some, I among them, believe that
the finest aromatic ever was Azzaro pour Homme (1978). You can tell it
was a perfume aimed at smart guys: the slogan "Un parfum pour les
hommes qui aiment les femmes qui aiment les hommes" is not for the
slow-witted. I wore it today for the first time in twenty years, and it felt
just as it always did: affable, slightly vulgar, completely unpretentious,
and overall just delicious. This fragrance is so good and historically so
important that I have met to date six perfumers who claim to have composed it (Gérard Anthony is officially credited), which puts it in the
same league as Giorgio and a few others for multiple attribution. Azzaro's other fragrances have mostly been disappointments, but all is forgiven. Just keep making this one. LT

Azzaro Women Now (Azzaro) ★ ★ ★ ★ *herbaceous floral* $

This fragrance is probably seeing a psychotherapist as I write. The strange bottle looks uncannily like those mysterious wet-shave razors for women, curvy, pink, and waisted. The fragrance is one part Déclaration, two parts Par Amour, i.e., a delicious, girly floral with designer stubble. It's very nice indeed, original and daring for a feminine, but I feel once it's had the operation it may be happier as a guy and will come back in a black spray can. I, for one, am going to wear it forthwith. LT

Baby Doll Paris (Yves Saint Laurent) ★ ★ *fruity floral* $

In the nineties, young women, to make their feminist mothers despair, enjoyed a brief fashion of carrying pacifiers as accessories and drinking out of baby bottles, while wearing a type of cutesy ruffled minidress called a baby doll. BDP was the first of a long line of fruity-floral Paris flankers, a strident, sulfuraceous grapefruit with a harsh, ammoniac feel, as if the wearer needed a diaper change. TS

Baby Grace (Philosophy) ★ *mimosa musk* $

Never to be outdone in cuteness, Philosophy's packaging explains, "If God has a face, surely it is that of a child, and if there is a place called heaven, it must smell like a baby." In its gale-force strength, Baby Grace reminds me of the lethally huge toddler in *Spirited Away*. Good news though: despite the vast diaper, the prevailing smell is merely a bad mimosa reconstruction. LT

Badgley Mischka (Badgley Mischka) ★ ★ ★ ★ ★ *gorgeous fruity* $$

The first time I met Badgley Mischka's fragrance was in a lab bottle tester at Bergdorf Goodman, a few months before its release. Sprayed on a blotter, the first thing that happened was a big, breathtakingly gorgeous fruity top note, which I promptly decided to forget about, since what doesn't have a big fruity top note these days? The second time I smelled it, I sprayed it from the real bottle (a set designer's idea of a classy bottle, with a metal nameplate making it look like an executive paperweight) and was immediately floored by a big, breathtakingly gorgeous fruity top note, with both lushness and freshness, reminding me of juicy edibles at the moment of maximum ripeness before everything goes to brandy— peaches, mangoes, lychees, pineapples—but fruity fragrances aren't my style, so I moved on. The third time I smelled Badgley Mischka, I sprayed it from a new tester for the purpose of writing about it, and the first thing I noticed was a really big, breathtakingly gorgeous fruity top note, but as I was feeling rather academic, having just been complaining about the prevalence of fruity fragrances, I focused instead on its similarities to Angel or Gucci's Rush, its lactonic woody drydown that unfortunately thins at the end, talking to LT about a possible link he smelled to Narciso Rodriguez for Her, and so on. The fourth time I sprayed it, it was after I'd written a dry, appreciative review, calm, sensible, and helpful, and it was evening, after dinner, with the lights out; I wanted to smell that big, gorgeous fruity thing again, now that the pressure was over. It rang out, came chorusing up from the skin in great clear peals like church bells on Easter morning, simple and perfect and sure, a message of straight-forward good news, and I imagine it's rather like this when the long-suffering hero looks up at the end of a string of confused romantic disasters only to discover that his longtime friend has all this time been the most beautiful girl in the room, and only familiarity prevented him from seeing it. Time to face the facts and hire a caterer—it's love. TS

Baghari (Robert Piguet) ★ ★ ★ ★ *orange chypre* $ $

The poetically named firm of Fashion Fragrances and Cosmetics Ltd has been doing a wonderful job of bringing back, as true to the originals as possible, the fragrances of Robert Piguet. Baghari is their third one, after Fracas and Bandit. I was waiting for this reconstruction: Baghari was great stuff to start with, perhaps the only Piguet fragrance endowed with anything resembling human warmth. Furthermore, I knew that Aurélien Guichard was in charge of the restoration work. A perfumer capable of composing Chinatown has everyone's full attention, particularly when doing a tricky technical job measured against a known reference. The result, I am glad to report, is perfect. Baghari is a dark, candied-fruit-and-spice fragrance given a dry lift and powdery freshness by a large slug of aldehydes. In florals, aldehydes act as a white background against which floral colors can shine. But a fruity-spicy aldehydic is quite a different beast and uses them, so to speak, in the *manière noire*. Aldehydes are, after all, at home in the intense orange-peel note of Baghari, where they were first identified. Like Guerlain's Vol de Nuit and Caron's Alpona, Baghari is half medicinal, half suggestive of edible medieval marvels such as Speculaas and panforte. Superb, and true to form. Now could we please have Futur? LT

Bahiana (Maître Parfumeur et Gantier) ★ ★ *woody citrus* $$$
Bahiana could have been a great fragrance had it not tried to be so "modern" (industry-speak for dull) in the top notes. It's a citrus that thinks it's a floral and then changes its mind to be woody. The idea is basically good, but the execution is too cheap and soapy. LT

Le Baiser du Dragon (Cartier) ★ ★ *failed oriental* $$
One gets the feeling that Cartier finds it hard to move on from its Art Deco heyday and is oddly incapable of reinterpreting that magnificent period in ways other than small-scale retro bling. Their choice of red for their recently unified packaging says it all: a heavy cinnabar, halfway between Chinese lacquer and opera plush, perfect for a menu binder in a pretentious restaurant. Give them credit, LBdD's chinoiserie is at least coherent from name to bottle, though the much-anticipated contents turn out to be a disappointment. Picture Shalimar without citrus, a dollop of sweet-green amaretto up top to give the dreaded cheap chocolate character of Must, plus a huge woody-rosy accord in the middle largely lost in the noise. For something so loud and rich, it runs out of puff early. This is a floral oriental trying so hard to get everything on board that the dragon ends up above maximum gross weight and has to abort takeoff. All in all, a puzzle. Then came a strange epiphany: I handed a smelling strip to my colleague Ian Smith, an analyst of thirty years'

standing with the defunct fragrance firm of BBA and one of the inventors of smelling gas chromatography. In his wonderfully syncopated London accent, he passed a judgment that has not so far been appealed: "That's nineteen-bloody-seventy-two Old Spice, that is." LT

Baldessarini (Hugo Boss) ★ ★ ★ ★ *woody fruity* $$
Named after Boss's boss, Werner B., this fragrance has remained curiously unnoticed considering its excellence. Part of the problem may be that the Hugo Boss perfume lineup is a model of confusion, and you'd need an audio guide to make sense of the Boss shelf at Sephora. Baldessarini is supposedly aimed at the Silver Surfer, not the cartoon character, but the man who is (a) on the wrong side of fifty, (b) has all his hair and plenty of cash, and (c) still gets daily opportunities to spread his genes. I manage the first of these criteria effortlessly, so I guess I'm allowed to wear it. Baldessarini is to perfumery what the script for *Toy Story* is to movies: an amazingly skillful, multilayered thing that can be enjoyed by everyone for entirely different reasons. Level 1: Splash it on, or better still enter a bathroom after someone else has, and it feels like a salubrious, sunny cologne. Level 2: Wait ten minutes, and it enters what musicians would call a development section where fresh woody and warm notes shimmer constantly like colored flakes in an opal. Level 3: Wait till the drydown, and you get a superb woody-fruity accord redolent of damascones and damascenones, those astonishing molecules that glow like stained glass and span the olfactory range from raisin to rose. Baldessarini's drydown is not new: it was first tried in Rochas's Globe (1990), a pioneering and commercially disastrous fragrance that tried to play by a different set of rules, by avoiding all masculine clichés, and ended up, like many of Rochas's efforts, an honorable failure. Behind Globe, there is the largely forgotten Gran Valor by the distinguished German firm of Mäurer & Wirtz (makers of the timeless Tabac [now known as Tabac Original] and these days little else of note). Baldessarini brings it all together and, successful or not, is one of the best fragrances in the pretty-barren field of masculines. LT

Baldessarini Ambré (Hugo Boss) ★ *crap amber* $$
This from the guys who did the wonderful Hugo Boss Baldessarini? A sad joke, indistinguishable from a hundred others. LT

Balkis (Parfums de Nicolaï) ★ ★ ★ *powdery rose* $$
This one appears to have changed somewhat between the version I smelled at the time of the first release two years ago and today. It is quieter, less fruity-rosy, less bright, and overall less interesting. This is one of Patricia de Nicolaï's more commercial fragrances and, while not offensive, fails to rise above a skillful, generic prettiness unworthy of this firm's great creations. LT

Balle de Match (Parfums de Nicolaï) ★ ★ ★ *green citrus* $
A competent but unexciting modern masculine in the woody-grapefruit style. Probably sells well and helps keep Parfums de Nicolaï afloat. LT

Balmain (Balmain) ★ ★ ★ *unisex chypre* $$
What was Balmain thinking? To bring out a retro green chypre in 1998 was either otherworldly or foolhardy: the genre had all but exhausted itself, the classics (Givenchy III, the first Scherrer) were selling poorly, and only the dated and skeletal Eau du Soir held up the ragged flag of this once-classic genre. Balmain is unusually green-aromatic up top, and overall makes a very presentable masculine in the manner of Guerlain's Derby, only drier. LT

Balmya (Balmain) ★ *fruity floral* $$
When in a hole, don't dig. Balmya is a fine piece of spadework, a fruity magnolia clone when none was needed. When is Balmain going to wake up? LT

Bandit (Robert Piguet) ★ ★ ★ ★ ★ *bitter chypre* $$
I'll start with a note of caution: I've owned several bottles of the original Bandit over the years, and this is not it. But read on. Reproducing mod-

ern versions of Germaine Cellier's masterpieces is both easy and hard: easy, because her perfumes had such bold, distinctive structures that even a pixelated version of Bandit, such as the last, dreadfully cheapened and traduced "original" version, was still recognizably the old scoundrel; hard, because Cellier was fond of using bases in her compositions, to the horror of other perfumers. Bases are mini-perfumes, prepackaged compositions that dispense you from reinventing the wheel every time you need a complex but recognizable note in your fragrance: peach, leather, amber, etc. Some, like Ambre 83, Persicol, and Animalis, are so rich and so good that you wonder why nobody just bottled them and sold them. The problem with Cellier's use of bases is that half of them have disappeared, so that even if the whole formula were to fall into your hands and you trekked to the address of the maker of Dianthiline 12 in Grasse, you'd likely find a time-share development instead of a little fragrance factory. Modern reconstructions of Cellier's perfumes are above all a work of translation of the original formula into things you can actually identify and buy today. In my opinion, this can be positive: these perfumes always carried a certain amount of excess baggage to compensate for the starkness of the basic accord. If it can be done elegantly, a cleanup is in itself no bad thing. One just has to get used to the idea that, as with vintage aircraft, what you see is a machine in which perhaps only the serial number plate subsists from the original, and every spar and rivet has been made from scratch. This version of the 1947 original is a bit like a reconstructed Bell X-1 supersonic aircraft: sleek, beautifully done, and a mite too clean, as if ready for a movie shoot. But the magic is all there: bitter, dark yet fresh, beguiling without any softness, and still several unlit streets ahead of every other leather chypre around. LT

Baume du Doge (Eau d'Italie) ★ ★ *milky anisic* $ $
Like Hypnotic Poison and Fahrenheit 32 before it, Baume du Doge aims for a milk-with-ice effect. After a semibrutal top note featuring a woody amber that should be serving time for assault, a few striking moments

of coherence are followed by an ugly, bare drydown as charming as a cement lot. TS

B de Boucheron (Boucheron) ★ *canned fruit* $$$
Tinned peaches against a Glade background. LT

b.e. (Becker Eshaya) ★ *fruity amber* $
A chemical haiku for people who dislike fragrance, b.e. sets a slightly sad peachy floral on a Pleasures-style musk with a touch of screechy woody amber. TS

Beach (Bobbi Brown) ★★★★ *lemony jasmine* $$
Predating Bond No. 9's similar Fire Island by several years, Beach is a mood-lifting breezy combination of French suntan lotion and a happily synthetic ocean breeze, achieving that much-desired but elusive cheap-and-cheerful effect. Easy to like. As the name suggests, it would smell its best accompanied by a corn dog with mustard. TS

Beat (Rimmel) ★ *Alizé belch* $
At last we have commercially available in the West the powerful passion-fruit odor of which all clean bathrooms in Southeast Asia reek, I assume because it encourages visitors to leave quickly. Exceptionally repulsive, even when considered solely against other airheaded fruity florals. TS

Beautiful (Estée Lauder) ★★★★ *classic rose* $
It is. With Bernard Chant (Cabochard) and Max Gavarry (Dioressence) contributing to its creation, this rich, tobacco-tinged rose from 1985 has a classic profile. You can smell, underneath the very eighties intense sweetness (YSL Paris uses a similar powdery, liqueur-like rose), a mossy chypre base of more depth and complexity than usual, pairing sweet amber with an intensely vegetal green. But it also has a very modern feel, with a bright, herbal, woody radiance that broadcasts an attractive

low hum all around. This said, it smells unfortunately dated, the way many things from the eighties smell dated now: heavier and less legible than current fragrances, but with up-to-the-moment synthetics preventing it from smelling older. Someday it may smell fresh again. TS

Beautiful Love (Estée Lauder) ★ ★ ★ *metallic tuberose* $
Silvery, lactonic, fruity tuberose from outer space. Well built, with a solid, seamless drydown from top to bottom, and interesting, but not quite nice. TS

Beautiful Sheer (Estée Lauder) ★ ★ ★ *pear floral* $
This light, soapy fruity-floral in the modern shampoo style has nothing to do with the original Beautiful. It is a proper, soft pastel scent to match your Laura Ashley curtains or your Impressionist prints. It's worth noting that, for this type of fragrance, Beautiful Sheer has an unusually persistent and well-crafted drydown. TS

Beauty Comes from Within (Creative Scentualization) ★ ★
large peony $$
What comes from within here is a big, powdery peony accord. It joins the marching band of six-foot fluorescent peonies already stalking Fifth Avenue any day. LT

Beauty Rush Appletini (Victoria's Secret) ★ *Jolly Rancher* $
Victoria's Secret has determined that its customers need (1) cleavage and (2) to smell precisely like dime-store candy. You may discern an implicit insult to the male mind in this pair of facts. TS

Beckham Signature Women (Coty) ★ *fruit varnish* $$
Signature? Just draw a cross here . . . and here. This sub-Angel (Thierry Mugler) from hell reaches for a mixture of spray paint and tinned fruit. Could turn out to be useful as a sort of methadone to wean solvent abusers off the good stuff. LT

Be Delicious (Donna Karan) ★ ★ ★ *tart floral* $
A departure from Donna Karan's usual sleek city style, and a wonderful one. Be Delicious belongs to the grand category of cheap and cheerful fragrances, of which perfumer Maurice Roucel has done several, including his terrific Missoni, which is closely related. Be Delicious looks like a green apple, but the fragrance smells like a friendlier variation on Roucel's fresh green floral, Envy, with mouthwatering fruity notes added. Unfortunately, the inventiveness doesn't last; after the top note, it settles into a pleasant but derivative Tommy Girl smell-alike. TS

Be Delicious Fresh Blossom (Donna Karan) ★ ★ *tart peony* $ $
Another throwaway flanker that starts in hair spray and ends in Tommy Girl. Strictly for teenage girls who daydream about shampoo advertisements. TS

Be Delicious Men (Donna Karan) ★ ★ ★ *grapefruit woody* $
One of these intensely vegetal green and citrus top notes, reminding me of both the Jardin scents from Hermès (the tomato-leaf sharpness of Un Jardin en Méditerrannée, the plasticky grapefruit of Un Jardin sur le Nil), but with a standard-issue Cool Water–type drydown. Appealing in an initially jarring but ultimately conventional way, the perfume equivalent of a fauxhawk. TS

Beige (Chanel) ★ ★ *vieille France* $ $ $
When I first heard of this upcoming fragrance, I wondered why the guys at Chanel chose to give it a derogatory name, and I assumed the end result would be sufficiently un-beige to be worth a chuckle. Not so: Beige really is the same color as the big computer monitor you just lugged to the recycling dump. It smells like a dated, dismal average of Ma Griffe, L'Air du Temps, and Climat and drags on like an interminable Sunday afternoon tea at Auntie Mabel's. Amazingly, it does not even possess that redeeming virtue of most Chanel creations: excellent raw materials. A total screwup. LT

Bel-Ami (Hermès) ★ ★ ★ ★ *leather citrus* $$

The original Bel-Ami (1986) was bold, strange, beautiful, and a resounding commercial flop. Taking advantage, one assumes, of some arcane European Union restrictions on aromachemicals, Hermès has reformulated it while hotly denying any change (of course). The new version is much woodier up top, with a coriander note that bears the handwriting of in-house perfumer Jean-Claude Elléna. Gone is the weird, dissonant, citrus-and-leather accord that made the original so attractively irresolute. The drydown now veers toward the musky sweetness of Caron's No. 3. The overall effect is very good and, for those who never met the original, completely convincing. Shame, though. LT

Believe (Britney Spears) ★ ★ ★ *sweet fruity* $

A green-colored take on the sugary fruity floral. Let us be grateful for small mercies, like a top note made slightly more interesting by a touch of black pepper and citrus, and a well-put-together tart-and-sweet sherbet accord, which holds itself together better than Ms. Spears. TS

Bella Belara (Mary Kay) ★ ★ *fruit salad* $

Huge, sweet-sour, jammy fruity floral, almost vulgar enough to be interesting but ultimately too crude to work properly. LT

Belle de Nuit parfum (Fragonard) ★ ★ ★ *plum rose* $$

Fragonard's version of J'Adore but double reinforced with a rich lemongrass-soapy rose. TS

Belle en Rykiel (Sonia Rykiel) ★ ★ ★ ★ *fruity amber* $

Composed by Jean-Pierre Bethouart, this feminine counterpart to the superb Yohji Homme is a skillful three-in-one fresh-fruity-oriental fragrance that must have required a lot of fine-tuning to work right. After a melodious two-tone woody-fruity start reminiscent of Montana's discontinued and excellent Just Me (not the Paris Hilton homonym), BeR seems to find a balance point exactly where minty lavender, dry amber, and woody-floral notes meet. An original interpretation of the current trend for Janus-like feminines built on a masculine drydown. LT

Bellodgia (Caron) ★ ★ *lemony geranium* $$
This is supposed to be the grand carnation of Caron—creamy florals and clove—but I have never smelled the original. Restrictions on the clove note of isoeugenol have forced Caron to reformulate, but unfortunately the job wasn't done well. This is not a carnation, but a lemony geranium, almost like pine in the top note, with the sour soapy drydown that Richard Fraysse, Caron's current perfumer, believes should be the ultimate fate of every fragrance. TS

Belong (Celine Dion) ★ *fruity amber* $
Some kind of hideous downmarket Coco Mademoiselle blending a cheap fruity floral you wouldn't be caught dead in with an unspeakable aftershave you wouldn't be caught dead near. This is the rare feminine bad enough to be a bad masculine. TS

Bel Respiro (Chanel) ★ ★ ★ ★ *green floral* $$$
Of the Big Six that Chanel let loose upon the world early in 2007, Bel Respiro (which I would freely translate as Easy Breathing) is perhaps the least demanding. What I like about it is that the top notes replicate almost exactly the lovely feel of the old Vent Vert at the exact moment when it changed gears from the green galbanum blast of the top notes to the blush-on-a-cheek softness of the floral heart. What I don't like about it is that it then proceeds to fade politely to beige. BR is beautifully put together, but I fear that, like Eau d'Issey, it may end up appealing to the phalanx of women who don't really like perfume. On a guy, though, it would be great. LT

Bendelirious (Etat Libre d'Orange) ★ ★ ★ ★ *iris cherry* $$
Henri Bendel only
The best of the Etat Libre d'Orange fragrances, which state a simple

principle without confusing the message with extra ballast or polish, have been perfumery's perfect pop art: for example, Jasmin et Cigarette (a portrait of a lady via one flower and one Marlboro Light) or Sécrétions Magnifiques (calling the bluff of every trite floral perfume that claimed it smelled of sex). The jolt of joy caused by spraying Bendelirious feels like a fundamental involuntary reflex. I laugh every time: yippee! In 1947, Vincent Roubert used peach to put color in iris's cheeks in the disappeared masterpiece Iris Gris. Now sixty years later, Antoine Lie has repeated the miracle with an exuberant note of cherry—cherry as in cherry candy, Cherry Coke, cherry ice cream, even the much-missed (by me) Cherry 7UP. Together, these materials have the satisfying cold-hot, old-new accord of a square of powder blue beside a square of signal red. They sing. Caveat: the heart and drydown are too strong and sweet and lack the magic of the first hour. But what an hour. TS

Benetton Sport Woman (Benetton) ★ ★ *mandarin soap* $
Given the unrelenting bleakness of the Benetton Sport fragrance line, one imagines the brief for this one must have read like an editorial in *Welding News*. Despite this and against all odds, the perfumer managed to produce a sort of mandarin version of Pleasures that, while not earthshaking, is inoffensive. LT

Bergamote 22 (Le Labo) ★ *light green* $$
If this is a bergamot, I'm a *Phallus impudicus*. Pale, little fresh-green fragrance, Pleasures written in six-point type. LT

Beyond Love (By Kilian) ★ ★ ★ ★ *tuberose tuberose* $$$$
I have never much liked tuberose compositions such as Oscar de la Renta or Fragile. It seemed to me that they achieved their effect only by clipping the wings of the central note itself. Not only is the smell of tuberose flowers wonderful, it isn't even, properly speaking, floral in the clean, vegetal sense of floral fragrances. Tuberoses smell of butter, rubber, leather, blood, and heaven knows what else. Using fresh flowers as a ref-

erence, much as Roudnitska did with muguet (lily of the valley) for Diorissimo, Calice Becker has composed a straight-up tuberose using the best absolute from India, with touches of other notes (magnolia, iris) used only to narrow the gap between the extract and the fresh flower. The result is the best tuberose soliflore on earth. LT

Beyond Paradise (Estée Lauder) ★ ★ ★ ★ ★ *symphonic floral* $
Perfumery becomes art only when it adds something to nature. Applied to florals, however, this banal statement hides a multitude of tricky technical questions. For a start, many flowers, such as gardenia and lily of the valley, yield no oil, and those that do, like rose, produce materials that bear little resemblance to the real thing. Doing a rose, lily-of-the-valley, or gardenia soliflore is therefore artistically as hard as it gets. But realistic florals, though they may be great achievements, should really be judged by a panel of bees rather than by humans. Women have no business smelling like flowers. Abstraction has always been the soul of great perfumery, and abstract florals, where floralcy is not tied to one flower or another, have contributed many of perfumery's greatest masterpieces—such as when a judicious mixture of jasmine and rose, as in the old Vent Vert or in Joy, immediately achieved a glorious choral effect in which individual voices were lost. Doing abstraction with aromachemicals is both trickier and more interesting. Composing a floral one molecule at a time is a formidable combinatorial task, made possible only because over time the problem, like a really hard theorem, has been split into lemmas tackled by different perfumers, and reduced to groups of materials that achieve this or that effect. The enormous artistic edge that chemistry gives perfumers is the ability, familiar to the gods of Olympus and to fairy godmothers when putting together a titanically gifted baby, to compose a personage from disparate inherited virtues: the rosy, grassy freshness of lily of the valley, the rasp of lily proper, the mushroom note of gardenia, the lemon of magnolia, the banana of ylang-ylang, the deep woody velvet of violets, the boozy sweetness of rose, the soapy edge of cyclamen, etc. Marshaling all these

molecular genes into producing something viable, even beautiful, is far from easy. It requires an eye and a nose for both the overall effect and individual detail: each molecule must at different times join up with others in different roles to achieve a graceful arc from top note to dry-down. Calice Becker's Beyond Paradise, coming as it does after a series of masterly approximations—her Tommy Girl and J'Adore (respectively, high noon and sunset)—hits to perfection the dappled, fresh light of early morning shining on the sort of impossible garden that Sweden-borg would have seen in visions and described in detail. Not sure about Beyond, but definitely Paradise. LT

People who become fixated on perfume, enough to start knowingly buying more than they can actually wear, frequently enter the kingdom through a side door: seeking the strange, the hard-to-find, the pearl be-yond price, the long-lost something-or-other. Their minds (and mine, once) tend to go blank when presented with an attractive abstract floral meant to appeal to the hoi polloi. Instead, what the collector of arcana tends to like in florals are legibility, meaning smells you could name from the garden, and imbalance, meaning smells that draw attention to themselves for being outsized or wrong, like avant-garde clothes with unlikely diagonal zippers or puffy volumes where you wouldn't expect. Yet, as I got used to sampling the more recherché florals, a couple of facts eventually emerged from the mass of data: first, as LT points out, balanced abstraction, not representation, is the greater and more diffi-cult art in florals, and second, most florals maintain their illusion only for a brief time, and thin out rapidly or fall apart into constituents, like those sculpture installations of seemingly unrelated objects that from a certain angle spell a word or draw a picture. What is so impressive about Beyond Paradise's masterful portrait of a gorgeously fresh, fictional, ideal tropical flower, possessed of most of the floral virtues, is that the image holds steady for hours of drydown. But the seamless end product doesn't tend to invite consideration of the stubborn perfectionism that must have guided its construction: it takes a lot of work to make something this accomplished appear this easy. Lovers of the exotic beach-fantasy florals put out by numberless niche firms should pick up the weird sci-fi rainbow nipple bottle at the Lauder counter someday and give it an honest try. This said, I confess I admire this fragrance mostly without loving it, which probably says more about me than about Beyond Paradise. I once blurted out about a beautiful, buoyant piece of Mozart's that LT was in the middle of thoroughly enjoying, "You know, man, this thing lacks hip action." At the risk of sounding cranky, my favorite old florals like Joy and Fracas seem all by themselves to conjure up a personal presence in the room, almost solid, someone whose sleeve you might touch. In the last analysis, what often leaves me cold with squeaky-clean BP-style modern florals is that they smell perfect and lovely but not alive—I grasp into space but there's no one there. TS

Beyond Paradise Blue (Estée Lauder) ★ ★ ★ ★   *green floral* $
I love the first BP, and this appears to be merely a variation with less of the darker, sweeter, J'Adore-like notes of the original, replaced by a green, grassy, slightly soapy accord. The symphonic BP structure was so good that BPB feels like a movement during which the cellos and double basses take a rest. Very beautiful in a squeaky-clean, ethereal sort of way. LT

Beyond Paradise Men (Estée Lauder) ★ ★ ★ ★ ★   *green woody* $
Never has the word *accord* been more appropriate than for BP Men. The discovery of the citrus-herbaceous note of dihydromyrcenol in the early nineties added a pale gray puzzle piece to fit somewhere at the junction of yellow citrus, blue lavender, and green melon. As long as differential volatilities are properly taken into account, very complex chords incorporating all these colors can now be created. BP Men and Nautica Voyage are perfect illustrations of this. What is special about BP Men is the way it works more like music than like fragrance. Wear it, and after a few hours you will find your daily life suffused by the same feeling of peace you get when you settle into an armchair after tidying your apartment from end to end. All other masculines (and most feminines) seem

loud, coarse, and bare by comparison. Its composer, Calice Becker, has miraculously found a way to bottle a never-ending dawn such as Concorde pilots used to see when flying westward, racing with the sun. LT

Bigarade Concentrée (Frédéric Malle) ★ ★ ★ *bitter orange* $$$
The name says it all: *bigarade* is bitter (or Seville) orange, the type used in proper English marmalade. The oil, familiar to perfume lovers as the bracingly resinous note in Caron's old Alpona, has an interesting mixture of citrus friendliness and resinous austerity. Elléna's composition cleverly emphasizes both aspects, at the expense of what to my nose is a slightly rubbery top note. Very pleasant, deliberately simple, but somewhat lacking in mystery. LT

Bill Blass Couture 3 (Bill Blass) ★ ★ *ginger rose* $$$
Watery little thing of no interest. LT

Bill Blass Couture 7 (Bill Blass) ★ ★ ★ *dry citrus* $$$
Inspired, if the word applies, by Light Blue but improving on the model. A skeletally dry citrus with a touch of spicy warmth. A sort of wearable *limoncello.* LT

Bill Blass Couture 8 (Bill Blass) ★ *fruity floral* $$$
C8 brings to mind one of the worst perfumes of all time, the first La Prairie (1993), a fragrance that made you wonder whether the people charged with compounding it got danger money. It recycles LP's venomously cloying fruity note, somehow shoehorned into a synthetic white floral in the manner of Tommy Girl, with an effect akin to dressing an elephant in a white tutu. LT

Billet Doux (Fragonard) ★ ★ ★ *classic carnation* $$
This reissue of a Fragonard classic for the eightieth anniversary of the firm comes in a gorgeous bad-taste gold Gloria Swanson bottle. It's a good, old-fashioned, straight-up carnation. LT

Black (Bulgari) ★ ★ ★ ★ ★ *hot rubber* $$

Some of the best fragrances in history are built on precarious equilibria between two contrasting ingredients: the vanilla-vetiver accord of Habanita, the citrus-amber of Shalimar. This widens their emotional keyboard and, when the job is properly poised, allows them to smell different from moment to moment and from mood to mood, as if they always had something new and apt to say. In other words, they smell interesting, as opposed to merely beautiful. A friend of mine used to say that one particular type of short-grain Carnaroli rice he used for risotto seemed to understand his intentions and to possess native intelligence. I can now extend this insight to perfume: Black is buzzing with brains. It was composed by one of the greatest talents in the business, Annick Ménardo of Firmenich. Binary accords having been exhausted, what she did was increase the number of dimensions by one. Black sets out boldly into space on three axes: a big, solid, sweet amber note; a muted fifties Je Reviens floral note (benzylsalicylate) as green as a banker's desk lamp; and finally a bitter powdery, fresh rubber accord such as one encounters in specialist shops or while repairing a bicycle tire puncture. These three tunes hit you in perfect counterpoint when Black is first put on. The remarkable thing about Black's structure is the absence of top notes or drydown. Ménardo has contrived to make the harmony independent of perfume time, but very sensitive to small variations in one's perception. At different times, Black will strike you variously as a battle hymn for Amazons, emerald green plush fit for Napoleon's box at the Opéra, or just plain sweet and smiling. It also has the combination of great bones and good skin characteristic of old-fashioned perfumery, while being entirely novel and modern. Some things strive to be classics; others simply are. Spend an evening with Black and you will know that its place is with Bandit, Tabac Blond, and Cabochard among the great emancipated fragrances of all time. LT

Black Angel (By Mark Buxton) ★ ★ *sweet woody* $$$
Cheap-smelling Egoïste-type thing, inexplicable in a no-holds-barred
niche lineup composed by Buxton. LT

Black Aoud (Montale) ★ ★ ★ ★ *rose oud* $$$
The Montale Aoud range is directly inspired by the Omani (and more
generally eastern Arabic) style of perfumery. At its best, the Omani
school produces stark, wonderful fragrances based on contrasts between
radiant, color-saturated rose and dark, saturnine materials, chief among
which is the famous oud, or agarwood. Oud (the untranslatable glottal
sound of the Arabic letter ʿayn has turned ʿūd into "oud" and "aoud") is
an oil extracted from aquilaria trees affected by noble rot. Agarwood
partakes both of top-notch sandalwood, in having a sour yogurt-like
aspect, and of patchouli, in an earthy wet side, but brings complex notes
of its own, ranging from fresh to honeyed and stretching to animalic.
Agarwood is extraordinarily variable from batch to batch, depending
on provenance and age, and must be a technical perfumer's nightmare.
It seems to provide an easier, less intrusive background than either sandalwood or patchouli. Black Aoud is an oud in the grand manner: a
huge, rutilant rose set against olfactory black velvet, beauty in a red
dress snatched by a masked Zorro. This is a style that was made popular
in the West by defanged versions like Sinan, Parfum de Peau, and Knowing, until restrictions on damascones made it hard to achieve the proper
degree of fluorescence in the rosy notes. While not hugely original, Black
Aoud is arguably the best example of the real thing available this side of
Muscat's perfume market. LT

Black Cashmere (Donna Karan) ★ ★ ★ *smooth clove* $$
Who remembers Shiseido's first Zen? Some of the quiet, suntan-oil ef-
fect of that wonderfully straightforward fragrance carries over into
Black Cashmere, but with a smooth clove note added to make it less
languid. Thank you DK for bringing it back, and in the most exquisite
packaging too. LT

Black Orchid (Tom Ford) ★ ★ ★ *cucumber chocolate* $ $
Big egos, like gases, expand to fill the space others give them, and Tom
Ford's name now takes top billing above the fragrance itself. Ford has
even gone on record stating he considers Black Orchid a classic, as if the
title were his to bestow. Black Orchid's idea, first seen a year earlier in
Chanel's Allure Sensuelle, is in itself very interesting, a novel take on the
androgynous style of Angel and its brood: take a typical Lauder heavy
balsamic structure (Youth Dew, Spellbound), add to it a shining layer of
fresh-watery notes, and connect the two by a light, dry cedarwood accord. But this cucumber-on-chocolate idea works better on a smelling
strip than in real life. Black Orchid, despite its impressive stature, remains curiously anonymous in use, its soul seemingly insufficient to fill
the opera gloves. The overall message is contradictory. On the one hand,
the word *black,* omnipresent these days, coupled with *orchid* suggests a
woman in her midthirties still wanting to scare her parents by appearing at the dinner table made up like Cleopatra. On the other hand, the,
er, classy bottle is very 1976 Joan Collins. Perhaps, like most adolescent
provocations, this is an homage, Ford's "Dear Mom" letter to the mainstream Lauder buyer. LT

Black Orchid Voile de Fleur (Tom Ford) ★ ★ ★ ★
Fracas gardenia $ $
A smiling, bonny tuberose halfway between Fracas and Private Collection Tuberose Gardenia. Fresh and lovely with a sleepy languor, simply
beautiful in all its parts. TS

Black Sun (Salvador Dalí) ★ ★ *woody oriental* $ $
If you're going to do a masculine named after the fearsome Dark Star,
show some respect and have the decency to put a little melancholia in
the composition, instead of merely doing a bad version of Jean-Michel
Duriez's warm, sunny, and smilingly wonderful Yohji Homme. LT

Black Tourmaline (Olivier Durbano) ★ ★ ★ ★ *incense vetiver* $$$
The lone good fragrance in Olivier Durbano's range is a severe, noble vetiver-incense with the solemn working demeanor of an undertaker offering the choice of ebony or mahogany. Initially, its hale crude backdrop of pine floor cleaner too insistently covers up anything that might be taken as unseemly, but mercifully it exits quickly. TS

Black Vetyver Café Cologne (Jo Malone) ★ ★ ★ *coffee cologne* $$
Raffish name, nice roasted caramellic top-note accord, a sort of Lutens Mini-Me, very pleasant nevertheless. LT

Black Violet (Tom Ford) ★ ★ ★ *dark floral* $$$$
The great perfumer Edmond Roudnitska, who had a French fondness for high-concept prose, wrote a little book about fragrance in the superb encyclopedic collection Que sais-je? His tone throughout is an emphatic plea for perfumery to be taken seriously as art. He goes on at length about the fact that perfume, to be more than a smell, must have a recognizable form, by which he meant it must tell a story. Roudnitska would, I think, have been appalled at the turn perfumery has taken recently, and I don't just mean endless little Barbie-doll florals. He probably would have felt that many niche fragrances today, though one peg higher than mere smells, were not proper perfumes, belonging instead to the category of bases, those one-liner, figurative chunks of smell that made cheap thirties fragrances so same-y. I once heard Yves de Chiris, great-grandson of the man who brought steam distillation to Grasse, unfairly dismiss the entire Lutens line as bases. But art proceeds as spiral motion: these days everybody wants sound-bite fragrances. I feel that the difference between bases and perfumes is one of dimension: with bases you sniff around in 2-D checking for accuracy, while with proper perfumes you look up and enjoy the view. This preamble brings me to the fact that Black Violet, unlike most of the others in this Tom Ford collection, has terrific form. It is definitely not black,

not very violet (though it is a wine-like woody floral), and has some of the dowdy sexiness of an old-fashioned wrap dress. But, by heaven, it lunges for you right from the start like the famous opening line to Burgess's *Earthly Powers:* "It was the afternoon of my eighty-first birthday, and I was in bed with my catamite when Ali announced that the archbishop had come to see me." From top to bottom, BV is the perfumery equivalent of a really good yarn. More of that. LT

Black XS (Paco Rabanne) ★ *woody amber* $
There are supposedly all kinds of wonderful classic oriental smells in here, like "praline" and "cardamom" and "tolu balsam," but mostly what you smell is a powerful, dry woody amber the size of Manhattan or, to be specific, as if Manhattan were trying to lift itself, spires first, into your brain via your nose. TS

Black XS for Her (Paco Rabanne) ★ ★ ★ *woody vanilla* $$
The slick Goth packaging, reminiscent of Anna Sui's kitschy but fabulous black plastic powder compacts, holds nothing more transgressive than a warm, woody, cotton-candy vanilla. Foody and uncomplicated—Hell's Angel–food cake. TS

Blanc Violette (Histoires de Parfums) ★ ★ ★ *harsh violet* $$$
A clever fit of three closely related fragrance materials: the familiar powdery confection of Choward's Violet Flavored Mints; the concentrated greenery of violet leaf; and the angular, modern, and loud violet nitrile, which smells of metallic artificial cucumber. Altogether they form a vicious violet made up for the disco, a fragrance in the spirit of Debbie Harry, with blonde hair and baby fat disguised by serpent green eye shadow and spike heels. TS

Bleecker Street (Bond No. 9) ★ *green watery* $$$
David Apel, who did Bond's Wall Street, revisits the fresh-violet-leaf

idea that Bond is so curiously fond of. The top note is watery and harsh, and the leafy-woody rest has a dreadful hiss like cheap speakers. TS

Blenheim Bouquet (Penhaligon's) ★ ★ ★ *citrus spicy* $ $
Named after the stately Vanbrugh-designed home of the Dukes of Marlborough, this is a pleasant but unremarkable citrus with a spicy-woody drydown. Elegant and fresh in an understated way, but could do with better-quality raw materials. LT

BLV "Blù" pour Homme (Bulgari) ★ ★ *spicy fresh* $ $
Somebody has attempted to dress up a laundry-soap musk with oriental gestures of sweet citrus and spice. It's cloying and strident, and reinforces the impression that masculine scents in blue bottles are not to be trusted. TS

Blue Agava & Cacao Cologne (Jo Malone) ★ ★ *birthday cake* $ $
This pairing is an awful lot like cake from boxed mix, although it makes a half effort to be interesting with a medicinal smoky vanilla note. TS

Bluebell (Penhaligon's) ★ *hideous floral* $ $
Repellent. LT

Blue Stratos (Parfums Bleu) ★ ★ ★ ★ *classic fougère* $
Blue Stratos used to be a Shulton fragrance until Procter & Gamble listed it for sale in 1995, whereupon it was snapped up by a British entrepreneur named Tim Foley for not a lot of money, and has been doing well ever since. Foley, a longtime wearer of the stuff, amusingly describes his first contact with P&G as "Give me my ball back." This is the classic hairy-chested naff fougère from 1975, the year when Barry Manilow sang "Mandy" and Svetlana Savitskaya set a new women's airspeed record of 1,667 mph in a tweaked Mikoyan Ye-133. For us old codgers, it's

memories. For the rest, it's a period piece. Either way, it is to fragrance what aspirin is to headaches: it's cheap and it works. LT

Blush (Marc Jacobs) ★ ★ *minimalist jasmine* $
A very thin jasmine relying mostly on green and indolic facets, and skipping the sweet, dreamy part, presumably to come across more fresh. Achieves a pale peach tea over time. For people who would like to wear Joy, except they prefer something less beautiful. TS

Bobbi (Bobbi Brown) ★ *green muguet* $
Directly inspired by Gucci's Envy, but nowhere near as good. LT

Body Kouros (Yves Saint Laurent) ★ ★ ★ ★ *licorice rum* $
A colleague of mine, of otherwise impeccable intellectual credentials, once confided to me that he enjoyed splashing his girlfriend with fragrance during sex and specified (somewhat redundantly I thought) "on the body," as if there existed tempting alternatives. Body Kouros smells nice and would be worthy of a warm welcome were it not a blatant ripoff of Jean-Michel Duriez's Yohji Homme, now sadly discontinued. What's funny is that BK was composed by Annick Ménardo, whose Lolita Lempicka served as an inspiration to Yohji Homme in the first place, and who was thus merely getting even. LT

Bois Blond (Parfumerie Générale) ★ ★ ★ *iris carrot* $$$
BB starts with a tremendous rooty blast of iris and a related dusty-anisic note I assume is carrot seed, mysteriously curtailed a few minutes later by an invisible conductor bringing a raised index finger to his lips and glowering at the players. Thereafter follows an agreeable but nondescript cedarwoody masculine. Pleasantly straightforward but a bit like paying full price for an EP single. LT

Bois d'Argent (Dior) ★ ★ ★ *almond woody* $$$
A lovely, light variation on Hypnotic Poison (also done by Annick Mé-

nardo), this "silver wood" evokes the very biblical pairing of milk and honey. One of a set of three released simultaneously by Dior, the others being Cologne Blanche and the fantastic Eau Noire. TS

Bois d'Arménie (Guerlain) ★ ★ ★ *sweet storax* $$$$
I love that charming French curiosity Papier d'Arménie: little strips of blotting paper for burning, impregnated with benzoin resin, that come in booklets with a distinctive green and yellow cover and instructions suggesting that they magically chase away miasmas of all types. I am also a fan of BdA's author, Annick Ménardo, the Firmenich perfumer responsible for Bulgari's Black. This said, and despite my best efforts, I cannot bring myself to love BdA. There is, within incense, benzoin, and myrrh, in addition to the uplifting resinous smoky note, a flat, melancholy, honeyed, baby-pee–like note reminiscent of phenylacetic acid. Resinoid compositions sometimes cancel it out, sometimes emphasize it, and it is very present in BdA. The sweet-powdery drydown is much better, and true to form if somewhat nondescript. If Duchaufour's Timbuktu did not exist, I would have loved this essay in ancient perfume materials. But exist it does, and every other incense fragrance pales before it. LT

Bois de Copaiba (Parfumerie Générale) ★ ★ ★ *heure bleue* $$$
This is PG's homage to Guerlain's L'Heure Bleue: less complex and interesting but of solidly good quality. Buy the original. LT

Bois d'Encens (Armani Privé) ★ ★ ★ ★ *incense animalic* $$$
Armani's commitment to a spare, Japan-inspired visual style is so fanatical one suspects he occasionally needs a break, and that his private apartments may be furnished in Barbara Cartland chintz for light relief. The Privé line is fearsomely expensive; exquisitely packaged in black, disconcertingly lightweight wooden bottles; and mostly not worth the money except for Bois d'Encens, a frankincense composition. I find frankincense, like vetiver, to be an olfactory moving target. I used to

occasionally attend vespers at the Russian Orthodox church in Nice, where the best choir on earth sang out of sight and the music settled on the spare congregation like gentle melodious snow. The place allowed one to smell all gradations of incense, from the peculiarly dry and smoky feel it gives at low concentrations (in the entrance, near the postcards representing Alexander II's son) to the dirty, burnt-lemon aspect it acquires when the Metropolite stands before you and swings the burner in your direction in a vain attempt to flush out the inner demons that brought you there. Like the real thing, Bois d'Encens never smells the same twice: sometimes as clean as winter air, sometimes disturbingly animalic. If you can afford Bois d'Encens, buy it: there is nothing else like it. LT

Bois de Paradis (Parfums DelRae) ★ ★ ★ *berry sandalwood* $$$
BdP is a big, busy, warm creation very much—as its name indicates—in the mulled-wine style of Bois des Iles but with added fruit to give the somewhat weird effect of sangria served piping hot. Very pleasant, but a little loud. LT

Bois de Santal (Keiko Mecheri) ★ ★ *thin woody* $$$
Genuine Indian sandalwood oil is in short to nonexistent supply these days, transforming the traditionally safe category of straightforward sandalwood fragrances into mostly failed approximations of the inimitably gorgeous real thing. This one unsuccessfully addresses the problem with a threadbare lashup of sweet, milky musk and a pale woody amber. TS

Bois des Iles (Chanel) ★ ★ ★ ★ ★ *sandalwood oriental* $$$
Anyone who has ever worn real Indian sandalwood oil straight knows that it is a perfume in itself: milky, rosy, ambery, woody, green, marvelous. What Ernest Beaux's plush Cuir de Russie did for leather, his cozy Bois des Iles did for sandalwood. Though I've never worn a sable stole, I insist it must feel like wearing Bois des Iles: a dark, close, velvety warmth,

sleepy and collapsingly soft. For once the marketing material has it right. Chanel says it smells like gingerbread in the drydown, and so it does, sweet with vanillic balsams and spice. But that description doesn't begin to communicate the depth of the fragrance: there are aldehydes sifting a powdery brightness over all, so that the fragrance feels sometimes like the brunette sibling of No. 5. There is the delicious top note of citrus and rose, with the fruity brightness of a cola. It is basically perfect and, though over eighty years old, seems as ageless as everything Chanel did in those inventive years. If you think of all the best Chanel fragrances as varieties of little black dress—sleek, dependable, perfectly proportioned—Bois des Iles is the one in cashmere. I have worn it on and off for years, whenever I felt I needed extra insulation from the cold world. TS

Bois de Violette (Serge Lutens) ★ ★ ★ ★ *woody oriental* $$$
Shiseido's Serge Lutens had just finished overseeing the creation of Féminité du Bois, which took its sweet woody cue from Caron's Parfum Sacré, itself derived from Chanel's Bois des Iles: resonant, strings-only chords almost devoid of time evolution. The woody-fruity structure of Féminité was first devised by the perfumer Pierre Bourdon, apparently on a visit to Marrakech, and then passed on to perfumer Chris Sheldrake, who developed it with Lutens looking over his shoulder to keep it as dark and transparent as humanly possible. The result was the fragrance that properly put Shiseido on the map. Unusually, Sheldrake and Bourdon generously credit each other with the basic idea. When Lutens decided to open his fragrance shop in the Jardins du Palais Royal in Paris, like a publisher he needed several titles to kick off his collection. Enter the technique known as overdosage, widely propagated by Bourdon, in which a backstage component in one perfume is moved to the forefront in a new composition, a sort of rotation in perfume space. From Féminité du Bois came four variations, three of which create new effects by bold-typing one of the components of the original: musk (Bois et Musc), fruit (Bois et Fruits), amber (Bois Oriental). The

fourth, Bois de Violette, differs because the woody-fruity violet smell of methyl ionone recapitulates and intensifies the rest of the fragrance. Its rotation takes place around the center; the stained-glass mandala is perfected by a violet gem around which everything dances. I remember stepping out of Lutens's purple shop into the perpetually quiet walled gardens, armed with this purple smell with a purple name, thinking I was carrying the most precious object in the world. Curiously, Bourdon went on to do a fifth variation in a different context. He apparently included one of his Féminité sketches as an afterthought into a presentation for Dior, and to his embarrassment they picked it, resulting in Dolce Vita. LT

Bois d'Iris (The Different Company) ★ ★ ★ *iris whiskey* $ $ $
The first fifteen minutes give you an unusually rich-smelling iris, with wine-like complexity in the rooty part, plus a deep chord that reaches from peppery geranium through violets, licorice, and hay, giving off a rich, caramel-woody aroma like a good scotch. As it dries down, it first pales to a pleasantly intense aged-wood smell with vetiver, but then starts to fall apart. A very good masculine nevertheless. TS

Bois d'Ombrie (Eau d'Italie) ★ ★ ★ *vetiver leather* $ $ $
This is an odd, original, very interesting, and arguably not entirely successful accord of vetiver, leather, smoke, iris, and burnt-sugar notes. It is unquestionably a great smell, but fails in my opinion to coalesce into a great fragrance. LT

Bois du Portugal (Creed) ★ ★ ★ *woody oriental* $ $ $ $
One of Creed's best, this is a classic woody oriental, close in intent but not in richness or quality to de Nicolaï's divine New York, which is at once cheaper and vastly better. LT

Bois et Fruits (Serge Lutens) ★ ★ ★ ★ *plummy wood* $ $ $
A variation on the beautiful fruity cedar theme of Shiseido's Féminité

du Bois finds the fragrance in an intense, spiced-liqueur mood, a Christmas fruitcake full of plums steeped in rum—a muted Dolce Vita. TS

Bois et Musc (Serge Lutens) ★ ★ ★ ★ *musky cedar* $$$
Under the direction of Lutens, Christopher Sheldrake moved Shiseido's unforgettable fruity wood of Féminité du Bois over a funhouse mirror to create a series of related woody scents, each time swelling one aspect to several times usual size to give a new character. Bois et Musc is a subliminal, watercolor version with a fresh touch, which makes cedar feel like a new kind of rose. TS

Bois Farine (L'Artisan Parfumeur) ★ ★ ★ *bread hologram* $$
With a name like that (Wood Flour), you'd expect the shock of recognition, and sure enough, what you get is an olfactory one-liner. I suspect this fragrance came out of the accidental discovery that heliotropin, married to a cedarwood note and what seems to be a touch of herbs as in Après l'Ondée, gives a striking, mealy, almost nutty fresh-bread note. It does what it says on the can, but once that trick is pulled seems to have little more in store. A fun but lightweight offering, typical of the whimsical, middle-period Artisan after Laporte's departure and before Nouvelle Parfumerie set in. LT

Bois Oriental (Serge Lutens) ★ ★ ★ ★ *gin woody* $$$
Another offspring of Féminité du Bois made more heavily ambery on one end and on the other end lightened with a splash of gin and tonic: this is a nice, big-boned variation that nevertheless doesn't really improve on the original. TS

Bois Rouge (Tom Ford) ★ ★ *woody spicy* $$$
I once asked Patricia de Nicolaï why she didn't bring out a concentrated version of her fabulous New York, and she replied that the parfum concentration didn't work because it was too *tassé,* too squat. Likewise, Bois Rouge is a little too dense all the way through to be properly legible. It's

only when the noise dies down in the end that you realize that it is none other than New York stretched to wide-screen format. LT

Un Bois Sépia (Serge Lutens) ★ ★ *fresh woody* $ $ $
Who smuggled this dim-witted sport fragrance into the Lutens line? The sudden absence of Indian sandalwood on the raw materials market is no excuse for this banal reformulation. TS

Un Bois Vanille (Serge Lutens) ★ ★ ★ ★ *roasted sweet* $ $ $
Since Bois des Iles, perfumers have been countering the dry austerity of woods with sweet, edible-smelling accords. Built on this principle, the densely packed aroma of Un Bois Vanille—wood, amber, rose, milk, vanilla, licorice—mimics one of the most complex smells on earth, the atmosphere of a coffee shop (which leads me to the unexpected acknowledgment that coffee is largely a woody smell). We love roasted aromas for their complexity, that four-hand chord they play in the key of smoke and caramel, and UBV smells deliciously roasted, reminding me of a story that M. F. K. Fisher tells about a woman whose favorite thing to eat is a little nubbin of chocolate on a pin, roasted black over a candle. Then out of this vast, complicated smell emerges a beautiful melodic line: a sweet, musky amber with an almond-anise twist. Like many fragrances from Lutens, it may be hard to wear, but it is absolutely worth trying. TS

Bond Girl 007 (Avon) ★ *fruity floral* $
I even put John Barry's "007 Theme" on the computer speakers to get myself in the mood, but no dice. Bond must have run out of buxom call girls with fake accents, because he is now prowling around high schools. The best thing about this deeply uninteresting little floral is the name of the Avon division that markets it: Abdulla G. Said, M.D. Binzagr Co., in the historic port city of Jidda, Saudi Arabia, a place where the faintest breeze from the perfume souk is guaranteed to blow this dust mote straight back into the Red Sea. LT

Borneo 1834 (Serge Lutens) ★ ★ ★ ★ *virtual chocolate* $$$
Apparently Lutens has determined that the first olfactory point of con-
tact between Europe and the Far East took place there and then, in the
form of the patchouli leaves used to wrap bales of silk. The patchouli
was intended to keep moths away from the precious fabric (insects hate
camphoraceous smells), but when the silk reached Western shores, ele-
gant ladies wanted more of the smell. In other words, patchouli's career
in perfumery is a rise from bug repellent to luxury goods, a trajectory
meteorically traced in the opposite direction by many contemporary
fragrances. As often happens with Lutens-Sheldrake creations, the first
sniff comes as a complete shock: the overwhelming impression is one of
dark brown powder. Seconds later one realizes that this nameless dust is
made of two components, patchouli and chocolate, skillfully juxtaposed
(how?) so that neither the earthiness of patchouli nor the familiarity of
chocolate prevails. Borneo 1834 is like Angel in reverse: instead of jump-
ing out at you, it sucks you into its shadowy space. All the materials used
are firmly rooted in the "orientalist" (aka hippie) style, yet the size,
grace, and complexity of the overall structure make it the direct descen-
dant of orientals proper like Emeraude and Shalimar. LT

Boucheron (Boucheron) ★ ★ ★ ★ ★ *massive floral* $$
Composed by Jean-Pierre Béthouart (he of Fendi Palazzo) in 1988, this
is the Athena Nike of all floral orientals. The genre lends itself to sensory
overload and thick orchestral scoring: imagine having at your disposal
the combined forces of Joy and Shalimar to play with, and you will see
how most perfumers end up with monsters intent on world domination.
But there is beauty to be found in that direction, the oversized, heavy
beauty of Art Deco marvels: Hoover Dam, Milano Centrale railway station, Moscow State University—stylized grandeur that offsets weight of
materials by simplicity of line. When it came out, Boucheron felt like a
Firmenich mission statement: we are an aromachemicals manufacturer
and can outdo nature as and when we wish. Boucheron, at the time, felt
100 percent synthetic and, amazingly, none the worse for it. Being near

someone who wears it is like having your picture taken next to a marble foot as big as a car. LT

Boucheron Eau Légère 2006 (Boucheron) ★ ★ ★ ★
transparent oriental $ $
Light versions of heavy perfumes seldom work. This is one of the notable exceptions, where the beautiful structure of the original has been preserved (by one of the perfumers of the model, Jean-Pierre Béthouart) but made lighter, more transparent. BEL 2006 has that elusive quality of radiance that every perfumer seeks: rest a smelling strip anywhere on your desk, and tiny but perfectly legible whiffs of the great Boucheron structure will waft past from time to time, as if the composition were set in type intended to be legible at any size. LT

Boucheron Eau Légère 2007 (Boucheron) ★ ★ ★ *floral oriental* $ $
In a commendably honest but probably self-defeating move, Boucheron includes in the box for BEL 2007 a small spray sample of the original. What the two fragrances have in common is complexity. But whereas the first one was a team of eight in harness led by an expert hand, the first half hour of BEL, while skillful, elicits the famous question of a child during a contemporary music performance: "Are they still tuning up?" When it finally settles down, BEL turns out to be not so much lighter as spicier than the original. Stick with the superb original; just use less. LT

Boucheron pour Homme (Boucheron) ★ ★ ★ *big lemon* $ $
A very solid if unoriginal citrus chypre in the Chanel Pour Monsieur style, with a pleasant aldehydic-waxy note and a powdery drydown. Careful with the dosage; this one is loud. LT

Boucheron pour Homme Eau de Parfum (Boucheron) ★ ★ ★
woody chypre $ $
A weird, fresh, dissonant accord with a strong citral-anisic top note that

adds up to a shiso mint feel. Reminiscent in structure and complexity of Chanel's Pour Monsieur, which is saying something, but less suave. Neither gripping nor memorable, but, as Anthony Powell would have put it, "immensely presentable." LT

Boucheron pour Homme Eau de Toilette Fraîcheur (Boucheron)
★ ★ ★ *pale citrus* $$
A gray, fresh, beautifully put-together, but faceless modern masculine, which works fine in a hardly-there-at-all sort of way. Brings to mind a rain shower of bowler-hatted men Magritte might have painted. Probably among the best of this anonymous breed, but it's hard to tell. LT

Boudoir (Vivienne Westwood) ★ *rose chypre* $$
A syrupy-sweet distortion of Miss Balmain that aspires to be a taxicab air freshener. (Should have been called Bidet, not Boudoir.) Sickening but not totally without interest. My first thought on smelling it was "At least it's not a fruity floral." Keeping standards high is a daily battle. TS

Boudoir Sin Garden (Vivienne Westwood) ★ *anemic floral* $$
It seems your sin is coveting your neighbor's begonias. This ridiculously named fragrance is a very pale heliotrope with laundry-like "fresh" musky overtones and the devil nowhere in sight. TS

Brandy (Brandy) ★ ★ ★ *apple cider* $
No great fragrance by any measure, there's still a naive charm about this spiced-apple concoction, which smells like shampoo from a seventies childhood and is named after a carriage horse in New York. TS

Breathe (Fresh Scents by Terri) ★ *floral musk* $
A white-floral musk that reminds me of those hard, business-card–sized handsoaps in budget hotels. TS

Breath of God (B Never Too Busy to Be Beautiful) ★ ★ ★ ★ ★
smoked fruit $
In 2007, LT reviewed two surprising, beautiful fragrances—Inhale and Exhale—that came in a box with the Parfum d'Empire scents but turned out to be from BNTBTBB. According to Simon Constantine, the brand's head of fragrance, he thought to combine the smoky vetiver of one and the delicious alien fruity floral of the other and call the result Breath of God. Such an experiment should be a hot mess. But it's a triumph, a walk through an autumnal landscape in shades of pencil gray instead of painterly gold, with the sweet biological rot of compost below and dry air touched with woodsmoke above. In structure it is reminiscent of the best of Serge Lutens's scents, straddling the dark cedar-violet of the Bois fragrances and epic florals such as Sarrasins and El Attarine, and it has an herbal air of archaic medicine or potions to ward off malice. Surreal combinations—lemon ham, grape leather, bubblegum tobacco, loquat vetiver—rise from its depths each time it comes to attention, hour after hour. Wearing it, I feel a sense of wonder that so late in the perfume game there still can be such profound invention. TS

Bright Crystal (Versace) ★ *nasty floral* $$
Hideously screechy. LT

Brin de Réglisse (Hermès) ★ ★ ★ *licorice lavender* $$$
Brin de Réglisse is a sweet aromatic fougère in the style of Yohji Homme, which Jean-Claude Elléna, perfume's minimalist master, stripped down to expose the basic structure: just the roasted caramel note you find in some lavender materials, plus dark, salty licorice and a sweet coumarin drydown. Although it seems to achieve what it intended, it feels more like an academic exercise than a pleasure. TS

Broadway Nite (Bond No. 9) ★ ★ ★ ★ *sweet floral* $$$
One man never read the memo dictating that ladies today ought to wear

only quiet perfumes that won't upset anyone at dinner; that necessary fellow is the great Maurice Roucel, perfumer responsible for the un-apologetically noticeable Insolence; 24, Faubourg; Tocade; L by Lolita Lempicka; and others, bless him. Here he used the basic rosy-fruity-heliotropin idea of Guerlain's soft and fleeting Chant d'Arômes but skipped the bashfulness. Instead, strident bright rose materials popular in the big-hair eighties (the effect of which LT has described accurately as "neon") plus a dose of aldehydes, as unrelenting as fluorescent over-heads in a city diner at 2 a.m., generate a steady pink glow. As you'd expect from something with a name like a budget dinner-theater expe-rience, it can come off garishly appealing in a cheerfully cheap way, as Roucel's Envy for Gucci did. But eventually you find out that BN comes from good family. The big brash way it presents what's essentially a sweet and tender idea reminds me of Caron's first Farnesiana, and the duration and complexity of its drydown story remind me of the mimo-sa-violet conversation of Insolence. If Bond No. 9's owner, Laurice Rahmé, wanted a fragrance that would light up its wearer like Times Square on New Year's Eve, complete with tender kiss at midnight, she absolutely got it. One of the better fragrances of the Bond line, and a good time. TS

Brooklyn (Bond No. 9) ★ ★ *citrus woody* $$$
Fuggedaboudit. This is not Brooklyn. Not that it matters: who wants to smell like Greenpoint? Gimmickry aside, it's a rough Eau d'Hadrien plus cardamom, vaguely related to Déclaration. TS

Brooks Brothers Classic (Brooks Brothers) ★ *masculine cliché* $$
What BB means by "classic" is a derivative mishmash of several fragrances that earned their makers a lot of moolah in the last two decades. LT

Brooks Brothers New York Gentlemen (Brooks Brothers) ★ ★ ★
citrus chypre $$
A largely successful attempt by Richard Herpin of Badgley Mischka

fame to compose a presentable citrus chypre on what must have been a measly formula budget. Okay as an interim measure if you like Chanel Pour Monsieur but have cash-flow problems. LT

Brooks Brothers New York Ladies (Brooks Brothers) ★ *vile floral* $$
They say Brooks Brothers was, at some point in the distant past, a quality outfit. Its present devotion to what the British aptly call the stuffed-shirt aesthetic is so lamentably aspirational it makes Ralph Lauren's Polo range look Rastafarian. This project was clearly conducted from the outside in: the fragrance comes in an expensive pink box that tries very hard to emulate packaging from fifty years ago. The money ran out with the cardboard budget; the bottle looks stamped out of pink Lucite, and the fragrance is simultaneously so awful and so dated that it would be considered unpresentable in a Thai roadside bazaar. LT

Brûlure de Rose (Parfumerie Générale) ★ ★ ★ ★ *edible rose* $$$
Distantly related to the brilliant Tocade (Rochas), this transparent caramel rose with a silvery sheen sits atop a clever fruity musk base reminiscent of Mûre et Musc but much quieter. Good stuff. LT

Brut (Helen of Troy Ltd.) ★ ★ *cheap fougère* $
Last time I looked, Brut was a Fabergé fragrance in a glass bottle with a cute chain around it. It now looks like mouthwash, comes in a plastic bottle, and belongs to a hilariously named outfit (had Helen been properly limited, Troy would have an airport). It smells sort of like the original, though the original itself had had several bits surgically removed over the years. It used to be a glorious sweet fougère that smelled at once clean and dirty and went on forever. Is it still Brutish enough for nostalgia? Only barely. But it costs almost nothing, so buy some, look in the mirror, narrow your eyes, and picture yourself with hair. LT

Bryant Park (Bond No. 9) ★ ★ ★ *fruity patchouli* $$$
If memory serves me right, there was a peculiar effect in L'Artisan's Vo-

leur de Roses in which the combination of rose and patchouli conjured up a hallucinated strawberry. Bryant Park builds on this effect with a thinner rose and more berries to make up for it. The end result is curiously tentative, given the flashy promise of the Pucci-inspired pink bottle, but not bad. TS

B Scent (B Never Too Busy to Be Beautiful) ★ ★ ★ ★ *Joy-ful rose* $
The rose here smells like half of Joy—an exuberant pink flower with a charming anisic sweetness—paired with a vivid lemony top note worth smelling again and again. Somebody at BNTBTBB is having a good time. TS

B Spot (Benefit) ★ ★ *green melon* $
Relives a moment in the nineties when a slew of melon-scented body sprays and lotions entered our lives masquerading as a modern idea of freshness. This one has an oily chemical feel and a sour, unpleasant drydown. TS

Bulgari BLV "Blù" (Bulgari) ★ ★ ★ *spicy floral* $
To quote the great biophysicist Max Delbrück, the only guy ever to get a Nobel for nothing in particular: "I don't understand this. It must be wrong." There is something interesting in BLV's weird mimosa-ginger accord, but incompletely worked out, as if the perfumer had hurried to the deadline and submitted a pile of Post-its instead of a manuscript. I hope Alberto Morillas holds that thought and makes it work fully at a later date. LT

Bulgari pour Femme (Bulgari) ★ ★ ★ ★ *violet mimosa* $ $
I wore this wonderful fragrance, attributed to Sophia Grojsman and Nathalie Lorson of IFF, one sultry New York summer, when the air felt so densely humid you thought you might be able to kick up and swim through it. Good and bad smells everywhere seemed to have not merely presence but weight, nearly combing your hair as they raked past. Bul-

gari pour Femme, wafting up from the cleavage—its obvious natural environment—seemed to clear that thickened air. I wondered then what it was about this sweet floral, in a crowd of hundreds at Sephora, that transcended the usual clichés. Today, the fragrance feels a little barer but more legible because of it. And so I can smell a surprisingly basil-like, watery-green violet leaf, weaving through the powder cloud of mimosa and jasmine like a cool breeze. TS

Bulgari pour Homme Extrême (Bulgari) ★ ★ ★ *woody spicy* $$
Mercifully not in the least *extrême,* rather an elegant watercolor-like composition of woody, herbaceous, pepper, and spicy notes where everything manages to remain in its proper place all the way through to the drydown, unlike most masculines of this type that feel like the perfumer was herding cats. LT

Bulgari pour Homme Soir (Bulgari) ★ ★ ★ *fresh oriental* $$
A nicely judged, quiet, and somewhat shy fragrance that plays on the contrast between a woody-citrus accord in the sports fragrance mold and a pleasant biscuit-like coumarin-vanillin drydown. Delicate and well behaved, no small mercies these days. LT

Bulgari Rose Essentielle (Bulgari) ★ ★ *shrill rose* $$
Like the schoolmarmish, sour rose of Stella, but without the fun sweaty patchouli bit that made it a passable masculine. TS

B•United Jeans Man (Benetton) ★ *watery citrus* $
The name brings to mind the copulating cartoon ducks of the parody "Fly United" poster from the seventies, and the fragrance brings to mind precisely nothing besides the paltry sum the formula must have cost. LT

B•United Woman (Benetton) ★ ★ ★ *soapy floral* $
Presentable if somewhat ditzy little fresh floral. Mall-rat juice. LT

Burberry London (Burberry) ★ *floral abomination* $$
The horror: this one comes wrapped in a piece of wool in Burberry's hideous trademark plaid. This is a white floral so vile that only A. A. Gill, who famously described Burberry Brit as "chav spit," could do it justice. Words fail me. LT

Burberry London for Men (Burberry) ★ ★ *herbaceous chemical* $$
Weird and interesting herbaceous accord reminiscent of shiso mint found in Japanese cuisine. The drydown predictably drifts toward the scary lavender-on-steroids note that seems to turn up everywhere at the moment. A little crude, but much better than average. Hideous plaid-covered bottle. LT

Burberry London for Men Special Edition 2008 (Burberry) ★
linden lavender $$
In 1999, Escada let loose upon the world a thing called Casual Friday, since mercifully discontinued. BLFMSE 2008 revives the horror: a six-foot-tall, man-eating lavender from hell. I can see the hand-drawn wobbly letters: "It lives again." LT

Burberry London for Women Special Edition 2008 (Burberry) ★
acid floral $$
This dismal piece of cynical dreck is unaccountably credited to the great Dominique Ropion. Rejoice: it's a time-limited flanker! LT

Byzance (Rochas) ★ ★ ★ ★ *tuberose incense* $
Closely related to Ysatis, a languorous floral oriental, in which a creamy soapy aldehydic rose holds together the lemony lilt of cardamom on one end and a touch of sandalwood and vanilla on the other: Rive Gauche with Indian ornaments, like a good French girl playing dress-up, as oriental as Ingres's *Odalisque*. Byzance used to have a dreamy, liquid, heavy-limbed feeling, with a fluid, silken amber in the top, the purifying feel of incense, and a full, fresh, salty rose in the center. Reformula-

tion has removed the amber, freshened it, and taken much of the weight out, giving it the damp shine of white bathroom tile, closer to Anaïs Anaïs or, more pointedly, Kouros without the swagger. It still smells very good, and would make a terrific masculine. TS

Cabaret (Grès) ★ ★ ★ ★ *woody rose* $ $
Divine surprise! I was not aware of the existence of this fragrance, despite it having been around since 2003. Given Cabaret's fugly bottle and Grès's recent Marlene Dietrich series, I was ready for the worst. Ten seconds after putting it on a strip, I was smiling beatifically, for this brilliant Michel Almairac composition turns out to be a landmark, among the first of the recent slew of transparent woody roses and one of the best. Looking back over the years, as TS points out, it all started with Almairac's Voleur de Roses (1993) for L'Artisan Parfumeur, which smelled great but did not quite work. Cabaret's combination of pink pepper and incense up top makes it wonderfully fresh, while a clean rosewater note and huge musk gives it a down-pillow softness that makes you want to go back every hour and spray some more. Makes a superb masculine. LT

Cabochard (Grès) ★ ★ *worn leather* $
I remember ten years ago sitting on the London Underground opposite Peter O'Toole. Despite the white suit and the cigarette holder, nobody seemed to recognize him. This Cabochard is much the same: ravaged by years of abuse, gaunt, bleary-eyed, prematurely aged, heartbreaking to those who knew Bernard Chant's masterpiece in its heyday. Cabochard was once the greatest leather chypre of all, with the Chant trademark of a stark structure filled in with a complex woodwind harmony of smoky balsamic notes. It was softer than Bandit, less fruity than Jolie Madame, and had a fallen-angel charm to it that made you nostalgic for a stranger past than the one you dared live. This is Cabochard chewed down to a frazzle by accountant moths. If you never smelled the original, you would think Cabochard was merely Eau du Soir with fence varnish added. LT

Cabotine (Grès) ★ *nasty floral* $

Cabotine seemed vile to me when it came out in 1990, and I had avoided it since then. However, I was fully prepared, in the light of what happened since, to find it presentable on reacquaintance. No such thing: it is a trite, acid floral distantly related to Ma Griffe, with a dollop of a monstrously powerful fruity note that should have been banned by the Geneva Convention (see the first La Prairie for the bunker-busting version). LT

Cacharel pour l'Homme (Cacharel) ★ *nutmeg citrus* $$

I remember feeling a sense of doom when this thing came out in 1981. To put it in context, the seventies had been about big aromatic fougères, arguably culminating with Azzaro pour Homme. The fougère genie was a relaxed, old-fashioned guy somewhere on the axis connecting Clark Gable to George Clooney, all easy smiles and pretend goof. In contrast, the guy in Cacharel pour l'Homme was what the French at the time would have described as *jeune et dynamique*, a razor-sharp little prat who thinks that putting the word *nouvelle* in front of everything will cure the world's ills. As it turned out, my dread was justified, because PH was appallingly successful. It inaugurated a long and still continuing trend of masculine fragrances so skeletally barren and cheap-smelling that they have long been overtaken in quality by spray starch and sneaker tamer. To be fair, the nutmeg note of PH was novel and unexpectedly long-lasting. It is now trite, though still interminable. LT

Cadjméré (Parfumerie Générale) ★ ★ ★ *coconut woody* $$$

An abridged cypress-coconut version of the woody lactonic structure of Laura Biagiotti's Roma, for those who lament its disappearance. LT

Calandre (Paco Rabanne) ★ ★ ★ ★ ★ *aldehydic floral* $$

Some years ago, the French perfumery world, distressed by the resemblance of Molinard's Nirmala to Angel and the impossibility of copyrighting a (usually secret) formula, tried to set up a commission of experts that would decide when a perfume was a copy. The idea foundered on the Rive Gauche problem: RG came a year after Calandre (1969) and smelled sufficiently similar that even a perfumer could briefly mistake their drydowns in isolation. Nevertheless, RG was in many ways an improvement on Calandre, richer, darker, more complex. Inexplicably, while perfumers were unanimously positive about Rive Gauche, opinions on Calandre went from disparaging (a mess) to fulsome (brilliantly simple). Events have, in my opinion, worked out in Calandre's favor. The Rive Gauche reformulation(s) have slightly obscured the structure that made it memorable, whereas it remains entire in the less ornate Calandre. Buy lots of it before someone messes with it too. LT

Calèche (Hermès) ★ ★ ★ *wan aldehydic* $ $

When you know this has been composed by Guy Robert, all it takes is one sniff, absent all other information, to know they've grievously messed with it. This is Calèche after three high-temperature wash-rinse cycles, a pale stain on a smelling strip. At this point, when almost all the life has been drained out of it, it could make a pleasant, nondescript masculine for guys who like to see a feminine perfume on the bathroom shelf without the responsibilities of it belonging to a real woman. LT

Calèche Eau Délicate (Hermès) ★ ★ ★ *subdued floral* $ $

If you consider that the real Calèche is already so attenuated as to be in need of last sacraments, you dread the possibility of a more delicate version. As it turns out, CED, while still resolutely discreet and proper to a fault, is a pleasant gray-beige woody floral with an uncommon and luxurious ambergris note. Like its big sister, probably better pressed into service as an unusual masculine than a boring feminine. LT

Caline (Grès) ★ ★ ★ *brilliant floral* $ $

Some pieces of classical music such as Liszt's "*La Campanella*" are of scant interest except as essays in right-hand articulation, full of exposed crystalline runs and figurations in the top octave, where even the grandest piano sounds like one with eight keys made for two-year-olds. Many modern white florals mine that artistic seam and are so focused on the treble as to bring to mind nerdy discussions about whether tweeters are best made of paper, beryllium, metal ribbon, or Mylar. Caline (funny, I thought that was a Patou trademark) is an excellent ribbon tweeter: loud, brilliant, and probably capable of ranging beyond what humans can smell or endure. Perfumes like this make me wonder whether there might be an olfactory equivalent of permanent hearing loss. LT

Calyx (Prescriptives) ★ ★ ★ ★ ★ *guava rose* $$
Sometimes, while reviewing yet another middling batch of perfumes and looking in vain for their reasons for being, I wonder if the problem is me, if critical thought has obliterated pleasure at last and my days as a hedonist are through. Naturally, the next bottle is always a stunner. Like all Sophia Grojsman's best works, Calyx is built on a bold, simple structure: fruity (with a high-profile role for the deliciously garbagey, over-ripe smell of guava) plus floral (powdery rosy) plus green (neroli and oakmoss). From top to bottom, Calyx maintains its perfect balance between clean crispness and rosy sweetness without ever falling into either camp completely. Grojsman has a knack for getting an idea absolutely perfect: there's nothing you could add or take away here, like a perfectly tuned choir out of which you cannot distinguish any individual voice. Furthermore, I can't remember another green fragrance so friendly. Chanel's Cristalle, for example, and Gucci's Envy never escape a narrow-eyed bitchy effect. For a scent of the eighties—1986, to be exact—Calyx also manages to smell incredibly fresh and modern, perhaps because it helped inspire the next generation of fruity clean florals, although none have really improved on it. It's one of those rare fragrances you could wear your whole life. TS

Canali Black Diamond (Canali) ★ ★ ★ *sweet apple* $$
Undoubtedly, this bright, crisp fruity scent smells good and gives the Cool Water genre a well-put-together variation erring on the pretty side.

But now that it's this pretty, and now that the genre is already a tiresome cliché for guys, it makes a powerful argument for a bit of cross-perfuming. Gals, try it on. TS

Canali Style (Canali) ★ ★ ★ ★ *woody smoky* $ $
It would appear that combining the austere, radiant smokiness of Timbuktu and the spicy complexity of Déclaration squares the circle at long last and lets skilled perfumers achieve a new style of balanced, solid, high-quality masculine. This is both less and more than the sum of its parts: much of the distinctiveness is gone, replaced by a somber monochrome hum. But if you believe that the height of manly elegance is a perfectly cut dark suit meant to go unnoticed, you will love this fragrance. LT

Can Can (Paris Hilton) ★ *remedial candyfloss* $
Can it, by all means. LT

Candide Effluve (Guerlain) ★ ★ ★ ★ *thyme jasmine* $ $ $ $
Guerlain has in recent years re-released one discontinued fragrance per year from its archives as a limited edition. Some have been lovely, but none have been the lost wonder we hoped would emerge from undeserved obscurity. It turns out that, in a half-intelligent design scheme, Guerlain generated multiple forms of several perfume ideas over decades, and then the natural selection of the marketplace weeded out all but the indispensable. Candide Effluve (1922) is a segment of L'Heure Bleue (1912), using the vanilla, thyme, and jasmine but none of the pale fruity anise and violets. The name, which actually means "clean redolence," makes a puerile Anglophone want to make a joke about feminine hygiene, but an ammonia-like, animalic side of the fragrance beats her to the punchline. Though this sweet floral may be interesting to collectors of Guerlain, it's hard to imagine preferring Candide Effluve to either L'Heure Bleue or even a modern complex jasmine like Enlèvement au Sérail. TS

Caravelle Epicée (Frapin) ★ ★ ★ ★ *smooth spice* $$$

The Frapin family has been making cognac for a long time and has recently ventured into fragrance. Caravelle Epicée is a very skillful, uplifting, languorous accord of cardamom, guaiac wood, and thyme, which plays in the same register as Habit Rouge but in a quietly transparent sort of way. Short-lived but delicious. LT

Cardinal (Heeley) ★ ★ ★ ★ *incense citrus* $$$

James Heeley is a minimalist British designer living in Paris. Cardinal is a high-quality, transparently radiant incense fragrance emphasizing the kinship of resins to citrus, very pleasant, quiet, and clean. If, as I do, you love Brian Eno's *Music for Airports* and don't mind hearing a repeated, meditative, pseudorandom musical phrase for hours, this one's for you. LT

Caresse (Fragonard) ★ ★ *apricot floral* $$

Though it claims to be a reissue of an old fragrance, it's a bland lactonic fruity floral (orange, peach) straight out of 2008. TS

Carnal Flower (Frédéric Malle) ★ ★ ★ ★ *shimmering floral* $$$

Ropion is one of the greatest perfumers alive, and it is interesting to see him work with a far larger budget than his employer (IFF) would normally allow him in a mass-market fragrance. The top notes of Carnal Flower are euphorically beautiful, a perfectly judged floral accord that shimmers between the healthy vulgarity of tuberose and the rich, mouthwatering freshness of jasmine. Unlike Elléna, Ropion is a perfumer of the classical school, and the underlying structure is tremendously solid, durable, rich, underpinned by powerful synthetics. Once the initial blast is over, Carnal Flower drifts curiously close to near-forgotten greats of the eighties, such as Ysatis (Givenchy) and Byzance (Rochas). A serious, luxurious, all-day fragrance from one of the masters. LT

Carnation (Mona di Orio) ★ *floral oriental* $$$
Di Orio describes herself in her press material as a "living Modigliani," which, desirable or not, is clearly delusional. She also says she studied with Edmond Roudnitska, but her creations suggest she paid little attention. The good news about Carnation is that it does not smell of cloves, as most attempts at that elusive flower do. The bad news is that after teetering for a few moments on the edge of something interesting, a sort of leathery Chinatown, it settles into an awful fruity-chemical mess. LT

Carolina (Carolina Herrera) ★ ★ *fruity amber* $
This was one of many humorless post-Angel fruity orientals, which, in a sort of evil shiatsu, found the most painful spot in the overlap area of sour berries and loud synthetic ambers and pressed hard. TS

Carolina Herrera (Carolina Herrera) ★ ★ ★ ★ *peachy tuberose* $$
In this gigantic floral, a powerful peach has been grafted onto a Fracas-sized tuberose. Loud, pushy, and generally marvelous good fun, like a feathered, spangled headdress for Carnival, it is nevertheless one of those eighties florals that made the next generation loathe fragrance. TS

Carré d'As (Parfums de Nicolaï) ★ ★ ★ *boring fougère* $
A Cool Water–inspired fougère, competently put together but unmemorable. Manifestly a range-filler from one of the greats of French perfumery. LT

Carthusia Uomo (Carthusia) ★ *citrus woody* $$
Supposedly based on an old monastery formula and released in 1948, but could have been slapped together last Thursday. TS

Ça Sent Beau (Kenzo) ★ ★ ★ ★ ★ *tangerine fougère* $
There are two known roads to creating a striking, top-notch perfume:

do either a virtuoso version of a known classic form (the silk satin ball-gown) or a brilliant invention (the Diane von Furstenberg wrap dress). Kenzo's appropriately named Ça Sent Beau (That Smells Beautiful) from 1987 navigates the latter route, thanks to perfumer Françoise Caron, whose earlier Ombre Rose for Jean-Charles Brosseau still stands as proof of the possibility of finding a novel structure using a few simple, familiar materials. Ça Sent Beau's achievement is especially striking when you compare it to Gaultier's Classique, built on similar materials (orange citrus notes and powdery, fresh woody musks): the Gaultier is stonking, costumey, heavy, reminiscent of the laundromat, while the Kenzo is trim, chic, and reminds you of nothing on earth. On a woman, it has an air of cheerful efficiency and charm; on a man, it's a good-humored alternative to Caron's Royal Bain de Champagne, a Brut with fruit. Kindly ignore the bottle, which looks like a plug-in nightlight from the Dollar Store. TS

Cashmere Mist (Donna Karan) ★ ★ *dull floral* $
Hard to say much about this salicylate accord, wan and gray. LT

Cašmir (Chopard) ★ ★ ★ ★ *strange oriental* $ $
Interesting dissonant oriental. The contrast between the peachy, lactonic top notes; the slightly flat, mimosa floral heart; and the woody-animalic drydown will be perceived as nauseating by some and attractive by others. In its own way, it's as daring as Rabanne's La Nuit was in its day. This one has to be worn by the right person to work properly. LT

Cast a Spell (Lulu Guinness) ★ *mini Angel* $ $
Dreadful little thing. LT

Casual (Paul Sebastian) ★ ★ *pale muguet* $
Very thin, simple lily of the valley, clean and fresh but unfortunately nearly identical in smell to some brands of scented toilet paper. TS

Cédrat Intense (Parfums de Nicolaï) ★ ★ ★ *citrus woody* $$
The citron (*cédrat* in French) is a massive citrus fruit, and oil from its peel is used in perfumery. This is an accurate representation, close to lemon verbena but not as bright. Pleasant but neither intense nor particularly interesting. TS

Cèdre (Parfums 06130) ★ ★ *"sport" green* $$$
The post code for Grasse is 06130, a city once known for fields of flowers, now for luxury condos. Appropriately, nothing in Cèdre smells of anything that required watering. A thin sport masculine, which makes rote gestures in the usual directions without knowing why. TS

Cèdre (Serge Lutens) ★ ★ ★ *sweetened tuberose* $$$
Cedar has long been Lutens's wood of choice, so it seems peculiar that his Cèdre should not be a cedar at all. It's a tuberose oriental, incredibly camphoraceous-indolic and with an intensely oily combination of balsams and woods at bottom, a kind of niche version of Amarige. TS

Cèdre Blanc (Heeley) ★ ★ ★ ★ *fresh cedar* $$$
Some of the ideas of Heeley's Cuir Pleine Fleur (the velvety vetiver) and Sel Marin (salty citrus) are redeployed here in a different form, in a cigar-box context. Arguably less distinctively original than its two congeners, but wonderfully elegant and wearable. LT

Cèdre Sandaraque (Parfumerie Générale) ★ ★ ★ *woody fruity* $$$
I would love this one but for the fact that it is a flawed twin of Patricia de Nicolaï's Vie de Château (ex-Cheverny) done on what feels like a lower budget. Get the real thing. LT

Cefiro (Floris) ★ ★ ★ *waxed lemon* $$
A no-holds-barred aldehydic citrus that smells intensely of citral (lemon peel) and waxy aldehydes up top, and becomes very quiet thereafter. Strikingly fresh and pleasant. LT

Celine Dion (Celine Dion) ★ ★ ★ *milky floral* $
There's really nothing wrong with this perfectly nice ambery floral, a breezy little cotton shift of a fragrance, slightly melancholy with the milky-metallic note of helional. TS

Celine Dion Parfum Notes (Celine Dion) ★ ★ ★ *fresh floral* $
Like the original Celine Dion, but with a greener, fresher top. TS

Central Park (Bond No. 9) ★ *menthol rub* $$$
Aqua Velva. TS

Cerruti 1881 (Cerruti) ★ ★ ★ ★ *citrus rose* $
Pleasantly, affably vulgar juniper-citrus zingy cologne with a soft, rosy balsamic background. Has a beautiful room-filling radiance and a lovely powdery drydown. Much imitated and still very good. LT

Ce Soir ou Jamais (Annick Goutal) ★ ★ *pear rose* $$
Jamais. This Eternity-wannabe, with all of its violets and the funky pear note from Petite Cherie, smells far too much like a glass of white wine that's been sitting out all night. TS

C'est la Fête (Christian Lacroix) ★ *very fruity* $
Some people never learn. Lacroix released his first perfume, C'est la Vie, in 1990. It was so awful that in the intervening seventeen years I've met only one woman who praised it, and she was chewing gum while talking. To everyone's relief, it bombed completely and was discontinued. You'd think that Lacroix would henceforth hire people with brains, stay away from clichéd declarative names, and lose the bottles with a stub of coral on top. Instead he revisits the scene of the crime with a fruity floral (how original) that feels like a mixture of Cabotine and Champs-Elysées and in which the only natural ingredient is likely the grain alcohol used to dilute it. Loud, vulgar, and moronic. LT

CH (Carolina Herrera) ★ *pepper strawberry* $ $

It's hard to decide whether it's the cloying strawberry or the mind-alteringly potent woody amber that offends most. T S

Chakra 1–7 (Aveda) ★ ★ ★ *organic mixture* $

These all-natural "body mists" are definitely not perfumes in the conventional sense, but they smell very nice. My favorite is 7. L T

My favorite is 1. If you've gotten used to bare, entirely synthetic fragrances, these are a reset button for your nose; they smell rich, fresh, alive, and then they go away, having restored you to factory settings. Happily, they also smell very good when you wear all of them at the same time. T S

Chamade (Guerlain) ★ ★ ★ ★ ★ *powdery floral* $ $

I lived near the Champs-Elysées, two streets up from the Guerlain store, when Chamade came out in 1969, and I remember it wafting out of door number 68 as people came in and out. It was, as someone said of the Concorde, a new shape in the air. In those days I didn't buy perfumes, and initially thought Chamade was two distinct fragrances: I would smell the drydown on passersby and find it wonderful, but it took me months to connect it to the nondescript floral green top note. Chamade is perhaps the last fragrance ever to keep its audience waiting so long while props were moved around behind a heavy curtain. The drydown, when it finally arrived, was beautiful, a strange, moist, powdery yellow narcissus accord that had the oily feel of pollen rubbed beween finger and thumb. The modern Chamade still smells great but gets to the point much faster and has a slight flatness I have noticed in recent Jicky versions, something milkier and more sedate in the vanillic background. Nevertheless, a masterpiece. L T

Chamade pour Homme (Guerlain) ★ ★ ★ *herbaceous floral* $ $ $

Don't tell me Catherine Deneuve was a guy all along. This is a fleshed-out remake of the unsuccessful Coriolan, with the same gray, herbaceous-woody start and more floral notes below. This slightly gloomy style of masculine has its origins in Dior's great Fahrenheit, now unfortunately hobbled by European Union restrictions on octyne esters. Not great by Guerlain standards, but still so much better than the average masculine fragrance these days that it would be churlish to pan it. LT

Champaca (Ormonde Jayne) ★ ★ ★ *green floral* $ $
Champaca is a handsome, well-built fragrance in a square-shoulders eighties style, compellingly botanical and synthetic in what feels like equal parts, giving a soft, slightly buttery floral a backbone of amber and a pleasantly rich, green-woody herbal aura. (Very similar to Calvin Klein's Truth from 2000, but with better materials.) It is also peculiar in sometimes smelling stronger farther away than up close, and would work beautifully in small quantities on a man. TS

Champaca Absolute (Tom Ford) ★ ★ *harsh floral* $ $ $
Having had the good fortune of smelling Peter Wilde's top-notch champaca flower absolute I can reveal that Tom Ford's fragrance captures very little of the real thing's luscious charm and in fact smells cheap and chemical after only a few minutes. Avoid. LT

Champs-Elysées (Guerlain) ★ *fluorescent floral* $ $
Until people stop buying it in error and Guerlain finally puts it out of its misery, CE will stand as a *monument aux morts* commemorating the fallen in the debacle that immediately followed the sale of the Guerlain family silver to Moët Hennessy Louis Vuitton (LVMH) in 1994. LVMH's success was based on the correct premise that the great French luxury brands were badly run and undercapitalized. It seemed, at least in the early days of the Guerlain purchase, to be based on the entirely incorrect notion that a brand could be used to flog anything because perfume was hot air anyway, and the punters couldn't tell the difference. (LVMH has since seen the error of its ways.) Enter Champs-Elysées, composed by

Olivier Cresp of Angel fame. But the gods were lying in ambush: Guerlain totally screwed up its first advertising campaign and had to put together a second, very expensive one in a hurry. The fragrance flopped in Europe but allegedly did well with its intended audience of trashy teens in the Far East, though the sour tone of Guerlain PR when discussing the matter suggests things may not have been all rosy. Personally, I don't care whether the nightclubs of Macau stink of it: it is still the second-worst perfume Guerlain ever made (see Mayotte for the first). LT

Chance (Chanel) ★ ★ ★ *floral oriental* $
Stunned by the success of Coco Mademoiselle and a little embarrassed by its crudeness, the Chanel crew went back to work and tried to do on purpose what they had first achieved by accident. Coco Mademoiselle 2.0, aka Chance, was the result. But if it's not worth doing, it's not worth doing well. Avoid this one, unless you're dating Piltdown Man. LT

Chance Eau Fraiche (Chanel) ★ *chemical floral* $$
What's known as pushing one's chance. Depressingly banal. LT

Chant d'Arômes (Guerlain) ★ ★ ★ ★ *tender floral* $$$
The original (1962) was Jean-Paul Guerlain's first fragrance after the retirement of his father, Jacques, and was a light, powdery-peachy confection strongly suggestive of a fresh start and a sweet young woman, as if the younger Guerlain had both found love and made a clean break with the past. I liked it for its caressing softness, and hated the rather nondescript floral-aldehydic that replaced it sometime in the early nineties. This one is changed again, but seemingly only halfway back to the original, and I still don't get the full dose of peach that made it so great. Much better, but still a little shy. *Camarades, encore un effort!* LT

Chaos (Donna Karan) ★ ★ ★ ★ *woody fruity* $$
Among the DK reissues, none was more eagerly awaited than Chaos, which caused a sensation when it first appeared and an even greater one

when discontinued a few years later. Maybe my memory is playing tricks, but I remember it being slightly different, less spicy fresh and fruitier. Never mind, it's still great. For those of us already smitten with Féminité du Bois (1992) and Dolce Vita (1995), Chaos was great news. It was the first to take Bourdon and Sheldrake's warm, languid, delicious woody-fruity idea as a starting point and make it less cloyingly sweet, more of a morning fragrance, a happy, straightforward unisex composition that feels as new now as it did then. LT

Charlie! (Revlon) ★ *green floral* $
A huge hit in the seventies, Charlie! was the most popular of that era's inexpensive fragrances for the new working woman, promoted by the first perfume ads to show a woman wearing pants. Whatever it smelled like then, today it smells like the latest reformulation of Vent Vert—a crude, sour white floral with some galbanum gamely trying to stand in for class. You can't expect a gal to fork over hard-earned money for this. TS

Charogne (Etat Libre d'Orange) ★ ★ *spicy oriental* $$
Charogne means "carrion," a brave name for a fragrance. The Web site explains, with the insouciance of youth, that the description pertains to a mature woman skilled in the arts of love. The fragrance is a spicy-balsamic accord, pleasant enough but without much interest—evidence that the art school one-liner tendency may be taking over Orange Free State, which would be a shame. LT

La Chasse aux Papillons (L'Artisan Parfumeur) ★ ★ ★
white floral $$
All perfume houses must have a white floral, because it sells, though I wish it didn't. White florals bring to mind Oscar Levant's famous quip "I knew Doris Day before she was a virgin." Unless worn by a man or simply sprayed in the air, they can evoke a schoolmarmy primness, a desire to apply bactericidal stovetop cleaners to all areas of human en-

deavor. A woman should not merely smell of flowers, unless they be strange (tuberose) or completely abstract (Joy, Beyond Paradise). Still less should a woman smell of florist, which is what most of the synthetic white florals do, unless the effect is deliberate and humorous as in Dazzling Silver. All this being said, the combination of mawkish name and steely muguet aldehyde accord of LCaP is perfect for the genre, and this fragrance is far better put together than most. LT

Cheap and Chic (Moschino) ★ ★ ★ *fresh floral* $
The name suggests something disposable; the whimsical bottle was designed to resemble Olive Oyl, not your usual fashion icon; but the fragrance is a pleasant variation on fresh, powdery-sweet peony, built on cozy laundry musks with an appealing creamy, almost buttery feel. It's similar to the less cheerful, more sedate Heavenly from Victoria's Secret, which came later. Funny how the same things rearranged slightly here or there can be nice or nasty. You could do a lot worse. TS

Chelsea Flowers (Bond No. 9) ★ ★ *light peony* $$$
Pale, bodiless spring floral, pretty in an antiseptic way, for women who would prefer to smell of nothing, only they're ever so slightly afraid that their nothing has a smell. TS

Chembur (Byredo) ★ ★ ★ *woody incense* $$$
Byredo is a Swedish niche outfit that launched five fragrances early in 2008. Chembur is an incense fragrance in the transparent Timbuktu-Sycomore style but less rich and interesting than its congeners and with too prominent a metallic note (helional). LT

Chêne (Serge Lutens) ★ ★ *pencil shavings* $$$
Chêne (Oak) shows Lutens and Christopher Sheldrake stripping their usual woody structure down to a lean smell of sawdust, less a fragrance than a proposal for further discussion. TS

Chergui (Serge Lutens) ★ ★ ★ ★ *tobacco oriental* $$$

Hay absolute, all by itself, is so insanely good it's a wonder nobody just dilutes it and slaps on a label. A perfumer friend of mine gave me for reference a few muddy, viscous drops from the top producer of natural materials in Grasse, Laboratoire Monique Remy, and it is a fantastically complicated smell, like the best pipe tobacco on earth, smoky and plummy with an angular, bitter vegetal pungency—basically, a naturally occurring Rochas Femme. I have it on LT's word that some years ago he brought some of the same material to Serge Lutens and blew his mind. Chergui seems to be based on that true story, a rich, soapy, cherry-pipe-tobacco scent suitable for a handsome, smiling fifties daddy on Sundays, sweetly balsamic with a heart of marvelous hay and a good dose of iris, but in the end such a familiar plot that I can't help but wish it had been truer to the source. TS

Cherry Blossom (L'Occitane) ★ ★ *berry floral* $

Another pink fragrance that smells like hard candy in your favorite flavor, "red," and this time disturbingly buttery as well. Hard to imagine anyone buying it. TS

Cherry Blossom Fruity (Guerlain) ★ ★ *powdery fruity* $$

The continental drift that has taken place quietly but relentlessly over the last twenty years has narrowed the gap between cheap shampoos and expensive perfumes to such an extent that the smallest lapse of judgment in fine fragrance within the genres favored by functional perfumery lands you squarely in El Cheapo. Oddly, once a formula has been cleverly slimmed by the unsung artists who do for $18 per kilogram what originally cost ten times as much, it is all but impossible to reverse the debasing of the coinage. CBF is an object study in devaluation: it smells 10 percent better than the stuff you'll find in the TraveLodge bathroom, and costs fifty times the price. No doubt some people find both smell and price reassuring, and expect no connection between the two. Depressing thought. LT

Le Chèvrefeuille (Annick Goutal) ★ ★ ★ *lemongrass tomato* $$$
Honeysuckle is impossible: you can make it happen in photorealistic
detail for an exciting half minute (see Demeter's Honeysuckle), but you
can't build a full perfume on it because it never holds together. That's
why Goutal's honeysuckle isn't one. Instead, it's a garden fantasy of cit-
ronellal and tomato stems, a tom yum soup without the fish. TS

Chez Bond (Bond No. 9) ★ ★ *diet fougère* $$$
Pleasant but thin sweetened herbal woody, only half there, as if you'd
tried to wash another aromatic fougère off. TS

Chic (Carolina Herrera) ★ ★ *fruity floral* $
Things, like faces, sometimes age in a cruelly tawdry way, none more so
than the precarious contrivance known as the fruity floral, that fixed
smile of perfumery that passed for cheerful three or four years ago and
now feels like a facelift gone so badly awry that the lips no longer meet
comfortably. LT

Chic for Men (Carolina Herrera) ★ ★ ★ *fresh mishmash* $
The British, inventors of wonderful put-downs like "stuffed shirt" and
"hidden shallows," would say that this fragrance "makes all the right
noises," and indeed it offers the full panoply of masculine clichés from
citrus to cardamom via woods and woody ambers. This is a medley of
every aspirational masculine ever made, a sort of *Reader's Digest* version
of the guy wall at Sephora. LT

China Rose (Floris) ★ *syrupy "rose"* $$
The name must refer to a Chinese takeaway in Newark, the cloying smell
to the air freshener in the ladies' toilet. TS

Chinatown (Bond No. 9) ★ ★ ★ ★ ★ *gourmand chypre* $$$
The endearingly plucky firm of Bond No. 9 has produced its first and so
far only masterpiece. Composed by the young Aurélien Guichard (son

of the great Jean of Roure, now Givaudan), it is one of those fragrances that smells so immediately, compellingly, irresistibly great that the only sane response is love at first sniff. Chinatown is at once oddly familiar and very surprising, as if the lyrics in a favorite love song had been rearranged to make a new poem, just as affecting but unplanned by the original author. On the one hand, Chinatown harks back to classic, haughty green chypres like Cabochard, Givenchy III, and the first Scherrer. On the other hand, it has an odd, almost medicinal note reminiscent of the mouthwatering dried-fruit smell of Prunol, a base originally composed by Edmond Roudnitska for the defunct firm of De Laire. The combination strikes a precarious but totally convincing balance between remoteness and affability that suggests a personality at once full of charm and dangerous to know. Some people find it too sweet. To my nose it smells like a corner of a small French grocery in summer, in the exact spot where the smell of floor wax meets that of ripe peaches. A treasure in a beautiful bottle. LT

Chloé (Chloé) ★ ★ *humdrum rose* $ $
"This ribbon, this little ribbon, took four months to conclude upon," Michele Scannavini, president of Coty Prestige, proudly told the *International Herald Tribune* about the bottle's beige bunting. They must then have spent four minutes concluding upon the fragrance: a dilute, dishearteningly synthetic muguet-rose good enough to grace a non-abrasive bathtub cleanser. TS

Borderline false advertising, since the 1975 Chloé was a big natural tuberose. LT

Chocolate Greedy (Montale) ★ ★ ★ *gluttonous chocolate* $ $
I am inordinately fond of extreme gourmand perfumes, but I admit they are attractive only if you have crossed wires in your hypothalamus and the sight of a pretty girl actually makes you salivate. This one is

great fun, a low-calorie *pavé au chocolat* against a quiet woody-floral background. LT

Chopard pour Homme (Chopard) ★ ★ *citrus woody* $$
Nasty cross between Cacharel pour l'Homme and Cool Water, with a weird boiled-beetroot note thrown in. LT

Chrome (Azzaro) ★ *watery citrus* $
Why, oh why do people want to pay real money to get the smell of their shampoo played louder, and in a form that doesn't even wash hair? LT

Chrome Legend (Azzaro) ★ ★ ★ *jasmine woody* $$
Masculine florals are back? The last time this happened nobody bought them and a fair few people lost their jobs. This one is a fresh, aldehydic woody-jasminy affair, not bad except that it begs a question: If you're going to do that, why not go large and wear Pleasures? LT

Chypre Rouge (Serge Lutens) ★ ★ *immortelle disaster* $$$
Neither much of a chypre nor obviously rouge, Chypre Rouge is a jarringly sharp arrangement of pine woods, dried herbs, and curry spices that unfortunately reminds you that most of these smells serve in nature to repel rather than attract. TS

Ciel (Amouage) ★ *bad floral* $$$$
Somebody please put a stop to this. Amouage's good fragrances do not deserve the company of this trivial white-flowers confection, even though the dismal structure is put together from unusually good materials. Interesting only to show that an expensive version of something cheap is still cheap. LT

Ciel pour Homme (Amouage) ★ ★ ★ ★ *animalic spicy* $$$$
God works in mysterious ways: Ciel pour Femme was trivial, but the

version for men (same name, same blue packaging) is as weird as it gets. The accord, and I say this without implied criticism, can only be described as urinous, suggesting that costus or Aldron went into the composition. I haven't smelled anything so startlingly zoological (without civet) since Dior's outrageous Jules, and I applaud it. I do not see how a woman, in the presence of a man wearing Ciel, could fail to immediately picture him in his underwear. The rest depends on circumstance. LT

Cinéma (Yves Saint Laurent) ★ ★ ★ ★ *sweet mimosa* $ $
With a name like that, and given YSL's distinguished tradition, you'd expect a wide-screen thing that would pin you to your seat. Nothing of the sort: Cinéma's volume button is firmly stuck on quiet, and the very pleasant composition smells halfway between powdery mimosa and warm apple crumble. So polite and apologetic, you wonder what it's trying to atone for. LT

Cinéma Festival d'Eté (Yves Saint Laurent) ★ ★ ★ *fruity amber* $ $
Perfectly passable vanilla amber in a pipe-tobacco way, fun big lumpy bottle the size and shape of a brick. But if you want this kind of thing for summer, we recommend Vanilia (L'Artisan Parfumeur) instead. TS

Cinnabar (Estée Lauder) ★ ★ ★ ★ *spicy oriental* $
If, as Cyril Scott believed, the devas control human evolution by putting ideas in the minds of artists, some archangelical management failure occurred circa 1977. Cinnabar, a stonking oriental named after a mercury mineral found in China, came out weeks after Opium, a stonking oriental named after a drug found in China and packaged in bottles the color of cinnabar. Cinnabar was (and is) good but not great and was rightly overshadowed by its twin. Now that everyone has grown thoroughly tired of Opium, it is worth smelling again. LT

Cirrus (Amouage) ★ *fruity woody* $$$
Alas, the very distinguished firm of Amouage has lost the plot with this one, another Cool Water remake of little interest. LT

Citron Citron (Miller Harris) ★ ★ *pine citrus* $$$
This was Lyn Harris's first fragrance, and what a timid start! An apologetically light, antiseptic-smelling citrus that lazy teenagers can spray around the kitchen to convince Mom and Dad they've done their chores. Amazingly, she went on from this to do one of the filthiest fragrances of all time, the fantastically unwashed L'Air de Rien. TS

City Glam for Her (Armani) ★ ★ ★ *rose chypre* $$
A skillfully done but clearly low-budget fluorescent fruity rose with a patchouli, interesting because markedly different from other cheap fruity florals. Surprisingly coherent berry-rose drydown. TS

City Glam for Him (Armani) ★ ★ *bare cologne* $
Urban glamor? A thin, soapy citrus floral like a twenty-four-hour antiperspirant formula. TS

cK Be (Calvin Klein) ★ ★ ★ *light fougère* $
CK One demonstrated brilliantly that a quiet citrus fragrance, like a pacifist movement, could make itself heard without resorting to violence. CK Be does the same with a fougère composition and, though less radiant, perfectly hits the spot for those who want a fragrance not just to evoke a faded memory, but to smell like one. LT

cK IN2U Her (Calvin Klein) ★ *fruity amber* $
OMG PU. Insanely strong fruit meets insanely strong woody amber. KTHXBYE. TS

cK IN2U His (Calvin Klein) ★ *7UP amber* $
IM IN UR BOTTLE BORIN UR GF. TS

cK One (Calvin Klein) ★ ★ ★ ★ *radiant citrus* $

CK One is not so much a perfume as a chemical time machine. Most fragrances happily operate on a logarithmic time scale, each successive phase occupying a span ten times longer than the previous one: six minutes of top notes, an hour of heart, and the rest of the day for drydown. But cK One takes a different tack, by stopping time altogether. In the eighties, this used to be called linear perfumery, and was usually applied to big-hair contraptions that, alas, froze the clock at 11 on a Saturday night. The rest of the time, they worked like heels and a gold lamé dress on the morning train to work. Instead, cK One takes a soapy, fresh top note and fleshes it out with a skin-toned ensemble of middle and drydown materials. Every one is picked for radiance, so the chord can be heard just as clearly thirty paces away as up close. The mix in the air is unvarying, and time forever stands still at 8 a.m.: the frozen morning of a day full of promise. LT

cK One Summer (Calvin Klein) ★ ★ *floral grapefruit* $

Eye-wateringly dull fresh grapefruit that smells like shower gel. LT

Clair de Musc (Serge Lutens) ★ ★ *musky floral* $ $ $

A pleasant but uncharacteristically nondescript and run-of-the-mill musk for Lutens, who, after all, gave us the no-holds-barred, lush animalic Muscs Koublai Khan. TS

Clean (Clean) ★ *passionfruit citrus* $ $

The fruity notes in this fragrance, the first in the now-far-too-large Clean line, remind me of those candies they string on necklaces, the ones that taste and feel like flavored chalk. TS

Clean Fresh Laundry (Clean) ★ *lime musk* $ $

A sniff is enough to put you off personal hygiene for weeks at a time. LT

Clean Lather (Clean) ★ *un clean* $$
Clean's worst fragrance. Yay. LT

Clean Men (Clean) ★ *messy citrus* $$
Clean has fulfilled at least one functional perfumer's Walter Mitty dream: "Look, Mum, fine fragrance!" This is the best of the Clean line, which means it's merely a bad fragrance. LT

Clean Provence (Clean) ★ *citrus musk* $$
I lived in Provence for eight years and mercifully never encountered this extraordinary accord of cheap gin-and-tonic and wet concrete. LT

Clean Shower Fresh (Clean) ★ *trash floral* $$
Clean does a white floral. Come back, Creed's Love in White, all is forgiven. LT

Clean Ultimate (Clean) ★ *citrus floral* $$
These Clean scents are like a party game: name that household product! However, this one's not vile, just tawdry. I feel pretty sure the top note is Dawn, the drydown Downy. It generates a sense memory of warm suds up to my elbows and resentment against my mother. Can be used to fool dates into thinking you're domestically inclined. TS

Clean Warm Cotton (Clean) ★ *citrus floral* $$
The devil grants your wishes, and his celebrity brand is called, of course, Clean. You, I, and everyone else have occasionally wondered why they didn't make a fragrance that smells like Bounce sheets, only stronger. Now we know why: it smells terrible, like Muzak played at Metallica sound levels. Hideous. LT

Climat (Lancôme) ★ ★ ★ ★ *abstract floral* $$
Created in 1967, Climat was born old, a laggard latecomer to the Ma Griffe tweedy-floral category. Smelling it brings to mind my father's ob-

servation, made roughly the same year, that women were forsaking gir-
dles and no longer looked tubular around the middle. Climat is still
cylindrical but, like smoking and Hermès scarves, has gained delicious
retro connotations. Ordinary Climat, like all Lancôme fragrances, had
been cheapened over the years and was a shadow of its former self. No
doubt "because you're worth it," L'Oréal has decided to spruce up a
handful of Lancôme classics and bring them back in proper spec. The
"Collection" version of Climat is excellent, much richer, and makes an
ideal grown-up fragrance for someone who clearly isn't. LT

Cocktail (B Never Too Busy to Be Beautiful) ★ ★ ★ ★
woody ylang $
A woody floral that smells like new sneakers. God, what fun! TS

Coco (Chanel) ★ ★ ★ ★ *elegant spicy* $ $
Coco has to be seen in historical context. In 1977, Saint Laurent's Opium,
composed by Jean-Louis Sieuzac, shook the world of perfumery. It
smelled astonishingly new, sensual, and distinctive, and the name and
packaging were spot-on. Thirty years later, it is still the textbook example of perfect top-down design. The idea was in the air: a few months
after Opium, Lauder released Cinnabar (similar smell, same color, same
Chinese theme), on which they had clearly been working independently
for some time. Cinnabar was eclipsed by Opium. Why? Because it merely
smelled good, whereas Opium held a bold, discernible structure within
its dark cloud of resins, spices, and balsams. In the next few years, everyone tried to go one better on Opium, with little luck. Coco (1984) was
the first to advance the game, in part by taking advantage of the recent
arrival of damascenones in the perfumer's palette. Damascenones have
spectacularly complex, dusky, and exotic dried-fruit odors. Like the lactones in Mitsouko sixty years earlier, they can be used to soften and
brighten a composition. Coco did this superbly, and to this day no one
has improved on it, though Krizia's Teatro alla Scala came close. That

said, Coco feels terribly dated and needs another decade or two to over-come its tired eighties image. Let's hope they still make it by the time people are ready to give it a fresh try. LT

Cococabana (Parfums de Nicolaï) ★ ★ ★ *coconut tuberose* $ $
Patricia de Nicolaï's creations have occasionally been criticized for be-ing very classical and somewhat unadventurous. Those who hold that view should smell Cococabana. The top note is a weird accord of tube-rose, green notes (mastic gum?), and sweet, creamy coconut. The bal-ance is precariously perfect for some time, especially on fabric, but eventually the lactones take over (they always do) and the drydown is a bit high-calorie. Very interesting nevertheless. LT

Coco Mademoiselle (Chanel) ★ ★ ★ ★ *floral oriental* $ $
By rights, this is the one that should be called Chance, because it hap-pened by accident. Chanel put CM together as a "flanker," a product designed to ride the coattails of a famous brand name while keeping PR on the boil. Not a lot of work went into it, and Chanel was, I am told, as surprised as everyone else when it became a runaway success. CM and its congeners arise from the systematic application of a trick first discov-ered by Angel (q.v.). This consists in mixing an intense, almost mascu-line spicy-oriental base with a strident floral accord. In the case of Angel, the effect is wonderfully androgynous and scarily over-the-top. Noth-ing takes the fun out of a filthy joke as surely as toning it down, and that's what CM is about. Perfumers love doing this stuff because it's easy: mix equal parts of Héritage and Allure, stir, and call in the evalu-ator. This style is a success for the same reasons that Respighi's *Foun-tains of Rome* is one of the best sellers of classical music: it's loud, impressive, and undemanding. But when mediocrity is easy, greatness becomes hard. These fragrances are as difficult to tell apart as the ladies at a Scala first night: all tan, makeup, and hair. Mercifully, this style is on its way out. LT

Coeur de Fleur (Miller Harris) ★ ★ *wall flower* $$$
This was one of the first four MH fragrances launched in 2000, and I found it, then as now, so boring that I ceased to pay attention to the brand for several years. It turns out I was wrong, and Lyn Harris has moved on since then and produced interesting fragrances. But this pale, polite, apologetic floral still strikes me as a non-event. LT

Coeur d'Eté (Miller Harris) ★ ★ *fruity lilac* $$$
Lilac fragrances struggle not to smell like air freshener, and Coeur d'Eté makes a valiant effort by buttressing this essentially flat floral note with herbal and berry touches. Smells nice while it lasts but eventually falls apart, ending up like scented tissue at the end. (Better on fabric than on skin.) TS

Un Coeur en Mai (Parfums MDCI) ★ ★ ★ *green rose* $$$$
Both Patricia de Nicolaï's own company and MDCI are classicist firms with distinctive, complex fragrances made with tremendous skill and top-notch materials, including several we give five stars. De Nicolaï in particular has a history of innovative work. It's odd, then, that for MDCI she has turned out two minor scents in a vintage apothecary aesthetic, pretty but unambitious. Un Coeur en Mai is a well-behaved tea rose with bright metallic highlights and a nostalgic fatty-musk, Camay-soap background, which makes the colors peach and white go striping through one's mind and recalls those dignified Regency canvases that slap even Sir Christopher Wren and George Washington with half a tin of rouge. TS

Cologne (Thierry Mugler) ★ ★ ★ ★ *steam clean* $
I assume that, when he's not pretending to be French to save trouble, Thierry Mugler travels with a passport that says *Forbidden Planet*. All his clothes and many of his fragrances have that oversized-pentagonal future-past thing, which makes you want to lie back in your magnetic hammock and ask Robbie to bring you a purple cocktail. His Cologne is

that rarest thing: a fun masculine fragrance. And like all good jokes, it's brief and to the point. Take an aromachemical that smells hissy like hot steam from an iron, and instead of putting a smidgen of it in a lemony-woody composition (fresh, bracing, blah, blah, yawn . . .), just use it almost by itself, accompanied by some pale floral-aldehydic notes. There you have it: triple-distilled essence of space-age barbershop. And it comes in a bottle big enough to last a Krell several days. LT

Cologne à la Française (Institut Très Bien) ★ ★ ★ ★ *great cologne* $$
To a former French schoolkid like myself, the words *très bien* have the beautiful, unattainable ring of the highest possible grade on your homework: *passable, assez bien, bien,* and *TB,* all in red ink. The founder of ITB charmingly asserts that the outfit once existed, and that he found the name in his grandmother's correspondence together with recipes for superior colognes. A good cologne is the perfumery equivalent of a postconcert encore: brief; familiar to the entire audience, which sighs with pleasure when hearing the first notes; and completely devoid of any ambition beyond transient joy. It is also one of life's absolute necessities, perfume for when you don't feel like perfume, before going to bed, to splash on your kids after the bath and introduce them to life's finer pleasures, etc. In short, cologne is a cleanser for the soul. ITB's Française is excellent, true to form, very lemony, and of superb quality; it does everything exactly as planned. A contender for best in class together with Chanel's. LT

Cologne à la Russe (Institut Très Bien) ★ ★ ★ ★ *soft cologne* $$
Very good indeed, like the other colognes from this firm, but with a softer coumarinic, vanilla, and tobacco background. LT

Cologne à l'Italienne (Institut Très Bien) ★ ★ ★ ★ *classic cologne* $$
Accurately named, a more Italian version of the classic cologne, closer to the Jean-Marie Farina effect with orange flower and petitgrain, as good as the Française but sunnier, with green instead of blue in the flag. LT

Cologne Blanche (Dior) ★ ★ ★ ★ *almondy cologne* $$$
One of the first things the designer Hedi Slimane did when he took over
Dior Homme was to bring out three "colognes" in large, plain hand-
some bottles. Only one, Eau Noire, was outstanding, but the other two
were far from bad and would have created more of a stir had they been
in less striking company. Cologne Blanche is a classic citrus on a he-
liotropin background, pale, indeed *blanche* all the way through. LT

Cologne du 68 (Guerlain) ★ ★ ★ *complicated cologne* $$
Feels like someone took three parts cologne, one part L'Instant Femme
and two parts L'Instant Homme, mixed them, and stirred well. Less
than the sum of its parts. LT

Cologne Grand Luxe (Fragonard) ★ ★ ★ ★ *lasting citrus* $
Though the lemon-herb top note is darker and less sparkling than the
usual citrus, this eau de cologne is trying to hold that note longer than
any other. Where most colognes tail off into a whisper of flower and musk
after ten minutes, Fragonard's high-quality Cologne Grand Luxe continues in this unusual husky voice for the full hour. Very good work. TS

Cologne Grand Siècle (Parfumerie Générale) ★ ★ ★
green lemon $$$
A good classic cologne with an electrifyingly zingy fresh blast up top,
incorporating green-bitter notes to great effect. LT

Comme des Garçons 2 Man (Comme des Garçons) ★ ★ ★ ★
candle smoke $$
This clever composition hinges on a series of subliminal associations
between materials, converging with poetic logic on an inventive accord.
The idea seems to be this: odd-numbered aldehydes (nine and eleven
carbons) have an intense snuffed-out-candle character with a citrus un-
dertone. Frankincense too has a citrus background, and is also suggestive of snuffed-out candles, though not through its smell but via its

presence in churches and its use as smoke. Put them together, as Symrise's Mark Buxton did, and you end up with an intricately synesthetic marvel. LT

Comme des Garçons 2 Woman (Comme des Garçons) ★ ★ ★ ★
woody rose $$
One day, time permitting and dramatis personae willing, I will trace back to its origins the startlingly novel and beautiful style of perfumery exemplified by Mark Buxton's CdG2W and Bertrand Duchaufour's Timbuktu. Looking at their recorded works, it is clear that (1) Buxton was composing transparent woody-balsamic fragrances like Jacomo's wonderful Anthracite Homme as far back as 1991, i.e., four years before Duchaufour's first fragrance, Amber and Lavender (Jo Malone), and (2) they worked together at Créations Aromatiques, where some interaction must have taken place. All credit to CdG for giving this deceptively minimalist style a space in which to take root and flourish. CdG2W is a transitional creature, a slimmed-down, ascetically spare version of the great fluorescent roses of the eighties (Parfum de Peau, Knowing). In its backdrop you can already feel the breath of dry wind that sweeps through Duchaufour's best creations. CdG2W is simultaneously rasping and caressing, like a person whose mood changes promise a rough ride, and has a decadent stridency that Duchaufour's noble, reflective creations bypass completely. It is, in short, both a beautiful fragrance and a landmark. LT

Comme des Garçons 3 (Comme des Garçons) ★ ★ ★ ★
woody floral $$$
A beautifully subtle creation by Mark Buxton in his trademark ultra-transparent woody-floral manner, at once quiet and radiant, without any particular overall color. Probably the best introduction to the genre for those who want a plausible alternative to not wearing any fragrance at all. I keep feeling that if Miyake had known Buxton, this would have been Eau d'Issey. LT

Comme des Garçons White (Comme des Garçons) ★ ★ ★ ★
cedar cinnamon $$
Mark Buxton is one of perfumery's great geniuses of brilliance on a budget, composing fragrances so satisfying that their cheapness is beside the point. His hugely influential compositions for Comme des Garçons are the prime example. CdG White arrived in 1996, the same year as both Kenzo Jungle fragrances, the year after Dolce Vita, and four years after the precursor to them all, Féminité du Bois. White uses the transparent cedar-rose fruit of FdB in a huge, innovative synthetic structure of modern woody and ambery materials that you feel more than smell, and which amplify the rest until it reaches the ceiling and the next room without ever seeming rude or loud. The final, ghostly drydown—a faded newspaper photo of itself—feels carefully spare rather than neglectfully bare. TS

Concentré d'Orange Verte (Hermès) ★ ★ ★ ★ *refined citrus* $$
The difference between lime and lemon has always struck me as more a difference in temperament than in mere smell. Much as an exactly chosen word in a poem causes a web of resonant meanings to light up in your mind, the choice of lime over lemon is a choice between two drifting continents of freshness, once close but now separated by an ocean. The perfumer's task is to supply a background appropriate to the local flora. New World Orange Verte brilliantly goes for the bitter green notes of galbanum. Like the superb Eau de Guerlain, which does the same trick with Old World lemon and verbena, Hermès's essay in bracing simplicity is a daily treat. (See also Eau d'Orange Verte.) LT

Coney Island (Bond No. 9) ★ ★ *woody citrus* $$$
Airy little accord of synthetic wood and tenacious citrus, fresh and pleasant from a distance (harsh and rather empty up close). TS

Confetto (Profumum) ★ *hand lotion* $$$$
Profumum does Hypnotic Poison. LT

Contradiction for Men (Calvin Klein) ★ ★ ★ ★ *citrus spicy* $
If one reluctantly accepts the canons of the modern masculine as a sort
of olfactory haiku, this one is laconically more expressive than most,
shifting delicately from a gray-citrus top to a woody-spicy heart and,
most important of all, to an interesting drydown that does not smell like
a shortage of cash, as most others do. Small mercies, but indicative of
talent and care on the part of the perfumers. LT

Cool Water (Davidoff) ★ ★ ★ ★ ★ *aromatic fougère* $
This beautiful 1988 composition made Pierre Bourdon famous and was
imitated more times, I'll wager, than any other fragrance in history save
Chypre. The problem with successful masculines is that you associate
them with the legion of aspirational klutzes who wore them for good
luck. Trying to assess CW without conjuring up the image of some
open-shirted prat with hair gel is a bit like the Russian cure for hiccups:
run around the house three times without thinking of the word *wolf.*
This said, unlike Chypre, CW belongs to the category of things done
right the first time, like the first Windsurfer and the Boeing 707. Countless imitations, extensions, variations, and complications failed to improve on it or add a jot of interest to this cheerful, abstract, cheap, and
lethally effective formula of crab apple, woody citrus, amber, and musk.
Now let women wear it for a decade or two. LT

Cool Water Wave (Davidoff) ★ ★ ★ *fresh floral* $
A testimony to the indomitability of the human spirit. I can just imagine the moronic brief ("fresh, bright, powdery floral"), the soul-
destroying back-and-forth to focus groups and consumer tests, the
sweaty palms all round at the thought that this fragrance might upset a
single soul, the joy when the final, faceless thing got accepted. And yet,
and yet: whoever composed this managed against all odds to give it a
small measure of originality, tiny little twists and turns too small to
register on the radar screen of the censors. The top note smells of hot
electronics and is odd, even alarming, but vanishes just before you can

ask "What was that?" and the heart has an unusually transparent, skillful freshness. It reminds me of a guy I used to know who would say "Screw you all" mezza voce in a cheerful tone when he came into the office, and everyone thought he was saying hello. LT

Cool Water Woman (Davidoff) ★ ★ *aquatic citrus* $
The masculine Cool Water was influential and great, but the feminine feels like a sport masculine: sour lemon, hissy sage, and something like fresh paper; so mean I winced when I smelled it. To end on a positive note, this could be an excellent scent for car wax. TS

Coriandre (Jean Couturier) ★ *rose chypre* $
Many classic rose chypres are long gone, but Coriandre (1973) is still around. The structure is unforgettable though crude: huge damascone rose materials, with their fluorescent fruity brightness, plus a patchouli-centered chypre base, pleasantly grassy and woody. Unfortunately, the current version trades the rich, forest-green resinous air of the original for a cheap-smelling, soapy-woody formula that smells like a spray deodorant for guys who don't care. LT

Coromandel (Chanel) ★ ★ ★ ★ *powdery patchouli* $$$
Of the six new Chanels launched early in 2007, this is the one that most clearly has Christopher Sheldrake's handwriting all over it. He recently returned to his alma mater at Chanel after nearly two decades at Quest, during which he was chiefly occupied with composing Serge Lutens's epoch-making line of fragrances. It must have been fun to see everyone, from Guerlain downward, gradually fall into step and pay him the sincerest compliment, imitation. Coromandel is, to my mind, Sheldrake's reinterpretation of Borneo 1834 done in the Chanel manner, muted, richer, less saturated, and less overtly oriental. It has enough patchouli in it to clear the air of Indian moths for a mile around, yet it manages to avoid any hippie earthiness by a trick I am sure every perfumer would

like to emulate. If there were such a thing as powdered white chocolate, it would smell like Coromandel. Wonderful. LT

Corps et Ames (Parfumerie Générale) ★ ★ *rose chypre* $$$
A fine instance of cut-and-paste perfumery: the top half of Rose de Nuit, the cheap half of Givenchy III, a bit of glue, and bingo! Another unnecessary fragrance let loose upon the world. LT

Cosmic (Solange) ★ ★ ★ ★ *oriental chypre* $$$$
The second collaboration between idiosyncratic jeweler Solange Azagury-Partridge and perfumer Lyn Harris (of Miller Harris), after their mega-oriental Stoned, is another mad three-ring circus of a scent. These gleefully overstuffed fragrances gratify that part of the soul fiercely opposed to the word "or" on menus: it is the greedy id that pounds the table and hollers, "Cheese *and* dessert! Chicken *and* beef! Red *and* white! Salad *and* fries!" The fantastic supersized genie who emerges from this heavy, silvered bottle is Diorella *and* Habit Rouge starring in a gorgeously overdone production to be staged with heavy velvet drapes, gilded everything, full symphony orchestra with twice the usual tubas, ladies and lads in silks, feather fascinators brushing the ceiling, and the balconies stuffed with princes showering coins on the unwashed perfume critics below. TS

Coup de Fouet (Caron) ★ ★ *spicy floral* $$
This, the eau de toilette version of Poivre, used to be lighter and more floral, but now that Poivre is itself lighter and more floral, Coup de Fouet feels redundant. TS

Courtesan (Worth) ★ ★ ★ *woody spicy* $$
A puzzling fragrance, this one is supposedly a feminine (and composed by the great Pierre Bourdon). In reality, it's more like an all-things-to-all-men masculine in the gingerbread style of Yohji Homme, but thin-

ner and less good, with a two-tone-whistle spicy cardamom-cinnamon start reminiscent of the sadly discontinued Just Me (Montana). Not bad, but unconvincing and thin, no doubt due to a skimpy formula budget. LT

Covet (Sarah Jessica Parker) ★ ★ *lavender chocolate* $
I suppose this could have been interesting on paper—a chocolatey fougère—but it comes off like an unfocused rehash of the flat, sweet, heavy Must de Cartier and relatives. The bottle looks like a Super Mario power-up. TS

Cozé (Parfumerie Générale) ★ ★ ★ ★ *herbal patchouli* $$$
A beautiful fragrance with a hippie heart: fresh herbs, amber, patchouli, and moss smelling of forest and import shop, an expansive feeling of simple good fortune, like pausing in the doorway between a happy home and a beautiful outdoor morning. TS

Cravache (Robert Piguet) ★ ★ *dry citrus* $$
To paraphrase Lloyd Bentsen: "I knew Cravache. Cravache was a friend of mine. This is no Cravache." The original, of which I own a couple of liters, was once brilliantly replicated before my eyes in fifteen minutes by Laurent Bruyère by mixing a leather base with some bergamot and a couple of other things he neglected to tell me about. The original Cravache was the most cheerful of leathers and the least hygienic of citrus fragrances. Unaccountably, given that it was worth reviving and required no special skills, the keepers of the Piguet name have chosen to create an entirely new fragrance, a pleasant dry citrus with no trace of leather. Nice but not in the league of, say, Eau de Guerlain and somewhat pointless. LT

Un Crime Exotique (Parfumerie Générale) ★ ★ *candle shop* $$$
I have no idea whether this was intentional, but UCE smells exactly like the dreadful monster breath of Yankee Candle shops: boozy fruit from hell. Wear it only if everyone around you has a lively sense of humor. LT

Cristalle (Chanel) ★ ★ ★ ★ ★ *citrus chypre* $$
Fragrance taxonomist Michael Edwards (his classification eclipses all others) puts Cristalle among the crisp citruses. This is unquestionably correct, but what makes Cristalle fascinating, like an intermediate life-form that shows evolution midway through morphing from one species to another, is that it also belongs somewhere in the green chypres (fresh mossy wood in Edwards's scheme). Considered as a citrus, Cristalle is far too solemn. Considered as a chypre, it has an unusual morning (possibly morning-after) feeling. There is a business-like briskness that suggests waking up from a night spent with a gorgeous stranger and finding her fully dressed and made up, ready to leave after nothing more than a peck on the cheek, leaving only a cloud of Cristalle as a contact address. Beautiful, and a little scary. LT

Cruel Gardenia (Guerlain) ★ ★ *Camay soap* $$$$
The cruelty here is toward the poor saps like me who, upon hearing the word "gardenia," are capable of trudging across town for a sniff of the rumor, only to be bitterly disappointed. However, let me treat the name as poetic license, put on my sober-reviewer cap—the one that says "be fair" at the front—and examine this fragrance on its own terms. Well, that was easy. This is a late-fifties formula (somewhere between a knock-off of Ma Griffe and Camay soap) found in a dumpster in Holzminden when Symrise decided to clear the archive. Would be perfect if the spray button said "sucker" each time you pressed it. LT

Cruel Intentions (By Kilian) ★ ★ *floral oriental* $$$$
Thin, uncertain thing with no discernible intent, cruel or otherwise. LT

Crystal d'Ambre (Keiko Mecheri) ★ ★ ★ *amber demonstration* $$$
Smell this one alongside Amouage's recent reissue of Ubar for a demonstration of the difference between a great fragrance and a good one. Like Ubar, Crystal d'Ambre makes use of an impressive, thundering animalic amber base that miraculously occupies only the top notes. Half of it

smells like the honeyed wood of oud and half of it smells like someone's been using the sidewalk for a toilet: end result, fantastic. Unlike Ubar, there's not much more. An ill-judged synthetic green floral appears after about an hour, and then exits in favor of plain labdanum. TS

Crystal Noir (Versace) ★ *white floral* $
This is described as a gardenia in the press material. No such thing, of course, merely a trashy white floral. The creative direction is by Versace. LT

Cuba (Czech & Speake) ★ ★ ★ *bay rum* $$
Inspired by the Bay Rum idea (bay leaves and juniper berries steeped in rum), Cuba starts with a strikingly camphoraceous, almost Tiger Balm top note, followed by an excellent woody-musky drydown with a slight animalic touch. Overall, an interesting trajectory and an unpretentious, refreshingly daring fragrance. Strongly recommended. LT

Cuir (Lancôme) ★ ★ ★ ★ *woody leather* $$
Part of the Lancôme Collection and bearing the same name as a classic fragrance, this is a very unusual and beautiful leather, devoid of the weight of ambery, smoky, and animalic notes that make most others sink on drydown. Instead, this one maintains a light, airy, woody, al-most vetiver-like translucency all the way through and feels more like rich suede than Connolly hide. Unlike other recent woody leathers, such as Armani's Cuir Améthyste, that tended to harshness, it feels as com-fortable as the real thing. Excellent. LT

Cuir Améthyste (Armani Privé) ★ *leather violet* $$$
I can see how Armani could fall into this trap: leather fragrances like Cuir de Russie have an automatic connotation of luxury goods, perfect for the ultra-luxe Privé line, and the iris chill at their center might be coaxed into plusher textures if it were switched for the chemically re-lated sweet smell of violets. In fact, Jolie Madame managed a violet

leather ages ago by pairing the bitterness of isoquinoline leather with an astringent violet accord. Sadly, Cuir Améthyste is a cage fight of powerful odors battling to the death—cloying, harsh, and confused. TS

Cuir Beluga (Guerlain) ★ ★ ★ *powdery amber* $ $ $
The release of the first three fragrances signed by outside perfumers (Cuir Beluga, Angélique Noire, and Rose Barbare) marked a turning point for Guerlain. For the first time fragrances were unequivocally attributed to their creators (Olivier Polge for CB), thereby ending two, perhaps three decades of economy with the truth. Guerlain also acknowledged at long last the influence of niche perfumery, specifically Lutens, in the structure of the fragrances, their cod-poetic names, and the tall rectangular bottle. Cuir Beluga's name, with its suggestions of large sofas and small portions of caviar, is no doubt intended to flatter a French fondness for naff luxury. The fragrance is basically a light, heliotropin vanillic amber with a touch of floral green notes in the heart and a smidgen of suede. It has a pleasant color and texture, and no discernible shape at all. LT

Cuir de Russie (Chanel) ★ ★ ★ ★ ★ *leather luxury* $ $ $
Leather notes in perfumery are due chiefly to two raw materials, smoky rectified birch tar and inky isoquinolines, the first natural and the second synthetic. They are not necessarily used together, and Cuir de Russie includes only the former. *Rectified* is a polite word for "cooked," and to this day in places such as Russia and Canada where birch is abundant, the sap is cooked in large pans until it turns black and fragrant. The results are pretty variable, but always deliciously complex: a lot of chemistry happens in a few minutes when things roast. Sadly, the use of birch tar is now restricted by the European Union, and I was afraid of what this would do to Cuir de Russie. The answer is not much. This superb fragrance still smells exactly as it should: to me, just like the interior of my stepfather's 1954 Bentley Type R, in the back of which I sat alone as a child, toying with the mahogany fold-out table on the seat

backs. What is remarkable is that this rich leather effect is achieved by mixing things that have nothing to do with tanned animal skins: ylang, jasmine, iris, all of which can be perceived in the top notes. There have been many other fragrances called Cuir de Russie, every one either too sweet or too smoky. This one is the real deal, an undamaged monument of classical perfumery, and the purest emanation of luxury ever captured in a bottle. LT

Cuir d'Oranger (Miller Harris) ★ ★ ★ *woody oriental* $$$
The thought of a mutant orange tree covered in hide has something alarming about it, but at least it tells you what the fragrance is supposed to be doing. CdO, while not bad, is chiefly interesting as a variation on Habit Rouge that makes you realize once again how small HR's demesne is. Some fragrances, like Chypre, open up territories the size of Russia, while some, like Pleasures, are more like France, with room enough for a dozen regions. Habit Rouge is like San Marino: mess with your weapon's aim by giving the knob a quarter turn, and you'll hit Rimini. LT

Cuir Mauresque (Serge Lutens) ★ ★ ★ *sweet leather* $$$
The great leathery classic, Caron's Tabac Blond, receives the Lutens treatment—more transparent, sweetened with jasmine and dried fruit. Lovely, but somehow less, and no match for, say, Knize Ten. TS

Cuir Ottoman (Parfum d'Empire) ★ ★ ★ *woody amber* $$
Tyrannies always look better from afar, and the Ottoman Empire seems to be in vogue at the moment, chiefly because it brought administrative incompetence, baggy trousers, and sentimental music to regions that would otherwise have been solidly Germanic. This leather is in fact barely a leather at all, more a sweet-woody tea-like composition. It is solid and beautifully crafted, but feels a little like the compulsory figures at skating: solid, precise, impressive, and unsurprising. LT

Cuir Pleine Fleur (Heeley) ★ ★ ★ ★ *floral leather* $ $ $
The name of this wonderful fragrance is a play on tanners' slang. Fleur refers to the outside layer of leather, bearing marks of hairs and scars, which is split with a blade from the inner layer, or croûte, to make two supple, thin sheets. Fleur, naturally, also means "flower." The structure of CPF is original enough to challenge common assumptions about this fragrance type. To be sure, it contains two ingredients typical of modern leathers: rectified birch tar for the rich smokiness and a leather base (Swederal?) to give a sweet, velvety suede feel. So far so good. But the great originality of CPF lies in the accompaniment: a complex, muted, fresh-green accord of violet leaf, citrus, and vetiver so skillfully woven that one perceives a composition in the painterly sense—perhaps a winter scene of rural Russia by Levitan, all muted colors with the shadows on snow rendered in a strange but exact purple. CPF should serve as an object lesson to all, from Hermès to Cartier, who hanker after a new type of beauty in masculine perfumes. LT

Cuir Venenum (Parfumerie Générale) ★ ★ ★ ★ *rye leather* $ $ $
Pierre Guillaume's best creations have a breezy intelligence and a deceptive clarity about them that first makes you smile, then shake your head in disbelief as you try to figure out what is going on. In CV, the combination of orange blossom and leather achieves an extraordinary effect. At the risk of putting off perfume lovers with preconceived ideas, I shall describe it as the wonderful aroma you get when you first bring your nose to a full glass of top-notch Belgian beer (Orval, Leffe) before drinking: a rich, floral, honeyed, bitter, mealy accord. It is odd that such an uncommonly appetizing leather should have been called Venenum (Latin for "poison"). LT

Cumbia Colors Man (Benetton) ★ *cheap shampoo* $
Only hard work and dedication can produce something as derivative and uninteresting as this. LT

Cumbia Colors Woman (Benetton) ★ *sour flower* $
Ghastly little squeaky-clean stunted floral. LT

Cuoio (Profumo di Firenze) ★ ★ ★ *woody spicy* $$$$
The name is Italian for "leather," of which Florence is the capital, and I expected a variation of Knize Ten. No such thing: the composition only contains small amounts of leather materials, chiefly perceptible in the drydown, and belongs to the mildly exotic style typified by Minotaure (Paloma Picasso) and Eau d'Issey pour Homme. Smells good, but a bit nondescript. LT

Curious (Britney Spears) ★ *syrupy floral* $
Before I go on, let me get this off my chest: I loved Britney. I loved her uncomfortably inappropriate *Rolling Stone* cover in her underwear when she was fifteen; her funny, slightly strangled-sounding, hiccupy vocals; the photo of her slouchy barefoot walk out of a gas station restroom; the shaved head; the junk food; the umbrella attack on the paparazzi; her unending declarations of confidence and resilience throughout—a pop princess living in a country music song. Curious was by reports the best-selling fragrance of 2004, netting $100 million in its first year. It comes in a blue faceted bottle dangling pink heart-shaped charms, designed to appeal to those women who refuse to change their preferences simply because they're of childbearing age. I hoped it would be insanely great. It was not. It smells of every crass fruity floral of the last five years blended together, a bland, inoffensive magnolia-and-cherries thing resembling children's cough syrup. It lasts forever, radiates like nuclear waste, and perfectly expresses the crude charms of its star. At long last, Britney is starting to depress me. TS

Curve (Liz Claiborne) ★ ★ ★ *blackcurrant peony* $
Though this combination of trendy blackcurrant and a bright aldehydic floral is competently put together, it feels sour and conventional despite

the surface cheer, like a person who dislikes you yet smiles with maniacal enthusiasm whenever you encounter her. TS

Curve for Men (Liz Claiborne) ★ ★ ★ *citrus fougère* $
Nothing out of the ordinary, but it smells good in the sweet, fruity-plus-violet-leaf fashion. TS

Cyprès Musc (Creed) ★ ★ ★ *woody green* $$$
Full marks to Creed for going out of their way to compose an unusual accord, very intense in a harsh, green, boxwood manner, with an almost sulfuraceous hard-boiled-egg note up top. Not my cup of tea, but definitely interesting. LT

Daim Blond (Serge Lutens) ★ ★ ★ *apricot suede* $$$
Unlike traditional leathers such as Tabu and Tabac Blond, which have felt rich and warm, Daim Blond (meaning suede, and not, as it sounds, an accursed towhead) feels arid and cool, a hollowed-out osmanthus-like idea of peach and leather but no soapy center; it unfolds a spare, long-fingered form whose intentions seem to mark a departure from the more straightforward orientalist scents of the Lutens range so far. TS

Daisy (Marc Jacobs) ★ ★ ★ *fruity floral* $
I'm sorry this pleasant, competent fruity floral (berries and white florals) isn't more interesting, because grabbing the white rubber Takashi Murakami daisies on the cap fills me with joy. TS

Dalí (Salvador Dalí) ★ ★ ★ ★ *huge floral* $
This early work (1983) by the great Alberto Morillas is a big, handsome, strapping floral chypre somewhere between Amouage and Bal à Versailles, though lacking the exquisitely rich texture of the former and the bold, striking structure of the latter. Very good nevertheless. LT

Daliflor (Salvador Dalí) ★ *fruity floral* $
Dalí, painter and jeweler of genius, author of a great book entitled *Scientific Archangelism,* all-around charlatan, and inventor of the celebrity brand, would have approved of this crass piece of nonsense as long as it sold well. Sadly, I don't think it will, unless migraine suddenly becomes fashionable. LT

Dalimania (Salvador Dalí) ★ ★ ★ *coconut fruity* $
I have an affection for the mildly creepy ruby-red bottle—a columnar shape rigged out of two noses and two sets of lips—and feel roughly the same about the fragrance, a joyfully tasteless cough-syrup fruity accord with a burnt-sugar vanilla and the robustness of one of Escada's annual fruities. TS

Dalimix (Salvador Dalí) ★ ★ ★ *citrus savory* $
A high-pitched smell of lemon made salty with a touch of herb. TS

Dalissime (Salvador Dalí) ★ ★ ★ *fruity floral* $
For a minute on the blotter, Dalissime has a delicious fruit punch prettiness that only the most hardened anti–fruity fragrance lovers could fault. But on skin, that top note vanishes rapidly, leaving behind a sharp white floral done in outline, composed of a fizzy-metallic woody amber, which smells like overheated electronics, and only the indole and cut-grass portion of a jasmine. TS

Damascena (Keiko Mecheri) ★ ★ *fruity rose* $$$
This upbeat, slightly shrill fluorescent rose with blackcurrant feels like part of a fragrance—an interval but not a chord. Specifically, it feels like part of Diptyque's L'Ombre dans l'Eau. TS

Le Dandy (Parfums d'Orsay) ★ ★ ★ *woody spicy* $$
D'Orsay, while never of the first rank, used to make some decent fragrances in beautiful bottles that can still occasionally be found in French

flea markets. This is a competent and comfortable woody spicy, somewhere between Déclaration (cardamom) and Yohji Homme (rum), set against a pretty conventional apple-amber background. Nice work. LT

Danielle (Danielle Steel) ★ ★ *acid floral* $
Black lace, pink background, nice bottle. As Slim Pickens says in *Dr. Strangelove,* "A guy could have a pretty good time in Vegas with this!" The fragrance is not all that bad. To be sure, it is a sour, pinched floral in the current manner and feels like the formula is only a few bucks away from being cheap enough for wall-socket air care, but it has a weird, papaya-like overripe twist in it that saves it from instant oblivion. LT

Dans Tes Bras (Frédéric Malle) ★ ★ ★ *sour heliotrope* $ $
On paper or fabric, Maurice Roucel's latest for Frédéric Malle is a flashy, high-concept combination of the sweet-and-sour, powdery-metallic structure of his Tocade and Broadway Nite, plus a huge dose of the wet-concrete smell of Cashmeran, all of which amounts to a confession that the smell of wet paint is delicious. On skin, however, the fragrance quickly fades into a quiet odor of unripe plums, tart and uninviting. TS

Dark Amber & Ginger Lily (Jo Malone) ★ ★ ★ *rose cedar* $
The combination of cedar, rose, and a milky floral sometimes causes a blurry sandalwood mirage to hover over all, or sometimes a hallucinated glass of Dalwhinnie. Simple, good, and a limited edition. If you missed it, there are other cigar-box cedars in the world, such as Krizia Uomo. TS

Datura Noir (Serge Lutens) ★ ★ ★ *tropical heliotropin* $ $ $
Datura, aka jimson weed, is a poisonous flower, occasionally used as a sometimes lethal hallucinogen, and clearly designed by Aubrey Beardsley, with long, white trumpet-shaped blossoms stretched umbrella-like upon supporting ribs, which, when twisted shut, form a curled-star aperture. The type that crowded the sidewalks of my old Brooklyn neighborhood

smelled like cheap lemon flavor. This is clearly unsatisfactory as a perfume idea, so Datura Noir is pure pipe dream, a tropical suntan-oil fantasy of cherry, coconut, and jasmine—trashy, sweet, and probably too heady, but pleasurably so in the summer heat. TS

David Yurman (David Yurman) ★ ★ *salty rose* $ $
A textbook example of perfumery economics wreaking havoc: just as you get interested in the rich, complicated top note of smoky florals with a sandpaper feel, the fragrance collapses into a tiresome, cloying rose that goes on forever and reaches the topmost floors of the house. They should have spent more time and money. It could have been fantastic. TS

Daytona 500 (Elizabeth Arden) ★ ★ *watery woody* $
I remember some years back asking for potato chips in a London pub, whereupon the barman said, "Which flavor?" and pointed to an impressive rack with twenty or so weird possibilities. ("Hedgehog" was one.) I asked for "burnt clutch and nitromethane," and he spun on his heel to find it before realizing I was having him on. Truth is, BC&NM would smell pretty interesting, far better than this fresh, wussy little thing that usurps the name of a gloriously scary race. What happened to real guys? My guess is they wear Mitsouko. LT

Dazzling Gold (Estée Lauder) ★ ★ ★ *bright floral* $
There is a curse on perfumes brought out in twos and threes, though it seems to fade with higher numbers. People will forgive a mixed lot as long as it is large, but will be merciless when only one of two sisters has charm. Dazzling Silver and Dazzling Gold were brought out together. Gold is in many ways a precursor of Beyond Paradise and shoots for what could have been a lush natural accord, if the absolutes of passion flower, lily, and orchid claimed in the composition had been available and used. In the event, it feels like an amateur rocketry attempt at put-

ting a satellite in orbit, when the second stage fizzles out due to lack of funds. LT

Dazzling Silver (Estée Lauder) ★ ★ ★ ★ *steely floral* $
This is the pretty but sharp-tongued sister of Dazzling Gold, a complex and very synthetic floral containing so much helional that it actually smells like a sucked silver spoon. The overall tonality is wonderfully otherworldly, like a mad florist's shop full of strange, alarming plants with flowers that look like sea creatures and leaves that reach out to sting. LT

Dear John (B Never Too Busy to Be Beautiful) ★ ★ ★ *lime pine* $
A warm woody citrus, pleasant and straightforward up top, that ends on a slightly oily note of ambrette seed. LT

Début (Parfums DelRae) ★ ★ ★ ★ *citrus chypre* $$$
As the son of the man (Edmond Roudnitska) and woman (Thérèse, a considerable perfumer in her own right) who made citrus interesting, Michel Roudnitska should excel at a brief involving prominent bergamot and lemon top notes. And sure enough, Début is in some ways an extreme variation on Diorella, or perhaps on Edmond's forgotten last work, Ocean Rain (1990) for Mario Valentino. The interplay between citrus, bitter notes, and floral sweetness is masterly and remains beguilingly unresolved until well into the drydown. I see this as more of an all-sails-to-the-wind masculine for those who have graduated from Eau Sauvage to Diorella and want to jump further still. LT

Déclaration (Cartier) ★ ★ ★ ★ *fresh spicy* $
It is instructive, with the benefit of hindsight, to follow the weight loss in Jean-Claude Elléna's style. He went from First (1976) to Rumba (1988), both heavyweights, then composed the magnificent (and doomed) Globe (1990) for Rochas, which already showed signs of a new

spareness. Déclaration, eight years later, was where his mature manner first showed itself. It is perhaps the most widely imitated fragrance since Cool Water, and almost every modern masculine owes something to it, sometimes an overt quotation of cardamom or juniper, but more often just the feel of the original, which is to fragrance what a glass of cold Sancerre is to wine: brisk, abstract, refreshing, a touch flinty, and altogether euphoric. Superb. LT

Déclaration Essence (Cartier) ★ ★ ★ ★ *fresh spicy* $ $
A skillful and interesting variation on the beautiful basic structure of Déclaration, with a strong resinous-animalic note of cistus in the core and a smokier drydown. Hard to choose between the two, but this one is a bit darker and richer, and I prefer it. LT

Délices eau de toilette (Cartier) ★ *vile fruity* $
Probably called Délices the way the Furies were called Kindly Ones, for fear of upsetting them. This is a woody-vanillic fruity so loathsomely potent and crass that I cannot find a bad word to say about it. On second thoughts, I can: it's not even vulgar. LT

Délices parfum (Cartier) ★ *fruity vile* $
There's a sketch by Billy Connolly where two Glasgow drunks go to Rome, enter a bar, and ask, "What does the pope drink?" The barman says, "Crème de Menthe," whereupon the two guys say, "Give us a pint," and spend the rest of the week puking up green in various fountains. Substitute cassis for mint, and you've got Délices parfum. LT

Delicious Closet Queen (Etat Libre d'Orange) ★ ★ *green woody* $ $
If a fragrance is going to have a punch line, it should be in the composition, not on the label. This is supposed to be a masculine for guys who wear pink silk undies, a type no doubt preferable to the Y-fronted varietal. But the fragrance is disappointingly Generic Guy, striped boxer shorts and all. LT

Derby (Guerlain) ★ ★ ★ ★ ★ *smoky wood* $$$
Derby is an oddity, the only case of a Guerlain masterpiece gone unnoticed. Released in 1985, it had very little impact, probably because of poor advertising and an ugly bottle. It was then repackaged and sold only at the Paris store, then briefly deleted, then reissued and now part of their lineup, one hopes permanently. Guerlain's gush and guff would have us believe that every one of Jean-Paul Guerlain's best fragrances is a paean to the *éternel féminin*. The truth is he's always been rather better at composing things for his own use, exhibits being Vetiver and Habit Rouge. Derby sits halfway between the confident swagger of HR and the dry restraint of Vetiver, on what might be described as the center of gravity of male fragrance. In structure, it is woody-balsamic with a touch of smoke. In radiance, it is like a Kirlian photograph of a healthy leaf, projecting a deep-green aura no farther than an inch, but suprisingly intense and durable up close. One of the ten best masculines of all time. LT

Deseo (Jennifer Lopez) ★ ★ ★ *coconut melon* $
Like two melodic lines that bump into each other and fall in love to their composer's surprise, Deseo feels like a fortunate accident. The frenetic interest of the last few years in fruity florals has forced perfumers to think like flavorists just at a time when flavorists were beginning to think like perfumers: witness the extraordinary recent progress in tropical-fruit mixes. What everyone seems to be rediscovering is the lost art of the cocktail; i.e., perfumery bases mixed and stirred for internal use. Deseo is a clever mix of sauvignon blanc and Baileys or, in perfumery terms, Envy and Rush. Separately, its components would respectively cause toothache and tooth rot. Together they work happily to produce a short-lived but superbly trashy perfume for eighteen-year-old girls on the prowl. LT

Design (Paul Sebastian) ★ *fruity shampoo* $
Heed the warning implicit in the packaging, which looks like a third-

world pastiche of classy gestures: gilded plastic in a fake Art Deco shape with a curly font. The poor fragrance is a thinned fruit-and-hay thing that smells like an old shampoo formula. How can such a thing have survived over twenty years? Was it good once and diminished later? I've only ever seen it at discount stores, in bulk. Hard to say. TS

Désir de Rochas Femme (Rochas) ★ *bleached rose* $
Thoroughly unpleasant fresh-rosy floral that whines like a dentist's drill and hurts almost as much. LT

Désir de Rochas Homme (Rochas) ★ *woody nothing* $
It is hard to imagine the decision process that leads to a fragrance like this, but let's try. Someone too high up in the hierarchy to be contradicted comes up with the novel notion of launching a definitively, crushingly dull fragrance. Eager to please her, minions reject, one after another, a dozen initial submissions that contain trace amounts of interest. At long last, after months of work, two talented perfumers, Béatrice Picquet and Jean Pierre Mary (responsible, respectively, for the superb L'Instant Homme and Yvresse), manage to hunt down and snuff out all remaining signs of life in their twenty-fifth attempt. They submit the twenty-sixth, which is officially declared DOA and chosen to propel Rochas's glorious name into the future. LT

Desire Blue (Dunhill) ★ *sugary soapy* $
It's blue—it must be sporty! Another soap-fragrance formula sold at a markup for clueless guys. TS

Diabolo Rose (Parfums de Rosine) ★★★ *minty rose* $$
This somewhat old-fashioned dense green rose comes with an unexpected smell of sweet mint, like those stiff, pillowy, pale pebbles waiting for you in a dish as you leave the restaurant, waiting twenty years for a taker. The whole makes a not particularly exciting but squarely well-done fragrance. TS

Diamonds (Armani) ★ *raspberry vanilla* $

When I was four and had a fever, I was prescribed a fruit-flavored liquid antibiotic, of which I had to swallow several tablespoons at a time. It took four adults to restrain me and force it into my mouth while I screamed. It tasted a lot like this. TS

Diamonds for Men (Armani) ★ ★ ★ *coffee fougère* $

The low-resolution, flamboyant top note of coffee and lavender is a copy of Yohji Homme by way of New Haarlem, which leads very quickly to the usual sweet-apple smell of a Cool Water fougère. Okay, if like a million others. TS

Dianthus (Etro) ★ ★ *creamy carnation* $$

Does the world really need a new carnation fragrance? This smells like one of those twenties bases that created and later exhausted this particular genre. See Bellodgia (Caron). LT

Dia pour Femme (Amouage) ★ ★ ★ ★ *classy floral* $$$

There is no question that Gold was a hard act to follow, and one imagines that many women would recoil at the sheer Wagnerian heft of it. Dia was likely put together for those who wanted a luscious floral smaller than size 59. Dia is beautiful though not wildly original, smells entirely natural aside from a touch of aldehydes, and breathes unalloyed quality for hours. The fresh, powdery drydown is especially good. LT

Dia pour Homme (Amouage) ★ ★ ★ ★ *dry wood* $$$

If your ideal of manly good looks is saturnine and demonic, say Niccolò Paganini or his modern counterpart Tommy Lee Jones, then this is the fragrance for you. Dark, dry, smoldering, it joins a small band of loners (among which are Guerlain's Sous le Vent and Morabito's Or Black) that actively dislike comfort, though it mellows a bit in the drydown. Very good. LT

Dilmun (Lorenzo Villoresi) ★ ★ ★ *citrus woody* $$$
A pleasant, simple neroli-orange-blossom cologne. TS

Dior Addict (Dior) ★ ★ *floral oriental* $$
A combination of cheap chocolate and dissonant heavy floral, this smells nasty from all angles. LT

I liked it very much in Macy's when I went there drunk one day, and told everyone afterward I had found the perfect bourbon vanilla with orange blossom, as if it had been a life quest. Sadly, the bourbon was all me. TS

Dior Addict 2 (Dior) ★ ★ *pink lemonade* $$
A light, sour citrus floral with too much in common with window cleaner. Try Par Amour Toujours instead. TS

Diorama (Dior) ★ ★ *fruity chypre* $$$
The present-day Diorama bears no relation whatsoever to the stupendous 1949 original, a sunny orange-peel version of Mitsouko, and is instead related to Diorella and Parfum de Thérèse, only less good. LT

Diorella (Dior) ★ ★ ★ ★ ★ *woody citrus* $$
Diorella came out in 1972, six years after Eau Sauvage, and has all the hallmarks of Roudnitska's mature style, as evidenced in Parfum de Thérèse: a rich, woody-floral accord at once sweet and bracing, very abstract and of no definite sex. I was trying to define the Roudnitska signature for myself, and all I could come up with was that it smelled like herbs, vitamin B, and lime. I didn't dare say it, but it had something oddly meaty about it. I asked my co-author, "If Guerlain were dessert, which course would Diorella be?" TS was unfazed: "Vietnamese beef salad," she said, which in my opinion is both sacrilegious and exactly right. Diorella was intended as a feminine and was the very essence of bohemian chic, with an odd, overripe melon effect that still feels both elegant and decadent. The modern version, no doubt fully compliant

with all relevant health-and-safety edicts since the fall of the Roman Empire, is drier and more masculine than of old, no bad thing since I have always seen it as a perfected Eau Sauvage and one of the best masculines money can buy. LT

2009 update. ★ ★ ★ ★. Great perfumery accords share with holograms the strange property of being damage resistant: the picture remains legible even though noise increases and fine detail is swept away. Diorella is one of those accords, and while the latest version is less caressingly decadent and lush than of old, it still conveys much of what made the original great. LT

Dioressence (Dior) ★ ★ ★ ★ *oriental chypre* $ $
Dioressence has been through so many different versions since its creation in 1969 by Max Gavarry and Guy Robert that, as the French say, a cat wouldn't recognize its kittens. When I first encountered it circa 1974, it was a big, lactonic affair, a sort of Gucci Rush with manners. Today it is a green chypre with a good barnyard note that smells like narcissus and brings it closer to, say, Chamade or Givenchy III. The present version is clearly of far better quality than a few years back, and it smells good, but I don't recognize old Auntie Dioressence in there. LT

2009 update. ★ ★. Insofar as this latest version is (a) not Dioressence and (b) no longer smells good, I see no reason why anyone should shell out for it. LT

Dior Homme (Dior) ★ ★ ★ ★ ★ *fruity iris* $$$
The Dior Homme bottle is strikingly solid, more beautifully made than one would expect. In fact, it is good enough to house a feminine perfume. This is quality stuff, and Dior Homme's new man in charge, Hedi Slimane, wants everyone to know. The fragrance? Composed by Olivier Polge, son of Chanel's Jacques, it takes its place among the half-dozen best masculines of recent years. In structure, it flirts with the virtuoso

modernist complexity of Hugo Boss's Baldessarini and the muted candied-fruit colors of Chanel's Egoïste. Where it differs is in an interesting, powder-gray iris top note and a drydown like an attenuated version of Chance with more tobacco. Refined, comfortable, and most of all a textbook example of successful top-down design. LT

Dior Homme Intense (Dior) ★ ★ ★ ★ *spiced apple* $$$
Essentially the same fragrance as Dior Homme, but intensified by much more of a delicious, sweet baked-apple smell. TS

Dior Homme Sport (Dior) ★ ★ ★ ★ *ginger soap* $
The name tactlessly (and probably correctly) suggests that wearers of the excellent original Dior Homme are lounge lizards in need of a workout. The bottle is a GTI version (with a red and black spray mechanism, for heaven's sake) of the original. Hedi Slimane, were he still in charge, would never have countenanced either for a second. The fragrance sheds all pretensions to languid weirdness and is a cross between Envy for Men (hot ginger) and any one of the Allure Homme fragrances (aspirational soap-on-a-rope). DHS is very pleasant, competently put together, and free of nasty surprises in the dry-woody drydown. The heart combines a sports-fragrance feel intended for the presentable young buck with a touch of the reassuring middle-aged torpor of the old Paco Rabanne. I find it a mite dull, though admittedly riveting compared to the competition. As such, it deserves to be very successful. LT

Diorissimo (Dior) ★ ★ ★ ★ *fresh muguet* $$
Diorissimo is the archetypal muguet, i.e., lily-of-the-valley soliflore. Bear in mind that no extract can be obtained from the natural flowers, so all muguets are reconstructions. The original 1956 Diorissimo established Edmond Roudnitska as the Mozart of postwar French perfumery. And Diorissimo was a truly Mozartian fragrance, with a catchy, jaunty presto tune like the overture to *The Marriage of Figaro*. How Roudnitska achieved it is the stuff of legend. In the garden of his house

in Cabris, near Grasse, he planted lily of the valley and used it for reference. The idea of Roudnitska on all fours among the little white bells, a smelling strip in hand, is delightful. A fundamentally important material to the original accord was hydroxycitronellal, one of a tiny number of hydroxyaldehydes in perfumery, which has much of the soapy, floral whiteness of muguet. Hydroxy, as it is familiarly called, is now restricted in use, though still present in the "list of allergens" on the present Diorissimo packaging. Today's Diorissimo is unquestionably different from the older version, though still a thing of great beauty. The best way to describe it, it seems to me, is as the voice of a great soprano close to retirement. The melody, the timbre are there, but some of the high notes are a little forced and have lost the effortless soaring, the liquid fluency of old. Up close, this thing shouts a little. But it has tremendous radiance and at a distance still works fine as likely the most distinctive fragrance of all time. LT

2009 update. ★ ★ . Diorissimo is going downhill rapidly; the latest version is harsher still. LT

Dirty (B Never Too Busy to Be Beautiful) ★ ★ ★ ★ *marine mint* $
Many people have cited my fondness for ELO's Sécrétions Magnifiques as a sign that I should retire to a sanatorium in the Pyrenees and take up bilboquet. I still think that the idea of associating a bilge-like marine note to a classic floral was at once inventive, humorous, and full of potential. Dirty confirms this with its brilliantly unexpected juxtaposition of an intense herbaceous minty note (more perilla than spearmint) and a bitter, faintly metallic saline note that smells surprisingly easy and natural. The sky blue of mint and the flint gray of the sea add up to a spacious, airy fragrance that feels as if it would encourage panoramic thoughts to go with the view. LT

Dis Moi, Miroir (Thierry Mugler) ★ ★ ★ *creamy floral* $ $ $
This very competently put-together fragrance is a fruity floral in which

both flowers (lily) and fruit (apricots and peaches) achieve a pleasant creamy texture. I see this as a cross between Badgley Mischka and Ivoire. Not bad at all. LT

Divine (Divine) ★ ★ ★ ★ *buttery floral* $ $
It's always heartening to see a small company break every rule and succeed. If Divine had been a draft business plan written by an MBA hopeful, the student would have failed. Location: Dinard, a sleepy little Breton seaside town across the water from beautiful Saint-Malo. (You can almost hear the Paris execs chuckling: "Dinard? You must be mad! Nothing *cheec* has come out of that part of the world since Anne de Bretagne left to marry our king in 1491!") Products: *grande parfumerie*, taking the big guys head-on. (What? No concept? No beach gravel in the bottles, no Celtic angle, no nautical gewgaws?) Product launch schedule: whenever the boss feels like it. (What? No flankers? No line extensions? Forget it.) *Eppur si muove*. The boss is a guy called Yvon Mouchel who ran a perfume store until he decided to make his own. His first was the eponymous Divine, a lovely, powdery, buttery floral-animalic that smells lusciously expensive and isn't. If you like your florals less than squeaky-clean, and want a perfume that feels like a spray-on version of an Alix Grès Grecian dress, look no further. Divine is as good as it gets in this direction. LT

Divine Bergamote (The Different Company) ★ ★ ★ ★
light citrus $ $
Bergamot is one of the most valued oils in perfumery, where it shines as an intense, resinous citrus-peel top note, and in tea, where it scents your Earl Grey. Jean-Claude Elléna's Divine Bergamote is an attempt to extend the material's bright but fleeting flash by seamlessly shifting from a broad, sunny top note of ginger and citrus we've seen in Ginger Essence to a middle section of orange blossom before fading to clean, slightly rosy musk. It works well and is as crisp as a winter morning, yet

frankly seems almost nonexistent. No one will smell it on you except in serious cases of invasion of personal space. In other words, another sheer, clean citrus ideal for people who don't like fragrance, but better than most. TS

Divin'Enfant (Etat Libre d'Orange) ★ ★ ★ *sweet woody* $ $
The name comes from a French Christmas song, with the child Jesus as DE. The fragrance is an orange-flower-and-coffee accord, interesting up top when the dissonance works, sweet and somewhat flat in the dry-down. LT

DKNY Delicious Night (Donna Karan) ★ ★ ★ *blackberry iris* $
What a beautiful idea! This is a fruity chypre in the style of Cartier's So Pretty, with a striking, deep-purple smell of blackberries and woody iris that exactly matches the inky color of the bottle. Sadly, it smells as if they didn't have the budget to do the idea properly—cheap, loud woody ambers and a thin synthetic floral section fail to fill out the structure—and I can only hope that they do it again, next time with feeling. TS

DKNY for Men (Donna Karan) ★ ★ ★ *lemony lavender* $
File this with the rest of the nondescript but nice clean-and-fresh men's sport fragrances based on citrus, lavender, and amber and sold in minimalist packaging. This one smells better than most, but still sort of mindless. TS

DKNY Men (Donna Karan) ★ ★ ★ *rice woody* $
Aromas journey between the cupboard and the toiletries cabinet all the time, and lately perfumers have been raiding the cereals. DKNY Men adds to a modern citrus-woody composition a small dose of the flat, low, humming warmth of basmati rice on the boil, plus a material that smells like steam-ironed laundry (see Mugler's Cologne). It's a smell of close quarters, dim light, half-asleep in the morning with the kettle on. Un-

fortunately, the whole thing is shot through with one of these woody ambers that feel like they're scraping the back of your sinuses with a rusty file, but at a distance it might work fine. TS

DKNY Men Summer 2009 (Donna Karan) ★ ★ ★ *woody citrus* $$
School of Light Blue, with the same top-notes-only overhang but a cleverer fougère supporting structure. Feels like a really good functional fragrance, but who would knowingly buy this and spray it on? LT

DKNY Women (Donna Karan) ★ ★ ★ ★ *sparkling citrus* $
In no way a proper feminine, and arguably not even a proper fragrance, DKNYW is an abstract composition that bristles with ideas and humor. Most of the fun is in the top note, a bubbly accord reminiscent of Lubin's lamented Gin Fizz that feels like it's about to sting you up the nose like CO_2 out of a soda can. What's interesting is that behind this frothing lemonade fountain there hides a clean white floral, almost unrecognizable in all that white noise. The drydown peters out somewhat, but who's going to complain about two hours of fun? Far better in my opinion as a fresh, jaunty masculine than as a feminine, where its irony is likely to be misconstrued as lack of warmth. LT

DKNY Women Summer 2009 (Donna Karan) ★ ★ ★ *fruit froth* $$
The fizzy, steamy, powdery accord of the original fragrance is still there, overlaid with a pale fruity floral. Curiously likable in a trashy, tinselly sort of way. LT

Dolce & Gabbana (Dolce & Gabbana) ★ ★ *creamy floral* $$
This was the first D&G fragrance (1992), a heavy-hitting aldehydic with a huge top note of carnation and floral heart. You'll find it rather nice if you're still around and conscious for the drydown. Few people are. LT

Dolce & Gabbana pour Homme (Dolce & Gabbana) ★ ★ ★
complex herbal $
If you're going to do a drone-clone, this is the way to do it. Complex enough that you don't get through it in five minutes, like the tough crossword in the daily paper. Pointless, but lots of guys enjoy it on the train to work. LT

Dolce Vita (Dior) ★ ★ *woody fruity* $ $
DV, released in 1995, was a luscious good-humored sister to the austerely beautiful Féminité du Bois released three years earlier by Shiseido. It was briefly discontinued and is now back in the Dior line. Alas, it has been appallingly reformulated and now smells like cheap maraschino liqueur. Find an old one on the interwebs if you can. LT

Domain (Mary Kay) ★ *fresh fougère* $
If Thierry Wasser and James Krivda of Firmenich spent more than fifteen minutes putting this together, they must have been interrupted. LT

Donna (Lorenzo Villoresi) ★ ★ *acetone rose* $ $ $
The top note is unmistakably nail-polish remover, the rest a standard, simple rose, somewhat sour. This, along with Uomo, was one of Villoresi's first fragrances, and it is hard to believe that on the basis of this he was encouraged to go on. TS

Donna Karan Essence Jasmine (Donna Karan) ★ ★ ★
jasmine jasmine $ $
Exquisite packaging (removing the spray cap is actually enjoyable, such is its micron-precise smooth fit). A nice high-quality extreme soliflore (jasmine). Looks great, smells great. Not properly speaking a fragrance, but so what? LT

Donna Karan Essence Labdanum (Donna Karan) ★ ★ ★
sweet resin $$
Perfumery would likely not exist at all without labdanum and its multi-faceted sweet-fresh resinous splendor. It is nice to be able to smell it unadorned, but DKEL lasts too short a time on skin to make it really worth it. LT

Donna Karan Essence Lavender (Donna Karan) ★ ★ ★
sweet lavender $$
Warm, slightly caramellic lavender accord; not as good as Caldey Island. LT

Donna Karan Essence Wenge (Donna Karan) ★ ★ ★
creamy wood $$
Most DK fragrances are built on a creamy woody-floral base reminiscent of the signature Caron background of Nuit de Noël, but quieter. This one adds an accord of cedar and sandalwood meant to approximate the smell of wenge, or African palisander. Very nice, but feels more like the smell of a room than a person. LT

Donna Karan Gold (Donna Karan) ★ ★ ★ ★ *lily amber* $
Although less likely to spark a trend than other florals on Calice Becker's CV (Beyond Paradise, J'Adore, Tommy Girl), Donna Karan Gold is one of the more assured feminines to drop into our mailbox in a long time. Lilies have a fascinating smell, mixing the familiar watery, green, indolic scent of white flowers with the smoky, brined scent of Easter ham, which, once you notice, you never forget. Using a smoke-like amber, Gold modulates between fresh and dry, glassy smooth and sandpaper rough. It somehow seems to cycle ever upward, like those audio illusions of tones that sound like they're climbing infinitely higher even though the series is actually repeating. The composition's minimal adornment lets you focus on this effect without distraction. Easily an everyday fragrance, and dry enough for a man to wear without feeling too camp. TS

Donna Karan Signature (Donna Karan) ★ ★ ★ ★ *woody floral* $ $
I had forgotten how good this fragrance was. DK's perfumes have had a complicated life and are less well known than they deserve. Part of the reason must have been the original packaging, which I am told did really well with Klingons. Now back in a uniform and splendid bottle, this is one of the best of the range, a creamy-woody fragrance with enough floral touches to feel rich and soft, but no definite color. Makes a wonderful masculine. LT

Don't Get Me Wrong Baby, I Don't Swallow (Etat Libre d'Orange) ★ ★ *clean floral* $ $
The name is a mildly amusing joke on contemporary squeaky-clean florals. The fragrance is a contemporary squeaky-clean floral. LT

Do Son (Diptyque) ★ *alleged tuberose* $ $
Coming out at roughly the same time as Carnal Flower (Frédéric Malle), Do Son never stood much of a chance with tuberose lovers. It didn't have the budget: the whole thing seems chemical and empty, and, after an okay fresh floral start, alternates between cloying and stale. TS

Douce Amère (Serge Lutens) ★ ★ ★ ★ *anisic woody* $ $ $
It's hard to think of any brand that has done more recently to expand the oriental genre than Serge Lutens. Back at least to Emeraude, orientals had always depended upon the richness of amber, for which you can flip to the A section of these reviews and smell all the Ambers and Ambres and Ambras therein. After Shalimar, Tabu made it safe for Youth Dew, Youth Dew made it safe for Opium, Opium made it safe for Coco, and so on. Then, working with Lutens, Christopher Sheldrake (now at Chanel) took Pierre Bourdon's original idea for Féminité du Bois and constructed an alternate oriental starting point based on the relatively less well traveled territory of feminine woody scents. They hit upon an accord of dried fruit, cedar, and cinnamon, with remarkable intensity and richness but without the weight of traditional amber. Lutens has

been busy populating this fertile frontier ever since. Douce Amère is an irresistible anisic oriental built on this structure, a more lighthearted sibling to Un Bois Vanille, for absinthe lovers. TS

Douceur de Vanille (Les Néréides) ★ ★ *musky biscotti* $ $
A nutty, sugar-cookie fragrance, but a bad fit with a particular rose and musk that veer off to one side and smell plasticky together. A more successful version of the same idea is found in Superworldunknown (B Never Too Busy to Be Beautiful). TS

Drama Nuuï (Parfumerie Générale) ★ ★ ★ *woody floral* $ $ $
Parfumerie Générale seems adept at a sort of prefab mix-and-match perfumery, in which existing standards are combined, as if they were bases, in often interesting and humorous combinations. This is a successful example, where an outrageously sensuous and dopey jasmine note is overlaid on a dry, cheap, and aspirationally sad masculine. The contrast between evolution's money-no-object perfumery and our el-cheapo one has seldom been so nicely illustrated. DN feels like Scarlett Johansson borrowing her dad's first interview suit (polyester) from years ago and, sleeves and flares turned up, looking great in it. LT

Dream (Fresh Scents by Terri) ★ *peach vanilla* $
Called a "fig vanilla" by Terri, it's more of a peach schnapps. Might make a charming handsoap, but hard to call it perfume. TS

Dream Angels Divine (Victoria's Secret) ★ ★ ★ *dry floral* $
It's illuminating to smell the two extant Dream Angels scents from 2000 compared to VS's recent concoctions. It seems VS used to cater to strumpets who wanted to be ladies, and now caters to ladies who want to be strumpets. DA Divine, from the former era, is a well-crafted, very dry woody fragrance, quiet and unobtrusive, far less sweet than DA Heavenly, a little mean in the way green florals can be, and utterly unflirty. TS

Dream Angels Heavenly (Victoria's Secret) ★ ★ ★ *lactonic woody* $
A sedate, low-key woody floral, slightly nutty, almondy, with a baby-powder feel, freshened up by a lemon-custard note. Stays close to the skin. Brings to mind long bedrest, puddings, and nurses. TS

Dreaming (Tommy Hilfiger) ★ ★ ★ (★ ★) *metallic fruity* $
An attempt to capitalize on the technical advances embodied in Calice Becker's Tommy Girl while changing the color balance from off-white to pink. Dreaming achieves this competently and delivers a fragrance that's squeaky clean and shiny, like a painting done with transparent nail gloss on polished aluminum. For adolescents. LT

I've smelled far better versions of this milky-metallic floral idea (see Bertrand Duchaufour's Flora Bella for Lalique), and this one is not helped by the addition of a sour fruit note like unripened mango. Unfriendly and unpleasant. TS

Drôle de Rose (L'Artisan Parfumeur) ★ ★ ★ ★ *fruity violet* $$$
This pale pink bottle holds an exuberantly girly scent: a rose with an old-fashioned powdery heliotropin sweetness and a modern bright freshness. It's a perfect alternative to those dreadful fruity-candy scents that are everywhere now, and much more forthrightly cheerful than anything else Olivia Giacobetti has done. To be worn while singing, "I feel pretty, oh so pretty . . ." TS

Duel (Annick Goutal) ★ ★ ★ ★ *matte maté* $$$
Maté, to those of you who haven't tried it, is what makes Argentineans and Uruguayans so much livelier than the rest of us, a substitute for tea or coffee that lasts six to eight hours, makes you forget lunch, and supplies a clarity of mind ideal for rash decisions. It smells like essence of twigs, somewhere between tea dregs and hay. Duel uses it as a central note, accompanied by wormwood, nutmeg, and leather. The effect is a

buff-colored aura, the sort of masculine fragrance that you can only smell at close range. Refined, warm, and comfortable. LT

Dune (Dior) ★ ★ ★ ★ ★ *fresh oriental* $
Forget suburban-gothic names, forget all the phony "noirs," from Angélique to Orris. True, menacing darkness is not to be found in upset-the-parents Alice Cooper poses, but in this disenchanted, ladylike gem. Loosely inspired by the excellent Venise five years earlier (Yves Rocher, 1986), Dune is a strong contender for Bleakest Beauty in all of perfumery. It is clearly headed from the very start toward that peculiarly inedible cheap-chocolate drydown that made Must, Allure (q.v. for a fuller account of the effect), and a thousand others, though Dune's is the best of the lot, dissonant but interesting. But the way it gets there is extraordinary, with a beguiling transparency, even freshness, particularly in the anisic carrot-seed top notes. It is hard to pin down what makes Dune so unsmiling from top to bottom: it's as if every perfumery accord had become a Ligeti cluster chord, drained of life, flesh-toned in the creepy way of artificial limbs, not real ones. Marvelous. LT

Dune pour Homme (Dior) ★ ★ ★ ★ *soapy citrus* $
A very good eau de cologne with a transparent, natural feeling in its leafy, lemon top note and sweet, soapy floral drydown. TS

Dunhill (Dunhill) ★ ★ *woody soapy* $
A somewhat loud and cheap-smelling fresh woody fragrance, with the familiar feeling of Father's Day soap-on-a-rope. TS

Dunhill Black (Dunhill) ★ ★ ★ *dry woody* $$
One of the current trends in masculines, and not the least successful, aims for a total absence of color, an effect reminiscent of the male choir of Ligeti's *Requiem*—so brilliantly chosen by Stanley Kubrick for the moonscape scenes of *2001*. In Black, this is achieved by a complex, over-

lapping cluster chord of a large number of woody, woody-ambery, violet-leaf, and dry-citrus materials, all at roughly the same volume and with the same volatility. The effect has the unrewarding complexity of noise, rather than the rewarding richness of music, but is nevertheless strikingly austere and clean. LT

Duro (Nasomatto) ★ *woody amber* $$$
The name means "hard" in Italian, as in "-on." The press material for Nasomatto says (my translation): "This perfume aims to intensify all aspects of masculine virility." Michael Edwards's database, normally precise about raw materials, says, "Scent of male virility accord." You've guessed it: this is a masculine, intended to celebrate the exuberant, unwarranted fondness Italians have for their weenies. So what does *cazzo* absolute smell like? Why wood, of course, followed by a huge synthetic woody amber that gradually takes over. Duro unusually combines the loud ineptitude of hippie confections with the brutality of cheap aromachemicals. Useful as a contraceptive, but little else. LT

Dzing! (L'Artisan Parfumeur) ★ ★ ★ ★ ★ *vanilla cardboard* $$$
Olivia Giacobetti is here at her imaginative, humorous best, and Dzing! is a masterpiece. Dzing! smells of paper, and you can spend a good while trying to figure out whether it is packing cardboard, kraft wrapping paper, envelopes while you lick the glue, old books, or something else. I have no idea whether this was the objective, but I have a few clues as to why it happened. Lignin, the stuff that prevents all trees from adopting the weeping habit, is a polymer made up of units that are closely related to vanillin. When made into paper and stored for years, it breaks down and smells good. Which is how divine providence has arranged for secondhand bookstores to smell like good-quality vanilla absolute, subliminally stoking a hunger for knowledge in all of us. L'Artisan Parfumeur is, for reasons unknown, planning to discontinue this marvel, so stock up. LT

Dzongkha (L'Artisan Parfumeur) ★ ★ ★ ★ *woody iris* $$$
Duchaufour has emerged as one of the best perfumers around today, and by now I await every one of his creations with impatience. Dzongkha resembles his earlier Timbuktu, but has a more classical musk-iris top note and heart overlaid on the smoky cedar background. It smells wonderful, airy, quiet, and salubrious, like incense burning under a starlit sky, with an overall effect close to Andy Tauer's L'Air du Désert Marocain but less intense. LT

L'Eau (Diptyque) ★ ★ ★ ★ *potpourri chypre* $$
Many fragrance brands, in their search for classiness, aim for an ancient apothecary aesthetic—Italian and English brands are especially fond of this schtick, which always seems costumey, like new mahogany-stained furniture trying to look old. Yet Diptyque manages to pull it off by being completely modern about it. L'Eau is their first fragrance, dating from 1968, and the first of their efforts to bring an English style of perfumery to France. This goal makes me think of Louis Menand mocking the best seller *Eats, Shoots & Leaves* with his quip "An Englishwoman lecturing Americans on semicolons is a little like an American lecturing the French on sauces." Still, the medieval-minded L'Eau is a fine argument for the case because it truly *sent bon*, like an ideal potpourri. It includes no sweetening amber filler or ballast, as it would if it were feeling French, but never ends up smelling fusty and characterless like actual potpourri laid out in gift shops. Instead, it centers around a rich accord of citrus, clove, and a fresh green angle related to orange chypres everywhere, and continues to smell beautiful in this newfangled old-fashioned way for hours. TS

L'Eau (Renée) ★ ★ *lemon melon* $
Quiet, confused, and, as its name indicates, watery. LT

L'Eau Bleue d'Issey Eau Fraîche (Issey Miyake) ★ ★ ★ *citrus sage* $$
The intense, savory note of sage from the original L'Eau Bleue meets up with an equally intense metallic citrus floral this time around. Instead

of falling apart immediately as expected, the two halves cleave firmly together. The effect somehow feels pungent while smelling only moderately strong, and smells markedly different from any other masculine I've encountered—striking, though not always pleasant. TS

L'Eau Bleue d'Issey pour Homme (Issey Miyake) ★ ★ *bare herbal* $$
Since Feu d'Issey and the subsequent Lite version, I've been waiting for the restless genius of Jacques Cavallier to get that weird milk/bread/hot-stone note just right. What you get first in L'Eau Bleue is a big blast of herbaceous sage-like notes, then the bread accord. Fifteen minutes later it shows signs of wanting to straighten up and fly right; the bread recedes and a pleasant talcum-powdery background shimmer makes an entrance. At this point all known laws of perfumery would lead one to think that the sage was the top note and the powder stuff the drydown. Not so: the powder fades, and the sage goes on and on, smelling increasingly bare and crude. LT

L'Eau Cheap and Chic (Moschino) ★ ★ ★ *aldehydic resinous* $
This sleek little number uses a big dose of some funny salty-anisic herb, like sage or tarragon, plus a smooth, translucent pine-resin smell and vetiver background to give its soap-powder floral a haunting twist, which for a while does a pretty good likeness of Serge Lutens's insanely wonderful (and not sold outside of Paris) La Myrrhe. A nice surprise. TS

L'Eau d'Ambre (L'Artisan Parfumeur) ★ ★ ★ *classic amber* $$$
In 1978, long before Ambre Sultan and all the current crop of niche ambers, Jean-Claude Elléna, under the direction of Jean-François Laporte, created this enjoyable hippie-friendly amber for L'Artisan Parfumeur. Rosy-fruity with a crisp beginning and a rich, boozy, powdery sweet drydown, it holds up well against the johnny-come-latelies, including its recent "Extrême" version, which is more like extreme cream soda. TS

Eau de Bonpoint (Annick Goutal) ★ ★ ★ *orange blossom* $
French teachers give out a *bon point* the way American teachers give out a gold star: nice job, kiddo! This is a straightforward cologne of neroli and orange blossom, which just smells good. TS

Eau de Camille (Annick Goutal) ★ ★ ★ *green floral* $$$
An excellent, crisp green floral in the spirit of Vent Vert, which would make a shiny, well-groomed cologne. TS

Eau de Cartier (Cartier) ★ ★ ★ ★ *violet leaf* $$
Ask a hi-fi buff what money buys you in sound reproduction, and she will say: good treble. Getting the sibilants and the cymbals right is what makes it possible to enjoy loud music. Eau de Cartier has the feel of full-range electrostatic speakers: at first you think it is overbright and a touch thin. But once you get used to it, you realize that there is a lot of airy detail in the crystalline timbre, and that it must have been devilishly hard to get everything so right: violet leaf, woods, citrus, all tinkling in the breeze like glass chimes. Excellent. LT

Eau de Cartier Concentrée (Cartier) ★ ★ ★ *violet leaf* $$
The Concentrée feels like one of those black-and-white photographs (still taken in parts of the Middle East as I write) where the photographer, using a watercolor brush, adds red to the lips and cheeks and brown to the eyes and hair. The original EdC was a steely gray gelatin-silver print, and this is the same thing in 1956 Politburo portrait style. Stick with the *diluée*. LT

Eau de Charlotte (Annick Goutal) ★ ★ ★ *soapy green* $$$
This combination of white florals and cassis feels like the type of cheap masculine that itself feels like a soap formula, although bizarrely EdC seems to be made of good materials. As time goes on, it gets more comfortable: an intensely jammy, leafy rose. TS

L'Eau de Circé (Parfumerie Générale) ★ ★ *unseemly Rush* $$$
PG does Gucci Rush. Slightly less blowsy and therefore less good. As usual, get the real thing. LT

Eau de Cologne (Chanel) ★ ★ ★ ★ *perfect cologne* $$$
There is a special pleasure to witnessing tired classics dusted off and played properly—for example, Carlos Kleiber's fresh-as-paint interpretation of Strauss's "Blue Danube" at his Vienna New Year concert. The cologne is perfumery's waltz and, like its musical equivalent, needs sweep, snap, and a touch of naughtiness to work properly. The recipe for cologne has been in the public domain for two hundred years, and I was very curious to see what Chanel would bring to this equation. Luxury versions of simple things often bring to mind Constant Lambert's quip "The trouble with a folk song is that once you have played it through there is nothing much to do except play it over again and play it rather louder." No such thing here, no doubled strings, no massed bands. Chanel has worked on the two ends of the fragrance. The lemon top note is given extra zing by a deliciously bright green-herbaceous note in the manner of Eau de Guerlain but less obvious, while the drydown uses an el-expensivo animalic musk (I'd guess Firmenich's Muscone) that harks back to pre–World War I masculines. All in all, simply the best cologne on earth. LT

Eau de Cologne du Coq (Guerlain) ★ ★ ★ ★ *lavender cologne* $$
A good cologne with a drop of Jicky in it. LT

Eau de Cologne Impériale (Guerlain) ★ ★ ★ ★ *lime cologne* $$
A good cologne with lime and lime-flower notes. LT

Eau de Dalí (Salvador Dalí) ★ ★ ★ *citrus floral* $
Deceptively simple, fresh floral that strikes an interesting balance between mouthwateringly acid citrus top notes and a discreet sweet-floral heart with animalic undertones. Not bad, and a plausible masculine. LT

Eau de FCUK (FCUK) ★ ★ *spicy woody* $

According to the PR folks, the old FCUK Him has been recast as Eau de FCUK, still enough to get the inner eleven-year-old giggling, but not gender-biased. You get a nice whiff of Indian spices and Tiger Balm, but it retreats into simple synthetic wood soon after. TS

Eau de Fleurs de Cédrat (Guerlain) ★ ★ ★ ★ *fresh citrus* $$

The citron (*Citrus medica*), or *cédrat* in French, is a big, funny-looking lemon with inch-thick white stuff between the rind and the small fruit in the center. The Eau smells great, fresh and concise. LT

Eau de Gentiane Blanche (Hermès) ★ ★ *orange blossom* $$$

After a thrillingly weird top note of raw peanut and green peppers, it is disappointing to find oneself moments later with a meek orange blossom. Clearly, the two colognes (the other is Eau de Pamplemousse Rose) made to flank the firm's signature Eau d'Orange Verte are not meant to be as original or coherent as the Hermessences or the Jardin fragrances. TS

Eau de Givenchy (Givenchy) ★ ★ *green floral* $$$

This 1980 fragrance belongs to a fresh, borderline sour, floral green genre (Jardins de Bagatelle, Eternity) that has always felt somewhat uncomfortable to me, like the sweep signal on old TVs, supposedly out of audible range but in fact right on the edge of it, the sort of thing that feels great when it stops. Considering how many screechy fragrances have been developed in the last ten years, it would be churlish to make this relatively comfortable one carry the can, but I still don't like it. LT

Eau de Grey Flannel (Geoffrey Beene) ★ ★ *gray citrus* $

Hard to see the point of this confection, a dull dihydromyrcenol accord overlaid with a timid replica of the green-citrus idea of the original (see Grey Flannel). LT

Eau de Guerlain (Guerlain) ★ ★ ★ ★ ★ *citrus verbena* $$$$
Eau de Guerlain is to citrus what the mandolin, with its doubled-up strings, is to a guitar. It is as if, by some arcane miracle of perfumery, the ivory and green notes of citron and verbena have been made to sing in harmony with the jaunty lemon-bergamot tune exactly a major third on either side, giving the whole thing a ravishing, nostalgic timbre. Even more miraculous, Eau de Guerlain has a coherent, fresh drydown that completely transcends the cologne genre. If you want citrus, there is simply nothing better out there. LT

Eau de Jade (Armani Privé) ★ ★ *expensive cologne* $$$$
Silly name, silly price. Armani Privé does a cologne, probably the biggest waste of money this side of Le Labo's Fleur d'Oranger 27. LT

L'Eau de Jatamansi (L'Artisan Parfumeur) ★ ★ ★ ★
floral spikenard $$$
Italian has the wonderful word *impegnativo*, perhaps best translated as "consequential," to denote things that one should not do lightly; by antonymy, *non impegnativo* denotes the vast and wonderful category of things that must be done lightly if at all. In the world of fragrance, there is (look carefully on your bathroom shelf) an empty parking spot for something that is not an eau de cologne yet not a perfume, something between the inconsequential cologne and the *impegnativo* perfume. This is, I believe, the slot best filled today by all-natural fragrances, be they Marrakech (Aesop), Grezzo (La Via del Profumo), Yatra (Aveda) or, the case in point, Eau de Jatamansi. EdJ announces its purpose clearly: a large bottle to signal an intent to use it liberally, plus a similarly scented bath line, a candle; i.e., all the hallmarks of private pleasures. It smells utterly delightful, despite suffering from some of the spice-market sameness that afflicts all natural fragrances. The structure, though not wildly original, is exceptionally skillful and subtle: fresh woody citrus up top; a caressing dollop of soft rose; and a background of, among other things, spikenard and incense. At no point in the fragrance's evo-

lution does it become bare or boring, and it ends on a woody-balsamic benzoin note that is beyond reproach. Composed by Karine Vinchon of Robertet (clearly a talent to watch), this is a great effort from an outfit that may yet turn out to be the Guerlain of the new century. LT

L'Eau de l'Artisan (L'Artisan Parfumeur) ★ ★ *lemon verbena* $$$
If you love Eau de Guerlain but want to pay more while getting a harsher, lower-quality fragrance, this one is for you. LT

Eau de Lavande (Annick Goutal) ★ ★ ★ *clove lavender* $$
What do you do to show off a good lavender? Goutal decided that a little vanilla, a little bergamot, a little spice would give it depth without changing its essential character. It works and lasts longer on skin than expected. TS

L'Eau de l'Eau (Diptyque) ★ ★ ★ *soapy oriental* $$$
A sort of conservation law dictates that there should at any time be at least one Victorian dandy fragrance out there, and since Penhaligon's seems reluctant to carry the burden, Diptyque steps in. This is a high-quality, manicured, no-hanging-nails version of Hammam Bouquet, loaded with the full range of raw materials that unquestionably make a pleasant masculine: lemon, petitgrain, lavender, orange blossom, and tonka bean against a muted background of spicy pomander. To me it evokes the disparaging side of the phrase "well groomed": a little too clean, a little too loud, as if keen to hide something. LT

Eau d'Élide (Diptyque) ★ ★ ★ *lavender amber* $$
A perfume critic's life has moments of embarrassing enlightenment: I was racking my brains (1) to figure out what this thing reminded me of and (2) to say something interesting about it if at all possible. The fog lifted all of a sudden when I realized that Eau d'Élide smelled exactly like the wet wipes I used on my children when they still wore diapers. A satisfying job and a great smell, but several notes short of a true perfume melody. LT

Eau de Lierre (Diptyque) ★ *watered gin* $$
Wan leafy green. For the fun of putting on perfume without the fun of smelling it. TS

Eau de Monsieur (Annick Goutal) ★ ★ ★ ★ *citrus mossy* $$$
A handsome, rich masculine with the comfortable feeling of natural materials: the crispness of citrus, a mossy chypre background, all made interesting by a touch of the fascinating caramel-curry note of immortelle. Five years after trying it here, Goutal took it much further in her brilliant Sables. TS

L'Eau de Néroli (Diptyque) ★ ★ ★ *powdery cologne* $$$
Whoever goes to Diptyque to buy an eau de cologne is probably also hoping for a Philip Glass cover of "White Christmas." Diptyque complies, with a fairly run-of-the-mill affair distinguished neither by quality of materials nor originality of accent. LT

Eau de New York (Bond No. 9) ★ ★ ★ *citrus cologne* $$
Perfectly pleasant, light lemony-floral cologne for boys and girls. That said, the only reason to choose this over, for instance, the far better Chanel Eau de Cologne (or even Jo Malone's Lime Basil & Mandarin) is because you like the adorable bottle. TS

Eau de Noho (Bond No. 9) ★ *mutant mimosa* $$$
Eau de Noho had a chance to be good with its interesting violet mimosa, like the ghost of Après l'Ondée looking for a witness in a green wilderness. Then a stonking violet leaf arrives to turn everything watery and harsh. Much too close to dishwashing detergent. This needed work. TS

Eau de Pamplemousse Rose (Hermès) ★ ★ ★ *vegetal cologne* $$$
Starting with Un Jardin en Méditerranée, Jean-Claude Elléna has created several fragrances for Hermès that use cut-grass, herbal, and tomato-leaf notes in a clever signature vegetable bouillon into which he chucks

things as various as leather (Kelly Calèche) and mango (Un Jardin sur le Nil). Here bitter orange peel helps his vegetal cologne extend a vividly realistic grapefruit top note, which though brilliant can't last longer than a few seconds. TS

Eau de Réglisse (Caron) ★ ★ ★ *lemon coffee* $$$
Apparently heavily influenced by the licorice of Yohji Homme, this simple, cheerful fougère begins with a refreshing, bold top note of lemon and roasted coffee, and resolves into a pleasantly anisic green drydown. Confusingly, the tall cylindrical bottle with italic type looks like an afterthought, as if they'd forgotten it needed a bottle until the last minute. TS

Eau de Rochas (Rochas) ★ ★ ★ ★ *patchouli cologne* $
In the way that Chanel Pour Monsieur spiked the citrus with a dose of a good mossy chypre formula, Eau de Rochas makes its already excellent citrus cologne memorable with a rich, woody patchouli that smells halfway between black licorice and incense. It gives the otherwise crisp citrus a dark, almost garbagey decadence reminiscent of Diorella. TS

Eau de Rochas Homme (Rochas) ★ ★ ★ ★ *woody citrus* $
A surpassingly zingy fresh citrus, distinguished by a clever note of myrrh in the drydown, which adds an odd lemony-resinous note of its own. LT

Eau de Rubylips (Salvador Dalí) ★ *sour floral* $
There is something nightmarishly prolific about Dalí fragrances (currently twenty-five in number, mostly trash): they seem to breed as fast as we can write them. EdR is one of the worst, hack work composed in what feels like five minutes, if that, by Michel Almairac. LT

Eau de Shalimar (Guerlain) ★ *cheap oriental* $$$
A short recap for those who missed the preceding installments of the Shalimar boob job. In the beginning (1925) there was a genius oriental

fragrance called Shalimar, the headiest confection of real vanilla, fresh citrus, and herbes de Provence. Some years ago (2003), a need was felt among the thinking heads at LVMH to make a version more accessible to the young. Mathilde Laurent, then in-house perfumer at Guerlain, was drafted in. She did a great job, and the late, lamented, and altogether beautiful Shalimar Eau Légère was born. Then she fell out with the boss (Jean-Paul Guerlain), who reissued the fragrance under his name with a slightly different and less pleasant top note the following year. Now comes Eau de Shalimar, comprehensively unpleasant from top to bottom: a loud, cheap, air-care synthetic-vanilla top note, with a caricature of the thyme-lemon oil accord thrown in, followed by a nasty musky, chemical accord reminiscent of a dirt-cheap knockoff of Habit Rouge mixed with Paco Rabanne pour Homme. To be avoided at all costs. LT

Eau des Merveilles (Hermès) ★ ★ ★ *salty orange* $$$
EdM is apparently based on an "idea" of ambergris reconstituted by mixing other materials (why not get the real thing?). It is a polite, slightly confused, muted fragrance with a pleasant orange start and a complex, salty drydown that feels like several fragrances at once. A similar saline effect was already achieved more forcefully and interestingly in Diptyque's Virgilio years ago. LT

Eau de Star (Thierry Mugler) ★ ★ ★ ★ *minty oriental* $$
Toothpaste Angel! Great! LT

Eau de Vert (Miller Harris) ★ ★ *flat green* $$$
Water of Green? Never make puns in a language you don't speak well. Somewhat confused and indecisive herbaceous-soapy affair, not very pleasant. LT

Eau d'Hadrien eau de parfum (Annick Goutal) ★ ★ *lemon wood* $$
When you have a fragrance composed entirely of citrus oils and moss

extracts, and industry allergen restrictions command you to strike out the limonene, citronellal, and oakmoss, you're screwed. The decent thing to do is discontinue, but it's not easy to ax a big seller. So you compromise. Eau d'Hadrien is far thinner—more lemon-scented dishwashing soap than lemon oil—and more floral than ever before, putting it into competition with richer colognes like Chanel's, for which it's no match. TS

Eau d'Hadrien eau de toilette (Annick Goutal) ★ ★ ★
woody lemon $ $ $
Goutal's steady best seller from 1981, which in private moments I like to call "Yo, Adrian," is in the eau de cologne style but even more subdued than usual, going from a pleasant, cool lemon to nearly imperceptible smooth woods with a basil tone. Deliberately understated, a good choice for antiperfume types. European Union restrictions on citrus oils threaten to put the kibosh on this one, so stay tuned. TS

Eau d'Hermès (Hermès) ★ ★ ★ ★ *animalic cologne* $ $
The devil, it is said, grants your wishes, in this case the widespread one for a simple-but-classy "cologne" for men. Eau d'Hermès takes a straightforward citrus-and-lavender motif and enriches it with plenty of lush, complex, silken woody notes and a fat dollop of animalic civet. It smells unquestionably great but feels a bit like modern luxury cars that insist on passé accents of burl walnut to signify old-fashioned luxury. One can only applaud the quality of the materials, but the overall effect has a monogrammed-slippers feel to it. This fragrance should be avoided by middle-aged men unless they habitually wear striped shirts with a contrasting white collar. LT

Eau d'Hiver (Frédéric Malle) ★ ★ ★ ★ *pale almonds* $ $
One of the dangers of the new French school of perfumery typified by Jean-Claude Elléna is the lure of bloodless overrefinement, what I would describe as Ravel's disease: wonderfully crafted, elegantly orchestrated pieces drenched in pale sunlight. These watery Elysian Fields no doubt

have their rewards, but earthy sensuality is not one of them: angels don't have sex. This being said, there is one fragrance raw material that just begs for this treatment, and that is the mimosa note of heliotropin. I have no idea how Elléna has managed to circumvent restrictions on the use of this material in the European Union, but the result is stunning: an elegiac, powdery, almonds-and-water accord that takes its place next to Guerlain's Après l'Ondée and Caron's Farnesiana among the fragrance Ophelias of this world. LT

L'Eau d'Issey (Issey Miyake) ★ ★ ★   *melon floral* $
What's the point of reviewing L'Eau d'Issey, I wonder, when each reader has known at minimum five people who wore it? But we would be remiss to leave it out. However, smelling this best-selling fragrance in earnest today is a shock. For one thing, it has a reputation as a very light fragrance but is instead extremely strong. The green floral bouquet at its core seems crudely friendly, like floral air fresheners you've known; the distinctive, airy, green melon–aquatic note of Calone, which made the fragrance seem so new in 1992, reminds us mostly of Windex now. It seems unfair that this fragrance should have lived while its more deserving cousin Feu d'Issey was put to the axe. It also seems counterintuitive that the preference for squeaky-clean, bland, fresh, faceless fragrances in frosted glass—cK One, Acqua di Gio, Light Blue—should have arisen while the main fashion, grunge, was to look as if you'd been sleeping under a bridge for months. But fifteen years ago, it was all part of the penitent ideal: goodbye to Mötley Crüe and their extraneous hair and umlauts, bye to shoulder pads and pointy-toed stiletto heels, bye to Opium and Giorgio. A straightforward, pleasant spring floral that smelled like glass cleaner, with a Japanese name and a simple conical bottle, seemed pure and unfussy, honestly generic. The story always told is that Miyake asked for a fragrance that smelled like water, despite water smelling, notably, like nothing. Nearly everyone I knew owned a bottle. There is little reason to own one now. If you love the eerie freshness of it, you could try the peculiar Cologne by Thierry Mugler or the unforgettably

crisp Silences by Jacomo, and if it's the conventional green floral at its heart that moves you, you can seek out, say, Cristalle or Private Collection and set sail for ever farther and more satisfying seas from there. TS

L'Eau d'Issey pour Homme (Issey Miyake) ★ ★ ★ *fizzy lemonade* $
A zingy little citrus with a weird turmeric astringency, the masculine L'Eau d'Issey actually works somewhat better than the feminine, smelling more interestingly dissonant, with that odd herbal intensity that Asian artificial fruit flavors often have. Surprisingly long-lived. Good clean fun, very similar in its hissing pop to DKNY Women. TS

L'Eau d'Issey pour Homme Intense (Issey Miyake) ★ ★
herbal citrus $
In more proof that there is no logic to fragrance names, the Intense version is in fact weaker smelling than the original, with a licorice-like vetiver background that gives it a nudge in an aromatic fougère direction. Though far from as good as the best of its kind, it could have been much worse. TS

Eau d'Italie (Eau d'Italie) ★ ★ ★ *milky metallic* $$$
Not really a perfume, more of a smell, this is the first appearance (2004) of an eerie, quiet little idea that Bertrand Duchaufour worked out more fully in the limited edition Flora Bella (2005) for Lalique. Instead of the citrus cologne you expect from an Eau de Something-or-Other, Eau d'Italie pairs metallic-watery-smelling materials and pale milky woods, giving a sad, wistful odor, like baby's breath. TS

Eau d'Orange Verte (Hermès) ★ ★ ★ ★ *good cologne* $
Packaged to look like a higher dilution of the Concentré (q.v.) but to my nose more Cologne-like, woodier, and with less lime on top. Good. LT

Eau du Fier (Annick Goutal) ★ ★ ★ ★ *leathery tea* $$$
A *fier* is a puffed up, show-off kind of guy, the perfect type to wear this

combination of leathers, leaves, and citrus, because it smells like nothing so much as the interior of a brand-new car. TS

Eau du Navigateur (L'Artisan Parfumeur) ★ ★ *coffee herbaceous* $$$
One of the fragrances in LAP's range that dates back to the Jean Laporte days (1982). One assumes the reason it is still around is that people buy it. Once again, Laporte was ahead of his time. However, EdN is very dated today, and interesting only for its roasted-coffee and leather notes, which make an intermediate life-form between then-prevalent aromatic fougères (Aramis and Azzaro Homme) and, later, fully developed creations like Bel-Ami (1986) and Yohji Homme (1999). It is vivid but slightly chemical, as is often the case even with Laporte's best creations. LT

Eau du Soir (Sisley) ★ *cheap chypre* $$$
Unpleasant green chypre. LT

L'Eau du Sud (Annick Goutal) ★ ★ ★ *basil cologne* $$$
I prefer L'Eau du Sud to Goutal's best seller, Eau d'Hadrien—with more herb and less lemon, it feels weightier, with a handsome, sleek, soapy texture, like a slippery object underwater you can't seem to get a grip on. TS

Eau Egyptienne (Cinq Mondes) ★ ★ ★ *savory spice* $$
Based on the ancient Egyptian perfume (and possibly medicine) *kyphi*, which was made trendy a few years back when the Egyptian Museum in Cairo commissioned a reconstruction from perfumer Sandrine Videault. Olivia Giacobetti's version, for luxury spa Cinq Mondes, is a pleasant though unextraordinary mixture of spices, very fleeting. TS

Eau Emotionelle (Agent Provocateur) ★ ★ *light chypre* $$
A lightening up of the rose chypre idea with more fruity floral notes. Fun for a bit, but really cheap and a little tiresome. TS

Eau Fraîche (Dior) ★ ★ ★ ★ *luxurious cologne* $ $
Colognes have something in common with dry martinis, in that the
search for dryness and distinction cannot take you further afield than
the basic structure will allow. All you're given to play with are the proportions and qualities of the raw materials. To get around this, Eau
Fraîche uses a trick common to Chanel's Pour Monsieur and Monsieur
de Givenchy, i.e., adding a touch of a beautifully balanced chypre to a
zingy cologne formula. It's as if lemons fresh off the boat from Sicily
suddenly started speaking with a languid sixteenth arrondissement
accent. LT

L'Eau Guerrière (Parfumerie Générale) ★ ★ ★ *reefer madness* $ $ $
It is really hard to dislike EG, which reassembles elements familiar to
those who enjoy Nasomatto fragrances, but in a more civilized fashion.
A concert of woody, camphoraceous, spicy, and citrus notes sings out
like mad for five minutes, after which the fragrance settles down to a
note strongly reminiscent of cannabis resin (yes, I inhaled). A very nice
hippie confection and a fun simpleminded masculine. LT

Eau Illuminée (Parfums DelRae) ★ ★ *sour cologne* $ $ $
Eaux de cologne are classically fresh, a style based on easygoing natural
materials: citrus, florals, herbs, woods. When composed with good materials and skill, as undoubtedly this one is, they tend to be the most
relaxed and unpretentious of fragrances. (See Chanel's Eau de Cologne
and the full line of Institut Très Bien for examples.) Something chafes in
this one, though. As much as it tries to act natural, it is finally too sour,
too green, too uptight. TS

Eau Lente (Diptyque) ★ ★ ★ ★ *spice floral* $ $
In C. S. Lewis's Narnian "Plato for Dummies," *The Silver Chair*, a witch
who rules an underground cavern, where a prince and several children
are held captive, tries to convince those who have spent too long in
darkness that there is no sun and no moon, save imaginary ravings in-

spired by lamps; no trees; no wind; no grass to be blown by it; no other world at all. The noble soul's great danger there is the slow fall of expectations to degraded local values. Smelling one of these original Diptyques after suffering through a stretch of confused, high-concept, low-budget niche fragrances is like breaking through a prison ceiling to find fresh air and stars. Eau Lente has the complexity and dry-woody air of a spice cabinet, plus a sheen of fresh herbs, notably a soapy-mint basil. It modulates first from transparent modern oriental to rich floral bouquet and then at last to classical resinous amber, like those hypnotic colored lights that slide from pink to cyan without anybody noticing. This first range of Diptyque scents has for decades been unlike anything else in perfumery: immediate, memorable, and profound, ancient in concept and eternally modern in execution. TS

L'Eau Neuve (Lubin) ★ ★ ★ ★ *camphor chypre* $$
A Tiger Balm chypre. Are they reading my diary? In a modern-hippie aesthetic reminiscent of Timbuktu, the smell is halfway between medicine and cologne, with a long, amazingly natural-smelling, excellent chypre drydown. Cheerful *Yellow Submarine*–style bottle. TS

Eau Noire (Dior) ★ ★ ★ ★ *everlasting flower* $$$$
Generally, when perfumes come in twos and threes, only one really works, and Dior Homme's three colognes are no exception. They are all competent and luxurious, but only Eau Noire, composed by Francis Kurkdjian, stops you in your tracks. Eau Noire is the first fragrance since Annick Goutal's amazing Sables to make overt use of helichrysum (immortelle), an odd, fenugreek-like smell halfway between curry and burnt sugar. The difficulty with immortelle is that it tends to take over the party with its big contralto voice. Goutal had set it in an oriental context, but Kurkdjian takes a different tack and goes for lavender. This fits nicely with a mental picture of sun-roasted garrigue, where both smells frequently coexist. Natural, warm, and comfortable, this is a very good neoclassical fragrance and much more than a cologne. LT

Eau Parfumée au Thé Blanc (Bulgari) ★ ★ ★ *aldehydic tea* $$$
Jacques Cavallier messes with Jean-Claude Elléna's original Thé Vert idea to keep the transparency while adding some brilliance. Not bad in that particular fade-to-white style, but a bit like chalk on blackboard. LT

Eau Parfumée au Thé Rouge (Bulgari) ★ ★ *sweet tea* $$$
Bulgari is pushing the line of EPT(x), where x is any pale color, for all it's worth. The Rouge is really not very good at all, sweet and cloying like low-grade tea with milk in a roadside diner. LT

Eau Parfumée au Thé Vert (Bulgari) ★ ★ ★ ★ *floral tea* $$$
In 1993, along with L'Eau d'Issey a year earlier, this fragrance most perfectly captured the groundswell of dislike for the marching-band monster fragrances of the eighties. It was also the fragrance that put Jean-Claude Elléna on the map, and deservedly so. Whereas L'Eau d'Issey was merely a huge floral with a ton of Calone added, this is a truly original, novel perfumery form, at once vivid and pale, a sort of cK One for grownups. It was designed for people who hate fragrance, and having smelled it on a phalanx of starved women pushing strollers around Chelsea, I find it hard to love. Very impressive nevertheless. LT

L'Eau par Kenzo pour Femme (Kenzo) ★ ★ *watermelon floral* $$
Watermelon flavor. Women want to smell like this? TS

L'Eau par Kenzo pour Homme (Kenzo) ★ ★ *citrus woody* $$
In 1996 when L'Eau par Kenzo was released, the fashion for watery fragrances was still going strong. While pleasantly green and competently put together, it is still a grievous yawn. TS

L'Eau Rare Matale (Parfumerie Générale) ★ ★ *presque rien* $$$
So rare it's practically not there. I may be anosmic to some towering material within this concoction, but to my nose it feels like an extenu-

ated version of Mugler's wonderfully hissy Cologne, like catching the tail end of a cymbal sound. Who would pay for this? LT

Eau Sauvage (Dior) ★ ★ ★ ★ ★ *citrus floral* $
I always forget how good this darned thing is. Part of the reason I don't wear it is that it reminds me of my youth. Also, it is a touch louder than I feel comfortable with. Eau Sauvage broadcasts itself quite far by being written in an intrinsically legible type, a sort of Garamond of smell. Great perfumers play with the cologne idea the way Prokofiev used eighteenth-century structures in his First Symphony: take the familiar and, as if it were one of those Transformers my son plays with, turn the horse-drawn carriage into a spaceship. What Roudnitska did to cologne here is threefold: (1) Add a slug of a pine-needles-and-rosemary accord, which the Italians did so well in postwar marvels like Acqua di Selva and Pino Silvestre. (2) Use his own trademark Vietnamese-salad accord (see Diorella for a fuller account). (3) Famously be the first to lubricate the whole thing with hedione, a floral material that can wet the driest lips. I've heard perfumers say there is so little hedione in Eau Sauvage that attributing ES's success to it was a bit like attributing Jascha Heifetz's skill to the Guarneri he played. Either way, a masterpiece. LT

Eau Suave (Parfum d'Empire) ★ ★ ★ *green chypre* $$
A somewhat conventional and disappointing green chypre in the Givenchy III mold, made with decent raw materials but a little bare and insistent on skin. LT

Eau Trois (Diptyque) ★ ★ ★ *frank incense* $$
Frankincense has a great smell, which is why it's been used since forever. Eau Trois is mostly frankincense, and smells great. LT

Eau Turquoise (Parfums de Nicolaï) ★ ★ ★ ★ *sage mango* $
The benighted girlish orphans known as fruity florals have been, in

their nauseatingly cute multitudes—like Henry Darger's baby-faced Vivian Girls—lost, abused, excoriated by the cruel grown-ups, and left leaderless in these woods for too long. Enter a cross-dressing heroine. I found it hard to believe that de Nicolaï intended to market this thing as a fruity floral, but there it is on their Web site, so it must be true. To the magical greeny-resinous nexus that binds mango, with its powerful note of pine resin, to cedar and oakmoss, there seems to be added an incredible note of fresh sage, which LT has noted smells slightly urinous. For women and men who wear Jules and Eau Sauvage. TS

Echo (Davidoff) ★ *woody citrus* $
To borrow John Redwood's description of his political friend William Hague, a perfume made for a "train-spotting nonentity with a surface gloss of management theory." LT

Echo Woman (Davidoff) ★ *screechy floral* $
Deeply uninteresting el-cheapo bright rose. LT

Eclat d'Arpège (Lanvin) ★ ★ *peachy amber* $$
Belongs to an extremely synthetic subset of fruity-amber fragrances (Costume National's Scent is another) that project a bland artificial warmth. Appealing (radiant, sweet) and repulsive (warm vinyl) in exact balance, but not very interesting. TS

Eclat de Jasmin (Armani Privé) ★ ★ *expensive floral* $$$$
They say that when someone has been starving for a long period you should reintroduce her to food gradually for fear of killing her. The Privé collection may be a testimony to an analogous phenomenon among perfumers. They have acquired such frugal, alley-cat habits from being under the thumbs of brands, the worst misers in all of art history, that when given access to a feast they gorge indiscriminately. This could have been a great fragrance with good jasmine and osmanthus, a fresh

top note, and a refined woody drydown. And instead, it is an expensively pointless, shapeless floral. LT

Ecume de Rose (Parfums de Rosine) ★ ★ ★ *cassis immortelle* $ $
The dusty, spicy smell of immortelle gives this watery, green, fruity rose a strange seaside air of sand and dry brush. (The name means "pink foam.") The more recent, marvelous Missoni Acqua is a clearer, more striking version of this idea. TS

Eden (Cacharel) ★ ★ ★ ★ *sweet green* $
I wrote this long ago: "A rare instance of finely tuned coherence between the celadon coloured packaging and the opalescent green smell. Love it or hate it, Eden is one of the most distinctive perfumes in recent years, with an extraordinary raspy-suave, peculiarly stagnant start, little or no evolution in time and tremendous tenacity. Owning it makes perfect sense, but wearing it is another matter. Eden is undoubtedly a brilliant, cerebral exercise in perfumery, but who wants to smell like wet cashmere?" Ah, Hédènne . . . Perfume journalists are still talking about the 1994 launch, which took place in some sort of aircraft hangar near Paris and involved a large artificial island surrounded by water, covered in real jungle, and populated by naked adolescents of both sexes. I'd tell you more, but I wasn't there. Eleven years later, I walked into my local pharmacy looking for plastic atomizer bottles and caught an unmistakable whiff of Eden in the air. Sure enough, the tester was on the counter. Now, instant recognition can be a clear sign of fondness for a tune, voice, face, and of course perfume. And, with the help of hindsight, serendipity, and ten years of ever-sweeter masculine fragrances, I managed at long last to answer the question I asked at the end of my old review: I do. LT

Edwardian Bouquet (Floris) ★ ★ *floral chypre* $ $ $
On paper, this handsome chypre has a classic galbanum profile: fresh, bitter green, slightly musky. On skin, it turns peculiarly and distinctly

urinous with a curdled-milk smell, and would invite speculations on one's continence. TS

Effusion Man (Iceberg) ★ *woody boring* $
You don't want this guy to turn effusive. EM smells like a formula that's been dug up from the shelf of failed briefs, circa 1986. LT

Effusion Woman (Iceberg) ★ ★ *pale orange* $
A modern watery-orange chypre in the manner of Eau des Merveilles, like a cocktail made with white wine and a touch of Campari. LT

Egoïste (Chanel) ★ ★ ★ ★ *candied fruit* $ $
I remembered Egoïste as a beautiful but slightly watery pastel confection of candied fruits and low-key woods, and this one surprised me. I've never smelled Bois Noir, from which Egoïste was derived, but I suspect this is closer to the original. This is now the most Guerlain-like of all the Chanels, full of thyme, lavender, and other herbes de Provence, a sort of Jicky spiked with Antaeus and rounded off with Bois des Iles in the dry-down. A perfect alternative to Mouchoir de Monsieur, sprightlier and less dandified. Go easy when wearing it, though: this is strong stuff. LT

Egoïste Platinum (Chanel) ★ ★ *sad fougère* $ $
Named like a credit card for tightfisted sugar daddies, this was never likely to be a good fragrance. In fact, it is quite extraordinarily bad for Chanel and aside from a fleetingly interesting floral-leather note up top, reeks of the sad male clone it was intended for. If you check into a decent hotel, chances are a freebie on the bathroom shelf smells at least as good as this. LT

El Attarine (Serge Lutens) ★ ★ ★ ★ *apricot wood* $ $ $
Paris boutique only
I detect in many of the recent Lutens fragrances a growing impatience,

a rising tone of voice, as if he felt hindered in getting his way, in reaching what has been all along his only goal: making us swoon. Since 2005 his fragrances have gotten louder and heavier, and also in some ways more essential, more original. He is taking greater chances and as a consequence has produced duds (Miel de Bois) as well as masterpieces (Sarrasins). There is also something admirable in his relentless Arab obsession. Who but the defiantly otherworldly would today produce a perfume named after a madrassa, in this case a magnificent one in Fez? El Attarine is a beautifully dense confection, a sort of supercharged version of his La Myrrhe with an enormous note of candied apricots in the heart, extended by aldehydes at one end and the duskiest woods at the other. It is easy, in the cold light of a gray London day, to underestimate this piece of what should properly be called costume perfumery. You certainly don't go shopping for fabric softener wearing this. But the planets do move, and an evening comes when you look up and notice they are in alignment. That night nothing else will do. LT

Eleganza Luminosa (Linari) ★ ★ *woody citrus* $$$
This is the least worst of the Linari line, and it hits all the right notes—fresh, floral, and woody—in the right order, which would be fine except for the fact that everyone else has already played that particular tune to death, from Narciso Rodriguez onward. A lazy, shoddy little thing. LT

Elige (Mary Kay) ★ *sour floral* $
I love Perfume French almost as much as Automobile Italian (Mazda Luce Legato), and *Elige* is a gem of a name, no doubt an attempt to rightfully enter the "masstige" market. The fragrance is a washed-out aldehydic floral that manages to smell as if the stuff has gone off even when fresh from the factory. LT

Elixir (Penhaligon's) ★ ★ *cinnamon rose* $$
Acrid, phony potpourri smell; very loud. TS

Elixir Charnel Chypre Fatal (Guerlain) ★ ★ *trashy "chypre"* $$$$

Gone are Guerlain's years of constipation, the five-year intervals between major releases. Counting flankers and reissues, thirteen new fragrances were launched in 2008, too many for any art director to supervise properly. The Elixir Charnel series bears all the hallmarks of the new Guerlain at its suburban worst: all overwrought names, tarty bottles, and a hopeless spice-up-your-love-life aesthetic. Even the colors of the fragrances come from a naff eye-shadow palette. The fragrance, composed by the greats Christine Nagel (Theorema and many other spicy-oriental marvels) and Aurélien Guichard (Chinatown, God bless him), is the olfactory equivalent of a makeover: looks good when you first smell it, then makes you feel like saying, "I liked you better with lank hair, in the bottle-green rollneck." This all-things-to-all-noses style has run its course and is poised to become something we will enjoy loathing for the next decade. LT

Elixir Charnel Gourmand Coquin (Guerlain) ★ ★
gingerbread overdose $$$$

Given that Jacques Guerlain was the greatest virtual pastry chef in history, Guerlain hardly needs to kowtow to a gourmand tendency it invented, perfected, and is now busy traducing. The trick of the old Guerlain gourmands was to smell like the sum total of a large household in which dinner, among other things, was being prepared. Thus did Mitsouko smell of floor wax as well as peaches, and Shalimar of fence-paint creosote as well as vanilla. As we discovered in the early nineties (who remembers Octée's disastrous chocolate?), straight-up foody perfumes were nauseating. At the very least, a gourmand should make you salivate rather than burp. This is why Spiritueuse Double Vanille was a mistake, and ECGC falls into the same trap. Smelling it brings to mind Casanova's story of the eighteenth-century aristocrat, deathly ill with indigestion, who sees a hungry mendicant and says, "I wish I was in your place, you rogue!" LT

Elixir Charnel Oriental Brûlant (Guerlain) ★ ★ ★ ★
woody spicy $$$$
Had Oriental Brûlant not suffered the curse of all things that come in threes, which is that the one good thing is wrecked by the two bad ones, it would have been a nice spicy oriental with an unusually fresh cedar-wood-incense start. As it is, with its silly name and flouncy bottle, it risks being overlooked, which would be a shame. Makes an excellent masculine, if you can bear your bathroom shelf looking like something out of Victoria's Secret. LT

Elixir des Merveilles (Hermès) ★ ★ ★ *orange chypre* $$
This perfume is so perfectly *bon chic bon genre,* as the French call the canon of bourgeois respectability, that, like some of Holbein's portraits, it hovers on the edge of caricature. Had I been in charge at Hermès, I would have laughed heartily, marveled at Elléna's skill, and sent him back to the drawing board. And that would have been stupid, because nobody will notice the irony, least of all the Hermès young woman it is aimed at. Elixir acts reassuringly old, wearing Granny's vast sapphire ring at the first ball of the season: although the beautifully sunny and very Italian top notes of orange, like a tan, hint at a recent holiday some-where expensive, the heart and drydown belong to Maman's solidly plush, prim chypre, more Givenchy III than Cabochard. This doomed creature ages twenty years in as many minutes on the back of your hand. The process has something affecting, like seeing someone young strug-gling to be alive, only to eventually drown in inherited comfort. As Ray-mond Queneau wrote of a character in *Pierrot Mon Ami,* "ravaged by tranquillity." LT

Elle (Yves Saint Laurent) ★ ★ ★ *woody rose* $$
If imitation is the sincerest form of flattery, Bertrand Duchaufour and Marc Buxton must be delighted that all their ideas about transparent woody florals are gradually finding their way into the mainstream, al-beit cheapened and brightened by the necessity of appealing to a young

audience the big firms clearly reckon to be made up of morons. Elle is one part Miracle, one part Comme des Garçons, and two parts Narciso Rodriguez. The most original thing about it is that Jacques Cavallier found a way to sneak in the bread-milk note that made Feu d'Issey so good and so strange. Not unpleasant, but a bit of a mishmash. LT

Ellie (Ellie D) ★ ★ ★ *green floral* $$$
A green, powdery floral in a sort of Laura Ashley, summer-picnic style. Very competently done with quality materials, but a bit too suggestive of straw hats and lace-up espadrilles for my taste. LT

Ellie Nuit (Ellie D) ★ ★ ★ *chocolate milk* $$$
Sometimes even the professional perfume reviewer is baffled by too much information. On first testing Ellie Nuit—knowing it was composed by Michel Roudnitska and that its official profile involved wood, fig, violet, coriander, etc.—I struggled to put a name to its silvery mystery and set it aside. Now suddenly the meaning of its bitter, chalky, milky scent crystallizes in a vision: I see the small tin of dark dust, the brown cartoon rabbit, the undissolved lumps floating in cold liquid. Nestlé Quik! TS

Eloge du Traître (Etat Libre d'Orange) ★ ★ ★ ★ *aromatic fougère* $$
Antoine Maisondieu has a Prokofiev-like talent for taking a known structure and giving it a quarter-turn twist in a completely unexpected, generally upward direction, while making sure that the result is perfectly crafted. This fougère is his Classical Symphony. Yes, we've been there before, and yes, it uses conventional forces, but be honest: Does it not instantly turn your blood to sparkling Shiraz? LT

Emeraude (Coty) ★ *cheap oriental* $
This one breaks my heart and makes me despair of capitalism. The original Emeraude (1921) was a masterpiece that predated Shalimar by four years (rumor has it that Coty sold the formula to Guerlain) and in my

opinion remained unequaled among orientals. I remember first smelling it on the very first scratch-and-sniff ad circa 1967, below a demure nude in black and white. I would have swapped the girl for an ounce of the perfume anytime. Some years ago, Coty had the original reconstructed by Firmenich's Daphné Bugey and handed it out to guests at some swank party to which I was not invited. I have managed to smell it nevertheless and can report that it is fantastic, and incidentally in full conformity with EU regulations. Were it released today, it would probably be a best seller within weeks. The Emeraude sold in drugstores is a cynical travesty of the real thing, crap value even at the bargain-basement price. LT

Emporio Armani He (Armani) ★ ★ ★ *woody amber* ⚱
Minty in the top note, a Cool Water built on a wan woody amber. TS

Emporio Armani She (Armani) ★ ★ ★ *woody peony* $
A fresh white floral plus powdery woods and something like almond milk, like Dream Angels Heavenly: basically, a nice laundry smell. TS

En Avion (Caron) ★ ★ *anisic floral* $$$
Unlike Guerlain's equally aviation-themed Vol de Nuit, which had all the daring of a dessert cart, En Avion truly was an adventurous fragrance. Its particular combination of orange blossom and anise made for a wild, airy sweetness, and its leather-amber base has always been as dry as woodsmoke. Reformulation has changed its proportions in favor of the floral: a big lemony rose now seizes all the attention, as out of place as a fussy lace dickie would have been on Amelia Earhart. Caron has traded beauty for normality. TS

Encens et Bubblegum (Etat Libre d'Orange) ★ ★ ★ ★ *woody rosy* $$
Curious outfit, this ELO: founder Etienne de Swardt is a tiresomely bad writer of cod-erotic copy, of which their Web site is full. (Sample: "When transgression is tinged with erotic guilt, the impish sexuality of this

childlike woman . . .") He is also, clearly, an excellent fragrance art director with a knack for great names and has, in the persons of Antoine Lie and Antoine Maisondieu, identified some major talent. Encens et Bubblegum is a wonderfully quiet, transparent accord of sweet rosy and woody resinous notes, like one of those classic fairy tales where a surface of cuteness hides a solemn, even alarming message. LT

Encens et Lavande (Serge Lutens) ★ ★ ★ *resinous lavender* $$$
This Lutens-Sheldrake fragrance was subjected to the most arduous test of all: my daughter (age five) spilled a full bottle on the sofa. I had to smell the drydown for over a year, and still liked it a lot. So nothing wrong there. But this test showed what I felt all along, namely, that E&L works better as *parfum d'ambiance* than proper masculine. LT

Encens Flamboyant (Annick Goutal) ★ ★ ★ ★ *cigarette incense* $$$
Following an iron law of perfumery that governs any three or more fragrances released as a set, Goutal's original three Orientalistes (the others being Ambre Fétiche and Myrrhe Ardente) consist of two duds and one success. This is the success. Frankincense's icy notes of lime peel and pine play a Nordic winter interrupted by an unusual tobacco note last noticed in Jasmin et Cigarette (Etat Libre d'Orange). If you've ever had a smoke on a cold day in the woods, you'll know why this is exciting. TS

Enchanting (Celine Dion) ★ ★ ★ *fruity vanilla* $
An average outing down a well-traveled road, this sweet berry floral is perfectly pleasant in its way, and avoids the careless harshness or cloying sweetness of so many in this genre. TS

Encre Noire (Lalique) ★ ★ ★ ★ *woody vetiver* $$
"Black Ink" is a clever conceit: the weighty black glass cube looks like an upscale inkwell sold in the sort of catalog in which every other object comes in pebbled leather, and the top note, with its smooth smell of wet paint, will be a delight for anyone who's ever dipped a pen in india ink.

The rest is a transparent, fresh vetiver in the modern style, crisp and green, grounded by a well-judged touch of woody amber. Subtle and handsome, one of the best clean vetivers around. TS

Endymion (Penhaligon's) ★ ★ *spicy woody* $ $
A soft and warm fragrance done in Penhaligon's customary knees-and-elbows style. I see no possible reason for choosing this over dozens of better and often cheaper perfumes. LT

Energy Man (United Colors of Benetton) ★ ★ *dull fougère* $ $
So boring and derivative it should be stored for future reference as the average perfume of 2008. LT

Energy Woman (United Colors of Benetton) ★ *citrus fruity* $ $
Blah. LT

English Breakfast (By Mark Buxton) ★ ★ *metallic bergamot* $ $ $
I quote from the press material: "It's 7 in the morning. An English man in Japan sitting in the Shinkansen is going to Kyoto. What does he do at this time? He opens his sushi/sashimi box for breakfast." I confess the joke is totally lost on me, but at least this herbaceous-metallic confection does not smell of fish. LT

English Fern (Penhaligon's) ★ ★ *classic fougère* $ $
Modeled on the great classic Fougère Royale: coumarin, lavender, oakmoss, musk. Except that Fougère Royale smelled divine and this smells rough. LT

English Leather (Dana) ★ ★ *sweet amber* $
The old stuff used to be one of those feminines in battle dress that somehow were deemed acceptable by men, and smelled fantastic, sweet, and sultry. This stuff is drier, woodier, not at all leathery, and much cheaper than the original. To be avoided. LT

Enlèvement au Sérail (Parfums MDCI) ★ ★ ★ ★ ★
peach jasmine $$$$
Despite the silly name (Abduction in the Seraglio, after Mozart's opera),
I love this fragrance, and sprayed it several times while writing this review to rewind it to the beginning and see the title sequence again, for it
is stunning. It starts with an intensely animalic floral top note; moves
on to a golden, seraphic chord of jasmine and peach in the fifties-revival
manner of 31 Rue Cambon (which, to be fair, came five years later); and
gradually settles to a classical, well-poised voice with a hint of a spicy-
woody rasp. You'll probably want to spray it on fabric to admire the
graceful trajectory in slow motion. LT

En Passant (Frédéric Malle) ★ ★ ★ *lilac heliotropin* $$$
Though this is a perfect example of Olivia Giacobetti's tendency, in flo-
rals, to a pallid, cold complexion, the perfume equivalent of a consump-
tive gothic heroine in need of a corset loosening, En Passant nevertheless
is a fine white-on-white painting, beginning in lilacs and ending in a
chilly little heliotropin that implies that what you had perceived "in
passing" was a person wearing Après l'Ondée. TS

En Sens de Bois (Miller Harris) ★ ★ ★ *woody iris* $$$
Another MH fragrance, another lame French pun: *en sens* (in the direc-
tion of) = *encens* = incense. Interesting composition, rooty as much as
woody, with a carrot-seed-and-iris combination that livens up what
might otherwise have been a rather flat accord, and with salubrious,
smoky woody notes in the background. A bit too sedate and pastel to my
taste, but skillful and agreeable. LT

Enslaved (Roja Dove) ★ ★ ★ *vetiver heliotropin* $$$$
Roja Dove is a longtime perfume aficionado who sells a small, personally selected range of fragrances from a tiny boutique on the top floor of
Harrods. He has begun issuing perfumes under his own name, crafted
by anonymous perfumers. Judging by the three we've tested—Enslaved,

Scandal, and Unspoken—he is more curator than creator, since they are blasts from the past, using good materials and Dove's own twist. Unfortunately, Enslaved is Habanita suffering through a badly muddled rose top note. TS

Envy (Gucci) ★ ★ ★ ★ ★ *green floral* $$

Maurice Roucel has a knack for putting together perfumes that feel haunted by the ghostly presence of a woman: Lyra was a compact, husky-voiced Parisienne, Tocade a tanned, free-as-air Amazon. These have another Roucel hallmark, the spontaneity of the unpolished gem. When subjected to the full grind of the marketing department, Roucel's style can become cramped and tends toward brilliant pastiches of classical fragrances: 24, Faubourg; L'Instant; Insolence. Envy is to my knowledge the only time when the balance between Roucel's magic and the real world gave rise to a work that, like a diamond, needed both heat and pressure to form. My recollection is that Envy was panel-tested again and again while Roucel adjusted it until it outperformed Pleasures, then at the top of its arc of fame. It is amusing to think that such a comparison between apples and pears could be expected to be meaningful. However, it did constrain the woman inside Envy to be at once seraphic and suburban, complete with the sort of suppressed anger that such a creature would feel at being reincarnated as a florist in eastern New Jersey. LT

Envy for Men (Gucci) ★ ★ ★ *ginger oriental* $

This lovely woody oriental is based, unusually, on a big ginger note. Ginger smells great by itself but tends toward shyness in composition and comes across as rather soggy. Envy made it work, and the result was both fresh-soapy and spicy in a completely convincing way. The present version seems harsher than of old, but I couldn't vouch for that. LT

Equipage (Hermès) ★ ★ ★ ★ *smoky wood* $$

Equipage was composed by the great perfumer, scholar, cook, and amateur jazz pianist Guy Robert in 1970, a year after his Monsieur Rochas (now replaced with a completely different fragrance under the same name) and in very much the same vein. How times change: Apparently the Rochas brief asked him to make a fragrance that smelled of "cold pipe," which he did using smoky woods and balsams. Equipage, though in a similar peaty single-malt style, is warmer, richer, and more sedate. This is a preeminent example of the "lived-in" style of masculine fragrances, those that convey a quiet, slightly rumpled, gentleman-farmer sort of elegance and can be smelled only if you're close enough to feel cheek stubble as well. Full marks to Hermès for not messing with this marvel. LT

Equistrius (Parfum d'Empire) ★ ★ ★ *iris musk* $$
Allegedly named after a racehorse owned by PdE founder Marc-Antoine Corticchiato (frankly, I would have sworn it was a zebra, what with the "equal striations"), this is a delicate iris-ambrette accord. Like most irises this side of Hiris, it's as effortlessly classy as a pale young girl with violet eyes. But this one does not have much conversation. Go chat up Chanel No. 18. LT

Erolfa (Creed) ★ *woody melon* $$$
I remembered Erolfa from fifteen years ago as thoroughly nasty and was not disappointed. This loud, messy, vulgar accord has lost nothing of its grating, nasal-voiced, preening-prat unpleasantness. Anyone who wears this by choice probably dreams of buying a black Audi TT with his year-end bonus. LT

Escada (Escada) ★ ★ ★ *fresh floral* $
The trashy, glittery packaging and cheesy bottle, with a fifties-teal juice and a surfboard-shaped footprint, like something designed to match the look of Disney resorts, lead you to expect another fruity throwaway, but you get instead a classic, subtle, crisp white floral, nearly good enough in this style to have been one of the latest Lauders, advertised with tanned blondes in white cottons. TS

Escale à Portofino (Dior) ★ ★ ★ ★ *almond cologne* $ $ $
Funny how places like Saint-Tropez and Portofino, which ceased to be
pleasant forty years ago, live on as legends of luxury. The name's implied
suggestion is correct: Portofino is now so crowded that the only way to
approach it is from the sea, on a boat you can sleep in. The fragrance is
a lovely cologne with a mouthwatering citrus top note; a strange bitter-
almond note in the heart; and an excellent, high-quality fresh-waxy,
aldehydic drydown in the grand manner. It was composed by François
Demachy, formerly of Chanel and now overseer of LVMH fragrances. A
set piece brilliantly executed. Why the trashy packaging? LT

Escape (Calvin Klein) ★ ★ *white floral* $
Escape used to be interesting, but CK has reformulated it. It started out
(1991) as an old-fashioned, almost dowdy floral overlaid with the extraordinary marine note of Calone, before everybody started using it.
No doubt feeling that Calone had lost its power to surprise (true), they
assumed that the old Escape was therefore obsolete (false) and turned it
into an all-things-to-all-androids fresh white floral as distinctive as a
pebble in a gravel pit. LT

Escape for Men (Calvin Klein) ★ ★ *woody citrus* $
Faceless fresh thing. I look forward to it being discontinued, at which
point there will be no Escape for men. LT

Escentric 01 (Escentric Molecules) ★ ★ ★ *woody incense* $ $ $
Perfumer Geza Schoen is an aficionado of Iso E Super, nominally a pure
molecule, in reality a complex mixture of isomers and impurities adding up to a soft, radiant, velvety woody note with amber aspects. Iso E
Super is everywhere, though perhaps not quite in the proportions
Schoen uses. His 01 is what perfumers would call an *habillage*, the sort
of composition that technical staff put together to showcase a new material and induce perfumers to use it. There are better incense fragrances

out there (Heeley's Cardinal, Armani's Bois d'Encens, Amouage's Jubilation XXV), but 01 is not bad. LT

Les Espionnes du Tsar (Roméa d'Améor) ★ ★ *floral amber* $$$
The Roméa d'Améor line, from its name inspired by pre-WWI Grandes Horizontales (Liane de Pougy, Cléo de Mérode) to its chinoiserie packaging and overwrought fragrance names, is an exercise in (one hopes) tongue-in-cheek rococo nonsense. The fragrances were composed by the great Pierre Bourdon, who sadly announced his retirement last year. I hope these are not his last creations. Espionnes du Tsar (oddly translated on the bottle itself as "Secret Heroines of the Tsar," whoever they may be) is a competent modern floral oriental of decent quality and little ambition that smells like a hundred others. LT

Esprit de Fleurs (Frapin) ★ ★ ★ *smooth citrus* $$$
Weird and misleading name for a woody citrus, pleasant enough and discreet. Frapin inhabits roughly the same territory as Heeley fragrances, except that Heeley figured out that if you speak quietly you must say something interesting. LT

Esprit du Tigre (Heeley) ★ ★ ★ ★ *Tiger Balsam* $$$
I remember the first time I smelled Tiger Balsam (known as Tiger Balm in the United States). It was the year Sputnik went up, I was four, and my father who suffered from migraines had been given a little tin by a fellow who shared his compartment on the Trans-Siberian Railway. Tiger Balsam was then unknown in Europe, and we eked out the remains of the half-empty tin as if it were a fabulous relic from the other end of the Silk Road. To this day, nothing so convincingly smells the part of the healer as this cheap but magical mixture of eucalyptus, camphor, and cajeput. Esprit du Tigre's top notes of wintergreen (very quiet) and camphor are brilliantly done, almost medicinal but mostly soothingly cool, and they dovetail perfectly into a heart note of cardamom and in due course to a drydown of vetiver and cinnamon. It is a rare pleasure to

review a fragrance in which the components are all present and correct, as advertised, of high quality, beautifully put together without any pretentiousness, and intended to smell simply, melodiously, quietly good. Bravo. LT

Essence (Marc Jacobs) ★ ★ ★ *white floral* $ $
Irresistibly brings to mind General Jack D. Ripper's line "but I deny them my essence" in *Dr. Strangelove*. This competent knockoff of Beyond Paradise clearly owes much to gas chromatography and mass spectroscopy. Isn't science wonderful? LT

The Essence (Porsche Design) ★ ★ ★ *woody melon* $ $
Porsche Design is an outfit predicated on the notion that if you stick to brushed steel and black rubber, and use only straight lines and circular arcs, you can't go wrong. Almost all its objects disprove this. The fragrance comes in what looks like a scale model of the Deutsche Bank headquarters. The contents mumble all the right noises expected of a masculine: citrus, wood, melon, even a late-arrival touch of warmth in the drydown. All of this happens against the pianissimo background music of a retro green chypre in the Givenchy III style. There is no question that this is a skillful composition and less poverty-stricken than most. But the dismalness of the brief reminds us that if it's not worth doing, then it's not worth doing well. LT

Essence of Man (United Colors of Benetton) ★ *shampoo citrus* $ $
Benetton fragrances (all forty) seem to be predicated on the concept "throw in enough crap, some will stick." None does. LT

Essence of Woman (United Colors of Benetton) ★ *white floral* $ $
Thin, tinny dreck. LT

Essential (Lacoste) ★ *citrus woody* $ $
Superfluous. LT

Essenza di Zegna (Ermenegildo Zegna) ★ ★ ★ ★ *citrus steam* $ $
Credited to both Alberto Morillas and Jacques Cavallier, which is like saying a concerto written by both Franck and Fauré, this fragrance is an oasis of quality in the depressingly bleak landscape of contemporary masculines. Restrictions on the price of compositions mean that whatever effects are achieved on the way to drydown are likely to be short-lived, so spray EdZ on fabric, not warm skin, to best appreciate it. It begins with a transparent citrus-cardamom accord that seems to allow, as unusually clear water would, a glimpse into the elegantly constructed woody drydown. Within this, like a puff of steam from a hot shower, there is a note of lived-in bathroom, but so faint as to be barely identifiable: is it wet hair, a damp towel, or something more animalic? Could it be the strange steam-iron note Morillas used in the Mugler Cologne? Whatever it is, it lends human interest to this refined, discreet, pale composition and lifts it far above its faceless congeners. LT

Estée (Estée Lauder) ★ ★ *bright floral* $
This is one of the Lauder fragrances you almost never see on the counter, and for once I can see why. Estée is an intense floral with woody notes, a little shrill up top and dowdy in the background. I have no idea whether the original Bernard Chant composition has been messed with, but I find no great pleasure in smelling it today. LT

L'Eté en Douce (L'Artisan Parfumeur) ★ ★ *linden musk* $ $ $
When Mercedes Ruehl's character in *Married to the Mob* said of Michelle Pfeiffer's, "She thinks her shit don't stink," Pfeiffer must have been wafting something like this laundry soap on steroids. It combines an eye-crossingly powerful musk and one of those intensely chemical-tasting tisanes of linden and orange blossom that you find in French supermarkets. Someone is bound to mistake it for "light and fresh." (Formerly known as Extrait de Songes, before Goutal complained on behalf of Songes.) TS

Eternity (Calvin Klein) ★ ★ ★ *loud rose* $

I have always felt that Eternity was a copy of something not worth copying, Jardins de Bagatelle. Smelling them together now, I see why JdB, though arguably better, was a flop and Eternity a success. They are both unpleasantly screechy and soapy, but at least Eternity does not pretend to be demure. LT

Eternity for Men (Calvin Klein) ★ ★ ★ *mandarin lavender* $

An interesting twist on the perennially pleasant citrus-lavender accord using the (musically speaking) flattened note of mandarin rather than straight citrus, or the corresponding sharp of lime. This is a very skillfully composed and likable fragrance, but I wish more cash had been spent on the formula. It smells good but cheap, which would be fine if the overall structure were unpretentious as in Cool Water, whereas it is distinctly aspirational. LT

Etra (Etro) ★ ★ ★ *milky floral* $ $

The year is 1998. What is probably the most remarkable fragrance of the decade, Miyake's Feu d'Issey, takes the perfumery world by storm. All rational beings, myself included, predict a huge success for that pathbreaking idea. Fast forward: it was a total flop, years ahead of its time and incapable of even generating the expected hordes of toned-down, less radical versions of itself. This is one of the few, which came out a year later and makes you hanker after the discontinued real thing. LT

L'Etre Aimé Femme (Divine) ★ ★ ★ *peach lily* $ $ $

The tiny French firm Divine occupies a specialty niche that wouldn't exist were the world sane: good mainstream perfumes aimed at the bourgeois perfume buyer; that is, a woman with her own cash, over age thirty-five, with a mind of her own and a settled taste, of the sort now completely ignored by big firms chasing the limited disposable income of twenty-year-olds who want a piece of Beyoncé. L'Etre Aimé Femme is a dry lily amber, as in Donna Karan Gold, but with a friendly dose of peach—a silly addition, like dressing up one of Karan's somber column gowns with a sparkly brooch. Fine intentions but crude execution. TS

L'Etre Aimé Homme (Divine) ★ ★ *sandalwood attempt* $$$
Sandalwood's combination of buttermilk sweetness and peppery dry wood sounds an inspired pairing for immortelle's weird half-maple-syrup, half-fenugreek smell. Sadly, L'Etre Aimé suffers from the thin, acid character of its synthetic sandalwood substitute, resulting in something that could be called Bois de Paradis Sport. Such fragrances should be put on hold until good natural wood materials become available again. TS

Euphoria (Calvin Klein) ★ ★ ★ *redcurrant candyfloss* $
Post-Angel perfumery is an exercise in forever having your cake and never eating it: what made Angel interesting was the contrast between the eat-me vanilla, candyfloss, and blackcurrant, and the "for external use only" floral base. Some perfumers borrowed the licentious spirit of Angel (Insolence), some the structure (Flowerbomb), some the sexual ambivalence (Coco Mademoiselle). Some, like Dominique Ropion, took Jacques Guerlain's approach when faced with a new François Coty idea: how can I improve on this? If you're as good as Ropion at handling complex formulae made from powerful aromachemicals, you can lower yourself into Angel's engine room and mess with the machinery so it works less like a Jean Tinguely sculpture and more like a Swiss watch. In Alien it almost worked, but in Euphoria the thing just hums along. I personally consider these two fragrances to be like a blue comedy act with all the expletives taken out so you can show it on airlines, whereas the whole point of Angel was precisely the raunch. Still, amazing work. LT

Euphoria Blossom (Calvin Klein) ★ ★ *light floral* $$
Supposedly tailored to the Asian market, which likes "lighter" fragrances, this is a competent pale floral of mind-numbing dullness. Muzak for the nose. LT

Euphoria Men (Calvin Klein) ★ *nondescript* $

"It's about passion that stops at nothing," not even flogging a crap fragrance for real money. LT

Exclamation (Coty) ★ ★ ★ *powdery rose* $

My junior high smelled like this, as junior highs have perhaps ever after, so I was afraid I'd have trouble being objective through a fog of nostalgia. No trouble: this is a loud, crudely charming, low-budget version of Sophia Grojsman's hallmark, a rose tricked out with the big, sweet woody-fruity smell of violets (ionones), which started with Paris (YSL). TS

Exhale (B Never Too Busy to Be Beautiful) ★ ★ ★ ★ *smoky roots* $

My reading of Exhale is that it is a vetiver accord that follows the domino principle: perfumery notes that agree with each other must have a number in common. This vetiver has been extended in the smoky direction by a dry, light smoky wood that smells like cypriol to me, and in the rooty direction by carroty iris notes. The whole structure has the spare, dark feel of Timbuktu, but less fresh, and the salubrious, antiseptic smoke of Lonestar Memories, but less tarry. It is overlaid on a quiet, slightly animalic musk accord of great refinement. A superlative modern masculine at a time when the world badly needs one. LT

Explorer (Ralph Lauren) ★ ★ ★ *green woody* $$

I have an endless supply of gray skirts, black T-shirts, blue jeans, taupe eyeshadows, and red lipsticks because they're so standard they inspire a sort of "oh, I need one of those" mindlessness in shops. Middle-of-the-road masculines like Explorer are designed on the black T-shirt principle: they hope you won't remember you have five just like it. TS

Extravagance d'Amarige (Givenchy) ★ ★ ★ *citrus wood* $$

What an odd thing this flanker is! Burdened with the name of one of the loudest fragrances in history, and what's more, labeled extravagant, it didn't stand a chance. This is a very nice, quiet, delicate composition, chiefly made up of a waxy tangerine note against a quiet woody background. LT

Fahrenheit (Dior) ★ ★ *woody leather* $ $
Fahrenheit should now be renamed after another temperature scale, maybe Réaumur or Rankine, because it is unrecognizable. It used to be a great citrus leather in the manner of Bel-Ami, overlaid with the gassiest, hissiest, most diffusive note of violet leaf in all of perfumery. Acetylenic esters have now been severely restricted (triple bonds smell wonderful but are chemically reactive), and what's left is a kind of Bel-Ami. Except that Bel-Ami itself has been messed with and Fahrenheit is arguably better than the modern version. Either way, nothing to celebrate. LT

Fahrenheit 32 (Dior) ★ ★ ★ ★ *minty vanilla* $ $ $
This fragrance is at once wholly unpretentious and completely successful, striking a wonderful equilibrium between tropical warmth and minty coolness. It has the muted, cozy feeling of a gloomy day somewhere really hot, with that strange, cheerfully doom-laden TV-documentary look you get by using a gradient filter that makes the sky look darker than it should. LT

Fairy Dust (Paris Hilton) ★ *fruity terror* $
Fruit punch top note. Sucker punch follow-up. TS

Fairytales (Lulu Guinness) ★ ★ ★ *fruity vanilla* $ $
A balls-to-the-wall vanilla-strawberry-candyfloss confection that made my kids exclaim, "Gummy bears!" So overwhelmingly cute that I think it would only work properly on a Clint Eastwood lone-avenger type, chewing cud and asking, "Who you calling sweet, punk?" in a hissy voice. LT

Falling in Love (Philosophy) ★ ★ ★ *blackberry musk* $
It would be tempting to criticize this harmless piece of fluff for being crude, adolescent, and cheap. And indeed, since Jean Laporte did a very

similar thing in 1978 with Mûre et Musc, it's also unoriginal. But a sort of artistic statute of limitations plus a sudden feeling of indulgence caused by the fumes of ethylene brassylate make me rather fond of this musky blackberry confection. It should, however, come with a warning not to be sold to anyone over eighteen. LT

Fancy (Jessica Simpson) ★ ★ ★ *fruity vanilla* $
A shocking lot of you swan around smelling like pie. Fancy is surprisingly competent and intense for its tooth-decaying genre and manages to project itself impressive distances, forcefully flinging odors of canned fruit and sugar syrup against walls and ceiling. Its top note is basically the closest you'll ever get to drowning in a vanilla-syrup factory accident while still living to tell. If you like this, go for Vanilia or Hanae Mori. TS

Fantasy (Britney Spears) ★ ★ *toxic vanillic* $
(I once had a fantasy of meeting Britney at a party, explaining the principles of feminism to her, and watching her thereafter dedicating her life to fighting the scourge of child brides around the world, or something like that. End non sequitur.) This is like spraying Glade on strawberry-flavored cotton candy. Liberace would have found the packaging a bit over the top. TS

Farnesiana (Caron) ★ *floral woody* $$$
I had the good fortune to smell a bit of perfectly preserved vintage Farnesiana from the bottle of a collector friend, who let me dip the corner of my silk scarf into it. For the next week I could smell it: a sweet, almond-vanilla floral, both powdery and fresh, with a chilly anisic whiteness—heliotropin and aubepine (mimosa and hawthorn). It was extraordinary because the smell itself felt tender and delicate, but it was also extremely loud. It's as if something that should only be heard quietly were amplified to stadium volume levels—like when the squeaking of fingers over guitar frets gets the close-mike treatment and starts to sound like percussion. A few years ago, Farnesiana transformed into a

pastry gourmand, all marzipan and custard. Then it transformed again: thinner, rosier, a kind of pale violet with wood glue. Indications are that Richard Fraysse is allowed to do these reformulations in the name of EU restrictions. I don't know what this is, but it's not Farnesiana. Fraysse should smell Parfums de Nicolaï's Mimosaique and recalibrate his notion of what this is supposed to be. TS

Fashion Avenue (Bond No. 9) ★ ★ *mimosa shampoo* $$$
A green, fresh mimosa (I'm always sure that some passionate botanist will phone me up on the subject of one of these skeletal florals one day and howl, "You moron, it's obviously linden," and my career will end, or something like that), pleasant with a clean musk drydown, but curiously functional for the price. TS

F by Ferragamo pour Homme (Salvatore Ferragamo) ★ ★ ★
pepper fougère $
Apple-lavender top note, then a quick change to a peppery-green drydown. Uncomplicated, cheap, but basically works. TS

Féerie (Van Cleef & Arpels) ★ ★ ★ *sweet berry* $$$
The gleefully tacky blue bottle topped with a steel Tinker Bell fairy on a twig clearly states the intention of VC&A to compete with Paris Hilton. They win this round, since the fragrance, a fruitier and less chypre variation of So Pretty, is a better trashy fruit scent than any of hers. But it seems a Pyrrhic victory. TS

Felanilla (Parfumerie Générale) ★ ★ ★ ★ *banana iris* $$$
The easy, straightforward manner of PG compositions is too often wasted on fragrances that are pleasant enough but have been done to death, in a territory bounded by Serge Lutens, L'Artisan Parfumeur, and Diptyque. But when focused, PG is hard to beat: they push the boat out and embark on novel fragrance ideas that work both immediately and durably. Felanilla embodies one such idea. No doubt

helped by the new, cheaper Biolandes iris that's coming onstream, they have discovered a very clever and, it would seem, entirely novel way of making iris smile: banana. An empirical law of perfumery is that materials will agree if they have a facet in common. Only the truly smart would have noticed that there is a potato-like, rooty, astringent aspect to slightly unripe bananas (more peel than flesh) that was just begging to meet up with iris but too shy to ask. Felanilla feels like a formula that virtually wrote itself: iris, said banana, wood, saffron, and vanilla, all applied with a light touch and an eye on a faded shade of custard yellow that suggests a well-worn tropical silk shirt. Unique and remarkable. LT

Féminité du Bois (Serge Lutens) ★ ★ ★ ★ *woody fruity* $ $
First, the bad news: FdB has been reformulated, no doubt for EU regulatory reasons, and it is unquestionably different. Now the good news: the reformulation is very skillful and preserves the form of the original except in the top notes, when smelled close up, and in a thinner drydown. That may not be good enough for all the *aficiòn*, but I for one feel it is better to have this than nothing. The original FdB was of pivotal importance, both to Lutens's artistic program and to perfumery in general. Caron's Parfum Sacré had gone some way in that direction, but FdB was the first fragrance to demonstrate exactly what its name conveys; i.e., that a woody fragrance could be made as feminine as any. Lutens relied on exceptional talent: both Pierre Bourdon and Christopher Sheldrake are credited with FdB, and Bourdon's original structure was apparently inspired by Lutens's beloved Morocco. The candied-fruit and wood structure, at once transparent, rich, warm and almost gaudy, was a masterstroke. Its versatility was demonstrated by the "Bois de" variations that followed, as well as by Dolce Vita three years later. It is a crying shame that regulatory pressure is destroying so much of fragrance's already fragile heritage. Until the industry fights back (don't hold your breath) or crowds take to the Paris streets bearing banners that say "Mitsouko" (keep breathing), there is little we can do about it. LT

Femme (Rochas) ★ ★ ★ *woody floral* $ $

Some deep principle seems to be at work here (see Arpège): when you cheapen the formula of a big classic feminine, it morphs into a masculine. This suggests that (1) boys' fragrances have always been cheap stuff and (2) girls have expensive tastes. Either way, Femme, now a shadow of its former self, has grown a mustache and might as well be called Homme. That said, nice woody floral with lactonic notes. LT

Ferré (Gianfranco Ferré) ★ ★ ★ ★ *aldehydic floral* $ $

Five years after doing Iris Poudre for Frédéric Malle, Pierre Bourdon polished the idea for Ferré. Slightly more vegetal than the Malle fragrance, Ferré is nevertheless a close match: powdery, woody-sweet in a violet way, and slightly too bright, like overexposed flash photographs. TS

Le Feu d'Issey (Issey Miyake) ★ ★ ★ ★ ★ *milky rose* $ $

The surprise effect of Le Feu d'Issey is total. Smelling it is like pressing the play button on a frantic video clip of unconnected objects that fly past one's nose at warp speed: fresh baguette, lime peel, clean wet linen, shower soap, hot stone, salty skin, even a fleeting touch of vitamin B pills, and no doubt a few other UFOs that this reviewer failed to catch the first few times. Whoever did this has that rarest of qualities in perfumery, a sense of humor. Bravo to those who did not recoil in horror at something so original and agreed to bottle it and sell it, but shame also, since they lost their nerve and discontinued it before it caught on. Whether you wear it or not, if you can find it, it should be in your collection as a reminder that perfume is, among other things, the most portable form of intelligence. LT

Feuille de Réglisse (Parfums 06130) ★ ★ *five spice* $ $ $

Though it rests on a crude, synthetic muguet-jasmine base, there is an interesting idea of five-spice powder here: that magical mixture of star anise, Sichuan peppercorns, fennel, cinnamon, and cloves that perfumes Chinese braised pork shoulders. A good idea that deserves better execution. TS

Feuilles de Tabac (Miller Harris) ★ ★ ★ *leaf brown* $$$
A warm-woody fragrance in the manner of the first Aramis, only more natural. The drydown is a bit screechy, and the balance between sweetness and sibilant woody ambers a touch precarious. LT

Fever (LUSH) ★ ★ ★ *rose jasmine* $
Once the powerful odor of cocoa butter subsides, since for some reason LUSH has chosen a carrier oil for its perfume solids that makes it difficult to discern the actual fragrance, Fever turns into a perfectly nice, old fashioned powdery floral of rose and jasmine, a little boring perhaps, but certainly okay for virginal types who keep lace-trimmed diaries. TS

F for Fascinating (Salvatore Ferragamo) ★ ★ *citrus jasmine* $
A poor excuse for adding yet more glass, shrink-wrap, and cardboard to the world. An undistinguished, wan citrus floral, like a homeopathic dose of Miss Dior Chérie. TS

Fig Tea (Parfums de Nicolaï) ★ *fruit nightmare* $
When I smelled Fig Tea years ago at New London Pharmacy in New York, I staggered away spitting curses. Since some of de Nicolaï's fragrances have been slightly reformulated to lighten their touch, I thought it might have been improved. No. TS

Figue Amère (Miller Harris) ★ ★ *bitter green* $$$
No-holds-barred galbanum-isoquinolines accord, as green-bitter as it gets. Of nostalgic interest to the *afición* insofar as it replicates nicely the first five minutes of the original Vent Vert. Except that after that nothing much happens. LT

Figuier (Heeley) ★ ★ ★ ★   *fig hologram* $$$
I've never been crazy about fig perfumes (Premier Figuier, Philosykos, etc.), though I will readily admit that the surprise effect is wonderful and that they are historically important in clearing the way for later watercolor gardens; e.g., Elléna's work for Hermès. In my opinion, earlier figs were only made wearable by being overly perfumy and losing some of the starkness of the fruit. No such thing here: Figuier is as real as it gets and as a result probably better as a room spray than as a fragrance. The weird green-camphoraceous-catty note of oximes (stemone? buchu?) is as clear as a bell, together with a dusty, earthy, geosmin note and the sweetness of the fruit's red flesh, partly due to the strange habanero note also found in Un Jardin Après la Mousson. There is no better fig reconstruction out there. A masterwork of hyperrealist perfumery. LT

Fiore d'Ambra (Profumum) ★   *nauseating amber* $$$$
Profumum does Ambre Sultan. Beware. LT

Fiori di Capri (Carthusia) ★ ★ ★   *indolic carnation* $$
Notable mostly for a massive dose of indole that will make you wonder if you stepped in something, FdC is a well-crafted, zaftig, but not very interesting sweetened floral, heavy and a little too simple for my taste. TS

Fire Island (Bond No. 9) ★ ★ ★ ★   *airy jasmine* $$$
Laurice Rahmé, the feisty, savvy businesswoman behind upstart niche firm Bond No. 9, asked the perfumer Michel Almairac to give her the scent of the old Ambre Solaire suntan lotion—the reference nostalgic smell of French beaches—so she could then hawk it in association with beaches in her adopted home of New York. I myself, an American born and bred, have no memories of French beaches yet nevertheless find this expansive, simple smell ideally beachy: crisp salt spray, creamy white florals, no complications, mere happiness. TS

First (Van Cleef & Arpels) ★ ★ ★ ★ *aldehydic animalic* $$
Before Jean-Claude Elléna caught a severe case of minimalism and never recovered, he engineered full-figured French florals in the most baroque high style, as here in First (1976). It's essentially a dark variation on Joy— and therefore less joyful. In contrast to Elléna's later style of doing everything with less, this is everything done with more: more aldehydes, more patchouli, more animalic notes, including the barnyard phenolic smells of narcissus and castoreum, extending deep into the quality drydown. It smells rich and humorless, an ideal perfume for intimidation. TS

First Love (Van Cleef & Arpels) ★ ★ ★ *floral oriental* $$
This flanker to VC&A's excellent First is initially a study in dissonance, proposing to pair a sharp aldehydic floral with a powdery vanilla-amber oriental. The two halves feel at first like two unrelated perfumes layered together. Slowly, they drift into a nicely dry, nutty middle space, colored with the diffuse pink light of milky-fruity lactones, where everything manages to smell good in a soothingly old-fashioned way, but less interesting than you might have expected. TS

Five O'Clock au Gingembre (Serge Lutens) ★ ★ ★
salty gingerbread $$$
Classic gingerbread is dense with honey, but Miel de Bois proved that too much of that in a fragrance smells like the men's loo at a bar on Friday night. Instead, here a pleasantly salty, meaty note (lily? civet?) lends a spiced-tea composition weight and saves it from smelling like Christmas-themed room spray, before it settles for the smoky vanillic smell of plain benzoin. TS

Fleur (Floris) ★ ★ *fruity peony* $$
Why does a venerable 270-year-old perfumery need a standard-issue, modern, loud citrus peony? Trashy and brash in the usual way. TS

Fleur de Cabotine (Grès) ★ ★ *floral fougère* $
Doing a "fleur" of the disastrous Cabotine is like making a fragrance inspired by Karl Rove's nickname. The result, though, is far funnier than the intent: basically Brut overlaid with Glade. I see no reason why trendy guys could not wear this to great advantage. LT

Une Fleur de Cassie (Frédéric Malle) ★ ★ ★ ★ *symphonic floral* $$$
Another Dominique Ropion masterwork. This is perfumery at its most symphonic, an accord so rich, shimmering, and complex that I defy anyone to come to a firm conclusion on it in less than a week. This fragrance makes most other stuff look amateurish: the top and heart notes constantly shift between floral, spicy, smoky, herbaceous (thyme), and powdery (almond) in a manner reminiscent of the chord modulations in Richard Strauss's tone poems, an endless dance of seamless color changes. A perfume like this is not merely the result of a good idea. It is meticulously worked out like a clock, every wheel clicking precisely into place to give the right effect at the right time, and all the machinery hidden from view beneath an unruffled, serene face. LT

Fleur de Liane (L'Artisan Parfumeur) ★ ★ *melon floral* $$
If you missed the melon-aquatic floral trend when it made the rounds the first time, L'Artisan Parfumeur offers you another chance to experience it in all its howling power. This type of scent has always been a little like a perky neighbor who cheers you up if you encounter her once, but after a couple of minutes of shrill exclamations starts to wear on your nerves. Impressive duration; impossible to wash off. Very similar to old aquatic masculines like New West and Kenzo pour Homme. TS

Fleur de Narcisse 2006 (L'Artisan Parfumeur) ★ ★ ★ *hay farm* $$$
Last time I looked, Laboratoires Monique Rémy in Grasse had cornered the world's narcissus market and produced a fabulously expensive absolute collected from wildflowers in France's Massif Central mountains.

This smells very much like it, a curious, rich farm-like smell of hay mixed in with fresh-floral and animalic notes. Interestingly, the European Union label bears a long list of materials, not all of which appear to be contained in narcissus absolute, so this is clearly a composition. It doesn't last very long on the skin and is interesting more as a fleshed-out wonder of nature than as a proper fragrance. Could be used as a warm, vastly overpriced tobacco-like masculine. LT

A Fleur de Peau (Keiko Mecheri) ★ ★ ★ *leather oriental* $$$
An old-fashioned leather, like Tabac Blond or Cuir de Russie, but without the plush or the excitement: in other words, a dry birch-tar with a balsamic backdrop, nice but not as good a modern leather as Lancôme's reconstructed Cuir. TS

Fleur de Rocaille (Caron) ★ ★ *lactonic floral* $$
For incomprehensible reasons, Caron has a fragrance named Fleurs de Rocaille and one called Fleur de Rocaille, which are pronounced exactly the same. The singular Fleur is a lactonic peony, if you can imagine, like the old Fleurs but with the freshness of synthetic lily-of-the-valley materials, and a thinner patchouli-woody base. Not all that pleasant. TS

Fleur de Thé Rose Bulgare (Creed) ★ ★ ★ *bright rose* $$$
Unquestionably smells like expensive rose extracts, i.e., not at all like live roses, more wine- and liqueur-like. Less complicated but of vastly higher quality than most contemporary synthetic roses, with a nice woody drydown. A perfectly good alternative to legions of modern air-headed florals. LT

Fleur d'Oranger 2007 (L'Artisan Parfumeur) ★ ★ ★ ★
orange blossom $$$$
One hates to encourage gimmickry—limited editions always bring to mind Hummel figurines. The fragrance's claim to spotlight one year's

harvest of a particular material, in this case the orange blossom output of a single producer in Tunisia, seems to draw a parallel to wine, though Fleur d'Oranger uses several materials, while wine should be grape juice, period. In accordance with the high concept, each bottle costs an astonishing $295 for 100 milliliters of eau de parfum. Nevertheless, this is pretty, bright, and far better than other soliflores like Jo Malone's or Serge Lutens's, with impressive radiance and lasting power. I would prefer more of a complex composition to showcase the material, like Institut Très Bien's Cologne à l'Italienne, but if you're mad about orange blossom and can't get rid of money fast enough, this is the one. TS

Fleur d'Oranger 27 (Le Labo) ★ *cologne ripoff* $$$$
A boring cologne at $50 for 15 milliliters, which according to my calculations is $1 per squirt. The French are known for their wry humor. LT

Fleur du Mâle (Jean Paul Gaultier) ★ ★ ★ *powdery fougère* $
This cheerful, clean powdery masculine smells of Irish Spring soap, baby bum, and shaving cream, a scent so evocative of bathroom rituals, you can nearly see the white tile and the steamed mirror. It feels like parody, but it sort of works. As with the original Le Mâle, the nude-male-torso bottle seems intended to limit its use to solely the very gay or the imperturbably straight. TS

Fleur du Matin (Miller Harris) ★ ★ ★ *garden floral* $$$
Pleasant, natural-smelling floral, beginning with a refreshing but fleeting galbanum top note like an homage to Vent Vert, followed by a moment of citrus as if it intends to become a cologne. Instead, it ends up a soft bouquet in the unfussy but unexciting English style. TS

Fleurissimo (Creed) ★ ★ ★ *floral bouquet* $$$
A big floral-aldehydic bouquet, a joyless Joy. Get the real thing: it costs the same and smells better, and you won't have to stare at Creed's hideous packaging. LT

Fleur Oriental (Miller Harris) ★ ★ ★   *joss stick* $$$
As in most MH products, more cod-French, this time with a spelling mistake. A nice, powdery oriental in the mini-Shalimar manner, though a bit thin in the drydown. LT

Fleurs de Bulgarie (Creed) ★ ★ ★   *real rose* $$$
FdB perfectly illustrates the fact that the perfumer's job consists as much in hiding the faults of the raw materials she uses as in bringing out their strengths. While unquestionably made with quality roses, FdB seems to be a compendium of all the rose off-notes, from metallic to musty, that make rose oil so frustratingly hard to use. LT

Fleurs de Citronnier (Serge Lutens) ★ ★   *failed cologne* $$$
A dry, woody-soapy neroli accord that feels like an unfinished eau de cologne. LT

Fleurs de Nuit (Badgley Mischka) ★ ★ ★ ★   *sweet jasmine* $$
Their first time out, Badgley Mischka unexpectedly perfected the much-maligned fruity-floral genre, and this time around they've warmed up the aloof crispness of the Beyond Paradise muguet-jasmine with a dash of caramelized sugar (ethylmaltol). Nothing new, but terrifically pretty—not the bright morning of BP, not the glorious sunset of J'Adore, and not the drama of the name's promised night, but a pleasant, golden afternoon. TS

Fleurs de Rocaille (Caron) ★ ★ ★ (★ ★)   *carnation floral* $$
Caron in its heyday was a curious outfit, capable of producing some of the starkest, most humorous fragrances of all time, such as Royal Bain de Champagne, Narcisse Noire and Tabac Blond, aimed at the sort of Art Deco Amazon who rode Pegasus to work. Mysteriously, though, it could also come up with Fleurs de Rocaille and Nuit de Noël, masterly but staid affairs that bring to mind well-to-do ladies outside the church after Sunday service, all voilettes and pillbox hats. Fleurs de Rocaille is

a floral carnation affair so prim and proper it feels almost disapproving and makes you check your shirt is not spilling out of your trousers. Needless to say, it was a huge success. My landlady in Paris when I was a student opined that there were two perfume houses in Paris, Caron and Guerlain. Guerlain, she said, was for *cocottes* (kept women), while Caron was for duchesses. To this day I wonder which, the reckless Oriane de Guermantes or her workaday successor Madame Verdurin, she had in mind. LT

Fleurs de Rocaille was once the reference lactonic floral, the milky, ambery bouquet of good things in modest proportions that any polite girl would be happy to wear to an event where her manners would be judged. Based on the most recent (2007) sample, it's now simply an entirely soapy affair from start to finish, much less lactonic, and converging on the sour rose Richard Fraysse loves so much. TS

Fleurs des Comores (Maître Parfumeur et Gantier) ★ ★ ★ ★
jasmine vanilla $ $ $
When Laporte left L'Artisan Parfumeur in 1988 and founded MPG, he immediately set out to replicate part of the collection he had so brilliantly devised over the preceding twelve years. Fleurs des Comores is his Vanilia II, a bit greener, with more of the heavenly overripe-banana note of ylang and less candyfloss, but basically the same great idea. It is a credit to his intelligence and hands-on approach that the press release, for once, instead of serving up complete swill, tells it like it is: "Evokes summer evenings and suntanned skin." Precisely. LT

Fleurs de Sel (Miller Harris) ★ ★ ★ ★ *seaside bouquet* $ $ $
The saline note in perfumery is elusive. I have come across it in a vetiver context (Virgilio) and in various marine-like oakmoss notes, as well as in pure ambergris tincture. Interestingly, Lyn Harris claims that in this fragrance it is due to ambrette seed musk, which in retrospect does have a weird celery-like salty feel. Whatever the origin, it works beautifully in

this elegant, highly original herbaceous-marine composition. This cannot have been an easy perfume to compose: all the notes are quite distinct and singing in harmony only through clever, careful balance. Further evidence of Lyn Harris's growing skill and ambition, and her best perfume so far. LT

Fleurs d'Ombre Jasmin Lilas (Jean-Charles Brosseau) ★
cheap floral $
A cheap and crude jasmine-lilac affair, ideal for what the professionals call air care. LT

Fleurs d'Ombre Ombre Bleue (Jean-Charles Brosseau) ★ ★
cheap floral $
Sometimes less is more, and sometimes less is less. The Brosseau range looks discounted from day one and smells like it too. This cheap abstract-floral accord smells of salicylates and synthetic wood, thereby achieving a kind of hot insulation effect reminiscent of the smell of large, valve-powered radios with a magic eye up front. If the names Allouis, Hilversum, and Kalundborg mean anything to you, you're in for a bit of unintended nostalgia. LT

Fleurs d'Ombre Rose (Jean-Charles Brosseau) ★ ★
grapefruit floral $
A cheap-smelling but cheerful citrus, of the style usually labeled "pink-grapefruit," which evolves rapidly into a repellent candied-orange smell with no relation to rose. Brosseau has a much-loved dark, powdery, liqueur-like rose called Ombre Rose, and this is 180 degrees from that. TS

Fleurs d'Ombre Violette-Menthe (Jean-Charles Brosseau) ★ ★
scented glue $
I thought this would smell like those square Choward's Violet Mints that come in grape-purple foil and taste perversely inedible. I love those.

Instead, it smells like fruity-scented glue, or that intense kelly green liquid soap you find only in public washrooms. TS

Fleurs d'Oranger (Serge Lutens) ★ ★ ★ *medicinal jasmine* $ $ $
Lutens chose to intensify the medicinal and indolic smells of orange blossom above all else, reminding me of the black, treacly loquat syrup my mother used to give me when I coughed. A touch of savory-sweaty cumin makes the whole thing seem smothering and unsettling, like the exhalation of a poorly ventilated alleyway in some unidentified Southeast Asian city. On skin, it eventually settles for a light jasmine drydown. TS

Flora Bella (Lalique) ★ ★ ★ ★ *milky metallic* $ $ $
You could easily overlook this sleepy little greenish violet floral on a bed of pretty fabric-softener–type musks, except for a few notable features: a dreamy, dense, milky note, which reminds me of a Filipino dessert of sweetened condensed milk poured over shaved ice; the sharp metallic sheen of helional, which LT has described elsewhere as smelling like a "sucked spoon"; and a surprising long-distance radiance without force, which seems to be Bertrand Duchaufour's stock in trade even when working in a mild-mannered, no-surprises style such as this. Silver, chilled cream, and a far-reaching transparent glow: it should have been called Luna Piena instead. TS

Floret (Antonia's Flowers) ★ ★ *sweet floral* $ $
Antonia's Flowers' first two fragrances (the eponymous AF and this one) are based on "living flower" technology, the name used by fragrance company IFF for sampling the air around a flower, analyzing the hell out of it, and then trying to re-create the mix that will give the same air around a person. This one is a reconstitution of sweet pea, and it feels like sweet pea after a nasty accident followed by reconstructive surgery. What woman is camp enough to want to smell of sweet peas anyway? LT

Florissa (Floris) ★ ★ ★ *aldehydic floral* $$

A competent aldehydic floral with a mock-orange note. Dull but pleasant. LT

Flower (Cynthia Rowley) ★ ★ ★ *big lily* $

A very competent, accurate lily soliflore, complete with that weird salami note that makes lilies smell so oddly appetizing. If Firmenich were to market a lily base to save perfumers the trouble of reinventing the chastity belt, this would be it. LT

Flower (Kenzo) ★ ★ ★ ★ *melon woody* $$

As George Santayana told us before we forgot who he was, those who cannot remember the past are condemned to repeat it. Yet sadly, of all the arts, perfume is the most amnesiac, not because its history is unworthy of note but because it's impossible to transmit: it doesn't photocopy well or burn to CD, and you can't hum or quote it. While most young painters have seen at least poster prints in the mall of Michelangelo's Adam, most young perfumers have probably never smelled the original Emeraude. Of course, Alberto Morillas almost certainly knew Caron's Royal Bain de Champagne by heart when he replicated it and added a splash of hedione to make Flower, but it seems nobody else knew, least of all me, until one day LT pointed out what it was and I gave a good solid smack to my forehead. Royal Bain de Champagne, a debonair, sweet, powdery wood with giddy flourishes of melon, muguet, and heliotropin, had suavity and humor, like a tap dance in a tux, the perfume equivalent of a Gershwin tune ("Fascinating Rhythm" would do). We are forgiven for not realizing Flower was a remake, however, since Royal Bain de Caron (the Champagne brand police objected to the original name) hasn't smelled like itself in a while. In effect, like those bronze Roman copies of ancient Greek sculptures, Flower manages to preserve a classic on the sly, long after the original was melted for scrap. TS

Flowerbomb (Viktor & Rolf) ★ *sugary floral* $$$
Post-Angel sweet-tooth fantasia that smells like a shop where you buy gummies by the pound. Someone will object, "But it's rosy!" True. TS

Flower by Kenzo Fleurs d'Hiver/Winter Flower (Kenzo) ★ ★ ★ ★ *mimosa amber* $$
The original, successful, and much-acclaimed Flower was a modern, less euphoric reinterpretation of Caron's Royal Bain de Champagne, a melony mimosa with a sweet, powdery background. I was initially a little taken aback by the blatant similarity, but then Caron screwed everything up by reformulating, which means that Caron founder Ernest Daltroff's idea lives on in the Kenzo, and only there. This winter variation works by rotating the original in odor space, so that foreground becomes background and vice versa. FKWF is now a powdery oriental with a mimosa facet, and the combination is surprisingly successful and well balanced, done without skimping on formula price. Nice work. LT

Flower Le Parfum (Kenzo) ★ ★ ★ *coffee vanilla* $$
Masquerading as simply a parfum extrait version of the original Flower, Le (Soi-Disant) Parfum is an entirely new fragrance, keeping the intensely powdery, woody-heliotropin section of the original but swapping out all of its beautiful coral-pink fruity florals for a dose of coffee and more vanilla. Now twice as heavy and mistakenly serious, it's handsome, but a little bit like a Jim Carrey film recast with James Earl Jones. TS

Flower Oriental (Kenzo) ★ ★ ★ *patchouli oriental* $$
Much like Hermès Eau des Merveilles, Flower Oriental is a strange modern creature, a heavy, old-fashioned woody oriental given amplified radiance via the unexpected floral freshness of hedione and the transparent herbal-woody fuzz of Iso E Super. This sheer cloud of modern effects fails to mask the bombast of the main event: one hell of a patchouli amber, to make even hardened head-shop hippies feel overwhelmed. TS

Folavril (Annick Goutal) ★ ★ ★ *citrus fruity* $$$
Interesting how a largely natural composition can smell so much like fabric softener. Might make a cheerful masculine. TS

Une Folie de Rose (Parfums de Rosine) ★ ★ ★ *aldehydic chypre* $$
The madness of this rose begins with aldehydes, like a big-boned awkward cousin to Chant d'Arômes, but grows up unexpectedly into the leathery patchouli-oakmoss of Miss Balmain. TS

Fool for Love (Ego Facto) ★ *spice floral* $$
All the mad luxury of five Yardley soaps at once. TS

Forever Elizabeth (Elizabeth Taylor) ★ *stale wreath* $
A name that sounds like a conclusion to a funeral eulogy applied to a chemical floral so thin and spare it may soon get one. LT

(For you)/parfum trouvé (Miller et Bertaux) ★ ★ ★
fruitcake cedar $$$
What could the name mean? *Parfum trouvé* means "found perfume," which makes sense, since this is basically a lighter version of Féminité du Bois with less depth and persistence. The *For you* leads me to believe that somebody's beloved was wild about FdB but couldn't find it because of Shiseido's incomprehensibly limited distribution. TS

Fou d'Absinthe (L'Artisan Parfumeur) ★ ★ *wood boring* $$$
Absinthe (wormwood) became all the rage a few years back because a sanitized form of the liqueur was made legal again after a seventy-five-year ban, whereupon it quickly turned out to be neither more nor less harmful or interesting than its anisic substitute, pastis. This fashion eventually percolated to perfume, where wormwood had been dormant for decades. It has a resinous smell of only scant interest, and FdA, despite a skillful composition, fails to rise to more than a herbaceous woody *Gemisch,* a sort of cheerful Paco Rabanne pour Homme. Let us

now move on to the unfairly neglected hops absolute, with its vegetarian animalic note, etc. . . . . LT

Fougère Bengale (Parfum d'Empire) ★ ★ ★ ★ *spicy lavender* $$
If this is a fougère, my local Indian restaurant is a florist. This is an intense, saturated reinterpretation of the lavender-curry (helichrysum) accord of Eau Noire, delicious from a distance and a little loud up close, but overall very pleasant. LT

Fracas (Robert Piguet) ★ ★ ★ ★ ★ *butter tuberose* $$$
A friend once explained to me how Ferrari achieves that gorgeous red: first paint the car silver, then six coats of red, then a coat of transparent pink varnish. Germaine Cellier would have approved. Her masterpiece Fracas, after going through a threadbare patch in the eighties, was revived by a U.S. outfit and spruced up to a quality approximating the original as far as possible, with the usual Cellier caveats of disappeared bases (see Bandit). To my nose, what makes Fracas great is a wonderful buttery note up top, which I attribute to chamomile, and a nice bread-like iris touch in the drydown. Pink and silver, with tuberose red in between. LT

Fraîche Passiflore (Maître Parfumeur et Gantier) ★ ★ ★
passion fruit $$$
Tropical fruit not only can be taken as evidence for the existence of a God but can raise the question of whether there might be several gods. Passion fruit and mango clearly hail from a different celestial continent than do peaches and pears. Questions for science to answer: How do fruits know when they're in exotic places? Who taught them to samba? No doubt the Fruity Genome Project will tell all. In the meantime, for the perfumer, exotic fruits pose a thorny problem: what makes a lychee, passion fruit, or mango plausible is the judicious admixture of foul-smelling things like dimethyl sulfide and other sulfur chemicals. Add too much, and you end up with durian; add just enough, and the stuff is

gone in seconds. Accordingly, the first five minutes of Fraîche Passiflore are heavenly, and the remainder merely nice. LT

Fraîcheur Muskissime (Maître Parfumeur et Gantier) ★ ★ ★
citrus musk $ $ $
Very clean citrus musk, intended as a feminine but more like an Edwardian masculine, quiet, refined, a touch perverse in a suitably low-key way, which brings to mind Beatrice Campbell's famous comment "Does it really matter what these affectionate people do—so long as they don't do it in the streets and frighten the horses!" LT

Frangipane (Chantecaille) ★ ★ ★ *woody floral* $ $
The Chantecaille scents are essentially light floral waters for women in beige lipstick and straightened hair. This is the most wearable of the lot, a sweet, woody-vanillic orange blossom that smells slightly bitter, like dilute chocolate, with a mildly off-kilter cucumber note lurking inside. Blandly pretty and just interesting enough to stand out without disturbing anyone, like a young socialite who takes a Latin dance course and ever after is known as the daring one in her set. TS

Frangipani Absolute (Ormonde Jayne) ★ ★ ★ ★ *fresh floral* $ $ $
One variety of the tropical lei flower known as frangipani smells like jasmine, another like peach. Ormonde Jayne's version finds a sunny halfway point between the two and miraculously manages to maintain a seamless impression of just-picked dewy freshness and intensity for hours, from the burst of its lemony start through its long, cool cedary drydown. TS

Frankincense and Myrrh (Czech & Speake) ★ ★ ★
frankincense myrrh $ $
The combination of these two resinoids of biblical fame is always interesting, because when smelled in solution as opposed to smoke, they seem to cancel each other's liturgical tendencies and come across as slightly dustier and dirtier, with a lemony angle to the mvyrrh and a

musky side to the incense. This very nice and very natural fragrance, for once, does exactly what it says on the can. LT

French Cancan (Caron) ★ *sweet floral* $$$
The story I've heard is that Caron created French Cancan to appeal to the American perfume buyer. On the basis of this insipid powdery sweet floral, we can assume they didn't think much of her. TS

French Connection Fragrance (FCUK) ★ ★ *citrus floral* $
I was told this was the fragrance formerly known as FCUK Her, presumably renamed because it wasn't that funny after all. This is a nice if short-lived eau de cologne in the lemon verbena direction. TS

French Lime Blossom Cologne (Jo Malone) ★ ★ ★ *green floral* $$
Pleasantly sweet-herbaceous little thing, unpretentious and agreeable. LT

French Lover (Frédéric Malle) ★ ★ ★ ★ (★ ★) *bitter green* $$$
Sold as Bois d'Orage in the United States
Perhaps the most disturbing and at once most interesting aspect of the smell of cigars is a sour, sharp note particularly evident in cold, half-smoked cheap cigarillos. I am not sure what molecule is responsible for it, though I suspect a pyrazine. This smell sits for me at a sort of vanishing point of olfactory perspective, or more exactly a high-pitched end of the smell spectrum, where all smells ring hard and dry like the rightmost three keys on a grand piano. In this region, provided it is smelled at low levels, cold-cigar smell feels the same as galbanum and some woody ambers, especially the wonderful amberketal. Bourdon has clearly figured this out. FL is brilliantly constructed from materials whose intersection lies in that weird region: incense, tree moss, galbanum, and pepper. Like it or not, FL smells like yesterday's shirt when you pick it up from the floor and sniff it—stale smoke, dried sweat, and all—wondering whether it will do for another day. Clearly, the French Lover needs a woman (and a washer-dryer) in his life. LT

I can't see all that for the eight-story-high woody amber standing in the way. TS

Fresh (Dunhill) ★ ★ *green woody* $ $
A very bare violet-leaf masculine with a slight smell of wood glue. TS

Fresh Patchouli (Jovan) ★ ★ ★ *banana patchouli* $
Patchouli is filled out here in two clever ways: first, its fruity-wine quality gets help from a banana-like floral note (ylang-ylang or jasmine?), and second, the fresh, woody, green side of patchouli is emphasized with wonderful notes of cut grass and leaves. Better and cleverer by half than the dozens of heavy-handed, head-shop–redolent niche variations on the theme. TS

Friends Men (Moschino) ★ ★ ★ *woody citrus* $
Interesting, fresh, fizzy-grapefruit composition in the manner of DKNY Women, but less striking. Without great ambitions but altogether agreeable and crisp, with a pleasant powdery drydown. LT

Frolic (Origins) ★ ★ ★ *fresh floral* $
It is hard to fault the execution of this *tutti fiori* little thing, which takes chemical-fresh, powdery cuteness to a level of competence it probably does not deserve. For twelve-year-olds, or to spray in the toilet. LT

Fruit de Bois (Jean-Charles Brosseau) ★ ★ *citrus woody* $
Incredibly cheap-smelling but passable lemon-soap scent. TS

Fuel for Life (Diesel) ★ ★ ★ ★ *fruity herbaceous* $ $
Cavallier's brilliant but unwearable herbs-from-Mars accord from L'Eau Bleue lives on in a completely different form in this fragrance, mixed with a weird, and very Japanese, camphoraceous-fruity idea first seen in Diptyque's Oyedo. This courageous, inventive, beautifully crafted fragrance will probably not do well because it fails to hit any of the known

buttons that would make its intended audience come back for more. Nevertheless, hope springs eternal. Full marks to Thierry Wasser and Annick Ménardo for producing a gem of modern perfume architecture. LT

I personally believe that this terrifically weird, left-of-center fruity has just the right balance of trendiness (mango sweetness) and brains (the funky herbal angle, the Angel-like camphoraceous feel) to appeal to the hipster girls that Diesel is after. It has the benefit of seeming both clever and dopey, the Lolita Lempicka effect. What's not to like? TS

Fuel for Life Men (Diesel) ★ ★ ★ ★ *modern fougère* $ $
The name sounds like a lottery for guys trying to ignore Prius ads, and the bottle, wrapped in a zippered, stitched distressed-canvas bag, conjures up third-world labor making frivolous objects for the idle rich. After all that, the fragrance comes as a pleasant surprise: it is none other than a brilliantly inventive variation on the purest, most classical fougère theme as seen in Brut and Canoe, enlivened with a sweet-woody-amber accord that somehow overlaps perfectly with the original structure without masking it. Nice work. LT

Fuel for Life Unlimited (Diesel) ★ ★ *sour fruity* $ $
The first two Diesels were pretty creative in a light, whimsical sort of way. This one is much less good and smells cheap and confused rather than cheerful. Why not abolish flankers? LT

Fuel for Men (Donna Karan) ★ ★ ★ ★ *citrus wood* $ $
If you like Cool Water and Allure Homme but hanker after something quieter and more melancholy, this one's for you. The reissue of DK's fragrances is a timely reminder of how far ahead of her time she was and how coherent her aesthetic has always been. Very good indeed. LT

Fumerie Turque (Serge Lutens) ★ ★ ★ *floral leather* $ $ $
With a face like a long-lost cousin of Cuir de Russie, Fumerie Turque

decorates a floral oriental with smoke and leather notes. Though it was once, if we remember right, a rich, delicious fantasy of pipe smoke, it sadly seems to have lost weight and smells more like a pale woody floral with a touch of bonfire than anything else. TS

Fumidus (Profumum) ★ ★ ★ *kippered peat* $$$$
There is a definite need for phenolic, smoky fragrances, and Andy Tauer has magisterially answered it with Lonestar Memories. This one is a peaty vetiver, nice if you don't know any better. LT

Funny! (Moschino) ★ ★ ★ ★ *fruity tea* $
What's funny here is how talent can infuse even the trite with surreptitious joy: in structure, this could have been yet another squeaky-clean fruity floral. But one of the delightful properties of intelligence is its ability to counter dumb questions with smart answers. In response to what was no doubt a witless brief, Antoine Maisondieu has produced a small gem of humor, freshness, and transparency. The core accord is tea with rose, overlaid with grapefruit and blackcurrant. The woody notes of the former balance the sulfuraceous bloom of the latter, and the thing sings like a happy barbershop quartet. LT

Gardenia (Chanel) ★ *not gardenia* $$$
Chanel's boutique fragrances are so good overall that there was a danger of the gods becoming jealous. Gardenia averts this calamity: it is a thoroughly unpleasant, loud airport-toilet floral, very nearly bad enough to grace the ranges of Creed or La Prairie. LT

Gardenia (Elizabeth Taylor) ★ *not gardenia* $
Most gardenias fail to replicate the flower. Some don't even try. This is one. LT

Gardenia (Floris) ★ ★ *not gardenia* $$$
Does not smell in the least like gardenia. Floris makes a big deal of its

unbroken tradition, 277 years and counting. Considering how undistinguished their range is, I would keep quiet about how long they've been at it, like an aristocratic family whose ancestry goes back twelve generations and has produced nothing better in four centuries than a judge at Crufts Dog Show. Hire a good perfumer and get on with it, instead of flogging this nonsense to Italian tourists. LT

Gardenia Passion (Annick Goutal) ★ ★ ★ *vegetal tuberose* $$$
According to Laurice Rahmé, now of Bond No. 9 but the distributor for Annick Goutal in the United States for many years, at one point she exhorted Goutal to create this fragrance for American women, because American women liked gardenias. The trouble was that Goutal reportedly didn't, which is possibly why Gardenia Passion is actually a tuberose, halfheartedly disguised in a veil of bitter green foliage like an uninvited dinner guest in red satin trying to sneak in by crouching behind a fern. TS

Garden Sensuel (Guerlain) ★ ★ *floral bouquet* $$$$
One of the problems of doing perfume in oil is that you have to be careful not to end up smelling like a deep fryer. Aside from the odd canola-oil backdrop, this is a dull, tasteful, quiet floral of no consequence. TS

Garofano (Lorenzo Villoresi) ★ *carnation booze* $$
A soliflore (*garofano* means "carnation") based on a roses-and-cloves–style base with an overwhelming liqueur-like intensity, misguidedly strong and sour, musty in the drydown, hard to imagine wearing. TS

Garrigue (Maître Parfumeur et Gantier) ★ ★ *aromatic fougère* $$
This one smells wrong to me: supposedly created in 1988, it smells very much like a standard-issue late-nineties masculine. I do not recall the earlier version, but I certainly don't think much of this one. LT

Gaultier2 (Jean Paul Gaultier) ★ *sweet milky* $$
G2 pursues a sweet barbershop smell of baby powder, a musk with milky-floral sweetness, yet played in an uncomfortably high register, oily-green smelling and indigestibly antiseptic. I found it nauseating. TS

Génie des Bois (Keiko Mecheri) ★ ★ ★ *green woody* $$$
A peculiar homage to the gorgeous, transparent fruity-cedar oriental of Shiseido's original (and now unavailable) Féminité du Bois, Keiko Mecheri's Génie des Bois attempts to add a huge dose of cut-grass green notes to the structure to freshen things up. It is now a fairly convincing impersonation of fresh cut wood, but not nearly as well balanced or haunting as its inspiration. TS

Ghost Cherish (Ghost) ★ *metallic floral* $
This is what I imagine a compounding accident at Robertet smells like. Q: How did the great Michel Almairac manage to do something this bad? A: He was given an inadequate budget. LT

Ginger Ciao (YOSH) ★ ★ *ylang basil* $$$
Those of a hippie sensibility may have been looking all their lives for this exact heavy-hitting exotic combination of coconut and the rich overripe-banana smell of ylang-ylang, but I find it too dense to be comprehensible, with a bit of funk like re-used cooking oil. A touch of soapy-green basil confuses instead of clarifying. TS

Ginger Essence (Origins) ★ ★ *ginger floral* $$
The soapy-fiery-medicinal smell of ginger root is unusual in feeling simultaneously cooling and warming, but it is apparently hard to sustain. The initial minutes of GE are invigorating, with a rosy background, but unfortunately the whole thing falls flat soon after. Fun while it lasts. TS

Ginger with a Twist (Origins) ★ ★ *ginger lemon* $ $
A takeoff on the original Ginger Essence, this "sparkling body cocktail" manages to intensify the enjoyable ginger effect with a lemony geranium booster. An improvement on the first, but short-lived and still somewhat flat in the drydown. TS

Ginseng NRG "Energy" (Jovan) ★ ★ *sporty soapy* $
Misprint: they meant GNR (generic), specifically in the laundry-soap genre. That said, you could spend a hell of a lot more on masculine fragrance and still get worse than this. TS

Giorgio (Giorgio Beverly Hills) ★ ★ ★ ★ *fruity tuberose* $ $
It is considered polite to deplore the excesses of the eighties (and to trot out Opium, Poison, and Giorgio as exhibits), much as one would disapprove of Tiberius, Caligula, and Nero and welcome the return to sanity represented by the Claudius (nineties) school of fragrance: pinched, mean, and full of sour probity. Yet insofar as perfume is more circuses than bread, I suspect many people harbor a sneaking fondness for the bad old days. Upon revisiting the scoundrels for this guide, I was struck by the fact that the problem was not that one was tired of cheap magic (witness the fact that Angel came later and did very well, and Insolence carries on the tradition), but that a new style was needed. Surprise fades fastest of all the emotions, and what is amazing is how long these contrivances kept us interested. The secret of Giorgio was the discovery of an accord that could stand up to a monstrously powerful tuberose while extending it in interesting directions. Two heroically strong aromachemicals were drafted: one being allyl amyl glycolate, an intense fruity-peppery ester reminiscent of pineapple, and the second a mysterious Schiff's base made between helional (a fresh, almondy, marine material) and methyl anthranilate (the Concord grape smell). Most Schiff's bases are colored because of the carbon-nitrogen double bond, hence Giorgio's bright yellow tinge. The result was a cute, twelve-foot-tall singing canary, at first impossible to ignore, and at length too big to love. But

if any composition embodies what makes half-natural, half-synthetic (i.e., classical) perfumery great, it is Giorgio. LT

Giorgio Red (Giorgio Beverly Hills) ★ ★ ★ *spicy floral* $
Zing! This is a brash, cheerfully cheap, spicy floral in the Paloma Picasso mold, with sour, soapy florals and a rough sketch of a chypre base: not very interesting, but it gives the right impression at a distance if walking by quickly. TS

Givenchy III (Givenchy) ★ ★ ★ ★ *green chypre* $$$
An earthy English friend of mine used to be fond of the expression "good, clean dirt," which she applied to situations that would have sent most people scurrying for tetanus shots. She would have loved this spruced-up reissue of G III: the leather and green chypres all have a curious lived-in quality that gives Bandit, Jolie Madame, and even the rather prim Y a special feel, as if one were simultaneously smelling several successive applications of the same fragrance on fabric without a dry-clean in between. G III was always the brightest and soapiest of the lot, but it still retained a faintly morning-after atmosphere. This long-awaited reissue is a wonderful thing, quite a bit drier and lighter than the original but none the worse for it, and quicker getting into the distinctive strings-only leafy-green heart, which goes on forever. Excellent, and a great masculine too. LT

Givenchy Gentleman (Givenchy) ★ ★ *worn leather* $$
This one has been reformulated. Once great, it is now a sad little woody leather. LT

Givenchy pour Homme Blue Label (Givenchy) ★ ★ ★
Tiger Balsam $$
Very nice Vicks VapoRub–type resinous medicinal start, followed by a woody-spicy drydown ending with a weird hay note. Interesting new style of masculine fragrance in the manner of Miyake's L'Eau Bleue,

though this one is better, more coherent, better built, and not in the least offensive. Smells a bit like you're nursing bronchitis by chewing herbal cough drops. LT

Glamour (Moschino) ★ ★ *sour floral* $
Michael Edwards classifies this one as "Floral Oriental (Fresh Citrus Fruity)," which is the perfumery equivalent of what a political wit once described as "extreme center." These are fragrances designed to appeal to the fondness for Kylie Minogue that inhabits all of us: small, cute, brightly colored, pert, and not particularly memorable. LT

Gloria (Cacharel) ★ ★ ★ *amber rose* $$
A sugary fresh rose with impressive radiance and a biscuity, almond-woody drydown. Very competently put together, but dopey. TS

Glow (J-Lo) ★ ★ ★ *metal floral* $
What's Glow about? "Capturing angelic, glistening sensuality," goes the blurb. More prosaically, J-Lo herself adds, "Something that feels like you just came out of the shower and you are the sexiest person in the world," which in my experience works best if you were that when you went in. That said, it is a nice, unpretentious squeaky-clean floral, with that weird sucked-silver-spoon sheen of helional, perfectly fine on a well-scrubbed sixteen-year-old. LT

Glow After Dark (J-Lo) ★ ★ *floral oriental* $
An AngelAllureChanceCocoMademoiselle clone of no particular interest, save that it also comes as a solid perfume in a pendant. Solid per-fume is a good idea and should be more widely available. Putting it in a metal pendant is not so good, because your greasy fingers will leave marks all over it. LT

Goddess (Baby Phat) ★ ★ *pale rose* $
Probably wants to be rose when it grows up, though it's hard to find where you've sprayed it a minute after you put it on. TS

Go Green (LUSH) ★★ *green citrus* $
With a limited palette of natural materials like this—mostly citrus, herbs, and vetiver—you'd think you couldn't go very wrong. But despite feeling made of good stuff, the balance feels off. It has the haphazard smell of those essential-oil preparations mixed to repel insects rather than smell good. By the way, how is a big, black plastic bottle environmentally friendly? The solid version seems less long-lasting. TS

Golden Amber (Becker Eshaya) ★★ *sharp amber* $$
A sweetly balsamic, woody-amber oriental, but thin and rather sharp, with some ill-judged fruity-floral notes. TS

Golden Goddess (Baby Phat) ★ *fruity floral* $
Short-lived sugary fruity blah in a hilariously cheap blinged-out bottle that looks like a toy designed by a six-year-old and made in China. TS

Gold Man (United Colors of Benetton) ★ *hissy patchouli* $$
Dreadful, cheap patchouli mixed with a battleship gray woody-citrus base. Could be used as a repellent. LT

Gold Woman (United Colors of Benetton) ★ *fruity mess* $$
Not properly speaking a fine fragrance. LT

Gomma (Etro) ★★★ *sweet leather* $$
Gomma means "rubber," and I half expected some version of Bulgari's Black. In the event, it is none other than a classic leather in the Knize Ten mold, but more floral. Composed by the great Edouard Fléchier, it is as good as this unambitious genre gets (but nowhere near the sublime heights of Chanel's Cuir de Russie). LT

Gourmandises (Keiko Mecheri) ★★★ *woody rose* $$$
Gourmandises bears a family resemblance to perfumer Yann Vasnier's Palisander for Comme des Garçons: It's a deconstructed woody rose us-

ing powerful synthetics for a strange, rich, but transparent effect, with an interesting smell of what may be davana—like tea and dried fruit—in the floral part. The structure is wonderful, but the materials feel less than top-notch, and one wishes a client would give him a bigger budget to play with. As it is, this is admirable work but a bit strident. TS

Gramercy Park (Bond No. 9) ★ *green soap* $$$
The press materials indicate I should be finding a lily in here, but I do not. Very bare herbal masculine. TS

Grand Amour (Annick Goutal) ★ ★ ★ *powdery hyacinth* $$
With an expansive, powdery radiance on par with Goutal's Heure Exquise and a winning, honeyed green floral as sweet as the air inside a florist's shop, Grand Amour has impressive ambitions, combining aloofness and warmth in search of that magical proportion that turns a starlet into a star. But Chamade does everything Grand Amour does so much better—the soap, the powder, the fruity rose, the silvery green sheen—that the whole excellent effort can't help but feel futile. TS

Les Grandes Amours du Taj-Mahal (Roméa d'Améor) ★ ★ ★
citrus floral $$$
Pleasant citrus fresh-floral of good construction and better-than-average quality. A bit of a yawn, but nicely done in a squeaky-clean soapy sort of way. LT

Les Grandes Prêtresses Incas (Roméa d'Améor) ★ ★ ★
floral oriental $$$
In the customarily overegged style of Améor PR, this fragrance is claimed to contain canna orchid despite the facts that (a) to my knowledge no such material exists, and (b) canna is a member of the ginger family, not an orchid. Be that as it may, the fragrance is an interesting hybrid between a pale floral and a spicy oriental. The parts are too well

known for their combination to strike one as entirely original, but one is always grateful for a fresh idea. LT

Grapefruit Cologne (Jo Malone) ★★★ *woody cologne* $$$
The programmatic name leads you to expect a holographic grapefruit opening blast, followed by a classic cologne structure. And that's what you don't get. To be fair, grapefruit is a lot harder to do than most people realize. For a start, a true-to-life accord can be obtained only by using sulfuraceous materials that are extremely hard to dose and perceived differently by different people: some will say grapefruit, some garlic. Second, the best long-lasting grapefruit material, nootkatone, is pretty expensive and quiet. Plan B is to do a woody-citrus accord with some green notes, as is the case here, and that works fine but lasts about as long as you can balance a broom on the end of your finger. Ten minutes after spraying, GC has turned into woody cologne, not unpleasant but completely unremarkable. LT

Great Jones (Bond No. 9) ★★★★ *citrus oakmoss* $$$
One of those handsome, traditional masculines, derived from the smokier Monsieur Rochas, that slide along a seamless path from bittersweet orange peel to dry, grassy vetiver-woods, avoiding on the one hand any gourmand or flowery flourishes or, on the other hand, that masculine weakness for monogrammed leather objects (see Mouchoir de Monsieur, Eau d'Hermès) that leads you to suspect a diagnosis of gout in later life. Instead, Great Jones is discreet and steady, beautifully reserved: the smell of a fellow you could count on. TS

Green, green, and . . . green (Miller et Bertaux) ★★★ *lemon leaf* $$
There was a lemon tree that grew behind my childhood home, and I used to pick its leaves and rub them between my fingers. A simple, lovely smell. Pleasant woody-floral drydown. TS

Green Irish Tweed (Creed) ★★★★ *fresh green* $$$
Probably the only truly great fragrance produced by this firm, it was

composed in 1985 by Pierre Bourdon, who three years later rehashed a similar structure in the hugely successful and endlessly imitated Cool Water. Green Irish Tweed feels as good as it ever did, with the brilliantly imaginative accord of Ambroxan (metallic amber), dihydromyrcenol (gray citrus), and octin esters (green violet leaf) sweetened by a touch of apple up top and sandalwood below. Brilliant, legible, perfectly balanced, immediately recognizable. LT

Green Tea (Elizabeth Arden) ★ ★ *lemony floral* $
It's a bit difficult to say why Arden needed to put out a green tea fragrance in 1999, six years after the much better Eau Parfumée au Thé Vert (Bulgari) established this particular style of airy, lemony floral as being "green tea," except that "Elizabeth Arden Green Tea" is much easier for most Americans to say than "Bulgari Eau Parfumée au Thé Vert." TS

Gregory (Fresh Scents by Terri) ★ ★ *metallic patchouli* $
Described on Terri's Web site as the "rugged, sexy flavor of every man," this was a potentially interesting idea of soapy patchouli with the smell of tin, unsuccessfully carried out. TS

Grenats (Keiko Mecheri) ★ ★ *green apple* $$$
Resembling mostly one of the hundreds of citrus and green-apple masculines we can't tell apart, Grenats has nothing particularly to do with pomegranates. Hard to see the point. TS

Grey Flannel (Geoffrey Beene) ★ ★ ★ ★ ★ *sweet green* $
Very few masculines have been more influential than GF, released in 1975. It is the halfway stop in the long journey that leads from Fougère Royale to Fahrenheit. While still properly herbaceous and inedible, its distinguishing feature is a top note in which fresh citrus components were married to the leafy green of violet leaf and galbanum resin in such a way that the fruit-juice quality of the citrus was completely gone, and

only its woody aspect survived. This weird accord was a precursor of the woody almost-citrus (dihydromyrcenol) of Cool Water, only far richer. What makes GF fascinating is the way the dry half of the fragrance is rounded off by a sweet-herbaceous coumarinic note that provides perfect balance and fit. All in all, and despite the fact that GF can occasionally feel a little crude, a masterpiece. LT

Grezzo (La Via del Profumo) ★ ★ ★ ★ *woody fruity* $ $
profumo.it only
Strange name, strange outfit, great fragrance. Dominique Dubrana is a French-born, self-taught perfumer who has set up shop in Italy and makes all-natural fragrances. He also sells (www.profumo.it) excellent dilutions of unusual raw materials such as ambergris and civet. Dubrana is a poet and scholar in, as far as I can tell, the Sufi tradition. His fragrances are all pretty good, but some, like this one, are exceptional and, amazingly, stand comparison with any non-natural perfume. All-natural fragrances are for the most part soggy herbaceous decoctions with the bone structure of a sea cucumber. Grezzo is a beautiful woody-fruity confection based on an accord that smells like cedar and apricots (osmanthus?). Not particularly long-lasting, but cheerfully delicious and great as both masculine and feminine. LT

Gucci (Gucci) ★ ★ ★ *woody oriental* $ $
Gucci, following the departure of Tom Ford, shows alarming signs of reverting to guido style, i.e., the Miami pimp-and-moll look of the bad old days: the bottle of Gucci looks pure eighties and even has a gold-plated miniature belt buckle hanging from it, more Guccione than Gucci. The fragrance, composed by the talented Antoine Maisondieu, is one of a breed of well-crafted, drop-dead-pretty but instantly forgettable woody orientals begat by Narciso Rodriguez for Her, a sort of olfactory Carmen Electra. The basic formula is a swirling cloud of woody, woody-amber, and spicy notes, and Gucci adds a fresh fruity top note and an interesting but short-lived white-floral magnolia accord. The

whole thing runs out of cash at about $t = 60$ minutes and thereafter feels like the morning after. LT

Gucci by Gucci Pour Homme (Gucci) ★ ★ *sararī man* $ $.
I can see where the inspiration for a thing like this would come from: a train platform at a railway station in a major city, afternoon rush hour, the day the clocks are set back, and it's dark when you head home (an hour's travel). No place to sit, too crowded to read, and the guy next to you has recently refreshed his aftershave. LT

Gucci Eau de Parfum (Gucci) ★ ★ ★ *indole oriental* $ $
What would otherwise be merely a pleasant, Tabu-like balsamic oriental has the unusual twist of an incredibly indolic orange-blossom floral, which gives it some of the familial intimacy of smelling your beloved's breath in the morning before toothpaste again makes him fresh as a stranger. A bit sleazy, but not bad at all. TS

Gucci Eau de Parfum II (Gucci) ★ ★ ★ ★ *sage floral* $ $
The surprisingly heavy bottle (prying the tractor-tire-sized cap off is no joke) holds a subtle pink floral of blackcurrant and violet, which manages, via the absence of sugar and the presence of a sober, savory herbaceous accord, to avoid any ditziness. Quiet and competent, smart without showing off, this is one of those fragrances that seems designed for the professional life—the discreet scent of the ideal assistant. TS

Gucci pour Homme (Gucci) ★ ★ ★ ★ *incense amber* $ $
Michel Almairac's brilliant composition did for frankincense what Envy Men had done for ginger a few years earlier, and started a trend of liturgical fragrances that shows no sign of fading. I love the smell of incense, and GpH does a great job of preserving its smoky freshness up into the heart. After such a striking couple of hours the drydown accord cannot help being more banal, but is pretty good nevertheless. Wear this one on fabric to make it happen in slow motion. LT

Gucci pour Homme II (Gucci) ★ ★ *tea fougère* $ $

This woody bergamot-and-violet-leaf composition is a game attempt at making a spiced-tea fragrance for men, but it feels oily and screechy. TS

Guerlain Homme (Guerlain) ★ ★ ★ ★ *rum wood* $ $ $

First, the good news: the fragrance smells great and the bottle looks fine. Now, the sad news: both are derivative. The fragrance is uncomfortably close in structure to the wonderful Yohji Homme (q.v.): the cool-warm balance; the presence of rum, mint, and an anisic note. On balance though, since Yohji is discontinued I'd rather have GH than nothing. As for the bottle, designed by coach builder Pininfarina (go back to work: the nose of the Scaglietti needs fixing!), it is a blatant copy of Dior Homme. Add to this, the name, and one wonders: is Guerlain hoping no one will notice? LT

I find GH sufficiently different from Yohji Homme to give me pause before recommending it as an alternative: the Guerlain is much paler and less profound, lacking the deliciously roasted quality that made YH so interesting. TS

Guerlinade (Guerlain) ★ ★ ★ *soapy floral* $ $ $

This fragrance (supposedly a republished 1921 original) bears the name of the legendary base supposedly added to every Guerlain perfume to give it an *air de famille*. If I may be forgiven a little pedantry, the name has illiterate silliness built into it, because French phonological rules dictate that the *a* in *Guerlain* should be retained in derivations, as in *Guerlanade*. The smell bears no relation to whatever the great Guerlains have in common. Guerlinade is a pleasant, slightly soapy floral of excellent quality, halfway between hawthorn and lily of the valley, and totally harmless. LT

Guess by Marciano (Guess) ★ ★ *caramel floral* $

One of the advantages of Italian and its dialects is the ability to turn nouns into expressive adjectives: *bagascia*, meaning "tart" (as in the profession) in Genoese becomes *abbagasciata* (tartified) and leads as needed to the untranslatable superlative *abbagasciatissima*, which conveys the stratospheric vulgarity of this fragrance. The list of "materials" includes curaçao; pink honeysuckle; and, God help us, dulce de leche. Nauseating. LT

Guess Man (Guess) ★ *chemical fresh* $
Tedious drone-clone, smells of fresh plastic VOCs. Claims to contain Siberian Blue Fir, whatever that may be. LT

Guess Woman (Guess) ★ *imitation tea* $
Shameless, blatant copy of Tommy Girl done with a gas chromatograph badly in need of calibration. LT

Gypsy Water (Byredo) ★ ★ ★ *sweet wood* $$$
What this combination of lemon custard and sandalwood has to do with the Roma, I can't begin to fathom. Essentially, take a big eighties woody floral like Ysatis, then remove the florals. It smells good though somewhat anonymous. TS

Habanita (Molinard) ★ ★ ★ ★ *vetiver vanilla* $
Molinard, like all the Grasse firms ending in *-ard* (like Fragonard and Galimard, old Germanic names dating to Lombard days) makes mostly cheap and cheerful stuff for its factory shop, and only one serious fragrance worth mentioning, the colossal Habanita. Allegedly composed by a Grasse pharmacist in 1921 (shades of François Coty's early days, when he learned fragrance composition making lotions in a pharmacy), it juxtaposes vetiver and vanilla in such a way that both disappear and are replaced by something that is not the sum, more like the vector product of the two. I once described it as Arthur Miller arm in arm with Marilyn Monroe, but in truth it would be their gorgeous hypothetical child. LT

Habit Rouge (Guerlain) ★ ★ ★ ★ ★ *sweet dust* $$
One of the most immediately and permanently appealing ideas in all of perfumery—the orange-flower-and-opopanax accord, soft and rasping like stubble on a handsome cheek, is a bit like beauty itself—immediately understood, never quite elucidated. The new version of HR, which may have undergone some cleanup at the hands of Edouard Fléchier, appears sparer, less laden with dandified frippery than previous ones. This emphasizes HR's most attractive aspect, the surprising but in retrospect self-evident character that is the hallmark of a work of genius. LT

Habit Rouge Sport (Guerlain) ★ ★ ★ *citrus spicy* $$
Given that Habit Rouge means "hunting pink," adding the word "sport" after it is nonsensical as well as depressing, and the critic feels a sense of dread at Guerlain's unrelenting naffness. HRS is to HR as Vetiver pour Elle is to the original Vetiver: the familiar masculine accord has been faded to what in Photoshop would be 50 percent opacity and merged with a citrus-floral base. The latter would no doubt be unremarkably ditzy by itself, but the combination is surprisingly pleasant, miles better than the other HR flankers and a plausible fresh, modern alternative to regular HR. LT

Hadrien Absolu (Annick Goutal) ★ ★ ★ *intense citrus* $$$
This concentrated version of the pale Eau d'Hadrien is better: a bright little citrus cologne, not as good as the best but far from the worst. TS

La Haie Fleurie (L'Artisan Parfumeur) ★ ★ ★ *jasmine solifore* $$$
Nice jasmine. LT

Halston Z (Halston) ★ ★ ★ *gray citrus* $
Strange bottle, like a large white blood cell in frosted glass. Bitter, completely linear woody-citrus accord with a solvent-like top note. Relentlessly overcast-gray and mute, ideal for strong, silent types and aspiring secret agents. LT

Halston Z-14 (Halston) ★ ★ ★ ★ *woody citrus* $
Opinions differ as to what Z-14 means. Was it the code name for a Firmenich captive molecule in the formula? Was it the perfumer's code for the variation chosen by Halston? Either way, this hugely influential fragrance, now almost forgotten and sold for very little in the most dismal places, was easily twenty years ahead of its time when it came out (1976) and is still wonderful today. It is at heart a classical chypre accord of bergamot, cistus, and oakmoss, which is overlaid with a very tight, woody-lemony structure. The remarkable thing is the way in which the dry, resinous woody notes enhance the turpentine aspect of the lemon aldehyde, citral, to such an extent that only the fizz of a lemon ghost is left without any cologne feel. A dark, dry, direct marvel. LT

Hammam Bouquet (Penhaligon's) ★ ★ ★ *woody floral* $$
A hammam is a Turkish steam bath, and this is a classic Edwardian (actually late-Victorian) unisex fragrance, with plenty of lavender and rose on a background of woods. The original formula must have been great in a languid sort of way, but the modern version feels a little harsh, no doubt because many materials are no longer obtainable or affordable. LT

Hamptons (Bond No. 9) ★ *oily woody* $$$
Anyone who would choose to wear this confused, harsh concoction is someone you would not invite for a weekend at your summer home. TS

Hanae (Keiko Mecheri) ★ ★ *fruity floral* $$$
Why would a niche outfit make a pedestrian fruity floral? This one is exceptionally cloying in a children's-cough-syrup way. TS

Hanae Mori "Butterfly" (Hanae Mori) ★ ★ ★ ★ *fruity oriental* $$
Hanae Mori's eponymous fragrance from 1994, with a terrifically trashy cotton-candy idea lifted straight from Vanilia, uses today's popular, cheerfully bright berry notes (a deliciously natural-smelling cassis plus a rosy strawberry), but places them in an unexpectedly classic woody-

floral setting rather than the Kool-Aid-colored body sprays they're used to. More exuberant and richer than the similar Hot Couture by Givenchy, but more subdued than its rose-vanilla cousin Tocade, HM is a bombshell gourmand, incredibly rich and strong, projecting far distances and intensifying with time. Go light on the spray. TS

Hanae Mori "Butterfly" Eau Fraîche (Hanae Mori) ★ ★ ★
sugared grapefruit $ $
This lightened version of the original keeps the sweet woody background but deletes some vanilla and replaces the berries in the original with a sharp pink grapefruit. The combination works, but better on paper than on skin, where it smells slightly rubbery. TS

Happy (Clinique) ★ ★ ★ *milky floral* $
The peculiar thing about Happy is how unhappy it appears: on the box, the lowercase type with the full stop brings to mind Droopy Dog with his tented, saggy face intoning, "I'm happy." The press agent at first seemed reluctant to send a sample, asking me anxiously when I requested it, "But what do you do if you dislike a fragrance?" At that point, I fully expected it to be terrible, but it isn't. Happy is a lovely, mild floral with soothing, milky tones of papaya against the hale, clean musks from Pleasures: nothing brash, nothing too manic, but I suppose people wouldn't buy it if it were called Sedate. TS

Happy for Men (Clinique) ★ ★ ★ *woody citrus* $
A pleasantly fresh citrus woody with some of the milky, slightly overripe papaya notes from the feminine version. What I like is that it isn't immediately recognizable as a masculine. It doesn't last, though, and fades to a pale woody amber. TS

Happy Heart (Clinique) ★ ★ ★ *aldehydic floral* $
A fresh, powdery aldehydic white floral with a smidgen of pine needles added. Smells like a really good fabric conditioner. LT

Harmatan Noir (Parfumerie Générale) ★ ★ ★ *mint wood* $$$
Perfumes with a mint top note always have a difficult transition at $t = 10$ minutes when the freshness runs out and something else must take over. Here the transition is smooth, to a pleasant but not particularly interesting herbaceous accord in a modern masculine manner. LT

Haute Couture (Hanae Mori) ★ ★ ★ *fizzy jasmine* $$
A bright, citrusy, aldehydic, sweet jasmine floral with classic references but modern lightness and a nose-tickling sharpness, Haute Couture reminds me in feeling of those terrific, fun, fruity, un-oaked New World sauvignon blancs—clear, acid, vivacious, good company. TS

Hei (Alfred Sung) ★ ★ *fresh green* $
The blue glass bottle, gray top, and simple shape warn you of an incoming sports fragrance, and sure enough: sneaker juice, though no worse than most. LT

Heiress (Paris Hilton) ★ *fruity floral* $
Hilariously vile 50/50 mix of cheap shampoo and canned peaches. LT

Heliotrope (Etro) ★ ★ ★ *powdery mimosa* $$
Heliotropin is closely related to vanillin, has an almondy floral vanillic smell, and is an ingredient of the abstract compositions that go under the name *mimosa* or *heliotrope* in perfumery books. To a French nose, it smells of a paper glue for kids that used to be sold in little pots with a small plastic ice-cream spoon to help you make a mess. This is one of Etro's most sedate fragrances in an eminently sensible range, and is perfectly nice if you like that sort of thing. LT

Héritage (Guerlain) ★ ★ ★ ★ *woody amber* $$
There was a brief period around 1990 when masculine fragrances tried on a bigger persona, akin to the faintly acromegalic men one sees in forties shirt advertisements: square chins, broad shoulders, big-boned

but graceful hands, wavy hair, affable but remote like warriors on home leave, good-looking enough to be gay, only straight. In other words, England on steroids. Naturally, Joe Blow was far from ready for this evolutionary leap, and a string of great nineties fragrances missed their target by miles: Zino Davidoff, Globe, Troisième Homme, Insensé, Bel-Ami. Héritage (1992), derived from Zino, was another failed try at making masculine fragrance stop dragging its knuckles on the ground: the fossil record shows no trace of a species intermediate between young buck and old fart, as if straight men aged without ever growing up and had no need of fragrances fit for heroes. Yet very few masculines are as instantly appealing as Héritage. Its huge brass chord spans several octaves from a woody-ambery top note to a powdery vanillic bass via a spicy center of great richness. The downside is tremendous radiance, bad news in a masculine. The curious thing is that fifteen years later, women are flocking to fragrances like Coco Mademoiselle and Narciso Rodriguez for Her that are basically Héritage in drag. If I were Guerlain, I would do a Chance with this one: delete the masculine, add a drop of jasmine, change the silly name (in French, it means both "inheritance" and "heritage") and bring it back as Héritière. Too bad Paris Hilton (Heiress) thought of it first. LT

Herrera Aqua (Carolina Herrera) ★ ★ *herbal amber* $
Everything's in place but unspeakably dull. This is the fragrance of a man you can't talk to for thirty seconds without checking your watch. T S

Herrera for Men (Carolina Herrera) ★ ★ ★ *immortelle citrus* $
An interestingly savory, curried version of an herbal sport cologne, like the playboy son of Eau d'Hermès. T S

L'Heure Bleue (Guerlain) ★ ★ ★ ★ ★ *dessert air* $$
When it comes to arranging a folk theme, the early twentieth century had Mahler and L'Heure Bleue, and we have Enya and Fleurs d'Oranger (L'Artisan Parfumeur, Lutens, etc.). The brilliance of L'Heure Bleue is to

cast fresh, shallow, sunny orange flower in a huge role, flanked by two giants: eugenol (cloves, carnation) and ionones (woody violets). Their chorus inexplicably achieves a mouthwatering praliné effect close to that lethal Torino delicacy, the Gianduja. This is Guerlain the virtual pastry chef at his best, with a fragrance that teeters on the edge of the edible for hours without missing a step. If you're Red Hot Riding Hood and a hungry wolf just rang the bell, this is the one for you. LT

Heure Exquise (Annick Goutal) ★ ★ ★ ★ *animalic iris* $$$
Goutal's style of refined, unobtrusive, classical florals can suffer from feeling too prim and well mannered, easy to admire but hard to love, like tightly tailored clothing that, while beautiful, makes it hard to walk. Heure Exquise is one Goutal that I genuinely love: a rich galbanum-and-iris composition close to Chanel No. 19 but, in contrast to the neurotic feeling of the Chanel, with a generous, warm backdrop of woody and animalic notes that feels like falling into a featherbed. TS

He Wood (Dsquared2) ★ ★ ★ *fruity fougère* $
Yes, it's another fruity violet-leaf masculine, and yes it smells pretty cheap. But Daphné Bugey has managed to make the old trick work by tweaking the balance carefully, to turn down the stonking synthetic woods and woody ambers and to turn up the vetiver until it meets the violet leaf halfway. Good show. TS

Higher (Dior) ★ ★ *fruity sporty* $$
Yes, please, next time aim higher. A sporty fougère with a hissy pear top note. TS

Higher Energy (Dior) ★ *citrus sport* $$
I've run out of things to say about these horrible sporty masculines. TS

High Intensity (Mary Kay) ★ ★ *sweet citrus* $
Boring, cheap, but not particularly offensive citrus-balsamic-sweet

confection intended for the male of the species. Smells like shampoo. LT

Hilfiger (Tommy Hilfiger) ★ ★ *dismal fougère* $
The more naturals they list, the less they actually use. Hilfiger is supposed to contain bergamot, grapefruit (pink), mandarin, pepperwood, absinthe, juniper oil, rosemary, papaya, jasmine, rose (tea), pepper (black), mahogany, curcuma, skin accord, cashmere woods, patchouli, sandalwood, suede note, moss, cistus labdanum (rockrose), tonka bean, and papaya. Actual impression: cheapo chemical mix somewhere between the new Dove soap and Cool Water. LT

Himalaya (Creed) ★ ★ *soapy pepper* $$$
Washed-out pink pepper confection, overexposed by three stops. LT

Hindu Grass (Nasomatto) ★ ★ ★ ★ *fresh spicy* $$$
If you speak as loud as Nasomatto, make sure you have something interesting to say. Hindu Grass is the only fragrance of the range that does: a lovely accord of cardamom; rose notes; and fresh, aromatic herbs. It's still an 8.5 on the Richter scale, but as a seismologist once pointed out to me, earthquakes can be entertaining if you're out of doors. Very nice provided you only put on the smallest spritz several hours before joining the company of humans. LT

Hindu Kush (La Via del Profumo) ★ ★ ★ ★
resinous oakmoss $$ *profumo.it only*
If your favorite part of Mitsouko is the resinous, floor-wax-and-church-incense start, here it is in the pure state, made with only natural materials and delicious, though not particularly long-lasting. LT

Hippy Fizz (Moschino) ★ ★ *lemon floral* $$
The "sparkling" press release makes clear that this is for the fragrance-phobic, and, sure enough, it smells like one of the latest Palmolives. TS

Hiris (Hermès) ★ *sad iris* $$$

Olivia Giacobetti is responsible for several masterpieces, including Dzing! and Premier Figuier, both for L'Artisan Parfumeur. Those are truly great insofar as she manages to break with her usual manner: delicate florals with a pale, sour note reminiscent of clothes washed with unscented fabric softener. Sadly, Hiris is part of this contingent, with the rooty iris note adding a remote, pinched temperament to the overall effect. 'Orrible. LT

Une Histoire de Chypre (Molinard for Aedes de Venustas) ★ ★
(★ ★ ★) *fruity chypre* $$$ *Aedes.com only*

What an odd project this is: the best niche-fragrance store in NYC teaming up with one of Grasse's egregiously trashy "-ards" (the other two being Fragonard and Galimard), to come up with Diorella on the cheap and with too much peach lactone in the drydown. This is the sort of stuff that, thirty years ago, might have been called Fiorella and sold in discount buckets or at kiosks outside Moscow Metro stations. LT

I don't think it's as bad as all that, but then again I'm fond of this style. At a distance, it gives a convincing impression of something very like Diorella but peachier, with a bit of chemical white noise. Up close, it's rougher, and I too would counsel getting the real Diorella or Frédéric Malle's Parfum de Thérèse instead. I'm a little disappointed, also, for personal reasons, because I'd hoped it would be the actual resurrection of Coty's long defunct Chypre, not Edmond Roudnitska's fruity take on it. TS

HM (Hanae Mori) ★ ★ ★ *lavender green* $$

(Dilly dilly.) This is one of these terrifying mutant fruity herbals that come on like lavenders on steroids, built out of screechy synthetics (woody plus green plus fruity), but in this version, at least the whole thing is nicely buttressed with fruity cassis and a garden's worth of girly flowers. When it comes to masculines, I've smelled much worse, although this is probably a bit more powerful than one would like. A ghost of Angel haunts the top note. TS

Homage (Amouage) ★ ★ ★ ★ ★ *incense rose* $ $ $ $

At the impossibly swank launch in Muscat of Amouage's two Jubilation scents, guests found, upon arrival in their hotel rooms, a limited edition bottle in a plain white box labeled simply Attar; i.e., "fragrance." When sampled, this anonymous thing turned out to be breathtakingly beautiful: at once lofty, tremendously radiant, and dizzyingly rich. Faced with such an apparition, most of us immediately look around for someone to share our impressions, and the more witnesses the better. I felt the usual mixture of pride and frustration at being in possession of a thing of beauty that few others could share. For company, I gave some to my eight-year-old daughter, who wears it on big occasions. Thankfully, this mysterious Attar, renamed Homage, is now available in limited distribution. The firm tells me it was composed in house, chiefly of Cambodian oud, Ta'if rose, and Omani silver frankincense, which is to say, the best and most expensive stuff around. Oman was making perfumes when Europeans only bathed once a year on doctor's orders. While there, I had occasion to sample, both in shops and in the wake of passing Omanis, the local style of oud, a fiercely elegant accord of rose and wood that radiates aquiline beauty. For Homage, the firm has gone one better on the usual composition and added not only frankincense, which fills the composition with stratospheric light and ice, but apparently some citrus oils to make it more pleasing to Western noses. Mine finds it irresistible. LT

L'Homme (Yves Saint Laurent) ★ ★ *woody citrus* $ $

If Pierre Bourdon had, over the years, got due credit and collected a buck for every bottle sold containing a Cool Water clone, he would be richer than Berlusconi and more famous than Edith Piaf. Thousands of young kids would grow up in French suburbs dreaming of becoming perfumers, the Collège de France would house the Perfumery School, and the Louvre the Osmothèque (with the Impressionists moved to a refrigerated basement in Versailles). LT

L'Homme de Coeur (Divine) ★ ★ ★ ★ *woody iris* $ $
What a great start: Yann Vasnier's brilliant composition begins with a beautiful fresh-peppery juniper-cypress accord, which smoothly morphs to a luxurious woody-iris second subject, against a fresh, slightly smoky background of vetiver. Superbly judged, rich, complex masculine, best worn on fabric to maintain its proportions and delay the drydown. LT

L'Homme Sage (Divine) ★ ★ ★ *spicy wood* $ $
A very nice structure but a little bony, reminiscent of Jacques Bogart's long-forgotten Witness (1992). The warm, spice-wood-resin accord is friendly but somehow feels intrinsically cheap no matter how much the actual formula costs. Like a street kid made good, fragrances of this type cannot shed a muscular crudeness that would work well on, say, James Cagney but be totally wrong on Cary Grant. LT

Honey I Washed the Kids (LUSH) ★ *orange vanilla* $
HIWTK began as a best-selling honey-scented soap for LUSH. Besieged with requests by customers to make it a fragrance, they did. It smells like supermarket candles in jars: less a fragrance than a headache force field. File with the Clean line of fragrances under the heading "Be Careful What You Wish For." TS

Honeysuckle and Jasmine (Jo Malone) ★ ★ ★ *sweet floral* $ $ $
Nice little low-key floral, no great shakes but true to its name. LT

H.O.T. Always (Bond No. 9) ★ ★ ★ ★ *camphor earthy* $ $ $
For unfortunate cultural reasons, big patchouli fragrances have to overcome the ever-present insinuation that the wearer is either (1) a user of bongs, or (2) covering up what the British call pongs—strong stinks. Therefore, fragrances that feature patchouli prominently, such as L'Artisan's Patchouli Patch or Gap's Om, tend to go subtle and emphasize the material's clean, natural outdoors smell—haystacks, not head

shops. H.O.T. Always is far from this kind of subtle, but neither does it make you think automatically of stoned kids on Haight. Instead, it smells like a massive dose of camphor plus freshly overturned earth, and hits you with an invigorating, sinus-clearing, icy whomp, which you smell powerfully at quite a distance and which lasts for ages. Terrific gutsy stuff, lots of fun, and totally impossible to wear politely. TS

Hot Couture (Givenchy) ★ ★ ★ *trashy raspberry* $
The faux-fifties packaging belongs to a "Lucky Star"–era Madonna aesthetic, the pun is a groaner (haute and hot! ho haut!), and a fun arti-ficial raspberry-swirl ice cream idea has been muffled by classy, ambery good intentions. Also, I thought this had been discontinued. What's going on? I notice they've redesigned the packaging, switching from beveled black glass to clear with pink liquid, and replacing the old Art Deco couture gown image with a girly pink label. I suspect Givenchy aimed high, hit low, and went with it. TS

Hot Leather (By Mark Buxton) ★ ★ *nasty leather* $$$
In 2005, Michel Almairac inexplicably "committed," as the French would say, an Armani Privé fragrance called Cuir Améthyste, whose first version was so nauseating that it was promptly revised to a slightly more acceptable composition. Buxton's Hot Leather is essentially that first version in its unpleasant glory. Stay well away. LT

Hugo (Hugo Boss) ★ ★ *unexciting lavender* $
Dull but competent lavender-oakmoss thing, suggestive of a day filled with strategy meetings. LT

Hugo XX (Hugo Boss) ★ *thin floral* $
Smells like shampoo. LT

Hugo XY (Hugo Boss) ★ ★ *watery green* $
Another unnecessary fruity-woody fougère derived from Fahrenheit

and Cool Water, this time featuring an "iced accord." Since water gets no cooler than that, this must be the end of this road. TS

Hummer (Riviera Concepts) ★ ★ ★ *sweet lavender* $
The whole idea of a perfume named after that overpriced tin can is so embarrassing and the bottle so wonderfully naff that I was praying for the fragrance to measure up to the concept. Alas, the random gods of perfumery struck again: it's not bad, a sweet woody lavender more suggestive of a Toyota Camry than of the Tonka of Bling. LT

Hyperessence Matale (Parfumerie Générale) ★ ★ ★ *lemon tea* $$$
HM confirms my general impression that Parfumerie Générale is trying to be, so to speak, a Jo Malone for people who actually like perfume. In many (perhaps too many) of his compositions, Pierre Guillaume explores a sunlit territory of citrus, herbaceous, and woody notes: more than a cologne but less than a fully committed, full-orchestra composition. HM is very pleasant, though perhaps a touch predictable. LT

Hypnôse (Lancôme) ★ ★ *drab oriental* $
What, if any, is the point of hiring perfumers of the caliber of Thierry Wasser and Annick Ménardo and then giving them a fabric-softener budget to put together a major fragrance? L'Oréal (owner of Lancôme) is a dismal, pennypinching outfit in this respect. But then again, maybe that's how the rich get rich and stay rich. LT

Hypnôse Homme (Lancôme) ★ ★ *cheap lavender* $
Maurice Roucel's masculines sometimes tend toward the crude (Musc Ravageur, Lapidus), and this is one of those: a big, synthetic-smelling lavender on a big, synthetic amber background, a sort of shampoo writ large. LT

Hypnôse Homme Eau Fraîche (Lancôme) ★ ★ ★
lavender fougère $
Nicely executed modern woody lavender. Somewhat unadventurous. LT

Hypnotic Poison (Dior) ★ ★ ★ ★ *almond oriental* $ $
HP is an essay in snatching triumph from the jaws of defeat. I am as surprised to find it beautiful as I would be if someone turned up in an all-brown outfit and contrived to be gorgeous. Every single note in HP, from the plum and coconut up top to the vanilla and coumarin in the drydown, with some heliotropin in between, is dark, velvety, and autumnally muted. And yet their sum total radiates in a way that only a great perfumer could have arranged, a double-bass sextet that swings. And lo! It was done by Annick Ménardo, which explains everything. LT

I Am King (Sean John) ★ ★ ★ *fruity woody* $ $
The interminably copied Cool Water was fruity to start with, a Drakkar Noir with a Carmen Miranda hat. It heralded the great green apple migration, in which the note went from signifying women's hair products (1970s) to men's toiletries (late 1980s). I Am King declares this fruit hat to be a crown. Cute and pleasant, but not regal. TS

Iceberg Homme (Iceberg) ★ *sad shampoo* $
That's him all right. Now put him back in the freezer. LT

Iceberg Twice (Iceberg) ★ ★ *herbaceous floral* $
Naff masculine mysteriously intended for women. LT

Iceberg Twice Men (Iceberg) ★ *fruity woody* $
Undistinguished demure fruity floral combined with a bellowing woody-amber note, reminiscent of the little girl in *The Exorcist* shouting in a deep male voice. LT

Ichnusa (Profumum) ★ *cheap fig* $ $ $ $
Profumum does Premier Figuier. Should have been called Ficus Tertius, given that Philosykos came second. LT

Idole (Lubin) ★ ★ ★ ★ *saffron suede* $ $

The fastidious orientals of Olivia Giacobetti treat lushness as if it were taxed and show a heavy debt to Féminité du Bois, whose hugely influential transparent rose cedar used the sweetness of violets and damascones to create a new kind of oriental: vanilla free. Here, as in her Safran Troublant for L'Artisan Parfumeur, Giacobetti is working with an idea of Indian dessert: those delicate confections of rosewater, saffron, cardamom, and milk next to which a sweet like crème brûlée is suitable only for grunting ogres who eat with their feet. But unlike the bolder, simpler Safran Troublant, Idole never seems strong at any dosage, perhaps due to an eerie driftwood gray note at its center, reminiscent of Timbuktu, which makes the fragrance float at the periphery of attention even when you smell it right under your nose. Beautiful, subtle work in one of the most striking bottles seen in years. TS

IF (Apothia) ★ ★ *just tuberose* $

Diluted tuberose absolute. If this is fragrance, I'm Ernest Beaux. LT

Ilang Ivohibe (Parfumerie Générale) ★ ★ ★ *jasmine vanilla* $ $ $

Straightfoward jasmine floral with a vanillic drydown. LT

Impact (Caron) ★ ★ ★ ★ *lavender vanilla* $ $ $

The original 1958 Impact smelled like a 50/50 mixture of Poivre and Tabac Blond. This one is a concentrated Pour un Homme, possibly with a slightly better grade of lavender, though I wouldn't swear on that. What makes it unusual is that it is a sort of EdP concentration, rare in a masculine. LT

Les Impératrices Japonaises (Roméa d'Améor) ★ ★ ★ ★
floral joss-stick $ $ $

Probably the best of the RdA line and certainly the most striking, Impératrices revisits the joss-sticks-and-flowers accord of Lancôme's Poême, but with better materials and a light, airy touch in both the oriental and floral aspects, which turn that bludgeoning brute into a graceful fragrance. This is a smell one would probably appreciate just as much in a candle, except candles seldom get this good. LT

Imperial Opopanax (Les Néréides) ★ ★ ★ *sweet fougère* $$
Not an opopanax, more a light, old-fashioned fougère of lavender, coumarin, and citrus. A good-quality, nostalgic daddy's-shaving-cream scent. TS

Incense Extrême (Tauer Perfumes) ★ ★ ★ ★ *incense citrus* $$$
Andy Tauer's outfit is niche fragrance at its best: low concept, high quality, modest packaging, decent prices. Incense Extrême is less incense and less *extrême* than you'd think. After the first Russian-church whiff, the clever accord with petitgrain and iris is old-fashioned in a waxy, soap-and-water cologne way and brings to mind grand-hotel bathrooms: black-and white tiles, brass fittings, and hot water more abundant than you get at home. LT

Incense Rosé (Tauer Perfumes) ★ ★ ★ ★ *pomander rose* $$$
When, for my sins, I was once art director of a small fragrance line, a character flaw made it impossible for me to do a good job: if it was any good, a fragrance was in some sense always so much better than nothing, that it seemed churlish to be a perfectionist and demand more from the perfumer. There is a simple joy in a good smell: the elementary delight of watching fireworks burst against a black sky. And so it is with Incense Rosé. I defy anyone not to feel a Mendelssohnian rush of innocence upon smelling it. The combination of rose, cardamom, and mandarin is so warm, so welcoming, you feel as if you've just heard a piece of good news you cannot quite remember. LT

Incensi (Lorenzo Villoresi) ★ ★ *menthol oriental* $$
You'd expect a straightforward church incense from a fragrance called Incensi, and it gets there eventually—a nice, dry, peppery, woody varia-

tion on the theme—but first, for reasons difficult to fathom, you must pass through a muddled floral oriental unnecessarily complicated with cinnamon and camphor. TS

Individuel (Mont Blanc) ★ *citrus green* $
A laundry-soap formula, apparently for individuals who can't yet afford the Mont Blanc pens. TS

L'Infante (Divine) ★ ★ ★ ★ *mimosa floral* $$
If you're going to do a no-holds-barred, girly, powdery floral, this is the way to do it: rich, compact, complex, held together by an intense but natural mimosa accord. A beautifully worked-out fragrance, perhaps not as immediately striking as some in the genre, but more pleasant than most in the long term. LT

Infini (Caron) ★ ★ ★ *lactonic floral* $
A classic lactonic floral, dark and milky ambery like Givenchy's original L'Interdit, nice in a retro way but with a peculiarly masculine drydown of wood and violet leaf, which may not have been in the original. TS

Infusion d'Homme (Prada) ★ ★ *cheap iris* $$
Man infusion? Macerating a whole guy in pickling alcohol is now against the law in some states. French raw-materials outfit Biolandes has figured out a way to make iris root age fast, and has thus lowered the price severalfold. As a result, everybody from Chanel downward is doing an iris. This one is a pale and misguided imitation of Lutens's Iris Silver Mist. Pale because the iris note is treated meanly, like three little caviar grains on a tiny canapé, as if the stuff were still wildly expensive. Misguided because the original, in its Wagnerian splendor, used every iris note known to man, including some nasty ones to overwhelm the poet in us, whereas Infusion chickens out: the drydown is generic soapy in a retro sort of way. Avoid. LT

Infusion d'Iris (Prada) ★ ★ (woody floral) $ $ $
The good news: this is, by comparison with other Prada fragrances, a well-mannered composition. The bad news: it contains no discernible natural iris note, and feels rather like a gray, nondescript woody masculine. LT

Inhale (B Never Too Busy to Be Beautiful) ★ ★ ★ ★ *fruity wood* $
Having run out of Empires, Marc-Antoine Corticchiato at long last lets his hair down and moves on from the luxurious but slightly formulaic pastiches of his "historical" line to weird, abstract compositions that reveal a far more inventive talent. Inhale and its companion, Exhale, are both delightful fragrances. Inhale is a very strange accord of citrus-orange woods, an ink-like stagnant background, and the camphoraceous gummy-candy note familiar to those who like Japanese fruit gums. The result is not unlike Oyédo, but clearer and more stately. It feels a bit like a date with a Klingon: at first the forehead ridges are disturbing, but soon enough smoothness seems so passé. LT

Inner Grace (Philosophy) ★ ★ ★ *green chypre* $
Devoid of Philosophy's usual toe-curlingly embarrassing copy on the back of the bottle, this fragrance is apparently dedicated to the late Dana Reeve, indomitable wife of Christopher Reeve and head of his foundation for the disabled. It is an odd, peppery-green abstract floral, a bit as if Givenchy III and Y (YSL) had been codistilled to extract only the top notes. It has the urgent, brittle quality of someone whose voice is pitched slightly high by chronic stress. Pretty good, if a little bare. LT

Insensé (Givenchy) ★ ★ ★ ★ ★ *masculine floral* $ $
Insensé is back! Givenchy must be commended for bravely reissuing marvels from its distinguished past, not least because they put most of its present offerings to shame. The reissues of III and Vetyver were a great idea, since the world cannot have too many vetivers and green chypres. But Insensé was a matter of far greater import. When it was re-

leased in 1993, it was one of the most original masculines in decades and that rarest thing, a floral for men. Michael Edwards's database lists only eight such (leaving aside lavenders), a tiny number if you consider that there are 659 aromatic fougères. Insensé was far too clever for its time, and bombed miserably, hindered by a wan, floppy-haired, bloodless advertising image that suggested it was a perfume for wusses. And in retrospect you can see why: despite doomed attempts to swim upriver, such as Globe (Rochas) and No. 3 (Caron), the early nineties were going in a completely different, far easier direction, toward spices and woods. Insensé is a remote relative of green chypres. Its composition is unusually complex and hovers between the herbaceous and the green-floral against a woody background, with a touch of the sweet musky character of Rabanne pour Homme. It is blessed with two qualities that are the surest mark of a good masculine: melancholy and mystery. It will likely flop again, so buy it now before Givenchy changes its mind. LT

Insolence (Guerlain) ★ ★ ★ ★ *floral oriental* $$

They got the name right. Insolence puts one in mind of the sort of person who, while intrinsically attractive, manages to antagonize everyone by lacking all social graces. Using toothsome Hilary Swank in the ads as a lapdancer from *Star Trek* is ludicrous. The dirty-dishes bottle is memorably silly. The Trésor-like hue of the liquid must have been decided by a color-blind anosmic. The fragrance itself starts with two minutes of the most disastrous top notes in living memory (hair spray and Violettes de Toulouse). What a shame, because it is a monumentally skillful thing. This is Maurice Roucel's homage to L'Heure Bleue, and bears the same relationship to its model as Godowsky's studies do to Chopin's Études: the structure of the original has been parceled up into tiny elements that are then set in motion like a flight of starlings, making a shape in the air that is recognizably L'Heure Bleue, but swirling, intermittent, teeming with decorative melismas borrowed from other sources. Jacques Guerlain's masterpiece is transfigured into something that lacks L'Heure Bleue's weight, poise, and softness, a ghostly creature of spangles and neon. It is legitimate to prefer the original, and to dislike Insolence's loud, brassy tone. But the art of perfumery is irrevocably advanced. LT

Insolence eau de parfum (Guerlain) ★ ★ ★ ★ ★ *Godzilla floral* $$$
In their haste to copy Angel, most perfume houses lost track of the fact that what made it great was not just the smell—that weird combination of patchouli, candyfloss, and blackcurrant—but the effect, the ta-da! moment, the euphoric surprise that a perfume could be so outrageous and still win. The first Insolence came close, except that the shock was spoiled by a violet-hair-spray top note that made it stumble as it cartwheeled onto the stage. When Guerlain PR offered to send me the new Insolence EdP, I inquired whether the formula was different. The young lady on the phone said yes with a knowing chuckle. And, by golly, it really is different. Guerlain has finally decided that this thing should not even try to be classy and has embraced it as the most deliciously vulgar perfume on the market today. Maurice Roucel's serious compositions are always complex, but there is so much going on here that it feels like a seventies action-movie poster, with a helicopter hovering over a burning building to the right, two cars jumping off a pier in the middle, a girl in a white dress being lifted out of a swamp in a guy's arms at left, and an erupting volcano in the background. The accord is tuberose, red fruit, orange blossom, and a green-peppery Poême-type note that fits perfectly in this context. All four are heavy hitters, and the combination is simply huge. There is something reckless, irreversible, cataclysmic about pressing the spray button on Insolence EdP, even when it is pointed well away from you. I put some on a smelling strip, left it on the table, and walked out for lunch. The perfume ran after me: enough had strayed onto the back on my hand to create a cloud of pink-neon trashiness that made me feel I was being driven to the local café in a stretch limo. When I came back, the strip greeted me heartily across the room. I know I will regret saying this (especially sitting next to it at dinners and concerts), but this Insolence is a masterpiece. LT

Insolence Eau Glacée (Guerlain) ★ ★ *soapy floral* $ $

There used to be a comic character on Italian TV called Fracchia, who would stand outside his boss's office and rehearse in a confident, stentorian voice the demands he was about to make: a raise, longer holidays, a corner office. He would then timidly knock on the door, answer the imperious command to enter, and crumple immediately to plead in a croaky, imploring tone to have his holidays and his salary cut. Insolence Eau Glacée is Guerlain's Fracchia: The Insolence franchise is so brash, loud, and vulgar that you'd expect this fellow to shout, whereas it mumbles like talcum powder done in the milky-floral style of Fahrenheit 32. Pointless and disappointing. LT

Inspiration (Lacoste) ★ *sad florist* $

More like Imitation (in this case of Dazzling Silver). LT

L'Inspiratrice (Divine) ★ ★ ★ *buttery floral* $ $

Yvon Mouchel, Divine's founder-owner, is passionate about perfume in a quietly determined way that commands respect. His tiny firm started in 1986 and probably would not exist today without the Web, which picked up in earnest about ten years later and allowed him to build enough of a customer base to release a fragrance almost every year since 2000. L'Inspiratrice, his latest, is a very sweet oriental which would be cloying were it not exceptionally, intensely powdery, a sort of liqueur-like concentrate of old-fashioned talcum powder. LT

L'Instant (Guerlain) ★ ★ ★ ★ *eclectic floral* $ $

It is no exaggeration to say that in 2003 the world was waiting for Guerlain to either die or redeem itself after the cynical Champs-Elysées (1996) and the disastrous Mahora (2000). Guerlain had in the meantime got the message that business as usual was not good enough, and called upon the great Maurice Roucel, of 24, Faubourg fame, to do their latest feminine. Expectations were high, and they were only partly satisfied. To be sure, L'Instant hits all the right notes, but it feels mellifluously empty, like an election-night victory speech of your favorite politician: "I shall endeavor to be a fragrance for all women" or "Together we will build a better floral," etc. It is possible, especially late at night and after several glasses of wine, to be moved by L'Instant's sleek, bland rhetoric. But, as Churchill said, "Tomorrow I shall be sober." LT

L'Instant Fleur de Mandarine (Guerlain) ★ ★ ★ *thin mandarin* $$
Loosely based on L'Instant, FdM follows the present trend, started by Eau des Merveilles (actually by Azzaro's Azzura, but who remembers that?) and extended by Cacharel's Liberté, for sun-drenched orange chypres that feel as sedately exotic as a Club Med catalog. But as always in fragrance, minor variations can cause a composition to hit the spot, and this one does, especially if used as a refined masculine in the style of the late and lamented Insensé. LT

L'Instant Magic (Guerlain) ★ ★ ★ *floral vanilla* $$
For a few wonderful moments, L'Instant Magic has a fresh, bright innocence of anise and vanilla, and comes off like an update of L'Heure Bleue. Right when you're beginning to think you'll get a bottle for your sister, all the fun ends and you're left with an entirely generic, faceless floral oriental with bad vibes. TS

L'Instant Magic 2008 (Guerlain) ★ ★ ★ *citrus floral* $$
Competent but boring powdery peony-citrus composition; less unpleasant than some but still completely unnecessary. LT

L'Instant Magic Elixir (Guerlain) ★ ★ ★ *radiant musk* $$
Okay, you say, enough with the classy chypres. What I really want is to smell like that whoosh that comes out of the dryer when I open the door! This is called in the fabric-softener industry the "magic moment," implying that Guerlain might have a sense of humor. TS

L'Instant pour Homme (Guerlain) ★ ★ ★ ★ *green citrus* $ $
It is hard to find fault with this one, created by Beatrice Piquet. For a start, the packaging is exquisite. For the first time in years a Guerlain has a look (slightly Chanel-inspired, but who cares?) at once distinctive, classy, and coherent. Now for the smell: on skin, it is like watching a perfect Olympic dive from the 10-meter board. It goes from fresh-citrusy in the manner of Shalimar Lite to a suave-sandalwood reminiscent of Samsara Lite via two half-twists, one of anise and one of vetiver. Elbows tucked in all the way, perfect entry, no splash. One immediately wants a replay in slow motion: spray it on fabric and marvel at how it's done. Another thing noteworthy about L'Instant pour Homme is that it smells good even in the thumbnail-sized versions of deodorant, shower gel, etc. It's like Barber's Adagio in quartet form: they've got the tune right. LT

Instinct (David Beckham) ★ ★ ★ *spicy vetiver* $
More proof that snobbery in perfumery is pointless, Beckham's fragrance is actually a solid, handsome piece of work, pairing aromatic citrus and spices with a lovely licorice-fresh vetiver, and much better than most of the dreary sport fragrances that distinguished brands condescend to sell. Furthermore, I can't stop playing with the magnetized cap. Genius, pure genius, Becks. TS

Instinct After Dark (Beckham) ★ ★ *grape citrus* $
A Cool Water with a surprising top note of purple soda. Too low budget to work, but interesting that Coty tried it. TS

Intense Euphoria Men (Calvin Klein) ★ ★ ★ *cantaloupe fougère* $ $
This perfume reminds me of that test for unconscious sexism involving a surgeon saying, "I cannot operate on this boy, he is my son," though the boy's father has been injured in the same car crash. (Answer: the surgeon is a woman.) If IEM were a feminine fragrance, everyone would find it okay: a little fruity, a little woody, a little herbaceous, so what?

But it's a masculine! And just as a guy gets compliments from female guests when he clears the table and does the dishes for the first time in eighteen months, this thing will be deemed awesome because it is so cute, so new century, so stay at home. In truth, it's not bad, and the top notes are fun, a sort of fruit salad drenched in Cool Water. It suddenly runs out of formula cash after an hour, leaving only synthetic sandalwood, so spray it on fabric. Bravo to the marketing people for courage. Please do this again, and next time make it interesting. LT

L'Interdit (Givenchy) ★ ★ ★ ★ *lactonic floral* $ $ $
These old milky, nutty florals from the fifties, with their abstract bouquets of spring blooms, would upset no one in church, but although they sound light and fresh, they relied on a dark amber fuzz to relay sweetness. L'Interdit, an excellent if boneless soft floral with nothing interdicted about it, comes so far in that salty, ambery direction that it approaches the dark chypre of Baghari. This touch of darkness in an essentially harmless floral reminds me of that closed-lipped smile in photographs of actresses of the time, which seemed to imply unspoken mysteries in what were essentially unmysterious beings. Givenchy tried to rerelease L'Interdit previously as a fruity floral, the equivalent nice girl's fragrance of today, but no one loved it. The 2007 is truer to the original, perfectly proportioned, well behaved, and of excellent quality, though much of its pleasure is the thrill of the retro, like watching a perfectly restored old black-and-white film and falling under the spell of that midcentury acting-school accent. TS

Intimately Beckham for Men (Coty) ★ ★ ★ *violet fougère* $
The biggest surprise of Intimately Beckham for the lads is the packaging: it looks for all the world like a crystal perfume bottle for a lady's vanity. Progress! The fragrance is a fairly straightforward descendant of Grey Flannel fougères: a sweet violet with the watery green of violet leaf and a touch of spice. Pleasant (though not natural) sandalwood drydown. TS

Intimately Beckham for Women (Beckham) ★ ★ ★ *white floral* $
This is a throwback tuberose that reminds us of the old florals like Oscar de la Renta and White Diamonds, appropriate for strapless gowns and charity dinners. Those fragrances tempered the weirdness of tuberose with sweet tobacco-like oriental notes, resulting in big-boned but beautiful effects. Victoria Beckham's fragrance, however, loses its floral lift on skin, where it comes off as a kind of muddled methyl anthranilate grape juice and woods, so it's best appreciated on fabric or a paper blotter. TS

Intrigant Patchouli (Parfumerie Générale) ★ ★ ★ ★
civet patchouli $ $ $
Intensely sixties animalic patchouli-oriental with a citrus top note. Agrees with purple velvet and too much makeup. Nice. LT

Intuition (Estée Lauder) ★ ★ *grapefruit floral* $
Intuition feels like people you want to like until they do the wrong thing halfway through the evening, like use the phrases "passed away" or "fast track." It's basically a good idea, a sort of hybrid between a spritzy masculine and a bright floral, with a lovely grapefruit note up top and plenty of well-crafted complicated stuff underneath, but ultimately you decide not to hire it. LT

Intuition for Men (Estée Lauder) ★ ★ ★ *boring amber* $
Reading the perfumery-for-dopes description of the accords on which this fragrance is based, one would expect an oriental built like Polyphemus: fully three layers of amber, one light, one essence, one drenched (really). After all that, the fragrance comes across as somewhat polite and disappointing. Intuition for Men belongs to the recent school of masculine perfumery in which artistic directors try their level best (probably to stave off terminal depression) to compensate for the poverty-stricken canons of the genre by choosing formulas of byzantine complexity and end up with fragrances not unlike the dinner-party bore

who works in insurance but is a specialist in Christian heresies in Asia Minor, second to fourth centuries CE. LT

Invasion Barbare (Parfums MDCI) ★ ★ ★ ★ ★ *spicy woody* $ $ $ $
This is the first and so far only fragrance by Stéphanie Bakouche, graduate of the French perfume school, ISIPCA, student of Patou's former magus Jean Kerléo, and clearly a talent to watch. On first impression, IB had one of those majestic woody-spicy baritone top notes that usually make me cringe in anticipation that the impressive breadth will soon run out of cash and give way to a skeletal drydown. After ten minutes I uncurled my toes and relaxed: this thing was not done on the cheap, and is in fact one of the top two or three fragrances in this genre on the face of the earth. The closest thing it brings to mind is Penhaligon's old and discontinued Lords, but IB is much better. If you want a distinctive, high-quality masculine less dandified than Mouchoir de Monsieur and less affable than New York, this is it. LT

Io Capri (Carthusia) ★ ★ ★ *spearmint woody* $ $
Creating a minty fragrance without making you think of toothpaste is a task beyond the reach of Carthusia. All the same, Io has a pleasing, slightly smoky woody-floral backdrop and a refreshing feel. TS

Iris (Profumo di Firenze) ★ ★ *short iris* $ $ $ $
Florence is where they used to produce iris root, so you'd expect a Florentine iris to be pretty good. This is okay rather than great, very much a standard-issue dead-poets composition with heliotropin. Five minutes later it's gone. LT

Iris 39 (Le Labo) ★ ★ ★ ★ *green iris* $ $
A very nice iris, all the more so because it is done in an unusual and interesting manner: instead of using its gray-powdery aspect as a corrective to floral optimism or leathery barbarity, it is used here in a patchouli-herbal-green context that emphasizes its wet, rooty, earthy aspects. Light,

natural touches all around, clearly a well-thought-through fragrance, and a worthy addition to the small band of irises worth wearing. LT

Iris de Nuit (Heeley) ★ ★ ★ ★ *ambrette iris* $$$
Chic, as opposed to mere luxury, arguably requires a mixture of the rare and the industrial, expensive and cheap, refined and rustic. The iris root note has such a propensity toward sadness (Iris Silver Mist) and pallor (28 La Pausa) that it needs some friends to drag it outdoors and compel it to have a good time. IdN achieves this by marrying expensive iris with the chemically related (and dirt-cheap) ionones of violets and a note I've always liked (a sort of iris with freckles), the inexpensive and cheerfully rooty carrot seed. IdN's top notes are extraordinarily wine-like, after which the composition settles to a gray velvet shade. Once again, as in all Heeley's perfumes, the composition is structurally sound, held together in this case by a lovely note of ambrette seed, a natural macrolide musk, which discreetly emphasizes both the silvery and fruity aspects of the other components. If there were such a thing as English perfumery—natural, quietly confident, refined—it would look something like Heeley's range. LT

Iris Ganache (Guerlain) ★ ★ ★ *iris amber* $$$
It's as if someone fixed what was wrong with Insolence—that top note of hair spray and terror—but lost what was wonderful. After a beautiful start, like Après l'Ondée with caramel, Iris Ganache gets stronger and sweeter, until all that's left is strident, oily amber. Too bad. TS

Irisia (Creed) ★ *green chypre* $$$
With no discernible note of iris, this is a green floral chypre of exceptional banality and unpleasantness, halfway between Givenchy III and Alliage, but without the grace of the former or the simplicity of the latter. LT

Iris Nobile (Acqua di Parma) ★ ★ ★ ★ *iris gardenia* $$$
At last a properly ambitious fragrance from AdP, not very iris-like but drying down to a beautiful clean gardenia accord, which is unusual. LT

Iris Noir (Yves Rocher) ★ ★ ★ *floral herbaceous* $

Yves Rocher, probably France's biggest cosmetics and fragrance firm and resolutely downmarket, is to be commended for (1) bringing out three ambitious, high-end fragrances; (2) giving the perfumers enough formula money to do a good job; and (3) selling the result for a reasonable price, less than $40 for a two-ounce bottle of EdP. From what I hear, these fragrances were intended as an introduction to serious fragrance for the average YR customer. Curiously, Yves Rocher has a distinguished track record in fine fragrance that has gone largely unnoticed. Their Venise was essentially Dune five years earlier, Ispahan an excellent floral oriental. Iris Noir uses all the right words in its name but turns out not to be an iris at all, rather a sage-like aromatic in the manner of Miyake's L'Eau Bleue, but less aggressive. Pretty good and an absolute bargain, in my opinion better as a masculine. LT

Iris Pallida 2007 (L'Artisan Parfumeur) ★ ★ ★ ★
blueberry pepper $ $ $ $

Despite the astronomical price of these limited edition Harvest fragrances, they're not quite the expected rip-off. L'Artisan Parfumeur has excelled in setting off these top-notch natural materials in simple compositions that reveal facets heretofore hidden. This gray-blue iris is made grayer and bluer by a dry note of black pepper at one end and a surprise touch of blueberry at the other. At a time when everyone is using iris by the bucket, this one stands apart. Stately, quiet, eerie. TS

Iris Poudre (Frédéric Malle) ★ ★ ★ *powdery fruit* $ $ $

The hugely talented and unusually articulate Pierre Bourdon revisits the theme of Iris Gris. Simply stated, the problem with iris-root smell is this: everyone loves its gray, nostalgic, romantic powderiness, but the stuff is, truth be told, as funereal as it gets. The great Vincent Roubert solved the problem in 1947 with Jacques Fath's Iris Gris by adding the lactonic peach base Persicol and endowing the grayness of iris with the pink shimmer of a pigeon's throat. Bourdon is less subtle, and his expertise in making resolutely sunny, fruity compositions very quickly dries iris tears. After a restrained initial gravitas appropriate to the occasion, Iris Poudre veers toward a happier disposition reminiscent of Bourdon's Dolce Vita. But then everyone knows that funerals make the survivors feel glad to be alive. A good fragrance, but not true to its name or material. LT

Iris Silver Mist (Serge Lutens) ★ ★ ★ ★ ★ *iris root* $$$
Long before everybody started doing irises and (mostly) pseudo-irises, Lutens had commissioned an iris to end them all from Maurice Roucel. The story goes that Lutens pestered the perfumer to turn up the iris volume to the max, and Roucel in desperation decided to put in the formula every material on his database that had the iris descriptor attached to it, including a seldom-used, brutal iris nitrile called Irival. The result was the powderiest, rootiest, most sinister iris imaginable, a huge gray ostrich-feather boa to wear with purple dévoré velvet at a poet's funeral. LT

Iris Taïzo (Parfumerie Générale) ★ ★ ★ ★ *clever iris* $$$
A deeply strange and rather wonderful combination of ripe fig (flesh, not leaf), bread-like iris, and honey-propolis notes that adds up to a sort of ectoplasmic Fig Newton. Humorous, original, and nicely executed, but somewhat short lived. LT

Isfarkand (Ormonde Jayne) ★ ★ ★ *lime woody* $$
After an exciting lime-and-pepper top note, which gives you the sensation of someone running about and opening all the windows in a gale, Isfarkand quickly settles for the low woody hum that characterizes all the Ormonde Jayne scents (perfumer Geza Schoen liked the material Iso E Super so much, he made a perfume called Escentric Molecule 01 consisting of nothing but), with a touch of floral. Someone needs to find a way to make the first few seconds last forever. TS

Iskander (Parfum d'Empire) ★ ★ ★ *woody citrus* $ $
Arab speakers interpreted the *Al* in Alexander as a definite article, and they couldn't pronounce the Greek letter *xi,* so he became Iskander, and apparently his name is still invoked in Persia to frighten children who will not go to bed. Iskander is a very nice woody-spicy fragrance in an eighties mold, somewhere between Derby and Jules. Well turned out and reassuringly luxurious, but not the stuff of dreams. LT

Island (Michael Kors) ★ ★ ★ *white floral* $ $
Is this island "beyond paradise" by any chance? A bright, radiant top note of citrus and white florals leads to an incredibly familiar destination, but a little screechier. Nicely done, although not very original. TS

Island Bermuda (Michael Kors) ★ *beyond purgatory* $ $
Michael Kors PR calls this thing a "breezy floral," which reminds me of *Tintin's* Captain Haddock standing at the helm, puffing contentedly on his pipe in a Force 10 gale he calls a *jolie brise.* This thing is a ham-fisted copy of Beyond Paradise and J'Adore, done with less money and less skill, and quite a bit louder. Awful. LT

Island Gardenia (Jovan) ★ ★ *tuberose actually* $
A fresh, Fracas-type tuberose with half the wallop: not at all a gardenia, it smells pretty good initially, then harsher and more chemical as time goes on. TS

Itislove (Salvador Dalí) ★ ★ *rose vanilla* $ $
Knockoff of the gorgeous Tocade, with harsh, mall-girl pink synthetic florals substituted for Tocade's deep, multifaceted rose. TS

Ivoire (Balmain) ★ ★ ★ ★ *soapy floral* $
Released in 1980, Ivoire was the first, and remains the best, of a clutch of dense, creamy, soapy florals that made it big just before the Poison-

Giorgio eighteen-wheeler trend ran these prim fragrances over. Ivoire has a classic, slightly nondescript, downmarket French chic about it, and comes in a pleasantly dowdy bottle. Balmain's new owners are reputedly looking hard at the whole line, so stock up in case they discontinue it. LT

Jade (Olivier Durbano) ★ *mouthwash fruity* $$$
Jade is the saddest of all semiprecious stones, looking like faded plastic when real. Rightly, it is here represented by an ill-judged mixture of Scope mouthwash and a fruity chypre. Fascinatingly bad. TS

J'Adore (Dior) ★ ★ ★ *peachy rose* $
When J'Adore was first released in 1999, it felt like a departure for Calice Becker, whose Tommy Girl was a fresh apple-tea floral that made every day feel like a morning after a rain. In contrast, J'Adore passed the snow glare of Becker's usual floral style through an amber filter, via a beautifully dark candied-plum note. The fragrance went from golden sunset to purple dusk by coming surprisingly close in the drydown to the dark, incense-like rose of Parfum Sacré. I use the past tense because things have changed, perhaps because LVMH no longer simply buys the finished perfume oil from Givaudan but now makes part of it in-house, under the management of François Demachy, formerly of Chanel. Today's J'Adore is a perfectly nice peachy, soapy rose floral with none of its former late-afternoon glow. It smells like one of its own knockoffs. *J'aime bien, mais j'adore pas.* TS

J'Adore l'Absolu (Dior) ★ ★ ★ ★ *jasmine rose* $$
This flanker to J'Adore uses more floral absolutes in the recipe: you can smell a richer rose, a touch of tuberose (missing from the original), and an excellent grassy-green jasmine, which all comes off smelling like a variation on Joy. While I like it very much, I find this gimmick of redoing a fragrance with high-quality naturals, as Givenchy did also with limited editions of Amarige and others, somewhat embarrassing: Do they really want to emphasize how cheap the florals are in the originals? TS

Jaïpur (Boucheron) ★ ★ ★ ★ *apricot tart* $ $

Sophia Grojsman has composed more masterpieces than seems fair, and the perfumes of her mature period in the nineties (Trésor, Yvresse) likely made IFF more money than the rest of the firm's work combined. Her late-manner "florals" are actually extraordinarily fruity, but in a peculiar way reminiscent of ripe, sweet, transparent fruit in syrup rather than the powdery lactonic notes of fruity chypres or the cute, sour berries of contemporary fruity florals. Jaïpur, like Grojsman's exactly contemporary Kashaya for Kenzo, is a majestic sweet-sour accord of apricots and plums overlying a complex woody-rosy heart. Kashaya's internal contrasts were so intense and well judged that the perfume felt as if it came out in stripes. Jaïpur is a lighter composition, with some of the gourmand attraction of Poison, but none of the indigestible chemistry. Jaïpur, in fact, smells like one of those highly ornamental and nevertheless delicious French yellow-plum tarts that are to pastry what Versailles is to gardens. LT

Jaïpur Homme (Boucheron) ★ ★ ★ *sweet powder* $ $

A pleasant, powdery oriental, a sort of cross between Shalimar Eau Légère and Habit Rouge. A bit too deliberately dandified for my taste, as if it were part of a set of things purchased in a hurry to celebrate being admitted to a country club. Go for New York instead. LT

Jaïpur Homme Fraicheur (Boucheron) ★ ★ ★ *earthy fresh* $ $

A very presentable if slightly pale vetiver top note with a touch of an earthy geosmin-like material in the drydown, set against a quiet green lavender-citrus accord. Composed by Annick Ménardo in what must have been an uncharacteristically irenic mood. LT

Jaïpur Saphir (Boucheron) ★ *gum ball* $ $

My eight-year-old son, who has an inherited fondness for trash, always gravitates, tugging me by the arm, toward the type of gumball machine that contains an oversized, brightly colored assortment in a big transparent sphere. Put the coin in, turn the handle, and there falls into your hand a soiled, dusty ball the size of a sheep's eye, which tastes like a cross between shampoo and taxi freshener. Jaïpur Saphir achieves the same effect without any of the fun. LT

Jamais le Dimanche (Ego Facto) ★ *marine dreck* $$
The press materials claim this land for incense. If this is incense, those felted scarves sold for $10 on New York's Sixth Avenue are pashmina. TS

Japon Noir (Tom Ford) ★ ★ ★ *spicy wood* $$$
JN is a fine piece of intricate perfumery counterpoint, a rich, compact, spicy confection with unusual fresh, powdery notes in the heart and a distinguished woody-floral drydown. At times I detect the same structure with a touch of osmanthus as in the legendary Nombre Noir (curiously also a Japan-inspired fragrance), but this one is more opaque and less affecting. Beautiful nevertheless, enigmatic, and well put together. LT

Un Jardin Après la Mousson (Hermès) ★ ★ ★ ★ *floral pepper* $$$
This is Jean-Claude Elléna's third Jardin, after the innovative Méditerranée and the somewhat sullen Nil. Elléna is a perfumer of great inventiveness and refinement, and this is a piece of work to admire as well as enjoy. The core accord, best enjoyed on skin for simultaneity of effect, is a remarkable idea: a combination of melon, capsicum, and peppercorns that, to my nose, adds up to the incongruously fruity note that distinguishes habanero chilies from mere hot ones. Elléna's skill here is didactic: as you smell it, the construction comes apart and flies back together like an instructional video, and the effect is delightful. On a paper strip or on fabric, the fragrance is rather different, with the notes peaking at different times in a succession of fresh, watery effects that holds the attention while remaining abstract. I have often complained about a slightly bloodless aspect of recent Hermès creations. In this case it is essential to the artistic effect and completely convincing: as often happens

with perfectly tuned fragrances, the mix is much stronger than it appears at first sniff. Excellent. LT

Jardin du Néroli (Maître Parfumeur et Gantier) ★ ★ ★
resinous orange $ $
A very good neroli, complete with the resinous, orange-flower-and-citrus aspects, against a nice woody-musky background. LT

Un Jardin en Méditerranée (Hermès) ★ ★ ★ *tomato stem* $ $
This was Elléna's first fragrance for Hermès (2003), and it is done in an odd transitional style borrowing elements from different worlds: the prevailing squeaky-clean florals of the day (Pleasures and its descendants); an incongruous, loud green top note of tomato stems (first done in Ricci's 1996 Les Belles) that hints at the paint-from-nature style of later Hermès works; and an odd quotation of Jacques Cavallier's superb but doomed Feu d'Issey (1998). Curiously, it is the focaccia note of Feu d'Issey that makes the whole thing work as a sunny, abstract composition, a sort of scrambled Dufy watercolor. Time gradually upsets the precarious balance of the parts, and the drydown is banal. LT

Jardins de Bagatelle (Guerlain) ★ ★ ★ *dry floral* $ $
A comical effect of perfumery's recent race to the bottom in terms of quality is that even the harshest, most chemical fragrances of earlier days now seem positively organic. Bagatelle (released in 1983) was for long my least favorite Guerlain before being dethroned by post-LVMH succubi like Mahora and Champs-Elysées. What is odd about it is that the fashion for acid, metallic florals has come back and JdB now takes pride of place, a grande dame among droids. Not great, but the very best of a lousy lot. LT

Un Jardin sur le Nil (Hermès) ★ ★ ★ *woody fresh* $ $ $
The involuntarily hilarious story of the composition of this fragrance was told by Chandler Burr in the *New Yorker,* with poor Elléna trudging

to a five-star hotel in Egypt for inspiration accompanied by a high-level Hermès contingent. The result of this pointless exercise is a curiously flat, shapeless, pale-green affair that initially smells a bit like a new plastic tablecloth, then settles to a pleasant woody-fresh drydown. LT

Jasmal (Creed) ★ ★ ★ *green jasmine* $$$
A simple, straightforward jasmine soliflore with a green top note. LT

Le Jasmin (Annick Goutal) ★ ★ *metallic jasmine* $$$
There's an excellent jasmine wasted in here, a combination of grassy green and creamy white floral, marred by a powerful woody amber with a sharp, peppery character. TS

Le Jasmin (Chantecaille) ★ *cucumber jasmine* $$
A green, indolic jasmine, dosed for some reason with a ton of the strange, peculiar, oily-metallic cucumber of violet nitrile. LT suggests that some people are more sensitive to the harshness of nitriles than others. To this reviewer, this fragrance is like nails on a chalkboard. TS

Jasmin 17 (Le Labo) ★ *crap jasmine* $$
A wan little jasmine so grievously defaced by a civet reconstitution (chiefly made of the fecal-smelling molecule skatole) that it manages to smell pretty dire all the way to the drydown. LT

Jasmin de Nuit (The Different Company) ★ ★ ★ *spicy jasmine* $$
When Jean-Claude Elléna left The Different Company to become the in-house perfumer at Hermès, his daughter, Céline Elléna, became the perfumer for TDC. Like several of the top perfumers from France, Céline is working in the family business (her grandfather was also a perfumer, making her a third-generation nose), but her style, judging by this, her first fragrance for the line, does not follow her father's low-calorie *nouvelle parfumerie*. A world away from the previous minimalist entries in this line, JdN is a heavily animalic jasmine, in the more-is-

more, heavy-handed, hippie-orientalist mold of Maurice Roucel's Musc Ravageur. I find it a little Norma Desmond in effect, but who's to say there's never a time for that sort of thing? TS

Jasmine (Keiko Mecheri) ★ ★ ★ *jasmine soliflore* $$$
An unambitious but nice jasmine soliflore, of the greener and grassier variety. TS

Jasmine (Renée) ★ ★ *white floral* $$
A boring "white flowers in a field" crowded with boring white flowers. LT

Jasmin et Cigarette (Etat Libre d'Orange) ★ ★ ★ ★ *floral ashtray* $$
Delightfully does what it says, with only one small quibble: had René Magritte smelled this fragrance, he would no doubt have exclaimed, "Ceci est une pipe!" The tobacco note in this fragrance reminds me not of a cigarette, but of the old Monsieur Rochas, which was designed to smell like a cold pipe. How times have changed. Smoking is now a sin, and some erotic magazines specialize in pictures of smoking women, making me think I should have stocked up years ago. LT

Jasmin Noir (Bulgari) ★ ★ *woody floral* $$
Noir is the new silly. This is the sort of industrial-strength, thickly scored, too-many-cooks (four perfumers, apparently) composition the French call *une soupe*. TS describes the genre as cough-syrup ice cream, and I agree. LT

Jasmin Vert (Miller Harris) ★ ★ ★ *elegant floral* $$$
In a world awash with perfumery dross sold as gold, a brand like Miller Harris that sells quality fragrances made with a high proportion of natural materials is a refreshing change. MH fragrances have been getting steadily better, denser, and more interesting over the years, and this complex, abstract white floral with narcissus is an accomplished

piece of work in an English summer-dress-and-rosy-cheeks style. Recommended. LT

Jasper Conran Woman (Jasper Conran) ★ ★ ★ ★ *citrus chypre* $$$
A bright, balanced, classic citrus eau de cologne with a dash of green, resinous, woody chypre in the manner of Chanel Pour Monsieur; a lemon top note that wakes you up like birdsong at sunrise; and a good soapy jasmine that keeps it all going. Feels like an all-grown-up version of L'Artisan Parfumeur's Thé pour un Eté. TS

Jazz (Yves Saint Laurent) ★ ★ ★ ★ *fresh fougère* $
Time flies: Jazz is nearly twenty years old. At the time of its release, it struck me as a timid, overly complicated, and rather cheap-smelling fougère, less confident than the classics of the genre (Azzaro, Calvin, etc.) and less adventurous than, say, the similarly artemisia-based Romeo Gigli per Uomo. Sometimes things improve with time because we get used to them, and sometimes Warren Buffett's maxim applies: "You don't know who's swimming naked until the tide goes out." The tide of masculines did go out, to reveal dozens of unprecedentedly dull "sport" fragrances, all in Speedos. Jazz now feels pleasantly rich, a little timid, and altogether charming, like a handsome guy (I picture Saint Laurent himself) wading into the waves in the buff without removing his specs. Very nice. LT

Jean Paul Gaultier "Classique" Eau d'Eté (Jean Paul Gaultier) ★
light citrus $$
Nearly imperceptible citrus-floral when sprayed on paper, smells like Elmer's glue on skin. Then it vanishes, practically on contact. TS

Jean Paul Gaultier "Classique" Eau de Toilette (Jean Paul Gaultier) ★ *fruit oriental* $
Gaultier's Classique may stand forever as the perfect triumph of packaging over contents. The striking bottle, with the shape of an armless

feminine torso like a dressmaker's dummy outfitted with frosted glass corset, is a direct copy of the famous torso bottle for the original Shocking by Schiaparelli. The tiresome fragrance, composed by Jacques Cavallier, who knows better, rivals Amarige in terms of diabolical intent: cloying notes of canned orange sections in syrup collaborate with powerful, powdery vanilla-musks to overwhelm. It manages, amazingly, to be both pungent and thin, like the far end of a cheap drydown. And it was a huge hit. TS

Jean Paul Gaultier Monsieur (Jean Paul Gaultier) ★ ★
verbena cedar $
Dilute, not very interesting citrus herbal. TS

Je Reviens Couture (Worth) ★ ★ ★ ★ *floral green* $
Couture is French for "not the ugly little bottle sold on the duty-free trolley in flight, the one that smelled like paint stripper." JRC has finally kept the promise implicit in its name—*je reviens* means "I'll return." Over the last thirty years, the Worth coinage had been so debased by accountants making the formula ever cheaper that this pillar of classical perfumery had become a sad joke. I do not have the sixties one at hand to compare, but it is vivid in my memory: a classic, muted floral-salicylate accord. Salicylates, kissing cousins to aspirin, have a strange, nondescript floral-green smell with smoky overtones, which smells perfumy in itself and works mysterious wonders in floral accords. The top note of JRC is unquestionably a proper, el-expensivo jasmine, and the drydown is fine. What's missing? The same that's missing in every modern version of fifties classics: nitro musks, without which this kind of perfume is permanently hobbled. All the same, welcome back. LT

Je Suis un Homme (Etat Libre d'Orange) ★ ★ ★ ★ *woody citrus* $ $
An excellent woody masculine in the general direction of Guerlain's Derby, but drier and with more citrus up top. Solid, nicely crafted, and lush. LT

Jewel (Alfred Sung) ★ ★ ★ *soapy floral* $

In this unambitious style, it's hard to achieve more than fair-to-middling glory. Jewel does all right for its genre, alternately smelling like Tide and a green muguet-jasmine floral. TS

JF (Floris) ★ ★ *green apple* $ $

Floris's signature men's fragrance, named after their founder, Juan Famenias Floris (shouldn't it be JFF?), is an extra-fruity, simplified Cool Water. I do like the invigorating mixed-citrus top note, but it doesn't last. TS

Jicky (Guerlain) ★ ★ ★ ★ ★ *lavender vanilla* $

Jicky is the oldest perfume in continuous existence: since 1889, the year of the Eiffel Tower, the Exposition Universelle, the first centenary of the French Revolution. This claim is occasionally disputed by phony pretenders to the throne, like Penhaligon's, Floris, and Houbigant (old names, new formulas) or complete fabrications like Rancé. Such durability cannot be a mere matter of luck: Jicky brought something new to perfumery, and that something still matters today, partly because much that has happened in between is far from good news. By the standards of postwar fragrance, Jicky is a marvel of simplicity, an object lesson in perfumery. The basic idea is lavender and vanilla. Lavender, then as now, was steam-distilled and not wildly expensive. Vanilla is another matter. When Jicky was being conceived, synthetic vanillin made by the Reimer-Tiemann process was just coming onstream, and the firm of De Laire in France had got the license on the patent. The first synthetic vanillin wasn't just cheap, it was different from the natural stuff, far sweeter and creamier. Aimé Guerlain wisely chose a mixture of synthetic and natural, one for power, the other for bloom. But De Laire's yellow vanillin was peculiar, because the German process left a small amount of cough-mixture guaiacol and other smoky phenols in the final mix, which is why Guerlain continued to ask for this special impure grade when the process was improved. Nowadays they just add a touch of rectified birch tar to get the effect. That effect is what Ernest Beaux hankered after when he complained that his vanillas always turned out like crème anglaise, and Guerlain's like Jicky. But vanilla and lavender are only part of the story. Jicky also contains a huge citrus note (think lemon cheesecake), Guerlain's trademark bouquet of French herbs (thyme, etc.), a big dose of civet and Lord (actually Jean-Paul Guerlain) only knows what else. Is the modern Jicky identical to the first one? Of course not. Is it an honest attempt to continue it? Yes. I cannot comment on pre-WWII Jicky, having smelled it only once, and then fleetingly. I can vouch for the fact that the Jicky of my childhood was raunchier, more curvaceous, less stately. What happened? Hard to say: it can't be the lavender or the vanilla, it can't be the citrus, the herbs, or the civet. As Holmes said, "When you have eliminated the impossible, whatever remains, however improbable, must be the truth." My guess is that what made the old Jicky smile were the irreplaceable nitro musks, most of which disappeared from European perfumery years ago because of alleged neurotoxic and photochemical problems. The modern Jicky is perhaps a touch smoother and cleaner than it really should be, but still a towering masterpiece. And one more thing: lest anyone think that unisex perfumes are a modern invention, this one was worn by both women and men ten years before an electric car, the Jamais Contente, broke the world speed record and hit 100 km per hour. LT

Jil Sander Pure for Men (Jil Sander) ★ ★ *woody citrus* $$$
Clean, dull, fade-to-white masculine sports fragrance. As distinctive as a lump of rock in a quarry. LT

Jil Sander Style (Jil Sander) ★ *woody floral* $$$
A woody-sweet white floral so derivative, so flat, so cloying that I gave up trying to find what it was an imitation of because it is a medley of half a dozen things (themselves derivative) I don't want to be reminded of. LT

John Galliano (John Galliano) ★ ★ *sweet aldehydic* $ $

A few years back, Galliano did a home fragrance of spice and incense that was so drop-dead, some fans sprayed it on their clothes and wore it on the town. "Make it a real perfume!" they cried. A vital part of the message must have been lost, since this baroque purple bottle is filled with an entirely unrelated powdery floral: part iris, part dry wood, part sweet lime blossom, pleasantly radiant in an Iris Poudre way, and reminiscent of the too-sweet drydown of Bendelirious, though it falls apart on skin. TS

John Varvatos (John Varvatos) ★ ★ *sweet fougère* $

For classicists, nothing beats the smell, on a man, of old-fashioned shaving cream. So though there's nothing out of the ordinary about this sweet, lime-peel soapy barbershop air, I do find it more appealing than the last twenty masculines I've smelled. However, the drydown gets cheap fast. Serious dandies wear Caron's No. 3 or YSL's Rive Gauche for men anyway. TS

Jolie Madame (Balmain) ★ ★ ★ *green violet* $ $

One of the all-time great leather chypres, Balmain's Jolie Madame was composed by the legendary Germaine Cellier in 1953, in those glorious postwar years when everyone still wore hats. Leathers veered between the plush and the butch: Chanel's Cuir de Russie, plush; Knize Ten, butch. Cabochard, plush; Cellier's own Bandit, butch. Jolie Madame was unusual in avoiding both plush and butch via a big fruity violet note that made what could have been a harsh, bitter leather in the style of Bandit instead the easiest to wear of the classic leathers, simultaneously girlish and tough, like a patent-leather Mary Jane. It was pretty but with plenty of spine: just about perfect. In fact, when I was asked by friends which perfume I'd choose if I were condemned by a heartless judge to marry one fragrance and stick to it, I said I'd take Jolie Madame, because it always seemed to hit the spot. But Balmain was bought recently by a firm that owns several other once-great fragrance brands, and a flood of bottles hit discounters, leading us to suspect inventory was being cleared because a repackaging or reformulation was coming. The packaging is the same as last year, but the smell is somewhat emptier: more chemical, amber-free, with a harsh green note that sticks out and begs for trimming. Right now, Jolie Madame is a fine violet with character, but she's not what she used to be. TS

Joop! Go (Joop!) ★ *citrus rosy* $
A slightly more floral version of a clean, green soapy sport fragrance (even the bottle is shaped like a bar of bath soap), in which you feel a perfumer is trying her best to make the most of a bad lot by sneaking in a few oriental flourishes under the required glacial freshness. Still not good. TS

Joop! Homme (Joop!) ★ ★ *violet soapy* $
Strange suggestion for a male fragrance: a sweet, animalic floral. Alas, it smells as cheap as floor cleaner, but it coulda been a contender. TS

Joop! Jump (Joop!) ★ ★ *apple shampoo* $
Sad Cool Water clone. LT

Jour de Fête (L'Artisan Parfumeur) ★ ★ *play duh* $$$
I have a hard time seeing the point of this kindergarten accord of vanilla and heliotropin, a sort of perfumery "duh" with no other virtue than bland, sweet pleasantness. Nice on a baby, I guess. LT

Jovan Musk for Women (Jovan) ★ ★ ★ *soapy musky* $
Coty's answer in 1972 to the hippie fashion for single-note oils (musk, patchouli, or sandalwood, generally) was Jovan Musk, a composition masquerading as a stand-alone material. It's actually quite floral, in a pretty lily-of-the-valley way, but the musk is nevertheless the main event: a hard-to-resist smell that broadcasts warm, friendly vibes all around. Still cheap, still cheerful. TS

Jovan White Musk (Jovan) ★★ *watery musky* $

There's something melancholy, metallic, and reminiscent of swimming pools in this flat little musky floral. TS

Joy Comes from Within (Creative Scentualization) ★★★
big meringue $$

CS is a small California firm run by Sarah Horowitz-Thran, and the Comes from Within line is a range of upmarket niche fragrances. The silly self-help names made me anticipate the equivalent of Windham Hill music, i.e., organically grown Rohypnol. Not so: these are competently crafted. JCfW is a big, plush, comfortable aldehydic-orange-flower-and-vanilla accord, very pleasant but not very original and much less interesting than Love (By Kilian). LT

Joy eau de parfum (Jean Patou) ★★★★ *floral aldehydic* $$$

I have it on completely trusty authority that no changes whatsoever have been made to the formula of Joy and Joy EdP save the inevitable adjustments that all fragrance firms make to deal with batch-to-batch quality fluctuations in natural raw materials. This said, I would not be particularly surprised if one day Patou was forced to follow suit and either reformulate the classics as Guerlain, Chanel, and everyone else has done or (unlikely for a P&G company) put a skull and crossbones on the bottle. I would urge all Patou fanatics to stock up against this eventuality. However, perfume lovers take note: what is sold as Joy EdP is the old Eau de Joy, a different formula from Joy parfum, and this was always so. The EdP uses lighter, fresher qualities of both jasmine and rose and more aldehydes. To my nose it comes across as more citrus-rosy, less abstract, and less dark than the parfum. This said, it is wonderful. LT

Joy parfum (Jean Patou) ★★★★★ *symphonic floral* $$$

There has been much talk about Joy being damaged by reformulation, and I have more than once been called names by Joy aficionados who swear blind that Joy has been changed and therefore I must be either corrupt or incompetent. Nothing is certain in this valley of tears, and Joy may one day be changed, so stock up if your life depends on it. But the sample of Joy I received in October 2007 straight from the Patou fountain smelled every last bit as good as it ever did, i.e., sensational. To call Joy a floral is to misunderstand it, since the whole point of its formula (Henri Alméras, 1930) was to achieve the platonic idea of a flower, not one particular earthly manifestation. Joy does not smelled of rose, jasmine, ylang, or tuberose. It just smells huge, luscious, and utterly wonderful. LT

Jubilation 25 (Amouage) ★ ★ ★ ★ *fruity chypre* $$$$
One imagines an Amouage brief to be a bit of a mixed blessing for the perfumer. On the one hand, money may not be an object, as was the case for Gold and Dia, enabling the use of stupendous raw materials that evoke ancient splendors. On the other hand, the thousand-and-one-nights aesthetic is a hostage to fortune, because Serge Lutens has been there already and rules over all the Emirates west of Medina. Lucas Sieuzac has taken the no-compromise route of composing a fragrance from a classical French template and suggesting the Orient only by giving it more weight and languor than it would otherwise have. His starting point seems to have been Diorella, that amazingly intricate yet perfectly legible accord that was the crowning achievement of Roudnitska's career. Except that Jubilation (if I may be excused an anachronistic simile) is Diorella revised by Jacques Guerlain, with more amber and woods than I thought could fit in there, and none of the dissonant spring-in-Paris freshness of the original. The result is luxurious, oddly familiar, and likable from the start, and it is only later in the story that one realizes that Catherine Deneuve is speaking fluent Arabic. LT

Jubilation XXV (Amouage) ★ ★ ★ ★ *spicy incense* $$$$
The two Jubilation fragrances released by Amouage, the Omani firm, for its twenty-fifth anniversary are a delightful surprise after the disastrous last few. Amouage is under new artistic directorship, and apparently

the perfumers were chosen "blind"—i.e., fragrance first, name later, which is unusual. XXV is for men, ideally composed by the orientalist Bertrand Duchaufour, and perfectly in character with the brief: a modern Arabian fragrance. It sits somewhere between Gucci Envy for Men (ginger) and Gucci pour Homme (incense) in tonality, but in my opinion is more interesting than either of its precursors. The uniquely clean note of Omani frankincense is exactly right—light, transparent, and dry—and the spicy surround is warm and natural, though those who are hypersensitive to woody-amber notes may stumble upon one in the drydown. LT

Juicy Couture (Juicy Couture) ★ ★ ★ ★ *tuberose floral* $$
Far classier than the wonderfully trashy packaging would lead one to suppose, this is a nicely crafted floral incorporating that rare thing, a delicate, transparent tuberose. Clearly inspired by abstract florals in the manner of Beyond Paradise, but one of the best in the genre. LT

Jules (Dior) ★ ★ ★ ★ *aromatic fougère* $$
The little-known Jules (*jules* means something like "main squeeze" in French) is one of the most adventurous, reckless fougères ever put together. Its top note of sage on a background of cedar will either delight or shock depending on whether sage smells aromatic or urinous to you. But it's not that simple: to me sage smells urinous and that is precisely why I love Jules. Like Caron's Yatagan and YSL's Kouros, it feels like you know your lover well enough to no longer bother closing the bathroom door. LT

Juozas Statkevicius (Juozas Statkevicius) ★ ★ *woody oriental* $$
Juozas Statkevicius is a Lithuanian fashion designer from Vilnius (go there if you can, it's beautiful). His fragrance starts as a good cedar-incense oriental in the Comme des Garçons style but, sadly, is marred by a dreadful cloying drydown. LT

Just Cavalli Her (Roberto Cavalli) ★ *airline sweets* $
A tired, sad, cheap little fruity oriental, which got to this particular
party four years late. As Michael Curtiz said, "Bring on the empty
horses!" LT

Just Cavalli Him (Roberto Cavalli) ★ ★ *soapy woody* $
Pleasant, clean, slightly melancholy little thing, in the ugliest bottle
since East Germany went under. LT

Just Me (Paris Hilton) ★ *barf-bag floral* $
I defer to the fragrantbodyoilz Web site: "The top presents an ethereal
halo with delicious notes of frozen Apple and juicy Peach Nectar
wrapped with dewy Muguet and a splash of wet Ozone. A luminous
bouquet of sensual floralcy is at the heart of this fragrance. Delicate
Mimosa Blossoms entwined with sheer Freesia and Night-Blooming
Jasmine petals, while heady, rich Tuberose provides depth and texture.
At it's base, creamy Sandalwood is infused with Oakmoss and laced
with feminine Ylang-Ylang blossoms. Musk rounds and softens the
scent while a touch of Pheromones creates a sensual energy and undeni-
able allure that makes this fragrance the perfect signature for Paris Hilton. Celebrity... Trend Setter... Model... Beauty... Socialite...
Star." All true, unquestionably, hideously true. LT

Just Me for Men (Paris Hilton) ★ *sad sack* $
Ideal for her sort of guy. LT

Karma solid perfume (LUSH) ★ ★ ★ ★ *orange patchouli* $
Of all the terrifying potent odors that thicken the atmosphere in and
around any LUSH shop, Karma seems to be the most popular and probably still the best, a friendly combination of orange, patchouli, and lavender with a touch of sweetness. A good hippie fragrance is hard to find:
Karma is blessedly without the bloodless pallor of so many nature-

loving fragrances and without the hippie stonk of headshop oils. Basically, this is just good. Also, I love perfume solids. TS

Kate Moss (Kate Moss) ★ ★ *fruity floral* $
Leaving aside jokes about what the beautiful and well-turned-out Kate Moss can currently smell given what she puts in her nose, the first surprise of her fragrance is the packaging. The bottle looks incredibly cheap and kitschy, like a drugstore nail polish for the middle school set—Coty clearly spared every expense. The simple fragrance is pretty good at a distance, a small-scale Badgley Mischka built out of a bare berry and a sketch of a rose, but less good and somewhat harsh up close. TS

Keep It Fluffy (B Never Too Busy to Be Beautiful) ★
creamsicle musk $
In the BNTBTBB package of fragrances we received in 2007, one showed up smashed in transit, covering its perfectly innocent brethren with a smell so crude, so cloying, we nearly chucked the lot unreviewed. This was it. Don't let it deter you from the others. TS

Kelly Calèche (Hermès) ★ ★ ★ *vegetable iris* $$$
With Kelly Calèche, you get two perfumes in one. The bad news is neither is great, and they don't talk to each other. On fabric or a blotter, the complex top notes immediately inform you that the first of these perfumes is one of Jean-Claude Elléna's vegetable-patch accords, first seen in 2003 in Jardin en Méditerranée: tomato stems, grass, warm hay, clean earth. But Jardin possessed hybrid vigor, to pursue the horticultural metaphor, and its disparate components helped each other, whereas here they do not. The second perfume, which takes over very rapidly on skin, is basically Dior Homme, a warm, balsamic iris accord that worked a treat in the context of the youthful, virile directness of DH, but makes little sense in a classy feminine. Overall, this is one Elléna creation where

overrefinement and ornamentation predominate over structure and purpose. Disappointing. LT

Kenzo Air (Kenzo) ★ ★ ★ ★ *pepper vetiver* $
I was half expecting this to be a joke and the bottle to feel empty, like those canisters of inert gas that they sell to preserve wine. Instead, this is the world's most lightweight vetiver, cleverly built out of a dry, peppery note of angelica, anisic notes, and an austere woody-amber material. Feels a little cheap, but wonderful. The bottle looks like the high-concept cap to an even bigger bottle. TS

Kenzo Amour (Kenzo) ★ ★ ★ ★ *inedible vanilla* $$
It's been a while (probably Opium in 1979) since I last saw such a textbook case of top-down design. The beautiful and very Japanese space-age Art Nouveau melamine bottle matches the fragrance so perfectly in weight, texture, and color, it is hard not to laugh the first time you see, then smell. This perfume could easily have been a disaster: if one had to describe it in plain words, it would be "Bulgari's Black without the Rubber," or "Je Reviens with More Vanilla," both very unpromising territories and long trampled to mud by hordes of perfumers. But Daphné Bugey, a talented perfumer who recently did confidential reconstructions of four Coty classics I'd swim a mile for, chose to dig at the hardest spot in perfumery and found gold. Kenzo Amour has the plushness of a vanillic amber without the flat crème-brûlée angle, and the contemplative, muted floral coolness of Je Reviens without the bitter, poisonous character of salicylates. In fact, the irresolution between "Eat me" and "Don't eat me" is what makes this fragrance great. LT

Kenzo Amour Indian Holi (Kenzo) ★ ★ *rose oriental* $$
An unsuccessful attempt to mate the monumental vanilla-floral-woody structure of Kenzo Amour to the berry-rose-pepper of Miss Dior Chérie. The offspring is sterile. TS

Kenzo Amour le Parfum (Kenzo) ★ ★ ★ *solvent vanilla* $$

As with Flower, Kenzo alters the formula for the parfum concentration, making it a flanker variation of the original. In this instance, an ill-judged dose of powerful woody-amber notes plus more intense vanilla synthetics distort the form till it breaks. Since Kenzo Amour was potent enough, a parfum feels superfluous anyway. TS

Kenzo Jungle "L'Eléphant" (Kenzo) ★ ★ ★ ★ *clove plum* $$

Féminité du Bois was the first of this new breed of transparent, fruity cedar orientals, and Dolce Vita gave the idea a more classical orchestration. Kenzo Jungle dropped both the sleek modernism of the Shiseido and the luxury plush of the Dior and made it fun, by using a heavy hand with the clove and other spices, and amping up the fruit considerably. That fruit was the popular base Prunol, sold by the company De Laire and used for decades in moderation to give things like Jolie Madame and Coco a touch of raisin, before Kenzo Jungle poured it in with abandon. Like an Opium for the nineties set, Jungle is loud but lively, prickling with good humor all around. TS

Kenzo Jungle pour Homme (Kenzo) ★ ★ ★ ★ *lactonic citrus* $$

This light, woody citrus feels like a safer nutmeg variation on the cardamom cologne of Cartier's Déclaration, but with a lovely buttermilk backdrop saving it from joining the pile of forgettable spicy sports fragrances. Instead, it's wonderfully relaxed and unpretentious. (I love the kooky zebra-mane brush cap on the bottle.) TS

Kenzo pour Homme (Kenzo) ★ ★ ★ *fresh herbal* $

In 1991, Kenzo pour Homme was the second fragrance to use the melon-marine note of Calone prominently, after New West and before L'Eau d'Issey. It's a gentle woody herbal—anise and cedar—with a pale, subliminal shimmer, for the generation that wanted fragrance to be antifragrance. TS

Kenzo pour Homme Fresh (Kenzo) ★ ★ *herbal pine* $ $
I'm not saying there's nothing charming about the orange-spice oriental lurking in this fresh woody flanker to the original Kenzo Homme. I'm just saying that it's basically soap that doesn't get you clean. TS

Kiki (Vero Profumo) ★ ★ ★ ★ *strange lavender* $ $ $
Vero Kern is an aromatherapist turned perfumer, a trajectory that in my experience usually yields faith-based disasters composed in the presence of crystals. She differs from most others in the field, however, in her willingness to learn from masters (Monique Schlienger and Guy Robert) and in clearly possessing a natural talent for perfumery. Kiki is a lavender in which the slight burnt-sugar off note of lavender absolute has been extended rather than masked, by an accord of caramel and opopanax that accompanies it from top note to drydown. The effect is fresh, slightly barbershop-retro, and altogether memorable. Strongly recommended. LT

Kingdom (Alexander McQueen) ★ *heavy cumin* $ $
This perfume reminds me of whimsical newspaper features from quiet news days of the seventies: "How many people can you get into a Mini?" with pictures showing faces and hands pressed against windows. The question here would be "How many notes can you shoehorn into the drydown of Allure?" and the answer is "One too many." When this perfume came out, everyone raved about the fact that it contained cumin, as if that provided an excuse for the fact that it was dull, heavy, and opaque. Mercifully, it flopped. LT

Kisu (Tann Rokka) ★ ★ ★ *floral chypre* $ $ $
Upmarket home-decoration firm Tann Rokka does two fragrances. This was their first, a nice woody rose in the manner of the late, lamented Nombre Noir, unfortunately overlaid on a banal green chypre structure, which eventually shows through. Best worn on fabric to make the pleasant part last longer. LT

Kiton Black (Kiton) ★ ★ ★ *woody green* $ $

Kiton's second masculine fragrance takes the usual violet-leaf woody accord we've seen a million times and tweaks the terrifically strange top note with a few tricks borrowed from the structure of Missoni: a hissy, sharp white floral and a dry, screechy, chocolate-like woody jangling at the outer edges, with a sweet violet middle section holding it together. It works until the woody amber takes over, as woody ambers always seem to do. TS

Kiton Man (Kiton) ★ ★ *citrus herbs* $ $

A light, unexciting woody citrus with herbal touches, made a little strange by one of those harsh citrus or floral synthetics that has the high, panicked feeling of a teakettle whistling at full blast somewhere out of sight. TS

Knize Ten (Knize) ★ ★ ★ ★ ★ *amber leather* $ $

As Alphonse Allais put it, "As time passes, one meets fewer and fewer people who knew Napoléon." Knize Ten, like the sole veteran of the Grande Armée who lived long enough to be photographed, must feel terribly lonely these days, for it is the only survivor of the androgynous, reckless, dandified twenties leathers. Its elder by five years, Tabac Blond (1919), recently died a death at the hands of International Fragrance Association regulations and Caron perfumer Richard Fraysse, and if you look around there are no pre-WWII leathers left standing: Kobako, Shocking, and no doubt many others, all gone. (Cuir de Russie does not count in this context, because it is primarily a stupendous iris floral with a leather accent.) Knize Ten was composed by François Coty and Vincent Roubert, respectively the man who invented all perfumery and the man who did Iris Gris. For a long period KT was out of stock, the firm did not know when it would come back, etc. I feared the worst. I cannot vouch for the exact resemblance of today's formula to the original. What I can say is (a) it smells wonderful, with all the proper requisites of a leather, including smoky and amber notes firmly in place; (b) it contains a splendid strawberry top note, which, by a classic piece of perfumery misdirection, kisses you on the lips just as you focus on the dry, dark background; (c) it goes on forever in a completely civilized manner; and (d) it does not cost the earth. Let me put it simply: everyone should own this perfume, because there is only one like it. LT

Knowing (Estée Lauder) ★ ★ ★ ★ ★ *mossy rose* $
Of all the big fruity roses from the seventies and eighties, Knowing is perhaps the most polished and most wearable. At the time, synthetic fruity rose materials like damascones and damascenones had changed the landscape of rose perfumes, making them bigger, brighter, stronger, practically glow-in-the-dark. The great idea of the rose chypres, beginning with the now-discontinued Sinan, was to set these intense materials against a classic resinous mossy base—rubies against green velvet—to make these mutant roses seem more civilized and less like the rose that ate Tokyo. The results were striking but sometimes exhausting in their power. Knowing (1988) came late in the game and learned the lessons of its ancestors: it piles on the mossy, woody stuff and lets the pink simply peek out. Worn in small doses, it's just right. TS

Kouros (Yves Saint Laurent) ★ ★ ★ ★ ★ *musky fougère* $
Twenty-seven years after its release, the structure of Kouros is still so novel, so immediately recognizable, and so impossible to imitate that it is probably a sporadic case in perfumery. It smells like the tanned skin of a guy with gomina in his hair stepping out of the shower wearing a pre-WWI British dandified fragrance: citrus, flowers, musk. It has that faintly repellent clean-dirty feel of other people's bathrooms, and manages to smell at once scrubbed and promissory of an unmade bed. The fact that all these images are conjured up by a fragrance in itself so consummately abstract is a testimony to the brilliance of its creator, Pierre Bourdon. Such things happen not by accident but only as the work of genius. LT

Krizia Uomo (Krizia) ★ ★ ★ ★ *cilantro cedar* $

Krizia was in some ways the Italian Yves Saint-Laurent, albeit vastly less inventive. Its fragrances had their heyday from 1981 to 1986, first with K, the fragrance that put Maurice Roucel on the map, then Krizia Uomo in 1984, and two years later Teatro alla Scala, a Coco-inspired oriental that smelled great and looked wonderful. The compositions are like Krizia's designs: derivative but beautifully executed, each arguably improving on its model. The nearest relative to Krizia Uomo was probably Antaeus, though distant echoes of Paco Rabanne pour Homme are perceptible as well. But never mind influences: Krizia Uomo is a beautifully constructed woody fougère that starts with a polyphonic citrus note, continues with an unexpected blast of cilantro, and ends on a rich, dry, warm accord of cedar, all the while deftly avoiding both crudeness and dandified languor. LT

L (Apothia) ★ *allegedly iris* $ $

Sour, sweaty, derivative little thing that could have been a failed Hiris submission. Shameful in an expensive niche line. LT

L (L.A.M.B.) ★ ★ *freesia pear* $ $

The scent equivalent of that acid shade of lime green that designers convince the public to wear roughly every six years, after we've forgotten the horror of the last time. TS

L (Lolita Lempicka) ★ ★ ★ *heavy gourmand* $ $

I once had a peculiar dream in which I was wandering the halls of a great château, empty but spotlessly luxurious. Many unlikely things happened, but one is relevant, which I relate here. At the end of one narrow hallway, a small round table held a plate in pure gold, on which sat a gluttonously thick slice of chocolate cheesecake topped by a single mint leaf. The voice of my ghostly host announced, "Allow me to introduce Mr. Roucel." *Enchantée.* To get to the point, a number of Roucel's fragrances (Insolence; 24, Faubourg; L'Instant; Musc Ravageur) have to my mind a feeling of something too rich to stomach, but lightened with a few fresh notes, usually his signature magnolia leaf. As part of this contingent, L is most closely related to Musc Ravageur, but with more of everything: more citrus to start, more vanilla, more pie spice, more chocolate, more musk, more. Impressive but indigestible, except to those hearty persons who always demand a second slice. TS

Labdanum 18 (Le Labo) ★ ★ ★ *hippie amber* $ $
Le Labo fragrances, like the elements of some Periodic Table of Cool, are supposedly named after their main raw material followed by the number of ingredients. Labdanum 18, named after the sweet-ambery resin of cistus, is a pleasant hippie amber in the manner of Ambre Sultan, differing chiefly in a couple of powerful synthetic top notes that its composer Maurice Roucel carried over from his Lapidus pour Lui. LT

Ladyboy (B Never Too Busy to Be Beautiful) ★ ★ ★ ★
earthy amber $
BNTBTBB fragrances have often turned out so weird, rich, and novel that one ends up approaching them as one would a difficult crossword, expecting whatever pleasure they provide to come only after a sustained effort of understanding. This one is no exception, with a strange faceless start that feels like a fragrance seen from the back and a heart note that eventually settles into an autumnal hum: a muted, sullen, basso profundo of linseed putty (labdanum), woodsmoke (oakmoss and fucus), and sweet amber (another facet of labdanum). Be warned: this is a fragrance that only works on skin, so ignore the smelling strip. LT

Lady Caron (Caron) ★ ★ *white floral* $ $
Big, boring, tuberose-rich white-flowers fragrance of no particular interest. LT

Lady Stetson (Stetson) ★ ★ ★ ★ *aldehydic floral* $
Really, if a fragrance like this doesn't make you happy, what will? Aspirational types still buying up Chanel No. 22 in search of the sweet alde-

hydic floral of their dreams, take note: we sprayed Lady Stetson on one strip, No. 22 on the other, and observed the following. While No. 22 is heavy immediately with the plush iris that only Chanel can afford to use at every opportunity, Lady Stetson sets out on an airy, slightly powdery peach. As time goes on, No. 22 gets ever sweeter, to the point of discomfort, while the Lady seems simply to relax. It's a well-balanced structure of just enough amber, just enough floral, just enough peach, just enough soapy citrus to pull up a smile each time it comes to your attention. This fragrance smells great without showing off, and truth to tell, I prefer it to the Chanel. Now, if only the bottle weren't so hideous. TS

Lady Vengeance (Juliette Has a Gun) ★ ★ ★ *soapy rose* $$
Lady Vengeance? Only if in reference to Mrs. Macbeth soaping up. A non-naughty schoolgirl's fragrance, clean in a lemony-woody way. A good fruity rose without guile. TS

Laguna (Salvador Dalí) ★ ★ ★ ★ *transparent fruit* $
Marc Buxton was far ahead of his time when he did this in 1991, but wasted a great idea on a trash brand that did not spend enough cash on the formula. This weird, remote, immediately memorable, fiendishly clever accord of spicy, fruity, and watery notes spawned hundreds of fragrances. It smells the way backstage singing sounds in opera, unseen and haunting. LT

Laguna Homme (Salvador Dalí) ★ *trashoid oriental* $
If you drive a Moscow taxi at night, this one's for you. LT

Lalique Eau de Parfum (Lalique) ★ ★ *peony oriental* $$
A terribly frumpy attempt at an old-fashioned, rich floral oriental: all the elements are there, but they feel shrill and lack character. TS

Lalique White (Lalique) ★ ★ ★ *cream pine* $$
There used to exist a lovely Shiseido masculine called Tactics, a galbanum-

aldehydic confection sold in a Courrèges-like white and silver bottle. I won the right to buy the last bottle of it by threatening to handcuff myself to the metal stairs in Lutens's Palais Royal store. Lalique White, while not quite equaling Tactics' snowy texture, nevertheless goes some way in that direction: richer, creamier, and more feminine than any contemporary masculine usually dares to be. It's as if creator Christine Nagel mixed three parts of Pino Silvestre with one part Balmain's Ivoire and hit the name right on the button. LT

Lanvin L'Homme (Lanvin) ★ ★ *citrus fougère* $ $
The fragrance equivalent of a stage whisper: a quiet accord, only loud as hell. LT

L.A. Style (Mary-Kate and Ashley) ★ *cut-rate Angel* $
The twins' highly styled mugs decorate boxes that look as if they contain hair color. Instead, this contains a fruity disaster with Angel training wheels. There are things just as cheap that smell better. TS

Lauder for Men (Estée Lauder) ★ ★ ★ ★ *animalic fougère* $
A small subset of masculines (Jules, Yatagan, possibly Kouros come to mind) contain materials, like costus, that basically smell of wet hair and skin oils and hover at the extreme edge of decency. Lauder for Men is one of them, a strapping citrus fougère with a stentorian baritone voice, which tapers down to an animalic tobacco note. Anyone who is not anosmic must surely find it irresistible. Loud but wonderful, likely great on a woman. LT

Lauren (Ralph Lauren) ★ ★ *muguet pretender* $
Shame on Ralph Lauren. Gone is that particular lovely, soapy, basil-green, woody violet-rose, that unobtrusive, fresh-faced, proper young lady's fragrance, which radiated sweetly once from the corridors of high schools everywhere. Now inhabiting that ruby red cube is this soulless little changeling, swinging from neroli to lily of the valley in a

flash, having obliterated one set of memories and refusing to inspire any more. TS

Lauren Style (Ralph Lauren) ★ *white floral* $
Hideously screechy and banal "fresh" white-flowers fragrance, with no discernible redeeming features. LT

Lavandula (Penhaligon's) ★ ★ *wrong lavender* $ $
A British firm with a traditional outlook like Penhaligon's owes it to itself to do a decent lavender. After all, some of the world's best lavender used to come from the United Kingdom (Lavender Hill in South London bears witness to this), and much of it still grows in Norfolk. The mind-set that produces a great lavender (see Caldey Island Lavender) is one of humility toward a wonderful raw material: get the best stuff; discreetly iron out the off-notes; add a good, quiet fixative; and let it be. Sadly, Lavandula fails on all counts. You'd expect at least the first five minutes to be smooth, but no: this is a chemical, bath-salts lavender from outset to drydown. A waste of money. LT

Lavender (Caldey Island) ★ ★ ★ ★ ★ *perfect lavender* $
Lavender is summer wind made smell, and the best lavender compositions are, in my opinion, the ones from which other elements are absent, and only endlessly blue daylight air remains. Everyone should own one to feel good as needed and as a reminder that, in the numinous words of my perfumer-chemist colleague Roger Duprey, "There is no such thing as an uninteresting ten-carbon alcohol." Lavender consists mostly of one such, linalool, and needs careful handling both during distillation and composition to remain true to its benign nature. Caldey Island Lavender was composed for the business-minded monks of Caldey, South Wales, by Flemish freelance perfumer Hugo Collumbien (now age ninety), and is simply the best lavender soliflore on earth. To find it, Google the name. LT

L de Lubin (Lubin) ★ ★ *acetone chypre* $ $

It's hard to account for the prominent note of nail-polish remover in L de Lubin, except by assuming they meticulously based their reconstruction on analysis of a bottle that had gone off: a smell of acetone is common in fragrances that have been sitting in light. The rest wasn't really worth resurrecting: a mean crisp green floral in generic seventies style, as if someone has tried to cover up halitosis by rinsing with Eau Sauvage. TS

Le De (Givenchy) ★ ★ ★ ★ *jasmine ylang* $ $

Originally composed by the legendary Ernest Shiftan (Wind Song, Brut, Detchema) and recently reissued after reformulation, this is a deliciously tropical white floral with an unusual sage top note and an enormous jasmine-ylang heart, with scads of raspy indole, as comfortable as a pillow-topped mattress. Such is the quality of the materials that you will like Le De even if, like me, you find this sort of floral generally dull. The name, btw, is pronounced Luh Duh, meaning "The De," whatever that may mean. LT

Lemon Sorbet (Etro) ★ ★ *woody citrus* $ $

Would have been okay by any other name, but is a disappointment. This is a citrus-woody-carnation accord, neither particularly lemony nor particularly fresh, presentable in a slightly dowdy, gray sort of way. LT

Lentisque (Parfums 06130) ★ ★ *musky turf* $ $ $

A nearly nonexistent thin green accord. Useful if you desperately miss mowing the lawn. TS

Let It Rock (Vivienne Westwood) ★ ★ ★ ★ *citrus oriental* $ $

Just when I was feeling sure that no Vivienne Westwood fragrance would ever be worth wearing, this hideous bottle shows up, its name looking like drunken lipstick scrawl on a mirror, capped, like all Westwood's fragrances, with the Holy Hand Grenade of Antioch. The fragrance is wonderful. It sits next to Shalimar Light in the category of modernizations of the Shalimar oriental: a bright, resinous citrus-peel top note, plus a combination of coumarin and heliotropin like a toasted almond biscotti. A beautiful, easygoing, well-made fragrance. ts

Let Me Play the Lion (LesNez) ★ ★ ★ *spicy woody* $ $
Incredibly, the top note of Let Me Play the Lion replicates exactly the wonderful smell of a Middle Eastern shop down the street where I buy my olive oil and coriander. It is a transparent, dusty, satisfying odor of cedarwood and a varied inventory of dried things. I find the rest of the fragrance less interesting, but perhaps I lack imagination: Is there a vast untapped market for perfumes that smell just like sawdust? ts

Liaisons Dangereuses (By Kilian) ★ ★ ★ ★ *rose jam* $ $ $ $
It is a surprising fact of fragrance chemistry that the removal of two measly hydrogen atoms from damascone, a molecule that smells of rose, "cooks" it to achieve a jam-like effect. Rose jam is one of the most delicious things ever and, aside from artichokes, one of the few opportunities we have of demonstrating our superiority over flowers by eating them. Liaisons Dangereuses is a sweet rose fragrance with the brightness of the rose turned down exactly halfway between fresh and edible. I am not overly fond of rose fragrances in general, except when worn by the flower itself, but this is an exceptionally beautiful example of the genre. If you hanker after a rose version of the golden-sunset shades of J'Adore (Calice Becker too), this is it. lt

Liberté (Cacharel) ★ ★ *hard candy* $ $
If your mouth has ever been roughly cratered along the soft insides of your cheeks from sucking too intently on an orange hard candy, you'll recognize the top note of Liberté. To augment the general air of grade-school nostalgia, you get a whiff of inflatable pool toys too. Unfortunately, in a depressingly common bait-and-switch, Liberté loses heart

after a winning start and relies on a strident, sugary woody-amber accord to carry it the rest of the way. In the end, sadly, sickening, but suited to a backyard birthday party for eight-year-olds. TS

Lierre Rose (Parfums 06130) ★ ★ ★ *tobacco tuberose* $$$
A very eighties mixed bouquet with a pipe-tobacco-like amber base, for fans of Oscar de la Renta and the like. Thin but does the trick. TS

Ligea "La Sirena" (Carthusia) ★ ★ *sub Shalimar* $$
A powdery patchouli oriental with citrus top notes, a bit of a mess. TS

Light Blue (Dolce & Gabbana) ★ *citrus "amber"* $
Lemon sorbet doused with rubbing alcohol, technically remarkable in that normally transient top notes are made to last an oddly long time. Trouble is, you want them to go away. If you hate fragrance, you're probably on your fourth bottle. LT

Light Blue pour Homme (Dolce & Gabbana) ★ *marine woody* $
Probably the worst masculine in production today, a combination of, it seems, only two armor-piercing notes that happen to be the most unpleasant in perfumery, marine and woody amber: plague and cholera at once. LT

Light Comes from Within (Creative Scentualization) ★
soapy floral $$
Batteries not included. LT

Light My Heart (Morgan de Toi) ★ ★ ★ *musky clean* $$
Though intended as a feminine, LMH is basically a barbershop masculine and none the worse for it, with a musky-sweaty feel that goes in the direction of Kouros but quieter and more subtle. Surprisingly good and well worth trying. LT

Lily and Spice (Penhaligon's) ★ ★ ★ *lily saffron* $$
Penhaligon's is a frustrating outfit: they are clearly capable of good top-down design, their range is coherent and not outrageously priced, and they have so far avoided the high-concept nonsense typical of niche firms and stuck to making decent semisynthetic fragrances like everyone else. But one wishes they would try harder: many of their fragrances are boring and trite, aimed, it would seem, at tourists who go to Fortnum & Mason to buy presents for the family back in Modena. Lily and Spice is one of their better offerings: a very solid lily soliflore with an unusual saffron note made very fashionable a couple of years ago by a Givaudan ingredient. Oddly, the cresolic spice combination gives L&S a leather aspect I have not encountered in lily soliflores before. Nice but still a bit dull. LT

Lily of the Valley (Floris) ★ ★ *fresh floral* $$
There is no natural LotV extract, so all perfumes that smell anything like the flower are reconstructions, some totally synthetic, some only partly. This one is not bad, but a bit lumbering and functional, as if it were intended to cover a bad smell rather than impart a pleasant one. LT

Lily of the Valley (Penhaligon's) ★ ★ *failed muguet* $$
Muguet gives no fragrance oil (low yield, unstable), and it is not entirely clear whether it contains an as-yet-unidentified molecule responsible for most of its glorious fragrance. Muguet is Prokofiev's "Peter" tune made smell: a lung-expanding frolic through green, light, rosy-fresh notes. I can think of no other character save vanilla that is so universally loved. This has cost it dearly: the best muguet materials are molecules that include both an aldehyde and an alcohol group, respectively supplying bite and soapy softness. Unfortunately these hydroxyaldehydes (hydroxycitronellal, Lyral) are not very powerful. This and their popularity have led them to be used in large quantities on lots of people and have therefore created allergies. Both have now been restricted in use, and hydroxycitronellal is a huge loss. It is therefore no longer possible to

do a good lily of the valley. Penhaligon's tries nevertheless and fails, obtaining instead a green honeysuckle. LT

Lime Basil & Mandarin Cologne (Jo Malone) ★ ★ ★ ★
citrus green $$$
Simply wonderful. A bracing, rich citrus accord with the intriguing grass-and-mint smell of basil, clear and bright as a morning after rain. Just when you think that LB&MC is going to wither and die quietly, instead it glides seamlessly into a classical herbal cologne finish close to Eau d'Orange Verte (Hermès), with a light floral touch and more radiance and tenacity than you'd expect. Comes off natural, clean and relaxed, and comfortingly old-fashioned. Freshly showered guys should wear this instead of the "sport" things they think they like. TS

Lipstick Rose (Frédéric Malle) ★ ★ ★ *violet rose* $$$
To my surprise, it did smell precisely like a wallop of the sort of waxy, powdery rose-violet scent in the fancy French lipsticks that your overly made-up aunt with all the cubic zirconia bracelets might have worn when hovering over you in a cloud of hair spray to give you a smeary kiss on the cheek. It's like a knockoff with reversed values—as if Cartier copied your rhinestone drugstore brooch. A fragrance with a sense of humor is hard to find, and this larger-than-life celebration of a small luxury instantly made me smile. TS

Little Italy (Bond No. 9) ★ *animalic Valencia* $$$
On the one hand, I appreciate that there is a dearth of perfumes with the inimitable brightness of fresh oranges. On the other hand, this is not much help. A big dose of civet tries to add interest but only intensifies the problem. TS

Liu (Guerlain) ★ ★ ★ *powdery jasmine* $$$$
Despite its magnificent Art Deco original bottle (now replaced by the "bees" bottle of the Parisienne line), Liu was always one of the dullest

perfumes Jacques Guerlain ever composed, and its return in 2005 was a bit of a yawn. It is a very rich, competent, powdery jasmine with an unusual, almost lemony lift in the heart notes and a graceful drydown. It feels like face powder writ large. LT

Lolita Lempicka (Lolita Lempicka) ★ ★ ★ ★ ★ *herbal Angel* $ $
With most of the many fragrances based on Thierry Mugler's Angel, the first thing you think on smelling them is "Hello, Angel." Not this time. Perfumer Annick Ménardo found the sole variation that stands on its own. In Angel, a loud fruity-floral accord of jasmine, mango, and blackcurrant, like cleavage set to trumpets, is backed up by a somewhat louche and curiously masculine sweet woody section centered on patchouli. Together they sing a husky-voiced come-on. Lolita Lempicka, the first and best of the post-Angel crowd, keeps the sweet woody stuff but skips the pushup bra; instead, it plays out a fresh anisic melody that begins in salty licorice and modulates through several leafy changes as refreshing as lime soda pop, playing Doris Day to Angel's Peggy Lee. The fragrance is snappy and smart, an ideal accompaniment for flirtatious banter delivered by prim girls in glasses. Furthermore, like Ménardo's Black for Bulgari, Lolita Lempicka is a clever feminine that clever men can easily wear. I once got on a subway train just as a pretty young man stepped off in a cloud of it. If it was his girlfriend's, I hope he was clever enough to nick it. Bonus: darling bottle. TS

Lolita Lempicka au Masculin (Lolita Lempicka) ★ ★ ★ ★
licorice cologne $ $
In perfume, the male of the species is always smaller than the female. I feared the worst when I saw the bottle for LL au Masculin, molded in a form midway between a piece of chewed ice and Ren and Stimpy's Log. Fear not: the lads have been well served by the same perfumer (Annick Ménardo) who did the feminine. LLaM is a beautiful anisic take on a woody cologne with a wistful dose of violets. It has a tender nostalgic

air, a bit overly romantic even, intimating that the wearer may be prone to desperate gestures, heartbreak, and a weakness for sappy song lyrics. The girls who dislike the Angelic angle in Lolita Lempicka might be tempted to wear this one instead. TS

Lolita Lempicka Midnight (Lolita Lempicka) ★ ★ ★ ★
anisic floral $ $
Same fragrance, but more intense everywhere, especially in the violet and spiced apple sections. Smells great. The bottle looks straight out of a Tim Burton movie. TS

Lonestar Memories (Tauer Perfumes) ★ ★ ★ ★ *smoky carnation* $ $
It has taken a generation for us to forgive smoky-phenolic smells their association with Lysol, creosote, and all the wonderful kippered smells that brought instant death to naive bacteria and eternal life to wooden fences. Andy Tauer is likely too young to remember that age, and has unabashedly put together a wonderful smoky base that he first used to great effect in L'Air du Désert Marocain. His second fragrance, LM is softer, a touch more carnation-like, and wonderfully warm while retaining a salubrious ambiance Joseph Lister would have approved of. Strange but nice. LT

Look (Vera Wang) ★ ★ *lychee floral* $
A convincing lychee top note is not enough to sustain interest in this dull watery-green floral. TS

Lotus Blossom & Water Lily (Jo Malone) ★ *harsh floral* $
One of two Jo Malone fragrances based on the Japanese incense ceremony, the other being Dark Amber & Ginger Lily. Something was lost in translation in this discordant fragrance, half cinnamon, half bare floral, with a sour, unwashed smell like the sort of person who clears out one end of the bus. TS

Louanges Profanes (Parfumerie Générale) ★ ★ ★ *sweet floral* $$$
A well-executed and deeply boring sentimental floral; the sort of stuff that would float out of a romance novel if it had a scratch-and-sniff patch to illustrate the scene where she wears a white dress at sunset. LT

Loukhoum (Keiko Mecheri) ★ *powdery candy* $$$
In 1998, there seems to have been a mini-fashion for the sweet, powdered candy called Turkish Delight by English speakers, *rahat loukhoum* in Turkey, since both Serge Lutens and Keiko Mecheri did fragrances based on it. Mecheri's is nigh unbearable, hideously sugary, powerfully musky, and cloyingly fruity all at once, with an overwhelming woody base. It is also diabolically long-lasting; a spray on a robe of mine lasted several washings over several weeks. TS

Loukhoum Eau Poudrée (Keiko Mecheri) ★ ★ ★ *pale almond* $$
One of two recent variations on Keiko Mecheri's popular Loukhoum fragrance. There is now a light version and a dark, and the less expensive, less pretentious one is better. Eau Poudrée shifts the emphasis to almond from sticky cherry and uses a brighter, more lemony rose and a sparkling Pleasures-like musk to lighten the load. Out of all this careful editing and tinting emerges a charming, guileless, fruity mimosa inadvertently close to Britney Spears's Curious but without the nasty edge. TS

Loukhoum Parfum de Soir (Keiko Mecheri) ★ ★ *fruity wood* $$$
Given that the original fragrance honored Serge Lutens with the highest form of flattery, it should be no surprise that the bottle for Parfum de Soir looks like a graphic artist spent half an hour mucking with the bottle for Nombre Noir. Eau Poudrée is the sibling with all the charm, because Parfum de Soir has inherited the heavy bones and flat personality that made Loukhoum such a drag. It sadly radiates a prematurely wrinkled aura of talcum powder and prunes that's too intense at any distance. TS

Loulou (Cacharel) ★ ★ ★ ★ ★ *jasmine oriental* $$
Classified by Michael Edwards as Soft Oriental, var. Rich, which is to say Large Baklava, var. Syrupy, this is a perfume that might be reckoned a little over the top even by a Bombay attarwallah. But the secret of Loulou, worked out by the great master Jean Guichard (how does it feel to be the guy who did Eden, La Nuit, and Asja?), is to add a mysteriously raspy note to the whole composition that makes you want to smell more, not push the plate away. When I first encountered it twenty years ago, it made me think of those Christmas tree balls made of purple glass sprayed with black dust, which look like silk and feel like sandpaper. Do not be misled by the fact that Loulou, when found, is likely to be cheap. This is one of the greats. LT

Louve (Serge Lutens) ★ ★ *cherry almonds* $$$
Louve starts with an audaciously intense morello cherry note that forces one to think of a Cherry Coke cocktail (such things apparently exist, perish the thought). The cherry transitions to a strange soapy heliotropin accord with wet-sawdust undertones, more akin to the smell of a confined space in which perfumes are stored than of a deliberate mix. Neither very good nor very bad, but completely baffling. LT

Love (B Never Too Busy to Be Beautiful) ★ ★ ★ *bergamot jasmine* $
A pretty, slightly airheaded composition of cheerful, natural-smelling sweet citrus and tropical florals, approaching Juicy Fruit gum. TS

Love (By Kilian) ★ ★ ★ ★ *vanilla meringue* $$$$
Given the existence of Vanilia and countless imitations, one would think that the vanilla-candyfloss lode would by now be exhausted. Not a bit: Calice Becker has composed a meringue perfume that aims not just for the smell of beaten egg white, sugar, and vanilla but also for the slightly enervating, dry, screechy texture of the meringue itself. She brilliantly used methylundecylenic aldehyde (Adoxal), a snowy aldehyde with the faintest hint of egg smell, to achieve both at one stroke. A deliciously bright, light, low-calorie take on a classic food theme. LT

Love (Ralph Lauren) ★ ★ *metallic fruit* $$$
A name like this, like Apple's me.com, makes you wonder how much they paid for the trademark. Which may explain why they were short of cash when it came to the fragrance, a trite woody-apple thing of no interest whatsoever. Avoid. LT

Love de Toi (Morgan de Toi) ★ ★ ★ *strawberry peach* $$
More candy flavors for teenage girls who don't mind smelling like they just spilled Fanta on themselves. This one has more of a coherent drydown than most: an apricot so spot-on you suspect they spray the same thing on packets of fruit. TS

Love in Black (Creed) ★ *iris cucumber* $$$
Like everyone else (see Infusion d'Homme), Creed is doing an iris using the newly affordable Biolandes extract. Sadly, whoever did this fragrance hates iris, because the muted, velvety gray-violet aspect of that melancholy raw material is blasted away by a screaming top note of violet nitrile and blackcurrant buds. Such is the sheer volume of this accord that it causes olfactory illusions, like the weird clicks one hears in an ambulance horn up close, and one ends up smelling incongruous things like cup noodles and linseed oil. Ah, I know why the ambulance is there: iris just suffered a disfiguring car crash. LT

Love in Paris (Nina Ricci) ★ ★ ★ ★ *peachy floral* $$
Conventional at a distance but odd in the details, what could have been an entirely boring floral isn't at all. First there is a clever, left-of-center quality to the top note, an astringent, medicinal fruity-clove accord reminiscent of the fluoride rinse my dentist makes me swish at every visit. From there, it moves to a surprisingly handsome, peachy dark golden floral in the J'Adore style, but lit up unexpectedly bright, like a night game played under klieg lights. An entirely unexpected, pleasantly salty, animalic-metallic note grows more evident as it dries down. Ex-

cellent work. Note to Nina Ricci: The typefaces on our bottle have the look of an automatic missing-font replacement. Call quality control. TS

Love in White (Creed) ★ *burial wreath* $$$
A chemical white floral so disastrously vile words nearly desert me. If this were a shampoo offered with your first shower after sleeping rough for two months in Nouakchott, you'd opt to keep the lice. LT

Lovely (Sarah Jessica Parker) ★ ★ ★ ★ *cute floral* $$
If logic applied, celebrity fragrances (i.e., projects that add an extra layer of exploitative cynicism on top of an already mountainous heap of contempt for the consumer) should be reliably awful. Many have turned out really good instead, suggesting that the gods of perfumery enjoy a little joke. Pavarotti for men was ace, the first J-Lo was presentable, Naomi Campbell was just fine. Now Lovely comes along. Naturally, I approached it with the proper furrowed brow of the critic-not-about-to-be-taken in by nonsense. Five seconds later, I was like Solly in *Monsters, Inc.,* clutching little Boo to his hirsute breast. This is a truly charming floral, about as edgy as a marshmallow and all the better for it, with a fresh, gracious, melodic chord somewhere between lily of the valley and magnolia, which cascades down like the tune of a music box while you sit there transfixed by the intrinsic goodness of nice girls dressed in white. Makes you want to buy furry toys. LT

The woody accord of patchouli and musk at the bottom of Lovely seems borrowed directly from Narciso Rodriguez for Her, which came out two years earlier. In a way, Lovely is a big improvement on NR for Her, with a much more presentable, worked-out white floral replacing the other fragrance's shrill orange-blossom section, but the result politely stays much closer to the skin than does its irrepressibly radiant predecessor. TS

Love Spell (Victoria's Secret) ★ ★ ★ *cilantro floral* $
The plain, slightly sour fruity-floral top note seems designed for young

ladies in their early twenties named Elizabeth who never wear black. But as the top note subsides, a collection of grassy botanicals, like a platter of Vietnamese salad herbs, lends appetizing interest to an otherwise pedestrian soapy peony floral. (See Diptyque's fantastic Virgilio for a better version of this trick.) After all that action, the drydown is ordinary peach. Still, not bad for a tarty panty brand. TS

Luca (La Via del Profumo) ★ ★ ★ ★ *anything anything* $$$$
profumo.it only
On my table there sits a bottle of a very nice fragrance with my name on it. It was composed by Dominique Dubrana of profumo.it, using a clever system you will find on his Web site. You choose the materials you want in the mix (and the price reflects which ones you picked), give him a few more indications, and he composes a fragrance for you. This is ideal for people who want a bespoke fragrance but do not have $100K handy. LT

I have a trio named Tania, all interesting variations on the resinous floral theme I gave Dubrana, an all-naturals perfumer who possesses an unmatched gut instinct for where to seek beauty in this exceptionally difficult subset of the art. TS

Luctor et Emergo (People of the Labyrinths) ★ ★ ★
almond heliotropin $$$
The unlikely name means "I struggle and emerge," the motto of the Dutch province of Zeeland. It's impossible for anyone who has survived an American childhood to smell this salty cherry-almond fragrance without thinking immediately of Play-Doh. Inexplicably, this limp teddy bear of a scent is a huge cult hit, but I find it melancholy, nearly depressing. I prefer Après l'Ondée, the old Farnesiana, or the mimosas of Parfums de Nicolaï or L'Artisan for my heliotropin fix—something less likely to send me into the fetal position. TS

Lulu (Fresh Scents by Terri) ★ *muguet musk* $$
An unsuccessful blend of a dry, woody lily of the valley with cloying sweet and musky notes. See Pure White Linen for what Terri probably meant by this. TS

Lulu Guinness (Lulu Guinness) ★ *half pint* $$
Thin screechy floral, a version of Beyond Paradise made for Moldavian railway stations, packaged in an opaque glass baby-perfume white bottle nearly identical to the one made (by the same firm, a year later) for Nanette Lepore. Nice creative work all around. LT

Lux (Mona di Orio) ★ *dire citrus* $$$$
The world's most expensive cheap lemon sorbet flavor. LT

Luxe Champaca (Comme des Garçons) ★ ★ ★
competent floral $$$$
Boring soliflore that smells good. Total rip-off. LT

Luxe Patchouli (Comme des Garçons) ★ ★ ★
everlasting flower $$$$
CdG has clearly been to the Le Labo School of Misdirection, because this is not a patchouli, but rather an immortelle, with the fenugreek/burnt-sugar note that makes that material so hard to use. Less refined than Eau Noire, less sultry than Sables, but still perfectly nice. Outrageously priced. LT

Lyric Man (Amouage) ★ ★ ★ ★ *woody rose* $$$$
One of the few things I remember from taking tai chi lessons many years ago was when my instructor asked me to push hard on his chest. I did, and it was like pushing gauze, so perfectly did his movement mirror mine. Similarly, Lyric is a fragrance that opens before you as you smell it, to give you the feeling of falling forward into a space: a dark, still air

of transparent rose, slightly sour wet wood, and powdery persimmon. A daring yet unassuming fragrance that carries a charge of mystery and silence. Recommended. LT

Lyric Woman (Amouage) ★ ★ ★ ★ *dark floral* $$$$
Great fragrances move me (and, I imagine, many others) to a sort of musical resonance. And in perfume as in music, progress largely consists of getting used to one novel dissonance after another. In this context, I can safely say that I have never smelled anything like the chord at Lyric's core. It is a rose, to be sure, cleverly extended at one end by a dry, dusty, woody accord in the manner of Lyric's land of origin, Oman. What happens at the other end is a complete surprise. Where one expects a spicy, earthy uplift in the contemporary manner, there comes instead a plangent, overripe note, the exhalation of forgotten fruit in a sealed room. The effect is initially almost unpleasant but soon becomes celestial. Thelonious Monk would have understood this fragrance instantly. LT

Lys (Parfums 06130) ★ *marine citrus* $$$
They gotta be kidding with these watery dregs: a fragrance that smells from the start like the sour hangers-on left when you wash off a bad floral. TS

Un Lys (Serge Lutens) ★ ★ ★ *green floral* $$$
A pretty, though somewhat ordinary, raspy white floral (jasmine, lily of the valley) freshened with green and sweetened with vanilla. The touch of ham that makes lilies so odd shows more on paper than on skin. TS

Lys Méditerranée (Frédéric Malle) ★ ★ ★ ★ *singing lilies* $$$
I remember once, at the height of summer, passing through the village of Saint-Emilion, where every vine is pampered like the mane of a dressage horse and every building stone orthodontically perfect, and entering the imposing village church. In a gesture of thanks for an act of

divine grace, someone had filled the church with large white-and-purple lilies, hundreds of them shouting their fragrance in the confined space. The smell was so intense that it distorted into something else, and it took me a while to figure out what. Then I suddenly saw it: salami. There is a fleshy, salty, hammy quality to fresh lilies that sets them apart from other white flowers. The two great perfumery lilies of the moment are Lys Méditerranée and Donna Karan Gold (q.v.). Lys Méditerranée is more true to life, with a wonderful, powdery rasp and that strange sensation that lilies give that the smell is about to fall apart into its component parts any minute. A brilliant study in painting smell from nature from the great Edouard Fléchier. LT

M (Mariah Carey) ★ ★ ★ *almond floral* $ $
Mariah Carey fans have nothing to worry about: the cheap-looking butterfly bottle contains a perfectly pleasant nutty-lactonic sweet floral, with the browned-butter smell that nice girls have liked since Fleurs de Rocaille, but done in the modern style, with lots of the cotton-candy note of ethylmaltol and without the lushness of natural florals. TS

M7 (Yves Saint Laurent) ★ ★ ★ ★ *oud wood* $ $
The recent fashion for oud (the noble rot of *Aquilaria* trees) took flight when YSL released M7, where the oud accord was center stage. It came with an advertising campaign featuring a hairy naked guy, a sight rated "beautiful" by my co-author. Real oud is a complex material, with honey, tobacco leaf, minty-fresh and castoreum animalic notes all mixed together. M7 does a good job at covering all the bases but cannot quite get away from a certain brown-study grimness inherent in oud itself. For some reason, possibly this excessive gloom, M7 was a flop. It did not deserve to be, and may yet turn out a slow but perennial seller like Guerlain's Derby. LT

M7 Fresh (Yves Saint Laurent) ★ ★ ★ ★ *spicy herbaceous* $ $
Adding the word *Fresh* to M7 is a bit like saying "profiteroles lite." It's

actually a completely different fragrance, which starts very promisingly with a complex spice accord, but soon veers off toward the herbaceous *bouquet de Provence* accord that perfumer Jacques Cavallier later used in L'Eau Bleue. Cavallier's recent work, inventive and well crafted though it is, gives the impression of perfumes made for smelling strips rather than for skins, and destined to remain brilliantly conceived smells rather than comfortable fragrances. LT

Madagascar Orchid (Lisa Hoffman) ★ ★ *heavy floral* $$
This, like other Lisa Hoffman offerings, is a quartet of four fragrances titled Morning; Daytime; Evening; and, disappointingly, Bedtime. One advantage of calling a fragrance Madagascar Orchid is the small likelihood that anyone will complain that it is not true to life, especially in the event that all four are dull, sweet florals of no particular interest. They are "designed to complement a woman's changing olfactive sensitivities throughout the day." I'm not a woman, but can think of no day when I'd like to smell any of them. LT

Ma Dame (Jean Paul Gaultier) ★ ★ ★ ★ *lemon vanilla* $$
What had every right to be a hideous ditz fragrance in the worst cutesy pink manner is instead a clever tart—*tarte au citron*. It's saved from dull foodiness by an inedible vinyl-raincoat smell and a savory tarragon-like note. Cheap, brash, and perversely catchy, like a throwaway pop song with terrible lyrics you're embarrassed to find yourself and everyone else singing when it plays at the drugstore. Much better than it had to be. TS

Madame Rochas (Rochas) ★ ★ ★ *aldehydic chypre* $$$
Whatever the old Madame Rochas may have been, this is merely a nice, cheap, soapy aldehydic chypre in a late-seventies style, using all the funny facets of aliphatic aldehydes—smoky candlewax and that part of citrus that feels like fluorescent striplighting in offices. The drydown is a rose not entirely unlike Rive Gauche. TS

Madison Soirée (Bond No. 9) ★ ★ ★ *soapy floral* $$$$
Yes, I know that this green-floral plus musk essentially smells like shampoo. The trouble is, I like it. Out of all the shampoo florals in the Bond range, this is the one I'd recommend you use to fake hygiene on a day when plumbing is on the fritz. Careful: big sillage. TS

Magical Moon (Hanae Mori) ★ ★ ★ *fruity oriental* $$$
We've been down this whimsical, post-Angel, post–Lolita Lempicka, delicious fruity cotton-candy road before, with Britney and Hilary and all their friends, although in this case the gourmand sweetness is toned down considerably by the immediate presence of big masculine woody notes. The result is more interesting and less teenage than you'd immediately suspect, a sort of woody floral in disguise. Instinct tells me this would suit perverse boys better than conventional girls. TS

Magie (Lancôme) ★ ★ ★ *aldehydic chypre* $$
I do not have access to old samples of Magic, but Lancôme's revived "Collection" version smells plausible, i.e., a plush, elegant, and somewhat dry aldehydic chypre in the classic French manner. It brings to mind a pouting model, hands on hips in opera gloves, wearing a hat, a spencer jacket, and a pencil skirt, with her feet at right angles to each other as if she were going up a ski slope. LT

Magie Noire (Lancôme) ★ ★ ★ ★ *dry woody* $$
Magic Noire (1978) and, as TS pointed out, its exact contemporary Mystère by Rochas were the last of a stylish breed before the tidal wave of syrup of the eighties started darkening the horizon. These were dry, woody aldehydic chypres with a serious mien and great bone structure. The raw materials have suffered at the hands of accountants in the intervening thirty years, and this has turned Magie Noire into a perfectly respectable masculine in the Or Black mold, but less grand. LT

Magnifique (Lancôme) ★ ★ *soapy orange* $ $
"The spicy impertinence of saffron, the smoky embrace of exotic nagar-mota wood." Where do they find the people who write this stuff? Still, the thought of a yellow risotto that talks back at you is funny. As for the smoky embrace, *timeo Helvetii et* nagarmota *ferentes*: it would appear that every time Lancôme and Firmenich achieve an essentially natural-free formula, they celebrate by talking up a novel raw material for press releases. For Poême it was blue poppy, and here it is nagarmota, aka the wonderfully smoky cypriol, no trace of which can be perceived in the fragrance. This faded, underpowered composition uses two recent must-haves, a saffron note akin to Givaudan's Safraleine and a boiled-sweets orange reminiscent of Elixir des Merveilles, but in low-budget fashion. So two-years-ago. LT

Magnolia Romana (Eau d'Italie) ★ ★ *citrus mimosa* $ $ $
An interesting idea: take the synthetic structure of Cacharel pour l'Homme, and then use it as a setting for the blowsy, good-natured, powdery heliotropin of mimosa. The result is a little depressing but probably meant for men too frightened to live their dream of wear-ing Bulgari pour Femme. TS

Magot (Etro) ★ ★ *fruity citrus* $ $ $
Sometimes, as is the case here, an interesting accord slips away from you and ends up smelling like bathroom air freshener. Jacques Flori clearly wanted a contrast between citrus-fresh and dessert-like warm notes, but the thing refuses to fly. The name, by the way, either means "treasure" or refers to a grotesque Chinese figurine, and the Deux Magots is a famous bar-brasserie in Paris where Sartre enjoyed a philosophical pas-tis or two a long time ago. LT

Ma Griffe (Carven) ★ ★ ★ *green chypre* $ $
Famously composed by the great Jean Carles after he had lost his sense of smell, Ma Griffe is a classic green chypre, less herbaceous than Givenchy

III, less dry than Y, more floral than most, and with a Miss Moneypenny spinsterish loveliness that works perfectly if you are nothing of the sort. The present version seems better than in recent memory. LT

Maharanih (Parfums de Nicolaï) ★ ★ ★ ★ *powdery orange* $$
This one had been described to me as an amber oriental, and being familiar with the Maharajah *parfum d'ambiance* I expected the female of the species to be heady and heavy. Wrong again: Maharanih reminds me of the practical joke once played on a famous conductor by his orchestra. They agreed among themselves to replace a climactic tutti by complete silence. When the moment came, the conductor expected a tremendous blast, got nothing, and fell forward off the platform. The initial citrus of Maharanih swirls quietly past you almost before you've had time to think. From experience, you expect a boulder-like amber accord to come rolling down next, but nothing happens. At which point you fall into this extraordinary, delicate, luminous orange-rose-and-incense composition, an extended-range Vol de Nuit that managed to fly long enough to see sunrise. LT

Maîtresse (Agent Provocateur) ★ ★ *throwback floral* $$
After an excitingly weird rancid-glue (or seriously dirty drawers) top note, it eases into a replay of some big, friendly, cheap woody-jasmine thing my mother wore in the eighties and whose name escapes me. I can almost hear the *Dynasty* theme song. TS

Les Maîtresses de Louis XIV (Roméa d'Améor) ★ ★ ★ ★
lily muguet $$$
Maîtresses claims to contain "Gloriosa Superba from the Forest of Brocéliande," the latter a place twenty miles southwest of Rennes in Brittany that the local tourist board insists is the forest of Arthurian legend. As for *Gloriosa superba*, the likelihood of it growing wild in Brittany can be gauged by the fact that it is the national flower of Zimbabwe. But never mind the PR folderol: Pierre Bourdon has come up with a very

interesting floral: an homage to his erstwhile mentor Edmond Roud-nitska situated halfway between Diorissimo and Parfum de Thérèse. It is enlightening to finally understand that the salty note of Diorella and PdT is due to the cresolic aspect of lily (what I call its salami note), while the dissonant creamy note of Diorissimo is a counterpoint between fresh lily of the valley and sweet vanilla. Very floral, very girly, and very nice. LT

Malabah (Penhaligon's) ★ ★ *woody oriental* $ $
Failed attempt by Penhaligon's to emulate de Nicolaï's New York (q.v.). Smells like a cheap pomander. LT

Le Mâle (Jean Paul Gaultier) ★ ★ ★ *powdery lavender* $ $
This light, soapy lavender scent has a pale, powdered-sugar sweetness, clean and innocuous, for the guy whose favorite tipple is sugared Celestial Seasonings tea. LT smells it as intensely musky, barbershop retro. TS

Le Mâle Eau d'Eté (Jean Paul Gaultier) ★ ★ *sweet lavender* $ $
A thin sugared lavender, like Jicky at homeopathic dilution. Incidentally, it is hard to imagine a straight man confident or metrosexual enough to keep this girlishly decorated male torso, complete with pert buttocks and crotch bulge, on his bathroom shelf. TS

Mandarine Mandarin (Serge Lutens) ★ ★ *floral oriental* $ $ $
If you took a picture of CK's Eternity and hand-painted it, the way photographers used to put color on black-and-white portraits to give them cherry lips, green eyes, and rosy cheeks, you'd get Mandarine Mandarin. Deeply strange, quite intense, and not particularly wearable. LT

Mandarine Tout Simplement (L'Artisan Parfumeur) ★ ★
mandarin flower $ $ $
A veteran perfumer once told me that De Laire's legendary mandarin oil, sold for a fortune in the days before everybody bought a gas chro-

matograph, was in fact orange oil with a smidgen of green galbanum and a touch of smoky rectified birch tar added, relabeled and priced at a thirtyfold markup. I have no idea how this one is done, but the mandarin effect, though pleasant, is very brief and followed by a flat orange-flower composition of no particular interest. If you like mandarin, go for Mauboussin's Histoire d'Eau Topaze (if you can find it), where the note is durable and brilliantly orchestrated. LT

Mandragore (Annick Goutal) ★ ★ ★ *bergamot violet* $$$
Isabelle Doyen has built several fragrances using a crisp cologne structure with a transparent violet-iris accord playing the floral part. I prefer her mouth-puckeringly tart maté fragrance, Duel for Goutal, to Mandragore's pale tisane—pleasant but a disappointment under such a provocatively witchy name. TS

Manoumalia (LesNez) ★ ★ ★ ★ *tropical floral* $$$
At last, a perfume composed by the elusive Sandrine Videault! I've heard her work praised time and again by eminent perfumers and could never get hold of her compositions, mostly small-scale affairs, among which is a reconstruction of ancient Egyptian *kyphi* that I'd walk to Cairo for (and which is where it was before someone stole it). She lives in New Caledonia, a former French *département* and now independent. Manoumalia is her essay on two local flowers, fagraea and Tahitian gardenia (tiaré). Neither is available as a natural material (low yields, wrong smell), so she did what her teacher Edmond Roudnitska did for lily of the valley in Diorissimo: compose with her nose, using the real thing as reference. I am, regrettably, not familiar with the smell of fresh Polynesian blossoms, but I can say this: Manoumalia feels like it comes from another world, at the exact antipodes of the sour, bony little creatures perfumery begets by the hundred these days. It is soft as lips, caressing like a sea breeze, and as lush as a sunset. This is what Guerlain's Mahora should have been, had it not got sidetracked on the way to Tahiti at CDG duty free. LT

Marc Jacobs (Marc Jacobs) ★ ★ ★ *white floral* $ $
This is supposed to be a gardenia, and isn't. It's a white floral with watery notes. The ingredients allegedly contained in the fragrance reach new heights of imagination: blond woods, crystal musk, and of course gardenia itself, from which no essence has to my knowledge ever been satisfactorily extracted. Still, it isn't bad, and as white flowers go, it is a pretty dignified affair, though without the grand sweep of the best in the genre, Beyond Paradise. LT

Marc Jacobs Men (Marc Jacobs) ★ *sad fig* $ $
Cacophonic mix of salaryman aftershave and a failed fig note. LT

Le Maroc (Tauer Perfumes) ★ ★ ★ *floral oriental* $ $
Pretty impressive first perfume: a rich rose-jasmine on amber, the perfumery equivalent of a spiced honey-date cake, with smoky, animalic facets to conjure up a thousand and one late nights of storytelling by the fire. Everything turns unbearably sweet after this lovely beginning, but Tauer's insistence on high-quality materials is evident throughout. TS

Marrakech (Aesop) ★ ★ ★ ★ *spicy resinous* $ $
The upmarket Aussie botanical cosmetics firm produces two fragrances, Marrakech and Mystra. They say Marrakech is an all-natural mixture of clove, sandalwood, and cardamom, and on that basis you'd expect either a stonking hippie fragrance or some mood-music thing to go with hot pebbles on your back. And you'd be wrong. Marrakech seems to be composed of materials of virtually identical volatilities, so it is completely linear, with no distinct top, middle, and drydown. It smells resinous-edible, in a rich, spicy, Christmas-pudding sort of way, but without any cloying sweet notes at all. I imagine the resin-based embalming fluids of ancient Egypt must have smelled similar to this; shame that the dead never got a chance to smell them. This is an archaic fragrance of biblical directness and beauty, something to wear while reading Nietzsche's *Zarathustra* or, better still, Henry Rider

Haggard's *She*. I am sure Ayesha would have dabbed it on before supper with Leo Vincey, not that she needed to. LT

Mary-Kate and Ashley One (Mary-Kate and Ashley) ★ ★
piña colada $
Cheap trashy fun with a fruity top and coconut-rum woody drydown, a nice effect that falls apart shortly after application. It's fine for a tween audience who doesn't know what "jasmine spice," the description on the box, would smell like. TS

Mary-Kate and Ashley Two (Mary-Kate and Ashley) ★ ★
peachy musk $
Weightless, fresh little shampoo-formula peachy florals like this are probably fine for Mary-Kate and Ashley's tween audience but no one else. TS

Un Matin d'Orage (Annick Goutal) ★ ★ *woody fig* $ $
Whoever composed this "stormy morning" must be, at the very least, hyposmic to a tremendous woody-amber note (Karanal? Ambrocenide?) that makes this fresh-green fragrance as comfortable as having your dental plaque blasted away by ultrasound. LT

Matthew Williamson Collection: Incense (Matthew Williamson)
★ ★ ★ *amber incense* $ $
It must no longer be enough for the hip designer of the moment to release one perfume; it shows a lack of seriousness. Instead, there must be a Lutens-inspired collection (see Tom Ford). Williamson is no newcomer to niche fragrance, his first release apparently having been an Incense, quickly discontinued before I got to smell it, and remembered fondly by perfume-fanatic friends who are always seeking that perfect dose of Russian Orthodox church in a bottle. This Incense may or may not be the old thing reborn, but it certainly fits in with its hippie-souled niche brethren, smelling sweet like Ambre Sultan with a big, pleasant,

pine-like dose of frankincense added. If you like this sort of thing, you will like this sort of thing, though to my nose it's not as rich, haunting, or strange as many of the other incenses we've reviewed. TS

Matthew Williamson Collection: Jasmine Sambac
(Matthew Williamson) ★ ★ ★ *fruity jasmine* $ $
Nice balance between camphoraceous floral rasp and bubble gum. TS

Matthew Williamson Collection: Pink Lotus (Matthew Williamson)
★ ★ *fruity floral* $ $
I'm not sure what pink lotuses smell like, but this is not altogether pleasant, with a shrill background white-floral material plus something metallic and watery green, like the water at the bottom of the vase, sweetened with a bit of peach. I don't find it adds up to much, although LT hazards you could interpret this as a gardenia. TS

Matthew Williamson Collection: Warm Sands
(Matthew Williamson) ★ ★ ★ *woody muguet* $ $
Lily-of-the-valley fragrances usually arrive crisp, green, and freshly scrubbed, so the note feels strange and new at first in this sweet milky setting, like unknown tropical fruit from the future, before it relaxes into a more straightforward lemony-green muguet. I wish that initial odd balance could be maintained and hope someone's working on it. TS

Mauboussin (Mauboussin) ★ ★ ★ ★ *fruity oriental* $ $
Mauboussin is a jeweler headquartered at Place Vendôme in Paris, and last time I passed by, every piece in the window involved several dozen perfectly identical yellow diamonds of roughly one carat each, which discouraged me from wandering in. Mauboussin's feminine fragrances (composed by Christine Nagel) have all been very good, and the packaging exquisite. This, their first one (2000), is what I would describe as an Italian fragrance: compact, handsome, rich, and sunny. It is an oriental situated somewhere between the first Kenzo Jungle and Fendi's Theo-

rema, with a skillful combination of warm, mouthwatering dried-fruit notes and clean, uplifting woody-resinous incense and olibanum. Nagel has since shown she could turn her hand to many other styles of fragrance. But the perfumes of that period established her, in my opinion, as the queen of biblically rich orientals, and this is one of her best. Superb sci-fi tetrahedral bottle. LT

Mauboussin Homme (Mauboussin) ★ *woody oriental* $ $
There is a wonderful word in French that denotes an average specimen of the male of the species: *beauf'*, short for *beau-frère*, i.e., "brother-in-law." This is his fragrance. LT

Max Mara (Max Mara) ★ ★ *sugared floral* $ $
Aggressively boring but competently constructed fresh fruity-floral with a sugar-cookie sweetness and no brains at all. Reduces IQ with repeated use. The scent probably started life as a room spray. TS

Maybe Baby (Benefit) ★ ★ ★ *peach muguet* $
A basically friendly, simple, peachy floral without pretensions—sort of Pears soap. Smells good then gently goes away. TS

Mayotte (Guerlain) ★ *nasty "floral"* $ $ $ $
Mayotte, named after the Comoran island, is none other than the dreadful Mahora (2000), LVMH's second lapse of judgment after the Guerlain purchase. It was dreadful the first time around, and has not improved since. To call this a frangipani is to insult the entire *Plumeria* genus. It smells like a $200 plug-in air freshener. LT

Méchant Loup (L'Artisan Parfumeur) ★ *watery herbaceous* $ $ $
Bad wolf? More like wet dog. LT

Mediterranean (Elizabeth Arden) ★ *fresh floral* $ $
A perfume that feels like it's the rolling average of the twelve immedi-

ately preceding launches. When taken to such a jaw-dropping level, lack of originality almost becomes an art form in itself. LT

Mediterranean Lily (Renée) ★ ★ ★ *soap lily* $$
A rather nondescript lily, pleasant up top and soapy thereafter. LT

Mediterraneo (Carthusia) ★ ★ ★ *woody citrus* $$
A good if overpriced lemony cologne with a pleasantly bitter character, and apparently one of the original Carthusia scents from 1948. TS

Me Myself and I (Ego Facto) ★ ★ ★ *vetiver tuberose* $$
The elder and younger Guichards (Jean and Aurélien) turn in an interesting composition related to Terre d'Hermès. It exploits a brashness in the herbal-green part of vetiver to bend the green-floral bit of tuberose in the same direction. I'd love to smell this on a bigger budget. TS

Mensonge (Fragonard) ★ ★ *ginger citrus* $
No set of fragrances numbering three or more, released simultaneously, can be without its dud, and this is Fragonard's: a crisp sport masculine of which the world has too many already. TS

Menthe Fraîche (Heeley) ★ ★ ★ *shiso mint* $$$
Mint (see Cartier's Roadster below) is hard to work with, being rather volatile and with connotations of toothpaste. Menthe Fraîche is a brilliant essay in mintiness, with an intense, almost nail-varnish-like ketonic note up top and an exotic accord of shiso, peppermint, and lemon verbena underneath, the whole thing cleverly glued together by a lovely, green, hissy violet-leaf note. Whoever did this was certainly not fooling around, and MF is easy to admire though arguably harder to wear. LT

Messe de Minuit (Etro) ★ ★ ★ ★ *incense pomander* $$$
Midnight Mass! As the French say, *tout un programme!* A heady accord

of patchouli, incense, and slightly animalic myrrh within a citrus composition that goes from fresh lemon to spicy orange-peel pomander. Unpretentious and very nice. LT

Métal (Paco Rabanne) ★ ★ ★ ★ *green floral* $$$
In 1974, Japanese monster-movie fanatics were introduced to a new villain: a robotic Godzilla double in gunmetal gray called Mechagodzilla. Five years later, in 1979, in an entirely unrelated but fortuitous event, Paco Rabanne gave fragrance lovers Mecha–Vent Vert, hereby known as Métal. It is at first a lovely classic green floral of pretty hyacinths, jasmine, and muguet—except for a massive, sharp, icy, metallic note that you feel more than smell, as if someone is blowing hard on one of those whistles that only dogs hear. As it goes on, the monster, shedding all reference to flowers and overtaken by a powerful oily green note, smells ever more poisonous. Impressive. TS

Metalys (Guerlain) ★ ★ *floral musk* $$$
Originally called Metallica until the band objected, and reissued in 2006 under this new name. Starts out as a rather chemical jasmine, veers toward upmarket hotel shampoos and after much confusion finally lands on a diffusive musky-coumarinic note vaguely reminiscent of Paco Rabanne pour Homme. Pointless. LT

Michael (Michael Kors) ★ *evil tuberose* $$
Shrieking hair-singeing horror, probably first rejected for use in industrial drain cleaner. One of the worst ever. TS

Midnight Poison (Dior) ★ *woody oriental* $$
The Poison series has given two masterpieces, the original and Hypnotic; two passable fragrances, Pure and Tendre; and now a Midnight dud that makes it clear why the bottle was shaped like a pumpkin all along. Composed by Olivier Cresp and Jacques Cavallier, this is a confused, meretricious, skimpy, trivial, borderline-insulting confection,

clearly predicated on the notion that the intended buyer has already donated her brain to science. I pray it flops. LT

Midnight Rain (La Prairie) ★ ★ *fruity amber* $ $
Another Angel without the jokes, this is a cloying grapefruit oriental in memorably tacky packaging best described as evil disco. TS

Miel de Bois (Serge Lutens) ★ *animalic floral* $ $ $
Phenylacetic acid smells like honey in dilution, like urine at concentration. Miel de Bois (Honey of Wood) gets the balance drastically wrong and smells like a New York sidewalk in July. A very small percentage of people find it floral and don't know why the rest of us are howling. TS

Mihimé (Keiko Mecheri) ★ ★ *wan rose* $ $
If you like pale roses, this might be your kind of thing: a watered-down heliotropin with a fresh, slightly plasticky lemon. TS

Mille et Une Roses (Lancôme) ★ ★ ★ *light rose* $ $ $
First launched as a millennial limited edition by Lancôme as 2000 et Une Roses, this soapy rose has come back a thousand roses lighter in name but otherwise the same. On paper, it has a fastidious, bloodless freshness, and on skin it comes off as a bland lemon-vanilla. Many rose lovers count it as a favorite, but to my mind it does nothing you can't get much better elsewhere: a better lemon-vanilla is Shalimar Light; a better good-natured girlish rose is Drôle de Rose; a better fresh-faced ambrette-seed rose is Chanel's No. 18. TS

Millésime Impérial (Creed) ★ ★ *metallic citrus* $ $ $
Creed's claim to being purveyors of perfume to various royal and imperial houses of Europe is dodgy: their use of the Three Feathers device (wisely minus the "Ich Dien" motto) on all their fugly packaging suggests they have a Royal Warrant from the Prince of Wales, which to our

knowledge is not and has never been the case. One is inclined to take with a pinch of salt the long list of deceased emperors and empresses that they allegedly helped smell better. Ditto the supposed trouble to which they go to obtain rare essences and extracts: slow, expensive, low-yield things like tinctures, which would make even Guerlain blanch. Creed's perfumes make abundant use of synthetic materials (see Green Irish Tweed) and are only slightly above average in use of naturals. Now to Millésime Impérial: *millésime* in French is a pompous word for "year," used by winemakers instead of *année*. I am not sure what Creed means by it, but it sounds good. The fragrance is a mini Green Irish Tweed with more citrus, utterly unremarkable. LT

Mimosa pour Moi (L'Artisan Parfumeur) ★ ★ ★ *fruity mimosa* $ $ $
Mimosa is a wonderfully unsophisticated flower, even in nature—fresh white floral with a powdery almond-milk sweetness, good natured, soft all over. Mimosa pour Moi does a beautifully convincing job of playing real mimosa in the top note, although the drydown eventually settles for a pleasant but unrelated fruity-violet musk. TS

Miracle (Lancôme) ★ ★ *pepper rose* $ $
Teensy-weensy cutesy-pie fruity floral of the worst vintage (2000), made notable only by a short-lived black pepper top note. LT

Miracle Forever (Lancôme) ★ ★ ★ ★ *candied floral* $ $
The perfumers at IFF have been digging so thoroughly in the post-Angel territory of Lolita Lempicka and Coco Mademoiselle and turned up so little of interest (see Flowerbomb and Armani Code) that we thought it was time they moved on. Then this little flanker, seventh in the low-expectations Miracle line—the other six miracles being the sort to invite apostasy—showed us up. The basic format is easy: a big fruity floral against an oriental base of woods and the cotton-candy smell of ethyl-maltol, which all makes for a loud, complicated, but crude smell. Mira-

cle Forever leaves out half the sugar and replaces the usual sweet rose or orange blossom with a green, slightly poisonous white floral, equally milky and soapy. It feels like the ice queen of Gucci Envy in a maudlin, huggy mood after a few martinis. In this category, we finally have a Best in Show. TS

Miroir des Envies (Thierry Mugler) ★ ★ ★ ★ *hazelnut floral* $$$
This spicy, milky floral was composed by Louise Turner and Christine Nagel, both experts at suntanned, smooth fragrances. It is simple in structure, reminiscent of Hervé Léger's fragrance in weight and texture, but with a very unusual twist to it: the heart note is an intense hazelnut accord, a sort of Nutella absolute I find very attractive. Nice work. LT

Miroir des Secrets (Thierry Mugler) ★ ★ *aldehydic patchouli* $$$
This perfume claims to be the first in history to mix aldehydes with a patchouli-musk accord. That may be so, but why then does it smell like a hundred others, and much less good than the great-grandad of this genre, Or Black? LT

Miroir des Vanités (Thierry Mugler) ★ ★ ★ ★ *Campari soda* $$$
It is not every day that one comes across a truly novel accord in perfumery, and this one had me puzzled for a while until I figured out what it reminded me of: Campari soda, in the conical red bottles, served with a slice of lemon. And sure enough, the list of materials includes bark from the cinchona tree from which quinine was derived, as well as citrus peel. The idea is original and euphoric, though the execution could be fuller and more polished. I'll wager that the young perfumer Alexis Dadier will (1) be widely imitated and (2) go far. LT

Miss Balmain (Balmain) ★ ★ ★ ★ *herbal leather* $$
When I was a kid, if I imagined what a grown woman was supposed to smell like, this was the kind of thing I would have conjured up as the Platonic ideal: a slightly acrid, pleasantly adult smell of hard leather, stubbed-out cigarettes, and face powder, much like that mysterious

bloom that I remember coming up from the bottom of Mom's best handbag. Although, like Balmain's Jolie Madame, Miss Balmain is technically a floral leather, she lacks her sister's fluid sweetness. Instead, her dry herbal rasp has the appeal of a throaty voice that catches on every third word, and smells a bit like Eau d'Hermès improved by going cheap. There's something charmingly put-on and ambitious about it that makes me think of the way I was at eighteen, in my new pink-and-white houndstooth jacket from the $10 store, putting on a grown-up voice when I worked as a receptionist during the summer months, smoking on my lunch break, all the while pretending I'd been doing it for years. TS

Miss Boucheron (Boucheron) ★ *fruity floral* $$$
Fermat's principle of least action at work. Take the fine Boucheron "ring" bottle, change the glass color from deep blue to pink and the spray button to turquoise, add *Miss* in front of the name to suggest nubile idiocy, and fill it with a mixture of materials common to the last two hundred fruity florals, while making sure none costs more than $18 per kilogram. Serve ugly. LT

Miss Charming (Juliette Has a Gun) ★ ★ ★ *berry rose* $$
With the dramatic brand name, I was expecting something more dangerous than this pretty little smell: a toy-poodle version of a modern green rose, cousin to Miss Dior Chérie and City Glam. Good nevertheless, with a surprisingly well constructed drydown. TS

Miss Dior (Dior) ★ ★ *dry chypre* $$
Miss Dior has been through more reformulations than I've had bad sushi, and by now I'll wager some people out there are nostalgic for a version that existed only between March and November 1992. The present Miss Dior is a dry, pinched, aldehydic chypre, ageless in a prematurely wrinkled way, and makes me think of pursed, painted lips hissing disparaging bons mots. LT

2009 update. ★ ★. Still awful. LT

Miss Dior Cherie (Dior) ★ ★ ★ ★ *patchouli strawberry* $ $

Some fragrances, like some people, give a deceptive, facile first impression, which they then contradict with subtle twists and refinements that anyone who tuned out after the first few minutes would miss. Dior's sweet flanker to their (now much diminished) classic Miss Dior is far better than you usually get in the fruity-floral category. Although its main accord of strawberry-rose-patchouli isn't as arrestingly pretty as that of its contemporary rival Badgley Mischka, it feels more carefully put together, seamless and balanced, done with one lump of sugar, not two. Still, this kind of fragrance never feels like the woman of the house, more like the nanny, even if she's getting her PhD. TS

Missoni (Missoni) ★ ★ ★ ★ ★ *kaleidoscopic floral* $ $ $

Maurice Roucel has, over the years, proved himself a master of compositions at both ends of the perfume time scale, i.e., harmony and melody. Tocade, his definitive essay in short-form perfumery, rang a single chord with very little time evolution, and was all the more remarkable for achieving a totally novel effect using only well-rehearsed raw materials. His various long-form compositions (24, Faubourg; L'Instant; Insolence), demonstrated a growing mastery of counterpoint, whereby the mind's nose, throughout the fragrance's exposition, could focus on layers floating at different depths. In a conversation some time back Roucel recommended I smell his Missoni, about which he was uncharacteristically positive. When the package came, I marveled at the poverty-stricken ugliness of the bottle, and wondered whether Roucel had once again, as with Alain Delon's Lyra, entrusted his best work to a goofy outfit. It seems Missoni got lucky. I have no idea whether they will still be around in ten years, but I'll make sure I have enough of this perfume to last me a lifetime. This is one of the most accomplished fragrances in years, combining in a uniquely convincing way both the horizontal and vertical elements of a perfume score. At first, you mistake it for an entirely delightful hybrid of Tocade and Beyond Paradise. Seconds later, you realize that it has progressed to another chord, still complete with top notes, heart, and drydown, then to another and another, all spanning a wide but entirely comfortable fresh-to-sweet range, all different. Halfway through, when you least expect it, Missoni springs a stunning modulation to a luminous, almost minty accord. The effect is an uncanny feeling that the perfume is alive, somehow composing itself as it goes along. Most other perfumes are rapidly fading photographs: this one is a movie. LT

Missoni Acqua (Missoni) ★ ★ ★ ★ *citrus cedar* $$
Perhaps I'll shut up about the work of Maurice Roucel one day, but not today. With his two fragrances for the cheerful stripey-knit brand Missoni, he has been extending certain appealing perfumery ideas he's developed for years, which have a stealth genius not always apparent at first contact. For some reason, he seems to do some of his best work for minor projects. Take this blue-bottle flanker, easy to dismiss in the store among a hundred similar others. Considered at leisure at home, what seemed an ordinary fresh fruity floral suddenly fans out into a panorama of miniature wonders, like those bound books of color postcards I used to love as a kid, which open a series of small windows on the sublime. After a top note that recaps the best of the last ten years of white florals, freshened with a good dose of citrus and tea, this fragrance spins the wonderful green, fruity lily-of-the-valley idea of Roucel's Envy for Gucci around a dusty, nutty, spiced note of what seems to be immortelle, also known as helichrysum or everlasting flower, playing freshness against dryness in perfect counterpoint. Immortelle is supposed to be difficult and strange. Then why is it so at ease here? In short, this is a friendly, well-proportioned, easygoing fragrance, unpretentious but full of ideas. TS

Miss Rocaille (Caron) ★ *sour peony* $$$
For the young who apparently deserve no better: tart peony top note,

green aquatic midpart, and I couldn't get to the drydown to report without washing. TS

Miss Sixty (Coty) ★ *cheap candy* $
Ideal if you intend to be a miss at sixty. Smells like a "complimentary" fruit cocktail with an umbrella in it. LT

Mitsouko (Guerlain) ★ ★ ★ ★ *reference chypre* $$
On every occasion when I am asked to name my favorite fragrance, or the best fragrance ever, or the fragrance I would take with me if I had to move to Mars for tax reasons, I always answer Mitsouko. This elicits, broadly speaking, three types of responses: perfumers yawn, beginners write the name down, and aficionados decide I am a staid sort of chap. In truth, it is a bit like saying that your favorite painting is the Mona Lisa (not mine, by the way). Mitsouko's history illustrates to perfection the twin forces of innovation and imitation that move perfumery forward. It was released in 1919, supposedly the result of a love affair Jacques Guerlain had with Japan or a lady therein. But there is nothing Japanese about Mitsouko aside from the name. It is, as has been said countless times before, an improvement on François Coty's Chypre, released to huge acclaim two years earlier. Chypre in turn was based on a three-component accord so perfect that it remains unsurpassed and fertile in new developments ninety years later: bergamot, labdanum, and oakmoss. They smell respectively citrus-resinous, sweet-amber-resinous, and bitter-resinous. Picture them as equal sectors making up a pie chart, sticking to each other via the resin. The resulting genre, now called a chypre, has two fundamental qualities: balance and abstraction. Chypre is long gone, but I've had occasion to smell both vintage samples and the Osmothèque reconstruction in Versailles. It is brilliant, but it does have a big-boned, bad-tempered Joan Crawford feel to it, and was a fragrance in whose company you could never entirely rest your weight. Jacques Guerlain was Juan Gris to Coty's Picasso, obsessed with full-

ness, finish, detail. To Chypre he famously added the peach note of undecalactone, quite a lot of iris and probably twenty other things we'll never know about. The lactone makes a huge difference: it works like a Tiffany lamp, adds a touch of muted warmth and color, and unlike esterbased fruit notes, lasts forever. The effect of Guerlain's additions is a ripening of the chypre structure into a masterpiece whose richness brings to my mind the mature chamber music of Johannes Brahms. Mitsouko is also a survivor, most recently having dodged a bullet aimed straight at its heart by the European Union's chemical phobia. It looked for a while as if it was going to be reformulated in a hurry. In the end, the great Edouard Fléchier brought Mitsouko into conformity with European Union rules and it still smells great, though it arguably lasts less long than the old one. LT

M Moi (Mauboussin) ★ ★ ★ *ectoplasmic floral* $ $
Contemporary pale florals are like voile curtains: telling them apart is left for professionals. The rest of us would (God forbid) require months of training and adaptation to discern variations in their cloudy, shadowless light. Choosing one is ultimately a matter of deciding whether one wants a warm or a cold gray, and how bright. M Moi (Aime-moi) is quiet and cold, wan and distinguished, and interesting only as a sort of perfumed disappearing act. LT

Mogador (Keiko Mecheri) ★ ★ ★ ★ *fresh floral* $ $
This modern floral uses indefatigably fresh, green notes of cut grass and lily of the valley to give its rose heart a massive lift in the Beyond Paradise style (same perfumer), thereby avoiding any of the old-fashioned chintz curtains effects that rose soliflores can have. As time goes on, it gets nearer and nearer the beautiful melon-jasmine of Cristalle and its ilk, without the meanness. In fact, this fragrance is exactly what Sécrétions Magnifiques is behind the bilge. In short, these are all familiar points, but very nicely joined. TS

Molecule 01 (Escentric Molecules) ★ ★ ★ *woody ambery* $ $ $
Perfumer Geza Schoen, who had a big hand in, among others, Ormonde Jayne fragrances, is apparently a devotee of a woody synthetic raw material called Iso E Super. Iso E Super (originally an improved grade of stuff called isoprecyclemone e) is a fragrance chemist's wet dream, the sort of stuff that gets you a very nice gold watch when you retire: moderately powerful, very complex in smell, woody, ambery, slightly musky, herbaceous, possessed of a mysterious velvety quality that makes all fragrances shine and flow. Schoen wanted a fragrance made with only one raw material, and chose this one. Helmut Lang had already been there with the pleasantly straightforward Velviona, using only Givaudan's exceptionally wonderful and quite cheap macrocyclic Velvione musk. Velviona was more truly monomolecular, whereas Iso E Super is a complex mixture of isomers. In other words, Molecule 01 is a composition, which sort of defeats the object of the exercise. It nevertheless smells okay. LT

Le Monde Est Beau (Kenzo) ★ ★ *green woody* $ $
Many recent fragrances suffer the same problem as recent movies: all the good parts are in the trailer. The top note of Le Monde Est Beau (The World Is Beautiful) is an uplifting, clever grapefruit construction, made of tomato-leaf and floral notes, but moments after spray it collapses into a nondescript, dull woody mess. Same awful bottle as the far better Ça Sent Beau. TS

Monsieur Balmain (Balmain) ★ ★ ★ ★ *citrus sandalwood* $ $
This superb fragrance was one of Germaine Cellier's sunnier works, perhaps because she relaxed into a crisp, easy manner when creating fragrances for men. Her idea of a guy, both in MB and in Piguet's extinct Cravache, seems low-key and elegant, a perfect foil for his reckless partner wearing Bandit or Fracas. Monsieur Balmain is also notable for being a faithful reconstruction (by Calice Becker) of the original. I had the good fortune of smelling a vintage MB recently, and everything is pres-

ent and correct in the modern version: the weirdly durable lemon, the excellent sandalwood drydown. One of the best citrus fragrances of all time. LT

Monsieur de Givenchy (Givenchy) ★ ★ ★ ★ *citrus chypre* $$$
This 1959 marvel by Francis Fabron (Baghari, Quadrille, L'Air du Temps) has just been reissued. I confess I never smelled the original, but the present MdG feels wonderful and lies, as it should, exactly on the line that connects chypres with colognes, near Chanel's Pour Monsieur but with more citrus. It has a surprisingly Edwardian rosy start before settling down to a deliciously quiet, understated woody chypre drydown. Timelessly elegant and discreet. LT

Montaigne (Caron) ★ ★ *orange woody* $$$
Caron has the reformulation bug bad, and its very eighties-smelling Montaigne has gotten a makeover. It now begins with an expansive, fresh, aldehydic and fruity jasmine with all the trimmings, but then fades out to a confused woody floral without much fun in it, which I was told smells almost exactly like the original. TS

Montana Homme (Montana) ★ ★ *dry lemon* $$
The bottle is intended to look like some ribbed ancient ziggurat but ends up looking like a stump of celery left in the fridge too long. The fragrance is a dry woody lemon of no interest. I remembered it as better than this, and suspect the formula has been changed. LT

Montana Mood Sensual (Montana) ★ ★ *powdery pepper* $$
A potentially interesting accord of pink pepper and heliotropin, marred by cheap execution. LT

Montana Mood Sexy (Montana) ★ *not tonight* $$
Sad, watered-down, cheap, skimpy thing that smells like the far drydown of a loud, concentrated nasty thing. LT

Montana Mood Soft (Montana) ★ *light oriental* $$
Uninteresting and mercifully weak vaguely oriental composition. Should have been called Brown Study. LT

Monyette Paris (Monyette Paris) ★ ★ ★ *coconut tuberose* $$
This is a big tuberose, meaning Mother Nature did most of the composition work, somewhat softened by a big dollop of coconut lactones, against a dry-woody base. Skillful and solid, if you like that sort of thing. LT

Morgan de Toi (Morgan) ★ *penny candy* $$
In French slang, *morgane* means "crazy," so this would be Nuts About You." Smells of bubble gum. I was going to say "cheap bubble gum," but then I remembered there is only one kind. LT

Moschino (Moschino) ★ ★ ★ ★ *heavy oriental* $$
Big, striking, heavy, joss-stick oriental, an overgrown cousin of L'Heure Bleue, or perhaps an Emeraude with more woods. Not bad at all, but another pin stuck in a territory so crowded with interesting fragrances that it is hard to get really excited about second-rank specimens. LT

MoslBuddJewChristHinDao (Elternhaus) ★ ★ ★ ★ ★
woody floral $$$$
Sold encased in a two-part heavy concrete block, this "Unfaith" fragrance is, despite the overwhelming artiness, one of perfumer Marc Buxton's finest works (he recommended I smell it). MBJCHD is likely the high-water mark of that beautiful style of perfumery Buxton and Bertrand Duchaufour invented independently, the transparent woody floral. Their best creations, from Comme des Garçons to Timbuktu, provide a unique frisson, at once archaic and sci-fi, that brings to mind Le Corbusier's wonderful description of Gaudí's unfinished cathedral as "a ruin of the future." Whereas Buxton's previous fragrances often had a steely sheen about them, MBJCHD's admission of floral gentleness into his usual woody severity is affecting as never before. A masterpiece. LT

Moss Breches (Tom Ford) ★ ★ *boring woody* $$$
A decently put-together, slightly dull sweet-woody confection distantly related to Guerlain's superb Derby, only vastly less good. Also, what on earth are "moss breches"? LT

Mouchoir de Monsieur (Guerlain) ★ ★ ★ ★ *rich lavender* $$$
I once met the distinguished biologist Miriam Rothschild at her country home and, during a visit to the guest toilet, noticed a pristine bottle of a long-discontinued cologne on the shelf. I complimented her on finding it, and she replied, with a wave of the hand, "Oh that? Dior makes it for me." Most people are probably unaware that until Guerlain put MdM (Gentleman's Handkerchief) on the general market a few years ago, in order to wear it you were faced with a stark choice: you had to be either the actor Jean-Claude Brialy or King Juan Carlos of Spain. Now that the palace doors are open, what's it like in there? Wonderful, that's what. MdM is basically Jicky with a touch more civet and lemon at either end, and about as studiedly dandified as a perfume can be. If you can wear it without thinking of Rupert Everett playing Beau Brummell, do so by all means. LT

Muguet du Bonheur (Caron) ★ ★ *green muguet* $$$$
The Muguet du Bonheur I always knew was of good quality but suffered from the tendency of lily of the valley, unless treated with great care as in the brilliant Diorissimo, to smell like household products. The current batch is greener, more like the current version of Vent Vert, not very good. TS

Mûre et Musc (L'Artisan Parfumeur) ★ ★ *fruity barbershop* $$$
The original M&M, released in 1978 when Jean-François Laporte was still in charge, was an idea of genius: take ethylene brassylate, a deliciously creamy synthetic musk with overtones of raspberries, and add a ton of fuzzy, fresh red-berry notes. The result was a fragrance of tremendous radiance and transparency, seeming at once hippie and yogurt-healthy. It was their best seller, and deservedly so, for years. For

some reason, the current version no longer has the same effect for me, though according to the company the formula has remained exactly the same since 1978. If you've still got the old stuff, hoard it or send it to me. LT

Mûre et Musc extrait de parfum (L'Artisan Parfumeur) ★ ★
sour berry $$$$
The virtue of the original Mûre et Musc was a transparent simplicity in perfect step with its pop art times: a bright berry, a fruity musk. What fun! Use as directed. In 2008, to celebrate the thirtieth anniversary of a huge seller, Bertrand Duchaufour assembled an ultraluxe version, formulated from top to bottom as a grand perfume. It's an interesting flop, illustrating how charm school can kill the charm. After a winsome if unexpectedly plodding Froot Loops top note, everything shuffles about trying to get to the point until coming to a loud, tenacious bitter-green drydown in which the happy sparkle of the original is totally lost. TS

Mûre et Musc Extrême (L'Artisan Parfumeur) ★ ★ *see above*
Same as M&M, only more so. LT

Musc for Him perfume oil (Narciso Rodriguez) ★ ★ ★ ★
fruity wood $$$
Perfume oils are rather taciturn compared to alcohol-based fragrances and need the warmth of the skin to make themselves heard. This very interesting composition uses the constraint to its advantage, to give an odd, melancholy, suntan-oil, wet-wood, and ripe-fruit effect related to Amouage's Lyric Man, but much quieter, so much that you search for it on the skin to understand it. Indistinct accords can sometimes be frustrating, but in this case the murmur works, as when an adult speaks in a very low voice and rowdy children around him quiet down. An odd, serene, and remote fragrance. LT

Musc Maori (Parfumerie Générale) ★ ★ *cocoa butter* $$$
There apparently exists a cocoa-scented fragrance that weight watchers spray on their wrist when hungry to induce satiety. Musc Maori has much the same effect. LT

Musc Nomade (Annick Goutal) ★ ★ ★ *fatty musk* $$$
Some musks sparkle; some have a metallic shine; some smell fruity, some oily, some sweet, nutty, milky, or woody. Perfumers usually use a few, in case, as usually happens, people are anosmic to one or more. What I smell of Musc Nomade hints at amber, ink, cedar, patchouli, and animal hide and feels like a faded backdrop seen behind Kenzo Fleurs d'Hiver. TS

Musc Ravageur (Frédéric Malle) ★ ★ ★ *hippie musk* $$$
Ravageur, in French, has a positive connotation suggesting the ravages made among sensitive hearts by irrepressible male beauty. Despite my admiration for Maurice Roucel, I do not share what seems to be a general enthusiasm for the fragrance. Yes, it is powerfully musky in an animalic barbershop sort of way. But the remainder of the composition works like a huge fig leaf to hide the musk's correspondingly large pudenda and turns out to be none other than Lutens's Ambre Sultan revisited, i.e., a Moroccan-market hippie amber about as subtle as a skunk joint. Further, even if the initial effect does have a sort of crude charm to it, the accord fades to a rather cheap drydown reminiscent of the far simpler and less swaggeringly pretentious Envy for Men (Gucci). Nice, but more flashy than good. LT

Musc Samarkand (Les Néréides) ★ ★ ★ ★ *powdery animalic* $$
An excellent illustration of the dirty-clean paradox of musk: an accord halfway between an objectionable animal pong evocative of someone wanting a bath and the lusciously powdery, fresh sparkle of laundry warm in a cloud of Downy. TS

Muscs Koublai Khan (Serge Lutens) ★ ★ ★ ★ *beastly musk* $ $ $
No other perfume musk comes close to this potent animalic antidote to the laundered age, not even the obsolete and unavailable natural musk tincture. Back before I learned to stop worrying and love the bomb, I reviewed Muscs Koublai Khan as "the armpit of a camel driver who has not been near running water in a week." The scent is the same but my horror is gone. The fragrance turns out to be a lost-world fantasy of firelit palaces, with the soupy, sleepy warmth of two beneath a quilt. The cozy animal smells of civet and castoreum, smoky balsams, and powerful synthetic musks all conspire to make you think of your lover in barbaric furs. On the blotter it seems rather frightening, but on skin it reveals an intimate, archaic smell of burnt beeswax candles, which is to this English major a more convincing Khan than Coleridge's—who "on honey-dew hath fed, and drunk the milk of Paradise." TS

Musk (Etro) ★ ★ ★ *musty musk* $ $ $
Musks are large molecules, near the maximum size limit for humans to detect, and everyone seems to be incapable of smelling one or more of the type. Etro's musk may have hit my blind spot, because all I can smell is Cashmeran, the wonderful IFF molecule that manages to smell like musk, spices, or wet concrete depending on, so to speak, the angle of the light. Here the wet concrete predominates, and the overall feeling is pleasantly musty rather than musky. LT

Musk (Keiko Mecheri) ★ ★ ★ *aldehydic musk* $ $ $
Musk fragrances as a rule can go in one of two directions: soapy clean (Jovan Musk) or animalic (Lutens's Muscs Koublai Khan). This one is a bit of a mystery. It has an odd, fishy, unwashed-hair aspect on paper, and on skin a surprising, smoky, waxy character, with slight tones of white flowers, as if it were a stealth aldehydic floral or an incense played at a whisper. All in all, a more complex and engaging fragrance than expected from the name. TS

Musk (Renée) ★ ★ *amber musk* $ $
A boring oriental in a field crowded with boring orientals. LT

Must de Cartier (Cartier) ★ *Russian chocolate* $ $ $
I remember as a child being fascinated by chocolate assortment boxes. The small ones embodied the basically good idea of stuffing a shell of milk chocolate (how? I still wonder) with mashed-up bits and pieces, e.g., praline, coffee, vanilla cream, even candied orange. But when the box became too big, say more than six by six little parking spots, all manner of hubris showed up: pineapple, crème de cassis, God knows what else. Of course, we all stuck with the ones that came in sensible colors: avoid apple green, yellow, and, most of all, stripes. Must is the perfume that brought into the world, in expensive liquid form, the full ugliness of the chocolates nobody wants. The basic accord of vanilla, flowers, and galbanum is so indigestible that you could use it as an appetite suppressant. Worse than that, the awful idea spawned a whole industry: Venise, Dune, and Allure, though vastly better, are related to this dreadful thing. LT

Must de Cartier pour Homme (Cartier) ★ ★ ★ ★ *animalic wood* $ $
There is something really appealing about this fragrance, probably because it is so hard to pin down. It feels like someone took the salubrious cedar of, say, Antaeus and added to it the animalic, almost urinous note of Yatagan. A temple that smells like a brothel: great. LT

My Dream (Grès) ★ *white floral* $ $
The troubled house of Grès, which after the death of Alix Grès was briefly owned by businessman Bernard Tapie, now appears to be in Swiss hands. The parent firm, Art & Fragrance, also owns Lalique and, God help us, Alain Delon and Jaguar fragrances. The new Grès goes beyond celebrity fragrance to create dead-celebrity fragrance. (Advantages: no fees or royalties. Disadvantages: no photo ops.) Or rather three

dead-celebrity fragrances dedicated to poor Marlene Dietrich, who is not here to complain, as she certainly would. My Dream is a totally uninteresting "fresh" floral, so intensely derivative that it feels as though the perfumer has even lost track of what it was he was trying to copy. LT

My Insolence (Guerlain) ★★ *butterscotch cherry* $$
How could the brand that has made L'Heure Bleue to spec for a hundred years put out this cynical, trendy, hastily-cobbled-together cherry-almond sugary oriental? It's as if Hermès decided to sell a glitter-vinyl shoe with a lucite platform heel. TS

My Life (Grès) ★★ *citrus almond* $$
Unlike the appalling My Dream, this "Hommage à Marlene Dietrich" has an interesting structure based on a weird accord of grapefruit, jasmine, and heliotropin but, sadly, feels as if it has trickled up to fine perfumery from some plug-in air-care thing. Very nearly good, and the idea may be perfectible. LT

My Man (Fresh Scents by Terri) ★★ *citrus herbal* $$
Inoffensive if vanishingly faint citrus cologne. TS

My Passion (Grès) ★★ *attempted chypre* $$
An unbalanced but not uninteresting fragrance, reminiscent of a Givenchy III without oakmoss. It smells like a Meursault left out overnight in a glass, feels strangely old-fashioned up top, but is manifestly missing a load-bearing strut and topples over during the drydown. LT

MyQueen (Alexander McQueen) ★★ *shrinking violet* $$
They say that a film script credited to several writers usually indicates a patch-up job. This may be true for fragrances: this one lists the dream-team of Anne Flipo, Dominique Ropion, and Pierre Wargnye. Aside from a nice old-fashioned violet top note, it is hard to see what

they were up to. The thing fades to a murky woody amber that seems to apologize for its presence and fades quickly. LT

La Myrrhe (Serge Lutens) ★ ★ ★ ★ ★ *resinous aldehydic* $$$
Judging by the name and the Lutens line, you would think La Myrrhe would be an updated straightforward incense or an amber oriental. Open the bottle and fall prey to total surprise. Gone is the familiar oriental apparatus of spices, vanilla, heavy tobacco, leather, and sandalwood, the whole Cleopatra kit and caboodle. Instead, Lutens and Christopher Sheldrake set the smoky balsamic resin known as myrrh against a radiant, rosy, modern aldehydic floral of incomparable crispness, kin to White Linen. By this unexpected route, the fragrance somehow manages to replicate the thrilling balance of incredible brightness and sweetness that Shalimar once had, before decades of adjustments deepened its voice. La Myrrhe has a pure, clear, unearthly tone with beauty and force, as if the fragrance could sing a clean high C as high as heaven and not show the strain. TS

Myrrhe Ardente (Annick Goutal) ★ ★ *root-beer antiseptic* $$$
One of Goutal's ambitious trio, Les Orientalistes, which represents an excursion beyond the brand's usual polite florals. Unfortunately, the myrrh is smothered on two sides: by a potentially interesting note of root beer and a violently powerful woody amber, which is always so difficult to dose. The reference myrrh fragrance remains Lutens's. TS

Myrrhe et Merveilles (Keiko Mecheri) ★ ★ ★ *sweetened myrrh* $$$
The marvelous biblical incense material myrrh found its greatest expression in La Myrrhe (see above), composed by Christopher Sheldrake for Serge Lutens in 1995. It was essentially a crisp aldehydic floral with an added sheen of mystery, a streamlined structure that lined up the bright, soapy aldehydes with similar aspects in myrrh. The Keiko Mecheri version from 1999 is built very much on the same principle, but adds a dollop of milky and amber notes that don't fit well with the rest. TS

Mystère (Rochas) ★ ★ ★ ★ *floral chypre* $ $

The mystery of Rochas is how a brand with so many good fragrances has failed to become better known. Now that they've been bought by Procter & Gamble, we wait and see if things improve or die trying. So far, so good for Mystère, back as good as ever in its optical illusion bottle, which makes you want to adjust your set. Smell it to experience what may be the quintessential late seventies chypre: a black-and-green descendant of Bandit, a smell as smooth as glass, with an excellent, silvery, icy bergamot top note, the twilit-forest feel of oakmoss and patchouli, and the quietest florals, which have lost all their sweetness and contribute only a damp, camphoraceous cool. It makes me think of that funny saying: cold hands, warm heart. T S

Mystra (Aesop) ★ ★ ★ ★ *green resinous* $ $ $

Aesop's second fragrance, according to the label, is composed exclusively of three gums: labdanum, frankincense, and mastic. This will make you no friends in the compounding plant, because nobody likes to mix large quantities of sticky brown goo. This perfume must be sampled on skin because the volatile fraction of the resinoids distorts the smell completely on a smelling strip. It is a wonderfully dissonant accord of salubrious, bittersweet, and green notes unlike anything I have encountered before. It has some of the bracing transience of bay rum, but more archaic, and smells clean and earthy in the drydown. Wonderful. L T

Nahéma (Guerlain) ★ ★ ★ ★ ★ *virtual rose* $ $

The first three minutes of Nahéma are like an explosion played in reverse: a hundred disparate, torn shreds of fragrance propelled by a fierce, accelerating vortex to coalesce into a perfect form that you fancy would then walk toward you, smiling as if nothing had happened. The consensus among experts is that this fragrance, Guerlain's greatest rose, is in fact done without using any rose at all. Guerlain formulas are usually too rich even for analytical chemistry to make sense of, but from what information can be gleaned, it would seem that the rose at Nahéma's core is a geometric locus bounded by a dozen facets, each due to a different ingredient. Whether that is true or false, accident or skill, it is certainly true that the unearthly radiance of Nahéma is without equal among perfumery roses, and so awe-inspiring that nobody even tries. LT

N'Aimez que Moi (Caron) ★ ★ *floral mishmash* $$$
A confused top note of rose liqueur, violets, clove, and green notes gives way to the standard-issue modern Caron soapy rose drydown. All the Caron fragrances are, via reformulation, converging to the same uninteresting idea. TS

Nameless (By Mark Buxton) ★ ★ *cheap fresh* $$$
Let me quote from the Web site: "Sitting on a terrace at the lake of Côme. Watching the boats sail in and out of the harbour, especially 'Riva's.'" That would be Lake Como, unless France has invaded Lombardy, and Rivas without the apostrophe (Riva is a brand of nice motorboats that had its definitive moment in the sixties). The fragrance measures up to this deathless prose, a naff little thing that smells of scented toilet paper. How did this happen? LT

Nanette Lepore (Nanette Lepore) ★ *fruity death* $$
In its own way, almost perfect: the most intensely sweet, cloying, syrupy fruity floral possible, radiating all the way down the block and lingering for years, causing pink fuzzy pom-poms to spontaneously erupt on shoes and sweaters all around your zip code. Vile, yes, but somebody in a jeweled cardigan has been waiting for it all her life. TS

Narciso Rodriguez for Her (Narciso Rodriguez) ★ ★ ★ ★
radiant woody $$
One of the hazards of taking perfumes seriously as works of art is that occasionally one risks missing the point. Some fragrances, while not advancing the art one iota, nevertheless work when used as directed: sprayed on an attractive woman. One was Givenchy's Organza, a banal

rehash of every vanillic cliché, but undemanding, lighthearted, and lethally effective. Another was Talisman (Balenciaga), which made vulgarity feel like a richly deserved holiday from good taste. The latest is Narciso Rodriguez for Her. Probed on the smelling strip by the discerning critic, it is yet another woody oriental that brings to mind the (accurate) description of Taneyev's musical compositions as "original like a match in a box of matches." But give Narciso Rodriguez to someone you like, and stand at attention as she sweeps past. You then realize that some fragrances, like gravitation, reliably generate an attractive force day in and day out, without fuss or explanation, though theories abound. LT

Memorable mostly for mating a big, somewhat masculine patchouli-musk to its harsh, chemical-smelling orange-blossom floral. TS

Narciso Rodriguez for Him (Narciso Rodriguez) ★ ★ ★
woody green $ $
Another variation on the watery violet-leaf theme, but with all friendliness removed. A dry, screechy, metallic top note seems carefully crafted to discourage approach, after which a small, cautious floral sweetness sneaks in. It's a well-made fragrance for mean, forgettable people. TS

Narcisse Blanc (Caron) ★ ★ ★ *sweet narcissus* $ $ $
Pleasant orange-blossom-and-narcissus floral, as powdery as a swansdown puff buried in talcum powder. Same soapy-rosy-woody drydown as nearly all the current Caron. TS

Narcisse Noir eau de toilette (Caron) ★ ★ *woody jasmine* $ $ $
Shed a tear for Narcisse Noir. Where is the darkness, the strangeness, the smell of the cold, damp ashes after a bonfire, the animal breath—the drama? It was for women in columnar gowns, marcelled hair, and red lipstick waving foot-long cigarette holders and making life memorably difficult for everyone. It was one of Caron's few truly indispensable

fragrances. It is now a pretty, safe little sweet jasmine and orange blossom. How can you ruin a man's life properly while wearing this? TS

Narcotic Venus (Nasomatto) ★ ★ *tuberose foghorn* $$$
I never thought I'd meet a tuberose that would make me hanker for the quiet of Amarige, but this is it. Blaring, unsubtle, a kind of scrambled Insolence without the skill or the fun. If you meet someone who wears this, run. LT

Nautica Voyage (Nautica) ★ ★ ★ ★ *floral masculine* $
Smelling NV is a bit like like finding out that your local Chevy dealer just landed the part of Evita at the Met. From start to finish it keeps up a reassuring baritone patter in a familiar low-key Cool Water style, but forgets itself at odd times to break into snatches of soprano arias from Donizetti. This is Missoni with chest hair. It was composed by Maurice Roucel at the same time, and it is fascinating to see the strange arpeggiato effect of the woody-fruity chord in a dark-suit context. LT

Navegar (L'Artisan Parfumeur) ★ ★ ★ *astringent lime* $$$
Very nice dry-green juniper-citrus accord, a sort of Eau de Guerlain under a cold shower. As crisp as it gets. LT

Nectarine Blossom and Honey Cologne (Jo Malone) ★ ★
sweet peach $$$
I love it when they get precise: nectarine, dear, peaches are so last year. Nice peach base, fit for an upmarket hair conditioner. LT

Néroli (Annick Goutal) ★ ★ ★ *tarragon citrus* $$$
Neroli is an intensely green oil that comes from steam distillation of the flowers of the bitter orange tree, the Seville orange whose peel makes the best marmalade. (Solvent extraction of the same flowers gives you the jasmine-like orange blossom. An extraction of the leaves is known as petitgrain; an extraction of the peel, bigarade. Useful plant to have

around.) Goutal's Néroli, true to the natural material, is a handsome classic citrus with a full, resinous timbre and a salty, herbal coloration, not as clean or bright as Eau d'Orange Verte or Lime Basil & Mandarin, but with a rustic feel that makes a nice alternative. TS

Neroli 36 (Le Labo) ★ ★ ★ ★ *pale floral* $$$$
Le Labo's fondness for misdirection in the names of its perfumes (see Tubéreuse 40) is cute and may serve some arcane didactic or commercial purpose. My guess is they simply scrambled the labels to see if anyone noticed. Neroli 36, composed by Daphné Bugey, does not smell of neroli (Fleur d'Oranger 27 does). It is a weird soapy-metallic floral, not unlike TDC's Osmanthus but without the peachy caress, and oddly reminiscent of Molyneux's extinct Vivre. An interesting fragrance, pale in color but somehow still vivid. Recommended. LT

Neroli Portofino (Tom Ford) ★ ★ *expensive cologne* $$$
Portofino is a heavenly little Ligurian harbor village, originally home to a hundred fishermen and now visited by roughly a million Milanesi tourists every weekend. Neroli is also the basis for the classic cologne. This one is good but not great, and definitely not worth the money, considering the competition—for example, Chanel's Eau de Cologne. LT

Néroli Sauvage (Creed) ★ ★ ★ *green citrus* $$$
Creed excels at conventional accords done with good raw materials, and this fresh, green, woody neroli is one. No great shakes, but works like it says on the can and smells good. LT

New Haarlem (Bond No. 9) ★ ★ ★ *coffee lavender* $$$$
A further gloss on Eau de Navigateur (L'Artisan), which was the first to put coffee in your cologne, Bond No. 9's bold New Haarlem by Maurice Roucel ain't half bad. It smells rich and deliciously roasted in the top note, and eases into a lightly woody but short-lived fougère later. I don't know if I'm a breakfast junkie or what, but I find this coffee thing hope-

lessly attractive, and until science proves me wrong, I will firmly believe that men who smell like this are the type to grow five o'clock shadows by 11 a.m. TS

New Tradition (Etro) ★ ★ ★ *floral masculine* $$$
This is an anglophile homage to the Jermyn Street dandy, complete with lavender, rose, oakmoss, and a very high-quality animalic musk, but it has a slightly washed-out barbershop retro quality that embodies the melancholy of the genre but not the humor. LT

New York (Parfums de Nicolaï) ★ ★ ★ ★ ★ *orange amber* $
If Guerlain had any sense, they would buy Parfums de Nicolaï, add PdN's range to theirs, trash fifteen or so of their own laggard fragrances, a couple of de Nicolaï's, and install owner-creator Patricia de Nicolaï in Orphin as in-house perfumer. She is, after all, a granddaughter of Pierre Guerlain and genetic analysis might usefully reveal the genes associated with her perfumery talent. As a control where the genes are known to be absent, use the DNA of whoever did Creed's Love in White. Smelling New York as I write this, eighteen years after its release, is like meeting an old high school teacher who had a decisive influence on my life: I may have moved on, but everything it taught me is still there, still precious, and wonderful to revisit. New York's exquisite balance between resinous orange, powdery vanilla, and salubrious woods shimmers from moment to moment, always comfortable but never slack, always present but never loud. It is one of the greatest masculines ever, and probably the one I would save if the house burned down. Reader, I wore it for a decade. LT

New York Fling (Bond No. 9) ★ *floral thingy* $$$
One of these pale but powerful peony things, evoking those moments when you're not sure whether the restaurant has put lemon in the tap water or if their dishwasher failed to rinse all the soap out of your glass. TS

Nicolaï pour Homme (Parfums de Nicolaï) ★★★ *green lavender* $
PdN does not do this fragrance full justice by calling it a lavender soliflore. If Thelonious Monk had been asked to play a lavender chord, it
would have come out like this. The combination of sweet, blowsy top-
grade lavender, bitter green galbanum, and sweet-green mastic resin gives
a wonderfully dissonant feel to the head notes, while the drydown resolves into a harmony reminiscent of the muted musky, herbaceous
beauty of Caron's No. 3. Highly original and very elegant throughout. LT

Night-Scented Jasmine (Floris) ★★ *white floral* $$$
A soapy lily of the valley with cut grass, plus a slightly sulfurous, buttery
feeling, in no way resembling jasmine at night. TS

Nina (Nina Ricci) ★★★★ *rainbow sherbet* $$
May be another meretricious fruity scent for teenage girls who want to
smell like candy, but it's hard to resist this delicious lime-vanilla top
note, with its psychedelic pastel swirl of rainbow sherbet. (LT wagers
that it replicates the fruit punch that started this whole trend: Escada's
long-defunct but unforgettable Chiffon Sorbet from 1993.) The friendly,
lactonic, sugary drydown is a little ditzy but far from disgusting, a real
achievement in this mostly careless genre. TS

No. 1 for Men (Clive Christian) ★★★ *powdery floral* $$$$
A floral masculine in the classic Victorian manner, very languid and
somewhat soapy. A touch boring, but commendable in its complete lack
of adherence to masculine clichés. LT

No. 1 for Women (Clive Christian) ★★★ *woody floral* $$$$
This one is billed as the World's Most Expensive Perfume, but that's a cheat:
the bottle is studded with a real diamond. One ounce of this stuff goes for
$2,350 at the time of writing. A simple calculation reveals how relatively
inexpensive a real WMEP would be: (1) Compose it entirely of iris butter
from Florence ($30,000 per kilogram). (2) Dilute that 1:5 in alcohol, and

tell the distiller to keep the change. (3) Sell it by the ounce at a fivefold markup. Result: roughly $750 a pop. Price aside, what's No. 1 like? A nice woody floral in the manner of Amouage Gold but vastly less grand. LT

No. 4 (Jil Sander) ★ ★ ★ *big spicy* $ $ $

A big, heavy, ambitious spicy fragrance in the Lauder (Youth Dew, Spellbound) manner, with a very interesting bergamot top note that gives it a basmati-rice-like smell and sustains interest for half an hour until it runs out of puff. What comes out afterward is very eighties (the fragrance was released in 1990): heavy and complicated in a well-crafted but not particularly interesting way. LT

No. 5 eau de parfum (Chanel) ★ ★ ★ ★ *aldehydic interrupted* $ $ $

It turns out that the EdP is a different fragrance from the parfum and the EdT, and was composed in the eighties by Jacques Polge as a modern version of No. 5. Nothing is less modern right now than eighties fragrance. I sprayed the EdP on my arm, and after the nice aldehydic start and floral heart, I started getting whiffs of Polysantol, the oily and prodigiously durable sandalwood drydown of Samsara. However good, such a latecomer synthetic has no business being in a 1921 idea: it's as if Ben Hur wore a Rolex during the chariot race. There seems no point in buying this if you want the real thing. LT

No. 5 eau de toilette (Chanel) ★ ★ ★ ★ *peachy floral* $ $ $

I confess I had until recently failed to understand the differences between the various versions of No. 5. Chanel's engine room tells me that the fragrance has been recast several times over the years, the parfum being the original 1921 formula. This smells like fifties work, with woody-violet notes up top and a lactonic peach drydown. This version is the one I associated with No. 5 all along, largely because I could never afford the others. It is exquisitely beautiful, the true precursor to their recent 31 Rue Cambon, and feels slightly more ladylike than the imperishably crisp real thing. LT

No. 5 Eau Première (Chanel) ★ ★ ★ ★ *aldehydic floral* $ $ $

I have always liked objects, such as carabiners and pin shackles, that come in a wide range of sizes without changing shape. The No. 5 collection will soon deserve to be sold by ship chandlers, since it now includes essentially the same thing in four sizes. The Eau Première is the most compact of the lot, with less emphasis on flowers and more on citrus, first fresh lemon and later warm orange-peel; so much so that it briefly comes within the orbit of Baghari before retreating into powder-puff plushness. This is abstract, classical perfumery at its best, revisited by people who do not see modernization as an excuse for screwing up. I still find 31 rue Cambon more immediately affecting, but the restrained elegance of this Eau Première is of the sort one never tires of. It would also make a tremendous masculine. LT

No. 5 parfum (Chanel) ★ ★ ★ ★ ★ *powdery floral* $ $

When I lived in Villefranche, a little harbor village near Nice, I would occasionally walk to the nearby marina to look at a thirty-foot wooden sloop parked halfway down the pier. It spent most of its life under wraps, surrounded by white fenders. It was one of a pair by a local boatbuilder called Silvestro, his last boat, and had taken fourteen thousand man-hours. When the owner was aboard, you could see it entire. It was more beautiful than an object has any right to be. In fact, it hurt to look at. Other such artifacts: a ladies' black and gray loafer I once saw in Lobb's window in London; the two-thirds-size platinum watch my doctor wears and about which he will reveal nothing; and now, more affordably, Chanel No. 5 parfum. Fragrances very occasionally achieve a compelling 3-D effect, as if you could run your hand along them in midair. The original Rive Gauche and Beyond Paradise are relatively recent examples, but they are still recognizably florals, made of soft, perishable matter. No. 5 is a Brancusi. Alone among fragrances known to me, it gives the irresistible impression of a smooth, continuously curved, gold-colored volume that stretches deliciously, like a sleepy panther, from top note to drydown. Yes, it contains rose, jasmine, and aldehydes in the same way that a perfect body contains legs and arms. But I defy all who smell this to keep enough wits about them to worry about the parts. LT

The beauty and fragrance industry has lied to women for so long, convincing us to fork over cash for crud in shiny packages, that at this point even pure quality has trouble getting taken seriously. Evidence: the persistent and silly question "Has Chanel No. 5 been a best seller because of the fragrance or because of its marketing?" Clever marketing can get us to buy something once, but rarely again. We don't wear Chanel No. 5 because Marilyn Monroe wore it; we wear it for the same reason that Marilyn did: because it's gorgeous. What marked No. 5 as different from its lesser known and largely defunct cousins was an advantageous mutation: an overdose of the bright aromamaterials known as aliphatic aldehydes, harsh alone, but lending an intense, memorable, clean white glow to the rest of the woody floral, which was similar in structure to dozens of others at the time.

Whether, as the legend goes, the slug of aldehydes was a serendipitous mistake on the part of a lab technician preparing a trial, or whether Chanel's perfumer, the brilliant Ernest Beaux, came upon the trick himself, it's impossible to know, but they changed fragrance forever. Yet many more aldehydic florals have entered the market since; they have trickled down to soap formulas to the point that we think of them as the smell of soap. Chanel No. 5 stands out more than ever. Why? Because the firm has done everything in its power to maintain its beauty, even as other famous perfumes have suffered slow attenuation of their former greatness. In a sense, what it once had in common with other fragrances is what helps set it apart now.

Chanel made the wise decision years ago to buy its own jasmine and rose fields and is otherwise known to be fanatic about sourcing materials. Amazingly, despite the fluctuating qualities of natural ingredients from year to year, by careful and constant tweaking, No. 5 continues to smell like No. 5. On my right wrist, I have a No. 5 parfum that predates the fifties, and on my left, a brand-new batch. The musks have changed (wow, those obsolete nitro musks smell grand), and the top notes on the vintage stuff are damaged (smoky off notes, a whiff of burnt butter), but after fifteen minutes these two are nearly the same scent: a masterpiece of modernist sculpture from 1921, one you can wear. It has none of the tasseled-velvet-pillow plush of Shalimar or Vol de Nuit, none of the edgy weirdness of Tabac Blond or Narcisse Noir, none of the drama of Fracas or Bandit. It is an ideally proportioned wonder, all of a piece, smooth to the touch and solid as marble, with no sharp edges and no extraneous fur trimming, a monument of perfect structure and texture. And some people think perfume is not an art. TS

2009 update. ★ ★ ★ ★ *aldehydic amber*
The disturbingly different contents of a parfum tester in Athens International Airport led me to buy a bottle in Selfridges to confer with LT on quality control. The good news: the Athens tester was probably off, and the new bottle still smells good, still like itself. The bad news: some mucking about in the woods and musks has altered the overall balance. The rose and ylang no longer come as far forward. You smell mostly an accord of aldehydic citrus and praline-like woods, until in the end it all begins to resemble the new Baghari too closely. It is still excellent, still recognizable, but not as seamless or as bright. The official story from Chanel is that, aside from the necessary elimination of nitro musks when they were banned, nothing has changed and nothing ever will, but watch carefully. TS

No. 18 (Chanel) ★ ★ ★ ★ *iris rose* $$$
No. 18 is built around a rose-iris accord, and neither material immediately suggests something edible. But humans, men in particular, are supposed to have a one-track mind, and mine relentlessly thinks about food. The superb grade of rose oil used in No. 18 has a strong, liqueur-like feel reminiscent of those berry distillates from Alsace that look like colorless vodka and smell fluorescent pink. Together with the powdery, carrot-like smell of iris, it creates an extraordinary note of fresh bread

with herbs that floats around you until you focus on it, whereupon it splits again into its delicious parts. A strange, bare fragrance, as beautiful as a freshly scrubbed young face. LT

No. 19 (Chanel) ★ ★ ★ ★ *green floral* $$
In the history of feminine perfumes, there seem to be two recurring motifs of femininity: let's call them the cloth mother and the wire mother, after Harry Harlow's famous experiment. The cloth mother is the soft, cuddly, big-bosomed, heavy-hipped ideal of the feminine, best represented by the warmly creamy, nutty classic florals like Fleurs de Rocaille, Detchema, and Arpège. Lovely and soothing in a slightly boneless way, these are easy fragrances to like. But the wire mother is angular, unkind, tough, and cold—scary and handsomely hollow-cheeked. Of the wire mothers of perfume (see Miss Dior, Ma Griffe, and Envy for examples), No. 19, first released in 1971, may be the cruelest. It's said that Henri Robert composed No. 19 for Gabrielle Chanel when she was in her eighties, and a striking and admirably dissonant portrait it is, from the silvery hiss of its nail-polish-remover beginnings to its poisonously beautiful green-floral heart. (Unfortunately, it now lacks its former leathery chypre intensity that used to increase with time, petering off instead into a clean vetiver ending similar to the anticlimax of the current Calèche.) For a fragrance with so many springtime references, all white blossoms and leafy greenery, No. 19 never lands you in any Sound of Music meadows. It keeps you in the boardroom, in three-inch stilettos and a pencil-skirt suit. Haughty and immune to sweetness, with a somewhat antiseptic air, this extraordinary perfume appeals to any woman who has ever wished to know what it is to be heartless. TS

No. 22 (Chanel) ★ ★ ★ ★ *sweet aldehydic* $$$
No. 22 is above all an exercise in heavy lifting. Aldehydes are said to give "lift" to a fragrance, meaning they offset the sweetness and heaviness of whatever else is in there. Like its Antonov namesake, Chanel's 22 goes for the maximum-payload record as follows: (1) Determine the largest

dose of aldehydes a human can stand without fainting. (2) Load it up with as much sweetness as the aldehydes can bear. (3) Round it off with a note of iris to make it look easy. (4) Stand back and watch the whole thing lumber off into the sky after a three-mile takeoff roll. LT

No. 88 (Czech & Speake) ★ ★ ★ *masculine floral* $$$
An irritating aspect of the British is their fondness for Instant Victorian, though to be fair it is done chiefly for export: letters with curlicues, use of mustachioed words like *uncommonly* or *exceedingly,* a touching faith in the continued existence of gentlemen and their requisites. As C&S's Web site fatuously explains, "Czech & Speake is the product of an unusual idea: the creation of a tradition." C&S went from bathroom fittings to perfumes, which is as if Boeing started making TV dinners. Nevertheless, their fragrances are well built and unpretentious, and certainly deserve a sniff. No. 88 is a solid masculine floral in the style of Penhaligon's Hammam Bouquet, perhaps a touch sweet and loud to my taste but pleasantly old-fashioned. LT

No. 89 (Floris) ★ ★ ★ ★ *woody rose* $$
Probably Floris's best extant fragrance, a woody-rosy masculine in the dandified Victorian style, quiet, powdery, and very civilized. A continuation of soap by other means. LT

Noa (Cacharel) ★ ★ ★ ★ *cilantro floral* $$
With perfumes as with people, money doesn't necessarily correlate with quality. Noa is a small-budget wonder, concentrated with ideas: a terrifically compelling, smoky green, woody top note that would make a clever masculine, a big dose of cilantro for a left-of-center herbal accent, and the creamy, fresh, frictionless feel of white bath soap. It smells great, unusual but unpretentious, and has the feel of a perfect everyday fragrance, since its low-key radiance has the great advantage of not speaking unless spoken to, at which point it always seems to have something different to say. TS

Noa Fleur (Cacharel) ★ ★ *woody floral* $ $
It is interesting to see a soapy feminine drift in odor space in search of powdery freshness, and in doing so come so close to a woody masculine that you half expect it to drop all cutesy-pink pretense, kick off the high heels, sprout ear hair, and lower its voice by an octave. L'Oréal is ruthless in market research and consumer testing. I wonder what questions to the panels elicited this strange answer. LT

Noa Perle (Cacharel) ★ ★ ★ *amber tangerine* $ $
This kind of cacophonous, hoarse-voiced citrus peony, in which everything noisily resists cooperating with everything else, feels like a girlish temper tantrum in a bottle. Noa Perle smells confused and loud, even like ketchup now and then, before the whole freakout ends and you're left with a pale, carefully crafted, powdery, milky-metallic drydown, wondering what all that was about. Love the optical illusion box. TS

Nocturnes (Caron) ★ ★ *aldehydic floral* $ $
Neither I nor anyone I've met has ever been able to account for the existence of Nocturnes, a floral aldehydic so predictably pretty it would be considered too normal for a Miss Texas lineup. LT

Noël au Balcon (Etat Libre d'Orange) ★ ★ ★ *gingerbread floral* $ $
To be classed with Tea for Two and Five O'Clock au Gingembre, the pleasant cinnamon benzoin top note has the tea freshness of the former and the salty-sugary denseness of the latter. Unexpectedly, the drydown heads toward pure white-floral territory. As always with this type, probably best as *parfum d'ambiance*, but nice. TS

Noir (Christian Lacroix) ★ ★ *generic guy* $
Murky, dishwater-colored hybrid between a defanged Fahrenheit and an Allure Homme done on the cheap. So boring that one imagines the whole chain of command, from perfumers to evaluators and marketing

people, having to drink Jolt at regular intervals merely to stay awake. The best of the recent Lacroix. LT

Noir de Noir (Tom Ford) ★ ★ ★ ★ *rose chocolate* $$$
Sophia Grojsman's wonderful, wildly weird 100% Love for S-Perfume was an ebullient, even embarrassing mix of fresh rose and milk chocolate. More discord than accord, it was destined to separate the reasonable fuddy-duddies among us from the helpless romantics. Noir de Noir, by Harry Frémont and Jacques Cavallier, rewrites the same idea in smaller, shyer script: less grand but still touching. TS

Noir Epices (Frédéric Malle) ★ ★ ★ ★ *spicy woody* $$$
Plant a clove in the center of a petri dish, leave it open a while, and watch the bacteria grow: they will keep a respectful distance from the spice in the middle. Many of the small molecules devised by plants to keep infections at bay have ended up in perfumery, and we seem to have an innate sense of the salubrious use to which they were put by evolution. Walking into a herbalist's shop and smelling the olfactory cacophony of these helpful elves is always a strange, uplifting pleasure. The top notes of Noir Epices have something of that, but worked out in a wonderfully elegant way that flirts with the medicinal, without, as so many "natural" fragrances do, simply falling into it. The woody-rosy drydown is distantly reminiscent of the late and much-lamented Nombre Noir, and has a splendid, stylish, natural radiance without any of the harshness typical of powerful synthetic woods and woody ambers. A beautiful fragrance from Edmond and Thérèse Roudnitska's son Michel (also a gifted photographer) and probably my favorite in the Malle range. LT

Noir Patchouli (Histoires de Parfums) ★ ★ ★ ★ *dark wood* $$$
Yet another brilliantly executed composition from HdP, interesting for its contrast between the pungent, almost sour notes of patchouli and a minty-smoky, surprisingly fresh drydown. Sits between the matte darkness of Or Black and the transparent night of Timbuktu. Excellent. LT

Noix de Tubéreuse (Miller Harris) ★ ★ *pink tuberose* $$$
Bubblegum tuberose, of no great interest as either candy or flower. LT

Nombril Immense (Etat Libre d'Orange) ★ ★ ★ *clean patchouli* $$
The huge belly button to which the name refers is, apparently, the
Omphalos around which the universe revolves when you attain patch-
oulic peace. The fragrance is fresh, dark, and pleasant and would be
very good were it not a manifest knockoff of Bertrand Duchaufour's
sublime Timbuktu. LT

Notorious (Ralph Lauren) ★ ★ ★ ★ *Campari cola* $$
Remember Ingrid Bergman's first line in *Notorious*? "The important
drinking hasn't started yet." Olivier Gillotin's old-fashioned fragrance is
a pub crawl, first through a bracingly chilly gin-and-Campari top note,
then to a whiskey-cola middle section modeled on Youth Dew. This is
good news: a mainstream designer's name on a handsome perfume for
grown-ups. More of that. TS

Notte Bianca (Linari) ★ ★ *thin wood* $$$
The name suggests a sleepless "white" night, ironic for something as
soporific as this fragrance. After a sub-Sycomore start of vetiver and
smoky wood, the cash runs out, and NB settles for a $15-per-liter accord
reminiscent of the unlamented Cacharel pour l'Homme, with a touch of
what smells like a bornyl ester more suitable for washing the sheets than
(not) sleeping in them. LT

Nouveau Bowery (Bond No. 9) ★ ★ ★ *lime basil* $$$
Pretty, fresh, natural-smelling herbaceous citrus, identical to Jo Ma
lone's Lime Basil & Mandarin. TS

Nuit d'Amour (Guerlain) ★ ★ ★ *peach floral* $$$$
This limited edition el-expensivo fragrance reminds us once again that
Guerlain does vulgar rather well. Now, if they would only remove the

obvious Trésor quotation from this otherwise unimpeachably peachy floral, then recycle the lovely, powdery heart into the next edition of Chant d'Arômes whence it came, I for one would be a happy guy. LT

Nuit de Cellophane (Serge Lutens) ★ ★ ★ *plum peony* $$
For all the austere goth-futurist chic of Lutens's visual aesthetic, in fragrance he has often succumbed (sometimes brilliantly) to dizzying vulgarity. See the suntan lotion of Datura Noir, the tooth-aching sugared cherry of Rahat Loukhoum, the flimsy lace doily of Sa Majesté la Rose, the big hair and acrylic nails of A La Nuit. Nuit de Cellophane is another dramatic lapse of judgment: a fruity floral derived from J'Adore, boiled down to a syrup, and in desperate need of dilution. Clearly, some osmanthus was harmed in the production, and in general the florals are much better than you usually get in this genre. But it never manages to overcome a depressing banality and feels a step down from the creativity of Sarrasins and El Attarine. TS

Nuit de Longchamp (Lubin) ★ ★ *retro floral* $$$
This reissue of a Lubin classic is a sad travesty that has the feel of those bargain-basement scents European firms make for markets that can afford only the cheapest compositions. It smells like hyacinth, i.e., chemical. The weird thing is that it appears to contain some decent naturals, a complete waste. LT

Nuit de Noël (Caron) ★ ★ ★ ★ *marron glacé* $$
I have never understood the exalted status Nuit de Noël enjoys in the hearts of perfumers. To be sure, it is the fragrance where the creamy marron glacé base that is to Caron what Guerlinade is to Guerlain finds its purest expression. To be fair also, the black crystal bottles with a golden frieze are the height of thirties chic. But in some ways it is the least Caron perfume of all Carons, with ample flesh but no discernible bone structure. I defy anyone to recognize it other than by a process of elimination: "That smells like a Caron; but it's boring; must be Nuit de Noël." LT

Nuit Noire (Mona di Orio) ★ *floral animalic* $$$$
A hilariously bad fragrance, in which a very powerful sweet air-freshener note is overlaid with a loud civet fart, adding up to a vividly cheap and unpleasant accord. LT

Nuits de Noho (Bond No. 9) ★ ★ *diet Angel* $$$
Angel without the chocolate and with all the white florals. Very strong and better from a distance than up close. TS

Les Nuits d'Hadrien (Annick Goutal) ★ ★ ★ *orange fennel* $$$
This citrus cologne reminds me powerfully of a particular salad I've made: thinly sliced fennel, orange sections, thyme, touch of olive oil. Good but too simple to be more than occasional refreshment. Good drydown, like a memory of a floral oriental. TS

Number One (Parfums de Nicolaï) ★ ★ ★ *dark floral* $$
This is PdN's first fragrance (1989) and it deservedly won a Société Française des Parfumeurs prize the following year. A very rich composition with a dominant tuberose note. Superbly done from top to bottom, with an excellent drydown, but not (to my mind) the stuff of dreams. LT

Numero Uno (Carthusia) ★ ★ ★ *orange chypre* $$$
Resinous, woody-green chypre with a sleek bitter-orange note, recalling classic feminines but happily intended for men. (Similar to the earlier Great Jones by Bond No. 9.) TS

Nutmeg and Ginger Cologne (Jo Malone) ★ ★ ★ *spicy citrus* $$$
Pleasant if short-lived little thing, more nutmeg than ginger. LT

N.Y. Chic (Mary-Kate and Ashley) ★ *grapefruit handsoap* $
The Olsen twins' scents are priced for the junior high set. This one smells like liquid handsoap, based, I assume, on the theory that it is better that pubescents smell like handsoap than what they usually smell

like. I would scoff more, but I harbored a thwarted desire to own Debbie Gibson's Electric Youth fragrance at that stage in life, and even the wisdom of age cannot ameliorate the feeling of having missed out. TS

Obsession (Calvin Klein) ★ ★ ★ *big oriental* $ $
A triumph of timing over substance. Composed by Bob Slattery in 1985, this fragrance filled a very large oriental-shaped hole in the market. Everyone was tired of Opium, Emeraude had long been a gas-station bauble, Tabu was nowhere. Shalimar would have been perfect, but it was old, and in any event Guerlain was in the middle of a fallow period, busy promoting Jardins de Bagatelle. Enter Obsession, a cross between the citrus of Shalimar and the green of Emeraude, big and cheap in an engaging, come-hither, faceless sort of way. No one knew any better, so everyone bought it. LT

Obsession for Men (Calvin Klein) ★ ★ ★ *cheap oriental* $
This fragrance should come in a kit together with a Playboy Zippo lighter, a voucher for a down payment on a '71 Challenger, and a pop-up atlas of contraception to be given to seventeen-year-old males who show promise. LT

Obsession Night (Calvin Klein) ★ ★ ★ *woody oriental* $ $
Interesting to see Jacomo's wonderful Anthracite Homme (1991, a Marc Buxton creation) come back in a bottle fortuitously of the same shape and size, but after a sex change. Not as good as the original, but better than nothing if you can't find the Jacomo. LT

Odalisque (Parfums de Nicolaï) ★ ★ ★ ★ ★ *fresh chypre* $ $ $
Every once in a long while a composition, steered away from known landmasses by the perfumer's fancy, lands on virgin territory and claims it for itself. What happens afterward depends on the twists of fate, fashion, and finance. Some islands, like Angel, soon attract crowds. Others,

like Odalisque, are the Kerguelen Isles of perfumery, unspoiled, wind-swept, and largely forgotten. Until Patricia de Nicolaï's unerring naviga-tional sense found it, few would have suspected that land could emerge in the sea between the shy, melancholy, bloodless florals typified by Après l'Ondée and the arch, angular green chypres in the Cristalle man-ner. And yet there was: Odalisque's superbly judged floral accord of jas-mine and iris, both abstract and very stable, allied to a saline note of oakmoss, initially feels delicate, but in use is both sturdy and radiant. It is as if the perfumer had skillfully shaved off material from a classic chypre accord until a marmoreal light shone through it. A unique, un-derrated marvel, and great on a man as well. LT

O de Lancôme (Lancôme) ★ ★ ★ *fresh citrus* $
Released three years after Eau Sauvage, reminiscent of Lubin's old Gin Fizz and halfway between the two, OdL, though originally a feminine, is by now a perfectly acceptable fresh-citrus masculine for those who want to escape the dreary dirge of modern sports fragrances and put five minutes of spritzy fun into their weekday mornings. LT

Odeur 53 (Comme des Garçons) ★ ★ ★ *woody soapy* $$$
Historically important but artistically unsatisfying, this fragrance started a minimalist one-line concept-art school of perfumery that has so far proved only a moderately good idea. This one was intended to smell of clean, and does that a million times better than the fragrances from the Clean brand, which just smell vile. But it begs the eternal ques-tion: *pourquoi pas rien?* LT

Odeur 71 (Comme des Garçons) ★ ★ ★ ★ *woody metallic* $$$
This was also known as "anti-perfume no. 2," the second installment in the art-school minimalist period of CdG. It is a pleasantly woody-metallic masculine accord, rather pale and washed-out, with an unusual, slightly sweaty note up top. What makes it interesting is that it smells as

if a complete guy had come out of the box, specifically a freshly shaven fellow who smokes in secret and has just chewed spearmint gum so you won't notice. Not bad at all. LT

Ofrésia (Diptyque) ★ ★ ★ *bright floral* $$$
A refined, fairly natural, somewhat boring freesia accord. A bit straw-hat-floral-dress for my taste, but fine within the genre. LT

Oh Baby (Fresh Scents by Terri) ★ *soapy floral* $
A strongly aldehydic-green, clean soapy floral profile, hugely popularized by the niche surprise-hit perfume Child, of which Oh Baby is a straightforward copy. TS

Oiro (Mona di Orio) ★ *floral oriental* $$$$
Third-world air freshener for the price of a flight to where they would sell it for 25 cents. LT

L'Oiseau de Nuit (Parfumerie Générale) ★ ★ ★ *amber wood* $$$
A competent amber from PG, reminiscent of both the endlessly imitated Ambre Sultan and Lagerfeld Classic, notable for a slightly greater emphasis on cedar notes, and therefore lighter and less sweet. LT

Old Spice (Procter & Gamble) ★ ★ ★ *powdery oriental* $
Aside from the wonderful smell, the thing I like best about Old Spice is the weird, thin little conical stopper on top of the opaque bottle. The fragrance is a delicious Tabu-like oriental, whose claim to be a masculine is based entirely on its transience. A man is a woman consisting entirely of top notes. LT

Olène (Diptyque) ★ ★ ★ ★ *white flowers* $$$
One of the many difficulties that nature has strewn in the path of perfumers is the vexed problem of indole. Indole is a small molecule made up of a hexagonal ring and a pentagonal ring fused together and contain-

ing nitrogen. It and its kissing cousin skatole are breakdown products of the digestion of food and are therefore found in feces. They are also found in large amounts in white flowers such as jasmine, ylang, etc., possibly to attend to the eclectic tastes of pollinating insects. In the textbooks, their odor is described as "fecal, floral in dilution," which is nonsense: they smell like shit when in shit, and like flowers when in flowers. By itself indole smells like ink and mothballs; skatole smells like bad teeth and that wonderful tripe sausage called andouillette. What, you ask, is the problem? If you measure the amount of indole in, say, jasmine oil and make up a synthetic mix with the same amount of the pure stuff, it will smell of mothballs whereas the natural one doesn't. Why? Nobody knows. But that is the main reason why white-flower reconstitutions seldom have the back-of-the-throat rasp of the real thing. Perfumers put in as much indole as they dare, but usually stop short of the full dose. Which brings me to Olène: a true-to-life, properly indolic jasmine. LT

Oliban (Keiko Mecheri) ★ ★ ★ *woody rose* $$$
This peppery variation on the old-fashioned rose chypre has the dense, slightly dusty feel of potpourri, despite its bright pink damascone notes. Handsome, but a bit of a throwback, and not nearly as engaging or polished in this arena as Estée Lauder's excellent Knowing. TS

Om (B Never Too Busy to Be Beautiful) ★ ★ ★ ★ *salted lemon* $
For the adventurous snacker, there is an irresistible shop in New York's Chinatown and all over Asia called Aji Ichiban, where you can buy in bulk from plastic tubs little candies packaged like firecrackers, flaking cylinders of mauve-tinted hawthorn candy, and a variety of dried salted things, from whole small fish to dark leathery lumps that look like ears of vanquished enemies but turn out to be preserved fruit. Slip a sliver into your mouth and your salivary glands cramp with violence. These concentrated tidbits smell curiously musty, with the kippered, hammy weirdness of all mummified foods, and somehow this pine-and-lemon fragrance does as well. Brilliant. TS

L'Ombre dans l'Eau (Diptyque) ★ ★ ★ *fruity green* $$

Despite the poetic name, this is not a melancholy watercolor illustration in brown and gray. Once you get past the arresting vegetal top note with its bright smell of snapped green bean, an intense berry jam comes to balance that high-pitched blast. It ends up sweet-and-savory, the way mango chutney is, and at certain distances plasticky, like a vinyl tablecloth. If you're looking for extremely vivid green, this is it, although it's a bit blunt for all-day wear. (Enjoyed it as a shower gel.) TS

L'Ombre Fauve (Parfumerie Générale) ★ ★ ★ ★ *woody oriental* $$$

I was recently reflecting on the mysterious fact that women seem to seldom steal Habit Rouge for themselves, and the possible reason: HR is far too feminine to be worth borrowing. In L'Ombre Fauve, the raspy, powdery accord of HR is reinterpreted in a more conventional floral-oriental context, and cleverly made to fit as a fresh note inside a woody, ambery structure. Interesting and very cleverly done, a new variation of a well-worn tune. LT

Ombre Rose (L'Original) (Jean-Charles Brosseau) ★ ★ ★ ★
powdery rose $

JCB's Ombre Rose was a deservedly huge success when it came out in 1981. Composed by the great Françoise Caron and released at the same time as her forgotten masterpiece Choc (Cardin), Ombre Rose was way ahead of its time, a powdery fruity-woody rose that has been imitated a hundred times since, often by perfumers unaware of what their model is. I'm not crazy about this type of fragrance, and Brosseau is a stack-em-high-and-sell-em-cheap sort of firm, but they were unquestionably the first to set foot on this particular planet inhabited by flesh-eating Barbies. LT

Omnia (Bulgari) ★ ★ ★ ★ *almond saffron* $$

Ignore the phalanx of lousy flankers in different colors: the original Omnia was genuinely innovative, one of the earliest fragrances to show that a combination of sweet, milky-nutty lactones plus the dusty, sour smell of saffron could mimic the satisfactions of sandalwood. It borrows heavily from the thriving race of cuddly, powdery almond-florals that went before it; truth to tell, Victoria's Secret Dream Angels Heavenly is an immediate family member. But this mild-mannered composition is rescued from boredom by (1) an astringent woody note, which makes what could have been a yummy little spiced almond unambiguously inedible, and (2) an underlying cheap citrus-woody cologne structure to remind you that you are wearing a perfume, not a flavor. Very good and clearly influential: see Idole and Tom of Finland for the niche offspring, Magnifique for the mainstream. TS

Omnia Green Jade (Bulgari) ★ *fruity musky* $
Ever wanted to buy every feminine fragrance under $30 at the duty free but lacked room in your suitcase? Now you can have a little of each mixed up at random in one bottle for convenience. Boring to the point of bad manners. TS

Omniscent (YOSH) ★ ★ ★ *plum tuberose* $ $ $
A camphoraceous, rubbery tuberose absolute plus a host of sweet fruity oriental notes: heavy and complex but without much character; could use a streamlining. TS

Onda (Vero Profumo) ★ ★ ★ ★ *rich leather* $ $ $
Onda is one of Vero Kern's three fragrances (Kiki and Rubj being the others). It is a beautifully crafted leather chypre with a strong vetiver note, smooth, rich, not overly tarry, with a rich farmyard hay-tobacco note that smells like narcissus to me, and a superb transition to a fresh-airy drydown that goes against the portly aging habits of most other leathers. Excellent. LT

Onde Extase (Armani) ★ ★ *creamy floral* $ $
An affably lush and totally derivative sweet-woody floral somewhere between Organza and Hervé Léger, but done on half the budget. LT

Onde Mystère (Armani) ★ ★ *spicy amber* $ $
Why is it that marketing people endlessly come up with sets of three fragrances when the trick is known to be as doomed as trilobites? Why is it that in those sets the oriental is always supposed to be inscrutably sensual? OM is a cheap, trashy oriental of no interest and a waste of the great Maurice Roucel's precious time. LT

Onde Vertige (Armani) ★ ★ ★ *woody citrus* $ $
I'm just back from Bangkok, where an alarming percentage of the truly pretty girls on public transport have five o'clock shadow, and it occurs to me that this perfume is made to measure for them: basically a woody-citrus masculine (Vie de Château springs to mind) bundled up inside a trashy floral. Very skillful work and probably a miracle given the formula cost, but far from wearable. LT

The One (Dolce & Gabbana) ★ ★ ★ *floral oriental* $ $
Probably the only wearable fragrance in the D&G range today, a modern floral oriental done with a very light touch, like a scaled-down Narciso Rodriguez for Her with fresh lily-of-the-valley notes in the heart. LT

Onyx (Azzaro) ★ ★ ★ *spicy fougère* $
Sold as Silver Black outside the United States
The brief on this one must have been "Do us another Azzaro pour Homme, the same only different, modern, etc." Pity the perfumer: How can you retain the essential simplicity and elegance of the aromatic fougère while adding decoration? Françoise Caron extended the original idea in two opposite directions: a fresh cardamom drydown and a peppery, gassy high note related to the octin esters of Fahrenheit. Nice work, and very wearable, but no reason to switch. LT

O Oui! (Lancôme) ★ *overexposed floral* $
This is a fresh floral in which every blindingly powerful floral aromachemical has been harnessed to induce a remarkable sensation of

bone pain that rises from the roof of your mouth to your forehead, similar to what happens when you eat ice cream too quickly. Chiefly of neurological interest. LT

Opium (Yves Saint Laurent) ★ ★ ★ ★ *spice king* $
Opium illustrates better than any other fragrance the peculiar phenomenon of love followed by rejection, known as fashion. It is unquestionably one of the greatest fragrances of all time, not only in terms of phenomenal success, but in having deserved it. Yet I would hate it if anyone wore it near me today. Why? Suppose you wrote down the basic requirements for a great fragrance: top of the list would come distinctiveness, then radiance, then (to keep out Amarige-like mutants) some sort of working relationship with natural smells. Opium has the first two in spades and passes muster on the third. But so do Shalimar, Chanel No. 5, and a host of other greats. What is it that makes Opium so dated, when fragrances fifty years older are fresh as paint? I believe the answer hinges on the faults of its qualities. The comparison with its almost exact contemporary and involuntary twin Cinnabar is instructive: both were inspired by the same vision, right down to country (China) and color (vermilion, aka cinnabar). There is something peculiar about spicy orientals: being made almost entirely of drydown materials, they lack time evolution, the arc of a fragrance that gives it life, and feel like broken wristwatches perennially stuck around 10 p.m. There the resemblance ends. Cinnabar was rich, warm, and fuzzy. Opium said one thing and one thing only, with tremendous force. While this was the most cogent statement ever made by balsams, one does tire of it. This, and not the quality of its raw materials, is what made Opium smell so fascinatingly solid in 1980 and now makes it smell tiresome. LT

Opium pour Homme (Yves Saint Laurent) ★ ★ *woody aromatic* $ $
As Talleyrand said, "Beware of first impressions: they are correct." The unusually tall and large bottle of OpH suggested something dilute within, and this turned out to be oddly in agreement with the smell. This

is an aromatic fougère in the manner of Azzaro Homme, revisited by Jacques Cavallier. It could have been good had he been given the means to flesh it out properly. As it is, nice proportions, but far too thin. LT

Opôné (Diptyque) ★ ★ ★ *big rose* $$$
Diptyque tries a clever trick with this one, i.e., to do a simple, natural, and spare version of the fluorescent roses of the eighties (Sinan, Parfum de Peau, Knowing, etc.). This is done by extending the spicy-woody aspects of rose with intense woody-fruity-floral aromachemicals like damascones and damascenones. I may be hypersensitive to these beasts, but I always find that while the first impression is stunning, this type of perfume invariably becomes strident with time. Opôné is a valiant attempt and better than most. It smells great up top and from a distance, but is simply too harsh up close for my taste. LT

Orange Blossom Cologne (Jo Malone) ★ ★ ★ *white floral* $$$
Malone's bright and soapy orange blossom smells very close to jasmine ("scads of indole," LT muttered in passing) but with a zesty twist, as seems to be the norm with recent orange-blossom soliflores. (Check, for reference, L'Artisan Parfumeur's recent limited edition, which cost an arm and a leg and smelled close to this.) TS

Oranger Alhambra (Armani Privé) ★ ★ ★ ★ *bergamot lavender* $$$
When you first smell older chypres in good shape, the harmonious, vivid accord of the top notes usually shows a strong family resemblance: you find citrus—bergamot or bitter orange—lavender, coumarin sweetness, a floral waiting in the wings. Then, after running its hand over the grand piano of your senses from sour to bitter to sweet, the fragrance moves to the main motif. The clever idea in Oranger Alhambra is to use merely the top of a classical chypre as the structure for a modern, streamlined cologne: Chanel Pour Monsieur meets Lime Basil & Mandarin. Excellent radiance, suave effect, faultless drydown. TS

Or Black (Pascal Morabito) ★ ★ ★ ★ ★ *dark fougère* $$
The firm of Pascal Morabito should not be confused with his parents' outfit, Morabito tout court, which also makes some fragrances. PM makes beautiful steamer trunks in black buffalo leather lined with salmon-colored silk, and the weirdest rings made of something that looks like plastic and is in fact synthetic sapphire encasing a precious stone. He's had these two fragrances (OB and Or Noir) for decades and to my knowledge has done absolutely nothing to promote them, beyond leaving them lying around in his hard-to-find shops. Or Black is an extreme fougère, smoky, dark, bitter, resinous-green, like triple-distilled Earl Grey, a step beyond even Rive Gauche pour Homme in its saturnine glory. Sensational. LT

Or des Indes (Maître Parfumeur et Gantier) ★ ★ ★
classic oriental $$
MPG does Shalimar. Get Shalimar. LT

L'Or de Torrente (Torrente) ★ ★ ★ *Campari vermouth* $
Torrente is chiefly known to the memorious French for having been the favorite couturier of Prime Minister Edith Cresson, easily the dowdiest politician of her era. L'Or is an oddly irresolute beast, complex without being satisfying, and smells more like a Negroni left in a highball glass than like a fragrance. Not bad, but probably better sprayed in a room than on the skin. LT

Or et Noir (Caron) ★ ★ *salty rose* $$$
A high-quality, complex, fresh lemony rose with bizarre off notes, including a bitterness like dark chocolate, a scorched smell like something burning, and wet dog. TS

Organza (Givenchy) ★ ★ ★ ★ *vanillic floral* $$
A fine instance of vulgarity done exactly right, Organza, right down to

its curvaceous bottle, brings to mind Harpo Marx rapidly outlining an hourglass figure with both hands, letting out a loud finger whistle, and grinning happily. This is a come-hither floral vanillic so direct, so straightforward, so cheerful that all reserve is instantly forgotten. The perfume critic snaps his laptop shut and accepts the invitation to dance. LT

Organza Indécence (Givenchy) ★ ★ ★ ★ *orange vanilla* $$
I was once in a sushi bar where the chef behind the counter, a feisty sixty-year-old Japanese, having ascertained that my companion was German, opined that he liked German girls because they were "tall," a word he accompanied by a cupping gesture of both hands to indicate large breasts. This reissued Indécence is unquestionably a tall perfume, a sort of Habanita with a woody-vanilla accord that feels warm and comfortable, accompanied by enough cinnamon and orange to make it mouthwatering. I remembered it as less sunny, less good than this. Maybe I was wrong the first time, or maybe the formula has im-proved. LT

Oriental Lumpur (Les Néréides) ★ ★ *green nutmeg* $$
Not an oriental, just basically boiled kale. TS

Original Santal (Creed) ★ *sweet oriental* $$$
A vile, cheap, cloying masculine that would be disheartening as the smell of the hotel shampoo in Ulan-Ude. LT

Original Vetiver (Creed) ★ *unoriginal woody* $$$
Deserves some sort of prize for managing to make whatever vetiver it contains almost imperceptible. LT

Ormonde Man (Ormonde Jayne) ★ ★ ★ ★ *green woody* $$
Masculine fragrances (masculine almost everything, come to think of it) rarely venture outside tried and tested stereotypes. Those who try

endure the wrath of God. People still shake their heads in disbelief at the brilliantly original Insensé (Givenchy, 1993), "A floral for men ..." It takes guts to cut loose. Ormonde Man, derived from their signature feminine, is a sultry woody floral that sounds a muted, tourmaline-green chord from top note to drydown. Hear it once, and you'll want it again. LT

Ormonde Woman (Ormonde Jayne) ★ ★ ★ ★ *forest chypre* $ $
Of the many feminine perfumes since Bois des Iles that have been composed around woody notes, the others that I can recall have been cozy, powdery-rosy, touched with mulling spices, with the warm furred feeling of a napping cat by the fire, or, more recently, hippie-inspired simple concoctions meant to evoke mostly the gorgeous smell of hard-to-get sandalwood oil. Ormonde Woman is the only abstract woody perfume I know that triggers the basic involuntary reflex, on stepping into a forest, to fill one's lungs to bursting with the air. This is a full-fledged perfume with all the sophistication of Bois des Iles and its ilk, but none of the sleepy comfort. Instead, it has the haunting, outdoors witchiness of tall pines leaning into the night—a bitter oakmoss inkiness, a dry cedar crackle, and a low, delicious, pleading sweet amber, like the call of a faraway candy house. Lulling and unsettling in equal measure, and truly great. TS

Or Noir (Pascal Morabito) ★ ★ ★ ★ *powdery rose* $ $
A surpassingly cheerful fruity rose in the exuberant, fluorescent seventies style, not mossy like Knowing but more like Montana's Parfum d'Elle: brightened with peach, zingy aldehydes, and a tremendously radiant musk. It has the effervescence and sweet soapy feel of the sort of cheap champagne you buy to mix with orange juice for breakfast (though it has a little bit of the associated headache as well). TS

Orris Noir (Ormonde Jayne) ★ ★ *peppery cedar* $ $
The name combines two of the biggest recent trends: orris (iris-root

butter) is showing up everywhere, and so are perfumes named Something Noir (or Black Thingamajig). The trouble is that there's nothing particularly iris or noir about this. Instead, it smells like lemon and pepper with an oily-woody background, slightly chemical and faceless, a rare misstep for the excellent Ormonde Jayne line. TS

Oscar (Oscar de la Renta) ★ ★   *woody floral* $
The current version of Oscar de la Renta's Oscar from 1977 is complicated but flat, zipping from a tobacco-tinged tuberose top note to a nondescript woody oriental that reminds me of the way my clothes used to smell the morning after a big night out—clinging remnants of perfume and stale cigarette smoke. Ysatis was a better, plusher version of this kind of thing, although I hear that Oscar was a big, impressive tuberose once. It isn't now. TS

Oscar Citrus (Oscar de la Renta) ★ ★   *fresh floral* $
Competent chemical fruity floral with a citrus top note. LT

Oscar Red Orchid (Oscar de la Renta) ★ ★   *stale floral* $
Competent chemical fruity floral without a citrus top note. LT

Oscar Red Satin (Oscar de la Renta) ★ ★ ★   *sugary woody* $
Red Satin is a simple, sweet, pleasant oriental in the current ditzy, post–Lolita Lempicka style, built on the burnt sugar note of ethylmaltol but with an odd green, oily floral feel (salicylates?), veering to a somewhat chemical woody-vanilla drydown. It's absolutely no relation to the original Oscar, but perhaps a second cousin to Kenzo Amour. TS

Osmanthe Yunnan (Hermès) ★ ★ ★ ★ ★   *milky tea* $$$
When Jean-Claude Elléna, now in-house perfumer at a little saddler's outfit called Hermès, first did the soapy suede-and-apricots scent of the osmanthus flower for The Different Company's Osmanthus, it was like one of those deceptively simple, pretty Paul McCartney melodies that

seem so obvious once heard, you suspect he finds them lying fully formed in the street. Elléna could have stopped there. We would have been happy. But instead, in Osmanthus take two, he adds a layer of smoked tea, which could have turned into simply a representation of traditional Chinese osmanthus-scented tea, in itself not a bad idea. But Osmanthe Yunnan also turns up an unexpected milky sweetness at the skin, which transforms what was cool and seen at a distance into something warm and welcoming up close. Put it this way: you'd enjoy Osmanthus wafting by, but you'll follow Osmanthe Yunnan to its source. It is a perfume of pure happiness. If you had asked me before smelling this fragrance if any of the minimalist compositions that Elléna has been turning out in recent years could be ranked in the top tier artistically, I would have said no, by design they'd top out at four stars when at their best; but I would have been wrong. Osmanthe Yunnan is beautiful from start to finish, distinctive, impossible to improve, unforgettable, unpretentious, and the best of Elléna's work for Hermès so far. TS

Osmanthus (The Different Company) ★ ★ ★ ★ *dreamy peach* $ $
Osmanthus is a Chinese shrub that grows well in temperate climates (I used to have one in my London garden) and produces small white flowers that smell deliciously soapy and apricot-peachy, a sort of datura without the menace. I find its combination of gentle softness and dry reserve irresistible. It often turns up in fragrance notes listed in press packs, but these are as trustworthy as Greenpeace press releases; that is to say, you seldom smell it. Shiseido's fabled Nombre Noir was an exception, where a touch of it softened an otherwise stark composition. Looking at the components of osmanthus oil, you can see how it's going to work: lots of lactones (peach and coconut), ionones (woody violets), and theaspiranes (camphor-cassis). Osmanthus, like vetiver and narcissus, is a ready-made fragrance, and the perfumer's skill consists chiefly in bringing it back to life from the sleep induced by solvent extraction. Jean-Claude Elléna did this in 2001, when he was the in-house perfumer at The Different Company, and captures it perfectly, with a touch of lemony notes up top to

give a delicious, almost gardenia-like effect, and a soapy-woody drydown. I use this wonderful fragrance the way some people carry familiar objects to set up in hotel rooms and make everywhere feel like home. There is a protecting genie in its little travel bottle, which hasn't failed me yet. LT

Osmanthus (Keiko Mecheri) ★ ★ ★ *powdery hawthorn* $$$
This is a subdued version of the lovely, intense hawthorn-mimosa of Caron's original Farnesiana, before they changed it from a floral to a gourmand. Powdery, fresh, sweet, pretty, and absolutely no relation to osmanthus, which has an unforgettable soapy apricot-suede smell. (See The Different Company's Osmanthus.) TS

Osmanthus (Ormonde Jayne) ★ ★ ★ *grapefruit floral* $$
A cheerful floral plus bitter citrus peel, sweetened with amber: the fresh fruity floral in the line, the equivalent of a pretty cotton sundress. Ormonde Jayne's least distinctive scent, it seems to have little to do with osmanthus but smells pretty good anyway. TS

Osmanthus Interdite (Parfum d'Empire) ★ ★ ★
dark osmanthus $$$
The Empire behind this fragrance is China, from which comes osmanthus. Marc-Antoine Corticchiato seems very fond of hay absolute, and the top note of Osmanthus Interdite, like that of Ambre Russe, smells overwhelmingly of coumarin and tobacco leaf. I love osmanthus in most of its incarnations, from Nombre Noir to Osmanthe Yunnan. I find Parfum d'Empire's version rich, solid, and true to high-quality materials, but nevertheless a little stolid, as if the aim was to make a textbook example of osmanthus rather than a great fragrance. Just short of wonderful. LT

Oud 27 (Le Labo) ★ ★ ★ ★ *animalic ink* $$
Some years back I got a crisply written e-mail from a young woman in

the United States who explained that she was selling her soiled panties on the Internet to pay for her (college, judging by her vocabulary) education. She deplored the fact that she couldn't scale up the process and asked me whether I knew of any material that would help. I replied that I was myself, for noncommercial reasons, on the trail of such a thing and that I would keep in touch. Oud 27 makes me think I may be getting warm. Three minutes into it, after a wonderfully bitter, inky blast at the start, Oud 27 becomes properly pornographic: a wet-hair note and a couple of macrocyclic musks of the kind found near the rear end of deer take over, adding up to a sensational sweet-animalic note. The composition then behaves as if it's been interrupted in midaction, hastily buttons up, and acts natural thereafter, nonchalantly pretending to be a woody fragrance. Great fun, brilliant perfumery, and, for once, really raunchy. LT

Oud Cuir d'Arabie (Montale) ★ ★ ★ ★ ★ *leather oud* $$$
Together at last! Oud and leather, two epic, battle-scarred, weather beaten action heroes of perfumery appear on the same bill. I imagine them pictured against the sun, in ankle-length dust coats, holding a shotgun and a whip, respectively. Full marks to Montale for doing a bite-the-bullet "you sure you want this?" fragrance that sums up all perfumery can offer that's at once rugged, inedible, and salubrious. LT

Oud Sensuel (Guerlain) ★ ★ *resinous floral* $$$$
Our brief trip to Oman was a revelation of the virile glory of the oud-doused male: a smell that seems animal, vegetal, and mineral all at once, and certainly objectionable to most people not used to it, making you think, among other things, of petroleum, meat, fish glue, and the resin's origin as a tree's reaction to a fungal infection. Paired with rose, it is sensational. OS is torn between admiration for this style and cowardice, resulting in a pointless gelded compromise: their Garden Sensuel with a touch of oud. TS

Oud Wood (Tom Ford) ★ ★ ★ *fresh woody* $$$

Oud, or agarwood, is the result of noble rot chewing up several species of *Aquilaria* tree, and it became all the rage a few years back when it was allegedly used in Saint Laurent's M7. I say *allegedly* because it is an expensive and highly variable material, and the trend for its use in masculine fragrances mysteriously coincided with the creation of several excellent synthetic agarwood bases. What does it smell of? Hard to describe, but to my nose good agarwood has something unique in its weird combination of honeyed sweetness and woody freshness. OW smells like natural oud to me, and captures this contradictory ready-made-fragrance character perfectly. Very good. LT

Outrageous (Frédéric Malle) ★ ★ ★ ★ *apple musk* $$$

Not in the least outrageous, but unquestionably brilliant, Sophia Grojsman's latest work brings to mind Cocteau's line, "Un homme profond ne monte pas, il s'enfonce" (A profound person does not rise, he goes deeper). I have always felt that a sure sign of genius was a search for simplicity. Grojsman now peels off layer after layer to show that mystery needs no veil to stay mysterious. There is something spare, spacious and solid about her recent creations such as 100% Love. The top note of Outrageous is remarkable, the smell of an orchard cellar in which crab apples are stored, followed by the steam-iron note from DKNY Women, which I believe is due to a macrocyclic musk containing an ether group, which gives it a hissy sheen. Direct, memorable, and odd. *Bravissima.* LT

Oxford & Cambridge Traditional Lavender (Czech & Speake)
★ ★ ★ *dry lavender* $$

Good to see the rival seats of learning united, if only on a "gentleman's cologne." This is a very nice lavender, all the more so because the perfumer resisted the temptation to buttress the top-middle note of high-quality lavender with long-lasting synthetics, and opted instead for a bracing slug of oakmoss. Nice work. LT

Oyédo (Diptyque) ★ ★ ★ ★ *concord lime* $ $

Every once in a striped moon there comes along an accord that you know you have never smelled before. The last two for me were Angel and Salon Rouge (the latter in the Mugler box for the movie *Perfume*). Oyédo is the latest, so delightfully weird that it drove me crazy like a Rubik's Cube of smell until I managed to half figure out how it's done. TS and I joined noses on this one, and she sniffed a vital clue: it contains an anthranilic ester smell like muscat gummy sweets from Japan. Once you mentally subtract that, the rest is clearly a turpentine-lime accord with a touch of green-smoky mandarin thrown in. Is it a perfume? No idea. Can it be worn? I'll give it my best shot. One thing's for sure: it's brilliant. LT

Paco Rabanne pour Elle (Paco Rabanne) ★ ★ ★ *fresh floral* $ $

A crisp, fresh jasmine in a simplified Beyond Paradise style with a peculiar, milky-metallic peach that gives it a slightly exotic, alien feeling. Undemanding but easy to live with. TS

Paco Rabanne pour Homme (Paco Rabanne) ★ ★ ★ ★

citrus woody $

Such a beautiful, crisp, bracing top note—an expansive herbal-citrus accord that brings *Sound of Music* mountain foliage to mind—is a relief in a wilderness of hideous, cheap masculines that smell like bottled evidence of lab accidents. But then, there is something melancholy and a little dank, like tea made with twice-boiled water, about the pale green animalic drydown, which is nevertheless very good in its way. This 1973 composition was one of the first aromatic fougères, a genre that would grow to include better and more memorable members, e.g., Azzaro pour Homme, Rive Gauche pour Homme, Yohji Homme, Or Black, and the much maligned Drakkar Noir. TS

Paestum Rose (Eau d'Italie) ★ ★ ★ ★ *woody rose* $ $ $

The Eau d'Italie brand was created by the owners of what looks like a seriously beautiful hotel, Le Sirenuse in Positano, south of Naples on the

Amalfi Coast. It is particularly delightful that a hotel should buck the trend and, instead of slapping their label on low-grade perfumed products, hire someone of the caliber of Bertrand Duchaufour to compose exclusive fragrances. Paestum Rose is a woody rose in the transparent, Japan-inspired manner of early Comme des Garçons fragrances— beautifully crisp, clear, and refreshing. LT

Palais Jamais (Etro) ★ ★ ★ ★ *woody citrus* $$
Etro did well in the early nineties to rely on the distinguished Grasse house of Robertet for their compositions: Robertet's stock in trade, high-quality naturals, agrees with the rich, Silk Road aesthetic of Etro. PJ is a very interesting dissonant accord of smoky birch tar and vetiver, set against herbaceous notes of sage and cologne-like top notes. Rich, coherent, and unpretentious. LT

Palazzo (Fendi) ★ ★ ★ ★ *lychee woody* $$
For some reason, LVMH made the brash decision in 2007 to kill all existing Fendi fragrances and start over with just one. Luckily, it's a good one. Palazzo performs the miracle of turning the unbearably syrupy floral-oriental structure of fragrances like Armani Code into something delicious and strange, weirdly fresh and rich at once, by using a secret weapon: a huge dose of a classic powdery masculine fougère (think Brut). A cross between Ça Sent Beau and Chinatown—it feels like wearing both pink lipstick and a striped tie. Great. TS

Palisander (Comme des Garçons) ★ ★ ★ *boozy wood* $$$
In a fruity-woody style similar to Chanel's indispensable Bois des Iles and Caron's Parfum Sacre, perfumer Yann Vasnier's Palisander (rosewood) focuses on aged wood's caramel, rum-like complexity, shading from sharp green to powdery amber. With a rounded, milky musk to smooth it out, the effect is slightly old-fashioned in a lovely way, with a texture like scented talcum bath powder that you put on with a big white ribboned pouf. TS

Paloma Picasso (Paloma Picasso) ★ ★ ★ ★ *floral chypre* $$
Though the herbal-jasmine-spice-oakmoss structure of Paloma Picasso (1984) is derived from previous sleek, green, serious chypre fragrances like Cabochard and Givenchy III, part of its considerable appeal is that it smells wonderful while still smelling confidently cheap—there's no effort to throw an extra pound of butter or more egg yolks in the cake. Instead, it gives an overall impression of one smart gal—comfortable, breezy, sharp, and fizzy in the jasmine section, and terrifically mossy-patchouli in the drydown, put together perfectly without making much fuss. TS

Paname (Keiko Mecheri) ★ ★ ★ *anise vanilla* $$$
Paname is a pretty little herbal-green anise on vanilla, that never achieves the kind of clever, flirtatious magic that Lolita Lempicka manages with similar parts. Instead, with Paname you get the fragrance equivalent of a glass of cloudy pastis, mild and soothing but not memorable. TS

Paprika Brasil (Hermès) ★ ★ *evanescent peppers* $$
Another of Elléna's refined compositions, this one overly so. PB is so translucent and wan you "search for it on the smelling strip," as perfumers say. The pepper-peppers accord works fine, but it does not sustain interest and ends up smelling like the capsicum off note in cheap Graves wines. LT

Par Amour (Clarins) ★ ★ ★ ★ *woody rose* $$
Clarins did well to go to the distinguished Grasse firm of Charabot for the composition of the Par Amour fragrances, because the formulas they delivered are exceptionally comfortable and natural. This one has a perfectly judged soft, quiet accord of cedarwood, rose, and blackcurrant buds, which reminds me of late and lamented (now reissued) floral masculines like Insensé. Reassuring without being dull, simple without feeling basic, and transparent but not wan. I'm promoting this one to my bathroom shelf with immediate effect. LT

Par Amour Toujours (Clarins) ★ ★ ★ ★ *mandarin rose* $$

It turns out that the dreadfulness of Baby Doll Paris and related fragrances isn't due to the basic idea—a fluorescent pink citrus rose—but its execution. When interpreted by talented perfumers with access to wonderful natural materials, the idea improves tremendously. Par Amour Toujours uses a striking mandarin accord, built of green herbs and orange peel, and a beautiful rose with the barest touch of dry spice. Its transparency and complexity without creamy sweetness (lactones, vanilla) remind me in an oblique way of the highest grades of Chinese oolong tea. A wonderful fragrance that transcends its style. TS

Le Parfum (Lalique) ★ *rock bottom* $$

The lack of mitigating circumstances makes this 2005 composition a paragon of all that is wrong with perfumery today: composed by one of the world's greatest perfumers (Dominique Ropion) and sold at a high price by a distinguished glassmaker, this fragrance should be at least bearable, if not wearable. Nothing of the sort. Vile, cheap, obnoxiously powerful, and repulsively chemical, it sits in a barren wasteland somewhere between Allure and Amarige. I hope to live long enough to see this sort of faceless dreck wiped off the face of the earth. Nice bottle. LT

Un Parfum d'Ailleurs et Fleurs (The Different Company) ★ ★ ★
citrus floral $$

Before Victoria's Secret narrowed its focus to hot pink thongs with rhinestone-studded silhouettes of lap dancers on them, their catalog mysteriously used to feature dozens of delightfully dowdy ankle-length white cotton nightgowns in eyelets and lace, with demure pearl buttons in pleated bodices, the models always photographed looking dreamy while standing in open French doors framing the verdant countryside—garments clearly intended for the woman whose erotic fantasies take place in Jane Austen novels. There's something of the chaste allure of those nightgowns in this old-fashioned, sweetly rounded, soapy neroli-and-linden floral, as if it were designed to inspire the wholesome marital pleasures we assume are enjoyed by those people who live in tiny, tidy towns and are usually described as "decent" or "modest." The name means "a perfume of elsewhere and flowers," according to LT, who understands it as little as I do. TS

Un Parfum de Charmes et Feuilles (The Different Company) ★ ★ ★
herbal floral $ $
The intriguing medicinal herbal top note with shades of Chinese muscle rub led me to expect something unusual, but this oddly named fragrance (A Perfume of Charm and Leaves) just develops more white florals and that's it: a pleasant, minty floral, well crafted but unexciting. TS

Parfum de Peau (Montana) ★ ★ ★ ★ *neon floral* $
Released in 1986, this was one of the first fluorescent woody roses, and (together with Sinan) it took the world, especially the Middle East, by storm. What made PdP different from tamer interpretations of the same theme, such as Lauder's Knowing, was Edouard Fléchier's use of an animalic, almost urinous top note. It puts this fragrance in the same category as Rabanne's La Nuit and Fléchier's later Une Rose: unpresentable florals. Garish and excellent. LT

Un Parfum des Sens et Bois (The Different Company) ★ ★ ★
woody incense $ $
Every niche perfumery wants an incense, because their target audience—difficult-to-please perfume addicts—adores it as the smell of holy places and far-off lands. The Different Company's version (the confusing name means "a perfume of senses and woods") is subtle, probably too much so, with dry, peppery woods settling like a felt blanket over a few bright green gestures. The result is too muffled to feel like religion, unlike the powerful Bois d'Encens, Timbuktu, or Andy Tauer's

L'Air du Désert Marocain. More of a smell than a fragrance, it's much closer in character to Isabelle Doyen's Let Me Play the Lion, another cautious woody more evocative of shops than trances. TS

Parfum d'Été (Kenzo) ★ ★ ★ ★ *green floral* $
A twist on fruity, green florals in the style of Calyx and Cristalle, Parfum d'Eté is more transparent while still incredibly radiant, leaving behind all classic rose references and opting instead for spare modern freshness. TS

Le Parfum de Thérèse (Frédéric Malle) ★ ★ ★ ★ *fruity jasmine* $$$
It is a testament to Frédéric Malle's connections and powers of persuasion that this private composition intended by Edmond Roudnitska, the greatest perfumer of all time after François Coty, as a present to his wife, Thérèse (no mean perfumer herself), should be made available to the rest of us. This is Roudnitska reveling in extraordinarily complex yet perfectly proportioned and legible compositions. This and its congeners Diorella, Eau Sauvage, and to a lesser extent Cristalle, on which he also worked, are variations on the same Mozartian theme of a tune shimmering between minor and major modes, between north light and noon glow. I still prefer the original Diorella (vintage, that is) to Le Parfum de Thérèse, and I think the overall idea is best stated in a less ambiguous way, as in the more melancholy Cristalle. Further, there is something slightly crude in this fragrance compared to Roudnitska's best that makes it less desirable than I would have liked. LT

Parfum Sacré (Caron) ★ ★ ★ ★ *peppery rose* $$
One of the better fragrances in the Caron range, Parfum Sacré was a beautiful essay on the richness of wood, developing upon the rosy-woody idea of Bois des Iles. Rose gave PS a wine-like fruitiness and depth, and a huge dose of pepper and incense gave it a dry, ethereal transparency. Today the tremendous richness is gone, although enough

parts in roughly the right conformation give the idea still. It was a sweet and rich oriental before, but in its current thin woody state, converging on an accord reminiscent of Acqua di Giò for men, it would probably make a much better masculine. TS

Paris (Yves Saint Laurent) ★ ★ ★ ★ *roaring rose* $
Fragrance, along with fashion and music, reached an unprecedented level of bombast in the eighties: the shoulder pads were wide, the hair was big, the music was mindless, and the perfume was far, far too strong—which is why everyone in the nineties took to wearing cK One and L'Eau d'Issey, as a sort of olfactory fast to atone for years of overdoing it. To this day many people believe they hate perfume because they only remember the Poisons, the Opiums, the Gloriglos, and Paris, the zenith (or nadir, depending on how you look at it) of the perfumer's rose. The word on this fragrance is that it is a rose composed of ionones, those wonderful materials that smell fruity, powdery, and woody all at once. Spray Paris on paper and it exhales an intense, rich, wine-like breath. It comes off as more of a vast bouquet than a soliflore, and reminds me of those bridal bunches some florists construct by reassembling the petals of a dozen blooms around a single center, creating a Frankenstein rose the size of a cabbage. An hour in, you have room to breathe at last, and find, in the cloud of sweet and woody notes, long streaming sections running through it like alternating pink and green silk ribbons: a tender powdery mimosa and a piercing fruity green. The great Sophia Grojsman (Yvresse, Trésor, Eternity, Calyx) put this one together, and it marks the absolute end of this particular road, the point beyond which it is not possible to make a louder, bigger, more complicated rose. From here on, it is only possible to innovate by taking away, not adding. A brilliant, beautiful monster. I sprayed it on thoughtlessly the first time I saw it in a department store and knew I had made a social misstep when I saw people cringing away from me in the street and on the company elevator. Buy it, but put it on at your peril. TS

Paris Hilton (Paris Hilton) ★ *silly floral* $
Competent but depressing woody-fruity-floral aimed at ditzes. LT

Park Avenue (Bond No. 9) ★ ★ *mimosa floral* $$$
One of several similar florals in the Bond line, this simple, cheap composition should be called something like Powder Fresh and should stop perspiration for twelve hours. TS

Pasha (Cartier) ★ *aromatic fougère* $$
If, God forbid, you took the lamentable Eau du Soir, removed from it the skeletal remnants of a chypre structure, and added some Lemon Pledge, you would come close to Pasha. The whole Pasha thing is such a disaster, from the bottle that looks like a Farangian dress codpiece to the hideous watches that manage to make a Santos look classy, it's a wonder Cartier hasn't discontinued the whole line. I'll bet it's big in Brunei. LT

Passage d'Enfer (L'Artisan Parfumeur) ★ ★ ★ *pine incense* $$
Olivia Giacobetti's incense fragrance for L'Artisan Parfumeur has a wicked name (Street of Hell) with a quotidian origin—the name of the street where LAP's offices are located. Name aside, the fragrance isn't wicked at all. Frankincense usually has a mysterious, rich, saintly smell, but here, paired with a light musk and somewhat screechy white flowers, it seems highly resinous and soapy clean; some people think immediately of Pine-Sol. A beautifully salty, woody transition after a couple of hours isn't quite enough to make it all worthwhile. For incense, try Armani Privé's Bois d'Encens or Serge Lutens's La Myrrhe instead. TS

Passiflora (Keiko Mecheri) ★ ★ ★ *passionfruit cocktail* $$
This simple rosy fruit cocktail of a fragrance is as unpretentiously crowd-pleasing and trashy as a glass of Alizé on ice—I see chandelier earrings and gold sandals and a fire juggler near the entrance. Not very interesting, but fun. TS

Passion (Annick Goutal) ★ ★ ★ ★   *camphor ylang* $ $ $
The temperate white floral is a pretty, thoroughly laundered and starched lily-of-the-valley type, presentable in polite company, whereas its tropical counterpart is a disturbing, intense night-blooming creature full of smells of meat, milk, rubber, and camphor, which bring out the big hairy moths. Passion is one of the strangest night flowers you can find: the banana-jam smell of ylang-ylang, an icy camphor-and-wintergreen accord that could grow icicles in your sinuses, and a thick lactonic note that seems to coat the whole thing in butter. It feels humid, narcotic, unsettling, like a moonless July night without a breeze. TS

Passion (Elizabeth Taylor) ★   *fog horn* $
Z-17 in drag. LT

Passion Boisée (Frapin) ★ ★ ★   *woody mandarin* $ $ $
A skillfully composed, pleasant, but ultimately insubstantial accord of mandarin and dry woods. LT

Passion for Men (Elizabeth Taylor) ★ ★ ★   *woody oriental* $
Sold in what is probably the saddest bottle in the industry, a perfectly pleasant incense-based oriental, composed almost twenty years ago. Dated but far better than one would expect. LT

Patchouli (Comme des Garçons) ★ ★ ★   *spicy patchouli* $ $
A big, smiling, intense, bracing accord of fenugreek and patchouli, curiously reminiscent of the drydown of fifties Italian masterpieces like Pino Silvestre. LT

Patchouli 24 (Le Labo) ★ ★ ★ ★   *strange leather* $ $
When I worked summers in the biology department at Moscow State University, there was, at the top of the building, right under the hot roof, a small, airless storage room. Left alone for so long with no company,

the vanillic sweetness of the decaying old books had struck up a phenolic conversation with the harsh chemicals in the jars and the fragrant refringent oils in which pickled specimens swam blindly. The smell was at once beguiling, salubrious, and toxic, and felt like a perfume composed for a fiercely intelligent librarian. Annick Ménardo's poetic genius has accidentally re-created that hot, secret space for me. I shall henceforth refer to this fragrance as Labo de Russie. LT

Patchouli Antique (Les Néréides) ★ ★ ★ ★ *earthy patchouli* $ $
What distinguishes patchouli from other resinous, woody materials in perfumery is its unmistakable smell of freshly overturned soil. The rest, when aged, is much like sandalwood, an impenetrably complex cloud of interesting vanillic, woody, ambery, fruity odors. Patchouli Antique is what it says on the label. It has a cold smell of the damp undersides of garden stones in a sweet woody setting, making for a folk tale of a fragrance, rustic and bizarre. TS

Patchouli Patch (L'Artisan Parfumeur) ★ ★ ★ ★ *fresh earthy* $ $ $
This wonderfully deceptive fragrance opens as advertised with a big piercings-and-tattoos patchouli note. But just before the word *airhead* forms on your lips, it takes an abrupt 90-degree turn toward what is likely the most simultaneously seductive and unwieldy note in perfumery, that of helichrysum (everlasting flower), a strange, fenugreek-like note of tremendous power that is as hard to hide in a composition as a giraffe under bedsheets. It's been done before, to be sure, most notably in the sensational Sables (Annick Goutal) and more recently in Dior's Eau Noire, but it's still nice to see that strange face in the crowd. Patchouli Patch's surprises aren't over yet, however: in a curious inversion of the normal fresh-to-warm direction of fragrance, the drydown, reminiscent of the firm's Timbuktu, is a superb woody accord which disperses these parched top notes with a night breeze. A very nice perfume indeed, though some may prefer the third movement on its own. LT

Patchoulissime (Keiko Mecheri) ★ ★ ★ *patchouli vetiver* $$$
With patchouli oils available in every hippie shop for not a lot of cash, it's a wonder that niche firms keep putting out their upscale versions in frosted glass. Still, this one has a pleasingly animalic, barnyard air of hay and stables. TS

Patchouly (Etro) ★ ★ ★ *patchouli cloud* $$
A nice patchouli, which smells earthy-woody-camphoraceous, as the darned thing should. Having smelled patchouli, over the years, on legions of people prone to nod their heads like the little dog dolls in the back of cars, I wouldn't miss this type of fragrance if it disappeared forever. LT

Paul Smith London for Men (Paul Smith) ★ ★ ★ *violet coumarin* $
A sweet, dusty lavender-violet on a woody backdrop like sugared milk. Nothing new, but nice. TS

Paul Smith London Woman (Paul Smith) ★ ★ ★ *citrus oriental* $
Paul Smith does Shalimar Eau Légère. Nice, but get the real thing. LT

Paul Smith Man (Paul Smith) ★ ★ ★ *cardamom leafy* $
Nothing wrong with this pleasant, lightly spiced violet-leaf affair, which, like its predecessor Déclaration, has a sweet floral-and-fruity aspect that means the wearer's girlfriend will sneak a spritz in the bathroom now and then. TS

Paul Smith Rose (Paul Smith) ★ ★ ★ *tea rose* $$
Amusingly, this competent but dull tea rose soliflore claims to contain the extract of a varietal named Sir Paul Smith. *Vanitas . . .* LT

Paul Smith Woman (Paul Smith) ★ ★ ★ *soapy floral* $
The fluorescent floral genre has begat so many closely related and gener-

ally unpleasant creatures that, having reviewed the odd hundred, one becomes very attuned to the smallest inflections of that brassy, nasal perfumery speech. This one is better than most, with a woody-floral balance that works nicely, and a vulgarly pleasant soapy note that suggests a well-scrubbed sixteen-year-old up to no good. To be avoided by all other human varietals. LT

Peau de Pêche (Keiko Mecheri) ★ ★ ★ ★ *peachy aldehydic* $$$
While this breezy little number is no Chant d'Arômes, its clear predecessor and still undefeated in the aldehydic-lactonic game, it (1) hits exactly the right balance between peachy cream and lemony crisp, and (2) seemingly goes on forever. Sadly, the original, tender, rosy peach of Chant d'Arômes never stuck around for long, fading unexpectedly to an interesting vetiver chypre after a time, but Peau de Pêche (Peach Skin), while simpler and cruder, is centered on an extraordinarily long-lasting musk that itself seems to have peachy and aldehydic facets. The scent smells impossibly consistent from start to finish. Two days and three showers later, it still radiates intensely and recognizably from the skin. TS

Péché Cardinal (Parfums MDCI) ★ ★ ★ *blackcurrant peach* $$$$
Oscar de la Renta's peachy tuberose worn with the lining turned out: all the flamingo pinks of a sunset after a volcanic explosion, with a balance of acid and sweet that any white wine would be proud to show off. Veers dangerously close to a shampoo smell but remains pleasantly jammy as long as it lasts, then fades to an unexpected smell of waxed wood floors. A good lowbrow departure from the classicist first batch of MDCI fragrances—the charming pigtailed little sister of the bunch. Beware the seriously aspirational pricing, even for the refill. TS

Perfect Kiss (Creative Scentualization) ★ ★ *chocolate floral* $$
Nice try, but don't kiss with your mouth full. This fragrance reminds me of the early nineties, when everyone (first among them Thierry Mugler) wanted a chocolate accord. And everyone soon found out that

the fatty coumarinic aspect of perfumery chocolate makes you feel like you've had way too much already, which is why dieters use it as a spray-when-hungry. The combination with a floral base here makes it even less appetizing: all in all, a fallen Angel, without the demonic laugh. LT

Perfect Man Alternative (Bella Bellissima) ★★★ *woody herbaceous* $$
BBC news presenter and voiceover actress Bella Crane has started a niche firm. This amusingly named fragrance is a nicely put-together herbaceous composition in the manner of L'Eau Bleue, but with a better drydown, no doubt due to a larger fragance budget. LT

Perles de Lalique (Lalique) ★ ★ ★ *woody rose* $$
Retro roses are in, judging by Agent Provocateur, Rose Barbare, and now the much subtler Perles de Lalique. Instead of going for an easy crowd-pleaser and pouring on the vanilla, PdL gives a surprising dusting of black pepper over the strawberries. For a while, it's stylishly androgynous and easy to wear, like roomy wool flannel trousers, and its rose-patchouli heart takes a page from Voleur de Roses (L'Artisan). But it drifts too soon into a familiar synthetic woody-amber drydown with the wet concrete smell of Cashmeran. TS

Petite Cherie (Annick Goutal) ★ ★ *pear floral* $$$
Feel some pity for this fragrance, which suffers two severe drawbacks. It should be a winsome, girlish scent of pears and spring florals, but one of its materials (possibly the violet nitrile that smells like cucumber) contains an aspect that smells harshly of wet dog to many people. The pear material is also highly unstable, which means this fragrance is notorious among fragrance fans for tending to smell very wrong a few months after purchase. TS

La Petite Robe Noire (Guerlain) ★ ★ ★ ★ *tarty fruit* $$$
Guerlain seems occasionally to indulge a Paul Valéry–like talent for giving clichés a stylistic twist that enables everyone to enjoy the trite afresh,

as if it were newly minted. Here the gourmand style is given the clever-clogs treatment. LPRN goes so far in the *tartelette aux fraises* direction that it ends up smelling exactly like those purely decorative tarts the French are so fond of, with fruit that looks like enamel, crisscrosses of buttery pastry like stained-glass lead, and oceans of transparent syrup poured over the whole thing. By rights I should hate this thing, but instead I enjoy its silliness. LT

Peut-Etre (Lancôme) ★ ★ ★ *musky floral* $$$
As a child endlessly nosing about my mother's bathroom, I was mesmerized by a brick of bath cubes she had forgotten beneath the sink, wrapped first in gold foil, then in paper strips illustrated with the flowers supposedly impersonated within. Their scents had faded and mingled into one subdued, blurred floral like this warm, timid, musky smell of uncertain intention. TS

Philosykos (Diptyque) ★ ★ ★ ★ *ripe fig* $$
Sykos as in sycophant, the fig-bearer. This is a very convincing impression of figs, with their delicious combination of near-urinous leafiness, sweet fruity background, and earthy freshness. Because it was composed by Olivia Giacobetti sometime after Premier Figuier, I used to mentally refer to this one as Second Figuier, but in truth it is the first proper fig in perfumery. Excellent. LT

Philtre d'Amour (Guerlain) ★ ★ ★ *floral citrus* $$$
Released in 1999 and now part of the Parisiennes collection, Philtre d'Amour (Love Potion) is a bit of a surprise. With a name like that, I expected something big and intoxicating. Instead, it is Guerlain's version of Cristalle, but with the top two blouse buttons undone. This would make a great masculine: a wonderful top note of dry, aldehydic citrus with a touch of a woody muguet alcohol; a bitter, resinous, almost ink-like background; and a very surprising banana-like note of ylang-

ylang in the drydown. An alternative to the delightful Eau de Guerlain if you want freshness but are not prepared to compromise on intelligence. Excellent. Note: Guerlain has to improve the packaging. Unfortunately, the plastic bottle tray inside the box smells of plasticizers, and that's the first impression you get when you open it. LT

Pi (Givenchy) ★ *sweet nothing* $
The reference example of a design screwup. Confused bottle, weird astronaut advertising, polite but desperately cheap and thin mandarin-amber fragrance capable of sustaining interest for about 3.14 seconds. LT

Piège à Filles (Ego Facto) ★ *disgusting musk* $$
It means "girl trap." Per LT, this is "blatantly inspired by Le Mâle" and "more like a *piège à cons*" (idiot trap). Whatever enormous musk he finds is invisible to this reviewer, who detects only a smell like the water at the bottom of the vase, plus a startlingly unpleasant cucumber-metallic note. TS

Pierre de Lune (Armani Privé) ★ ★ *sad iris* $$$$
When all is smelled and done, what I like best about the Privé collection (apart from not having to shell out for it) is the impossibly light bottle. Considering Pierre de Lune benefited from what must have been a lavish fragrance budget, it weighs in at much less than the sum of its parts. It undoubtedly contains lots of good iris but does what iris (e.g., Hiris) compositions will do when in an ornery mood, i.e., go all sour on you and smell like raw potatoes. LT

Piment Brûlant (L'Artisan Parfumeur) ★ ★ ★ *floral green* $$$
A scaled-down Vent Vert done using tomato stems and capsicum as the green top note instead of the tall grass of galbanum. The floral heart is perhaps not quite enough to sustain interest once the initial blast is over, but it never becomes offensive. Nice work. LT

Piment des Baies (Miller Harris) ★ ★ ★ *lime agave* $$$
Very pleasant if somewhat spineless woody-peppery confection with a
citrus start. Smells amazingly like a margarita up top. LT

Pink Beach (Victoria's Secret) ★ *canned fruit* $$
Strong, syrupy fruity floral for girls who want to smell like Kool-Aid. If
you like this kind of thing, your thong is probably showing above your
jeans. TS

Play (Comme des Garçons) ★ ★ *woody marine* $$
A clean, woody-spicy accord that might have been interesting had it not
been spoiled by a big dose of Calone. LT

Play (Givenchy) ★ ★ *orange wood* $$
Givenchy's relentless pursuit of totally naff design reaches a new high
with the bottle for Play, which tries to look like an iPhone, only much
larger, reminiscent of the Soviet joke, "We have the biggest microcir-
cuits in the world." The fragrance is an undecided, incomplete thing, as
if Habit Rouge had been folded eight times over, cut with scissors, and
opened up again shot through with holes. Half-oriental, half-woody,
and entirely watery, Play makes you want to hit Stop. LT

Pleasures (Estée Lauder) ★ ★ ★ ★ ★ *snowy floral* $
In retrospect Pleasures (1995) turns out to have been a tipping point in
the history of perfumery, the storming of the fine-fragrance Bastille, the
moment when lowly soap finally overthrew the ancien régime and took
possession of its empty palaces. Its revolutionary precursors Chanel No.
22 and White Linen illustrate the struggles of this wish on its way to
fulfillment. Aldehydes have always been powerful and cheap, floral
bases as well, so soap perfumery made abundant use of low-cost versions of Joy, No. 5, etc. Quality soaps got very good at this, and the advertising (Lux, Camay) started showing demurely bathing blondes up to

their neck in white foam worthy of smothering a refinery fire. The soap makers never had the guts to do a fine fragrance scented just like the bar (my prediction is that a Dove EdP would sell well), so it was left to the fine-fragrance people to fake plebeian pleasures. But proper perfume's courtly manners gave it away, and the rose was always too good (White Linen), the musks too sweet (No. 22). By the early nineties two things had happened. First, the relentless impoverishment of fine-fragrance formulas narrowed the gap dangerously with functional fragrance, a recipe for class unrest. Second, the great fragrance company Firmenich developed musks (Muscenone, Habanolide) that fortuitously possessed a soapy, snowy sparkle reminiscent of aldehydes. All of a sudden it became possible for perfume to outlast soap without veering off course. Karen Khoury at Lauder, and Alberto Morillas and Annie Buzantian at Firmenich seized the moment: Pleasures. It caught the mood of women tired of loud eighties fragrances. They just wanted to smell clean, and not just transiently, but all day, broadcasting the spotlessness of their intentions. The message was that nothing had been deliberately added, that the pleasant, white radiance was just squeakiness writ large. Unfortunately, the scrubbed bareness of Pleasures begat a faceless breed that is still with us, but one can hardly blame a pioneer for spawning lesser imitations. LT

Pleasures Exotic (Estée Lauder) ★ ★ ★ *peach aldehydic* $
Competent peachy floral. Like turning up at Pleasures ski resort in summer: the shiny snow is gone, and the greenery is a little threadbare. Get Chant d'Arômes instead. LT

Pleasures for Men (Estée Lauder) ★ ★ ★ *fruity fougère* $
The good news is that this one is not a drone clone and, though clearly inspired by Cool Water, smells much more like a feminine. The bad news is that it's a bit chemical. Above average, but could have been much better still. LT

Pleasures Intense (Estée Lauder) ★ ★ ★ *green honeysuckle* $
Less intense than Pleasures. LT

Pluie d'Aromes (Cinq Mondes) ★ ★ ★ *happy spraying* $ $
Let's be fair: the spa line of Cinq Mondes is not in the business of fine
fragrance in the same way Guerlain is. But let's also be fair: their line of
eaux de toilette, nominally representing the spa rituals of various exotic
places, are very pretty compositions, reasonably priced, and made of
better stuff than many fine fragrances—and they even have drydowns.
The standouts are L'Atlas, a fortified jasmine plus orange blossom lush
enough to impersonate a frangipani, and Kyoto, an excellent fresh-
metallic tea rose that I prefer to the Creed equivalent. Siam is a bright
sweet-lemon citrus, Java a sleek eucalyptus. The only dud is Bengalore,
a pedestrian floral vanilla. Perfumer Olivia Giacobetti is credited with
all. TS

Plus Que Jamais (Guerlain) ★ ★ ★ ★ *disenchanted chypre* $ $ $
Plus Que Jamais was created by Jean-Paul Guerlain to commemorate
the new store at 68 Champs-Elysées and was described to me as a reca-
pitulation and celebration of all the Guerlain themes of the past. That
sounded a bit like a near-death experience, when the entire life of your
company flashes before your nose. I was prepared for the worst. Not so.
Plus Que Jamais is symphonic rather than melodic, in the grand French
manner of Yves Saint Laurent's Y or Van Cleef's First, and turns out to
be at once affecting and very elegant. The general tone is of a green floral
chypre and, like many of that breed, has the faintly uncomfortable
screechy feel of silk on silk. The only older Guerlain it reminded me of
was the least Guerlain of all, Jardins de Bagatelle. But whereas JdB was a
little crude, this one is refined in the extreme and has an autumnal chic
that is hard to resist. LT

Poême (Lancôme) ★ *horrid floral* $
The great perfumer Guy Robert once told me that in his opinion the

success of chypre fragrances was due in part to the fact that they agreed with food and wine. This prompts the following: name three fragrances incompatible with eating. Easy: Amarige, Spellbound, and Poême. What do they have in common? They scream like a factory siren at ten paces. They are so blatantly, horribly chemical that the message your nose sends to your brain is "Run for your life." Poême came five years after the other two, during which Jacques Cavallier figured out how to up the ante by combining the worst of Amarige (the hideous tuberose), the worst of Spellbound (triple-distilled oil slick), and a novel, uniquely unpleasant, peppery-floral chrysanthemum note all its own. Very few fragrances' bottles actually stink before being sprayed, merely upon opening the sealed package. Poême is one. LT

Pois de Senteur (Caron) ★ ★ *soapy floral* $ $ $
Polite, dull little soapy-woody floral. TS

Poison (Dior) ★ ★ ★ ★ ★ *huge tuberose* $
Reviewing Poison is a bit like road-testing an Abrams M1 tank in the evening rush hour. People just seem to get out of your way, and if they don't, you just swivel that turret to remind them you're not kidding. This is the fragrance everybody loves to hate, the beast that defined the eighties, the perfume that cost me a couple of friendships and one good working relationship. It is also unquestionably the best dressed-up, syrupy tuberose in history, and in my opinion it buries Amarige and the first Oscar de la Renta in the "make it a night he'll never forget" category. Every perfume collector has to have this, but please never, ever wear it to dinner. LT

Poivre (Caron) ★ ★ *spicy floral* $ $ $
Poivre was once a terrific spicy oriental, with a nose-tickling smell of cinnamon red hots plus carnation and a good, rich amber to anchor it. Now less picante, more rosy, it's middling and pointless. TS

Poivre 23 (Le Labo) ★ ★ ★ *balsamic thyme* $ $
Poivre means "pepper," and as you'd expect from Le Labo the fragrance is not particularly peppery, but rather a warm, woody-balsamic thyme composition of good quality yet only moderately interesting. LT

Poivre Piquant (L'Artisan Parfumeur) ★ ★ ★ *pepper peony* $ $ $
This is perfumery with a sense of humor. Since Angel, it has become possible to marry floral bases with just about anything. PP plonks an intense green peppercorn note like a racy pillbox hat on top of an endearingly shy, very girly peony accord. Not particularly deep, but a wonderfully skilled exploration of the unexpected. Great fun. LT

Poivre Samarcande (Hermès) ★ ★ *vanishing act* $ $ $
Another evanescent Elléna creation, this one so fleeting I had to spray it on twice to keep it in mind while writing this sentence. If, God forbid, the present trend continues, calculations indicate that Hermès should be releasing unscented Vodka Novosibirsk anytime soon. LT

Polo (Ralph Lauren) ★ ★ ★ ★ *dry oakmoss* $
A friend of mine reported that the girls at his high school were so fond of Polo that they poured it in their laundry in an attempt to smell it endlessly every day. While I think that's a rather expensive substitute for fabric softener, I can see their point: this stuff smells fantastic. A sleek, grassy-patchouli, mossy-woody scent, dry and smoky from one angle, sweetly resinous from another, Polo has a relaxed, expansive feeling in a comfortingly conservative way, like short hair combed neatly in a straight side part on a fellow otherwise charmingly shabby. No wonder some men have worn it all their lives. TS

Polo Black (Ralph Lauren) ★ *sage lavender* $
Another sclarene-based lavender-on-steroids affair, this smells like a cheap body wash equipped with a megaphone. LT

Polo Blue (Ralph Lauren) ★ *citrus woody* $
Disproves the aromatherapeutic notion that citrus notes make you cheerful. TS

Polo Double Black (Ralph Lauren) ★★ *sweet fougère* $
I like the idea that black can be doubled, as in Double Stout. This said, the fragrance is what the local street kids in my trash neighborhood are wearing, and I don't feel any particular kinship to their tribe. LT

Polo Sport (Ralph Lauren) ★★★★ *lavender pineapple* $
The basic Cool Water fougère accord that spawned hundreds of copies is the fresh, slightly faceless, citrus-lavender-woody material of dihydro-myrcenol given congeniality by a crisp, delicious apple and the intensely watery green smell of violet-leaf materials. Polo Sport is one of the few variations that introduces a twist worth the effort: instead of the expected green apple, a sweet-and-sour pineapple. It deepens and sweetens the structure—even more citrus, even more green until it feels too intense to bear, a fougère with sun glare. TS

Pomegranate Noir Cologne (Jo Malone) ★★ *woody fruit* $$
The word *noir* these days is liberally sprinkled on perfumery labels, as GTI used to be after car model names, to indicate something with a bit more character than you thought you could afford. The top note of PNC, devoid of any connection with pomegranate, is a thin fruit-jam-and-wood-shavings accord, not bad but a touch skeletal. Five minutes later, the fragrance feels like it's run out of puff and smells like Fernet Branca dregs left in a glass overnight. LT

Poopoo Pidou (Ego Facto) ★★★ *rice oriental* $$
Among formulas with budgets this low, this pretty sketch by Dominique Ropion is a standout. The top note is a perfect olfactory postcard of an evening in Thailand: the roasted, homey smell of rice and a floral accord half lemongrass, half jasmine. Quickly afterward comes a gentle, cuddly

wood-vanilla-musk. In all, an interesting variation on the concept of Kenzo Amour. TS

Possibilities (Ann Taylor) ★★ *woody amber* $
After the cheerful, modern fruity-woody top note quickly disappears, you're left with a citrus with woody amber in the Light Blue style but thinner. TS

Potion solid perfume (LUSH) ★★★ *clove carnation* $
The first thing that strikes you when you unscrew the container is a wallop of clove. The rest is a carnation, straightforward and unambitious. TS

Pour Monsieur (Chanel) ★★★★★ *masculine chypre* $$
Pour Monsieur should by rights be sitting under a triple-glass bell jar next to the meter and the kilogram at the Pavillon de Breteuil as the reference masculine fragrance. Technically, it is a fresh chypre, and embodies to perfection the accord of fresh bergamot, sweet labdanum, and austere oakmoss that defines the genre. But beyond that, it also defines the exact timbre and volume that a classic masculine fragrance should adopt: a warm, relaxed, confident voice, quietly melodious and in which you can hear a smile. Listen to it carefully, and you won't need to read Baltasar Gracián's *The Art of Worldly Wisdom*. LT

Pour Monsieur Concentré (Chanel) ★ *sweetened chypre* $$
Avoid this one: it is not a more concentrated version of Pour Monsieur, but a sweeter, more vulgar, more invasive thing that misses the point of the original without making an interesting new one. Get Caron's Troisième Homme instead. LT

Pour une Femme (Caron) ★★ *fruity chypre* $$
A brash sweet amber with cooked fruit, always somewhat overdone in the 1000 (Patou) style, but good for what it was worth. It's invaded now

with a screechy woody-rose drydown that seems completely incompetent and that I do not remember from before. TS

Poussière de Rose (Parfums de Rosine) ★ ★ ★ *cedar rose* $$
A Féminité du Bois with less wonder (less raisin, less cinnamon) and more rose. TS

Prada (Prada) ★ ★ ★ *amber patchouli* $$
Miuccia Prada is a genuine fashion visionary, but she shows no similar knack for perfume. Her first fragrance is an amber patchouli oriental as dense as lead. It shares a large segment of Angel's DNA, but lacks the fluorescent disco of Angel's fruity floral section. Instead, it gets into hippie head-shop territory, with a heavy overripe floral like the smell in your leather purse when you've had a banana in it since yesterday. TS

Prada Tendre (Prada) ★ ★ *floral oriental* $$
A sad attempt to cash in on all current fashions at the same time by mixing Narciso Rodriguez for Her with a nondescript acid rose and topping the whole thing with an unpleasant woody-amber note that simply refuses to go away. LT

Prelude to Love (By Kilian) ★ ★ ★ *iris lemon* $$$$
Mighty long prelude, threatening to last all blessed day unless you find love at the office. Forget the silly name, this is a sober, classy morning cologne embellished by a touch of iris, a sort of burl-veneer version of Mugler's, nice in a bathroomy, well-scrubbed, rosy-cheeked way. LT

Premier Figuier Extrême (L'Artisan Parfumeur) ★★★★
green floral $$$
Premier Figuier was the fragrance that put Olivia Giacobetti on the map, and deservedly so: its fig-leaf note (stemone, one of the few oximes in perfumery) was an overdue natural in perfumery, and pleasantly jarring. PFE feels to me less fig-like than the first one, though still robustly green all the way through. It occurred to me while smelling it that the reason for its richly deserved success is not so much the novelty of the composition but its classicism: this is the next generation of Ma Griffe, naughty and tweedy in equal parts. Did Miss Moneypenny have a daughter? LT

Premier Jour (Nina Ricci) ★ ★ *citrus floral* $$
Sometimes when you look up recipes on Epicurious.com you see home cooks leaving feedback somewhat like this: "I replaced the bread-crumbs with toasted chopped almonds, the spaghetti with some left-over oatmeal, the parsley with some dandelion, and then I added extra garlic. This recipe is terrible. I would not make it again." Premier Jour feels like a perversion of a lactonic floral recipe: yes, there are green florals; yes, there are musks; yes, there are ambers; yes, there is a nutty-milky aspect—but they feel like all the wrong ones. I would not make it again. TS

Prends Garde à Toi (Ego Facto) ★ ★ ★ *envious hyacinth* $$
A chilly green hyacinth borrowing from both Envy and Jules, with the prim standoffishness of the one and some of the ammoniac, cat-piss-

like discord of the other. A skillful reworking of an entertainingly vicious floral. TS

Princess (Vera Wang) ★ *tooth decay* $
Stupid name, pink perfume, heart-shaped bottle, little crown on top. I half expected it to be really great just to spite me. But no, it's probably the most repulsively cloying thing on the market today. LT

Les Princesses de Venise (Roméa d'Améor) ★ ★ ★ *fruity floral* $$$
Smelling the RdA fragrances one after the other eventually reveals Pierre Bourdon's game plan: virtuoso variations on the modern floral oriental. Princesses is a fruity floral with very interesting ideas dotted around throughout: top notes of grapefruit and blackcurrant, a white-flowers-and-lily core, and a green-woody background, all done with great skill. And yet, despite the artistry, the whole is not quite convincing and gives an impression of cheapness, which suggests that a higher formula cost might have delivered a great fragrance. LT

Private Collection (Estée Lauder) ★ ★ ★ ★ *floral chypre* $
Even snobs who turn up their noses at any perfume originating outside continental Europe must give this classic from 1973 its due. It smells to me like a bridge between the French tradition of rich floral chypres and Lauder's own very American soap-powder-bright White Linen. Private Collection was supposedly solely Lauder's personal fragrance until admiring friends convinced her to sell it. If true, it's proof the lady had good taste: it manages to offset exactly an intensely powdery, rich, sweet, floral bouquet with a handsome, dry, woody style, which reminds me of my rule for dresses, such that the more frou-frou the print, the less frou-frou the cut should be. Thus you get your girliness and you get to be a grown-up too. Beautiful, sunny, and confident, with both radiance and tenacity, this fragrance sits easily next to the big French classics on the shelf. If you've never tried a Lauder perfume, this is a good place to start. TS

Private Collection Amber Ylang Ylang (Estée Lauder) ★
vanilla syrup $$$$

Undigestible vanilla-pastry fragrances are a special problem in perfumery, where Shalimar demonstrates the correct solution and Spiritueuse Double Vanille a flunking error. PCAYY should have studied harder before giving this answer: a slow-moving fog of overpowering vanilla and maple syrup clotted with an enormous, sticky yellow dose of ylang-ylang, like drowning in a vat of bananas Foster. Polished, rich, and blithely aggressive. TS

Private Collection Tuberose Gardenia (Estée Lauder) ★ ★ ★ ★
real gardenia $$$

Michael Edwards's database of fragrance lists 23 fragrances called Gardenia and fully 344 that claim to contain the flower as an ingredient, which is good going, given that there is no such thing. Some believers in the Big Lie theory (if you're going to fib, go whole hog) go even further and list pink, green, or even black gardenia among their notes. The truth is that gardenia is a reconstruction, and few fragrances actually achieve the flower smell that I rate as the most irresistible and impossibly pretty on earth. This beautiful creation by Firmenich's Harry Frémont is one of them. The tuberose note in PCTG is very quiet, while the rest of the fragrance is an utterly lovely gardenia accord on a refined, radiant white-flowers background. The gardenia effect does not (and cannot) stretch to the drydown, and is much richer in the parfum than the EdP. Both are probably best sprayed on fabric. While it lasts, however, this is one of the prettiest tunes your nose has ever heard. LT

Promesse (Cacharel) ★ ★ ★ *fruity floral* $$

By now we can take it as given that the basic melody of fruity florals is hopelessly moronic, the perfumery equivalent of a door chime. All the poor perfumer has to play with when handed a nitwitted brief like this one is timbre: the tiny changes in quality and complexity of a composition that make the difference between harsh and comfortable. Promesse sticks faithfully to the pink mission statement but struggles (fully three perfumers are credited with having composed it, always a bad sign) to inject some interest in a plot that even Barbara Cartland would have deemed too girly. The first five minutes are pleasant, even interesting, like a mini EnJoy, a small swirling cloud of notes the color of lipstick. Then the money runs out, the music stops, and the thing goes back to the heavy-lidded torpor of a gum-chewing airhead in a discount store. LT

Promesse de l'Aube (Parfums MDCI) ★ ★ ★ ★ ★ *peach rose* $$$$
I've said it before and am happy to repeat it: there is nothing quite as good as a good chypre. Francis Kurkdjian, given what feels like an unlimited formula budget, has done an exceptional job in a completely classical manner. The tune of this fragrance (the name translates as Dawn Promise, after Romain Gary's autobiographical novel) may not be hugely original, but the orchestration will bring tears to your eyes. Everything is right: the proportions, from solar top note to deep drydown; the weight, solid but not heavy; the sweep, majestic and caressing. This is an homage to the fifties, done in the lithe, modern, apricot-fuzz manner of 31 Rue Cambon, which it predates by several years. Superb. LT

Provocative Woman (Elizabeth Arden) ★ *citrus floral* $
The name is simultaneously so stupid and so inappropriate to the fragrance that one wonders which of the two moronic ideas came first. A shrill little floral that feels like music heard through someone else's earphones. Nice bottle. LT

Pulp (Byredo) ★ ★ ★ *blackcurrant fig* $$$
Ignoring the archaic cinnamon-nutmeg orthodoxy, there are two major schools of modern dessert theory: chocolatism and the berry-lemon heresy. For adherents of the latter, the ideal end of a meal is a mouthful of blackcurrant (cassis) sorbet, the most intensely fresh and sour berry possible, with an almost ammoniac, slightly sulfurous green character.

The green fig-leaf note of stemone cleverly augments the cassis-with-a-side-of-cassis effect. Overall, it still smells more like a very good candle but should satisfy fans of a kir royale. TS

Pure (Alfred Sung) ★ ★ *soapy floral* $
After a strawberry top note, you find a pale, slightly sour, aldehydic floral, a distant poor relation of White Linen. TS

Pure (Dunhill) ★ ★ *brine floral* $$
The awkward Art Deco bottle, based on a curved, asymmetrical hip flask made by Dunhill, holds an appealing fragrance idea far more interesting than expected from the dull name: a metallic, oyster-like floral. Before you can get to really like it, a fresh, hideously potent woody amber takes over. TS

Pure (Jil Sander) ★ ★ ★ *fresh floral* $$$
A nice I'm-not-here-please-ignore-me-I'm-not-a-fragrance pale floral, like a million others but in the ninety-fifth percentile. One of the notes it allegedly contains is "pure air accord," and that about sums it up. LT

Pure Grace (Philosophy) ★ ★ ★ *soapy floral* $
Described on the back of the bottle as the clean smell of soap and water (surely only the former), this pretty much does what it says and in small doses gives a convincingly scrubbed, rosy-cheeked impression. The sort of thing Clean Perfume would do if it wasn't anosmic. LT

Pure Intense (Jil Sander) ★ ★ ★ *citrus woody* $$$
A clean, fresh, transparent woody-citrus affair typical of sports fragrances of the last decade, all of which suffer from the same problem: their accords are based on short-lived top-note materials, and these are telescopically extended into the heart and drydown by synthetic look-

alikes that smell very bare and chemical. If you like this sort of thing, get cK One, the only one that got the structure exactly right. LT

Pure Poison (Dior) ★★★★ *woody jasmine* $$
With a radiance covering roughly three city blocks, Pure Poison is a no-holds-barred floral oriental, which feels, like its forerunner Ysatis, like a simple tune played on a cathedral organ. This is a massive, sweet orange-blossom-and-jasmine affair, plus candied orange peel, with a few big woody notes to let people know you mean business. It feels designed for the woman who wears a Wonderbra and no discernible blouse under her suit. TS

Pure Purple (Hugo Boss) ★ *cherry syrup* $$
Smells exactly like the synthetic flavor used in codeine syrup, but induces a hacking cough instead of relieving it. LT

Pure Sport for Men (Benetton) ★ *no fragrance* $
This fragrance is so close to nonexistence that you wonder what the compounding of the oil looks like: guys in blue overalls transporting invisible drums on forklifts and pretending to pour them into empty vessels before giving the resulting air a good stir and carefully partitioning it into empty drums labeled Benetton while quality control takes a sample and makes sure the gas chromatograph trace is completely flat. LT

Pure Sport for Women (Benetton) ★ *undetectable floral* $
The hideously garish Barbie-pink packaging leads you to expect something soapy and cute. Instead, you find almost nothing on the smelling strip. This is an executive summary of a fragrance, a one-liner that cuts straight to the (undistinguished) drydown of a dull, dry floral. Should have been called Pure Solvent. LT

Pure Turquoise (Ralph Lauren) ★ ★ ★ ★   *lactonic fougère* $ $

A sly fragrance that takes the herbal, violet-leaf fougère, standard in men's fragrance since at least Grey Flannel, and fleshes it out with a nondescript, slightly metallic, nutty-lactonic white floral to create the equivalent of one of those optical illusions that looks to be either a goblet or two faces in profile, depending on whether you concentrate on the white or the black space. If you think of Pure Turquoise as a feminine, it smells like a lily of the valley set in sage, and if you think of it as a masculine fougère, it smells like a huge improvement on L'Eau Bleue. It smells great both ways, but especially as a delicious, strange masculine, particularly because it fades soon to a murmur perhaps too quiet for a satisfying feminine. T S

Pure White Linen (Estée Lauder) ★ ★ ★ ★   *dry muguet* $

In my mind, an update of the gorgeously soapy classic White Linen threatened to be simply yet another modern meditation on the joys of handsoap, as so many soapy florals have been since. But Lauder has been characteristically careful with the White Linen name. So after a lovely fruity-floral top note in the current style, instead of fading off to nothing via a clean musk as is the norm, Pure White Linen comes to an interesting woody-herbal lily-of-the-valley drydown, with the same slightly sour cast that White Linen has, though with a transparent effect much closer to Pleasures. Overall, radiant, easy to wear, and a good extension of the original. T S

Pure White Linen Light Breeze (Estée Lauder) ★ ★   *soapy floral* $

Pleasures with sweeter florals and the damp-cold glisten of hedione, a cliché that deserves its own name by now: laundry of the valley? T S

Purple Fantasy (Guerlain) ★   *citrus floral* $ $ $

Purple, yes, as in prose. But no fantasy whatsoever. Instead, an Allure clone with a sour floral accord up top. Dismal. L T

Purple Label (Ralph Lauren) ★ ★ *leafy wood* $ $
The packaging (purple embroidered label stuck on cardboard pinstripe) is already naff enough, though the deep purple of the bottle is pleasant to look at. The fragrance is a dry, green-spicy confection of no particular interest, and clearly no compelling need propelled it into existence. But the press release is truly something. Purple Label is supposedly made up of three accords. Top: Personal Wine Cellar accord. Middle: Man's Club accord. Drydown: Classic Car accord. I think I'm going to Ralph. LT

Purplelight (Salvador Dalí) ★ ★ *green muguet* $
A pleasant, pale, nondescript milky white floral plus clean musk. So light it seems embarrassed to be there. TS

Purple Lips (Salvador Dalí) ★ ★ *fruity oriental* $
Sub-Flowerbomb. LT

Purple Patchouli (Tom Ford) ★ ★ *harsh floral* $ $ $ $
With a name like that, a fragrance needs to work hard to be taken seriously. In the event, PP is neither particularly purple nor notably patchoulant. It reminds me of the series of striking accords Christophe Laudamiel composed for the Mugler boxed set based on the film *Perfume*. These are what I would call smelling strip fragrances. Like the clothes in a couture collection, they embody interesting ideas that you could never actually wear, but that you hope will eventually find their way into worked-out stuff. PP is an odd neoclassical creature, a green chypre in the Givenchy III manner overlaid with a rasping floral accord reminiscent of those sticky spring blooms that smell halfway between fish skin and honeysuckle. LT

Pursuit (Dunhill) ★ *spicy sporty* $ $
The usual soap formula, this time with a touch of cinnamon. Like Old Spice, but not as good. TS

Putain des Palaces (Etat Libre d'Orange) ★ ★ ★ *floral leather* $ $
Trashy name (Hotel Whore), interesting fragrance: a mix of standard-issue powdery bonbon fruity floral and a woody-leather base. Not completely worked out, and a bit like wearing two perfumes at once, but not bad. LT

Quand Vient la Pluie (Guerlain) ★ ★ ★ ★ *root-beer iris* $ $ $
Despite the name (When the Rain Comes), Quand Vient la Pluie is most closely related to L'Heure Bleue, not Après l'Ondée. It joins Insolence and Iris Ganache among Guerlain's several recent attempts to update L'Heure Bleue's probably unimprovable anisic floral oriental. But QVlP is an excellent modernization: it smells deliciously fresh and bright in the top note, with an unusual, intense lime sweetness to the floral bouquet, and moves through a handsomely old-fashioned balsamic stage before a delightful anisic-vanillic drydown remarkably reminiscent of root beer. Balanced and beautiful throughout, this is a fragrance true to Guerlain, and full of charm and good humor. TS

Quand Vient l'Eté (Guerlain) ★ ★ ★ *dry floral* $ $ $
The name dates back to 1910, but the fragrance has been "reorchestrated" by Jean-Paul Guerlain for the 2005 reissue. If the accord is indeed representative of the 1910 original, then the ascent of Eternity and Jardins de Bagatelle has just been extended seventy years by this archaeological find. I'm of two minds about the fragrance: on the one hand, I am not fond of this style, a slightly sour, metallic (helional) floral accord that smells like a sucked silver spoon. On the other hand, this one is beautifully executed and has a prim, starchy prettiness that suggests Edwardian TV drama and passions corseted to the bursting point. It brings to mind Ambrose Bierce's definition of garters: "An elastic band intended to keep a woman from coming out of her stockings and desolating the country." LT

Quel Amour! (Annick Goutal) ★ ★ ★ ★ *pomegranate lilac* $$$
If, despite all our entreaties, you have your heart set on buying a pink fruit-salad fragrance, perhaps you will at least get one that isn't entirely airheaded. Take Quel Amour!, for example, which manages to be engaging beyond what you'd expect from its loud, air-freshener spring floral and medley of red fruits. The pairing feels brash, trashy, but really clever, the Erin Brockovich of fruity florals. TS

Quelques Fleurs L'Original (Houbigant) ★ ★ ★ *dull floral* $$$
One has to regard with some suspicion a perfume that claims to be the "original" version, much as one does those who preface a statement with "I'll be honest with you." It was a 1912 composition, and it is pretty clear that easily half the materials in the current version did not exist in 1912. I would be prepared to forgive everything in the name of progress if the fragrance were remotely interesting. But it is as dull as a floral can be, an olfactory dumb blonde that would work well only as an air freshener. LT

Quelques Fleurs Royale (Houbigant) ★ ★ *floral aldehydic* $$$
How the mighty have fallen. Houbigant, one of the oldest firms in the business, has for decades now been largely a joke, despite valiant attempts at bringing back Quelques Fleurs and now this Royale version. QFR is an odd mixture of cheap and expensive, a basically vulgar formula made with cheap synthetics with a dollop of decent floral materials added as an afterthought. Shapeless and uninteresting despite a promising start. LT

Quercus (Penhaligon's) ★ ★ *dry citrus* $$
Depressingly awkward and angular citrus floral that smells, above all, cheap. LT

Querelle (Parfumerie Générale) ★ ★ *dry woody* $$$
A pleasant but unambitious woody that soon settles into what feels like

the drydown of Antaeus but without the story so far. Like reading the torn-off second half of a thriller found on a train seat. LT

Racine (Maître Parfumeur et Gantier) ★ ★ ★ ★ *vetiver citrus* $ $ $
This vetiver is one of the best straight-up interpretations of this wonderful material, and allows a little time travel by smelling exactly halfway between the Guerlain and Carven vetivers circa 1972. Look no further. LT

Rahat Loukhoum (Serge Lutens) ★ ★ ★ *powdery candy* $ $ $
Even surpassing Datura Noir, Rahat Loukhoum is the most unabashedly trashy fragrance in the Serge Lutens line, for the big-sunglasses-and-stretch-velour crowd. Basically, if you want to smell like baby powder and cherry syrup, this is probably the best way to do it. TS

Ralph (Ralph Lauren) ★ ★ ★ *apple floral* $ $
Though dominated initially by the overwhelming smell of green-apple candy, Ralph is built on a pretty, crisp floral structure and, unexpectedly, made to last. TS

Ralph Cool (Ralph Lauren) ★ ★ *fruit schnapps* $ $
Up top, this smells uncannily like Alsatian Framboise schnapps. Amazingly, it does all the way through. If that's what you want to smell of, no one is going to stop you. LT

Ralph Hot (Ralph Lauren) ★ ★ ★ *maple syrup* $ $
A pleasantly dry, milky-nutty-woody gourmand, like Kenzo Amour with a side of pancakes. TS

Ralph Rocks (Ralph Lauren) ★ ★ ★ *orange praline* $ $
Like a Tiki theme party in a bottle, this terrifically brash, trashy orange blossom and woody-coconut concoction is worthy of a Malibu rum and Coke half-price special all night. I wish that part lasted longer than ten

minutes, but even the relatively mild milky-sandalwood drydown has a louche appeal. TS

Realm Men (Erox) ★ ★ ★ *woody oriental* $
You gotta love this, literally. The package says "contains human pheromones." On the back, in small print (I nearly had to put on reading glasses, maybe pheromones are wasted on me), it says, "Only Realm adds this extra dimension of human pleasure." Let's hope it's not one of those tiny rolled-up dimensions that string theories are all about. And after all that, the fragrance is very nice and a bargain at the drugstore price, a woody oriental not a zillion miles away from New York (Parfums de Nicolaï) but far cruder. For those who would choose a '67 Mustang over a Quattroporte of the same vintage. LT

Red Delicious Men (Donna Karan) ★ ★ ★ *woody tisane* $$
When I mistook this bottle for the women's fragrance, I decried it as unpleasant, but when I realized it was for men, I suddenly thought, "Oh, not bad!" If you're looking for a sociology thesis on gender differences, there you go. That said, there is an interesting prominent note of davana in RDM, a dried-leaves-and-fruit smell that comes off like a flavored tea (Constant Comment came to mind) set against a gray woody backdrop—appetizing and friendly, if a little flat. It reminds me of the exciting but unwearable davana-sandalwood accord in Christophe Laudamiel's extraordinary Salon Rouge for the *Perfume* movie coffret; here, though, the combination, in exchange for becoming wearable, has lost the excitement. Better on fabric than on skin, to appreciate the fruit without being overwhelmed by wood. TS

Red Delicious Woman (Donna Karan) ★ ★ ★ *cruel floral* $$
Donna Karan's Red Delicious, the sequel to her green-apple Be Delicious, turns out to be the evil twin of the wonderful Missoni from the same year. Both RDW and the Missoni were done by Maurice Roucel, and both illlustrate the way a talented perfumer can make a cheap com-

position smell interesting. RDW begins with a lovely fruity top note that smells like pure sunshine, but instead of the gently cycling panorama of happy surprises that characterizes Missoni's kaleidoscope, the next thing that lurches into view is a stonking huge white floral with a disturbingly animalic background—is that Camembert? Things only get weirder: delectable and painful in turns, RDW excels in drawing you near with a fresh, juicy lychee scent only to zap you with a jolt of powerful, painful muguet aldehydes when you get too close. There's no place to rest with this one. Basically, it's a taser lollipop. LT

Red Door (Elizabeth Arden) ★ ★ ★ *oriental rose* $
Really, this fragrance could be called Opium Paris, since the bottle design borrows the chinoiserie from the former, and the juice is a thinner version of the latter's dense rose liqueur, set against a drier spiced-woody backdrop. But then Arden would have to pay YSL royalties. A handsome bludgeoner in high-eighties style, Red Door (1989) was among the last of a big-boned kind. TS

Red Roses Cologne (Jo Malone) ★ ★ ★ *boozy rose* $$$
Question 15 (10 minutes). Complete this syllogism: "Roses smell good. This smells of roses. Therefore _____." LT

Red Vetyver (Montale) ★ ★ ★ *citrus vetiver* $$$
Not particularly interesting vetiver. LT

Reflection (Amouage) ★ *white floral* $$$
Launched in 2007, this is a fully worked-out example of what I call the overexposed white floral, a freesia composition so blindingly pale that smelling it makes you reach for sunglasses. I think I would hate on sight any woman who wore this knowingly. Amouage is diluting great artistic capital with unnecessary fragrances. LT

Reflection Man (Amouage) ★ *woody vanilla* $$$
Having met the female of the species, I was dreading this one. It turns out to be a sedated Habanita, a milky vanillic oriental like a giant marshmallow, with a cedar-vetiver drydown that struggles unsuccessfully to put some spine into it. Definitely not a good masculine, but could be fun on a woman if she likes trashy ambers. LT

Remix for Her (Armani) ★ *fruity floral* $
A trite, canned-fruit-salad confection of no interest except to illustrate the cynicism and idiocy of its makers. LT

Rêve en Cuir (Indult) ★ ★ *spicy oriental* $$$$
One part Féminité du Bois, one part Jungle Elephant (Kenzo). Overdone and overpriced. LT

Reverie au Jardin (Tauer Perfumes) ★ ★ ★ *woody fruity* $$$
There's a striking difference between steam-distilled lavender essential oil, the familiar, clean herbal smell we know from aromatherapy products everywhere, and solvent-extracted lavender absolute, a thick green liquid that smells much more fruity and floral, almost candied, close to the tipsy breath of chamomile absolute. Andy Tauer's effort at creating a full feminine perfume around lavender seems, to me at least, to focus on the more unusual character of the absolute. Reverie strikes you as quite pretty from a distance, with tremendously powdery, fresh floral radiance, and up close, it seems dense, even chewy, like those surprisingly intense Middle Eastern sweets flavored with rosewater and what seems to be half the world's production of honey condensed into a two-inch square. But the fragrance has two faces: one smiling, one grimacing. The reason seems to be that the handsome, resinous cleanliness of Tauer's signature smoky-amber accord can turn strangely functional-smelling in the presence of a few powerful synthetics, which amplify and extend the lavender effect at the cost of a cloying harshness that becomes more apparent with time. Overall,

Reverie is a metamorphic creature straddling two states at once, like that famous drawn illusion in which a lovely young woman's smooth cheek and choker necklace double as the hooked nose and grin of a crone. TS

This unique and mysterious "Dr. Tauer and Mr. Hyde" effect is apparent to me too. LT

Rien (Etat Libre d'Orange) ★ ★ ★ ★ *animalic leather* $ $
Smelling Rien (Nothing) makes you realize that there is currently no other unsweetened civet leather out there, a strange omission given the current niche interest in both categories. I love leathers, always find them too sweet, was crazy about Bandit because it was bitter, but would have preferred it undressed, i.e., with the chypre houndstooth tailleur dropped to the floor. I guess I'm the ideal customer for Rien. LT

Le Rivage des Syrtes (Parfums MDCI) ★ ★ ★ *sweet orange* $ $ $ $
The second MDCI fragrance by Patricia de Nicolaï is a durable candied orange-peel note with a background woody sweetness. Nice, but merely nice. TS

Rive Gauche (Yves Saint Laurent) ★ ★ ★ ★ ★ *reference rose* $
Probably the best floral aldehydic of all time, Rive Gauche was composed in 1969 by Jacques Polge of Chanel fame and overhauled in 2003 by Daniela Andrier and Jacques Hy at Givaudan. I have no idea why YSL messed with it, and on principle I regret any change or modernization of such a masterpiece. The balance between citrus, rose, and green notes set against a dark resinous background in old RG was wonderful. I have an old (circa 1980) sample and the new one. Comparison is made easier by the fact that the beautiful light-proof metal atomizer is the best possible container for long-term conservation. Old and new diverge right from the start: old RG has a strong tarry note up top that sets the dark, dramatic tone for the whole composition. The heart is very similar in

both, and the "form," as Edmond Roudnitska would have said, is unchanged. New RG is lighter, brighter, fruitier. Some of this may be due to instability of the citrus aldehydes over time in the old version. The perfumes converge for about an hour. Old RG has some weird, plasticky off notes in the heart, and the new one doesn't. Thereafter, all the way to the drydown, they follow parallel tracks a small distance from each other, and in my opinion the new one keeps level. If I had to describe the difference in overall effect, I would say old RG was more medicinal, the new one more edible. Both are excellent. Try the new, but if you really prefer the old, it will be available for years to come on eBay and other Web sites. LT

Rive Gauche pour Homme (Yves Saint Laurent) ★ ★ ★ ★
brilliant fougère $$

It took guts to come up with an aromatic fougère in 2003, when the species was reckoned extinct except for retro revivals like Klein's Calvin, first issued in 1979. To recap: the fougère genre is named after Houbigant's Fougère Royale (Royal Fern) of 1881. It has gone through so many incremental transformations since that it feels no more like the original than a modern Merc looks like the 1886 Benz "Patent" motorcar. This one is a descendant of Drakkar Noir, an excellent fragrance that was much maligned by Frenchmen after becoming, for some reason, a lesbian emblem in the eighties. It is less aromatic than most of its congeners, and completely devoid of sweetness. The bitter-nutty coumarin theme of fougères is here treated in a very dry-woody, almost smoky manner, but with a faint background of fresh talcum powder that stops it from falling into the gaunt style of, say, Morabito's Or Black or Armani Privé's Bois d'Encens. A wonderfully dark, stylish, modern masculine fragrance, as discreet and satisfying as a well-cut black suit. Superb black and brown metal atomizer. LT

Riverside Drive (Bond No. 9) ★ ★ ★ *leaf zilla* $$$
The compositions that Maurice Roucel has conjured up for niche firm

Bond No. 9 are evidence that he's in no danger of running out of ideas. Sometimes these ideas seem painted with a six-inch-wide brush— impressive from afar, but jarring or a touch crude up close. Riverside Drive's powerful spray of greenery, in a leaf-and-lavender accord Roucel has played with elsewhere (see his thing for Nautica), impresses your neighbor three doors down but shocks the one next to you. TS

Roadster (Cartier) ★ ★ ★ *warm mint* $$$
After a couple of years in purdah in the bespoke perfumery division (pray for an end to that nonsense), Cartier's in-house perfumer, Mathilde Laurent, was encouraged to submit a proposal for a fragrance intended for mass distribution. The motto was apparently "new freshness," a concept that has the effect of making one instantly feel as tired as the brains that came up with it. Nevertheless, Laurent's submission won. Her idea was to use mint as a top note, usually a no-no in fragrance because the suit who writes the checks will invariably mention toothpaste at some point. And mint is tricky: its menthol note is a coolant and lasts only seconds, while the remainder—i.e., what distinguishes mint absolute from menthol crystals—is more generically herbaceous. If only the laws of physics could be repealed and menthol could be made to stay, say, as long as linalool, then it might be possible to do a Jicky with mint instead of lavender. Your fearless reviewer, trusting that the EU has by now tested everything on animals, sprayed Roadster inside his mouth and can report that there is very little menthol in there. Nevertheless, the top notes briefly possess an arresting freshness, as if Guerlain's mole gray L'Ame d'un Héros had decided to wear a bright blue tie. From there, things evolve quite rapidly, first to a radiant cedarwood masculine of the furrowed-brow-and-gold-watch persuasion and then, as if Laurent was trying to inject some sunset glow into that character, to a warm Ambre 83 accord reminiscent of her Attrape-Coeurs. The whole thing works well enough, and in the context of contemporary masculine perfumery is tantamount to an upgrade to business class. Nevertheless, I expected better. LT

Roberto Cavalli (Roberto Cavalli) ★ ★ *woody rose* $ $
As a perfumer friend says, "You can't find it on the smelling strip." A well-constructed but hopelessly pale floral woody, as instantly forgettable as a list of two hundred random sixteen-digit numbers. LT

Roberto Cavalli Oro (Roberto Cavalli) ★ ★ ★ *orange cloves* $ $
Cavalli's glam-trash style does not agree particularly well with this woody oriental, though the fragrance does exhibit a traditional Italian overreliance on spicy and citrus notes and comes across as a sort of dandified pomander. LT

Rochas Man (Rochas) ★ ★ ★ *spicy fresh* $
Packaged in the most suggestive bottle since Fabergé's 1976 Macho, this Maurice Roucel composition has his trademark warm-fresh contrast and straightforward full-throttle manner. It is remarkably close (convergent evolution, not influence) to the exactly contemporary and more refined Yohji Homme, now sadly discontinued. If you can't find YH, get this. LT

Rock Crystal (Olivier Durbano) ★ ★ *thyme incense* $ $ $
A dose of thyme lends a savory, complex warmth to this fresh but thin citrus-incense fragrance. Good idea up top, but it peters out in the drydown. TS

Rock'n Rose (Valentino) ★ *fruity floral* $ $
A little rose and lychee affair, as enticing as pink nylon nighties sold in sex shops. LT

Roma for Women (Laura Biagiotti) ★ ★ ★ *vanilla indole* $ $
Roma lies on the line that connects Dune to Must de Cartier via Allure, Venise, Trouble, and all points West. In Roma the vanilla-indole drydown is brighter, simpler, and friendlier, a cheerful Dune-made-easy that works surprisingly well. LT

Romance (Ralph Lauren) ★ ★ *pink floral* $ $
A reprehensibly dull and not even pleasant soapy floral with sugary gestures, for the kind of young women who get their hair cut precisely the same as their friends and shop from the same catalogs, so even their boyfriends can't tell them apart at ten paces. TS

Romance Eau Fraîche 2008 (Ralph Lauren) ★ *watery lemons* $ $
On a river path in North London, we passed two bundled-up, brisk Englishwomen, one of whom shouted roughly at a dog sniffing another's bum, "No romance, you two!" There's no romance in this either. TS

Romance Men (Ralph Lauren) ★ *fresh nothing* $
About time somebody gave women that order, which reminds me of Peter Cook wondering if "Gentlemen, lift the seat" was an invitation to upper-class larceny. The fragrance is so unmemorable that the only appropriate review is "It has a smell." LT

Romance Men Silver (Ralph Lauren) ★ ★ *woody fresh* $
In the vast, desolate landscape of modern masculines, this is far from the worst, but it is hard to imagine someone sentient actually preferring this to anything else: it would be like falling in love with one particular dollar bill. LT

Roots Spirit (Roots) ★ *citrus musk* $
Rigorously forgettable in a Light Blue kind of way. TS

Roots Spirit Man (Roots) ★ *woody citrus* $
Faceless drone-clone juice. LT

Rosa Flamenca (Parfums de Rosine) ★ ★ ★ ★ *turpentine rose* $ $ $
I have no idea what connection lies between paint thinner and flamenco, but I'm willing to accept there may be one. This fruity-woody rose, with its expansive accord from turpentine to dry amber, feels like a Serge

Lutens fragrance that ran away from home, and reminds me of a fantastic dress I once had, a sheer brown mesh layer over a shocking pink sheath: from a distance, merely a deep wine color, but up close, a startling contrast. Clever and striking. TS

Rose (Caron) ★ ★ ★ *rose liqueur* $ $
Being an enthusiastic cook, I once bought a couple of Filipino cookbooks to remedy my embarrassing lack of knowledge of my father's native cuisine. Yet the books languished unsplattered, since whenever I read the list of ingredients for any dish, I could think of about five better ones I could make of the same stuff. Which brings me to this Caron. All expensive rose soliflores boast of sourcing only the best natural rose essences to capture the beauty of the flower, but somehow they all tend to smell a bit like this: part lemon soap, part wine vinegar, part green (as in boiled vegetables). It smells like quality ingredients, but I can't help but feel they deserved a better recipe. TS

Une Rose (Frédéric Malle) ★ ★ ★ ★ *angry rose* $ $ $
Edouard Fléchier is a top-class perfumer currently at Guerlain, but Une Rose was composed when he worked with the distinguished natural-materials firm of Mane. In a corner of Mane's Art Deco factory high on a hillside above Grasse is a special stainless-steel still where Rose DM is made in very small quantities. DM stands for *distillation moléculaire*, a pompous name for high-vacuum, low-temperature distillation. Treating roses gently pays dividends: Rose DM is a heady, liqueur-like material seemingly devoid of the heavier notes of steam-distilled rose oils, with a top and heart like no other—dry, silken, peppery. In the grand brutal manner you'd expect from the guy who composed Poison, Fléchier marries this most refined of raw materials with the most angular woody amber known to man, a Quest molecule called Karanal. This is a risky gamble. For a start, woody ambers have no fixed intensity but seem to get stronger with time and with exposure. The first time I smelled Karanal, it was odorless, while now even a touch feels strong. Then there

is the fact that Karanal smells urinous, not ambery, to a small subset of women. Undaunted, Fléchier adds what he calls a "truffle" accord, a soft, earthy-creamy base to complete this odd, cantilevered structure. The result is a remarkable, angular, uncompromising fragrance endowed with the alarming beauty of an angry Carmen. LT

Rose 31 (Le Labo) ★ ★ *not rose* $$
This aldehydic carrot juice was, unaccountably, composed by the brilliant Daphné Bugey, of Firmenich, who did Kenzo Amour and four sensational (and as yet unavailable) Coty reconstructions. Is Le Labo some sort of rehab where perfumers go when their noses are tired? LT

Rose Absolue (Annick Goutal) ★ ★ ★ *rose liqueur* $$$
I'm always disappointed by rose soliflores: the material seems impressively complex but too sour to enjoy, like those wines that taste like they'd rather be vinegar. However, if you like that sort of thing, you'll probably love Rose Absolue, which is made of top-notch natural rose materials, which I can't help but feel would be put to better use elsewhere. TS

Rose Absolue (Yves Rocher) ★ ★ ★ *fresh rose* $
Rose Absolue is by far the best of Yves Rocher's latest set of three upmarket fragrances (the others being Voile d'Ambre and Iris Noir), a comfortable, lemony-powdery rose that feels strikingly real, like the headspace rose reconstructions of the eighties, on a background of tonka and patchouli. Far better than one has any right to expect given the bargain price of less than $40 for two ounces. LT

Rose Alexandrie (Armani Privé) ★ ★ ★ ★ *resinous tuberose* $$$
The blend of old-fashioned and modern in Estée Lauder's still popular Beautiful has come to smell somewhat dated. Rose Alexandrie solves this knotty problem in true Alexandrian style: with a drastic cut. The

half of Beautiful that stays is a brilliant, candied, slightly metallic, tuberose-rose with a resinous green background—a floral midway between Fracas and Knowing—while the half that's left out is the powerful, powdery-woody, ambery-mossy bit that was basically Cabochard. It still has the spotlit movie-star smile of a classical rose chypre, but its feeling of transparency is excitingly new. The drydown is a comfortable slide into fresh musk. Appropriate anywhere that fire-engine-red lipstick is. Now, if you will forgive me a curmudgeonly excursion, let me point out that Rose Alexandrie could have been a Lauder fragrance of twenty years ago, when you could count on a fragrance priced for ordinary humans to be this coherent from top to drydown and made of stuff this good; you didn't have to pay nearly $200 a bottle, journey to a big-city Saks, and deal with some guy in a black turtleneck. TS

Rose Barbare (Guerlain) ★ ★ ★ *ambery rose* $$$
When, following years of rudderless drift after the LVMH purchase, Guerlain finally got a grip on things, they tried to make up for lost time by going upmarket, bringing back some classics, refurbishing and expanding their store at 68 Champs-Elysées, and releasing niche fragrances to regain the artistic high ground. The niche line comes in tall rectangular bottles borrowed straight from Lutens (you get a pained silence when you sadistically point that out to Guerlain PR). Rose Barbare, composed by Francis Kurkdjian, was in the first batch of three. It is a clever, high-quality remake of the fluorescent woody damascone rose of Sinan, Montana's Parfum de Peau, and Lauder's Knowing. RB has all the qualities and faults of the style: 'big boned, handsome, striking, but a little tiresome in the long term. This is among the best, with an intense pepper note that prevents the drydown from becoming too strident. In the same manner, I find Fléchier's Une Rose (Frédéric Malle) more *barbare,* and more interesting. LT

Roseberry (Parfums de Rosine) ★ ★ ★ *blackcurrant bud* $$$
Natural oil of blackcurrant buds has an intense, complicated smell, pulling together the expected fruity cassis, a bright cut-grass green, hissy ammonia-like notes described by perfumers as like "cat piss," and an unmistakable air of sulfur. Roseberry uses all of it at full volume, although it feels more like room spray than like personal fragrance. TS

Rose d'Amour (Parfums de Rosine) ★ ★ ★ ★ *rose chypre* $$$
This cold, dense composition, marked most in the top note by the barn-yard smell of narcissus, seems at first reminiscent of the atmosphere of rooms that have gone unventilated too long. After a time the windows open, and it settles into a handsome, easy green soapy style related to Rive Gauche. It could make a fine masculine. TS

Rose de Feu (Parfums de Rosine) ★ ★ ★ *green rose* $$$
A big green rose with a touch of a Shalimar-like citrus vanilla in the top. It has no particular problems but no particular interest either. TS

Rose de Nuit (Serge Lutens) ★ ★ ★ ★ *rose chypre* $$$
A classic, retro rose chypre in the clean, green, patchouli-focused seven-ties style of Coriandre and cohort, with a magically translucent floral freshness washing it smooth like a river pebble. Adding a ton of osman-thus would bring you close to the ruby translucence of Lutens's legend-ary and defunct Nombre Noir, but instead you get a ton of the rich, green smell of galbanum with your roses. The difference between Nom-bre Noir and Rose de Nuit is the difference between the violet glow of white objects under black light and the same seen under a full moon; in fact, come to think of it, rose chypres seem to reveal a secret kinship between the Parthenon and the disco. They share genes, also, with their green mossy masculine brethren—a bit of Paco Rabanne pour Homme lurks in here. Excellent. TS

La Rose de Rosine (Parfums de Rosine) ★ ★ ★ *nostalgic chypre* $$$
This has the face of a long-gone fragrance, a very old-fashioned, ambery green chypre, like Ma Griffe or Miss Dior, a fragrance for efficient ladies coming out of large cars on their way to impress each other, men being always beside the point. It gets less and less friendly with time. TS

Rose de Siwa (Parfums MDCI) ★ ★ ★ *pale rose* $$$$
A big, linear, pale fresh rose. Nicely done and somewhat dull. LT

Rose d'Eté (Parfums de Rosine) ★ ★ ★ *apple mimosa* $$$
This crisp little number is a sweeter, denser, more powdery take on Tommy Girl. TS

Rose d'Homme (Parfums de Rosine) ★ ★ ★ ★ *floral masculine* $$$
A nicely done, sweet, woody orange blossom for boys: basically, Habit Rouge. TS

Rose Ikebana (Hermès) ★ ★ ★ *polite floral* $$$
I always associate ikebana with other anal-retentive Japanese rituals, like combing sand, picking on trees smaller than you are, and taking forever to brew a cup of tea. These are pastimes for depressed middle-aged women of means. Hermès's flower arrangement is as dull and effete as the real thing, just a nice little rose against a nice woody background. As a relative of mine once said, slumping in an armchair after visiting three Grasse factories awash with roses: "Un peu de merde, s'il vous plait!" LT

Rose Intense (Parfums de Nicolaï) ★ ★ *plasticky milky* $$
This is Patricia de Nicolaï's version of a transparent woody rose in the Mark Buxton style. Out of classical habit, she has fleshed it out with lactones, exactly what it didn't need. Like pouring cream into lemonade. TS

Rose Opulente (Maître Parfumeur et Gantier) ★ ★ ★ *huge rose* $$$
The time has come for me to make a confession. I find roses as flowers pleasant but boring, I like rose in abstract florals, and like TS I find rose soliflores uniformly dull, often borderline unpleasant. This one is excellent and clearly contains scads of high-quality natural rose. But who, aside from bees, would have any interest in someone smelling like this? LT

Rose-Pivoine (Parfums de Nicolaï) ★ ★ ★ *brassy peony* $$
A wonderfully fresh, luminous, and (relatively speaking) natural rose-peony accord, probably the best in this very fashionable and mostly air-headed genre. Shows that talent can transform even the banal. LT

Rose Poivrée (The Different Company) ★ ★ ★ *fruity rose* $$
I could be wrong, but I think I smell a big reformulation. If memory serves me right, Rose Poivrée (Peppered Rose) was once entirely un-presentable, with a heavy dose of the fecal-animalic note of civet and not much rose. I remember it well, because I brought it to dinner with a (gay) male friend of mine who has an interest in perfume, and we both had the same reaction: dirty male underwear. It was exciting, awful, wrong, hilarious, and great. Now, fast-forward to this fragrance of the same name but new vintage. It is a lovely, fresh, high-quality rose with wonderful fruity facets of lychee and raspberries, fruitier on skin and more pink pepper (spicy-herbal, if you like) on paper and fabric. Friendly and robust, one of the better rose soliflores I've en-countered, but, if you don't mind my saying so, I remember when this fragrance had balls. TS

Rossy de Palma (Etat Libre d'Orange) ★ ★ ★ ★ *edgy rose* $$
Some geranium and tea roses, most notably the original Tea Rose and Lutens's Rose de Nuit, achieve a teeth-on-edge effect akin to the grippy froufrou of a fold of crepe rubbed between thumb and forefinger.

RdP joins them: the balance of lemony, hissy green, and smoky notes in this soliflore is nicely judged and works to make this rose edgily uncomfortable, as if asked to sit on a bar stool while wearing a very short skirt. LT

Rouge (Christian Lacroix) ★ ★ *grapefruit milk* $
Remember the scene in the movie *Heathers* in which Winona Ryder's character proposes making another character vomit by serving her a mixture of milk and orange juice? That's the top note here: a small, sad, grapefruit-flavored version of the grand Gucci Rush. Resolves into a mild woody rose of no great distinction. TS

Rouge (Hermès) ★ *floral oriental* $ $
Hermès perfumes went through a bad patch before their recent revival. Rouge smells confused and heavy on the stomach, as if someone had mixed the cheap chocolate notes of Cartier's Must with a flat imitation of Chamade's powdery drydown. Like guests at a misconceived dinner party, the raw materials talk past each other and eventually get into a drunken argument. An embarrassing mess, which Hermès would do well to discontinue. LT

Rousse (Serge Lutens) ★ ★ *anise clove* $$$
Another Lutens from the *période bizarre:* a mulled-wine accord made with clove and cinnamon mixed with an intense rooty-anisic (carrot-seed?) note, adding up to one fine mess. LT

Royal Bain de Caron (Caron) ★ *metallic fruity* $ $
Once called Royal Bain de Champagne, until the region of Champagne complained, RBdC was a masculine fragrance of such tremendous style, humor, and confidence that wearing it seemed guaranteed to make anyone briefly resemble Fred Astaire. You can find a nearly exact replica in today's Flower (Kenzo), but not in today's RBdC, which is a thinner,

metallic fruity scent, reminiscent of the original sweet, powdery melon fougère, but far from good enough to pass you off as aristocracy at the charity ball. TS

Royal Pavillon (Etro) ★ ★ *heavy floral* $ $
An overloaded, floral sweet-green composition that manages to smell cheaply synthetic despite likely being mostly natural. Indigestible, heavy, and confused. LT

Royal Scottish Lavender (Creed) ★ ★ ★ *spicy lavender* $ $ $
I love lavender in exact proportion to its simplicity, and feel that it no more needs bolstering than a pashmina scarf needs whalebone stays. The rather good lavender in here is completely flattened by a powerful woody-spicy accord, like a choirboy trying to keep up with the Three Tenors. LT

Le Roy Soleil Homme (Salvador Dalí) ★ ★ *sweet herbaceous* $
A blatant remake of Eternity for Men, arguably better in the drydown. LT

RSVP (Kenneth Cole) ★ *woody amber* $ $
A cheap clone of Envy for Men that comes laden with one of those mutant woody-amber drydown notes (Karanal? Ambrocenide?) that are so diabolically intense and high-pitched they could be used to make people confess to crimes they did not commit. LT

Rubj (Vero Profumo) ★ ★ ★ ★ *pale rose* $ $ $
Rubj is Vero Kern's floral, a pale, saline, but entirely comfortable accord of jasmine and rose. Its character is reminiscent of de Nicolaï's Odalisque, only slightly warmer and fruitier. Recommended. LT

Rubylips (Salvador Dalí) ★ ★ ★ *woody fruity* $
The top notes of this strange fragrance (credited to three Firmenich

perfumers, a sure sign of a snaggy project) are very interesting in the manner of Oyédo and Inhale, with a citrus-woody Japanese-gummy accord that works beautifully and commands full attention for five minutes. The thing then snaps shut like a fan and carries on as a fresh floral of no particular interest. LT

Rumeur (Lanvin) ★ *white floral* $$
Baseless. TS

Rush (Gucci) ★ ★ ★ ★ *lactonic chypre* $
Has anyone ever made a more perfect fragrance for a night out? Tom Ford reportedly took about two seconds to say yes to the formula after smelling it, and if anyone seems to take longer, hand him a deconges-tant. When this milky, woody, peachy-jasmine in its opaque red plastic rectangle arrived in shops, it had a bit of the shock of Dylan going electric: though Rush had the bone structure of the kind, cuddly lactonic florals that had kept nice girls smelling good for decades, it came in a joyful fuzz of hair spray and noise, with a delicious, dissonant Habanita-like base of patchouli-vetiver-vanilla putting a growl in its voice. This is not a fragrance for office, theater, or fine dining; it announces its sloppy good mood for miles about, and woe to anyone in the vicinity who planned on using his sense of smell for anything else. This is large-scale outdoor art. And what's more, though it smells so new, so confident, so reckless, so of-the-moment, Rush manages at every stage to feel cozy and alive, never a cold stranger—this creature may be from outer space, but its blood is warm. TS

Rush II (Gucci) ★ ★ *fresh rose* $
As if to apologize for the behavior of its Amy Winehouse older sister, Rush II is a pale tea-rose accord with a weird banana-peel note, of no great interest. This is the kind of fragrance that you sniff around for on the smelling strip as if trying to find a clue to its structure, only to realize after a while that it is a one-liner, and a dull one at that. LT

Sables (Annick Goutal) ★ ★ ★ ★ *immortelle amber* $$

In 1985, Goutal came out with Sables, which many (including me) reckon to be her best fragrance. Rumor has it that it was composed by Goutal for her husband, lucky man. It is an object lesson in the use of the difficult burnt-sugar/fenugreek note of immortelle (aka everlasting flower or helichrysum). Immortelle always sticks out, like a giant César thumb sculpture, of any composition, so Goutal chose, simply and cleverly, to give it a pedestal of very conventional sweet amber on which to show off. I had not smelled it for some years, and the present version seems a touch drier, less sweet than the old, and all the better for it. A wonderfully original and satisfying fragrance. LT

Sacrebleu (Parfums de Nicolaï) ★ ★ ★ ★ *dusky oriental* $$

If you travel at night on Europe's railways, near big stations you can sometimes see lights the size of a teacup nestled between the rails, shining the deepest mystical blue-purple light through a filthy Fresnel glass. They appear to be permanently on, suggesting that the message they convey to the train driver is an eternal truth. Since childhood I have fancied the notion it may not be a trivial one like "Buffers ahead" but something numinous and unrelated to duty, perhaps "Life is beautiful" or some such. Sacrebleu has the exact feel of those lights, a low hum that may be eclipsed by diurnal clamor but rules supreme when, at 3 a.m., you know you are looking into your true love's eyes even though you can't see them. LT

Sacré Coeur (Ego Facto) ★ *citrus herbal* $$

A cheap derivative of L'Eau Bleue, itself not exactly big budget. TS

Safari for Men (Ralph Lauren) ★ ★ *aromatic fougère* $

Sufficiently trashy to be wearable if the effect you're after is "Burt Reynolds on a bearksin rug." LT

Safran Troublant (L'Artisan Parfumeur) ★ ★ ★ ★
saffron vanilla $$$
A simple test to detect a non-native French speaker is to have him or her say "un bon vin blanc." One or the other of those nasal vowels is bound to trip you up. I imagine many people will be pointing to Safran Troublant rather than asking for it. Just act familiar, and call it ST. It is based on a very novel and interesting idea, an accord of rose, vanilla, and saffron I have never encountered before. What is odd is that the saffron, though not particularly milky on its own, has a cream-like effect on the other notes and gives this fragrance the caressing, almost moist feel and color of the best chamois leather. Seemingly uncomplicated, but high art at heart. LT

Saks Fifth Avenue for Her (Bond No. 9) ★ ★ ★ *peach tuberose* $$$
Essentially a remake of the wonderfully peachy-bright tuberose of Fracas and Carolina Herrera, but with a ton of the smoky, blown-out-candle smell of the peach lactone material, which usually vanishes in composition. Mistake or not, I rather like it. TS

Saks Fifth Avenue for Him (Bond No. 9) ★ *woody amber* $$$
I'm not a fan of the curiously large number of Bond masculines that seem to follow this overdone, bare modern theme: a powerful woody amber, a citrus, a screechy synthetic lavender. Given that the brand has produced Great Jones and New Haarlem, they're clearly capable of doing better for the guys. TS

Sa Majesté la Rose (Serge Lutens) ★ ★ ★ *crisp rose* $$$
Her Majesty the Rose is a literal, crisp rose with a garden air in the sexless English style, via lots of soapy-lemony aldehydes and citronellol. I imagine it repels mosquitoes well, but whether you love it depends on how you feel about straightforward roses. (I prefer them on the stem, myself.) TS

Sampaquita (Ormonde Jayne) ★ ★ ★ *light jasmine* $ $
A polished but soft, boneless floral, with a soapy lily of the valley playing lead in a grassy, fresh white-flowers accord. I'd expect a fragrance named for a type of jasmine (sambac) to be much more specific than this, but it still smells nice, though not necessary. TS

Samsara (Guerlain) ★ ★ ★ ★ *sandalwood jasmine* $
As with *Star Wars: Attack of the Clones*, the case of Samsara is fascinating first because it was so bad, second because it was so big, and third because it was happening to a beloved franchise. Samsara, appropriately enough, is named after the Hindu cycle of death and rebirth, and it was both a beginning and an end in the Guerlain story, a fragrance in which the things that had always gone right were tainted by the things that have gone wrong since. It was meant to be Guerlain's entry in the Opium-Cinnabar sweepstakes, the prize being the heart and dollar of the eighties perfume buyer with her love for costume-drama orientals in red bottles. Guerlain should have been ready for the challenge, since it already had a couple of glamorous classic orientals in Vol de Nuit and Shalimar, but what Guerlain wanted was something modern, and by modern, they meant something you could smell a quarter mile away. Samsara was sweet, complicated, and loud. It was the signature scent of my best friend from college, she being a larger-than-life personality for whom a perfume with a reach smaller than the Metropolitan Opera House would have felt too demure. (I realize she may never speak to me again after reading this review.) I had long written Samsara off as bombastic and unsubtle when I picked it up to review it today. Hindsight humbles. It is, in every sense but one, a Guerlain in the classic style, with top-notch, rich jasmine and ylang-ylang playing the full, vast white-floral chord from banana to licorice and grass, and tons of the delectably complex burnt-sugar amber we loved so much in Attrape-Coeur: in other words, high-quality materials working in concert to provide a lovely plush effect. Except for that sandalwood. I'm told that Samsara used to feature quite a bit of excellent real sandalwood from India as

well as the pottery-shattering synthetic Polysantol for which it is infamous: a smell so thundering you can almost hear it coming if you put your ear to the ground. Mysore sandalwood is now all but unattainable, due to Indian government regulation of the endangered source, so Samsara seems to have gotten only more synthetic. Sadly, beyond the beautiful florals lurks an indigestibly heavy, artificial praline-and-coconut confection, like those evil cookies the Girl Scouts sell called Samoas: they give you a stomachache while you're just looking at the box. Rumor has it, contrary to the official company story, that Samsara was the first Guerlain fragrance composed by an outside perfumer. True or not, Samsara felt to many like an irreversible break with tradition, confirmed by the subsequent (awful) releases of Mahora and Champs-Elysées. TS

Sandalwood (Floris) ★ ★ ★ *dry sandalwood* $ $
Like it says, this is sandalwood: dry, faintly lemon-rosy, and without the creamy side of the material. Heavily synthetic but decent. TS

Floris used to make a great, sweet, powdery natural sandalwood until, I believe, the eighties, and it was by a mile their best fragrance. Due, one assumes, to difficulties in supply and/or rising prices, it was discontinued. This revival is clearly a synthetic and I am almost completely anosmic to it, which suggests it may be an isobornyl cyclohexanol. LT

Sand and Sable (Coty) ★ ★ ★ *peachy lilac* $
I feel like one of those Impulse body spray ads: If you like Carolina Herrera, you'll love Sand and Sable! This floral is a lot cheaper, however, starting with a Fracas-like tuberose but diminishing fast to a bare lilac. Stays likable a long time, but in a pushy way. We all have friends like that. TS

Sander for Men (Jil Sander) ★ ★ ★ *dry wood* $ $
This Jacques Cavallier creation from 1999 piles on the dryness a mile high. Let me quote from the list of materials that make up this ramrod-

straight fragrance: cardamom, clary sage, pepper, geranium, violet, cypress, spearmint, cedarwood, guaïac wood. With that kind of CV, you don't expect much languor. This is the last smell you remember before the wearer fires you. LT

Sanguine (Keiko Mecheri) ★ ★ *fresh citrus* $$
This fresh, bright orange-peel scent is pleasant but thin, no match for truly wonderful citrus fragrances like Eau de Guerlain or Chanel's Eau de Cologne. TS

Santal (Floris) ★ ★ *spicy woody* $$
A bare, woody-spicy fragrance very much in the nineties masculine mold, cheap and boring. LT

Santal Blanc (Serge Lutens) ★ ★ ★ *fruity sandalwood* $$$
Between this and Lutens's Santal de Mysore, I'll take this more lighthearted study of sandalwood's charms, with its bright, fresh floral shine and raisin sweetness. TS

Santal de Mysore (Serge Lutens) ★ ★ ★ *rum cask* $$$
Sandalwood oil from Mysore, India, was for a long time both fairly cheap and gorgeous—which is probably why it was overharvested to the point of needing government protection. I have a small reference sample of the real thing, with its inimitably creamy, tangy smell of buttermilk. I have no idea if Santal de Mysore manages to use any of it or if it depends on the Australian sandalwood (totally different plant and material) or synthetics, because it aims to cover any gaps with an overpowering coconut-and-caramel accord reminiscent of Samsara, a tropical fantasy of rum in oak barrels for armchair pirates. TS

Santal Impérial (Creed) ★ ★ *not sandalwood* $$$
There is so little legally obtained sandalwood left in India that any "santal" fragrance, no matter how highfalutingly named, is usually made

today of Australian sandalwood (nice but totally different species) or a combination of synthetics (cheap, fairly pleasant but basically sweet woods rather than real sandalwood). This seems to fall into the latter category. I think a moratorium should be put on all sandalwoods until they find a reliable supply of the real stuff. LT

Santal Noble (Maître Parfumeur et Gantier) ★ ★ ★
modern sandalwood $$
Indian sandalwood is nigh unobtainable at the moment, and this one is clearly the Australian variety, which smells good but nothing like the real thing. LT

Santos (Cartier) ★ ★   *woody oriental* $$
A strange beast, in a style that has aged badly. A sweet, woody oriental, a sort of hairy-chested brother to Paco Rabanne pour Homme. Neither very original nor very pleasant. If you like this stuff, get Yatagan. LT

Sarrasins (Serge Lutens) ★ ★ ★ ★ ★   *leather floral* $$$
It is said that the young Belgian composer Guillaume Lekeu fainted upon hearing for the first time the fourth chord of Wagner's *Tristan* and had to be carried away on a stretcher. Were he around today, cured of Wagner and now passionate about fragrance, I would have him sit down before smelling the first few minutes of Sarrasins, and would keep some 4711 handy to revive him if needed. Sarrasins (Saracens) starts with a tremendous blast of properly indolic jasmine. Just when you are finished saying "Very nice" and are beginning to form the thought "Where is this white floral going next?" it briefly modulates to what you think is going to be a dark, minor-mode leather note and immediately afterward startles you with a refulgent blast of apricots. The leather-apricots accord smells to me like osmanthus, and the duet with jasmine then carries on satisfyingly for hours. I've been a Lutens fan from day one, but of late had trouble liking several fragrances that felt oddly loud, even crude. This one is in a completely different league in both intent and execution,

an ambitious, abstract, large, rich, sweeping thing of beauty that smells fantastic on skin, is devoid of any overt orientalism, and could just as well have formed part of the new Chanel collection. A minor word of caution: the fragrance is colored an intense purple and stains paper and fabric almost as wine would. LT

Scandal (Roja Dove) ★ ★ ★ *rose tuberose* $$$$
Here is the Fracas tuberose perfume taken to the absolute limit, made preposterously intense by way of a liqueur-like rose streaked through with apricot and raspberry. It is enormously rude and will cause everyone sitting next to you to push his plate away after one bite and to lean back while talking to you as if you've clutched him in a tango. Good materials, very competently done, but frightening. TS

Scarlett (Keiko Mecheri) ★ ★ ★ *green woody* $$$
This is a poisonously green-smelling masculine, with an alarmingly bitter neroli accord paired with a friendly spice-and-wood oriental, like a fellow who wants to shake your hand specifically to crush it. TS

Scent (Costume National) ★ ★ ★ *fruity amber* $$
The generic name must be tongue in cheek, because this Scent seems rigorously standard by current measures: fluorescent pink berries, a tea backdrop for that fresh and clean feeling, and a crowd-pleasing synthetic drydown of sweetened woody amber, sheer as flesh-colored nylons and guaranteed to broadcast friendliness. Admirably, it does do that, at length and at a distance, though occasionally it begs the question: Is there such a thing as absolute of plastic beachball? TS

Scent (Theo Fennell) ★ ★ ★ ★ *saffron musk* $$$
Theo Fennell is a British jeweler who sells, among many other essential and desirable things, a solid silver lid for a Marmite tin. His Scent, composed by Christophe Laudamiel, is a wonderful surprise. Pitched as an "old-fashioned" fragrance, it is in fact nothing of the sort, rather a mod-

ern masterpiece. It starts with a remarkably creamy-fresh and radiant accord of saffron and musk. Just when you think "That's really nice, whatever next?" it turns into a Guerlain Transformer. First a lavender-vanillic note kicks in that makes it sidle up to Mouchoir de Monsieur. An hour later it has morphed into a warm woody-powdery fragrance (say Attrape-Coeurs). Later still an intense woody-ambery accord brings it perilously close to Héritage and therefore to all the Héritages-in-drag current at the moment, like Chance. At this point TS and I were ready to watch it drive off that cliff and fall into nasty-drydown hell. It teetered on the edge for a while, retreated, and, amazingly, went back after twenty-four hours on the strip to the musky-saffron accord of the start. All the while, it amply satisfied the Guy Robert criterion: "A perfume must smell good." It is hard to say whether Scent Is better as a masculine or a feminine. Either way, original, memorable, and technically brilliant. LT

Scent 79 Man (Jil Sander) ★ ★ ★ ★ *cigarette wood* $ $
A languid, chilly smell of damp-leafy green notes, dry wood, and un-smoked cigarette that could make you nostalgic for the days when people smoked in bars. Perfumer Mark Buxton has composed that modern anomaly: a well-crafted masculine. Directly descended from the "cold pipe" of Monsieur Rochas, 79 is a welcome throwback to a more debonair sort of fragrance and makes me think wistfully of five o'clock shadows and that mesmerizing, moving sculpture of tension lines and curved bulk that is a masculine forearm. A fragrance for men who own no baseball caps. TS

Scent 79 Woman (Jil Sander) ★ ★ ★ ★ *fruity galbanum* $ $ $
Since this guide was first published, we've received many e-mails from readers desperate to replace a vanished perfume-love, usually from the seventies or eighties, either discontinued or reformulated, and of the creamy-green floral genre (see Ivoire and relations) that has been out of fashion for roughly twenty years. Some genius at Jil Sander may have

been intercepting our e-mails when he or she told Evelyne Boulanger at Symrise to reincarnate such a floral in the modern mold, which is to say, with fruit added. A slug of cordial is not always perfume poison; much as Chinatown refurbished the old Givenchy III format with a glorious dose of peach and vanilla, Scent 79 redoes Chanel No. 19 with the same. Hallelujah, it works and is gorgeous. TS

Scent of Peace (Bond No. 9) ★ ★ *fruity floral* $$$
Bond No. 9 aimed for an unpretentious crowd-pleaser with this cheerful grapefruit-and-cassis floral. If you've always wanted to smell like shampoo but your fear of running water prevented you from realizing your dream, this is for you. TS

Sea and Sun in Cadaqués (Salvador Dalí) ★ *metallic grapefruit* $
Smells like ether up top, but sadly does not lend itself to solvent abuse. LT

Sécrétions Magnifiques (Etat Libre d'Orange) ★ ★ ★ ★ ★
nautical floral $$
Stupendous secretions! The Dada name had me drooling. The fragrance is both less and far more than I expected: It is not an animalic (supposedly) raunchy thing that works on the assumption that we collect soiled underwear or frequent the same nightclubs as cats and dogs. It is, however, an elegant fresh floral in the manner of Parfums de Nicolaï's Odalisque, given a demonic twist by a touch of a stupendous bilge note, which, my vibrational nose tells me, can only be a nitrile. I remember years ago mounting an impassioned defense of a forgotten Quest material called Marenil, which smelled just like that: oily, metallic, entirely wrong, and begging to be used intelligently. I'm delighted to see it was possible. LT

Secret Obsession (Calvin Klein) ★ *fruity wood* $$
When asked "what makes a great fragrance?" I mumble something about great fragrances being abstractions greater than the sum of their

parts and having recognizable soul and competent construction. And then there are Poison and Amarige, which meet these criteria but not the vital one: *un parfum doit sentir bon.* Meet another horror of distinction. Secret Obsession is a plastic-flavored, toxic mystery fruit related to viscous neon-orange home fragrance oils of bad times past; it brings to mind things people once sprayed on shag carpets in dorms to cover up the smell of vomit, and which made you miss the vomit; it triumphs over all other local odors; it makes you Google "migraine treatment" and "environmental hazards perfume." That said, though you could argue that it derives from the rose-pepper-wood of Parfum Sacré, it is uniquely ugly at any distance, therefore ideal for people who buy perfume and "don't want to smell like everyone else." Try this and ask yourself: are you sure? TS

Secret Wish (Anna Sui) ★ *fruity floral* $
A secret not worth keeping. LT

Sel de Vetiver (The Different Company) ★ ★ ★ ★ *savory iris* $ $
A beautifully done, rich, rooty accord of iris, patchouli, and vetiver, with a mysterious salty smell like hickory smoke, which drifts in and out of the scene. The whole has an earthy, vegetal, outdoor air, with more than the expected radiance. Curiously, to my nose, SdV, credited to Céline Elléna, has a lot in common with Terre d'Hermès, which her father did the same year (2006), but they develop differently, with SdV following a crisp, green narrative, and Terre d'Hermès headed in a stronger, nutty-coumarinic direction. TS

Selection (Hugo Boss) ★ *powdery woody* $
The name brings to mind old Sheffield knives, the lowest grade of which was "Selected Steel." Not a bad structure, but a desperately cheap formula. A bare, woody-powdery confection ideal for the man who wants to be as similar to the next guy as freshly minted subcompacts in the factory parking lot. LT

Sélection Verte (Creed) ★ ★ ★ *fresh citrus* $ $ $
A very nice fresh-citrus accord consisting mainly of high-quality lemon oil, verbena, and what smells to me like a touch of bouquet de provence. Unpretentious, straightforward, and zingy. LT

Sel Marin (Heeley) ★ ★ ★ ★ *salty vetiver* $ $ $
We've seen this fresh-salty, bracingly marine idea of citrus, helional, and vetiver before, notably in Diptyque's Virgilio and Miller Harris's Fleurs de Sel, but in truth I think this iteration is the best so far. LT

Sensations (Jil Sander) ★ ★ *floral oriental* $ $
A boring, white-floral oriental with fresh notes, indistinguishable from a hundred others. LT

Sensi (Armani) ★ ★ ★ *woody jasmine* $ $
In the polite manner of YSL's Cinéma, Sensi is a mild floral oriental of woody jasmine with a nice lime top note, adjusted carefully—you imagine a music producer moving all the sliders on the board to exact center—to hit the middle of the road. It's like beige trousers: comfortable, flattering, and unlikely to offend, but unlikely to inspire either. TS

Sensuous (Estée Lauder) ★ ★ ★ *lily sandalwood* $ $
Lauder has long been synonymous with so-called "icy" blondes and abstract, squeaky-clean white florals. Aside from Youth Dew, its orientals (Cinnabar, Spellbound) have always been less assured. This time, to ease the transition, the advertising mixes blondes with brunettes (two each) to signify that New Hampshire and tennis legs have not gone out of style. The four beauties are wearing the same morning-after guy's shirt, lucky man. The message is half prim, half sexy. The fragrance has a tan, creamy texture in which a lily note meshes with vetiver and synthetic sandalwood—synthetic because natural sandalwood oil is, because of restrictions due to overharvesting, missing from the perfumer's palette. Sensuous suffers for it. As always with Lauder, the radiance is

perfectly calibrated and gives a faithful impression at fifteen paces without being loud. However, up close the fragrance disintegrates over the first hour into a bare array of disconnected things failing to cohere: white floral, synthetic wood, praline-like amber. All told, thin and lacking in mystery. LT

Sentiment (Escada) ★ ★ *fruity floral* $
A typical object from the turn of the century: the standard fruity floral. It's pink. It's fruity (grapefruit, red berries). It's floral (rose, violet). It's not sugary enough to be a gourmand, but it's a little sugary. It's harsh, trashy, and sort of awful, a first cousin of Baby Doll Paris. Future civilizations will not understand. TS

Sentiment pour Homme (Escada) ★ *spicy woody* $
Something dull seen occasionally through a wall of white noise. To choose this as your personal fragrance could only be a cry for help. TS

Serge Noire (Serge Lutens) ★ *camphor clove* $$$
Serge, as well as being Lutens's given name, is a type of fabric (in France, generally of silk), so *serge noire* is, roughly, a black twill. You would expect an eponymous fragrance from the dramatic Lutens to be his ultimate personal statement of what a fragrance should be: i.e., a hell of an oriental. Instead, this is an oriental from hell. Serge Noire, in one go, collects all the faults of the Lutens style. It is violently powerful, as is his Gris Clair; concentrates exclusively on the indolic, rubbery, mothball-camphor off-notes of florals, as in Miel de Bois and to lesser extent Fleur d'Oranger and Tubéreuse Criminelle; is cloying, as is Cèdre; has clove in such quantities that you think of dentists; and indulges to the hilt all the hippie clichés of spices and woods, creating an overwhelming funk reminiscent of Chinese herbal cough syrup. All the same, there is a set of values for which this fragrance is the zenith and not the nadir, but I am not a cultural relativist, and I say this is a disaster. TS

Seringa (Floris) ★ ★ *loud floral* $$
A mock-orange floral. Who on earth would want to smell like this? I'm
sure even the flowers, given a choice, would switch fragrance. LT

Serpentine (Cavalli) ★ *fruity amber* $
An off-brand whiskey sour poisoned by your enemies. Run away. TS

S-eX (S-Perfume) ★ ★ ★ ★ ★ *space leather* $$
Felice Bianchi Anderloni, founder of the legendary coach-building firm
Carrozzeria Touring (1926–66), was of the opinion that luxury and chic
were to a large extent mutually exclusive. In many of his forties cars, he
covered the dash with leather and overlaid it with lucite, thereby achieving a properly modern effect that put most other attempts at automotive
elegance to shame. Christophe Laudamiel, it seems to me, shares Anderloni's impatience with the merely plush. S-eX is a leather fragrance in
the grand manner of Cuir de Russie: rich, smooth, and suitably soft,
only overlaid with a shiny plastic accord that obliterates the retro feel
common to most leathers and turns it into the smell of a machine nobody has yet had the good fortune to strap himself into. LT

Sex Appeal for Men (Jovan) ★ ★ ★ ★ *herbal oriental* $
Here is more evidence of the glorious world predating the Great Fall that
occurred in perfumery circa the 1980s. Sex Appeal for Men, dating from
1976, is, to all appearances, an embarrassing artifact of silly seventies
marketing. Inexplicably, I love the ridiculous blue box, which must have
changed little in the last thirty years, with its retro typeface and bold
claims of raw biological effectiveness. Example: "This provocative stim-
ulating blend of rare spices and herbs was created by man for the sole
purpose of attracting woman. At will. Man can never have too much."
(You can almost hear members of the wearer's family shouting, "Put the
bottle down! You have too much!") Mesmerized, I read all of the text in
earnest several times and was ready for the fragrance to be abominable.

It is delightful, a fresh, handsome lavender-and-amber oriental with an affecting, aromatic anisic-woody drydown, which offers the additional satisfaction of costing $20 for three ounces at standard retail. You know, this is what guys who smelled bad used to smell like. It smells great. Whatever happened to us? How have we fallen so far? Was it Watergate? Was it Samsara? Was it cable TV? When will cheesy guys smell good again? T S

Séxual (Michel Germain) ★ ★ ★ *rose oriental* $ $
Despite our sincere protests, the fragrance industry will probably always sell itself as part of the flirtation arsenal. It moves product, after all. Still, there's nothing particularly sexual about Michel Germain's Séxual. Instead, it's an all-out heavy, classic rose, fruity up top, heavy on the eugenol, and cognac-like on the bottom. For rose lovers, it's not bad, but for Sophia Grojsman, who composed Séxual along with perfumer Carlos Benaim, it's nice work, but probably one of the less interesting entries in a rosy repertoire that includes Paris and 100% Love (S-Perfume). T S

Séxual pour Femme (Michel Germain) ★ ★ *sugary fruity* $ $
Another in a seemingly endless series of recent pink, sugary bubblegum florals, as relentlessly perky and brainless as a Stepford wife. T S

Séxual pour Homme (Michel Germain) ★ ★ ★ *herbal soapy* $ $
There's nothing unusual about this classic-smelling masculine, which freshens up the old, reliable soapy green-herbal genre with a touch of the gasoline-and-violets smell of more modern fougères. But it does have a better than-average herbal top note, and holds the tune together well from start to finish. T S

Sexy Darling (Kylie Minogue) ★ *floral dreck* $
Those scoundrels at Coty have been minting money with moronic celebrity fragrances instead of reissuing the great classics. I have many

times stated on record that celebrity pongs are on average not worse than most. Sexy Darling may cause me to rethink: this is so repulsively stupid a composition that I pity the poor girls who will get it as a present and wear it proudly. I know they're thirteen, but think of the damage done. LT

Sexy Little Things (Victoria's Secret) ★ ★ *sugared strawberries* $
Awful, Barbie-pink fruity floral, too garish even for child beauty pageant contestants. Should get one star, but the box whistled at me when I opened it. They get one more for making me laugh. TS

Shaal Nur (Etro) ★ ★ ★ ★ *warm vetiver* $ $
The work that Robertet's Jacques Flori has been doing for Etro in the last two decades is consistently of high standard and deceptively simple. His are complex, classical compositions. To be sure, they are done in an orientalist manner, but without falling into joss-stick or medicinal manners. The best ones achieve a Guerlain-like symphonic richness which, in my experience, results only from great raw materials and skill. Shaal Nur is a woody-warm vetiver, not a million miles from Vol de Nuit but leaner and drier. Very nice. LT

Shalimar (Guerlain) ★ ★ ★ ★ ★ *reference oriental* $ $
I hadn't smelled Shalimar on my hand for years before sitting down to write this, and it was quite a shock to do so. The previous memory had faded to its amber-vanillic drydown, that plush, plum-red velvet whiff that says "evening in Paris" as surely as catching a glimpse of the Eiffel Tower lit up for New Year's. Shalimar reminds me of those weird, garish paint schemes, all bold strokes and vivid colors, used on WWI battleships to make them invisible from a distance. Up close, it is intensely woody-smoky, with huge animalic notes, a sort of Jicky wound up like a seven-day clock. From afar, it is a vanillic amber with merely exceptional reach. Shalimar's effectiveness in the middle distance, like the

range of a gun, tells you what sort of damage it is meant to inflict. It is not intended for the man who smells it too soon, arm in arm on the way to the taxi. Neither is it a proper boudoir fragrance, a sort of extended dessert. Instead, its uniquely sweet, penetrating tune is supposed to deftly command attention at a dinner party, not so loud that you don't know where it's coming from, not so quiet as to be easily outgunned, above all on excellent terms with the food to come. LT

Shalini (Shalini) ★ ★ ★ ★ *fresh tuberose* $$$$
The blurb says Shalini is a "celebration of the emergence of a woman's inner butterfly"—perish the thought. The fragrance, composed by the great Maurice Roucel, is a sleek tuberose-based white floral with a deliciously bitter-fresh, almost fougère-like heart. While very good, it is simply not worth the money. Shalini attempts to settle in that weird part of the lift-versus-drag curve of economics, where the more you charge the more you sell. The 2.2-ounce parfum in the cheesoid neo–Nina Ricci bottle costs $900, though the 1 ounce is more reasonably priced at $400. Only nine hundred bottles were made, so hurry. Or rather, don't. LT

Shanghai Butterfly (Nanette Lepore) ★ *isopropyl alcohol* $$$
Just in case you think this chilly little synthetic amber in the Light Blue style is fabuloso, go home and smell the rubbing alcohol in your medicine cabinet. You could wear that and save cash. Cute bottle, though. TS

Shania (Stetson) ★ ★ *fresh rose* $
A very bare, soapy citrus rose, touch of powder. Not horrid, but not good either. TS

Shania Starlight (Stetson) ★ ★ *citrus floral* $
A weird, green, bare floral with a big citrus top note. You get the feeling it wouldn't be pretty even if they'd had the budget to do it right. TS

Shedonism (Origins) ★ ★ ★ *light tuberose* $$
Never mind the name, which is trying so hard to be hip that it ends up corny—or maybe it's so corny it ends up hip (not being able to tell signifies my having drifted beyond the reach of the zeitgeist). This is a perfectly nice sheer tuberose, nutty-sweet and friendly in the middle, woody in the drydown, and, come to think of it, aside from the top note, nearly identical to the wonderful (and quickly sold out) limited edition Azurée body oil by Tom Ford for Estée Lauder in 2006. Lauder owns Origins and has also released a Lauder scent (Azurée Soleil) based on the oil, in its understandable effort to milk a sleeper hit for all it's worth. TS

Sheer (Matthew Williamson) ★ ★ *woody floral* $$
A powdery-woody laundry-aisle spring floral, in the style of Gaultier's Classique but duller. TS

Sheer Halston (Halston) ★ ★ *melon muguet* $
Although it's a little screechy, this 1998 lily of the valley (of the harsh, not the soft, sort), with its fruit cocktail decorations, does presage the squeaky-clean, "tropical" white florals like Beyond Paradise, which came out a few years later. Unfortunately, it rushes to an unpleasant, bare drydown. TS

Sheer Obsession (Calvin Klein) ★ ★ *suntan lotion* $
A dull, light, cinnamon-vanilla floral oriental, pale beyond detection, not as good as Vanilla Fields. TS

Sheer Stella 2007 (Stella McCartney) ★ *sour floral* $$
A fresh floral that seems to be made entirely from off notes. It manages to combine the boozy wine-dregs aspect of rose, the sweaty-sour feel of green jasmine, and the cheap-laundry side of modern musks. LT

She Wood (Dsquared2) ★ ★ ★ *citrus heliotropin* $
Packaged in wood. Wood in the name. No discernible wood in the fragrance. Perfumer Daphné Bugey has skillfully turned this lemony mimosa into a breezy good time, despite a rough woody amber and what feels like a small budget. It works best in passing, a flowered breeze caught at a distance. Guys could easily wear this instead of the far more expensive Baume du Doge, if they want to play with mimosa. I promise: you barely see "she" on the bottle. TS

Shiloh (Hors là Monde) ★ ★ ★ ★ *gunpowder rose* $$$
Nothing wakes up the pedant in me like inaccurate, pretentious copy in perfume press packs. The makers of Shiloh claim that Hors là Monde is pronounced like Orlamonde and refers to a "beautiful quaint castle" overlooking the French Riviera. Having lived for four years next to said castle, I am in a position to reveal that it is in fact Maurice Maeterlinck's Villa Orlamonde, now a hotel near Nice called Palais Maeterlinck, and that the "là" in Hors là Monde is up there with "Professeur de Parfums" in the annals of mangled French. This said, Shiloh is a sensationally uncompromising fragrance made for those who thought Sinan was soft, Parfum de Peau wimpy, Coriandre a cop out, and Knowing way too quiet. Michel Roudnitska's Shiloh takes the fluorescent woody rose to an extreme that simply cannot be outshone. If Hellboy had an equally brick-red sister, she'd be splashing it on. LT

Sicily (Dolce & Gabbana) ★ ★ *oleaginous floral* $$
Indigestible soapy floral with a weird, rice-like bergamot top note, a sort of sun-faded Bal à Versailles. LT

Sienne l'Hiver (Eau d'Italie) ★ ★ ★ *spiced iris* $$$
Coming out the same year (2006) as Dzongkha for L'Artisan Parfumeur, Sienne l'Hiver, also made by Bertrand Duchaufour, is another variation

on dry woody iris. Sienne l'Hiver could be a classic chypre, somewhere between the oriental spice of Opium and the green hiss of Ma Griffe, but laid out in the sun for a week until totally dry. It feels, in that spot behind the eyes where all perfume overdose headaches live, much stronger than it smells, with tremendous radiance at low power. I prefer Dzong-kha's nutty richness to the dissonant metallic edge of this one, but kudos to Eau d'Italie for a line of consistently unusual, well-worked-out fragrances. TS

Silk Touch (Max Mara) ★ ★ ★ *sour floral* $$
Wholly unoriginal citrus-woody floral, of interest only for a sage-like herbaceous heart note that would make it a tolerable masculine if nothing else were at hand. LT

Silky Underwear solid perfume (LUSH) ★ ★ *cocoa butter* $
Like many people, I loved LUSH's Silky Underwear body powder, which was pretty much scented cornstarch with some cocoa butter added, and thought it was due to the fragrance. As a solid fragrance, an essential cheapness shows through. Turns out I loved the cornstarch. TS

Silver Cologne (Amouage) ★ ★ ★ *complex cologne* $$$$
I assume the term *cologne* refers to the dilution, because this is not the usual accord. As befits a classic masculine fragrance, SC has a transient, spicy start reminiscent of Caron's Yatagan, whereupon the volume is immediately turned down in time for an odd, mimosa (heliotropin) heart note and later a discreet, citrusy chypre-like drydown. Unconventional, natural, and very pleasant. Strongly recommended, a good alternative to Chanel's Pour Monsieur. LT

Silver Mountain Water (Creed) ★ *fresh metallic* $$$$
An unpleasant, hissy-metallic "fresh" fragrance with a strange note of wood glue amid the din. LT

Silver Musk (Nasomatto) ★ ★ *large musk* $ $ $
Musk molecules usually contain between fourteen and sixteen carbon atoms, close to the maximum size a molecule can have and still bind to olfactory receptors. Musks therefore lie at the ragged edge of human perception, and most people will be anosmic to one or more of the commonly used ones. Perfumers usually mix a few to make sure one comes through. Whatever the mixture in Silver Musk is, I can hardly perceive it. Interesting, however, to document the strange olfactory phenomenon akin to blindsight whereby one knows something is there without perceiving it. LT

I probably smell it entire: it's a cheap fougère that makes you automatically say "shaving cream" plus a weird metallic musk. TS

Silver Rain (La Prairie) ★ *Angel clone* $ $
Caution: two different compositions bear this name. These were my comments on the first Silver Rain when it was released: "Aside from dead octopus and isonitriles, the worst smell in the world has to be the tutti-frutti cloud emanating from scented candles in downmarket gift shops. Bottling that loathsome effluvium and selling it for real money does not, on the face of it, look like a good business plan. Yet that is just the bold step taken by the Swiss firm of La Prairie with Silver Rain. Their first fragrance a decade ago was also fruity, so powerful that I put the bottle out of reach of my kids for fear that if they spilled it we'd have to pack up and find another home. Full marks for design coherence, though: this one fully lives up to its plague-of-Egypt name." Others, not least buyers, must have felt the same. SR has been changed. The latest version is an Angel clone, trivial but bearable. LT

Silver Shadow (Davidoff) ★ ★ *woody orange* $
I am an admirer of Francis Kurkdjian, and I dimly see what he was trying to do here: an intense, resinous orange accord on a balsamic back-

ground. But I feel he was not given enough cash to pull it off, and the result smells cheaply hollow. LT

Sira des Indes (Patou) ★ ★ ★ ★ *floral swirl* $$$
Patou in-house perfumer Jean-Michel Duriez is the master of euphoric, swirling top notes (EnJoy, for example), and Sira is no exception. Sira works beautifully in the first twenty minutes, full of rich contrasts between ylang-ylang, frangipani, and animalic notes. Unfortunately, it then settles into a high-calorie tan monochrome not a million miles from Samsara, which, while easy on the nose, lacks conversation. A fragrance one imagines worn at the evening beach party, complete with sarong and hibiscus flower tucked behind the ear. Good stuff, but a bit holiday-of-a-lifetime. LT

Six Scents No. 1 (Six Scents) ★ ★ ★ *passion grapefruit* $$
The story of Six Scents: "A collection of scents that were created by six renowned perfumers working with six celebrated designers. . . . A percent of the net proceeds will go towards awareness and funding for the Designers Against AIDS." No. 1 has a lovely, sparkling tropical-fruit-and-grapefruit top note, a mite bright in the background, a sort of adolescent version of Pamplelune. LT

Six Scents No. 2 (Six Scents) ★ *blankety blank* $$
The designer here, Bernhard Willhelm, chose to emulate Issey Miyake in one of the master's senior moments and requested a fragrance that smelled of water. Like Miyake, he was quite properly fobbed off with a mixture of musk and Calone. LT

Six Scents No. 3 (Six Scents) ★ ★ ★ ★ *woody green* $$
Clever capsicum and wood accord not a million miles away from the first five minutes of Joop!'s wonderful (and now discontinued) What About Adam; pleasant and sprightly. LT

Six Scents No. 4 (Six Scents) ★ *pine citrus* $$
Nothing priced like something. LT

Six Scents No. 5 (Six Scents) ★ *pale stale* $$
Smells like martini dregs. LT

Six Scents No. 6 (Six Scents) ★ *chemical green* $$
For those who take their 2,4-dimethyl cyclo-hexene-3-carbaldehyde neat. LT

Skin Musk (Parfums de Coeur) ★ ★ ★ *sweet musky* $
When I was twelve, I had two fragrances: Chanel No. 5, the aspirational scent I saved my allowance to buy, and Skin Musk, the one I actually wore. This simple, cheap, good smell served in the fraught social circles of junior high society to let potentially hostile tribes know that you approached unarmed. Today it's made by Parfums de Coeur and still smells great in a low-key, unchallenging way: a long-lasting, fresh, powdery musk with a tender amber tone. TS

Snowpeach (Renée) ★ ★ *thin peach* $$
These guys would do well to order a sample of Pierre Nuyens's insanely great Peach Juice base, now at Givaudan: it would save work and show them how to do it properly. LT

Sogni di Mare (Antonia's Flowers) ★ ★ *dissonant green* $$
An odd, sweet-sour confection of vanillic and fruity-green notes, undemanding and pleasant, the sort of thing that my daughter (age seven) would love. LT

Soir de Lune (Sisley) ★ *woody rose* $$
Unextraordinary woody floral. LT

Soleil de Rochas (Rochas) ★ ★ *tropical fruity* $
A screechy sweet-and-sour floral in the current style: candy fruit flavors and a sugary orange blossom. TS

Solo Loewe Eau de Cologne Intense (Loewe) ★ ★ ★
melon fougère $ $
A prim and elegant French friend of mine took samba lessons and explained to me that moving her hips had proved beyond her because even a millimetric oscillation "made her feel like a whore." Masculine fragrances have a similar problem: they must signal modernity, adventurousness, and originality by movements so small that nobody will suspect girliness, with the effect that nobody notices them. If you are attuned to these microexpressions, SL is pathbreaking. Otherwise, it's just another boring guy thing. LT

So New York (Bond No. 9) ★ ★ ★ *sugar Angel* $ $ $
Bond offers two fragrances based on Mugler's much-copied Angel: Nuits de Noho, which is the white-floral heart of Angel, and So New York, which is the chocolate-and-fruit part. Neither is as interesting as Angel itself, but they're probably aimed at fussy people who nearly liked Angel except [fill in the blank]. TS

Songes (Annick Goutal) ★ ★ ★ ★ *woody jasmine* $ $
A neoclassical fragrance that radiates perfect mastery of time, Songes begins with a glorious natural jasmine accord and moves through a series of scene changes, coming close to a woody-powdery core distantly related to Habit Rouge, and eventually settling into a rich, long-lasting wood-vanilla white-flowers drydown of great refinement. Another Goutal classic. LT

So Pretty (Cartier) ★ ★ ★ ★ *blackcurrant chypre* $ $
After Escada made the world safe for big fruity florals with their Chiffon Sorbet in 1993, everyone started looking to the punch bowl for ideas. So

Pretty (1995) is Cartier's upmarket version of what was an essentially downmarket idea: a lovely rose slumming it with the Body Shop's Dewberry. Yet, unlike the condescending variations to come in the fruity-floral genre, this one isn't scumbled up with a hideous mess of a drydown. Instead, aside from that berry, it adheres to a classic peachy-powdery recipe—this is a Mitsouko with a shot of crème de cassis. TS

Sottile (YOSH) ★ ★ ★ ★ *tea rose* $$$
Neither I nor LT is any fan of rose soliflores, but if you're in the market for a tea rose, this is absolutely perfect: lemony fresh and pleasant, with a soapy cleanness from lily of the valley and just enough clove to give it a tingle. It has none of the pucker-mouthed vinegary aspect that makes other rose soliflores so uncomfortable to be around. TS

Soudain (Fragonard) ★ ★ ★ *salty citrus* $$
A light citrus herbal cologne, with a suite of herbs (to my nose, basil and bay) that give it some of the savor of salt-preserved lemons. TS

Sounds & Visions (By Mark Buxton) ★ ★ *dull fresh* $$$
A cheap-smelling, sad little "sports" fragrance that has no business coming from Buxton and being sold at this price. LT

Sous le Vent (Guerlain) ★ ★ ★ ★ *dry chypre* $$$$
I had prayed for a reissue of Sous le Vent for twenty years, since I smelled a sample of the old stuff on a friend's shelf. I remember a rich, aquiline green chypre in the manner of Piguet's Futur, a Katharine Hepburn sort of fragrance, great with a houndstooth jacket and two-tone shoes. The reissue seems very different from my recollection, and I am not sure whether my memory or Guerlain's is at fault. The modern SlV is a spare, lanky fragrance composed of beautifully judged distinct notes with plenty of air in between: dry citrus, green galbanum, oakmoss, dry woods, and a surprising soft spot of ylang-ylang that comes in and out of focus as the fragrance evolves. Stylish, entirely devoid of any typically

Guerlain curvaceous clichés, but in the last analysis at once very handsome and a touch dull. LT

Les Souveraines d'Egypte (Roméa d'Améor) ★ ★ *amber floral* $$$
Crème brûlée doused with L'Air du Temps. LT

Spellbound (Estée Lauder) ★ *medicated treacle* $
Powerfully cloying and nauseating. Trails for miles. Frightens horses. Gets worse. TS

S-Perfume (S-Perfume) ★ ★ ★ *subliminal musky* $$
The original was called Jet-Set and was created by Alberto Morillas for Nobi Shioya (Sacré Nobi), a sculptor fascinated with perfume. I never smelled the original, but Christophe Laudamiel has "remixed" the scent to make S-Perfume, mysteriously illustrated with a line drawing of a spermatozoon curled like an integral sign, swimming for the top. Laudamiel must have been sculpting effects on a nanoscale, since the impression is of a vanishingly quiet musk, but beautifully complex once you get into it: fresh floral, lactonic fruity, powdery-woody, with a slightly waxy impression, a top-to-bottom composition occurring at the threshold of detection, like a symphony playing at frequencies only children can hear. TS

It says on the package: "S-perfume is not recommended to people who are anosmic to Galaxolide." I am hyposmic to it, so I cannot report on the fragrance, which I find very weak. LT

Spigo (Profumo di Firenze) ★ ★ ★ ★ *excellent lavender* $$$$
Someone once told me a story about the perfumers at Chanel gathering to evaluate manufacturers' samples of solvent ethanol by diluting them with distilled water in a brandy glass, swirling the mix around, and smelling the impurities as they took flight to escape the flood. Lavender (chiefly another alcohol, linalool) is similar in that small amounts of

impurities decide whether the smell is pleasant or not after the first blast. The way to evaluate a lavender, therefore, is to put a copious amount on one's forearm, wait five minutes, and smell the dry residue. It should not contain any harsh notes. Surprisingly few lavenders make the grade, but this one certainly does, with no bad news in the drydown, just a discreet warm-rosy-citrus background. Simple stuff, but very nice. LT

Spiritueuse Double Vanille (Guerlain) ★ ★ *bad vanilla* $$$$
Anyone who has bought vanilla in pods knows that they do not smell very good up close, with dissonant fruity, rum-like notes that make you feel like skipping lunch. Guerlain obligingly magnifies all the negative traits of vanilla in this pointless, loud, and misconceived confection. LT

Spiritus/land (Miller et Bertaux) ★ ★ ★ *soapy woody* $$$
This is a low-key aromatic fougère, a little wood and a little patchouli with a brushup of spice: an old-fashioned, simple formula, pleasantly reminiscent of Dad's soap-on-a-rope. TS

Sport (Benetton) ★ *wet weekend* $
Reviewing masculine sport fragrances is a bit like attempting to write short stanzas about individual matches in a matchbox. This thing is as gray and nondescript as the packaging, and appears to contain only one ingredient, a sour little synthetic laundry musk. LT

Spring Flower (Creed) ★ ★ ★ *fruity floral* $$$
Given that fruity florals are (1) legion and (2) with few exceptions, like Badgley Mischka, uniformly ditzy, expectations are low. This one goes to the middle of the pack: it is adequately done, smells more natural than the worst, and does what the hideous pack implies, i.e., create a pink-colored cloud of soapy candyfloss. LT

Spring in Paris (Celine Dion) ★ ★ ★ *fruity floral* $
A pleasantly tart version of the ubiquitous fruity floral. There's something appealing about the contrast between milky and sharp here, similar to the marvelous, massively lactonic fruity-floral chord of Badgley Mischka. TS

Stargazer (YOSH) ★ ★ ★ *boxwood lily* $$$
A strange green floral of trimmed hedges and white flowers, with a poisonous air. Something in it makes me think of a purple cough syrup my mother used to force me to drink. That said, I rather like it. TS

Starwalker (Mont Blanc) ★ *citrus woody* $$
Astronauts report that it smells terrible aboard the space station, what with the small space, recycled air, and bodies close together. It'd be more nauseating, however, if they were wearing this. TS

Stella (Stella McCartney) ★ ★ ★ *salty musk* $
A floral musk in the style of Narciso Rodriguez for Her and Sarah Jessica Parker's Lovely, but with a tight-lipped rose instead of come-hither white flowers, Stella is a fragrance for women who programmatically say no. Judging by the press materials and the resulting scent, I suspect McCartney went in proclaiming a fondness for roses and a long list of "do not" commandments—do not be loud, do not be sweet, do not be heavy—because after the slightly harsh peony start, it gets apologetic: a muted, salty patchouli-musk designed to avoid complaints because it's not obviously perfume. Okay on a guy, I'd wager. TS

Stella in Two Amber (Stella McCartney) ★ ★ ★ *floral musk* $$
My expectations were low for this half of the Stella fragrance (see Stella in Two Peony for the other). Surprisingly, the simple rose-amber fragrance within the unexpectedly heavy, tiny metal compact is affecting, if unoriginal: a romantic, slightly powdery, nostalgic sweetness like

those horribly twee Irish melodies that get you choked up against your will. Then I realized: it's close to the old standby Ombre Rose, though less radiant and a little thin, as if it were whistling a tune you first heard played by a full band. As time goes on, it makes me think a little of Old Spice. TS

Stella in Two Peony (Stella McCartney) ★ ★ ★ *woody floral* $$
Weird idea, this one. According to the Web site, perfumer Jacques Cavallier took the original Stella fragrance and split it into halves, respectively named Peony and Amber. The stuff comes in a square bottle the color of what in Milan they call *trasù* (red-wine vomit). The fragrance is hilariously off-message, actually a pretty good, slightly sour masculine not a million miles from L'Eau Bleue (the Web site acknowledges this, calling it a "more masculine yet sexy signature") despite the brassy top notes. Who will wear this? Girls won't want to, and guys won't dare. Shame, because it would have made a pretty good submission for the next Masculine Floral Revival, due any day now. LT

Stella Rose Absolute (Stella McCartney) ★ ★ ★ *frowning rose* $
This misnamed fragrance, with its subdued, melancholy woody aura, is like the original Stella, only more so. On paper, it gives a lemony rose with patchouli-incense undertones, but on skin it seems more like the smell of hair that needs washing. Vaguely related to Voleur de Roses, but with the prim asexuality of a stereotypical maiden aunt (hair in bun, wire-rim spectacles, clothes the color of dishwater), this kind of thing is probably better on a guy, or at least sprayed on fabric. TS

Stephanotis (Floris) ★ ★ ★ *floral bouquet* $$
The wedding-bouquet flower is represented by this solid if uninspiring mixed floral of mostly carnation and jasmine, with a pleasant warm-candlewax background. Supposedly dates from 1768. TS

Stephen Jones (Comme des Garçons) ★ ★ ★ ★
aldehydic poblano $$$

A perfumer friend of mine once brought me samples of the aldehydes used in Chanel No. 5, and I made the mistake of uncorking them at dinner, despite pleas for me to stop. These blindingly bright aromachemicals, when pure, smell simultaneously of lemon peel, incense, and blown-out candles, effects generally lost in floral settings. The mad fragrance that hatter Stephen Jones has done with Comme des Garçons cheekily plays these off-notes up, not down, to make an aldehydic sweet floral of thrilling weirdness, a Chanel No. 22 with a top note of fried green peppers and overheated inkjet printer. So bright it makes White Linen look in need of a hot wash. TS

Stetson (Stetson) ★ ★ ★ ★ *floral oriental* $

How often does a perfume make you giggle uncontrollably? Stetson, bottled since 1981, is plainly for men. The box is a sober, manly box in two stony, manly colors. There are pictures of manly cowboys lassoing (manly) horses. The manly promo copy on the manly back says, "The legendary fragrance of the American West. A rich, masculine blend of rugged woods and spice." Well, shine my spurs, this is a masculine? I could've sworn it was a crisp, classical feminine oriental in the style of Tabu and Youth Dew, with that classic Coca-Cola brightness, an animalic jasmine to fill it out, and powdery, leathery balsamic woods to finish: an old-fashioned structure that still works a treat. It's gorgeous, as rugged and masculine as the lingerie level at Saks Fifth Avenue, and about ten bucks per ounce. I'd truly love a man who wore this, but in the absence of one, I'll gladly wear it myself. TS

Stetson Black (Stetson) ★ ★ ★ *green woody* $

It's yet another green-apple, leafy masculine. All the same, sweet spice and balsamic touches and restraint in the region of strident woody ambers make it better than many others in the genre. Sadly, the Stetson Black man is clearly a more timid, conformist creature than the delightfully transgressive original Stetson man. TS

Stetson Untamed (Stetson) ★ ★ ★ *toasted marshmallow* $

I'm not exactly sure what there is about this woody, nutty scent, with its reassuring smells of cardboard and cotton candy, that is either feral or related to sexy cowboys, as the box indicates it should be. It's cozy, though, and easy to imagine on the big, harmless guys that women call "teddy bears." TS

Stoned (Solange) ★ ★ ★ ★ *patchouli vanilla* $$$$

This hybrid of Habanita, Shalimar, and Vanilia attempts the ultimate amber oriental by combining features of past greats. This means, along with the usual vanilla and balsams, you find powdery heliotropin, patchouli, citrus, and crisp vetiver modernized with a big dose of cotton candy. Attractive, rich, sweet, and plush as anyone could want, but terribly familiar and somehow out of focus from all angles. In other words, this is loving pastiche, but not as distinctive as its forebears and much more expensive. It claims to be mixed with "diamond dust," which has no perceptible effect, though I haven't tried to sharpen the kitchen knives with it. TS

Story (Paul Smith) ★ ★ *thin vetiver* $

A clean little vetiver, pleasant enough but lacking a plot. LT

Straight to Heaven (By Kilian) ★ ★ *unfinished oriental* $$$$

Skimpy, dull little composition marred by a big dose of a woody-amber synthetic that feels like an ultrasonic dog whistle right next to your ear. LT

Sublime (Jean Patou) ★ ★ ★ *vetiver amber* $$

Sublime was a masterpiece in the grand manner, in my opinion Jean Kerléo's finest work. It is based on a precarious balance between two boulder-sized accords, one being the creamiest, sweetest vanillic amber imaginable, the other a lofty, fresh woody-amber vetiver composition. I cannot make sense of the Sublime sample Patou just sent. On the one hand, everyone at Patou swears blind it has not been messed with. On the other hand, it seems wrong, incoherent, less stately at both ends, as if the two boulders had been replaced with papier-mâché rocks of the sort that stagehands push around during operatic scene changes. The overall thing is the same size as the original, but the grandeur is gone. LT

Summer (Kenzo) ★ ★ ★ *milky mimosa* $
An evanescent little milk-powder floral with a hint of peanut: melancholy, pale, peculiar. TS

Sun (Jil Sander) ★ ★ *heavy oriental* $
Jil Sander perfumes are usually pretty good, but this one is an exception, a Loulou-like oriental accord that feels heavy and overripe from start to finish. LT

Sung (Alfred Sung) ★ *jasmine diaper* $ $
If memory serves me right, Sung was really wonderful once. I wore it when I was sixteen or so, and I found it immediately impressive and broadly appealing, like a six-foot floral arrangement for a hotel lobby— likable and noticeable with no motive but to say hello in a hearty tone. I recall it as a soapy-green jasmine bolstered by tobacco and woody notes, which went well with the smell of my suede jacket. Why do the bastards change things? Why? Today, a ton of animalic, overtly fecal notes try to make up for lost complexity, but they just end up smelling poopy. I miss my Sung. TS

Sunset Heat (Escada) ★ ★ *mega fruity* $ $
Is this my type of fragrance? No. Is it fun? Yes. A big tropical-fruit salad, initially pleasantly acidic and crisp, with an unfortunate, overly sweet drydown, because no party lasts. TS

Sunset Heat for Men (Escada) ★ ★ *fruity man* $
Cool Water knockoff with a complimentary tropical-fruit-cocktail top note, for men who don't mind downing drinks with small paper umbrellas in them, for as long as their hair gel holds. TS

Superworldunknown (B Never Too Busy to Be Beautiful)
★ ★ ★ ★ *delicious oriental* $
Nearly everything at first glance is wrong: the ragged seam on the cheap glass, the loosely glued colored-plastic gems peeling off the cap, the terrible name, the ridiculous-sounding brand (which is a spinoff of LUSH, the company responsible for making mall air unbreathable with its ghastly overpriced, overfragranced soaps). This is why when you put on Superworldunknown you feel giddy disbelief, as if Venus were suddenly emerging from a Manila trash heap. Superworld is a beautifully constructed, classical oriental descended from Emeraude via Theorema. It blooms from an old-fashioned dissonant top note of mucilage to a golden, gingerbread amber heart of balsam and spice inflated by a modern musk with a note of fruity plastic entirely welcome here. If I ran the world, this is how fragrance would work: all the money spent on the juice, the bottle a mere afterthought, not the sad, common reverse. These people are getting it right. TS

Sweet Lime & Cedar (Jo Malone) ★ ★ *lime musk* $ $
Lime leaf is usually the soul of freshness, but here it smells peculiarly harsh and dries down quickly to a potent, functional-smelling sugary musk. Jo Malone is ruining its reputation for doing light fragrances. TS

Sweet Paradise (Morgan) ★ *mango syrup* $ $
For ditzy teens who want to smell like tinned fruit. LT

Sycomore (Chanel) ★ ★ ★ ★ ★ *smoky vetiver* $ $ $
The dream team at Chanel seems to delight in applying superior skills to existing ideas they deem worthy of perfecting: Coromandel was a

reorchestration of Lutens's Borneo 1834, and of course their Eau de Co-logne is a "here's how we do it" object lesson to every perfumer since the 1750s. Sycomore is, in my view, a magisterial gloss on Bertrand Duch-aufour's Timbuktu. The latter introduced an Altoids-like idea to per-fumery, consisting of a minty-licorice coolness combined with a radiant crackling-wood-fire note. What Polge and Sheldrake seem to have real-ized is that this accord offered a solution to the age-old problem of vetiver: too little and it gets lost in composition, too much and it always smells the same. Vetiver has both an anisic aspect and a smoky one. Cleverly flank it with Timbuktu's two companions, add a big slug of sandalwood, and vetiver finds itself in worthy company at last. Together they make a strange, very natural accord that shifts from shade to shade of deepest olive at each sniff. There is a tension, a dark mystery, to Tim-buktu, which Sycomore does not try to emulate: it is content with merely being the freshest, most salubrious, yet most satisfyingly rich masculine in years. If putting it on does not make you shiver with pleasure, see a doctor. LT

Tabac (La Via del Profumo) ★ ★ ★ ★ *tobacco leaf* $$
Some years back I lived for a time in North Carolina and used to go shopping at Fowlers in Durham, one of the finest food stores in the world. Durham is home to half a dozen tobacco companies, including Lucky Strike. On some days, the downtown streets smelled so wonder-fully of tobacco that the whole place felt like it had been carved out of a giant gingerbread. Tabac approximates that beautifully, without being overly sweet or honeyed. A deliciously comfortable masculine. LT

Tabac Blond (Caron) ★ *woody floral* $$$
The booklet that Caron produces to explain its range describes its cur-rent perfumer, Richard Fraysse, as having a preference for "classic" fra-grance, and says he "professes a preference for the softness and fullness of feminine fragrances." This is ghastly bad fortune, because Ernest

Daltroff, Caron's brilliant founder, had a broader concept of the feminine than simple softness and fullness. Women are more than the sum of their bosoms, after all. Tabac Blond in 1919 was a tribute to that shocking modern creature: the woman who smoked. It was a terrific, edgy, weird leather chypre, closely related to the great Knize Ten and on the way to Cabochard. Like Knize Ten, it placed smoky and bitter leather notes in a bracing, green herbal chypre structure, sweetened with just enough amber to make it palatable. It got sweeter in the last twenty years or so—one friend quipped on smelling it, "Who put this Cinnabon in my Tabac Blond?"—but was still fantastic. And then sometime in the last few years, Fraysse instituted a smoking ban in Tabac Blond. The top note might seem deceptively right, smelling like a top-shelf whiskey, but once that's gone, you're left with a powdery, ambery rose related to the iteration of Arpège that Fraysse the younger worked on, but not as good. At least it's not like the version we smelled in Harrods a few months ago: a cheap green chypre like Eau du Soir. I'm not sure what's going on with these variations. All I know is I loved Tabac Blond. Can't Fraysse instead go ruin some perfumes that weren't interesting in the first place? TS

Tabacco (Profumo di Firenze) ★ ★ ★ ★ *lit pipe* $$$$
My first thought on smelling this was, "Here we go, another pipe-tobacco accord based on wood, rum, and tonka bean." Two minutes later, I marveled at the coincidence (I was sitting in a hotel courtyard at the time) that someone near me had just lit up a pipe. I looked around, saw no one, and realized I'd been had: such is the strong association between incense and smoke that, for once, Tabacco supplies it without fire. Nice work. LT

Tabarôme (Creed) ★ ★ *not tobacco* $$$$
I expected a warm, coumarinic tobacco accord and found instead a harsh sports fragrance pervaded by a hugely powerful woody amber on a woody-citrus background. Mislabeled and pointless. LT

Tabu (Dana) ★ ★ ★ *cheap oriental* $

All you can expect from an el-cheapo firm like Dana is what the French would call *beaux restes*. And that's what you get: Jean Carles's prodigious, balls-to-the-wall accord used to contain every note known to man as of 1932. Tabu was the Genghis Khan of orientals: break a bottle in your luggage and you wouldn't need the Golden Horde to clear your way. The modern version still has swagger, even looks dark and mean, and stains fabric like mad, no doubt due to the presence of a powerful Schiff's base in its composition. But it is now simply too cheap to bid credibly for a place among the great orientals of all time. LT

If you can find a sufficiently old bottle in a yard sale or an auction, it's usually cheap and worth having for fun and for reference: a sensational oriental with the deliciously anisic note of root beer set against powdery woods and leather. TS

Ta'if (Ormonde Jayne) ★ ★ ★ ★ *peppery floral* $ $

Ta'if, named after a Saudi city on the Hijaz plateau, famed for its roses, is a huge, self-confident floral-oriental, lit up like a film set. It kicks off with a remarkable pepper-saffron accord before settling down to a fluorescent floral heart in the manner of Caron Montaigne. Wear it when the desert wind blows, as Raymond Chandler put it, "one of those hot dry Santa Anas that come down through the mountain passes and curl your hair and make your nerves jump and your skin itch. On nights like that every booze party ends in a fight. Meek little wives feel the edge of the carving knife and study their husbands' necks. Anything can happen. You can even get a full glass of beer at a cocktail lounge." LT

Tam Dao (Diptyque) ★ ★ ★ *wood furniture* $ $

My new oak kitchen table arrived smelling like this: dried cut wood, the lime brightness of turpentine. While Tam Dao's smoky cedar is in the style of the incense woods in Dzongkha (L'Artisan), it's a much more modest, straightforward invention. (If I recall correctly, it was a creamy sandalwood when it was released, but sandalwood is in short supply these days, and things have changed.) Not really a perfume, more of a lovely smell. Probably best sprayed in your closet or on your pillow than on yourself. TS

Tangerine Vert (Miller Harris) ★ ★ *citrus cologne* $$$
A bright citrus cologne similar to but not as good as Concentré d'Orange Verte (Hermès). TS

A Taste of Heaven (By Kilian) ★ ★ ★ ★ *lavender vanilla* $$$$
Kilian Hennessy, fragrance professional and scion of the distinguished Cognac family, has decided to go it alone and start his own niche firm on a sort of Amouage Gold principle: cost no object in the choice of ingredients, period. Four of his first five fragrances have been composed by the great Calice Becker (J'Adore, Beyond Paradise, etc.). Aside from being good news, this indicates the extent to which perfumers working for the Big Five find daily life frustrating, and do unpaid work for niche firms as a temporary escape from the daily grind of big briefs. A Taste of Heaven is a completely straightforward no-holds-barred vanillic lavender using ace raw materials (lavender absolute, with its burnt-sugar helichrysum note and lovely chartreuse color), a twist of wormwood, and a salubrious drydown of oakmoss. If you love Caron's Pour un Homme, but would like an extra edge of richness and complexity, this one is for you. LT

Tea for Two (L'Artisan Parfumeur) ★ ★ ★ *cinnamon smoke* $$
That wonderful Indian concoction of spices, tea, and milk known as chai was one of those food fads that, like some sort of starlet of the palate, had its brief moment of fame before we all moved on to pomegranate juice. In 2000, Olivia Giacobetti used the theme as an excuse for a transparent spice oriental, dry and plain, with the bare minimum of sweetness, a touch of leathery smoke, and a well-judged hole where the amber usually goes. Probably a better room fragrance than a personal perfume and, judged as an attempt at modernizing the oriental genre,

completely trounced by Fendi's (depressingly discontinued) Theorema (1998). Still, not bad. TS

Tea Rose (Perfumer's Workshop) ★ ★ ★ ★ *green rose* $
Composed in 1972, Tea Rose was the first fragrance signed by the great Annie Buzantian (Pleasures), and was in many ways the first niche fragrance: the Perfumer's Workshop did nothing but fragrances, had a small range, was fairly hard to find, and had a devoted following. Tea Rose was and is a rose soliflore that illustrates how complex a composition must be before it can actually claim to smell of rose. The rose it depicts is huge, painted in watercolor, and has the species name written below it in cursive. LT

Le Temps d'une Fête (Parfums de Nicolaï) ★ ★ ★ ★ ★
green narcissus $
Guy Kawasaki once said that he believed in God because he could see no other reason for the continued existence of Apple Computer, Inc. Now that Apple is out of the woods, I shall redirect my prayers toward Parfums de Nicolaï. Patricia de Nicolaï, owner and perfumer, is one of the unsung greats of the fragrance world, and her superb creations survive in spite of inept marketing, absurd names, and the incapacity of the outfit to settle on a single shade of blue for their packaging or to hire a designer that will finally put their dowdy image out of its misery. This is their latest feminine, and it signals a departure from their ill-advised attempts to make more commercial fragrances. Le Temps d'une Fête is irresistibly lovely. Furthermore, it fills a gap in my heart I didn't know existed. I have always been impressed by the structure of Lancôme's Poême but dismayed by its cheap, angular execution. Conversely, I have always loved Guerlain's Chamade but deplored a slight lack of bone structure, particularly in the latest version. Le Temps d'une Fête marries the two and achieves something close to perfection, rich, radiant, solid, with the unique complexity of expensive narcissus absolute braced by olfactory bookends of green-floral notes and woods. Very classical, and truly wonderful. LT

Terre de Bois (Miller Harris) ★ ★ ★ *clean vetiver* $$$
Despite the silly, unevocative cod-French name, this is a very presentable, natural lemony-herbaceous vetiver of moderate staying power. LT

Terre de Sarment (Frapin) ★ ★ ★ *spicy citrus* $$$
Dry *sarments* (wine shoots) make great fuel to toss on a fire when grilling meat: they burn with a sooty flame that coats the food with a delicious smoky aroma. TdS is a very civilized fragrance not a million miles away from Frapin's Caravelle Epicée, with citrus top notes against a warm, spicy background. It has the hallmarks of the firm's compositions so far: handsome, graceful, but way too shy. Frapin needs posture and elocution lessons. LT

Terre d'Hermès (Hermès) ★ ★ ★ *fresh bergamot* $$
A delightfully fresh grapefruit-geranium confection, with no *terre* in sight. Harmless and pleasant at all times. LT

Thé Blanc (L'Occitane) ★ ★ *crisp oriental* $
White tea, which this is supposed to smell like, has a pale, leafy smell: pretty dull for a fragrance. That's probably why L'Occitane opted for this sweetened, sheer oriental mishmash, a cloying dessert smell of cardamom and citrus peel. I believe there's a handsoap in a certain airline's lavatories that smells exactly like this. TS

Thé Brun (Jean-Charles Brosseau) ★ ★ *smoky green* $$
An interesting greasy woodsmoke idea that doesn't smell good, because too bare. Too bad. TS

Thé pour un Eté (L'Artisan Parfumeur) ★ ★ ★ ★ *quiet jasmine* $$
Lovely fresh high-quality jasmine, very quiet and transparent, perhaps best on a man if he dares. LT

Thé Vert au Jasmin (L'Occitane) ★ ★ ★ *fruity jasmine* $
Satisfyingly soapy, fruity jasmine, with an uncanny resemblance to what the name describes (green jasmine tea). I've always loved jasmine tea, so I don't mind the literalism, although I think I'd enjoy it more as a room fragrance. TS

Thundra (Profumum) ★ *sour patchouli* $$$$
Thundra is a thoroughly unpleasant accord of patchouli and what smells to me like gum and opopanax, adding up to a dissonant, sour, loud bang-on-a-can thing. Tenacious as hell and truly repellent. LT

Tiare (Chantecaille) ★ ★ ★ *scorched flower* $$
Instead of settling for a fresh and clean white floral, this raspy, sharp green lily unexpectedly circles around a strange burnt sugar note. Interesting, though a touch bare. TS

Tiempe Passate (Antonia's Flowers) ★ ★ *big rose* $$$
A nicely put together musky rose. The name (Neapolitan for *tempi passati,* times past) led me to expect a deliberately old-fashioned fragrance. Instead, it has a modern feel, particularly in the drydown of synthetic musks. LT

Tilleul (Parfums d'Orsay) ★ ★ *linden musk* $$
Perfumery linden, though it wants you to believe it's like mimosa with a twist, is instead a citrus-muguet lash-up that belongs in Barbasol shaving foam and makes mixed-floral tisanes remind you of detergent. Tilleul might lend an old-fashioned just-soap-and-water charm to the right guy, but mostly it's a brute of a smell and brings to mind Olivia Giacobetti's other laundry-soap disaster, L'Eté en Douce. TS

Timbuktu (L'Artisan Parfumeur) ★ ★ ★ ★ ★ *woody smoky* $$
When I first encountered Timbuktu during a visit to an Artisan Parfumeur shop, I made the mistake of smelling it after revisiting some of

my favorites from the firm's distant and more recent past, like Dzing! and Vanilia. By the time I got to Timbuktu, my nose was tired, and I found it nondescript, almost odorless. Nevertheless, I took some home for further inspection. How wrong I was! Timbuktu is probably the first true masterpiece of what, by analogy with nouvelle cuisine, I would call *nouvelle parfumerie*. This school, whose chief exponents are Jean-Claude Elléna and Bertrand Duchaufour, is characterized by complete transparency, an unusually high proportion of high-quality naturals and what might best be described as the absence of a brass section in the orchestra. This strings-and-winds orchestration gives perfumes that never shout. Timbuktu has a tremendously melodious and affecting start of vetiver, sandalwood, and incense that seems quiet until you realize that, like modern sound systems that can pipe music into every room, one spritz fills a house with an odd, distinctly perceptible, but almost infrared shimmer of woody freshness. No perfume has ever privileged radiance over impact quite to this extent. The central accord in Timbuktu achieves what I thought impossible: a durable dry-woody note without the electric drydown screech of modern synthetics. Bertrand Duchaufour explained to me that part of this effect is due to the use of a rare essential oil from India called cypriol. Having obtained samples from Robertet, I can testify that cypriol, extracted from the sedge *Cyperus scariosus,* is quite something: a smoky note without a trace of oiliness or tar, the smell of crisply burned dry wood on a bonfire. But Duchaufour was being modest: no single raw material ever "made" a fragrance, and he should take full credit for a masterly composition. Timbuktu is the only modern fragrance that replicates, albeit by a completely different route, the bracing, euphoric freshness first bottled in 1888 by Paul Parquet as the defunct but immortal Fougère Royale. LT

Tobacco Vanille (Tom Ford) ★ ★ ★ *honey tobacco* $ $ $
Most people seem unaware that tobacco is heavily flavored, none more so than the pipe tobaccos that smell so much better in the pouch than

when smoked. TV reproduces the smell of Dutch pipe tobacco to perfection, and illustrates once again the fondness of our noses for complexity and richness. It is an essay in dried fruits and honey, and amounts to a more bearable version of Lutens's foghorn-like Miel de Bois. Smells great, but feels more like a cozy *parfum d'ambiance* than a real fragrance. LT

Tocade (Rochas) ★ ★ ★ ★ *rose vanilla* $$
It is far too early yet to sum up Maurice Roucel's achievements, since he seems to come up with new wonders regularly, but I would be very surprised if Tocade did not figure among his top three perfumes even twenty years from now. When it came out in 1994, Tocade went against the grain of the two major tendencies at the time, the outrageous and the apologetic, exemplified respectively by Angel and L'Eau d'Issey. Tocade's simple, compact prettiness felt so deceptively familiar that many failed to grasp how original it was. It was a floral oriental among many. It did not use any weird novel molecules. It made no mystery of its intent, which was to have some harmless fun with rose and vanilla, perhaps the two materials most frequently used by perfumers. And yet: if the devil is in the details, so are the angels. Tocade's rose was unlike any other, with the iridescent gleam of nail varnishes that change color depending on viewing angle. The vanilla too was weird, perfectly judged between ice cream, smoke, and candyfloss. Everything, from the juicy top notes to the butter-cookie drydown, meshed together perfectly, gracefully, happily, to give a perfume with vivid eyes, a ready laugh, and pretty dancing feet. LT

Tokyo (Kenzo) ★ ★ *milky woody* $
The apologetically mild fragrance within is no match for the streaks of urban light blasting across the packaging. Nicer on skin, in a kind of baby's-breath way, than on paper or fabric, where the potent woody amber tramples everything. TS

Tolu (Ormonde Jayne) ★ ★ ★ ★ *herbal oriental* $$
When Linda Pilkington opened her own perfumery in London in 2002, niche brands were serving novelties to the specialty buyer, mainstream perfume tended to give you the choice between loudly trashy or whisperingly apologetic, and the old classic perfume houses seemed to be having an identity crisis. In the same way that Diane von Furstenberg leaped on the fact that "no one was making a little bourgeois dress" in 1976, Pilkington must have realized that nearly no one was making the kind of polished perfume that adult women like to wear and fragrance companies used to be expected to make. Enter Ormonde Jayne. Tolu is the kind of fragrance Guerlain or Caron would be turning out regularly if all was right in the world: a rich floral amber, animalic and sweetly balsamic but never heavy, with a bright herbal-woody accord washing it in silvery light. This is a comfortable oriental in the classic mold, but with a completely modern feeling of open air, a subtle, sunny, dry atmosphere, as if Mediterranean gardens lay just out of sight. Highly recommended. TS

Tom Ford for Men (Tom Ford) ★ ★ ★ *fresh oriental* $$
The good news is the fragrance smells nice. The bad news is that it's a straight-up rehash of the excellent Baldessarini. Get the original. LT

Tom Ford for Men Extreme (Tom Ford) ★ ★ ★
chrysanthemum fougère $$$
The tenderly blurred, dreamy, androgynous top note of pepper and bitter, fresh flowers, with a clean, humid atmosphere like a hot bath, seems a nod to Anaïs Anaïs: very daring in a masculine. The rest, a fine but thin woody-lavender fougère, toes the expected line. TS

Tommy (Tommy Hilfiger) ★ ★ ★ *woody cardamom* $
The first Hilfiger fragrance was innovative when it came out in 1995 and has been imitated to death since. Up top, it smells like the breath of

someone who just drank an espresso and then chewed a cardamom seed. Curiously, neither ingredient is listed on the press pack, and instead we have a hilarious gallery of cod Americana: "Iowa lavender," "grass (blue)," and "Atlantic driftwood." It's a wonder they forgot banjo absolute and Grand Teton juice. Tommy dries down to a gray hissy musk and woody citrus. In its unaffected simplicity, and despite its depressing sport fragrance style, it is among the best of a bad lot. LT

Tommy Girl (Tommy Hilfiger) ★ ★ ★ ★ ★ *tea floral* $
No fragrance in recent memory has suffered more from being affordable than Tommy Girl. It's as if it were deemed less desirable for being promiscuous. Despite all the historical evidence to the contrary (Brut, Canoe, Habanita, and the first J-Lo), the world is still crawling with naive snobs who'd rather believe their wallet's loss than their nose's gain. Tommy Girl's origins were explained to me by creator Calice Becker, who was brought up in a Russian household, with a samovar always on the boil and a mother with a passion for strange teas. At Becker's instigation, the legendary chemist Roman Kaiser of Givaudan sampled the air in the Mariage Frères tea store in Paris to figure out what gave it its unique fragrance. From this a tea base was evolved, in which no one showed much interest. The idea waited several years until Elléna's excellent but only remotely tea-like Eau Parfumée au Thé Vert (Bulgari) came out in 1993. Its success made it possible for Becker to submit a tea composition for the Hilfiger brief. She won it, and eleven hundred formulations later the perfume was finalized, in collaboration with a brilliant evaluator who went on to study philosophy. Tea makes excellent sense as a perfumery base, since it can be declined in dozens of ways, as flavored teas will attest: Soochong, Earl Grey, jasmine, and so on. In that respect it could serve as a modern chypre, a mannequin to be dressed at will. Tommy Girl clothed it in a torero's *traje de luces,* a fresh floral accord so exhilaratingly bright that it could be used to set the white point for all future fragrances. Remarkably, late in the project, Hilfiger's PR firm asked Becker to give them some reason to label the

fragrance as typically American. Quest's resident botany expert was called in, and to everyone's surprise found that the composition fell neatly into several blocks, each apparently typical of a native American botanical. So it goes with projects whose sails are filled by the breath of angels. LT

The composition miraculously turned out to fall into accords typical of native American botanicals? Put me on record as skeptical. Tommy Girl smells great, though, and has been copied relentlessly. TS

Tom of Finland (Etat Libre d'Orange) ★ ★ ★ ★ *saffron cologne* $ $ $
Once cheap and abundant, sandalwood now costs a fortune and, for the commercial perfumer, might as well not exist, so the mysterious dusty-milky smell of saffron, in the form of a newish Givaudan material called Safraleine, has been playing understudy with occasional success. This saffron-lemon cologne has the unerring crisp dryness of the old Monsieur Balmain and brings to mind clear mountain weather with visibility to China or the feeling of cool hands on a fevered forehead. (Sadly, or happily as the case may be, the bottle shows only the name and none of the homoerotic imagery of the marketing and packaging.) TS

Trésor (Lancôme) ★ ★ ★ ★ *powdery rose* $
I once sat in the London Tube across from a young woman wearing a T-shirt printed with headline-size words "ALL THIS" across her large breasts, and in small type underneath "and brains too." That vulgar but wily combination seems to me to sum up Trésor. Up close, when you can read the small print, Trésor is a superbly clever accord between powdery rose and vetiver, reminiscent of the structure of Habanita. From a distance, it's the trashiest, most good-humored pink-mohair-sweater-and-bleached-hair thing imaginable. When you manage to appeal to both the reptilian brain and the neocortex of menfolk, what happens is what befell Trésor: a huge success. LT

Très Russe (Institut Très Bien) ★ ★ ★ ★ *coumarin floral* $$
The original Cologne à la Russe was an excellent orange-blossom varia-
tion on the cologne theme, distinguished by having the square, solid feel
of materials good enough for Guerlain (Habit Rouge, to be exact). The
eau de parfum version, with more of everything plus the sweet nutty-
hay smell of coumarin, smells up close like the creamy, soapy cologne,
yet at a distance gives a beautifully crisp, sweet floral radiance that you
might mistake in passing for L'Heure Bleue. It smells great. Comfortable
and well made, this sort of classical fragrance is built on the principle
that classics aren't classic because they seem old but because they seem
always new. T s

Tribute (Mary Kay) ★ *fruit bomb* $
Depressingly sad and cheap fruity floral. TS said it smelled like a flavor
of Slurpee, whatever that may be. LT

Le Troisième Homme (Caron) ★ ★ ★ ★ ★ *jasmine fougère* $$
For eye candy, both men and women look at women: men are simply not
decorative, as everyone knows. Except once in a great while comes a
disastrously beautiful boy who turns every head in the street, even if his
hair is overgrown, his grubby clothes fit badly, and he's oblivious to the
attention as he goes about his ordinary life—he breaks more hearts running out innocently to buy milk than we ordinary mortals manage to
bruise in a callous lifetime. Such boys, with their long dark eyelashes,
smooth cheeks, and perfect slender bodies, are called "pretty as girls."
Le Troisième Homme, named after the Orson Welles film and known
for a time as No. 3, is a boy like that, a type of beauty described poorly
as androgynous, when what we mean is that it is beautiful before it is
anything else, including male or female. I smelled it for the first time on
a woman and it caught my heart, the way a stray branch in the woods
catches the sleeve of your sweater, and I realized I loved it because of the
pitch of my voice when I asked for its name. I've never smelled it on a
man and wonder if I ever will: Accidents of nature are forgivable, but

how many men can pull off deliberate prettiness? Buy it even if you never put it on. TS

Trouble (Boucheron) ★ *dismal oriental* $$
This is what French perfumers call *une soupe:* a murky broth the color of mud in which float shreds of past fragrances, chiefly Allure and other creatures from that grim, inchoate tribe. An artistic failure and, mercifully, a commercial belly flop. LT

Trouble Eau Légère (Boucheron) ★ *indigestible oriental* $$
Considering the unnatural disaster that was the parent fragrance, the name of TEL reminds me of the famous headline "Small Earthquake: Not Many Dead." This is one of those accords that makes you feel like you've mixed the wrong things in a five-course dinner, made a fatal mistake with that second helping of mint ganache washed down with Baileys, and are urgently in need of a breath of fresh air. LT

True Star (Tommy Hilfiger) ★★★ *white floral* $
Standard-issue, well-crafted white floral of no consequence. LT

Truly Pink (Vera Wang) ★★ *huge rose* $$
An overwhelming rose reminiscent of the classic Tea Rose but frillier and girlier. On the plus side, it clearly contains a fair bit of good natural stuff. On the minus side, who on earth would actually want to smell like this? Spray it on your Barbie doll, make her happy. LT

Truth (Calvin Klein) ★★★ *floral oriental* $
Truth, released in 2000, suffered from a fatuously pretentious name and a confused advertising image, and was not a great success. The clean, simple bottle led one to expect something squeaky clean. The fragrance was, like most truths, not simple. The first impression is one of striking balance and clarity in the complex top notes, after which Truth proceeds on two parallel levels all the way to drydown: a green, sharp,

florist-shop floral accord above, reminiscent of Lauder's excellent but equally unsuccessful Dazzling Silver (1998), and a creamy woody-oriental accord below that that prevents the fragrance from becoming too bright and screechy. I see it as an attempt to re-create a modern, more transparent version of early-eighties soapy florals like Ivoire. In the end, it was probably too complicated and too grown-up for its intended audience. Very good nonetheless. LT

Tubéreuse (Annick Goutal) ★ ★ ★ *rubbery flower* $$
A tuberose for purists, this floral presents the material in all its unpresentable glory: rubber tires, steak tartare, Chinese muscle rub, and all. TS

Tubéreuse (L'Artisan Parfumeur) ★ ★ ★ *giant tuberose* $$$
A huge, somewhat chemical tuberose, buttressed by wide-load floral notes in a drydown that comes surprisingly soon. Not what you'd call subtle, but what tuberose is? I still prefer Beyond Love (By Kilian) for its greener, more faithful, more stable picture of this man-eating flower. LT

Tubéreuse (Caron) ★ ★ ★ *peach tuberose* $$$
In 2003, Richard Fraysse, Caron's current perfumer, made his contribution to Caron's "urn" fragrances, the ones they keep in what look like giant glass samovars, for the staff to decant into the crystal bottle of your choice. They include some of the great classics: Tabac Blond, En Avion, Farnesiana, Alpona, and so on. So what did Fraysse decide to contribute to this distinguished company? A competent Fracas, but flatter and less cheerful. TS

Tubéreuse 40 (Le Labo) ★ ★ *not tuberose* $
Labeling a bottle "Tubéreuse" and then putting an ordinary orange blossom inside reminds me of that urban legend about the Japanese spending thousands of dollars on rare, strange-looking, specially bred poodles that turn out to be sheep. The Japanese are smarter than that,

but Le Labo's customer, apparently, is not supposed to be. (Sold only in the New York City store, for incomprehensible reasons.) TS

Tubéreuse Criminelle (Serge Lutens) ★ ★ ★ ★ *menthol tuberose* $$$
If Ethel Merman were a floral, this would be it—loud, proud. Tuberose absolute usually contains, especially at the start, disturbing aspects of rubber and rotting meat. While most fragrances disguise or eliminate these potentially unpleasant effects, this one amplifies them: an icy blast of camphor, a salty, bloody smell, and a white-floral bouquet so indolic you think it must be a mistake, getting stronger by the minute. Terrific. TS

Tubéreuse Indiana (Creed) ★ ★ ★ *white floral* $$$$
Crude white floral whose bareness is not redeemed by superlative quality. LT

Tuberose (Renée) ★ ★ *thin tuberose* $$
It must have got to the point where perfumers, when asked for a tuberose, simply say, "Fracas or Amarige?" This one is an Amarige. LT

Tuberose Cologne (Jo Malone) ★ ★ ★ *light tuberose* $$
You really feel for tuberose when you see it dragged through the Jo Malone School for Girls: "Still too much tube, dear." Fracas diluted tenfold. LT

Tuscan Leather (Tom Ford) ★ ★ *new car* $$$
There are two converging trends at the moment, one toward light, unsweetened leathers, the other for early perfumery, e.g., the scents brought to France from Florence by Marie de Médicis. Ford's Tuscan Leather, with its transparent, woody smoky tones and light fruity touch in the background, is a good introduction to the genre, though in the same style I prefer Lancôme's Cuir, richer and more satisfying. An interesting

aspect of these fragrances is that the accord approximates a vetiver, even when that raw material is absent. (If only Patricia de Nicolaï could be persuaded to do a fragrance version of her sublime *parfum d'ambiance Vétiver de Java!*) LT

Tuscany per Donna (Aramis) ★ ★ ★ ★ *peony oriental* $
This is essentially a classic woody rose with a delicious orange-peel-and-amber oriental base, but what makes it new is a sharp, fluorescent pink, sulfurous grapefruit-peony in the modern style, which turns the whole thing excitingly garish and a little sweaty. I perceive it as swinging constantly from a comfortable, sugared floral to a twanging citrus-herbal, as if it spoke with a diphthong-heavy accent all its own, half old country and half new, a perfumery Brooklynese. Gotta love it. TS

Tuscany per Uomo (Aramis) ★ ★ ★ ★ *herbal patchouli* $
God bless Estée Lauder for not hating men, as other firms in the fragrance industry seem to do, judging by the stuff they call masculine perfumery. Lauder's masculine brand, Aramis, has been doing guys the great favor of making Tuscany per Uomo since 1984: a relaxed, lovely fougère with plenty of naturals, centered on the marriage of a grassy, herbal patchouli with a touch of friendly florals and amber resins taken straight out of feminine chypres. It's a variation on far richer, stranger masculines—see Jules (Dior)—but that makes it far more wearable because its strangeness has been carefully reduced. It may be less interesting for that reason, but also much easier to fit into ordinary life. Unlike the race of meaner, stingier masculines that has come through since, Tuscany has an open-collar ease and generous airy feel, with plenty of room for big gestures, without ever overwhelming either wearer or passerby. Smelling this all day would be no hardship, making this an ideal fragrance to give to a man already in your life. TS

Twill Rose (Parfums de Rosine) ★ ★ ★ ★ *animalic animalic* $$$
Do not be fooled by the complicated opening credits, all galbanum and cut grass. This picture is headed one way and one way only: the Sy-

narome base Animalis, a complicated mixture of musks and beastly notes like civet and castoreum and who knows what, a sort of Muscs Koublai Khan barbarian with a splash of aftershave. TS

Two Hearts Beating as One (B Never Too Busy to Be Beautiful)
★ ★ ★ *ylang jasmine* $
The awfulness of some of the names that come out of BNTBTBB is unprecedented in the history of fragrance and, for that matter, human industry. THBAO is a good if crudely lashed up inky-indolic jasmine-rose with a bit of the pineapple-cheesy smell of ylang-ylang. TS

U4EAHH! (YOSH) ★ ★ ★ *pear apple* $$$
This is a cheerful mix of fruit flavors—watermelon, pear—that ends up smelling to me like nothing so much as those green-apple candies I ate as a kid, the ones that turn your tongue the color of alien blood. Surprisingly, it stays coherent a long time. TS

Ubar (Amouage) ★ ★ ★ ★ ★ *humongous floral* $$$
I remember years ago seeing an IMAX movie at the Air and Space Museum in DC: it started out with a little grainy black-and-white film of a biplane taking off, and just when you were beginning to wonder why you'd shelled out twenty bucks, the screen turned to color, widened to a huge hollow sphere, and you were flying above a forest in turning-leaf colors above a Pitts S2 painted in shiny red and white. Even the sound was gorgeous. Everyone went "aah" and I shed forty years in ten milliseconds. After smelling several dozen pigeon-toed, rickety modern fragrances designed by depressive accountants, encountering Ubar was a similarly joyful experience. This thing is so huge, gleaming, overengineered, and chock-full of counterrotating planetary gears that you feel all you can do is let it tower over you while you walk around it and kick the huge tires. Ubar is technically a floral oriental, but the flowers are XXXL in size and the Orient has been scaled accordingly. If the old Dioressence had an illegitimate child with the first Rush, it would smell

like this: a huge purple and romantic rose in the manner of the lamented Nombre Noir; a ton of creamy lactones; a whale's worth of animalic amber. Ubar joins the small club of nuclear-tipped fragrances: Poison, Giorgio, Angel, Amarige. Use it carefully, for once you spray it on there's no going back. LT

U by Ungaro for Her (Ungaro) ★ ★ *rosy citrus* $
It took four perfumers, and good ones at that, to produce this measly nonentity? Doesn't IFF have a hundred like this on the shelf? Ungaro used to do pretty good stuff in the eighties, but this is pathetic. LT

U by Ungaro for Him (Ungaro) ★ ★ ★ *lavender musk* $
This composition is as messy as an eighteen-year-old guy's bedroom and tries to recapitulate every recent masculine cliché while sticking to a tight formula budget. Nevertheless, it has a cheerful cheap-aftershave directness that could work on a goofy, pretty boy. LT

Ultraviolet (Paco Rabanne) ★ *medicinal fruity* $ $
The bathrooms in hell smell like this. Aggressively, blindingly horrible, the worst part of fake grape flavor bolstered by the strongest artificial sweet amber concocted by man or devil. I want to cry. TS

Ultraviolet Man (Paco Rabanne) ★ *green sugary* $
Green violet leaf and sugar: Why? The bottle seems modeled on a staple gun. TS

Umé (Keiko Mecheri) ★ ★ ★ *woody floral* $ $ $
Like Badgley Mischka distorted in a funhouse mirror, this fruity-floral oriental pushes the lovely milky-rosy accord at its heart behind a loud synthetic wood background that amplifies everything but sacrifices gracefulness. TS

Unbound (Halston) ★ ★ *chemical floral* $
I use a fabric softener called Lenor April Fresh, a perlaceous blue liquid that looks like alien blood and smells like alien soap. Unbound, in a clear instance of trickle-up from functional to fine fragrance, smells very much like it, though heavier and less concise. Cheap and cheerless. LT

Unbound for Men (Halston) ★ ★ *spicy fresh* $
Yet another affable coriander sport fragrance, this one with a faint cod-liver-oil note. To be missed. LT

Unforgivable (Sean John) ★ ★ *dry amber* $ $
Presentable but dull Cool-Water-on-a-budget, with more oakmoss than usual in the drydown. LT

Unforgivable Black (Sean John) ★ ★ *woody fruity* $ $
Smells like fifty masculines mixed together. Boring. LT

Unforgivable Eau Fraîche (Sean John) ★ ★ *7UP woody* $ $
Unforgivable with a top note of lemon soda. Who ordered this? TS

Unforgivable Woman (Sean John) ★ ★ *fruity floral* $ $
Pleasant, well-crafted, and otherwise unremarkable fruity floral (peaches and apricots) that is woodier, less sweet, and less aggressively fluorescent than the average of that species. LT

Unforgivable Woman Black (Sean John) ★ ★ ★ *dark fruity* $ $
Given the swagger of Sean John women's clothes, this oddly muted fruity-woody fragrance is a pleasant surprise. Similar in intent to Amouage's Lyric Woman and Narciso Rodriguez's Musc but darker. Makes a nice masculine. LT

Unforgivable Woman Eau Fraîche (Sean John) ★ ★ ★ *melon rose* $$
An old-fashioned floral combining the last-night's-chardonnay rose of Eternity with the powdery, woody-melon structure of the old Royal Bain de Champagne (see Kenzo Flower). However, it lacks the life-affirming vulgarity of either and feels unnecessary. TS

The Unicorn Spell (LesNez) ★ ★ ★ ★ *green violet* $$$
LesNez is a small Swiss perfumery firm hoping, like Frédéric Malle, to present perfumes the way a publisher presents books, as the artful achievements of brilliant authors. Note, however, that many books are saved by good edits, which in the realm of perfume translates to art direction and evaluation, no small skills. So far, the LesNez fragrances seem unevenly edited. Unicorn Spell, despite an unforgivably precious name, is the best of the bunch, possibly because variations on its excellent fresh violet-iris theme have been edited twice before, in perfumer Isabelle Doyen's wonderful Duel and Mandragore for her main employer, Annick Goutal. Less reserved than either of those, Unicorn is a surprisingly affecting violet, miles away from violet's usual sweet, powdery context, with a bright, persistent, resinous leaf-green freshness, which reminds me of that fresh smell after a rain called, delightfully, petrichor. (Or perhaps I'm just thinking of Après l'Ondée.) TS

United Colors of Benetton Man (Benetton) ★ *drone cologne* $
Michael Edwards's Fragrances of the World database lists fully twenty-nine Benetton fragrances, a remarkable effort considering none of them appear to be much good. This one is among the most mediocre of that entire bunch. LT

United Colors of Benetton Unisex (Benetton) ★ ★ ★ *steam clean* $
The whole idea of a clothing company adopting shock advertising tactics to shake the world out of its supposed complacency is so nauseating that I imagine it turned many people away from buying Benetton's shabby clothes, no bad thing in itself. This unisex fragrance (all fra-

grances are unisex) composed by Firmenich's great Alberto Morillas is none other than a tame version of his wonderfully humorous Mugler Cologne, complete with hissing steam-iron note but less extreme. LT

United Colors of Benetton Woman (Benetton) ★ ★ ★
ambre solaire $
A strange and potentially disastrous cross between furniture spray polish and beach tanning oil. I happen to like both, and find their surprisingly successful combination in this fragrance very pleasant. LT

Unspoken (Roja Dove) ★ ★ ★ *patchouli floral* $$$
A little museum piece, which LT reckons smells most, in his memory, like Houbigant's long-lost Parfum Idéal (1900). After a huge (and vile) patchouli top note, which threatens to stop the bus at Woodstock, it settles to a pleasant rose-floral bouquet plus citrus, with that patchouli, now mollified, humming along in back. Old-fashioned but not uptight, made of good stuff, in general this smells all right if uninspired. One reason Dove's scents smell somewhat fusty is that they do not employ enough of what a graphic designer would call white space. At its best, Unspoken's floral aspect reminds me of our beloved Lady Stetson, though I like the Lady better. TS

Uomo (Lorenzo Villoresi) ★ ★ ★ *woody incense* $$
The hard part about reviewing LV fragrances is finding one that is neither vile nor trivial. The majority are one-liner hackneyed old recipes: incense, musk, patchouli, vetiver, wild lavender, etc. These never rise to Etro levels of composition and are firmly stuck in try-this-at-home territory. Those that try harder usually fail with a loud bang. Villoresi likes his fragrances heavy, and many of his compositions are of the sort that would make me leave a dinner table or concert seat if worn nearby. Only a few turn out to be bearable. Uomo is a woody incense, pleasantly dry and transparent, and not bad at all. LT

Uomo? (Moschino) ★ ★ *sweet soapy* $
No need for the question mark. This thing is so generic-guy that no doubt should remain as to its intended audience: the lad who wants to be indistinguishable from other lads. By no means the worst in this category, but still eye-wateringly dull. LT

Usiku (Jo Wood Organics) ★ ★ ★ *herbaceous spicy* $ $
The pleasant-smelling Usiku confirms once again that, with few exceptions, you can have natural fragrances in any color as long as it's brown. LT

Valentino (Valentino) ★ *dire vanillic* $ $
Interesting dissonant floral-vanillic accord, marred by what smells like bargain-basement execution. LT

Valentino pour Homme (Valentino) ★ ★ *dry woody* $ $
A pleasant, dry, gingery woody fragrance with a good, slightly waxy vetiver drydown. Not bad. LT

Van Cleef (Van Cleef & Arpels) ★ ★ ★ *heliotrope oriental* $ $
A good, square, solid floral oriental: a bouquet in the old-fashioned clove-touched style, with a feeling of dried flowers, plus a pleasant almond-anise-coumarin drydown. Although done in 1993, it feels about ten years older. TS

Vanilia (L'Artisan Parfumeur) ★ ★ ★ ★ ★ *candyfloss vanilla* $ $ $
There's Bad Vulgar (Louis Vuitton handbags, wood veneer in a brand-new car), there's Good Vulgar (flames painted on aircraft engine cowls, John Barry's James Bond theme), and then there's Great Vulgar: Vanilia. Jean-François Laporte was, as always, far ahead of his time in 1978 when he grabbed the wrist of whoever was weighing out the candyfloss (ethylmaltol) in his new vanillic amber and forced in ten times more than anyone had ever dared. In fact, thirty years later nobody has caught up

with the unfettered, hilarious, boisterous beauty of Vanilia. It's as if Shalimar met Andy Warhol and came out far trashier and happier. This perfume is so totally devoid of chic it has become the reference holiday from propriety and convention, and by association the purest exemplar of summer fragrance. Enjoy it with a banana float, a sunburn, and really loud music. There will always be time for refinement later. LT

Vanilla Fields (Coty) ★ ★ ★ *suntan floral* $
Ten or fifteen years ago vanilla fragrances seemed to take over the world, and every other woman walking by smelled like an ambulating bakery. I'd always written off Vanilla Fields in the drugstore as probably belonging to this phalanx, but I was wrong. Like Vanilia before it, but less edgy, Vanilla Fields is secretly a woody floral: a sweet little ditty of summer afternoons—a cozy, milky suntan-oil smell—simple and likable, a fine cheap thrill. It gets woodier and sweeter (and a little bare) with time. TS

Vanille Exquise (Annick Goutal) ★ ★ *smoky vanilla* $$$
Goutal's sales reps like to let you smell a fragrance sprayed in its bottle's cap and left to evaporate for a time. Smelled this way, it was a rich crème brûlée scent. On skin I was surprised to find it contained a violently powerful woody amber that gave an impression of burning hair. TS

Vanille Galante (Hermès) ★ ★ ★ ★ *vanilla jasmine* $$$
There is a wonderful René Magritte painting depicting a large carrot, a wine bottle, and a wine bottle whose top half has turned into a carrot. It is titled *The Explanation*. Elléna does the same thing in VG with vanilla and ylang-ylang, brilliantly dovetailing the medicinal, cough-syrup notes of vanilla absolute (no vanillin here, thank God) into the strange petroleum smell of benzyl acetate, a main component of jasmine and ylang. The sum total bottle-carrot is actually a sort of lily soliflore. It's so simple and straightforward you wonder why no one has done it quite this way before. LT

Vanille Tonka (Parfums de Nicolaï) ★ ★ ★ *vanilla carnation* $ $
I will never say it enough: Patricia de Nicolaï is one of the best perfumers around, and almost all her creations bring to mind the French word *seyant* (somewhere between "attractive" and "becoming"), a relaxed elegance and softness that used to belong only to Guerlain. This said, VT is her Vol de Nuit, a sort of cross between the balsamic darkness of Sacrebleu and the silken carnation of Number One, very much in the house style but less distinctive than her best. LT

Velocity (Mary Kay) ★ *lemon floral* $
Functional citrus/white-floral thing, very nearly good enough for a window cleaner. LT

Velocity for Him (Mary Kay) ★ ★ ★ *fresh citrus* $
There ought to be a separate category at the FiFi industry awards for Best Top Note, and Velocity for Him would likely do well: tomato stems and mandarin is an unusual opening gambit to a conversation and, in the context of a Mary Kay fragrance, far brainier than one has any right to expect. LT

Velvet Gardenia (Tom Ford) ★ ★ ★ ★ *real gardenia* $ $ $ $
Synchronicity, as the Gnome of Zurich would have said: just a few days before receiving this fragrance, I was complaining to a perfumer friend that there were no good gardenias around, when she said she'd smelled one that really worked, "with a proper mushroom note in it." This puzzled me, but there were no gardenias at hand to check, and I stored it under remarkable factoids. When I first smelled VG, I saw the light. Yes, gardenia makes you think that it's just a white flower, though sweeter, lemonier, fresher, more indolic, altogether prettier than the others. But the real secret to gardenia is a huge mushroom note which, once recognized, stares you in the face for the rest of your life. It's a bit like finding out that Audrey Hepburn had huge feet, which she did. VG is one hell of a gardenia, but it suffers from a problem that all perfumes and no flow-

ers have: flowers push the stuff out continuously, spray bottles only intermittently. If you want VG to say "gardenia" for longer than five minutes, spray it on fabric, not skin. LT

Velvet Hour (Kate Moss) ★ ★ *floral amber* $
Timid, bad green-floral top note leading to a passable mini-amber drydown, complete with interesting tiny animalic note. TS

Velvet Rope (Apothia) ★ *fruity mess* $ $
Mix equal parts strawberry Fanta, orange Fanta, and Malibu rum. Add a morello cherry. Cocktail is complimentary. Ladies free after 7 p.m. LT

Vent Vert (Balmain) ★ *green floral* $
I am sorry to report that Vent Vert is dead. The original, composed by Germaine Cellier in 1947, was an extraordinary thing, fully deserving of the fame and fortune it brought Balmain. It started with a sensationally bitter green-galbanum accord, which lasted long enough for the set piece behind it to be moved into place ready for smelling. As the green faded, the most beautiful, golden rose-jasmine accord took over and lasted for days, fading to a fresh powdery drydown that no modern perfume can even dream of. It was modernized in 1991 by Calice Becker. Why? Because Cellier used to fill in her stark accords using lots of bases (ready-made modular compositions), which were getting increasingly hard to source. When Becker was given the original formula, she unfolded it into its components by looking at the composition of each base (some of it re-entrant: base A used base B and vice versa). In the last analysis, she found that the original Vent Vert contained upward of eleven hundred components, which she reduced to thirty-odd. The 1991 Vent Vert, while less symphonic than the original, had some of the charm of familiar music played by a smaller ensemble: the newfound clarity made it possible to appreciate the tune to the fullest. Not the real thing, but a very good effort. In 1999, the formula was changed again by Nathalie Feisthauer and this time completely defaced. Instead of a three-

course meal, you get an airplane tray. Everything comes at once, and all in miniature. Vent Vert (version three) has become a linear perfume, with little time evolution save a terrible cheapening of the formula as time goes on and the money runs out, a sort of dollar dance in reverse. Worse still, the underlying structure is now a trashy green chypre in the loathsome Eau du Soir mold. LT

Vêpres Siciliennes (Parfums MDCI) ★ ★ ★ *candied orange* $$$$
As a rebuke to stomach-turning boiled-sweet scents like Liberté, VS demonstrates how sweet orange with amber can be classy rather than trashy. It feels like an excerpt from a big eighties floral oriental, an Oscar de la Renta without the tuberose or a Boucheron without the oomph. Absent the lift it would get from a good floral heart, the fragrance is uniformly dark, dense, and syrupy in a fashion similar to Serge Lutens's Fleur d'Oranger, with little radiance, and headed toward a flat amber drydown. Carefully done but a touch monotonous and murky in mood, as if the daylight has faded but you haven't remembered to turn on the lights. TS

Vera Wang Bouquet (Vera Wang) ★ ★ ★ *waxy rose* $$
Perfumer Loc Dong has been allowed to put forth an unusual proposal in a mainstream floral: an ugly top note followed by a good fragrance. The first spray smells like a cheap Beyond Paradise copy made of shampoo and neurosis, but it improves into a waxy-lemony, rose-jasmine bouquet, still derivative but not bad. TS

Vera Wang for Men (Vera Wang) ★ *soapy nightmare* $
Smells like something that might be called Mountain Glen, which you'd plug into a wall socket. LT

Verbenas of Provence Cologne (Jo Malone) ★ ★ ★
herbaceous citrus $$
Scaled-down version of the superb Eau de Guerlain, very pleasant for the first ten minutes and very thin thereafter. LT

Versace (Versace) ★ ★ ★ *white floral* $

Any fragrance that lists among its component materials Azalea Snow-bird, Azalea White Lights, Angelwing Jasmine, and Cashmere Wood Complex clearly can't handle the truth. What is it hiding? Perhaps the fact that it is a banal but very well-crafted white floral, notably devoid of both imagination and the screechy unpleasantness common to the genre. I cannot imagine who would want such a thing, but then, I don't use Botox. LT

Versace Jeans Couture Man (Versace) ★ *woody nothing* $

Versace Jeans is the downmarket (cheap) Versace brand, and this is a downmarket (cheap) fragrance of absolutely no interest whatsoever. Mercifully, it does not last. LT

Versace L'Homme (Versace) ★ ★ ★ ★ *citrus "ginger"* $

This fragrance was one of the best of the lot when it was released in 1984 and still smells great. The structure hits a lot of buttons simultaneously: big citrus blast, interesting core note of ginger as in Envy Men (not on the list of materials, may be an olfactory illusion), lovely "dirty" background in the manner of Jules and Kouros. A bit loud, a bit hairy chested, but really nice if you can pull it off. LT

Versace Man (Versace) ★ ★ *woody amber* $

A dry, woody, peppery oriental, confused and bare. TS

Versace Man Eau Fraîche (Versace) ★ *screechy citrus* $

Light Blue, but with the light off. LT

Versace pour Homme (Versace) ★ *laundry musk* $ $

A comparison of this dreadful thing to Versace L'Homme charts the precipitous decline of mainstream perfumery in the last twenty-five years: VpH is yet another tired Cool Water/Allure cliché overlaid with screaming laundry musks. Truly vile: a contender in the hotly contested "worst masculine since Duc de Vervins" category. LT

Vert d'Eau (Les Néréides) ★ ★ *green muguet* $$
Light-green floral with a citrus top, as wan and noncommittal as all the bit-player flowers in nature with names nobody ever bothers to learn. TS

Verte Violette (L'Artisan Parfumeur) ★ ★ *cucumber tea* $$$
VV goes from a powerfully cucumbery violet-leaf top note to a milky, metallic powdery floral paired with bitter green, which reminds me of a strong cup of Lipton with milk. Either it is confused or I am. TS

Vert Pivoine (Histoires de Parfums) ★ ★ ★ *woody floral* $$$
Interesting object lesson in bright woody-floral (peony) accords that avoids the customary klieg-light harshness of the genre. LT

Verveine (Heeley) ★ ★ ★ ★ *lemon verbena* $$$
In French bars and restaurants, infusions are served in large, thick-walled, frequently octagonal cups and, particularly when ordered after a slap-up meal spanning pan-fried frog's legs to profiteroles, have the feel of an absolution from sins of recent commission. Verveine is especially effective, with its semiprecious color of liquid peridot and the little paper tab that says "du Velay," a caressingly named, mysterious, and so far unidentified region from which all verbena apparently originates. Heeley's Verveine perfectly captures the plangent, minor-third feel of verbena in a fresh, floral context. Compare and contrast this with Eau de Guerlain, where a similar idea is arrived at from a sprightly citrus direction. LT

Very Irrésistible (Givenchy) ★ *woody floral* $
Everyone seems to be chasing a share of Allure's pot of gold these days,

and Very Irrésistible's advertising budget is so vast that it may succeed. Not that it deserves to. Allure was the Windows 98 of fragrance: bland, ugly, and successful only in terms of a vast installed base. VI goes beyond that: it is so nondescript, so cheaply derivative, so utterly devoid of beauty that it achieves a kind of bleak perfection. It is a perfume designed to be worn on a rainy Tuesday morning, standing in a crowded suburban train full of people on their way to work, each nursing a sleepy dream of early retirement while avoiding the others' glances. LT

Very Irrésistible for Men (Givenchy) ★ *fresh woody* $
Nothing of the sort, my dear. Despite the accent on the *é*, which suggests a refined Charles Boyer diction, this is about as trite a piece of perfumery as it is possible to do. If it were a Lynx deodorant, with an $8-per-kilogram perfume-oil budget, I would hail it as a masterpiece. As a proper fragrance, it is a sad joke, with a skeletal bitter-green accord up top and a loathsomely powerful woody-herbaceous thing beneath. I look forward to smelling cheap imitations of this in the markets of the Middle East, assuming anyone bothers: I wager they will be better than the original. LT

Very Irrésistible Fresh Attitude (Givenchy) ★ *woody citrus* $
Hilariously misconceived and loud. An attempt at grapefruit has been made by adding a huge sulfurous note of tropical fruit (oxane) that makes it feel like you're trying to cover up a smell of dope by spraying cheap aftershave. If you can ask for it by name without laughing, you're the ideal guy for it. LT

Very Irrésistible Sensual eau de parfum (Givenchy) ★
woody floral $
Brighter beginning, same sad end. Strawberry-flavored hemlock. LT

Very Pretty (Michael Kors) ★ ★ *shrubbery melon* $$
A thin slice taken out of Parfums DelRae's Amoureuse. This is a vast

improvement over the original Michael Kors tuberose of terror but still too close in spirit and budget to a functional formula. TS

Very Sexy for Her (Victoria's Secret) ★ *sour metallic* $
I have been racking my brain, trying to understand how one of the most unpleasant fragrances ever made was developed and brought to market. It consists of a loud metallic note (which you can replicate at home by chewing on a piece of aluminum foil) plus the sourest woody amber ever and a whiff of stale pizza. Let us charitably assume that its self-proclaimed sexiness has to do with the personal memories of some Victoria's Secret executive who falls helplessly into erotic fantasies in the presence of chemical spills and has mistaken this for a universal experience. Are people buying this? This fragrance and Givenchy's Very Irrésistible lead one to believe that *very* is actually perfume industry jargon for "not at all." TS

Very Sexy for Him (Victoria's Secret) ★ ★ *green woody* $
Although there is nothing particularly interesting going on in this clean, violet-leaf masculine, which smells like hundreds of others, it is, unlike its feminine counterpart, not hideous. TS

Very Sexy Hot (Victoria's Secret) ★ *mango raincoat* $
Happily, this fragrance has nothing to do with the original Very Sexy. Sadly, it is a barely-there fruity floral that smells mostly like PVC, which I would describe in greater detail, only there is no greater detail. TS

Vetiver (Annick Goutal) ★ ★ ★ ★ *salty vetiver* $$$
Every vetiver has its twist, this one particularly surprising. Having just recently thought long and hard about L'Air du Temps, I found, on smelling the top note of Goutal's Vetiver, that it had a familiar face. Its salty, seaside air feels incongruously like a fifties floral, turning this traditionally austere masculine material unexpectedly dressy, an evening gown done in gray super 120s. TS

Vetiver (Creed) ★ *not vetiver* $$$
Creed has, as my father would have said, gone where the hand of man never set foot, and made a vetiver that does not smell of vetiver, which is a shame because (1) vetiver smells good, and (2) whatever is in there instead does not. LT

Vetiver (Etro) ★ ★ ★ ★ *smoky woody* $$
Another of Jacques Flori's quietly masterful compositions for Etro, a proper licorice-and-earth vetiver, surrounded by a rich herbaceous-woody accord with a fresh, smoky drydown. Nice work. LT

Vetiver (Floris) ★ ★ *citrus vetiver* $$
A dry, fresh vetiver with a nice bourbon note up top and an overly simple grassy drydown. TS

Vetiver (Guerlain) ★ ★ ★ ★ *reference vetiver* $$
Though it is much thinner and drier than the original (about which I could write volumes), and despite the far greater choice available today than thirty years ago, this is still one of the best vetivers around. I still prefer the perversely confidential Vetiver pour Elle because of its greater complexity. LT

Vetiver (Lorenzo Villoresi) ★ ★ *vetiver vetiver* $$$
A very simple vetiver, initially citric, then herbal and woody, then, quickly, nothing. TS

Le Vetiver (Lubin) ★ ★ ★ ★ *incense vetiver* $$
Add another excellent vetiver to the pile. This one is unfussy and well proportioned, made of good stuff, with an impressively rich citrus-herbal top note washed clean by calm cold-smoke air similar to the cypriol in Timbuktu. The drydown is a sleek pine-incense vetiver colored lightly with clove. Smooth and resinous, close to those charming, open-

shirted Italian masculines, such as Krizia Uomo and Tuscany per Uomo, but with enough buttons done to avoid frightening your mom. Relaxed, handsome, one tanned wrist on the steering wheel, top down. Groovy bottle. TS

Vetiver 46 (Le Labo) ★ ★ *church incense* $ $
If you're familiar with Le Labo's scrupulous attention to labeling, you'd expect this not to smell of vetiver, and you'd be right: it smells of floor wax and cold incense, pretty much the sensation you get when you pass the second of the two airlock doors that prevent angels from escaping and enter a small, old, and well-kept Catholic church. LT

Vétiver Babylone (Armani Privé) ★ ★ ★ *woody citrus* $ $ $
Does not significantly smell of vetiver. For the first hour, it's a remake of Terre d'Hermès with the sparkle removed. Nice grapefruit-citrus top note, basically inoffensive milky-metallic-wood drydown, with a sporty structure that LT assures me is derived ultimately from the eighties predecessor of all these sad citrus-wood masculines—Cacharel pour l'Homme. I can't figure out who would spend this kind of money on something that smells so cheap, no matter what the actual cost of materials. TS

Vetiver Dance (Tauer Perfumes) ★ ★ *woody floral* $ $
Andy Tauer, a remarkable self-taught perfumer, works in a simultaneously ancient and modern aesthetic: balsams, wood, rose, herbs. His Vetiver Dance is an effort in the style of transparent woody scents like Elternhaus's MoslBuddJewChristHinDao and the grapefruit-vetiver of Terre d'Hermès. But Tauer's scent suffers first from the wrong rose—an opaque, metallic, sugary-powdery affair—and second from too many powerful materials upstaging each other until they fall into the footlights. This sort of fragrance needs to whisper, not shout. TS

Vetiver Extraordinaire (Frédéric Malle) ★ ★ ★ ★
angular vetiver $$$
The vetiver weed is unusual among perfumery materials in (1) having
no synthetic counterpart worth smelling and (2) being so distinctive in
personality that nearly all fragrances in which it is a majority compo-
nent are named after it, on the grounds that it would be futile to pretend
otherwise. When I was eight years old, my mother used to send me
down the rue Dauphine to what today would be termed a collectibles
shop specializing in Caribbean goods, to buy little bundles of the dried
roots. Let one thing be clear: no bottled vetiver to date comes close to
the dry, dusty, austere, yet fresh smell of the roots themselves. It is as if
only a withered solid could take on the role. Extracts of vetiver, of which
there are many, always tend toward an oilier, almost licorice-like note.
The problem seems to be that what we smell in the roots is slimmer, not
fatter, than what is extracted, so that adding other things is unlikely to
help. Vetiver has been married with a huge variety of partners ranging
from ginger to vanilla. Here Dominique Ropion performs an interesting
trick akin to an optical illusion by adding lead-pencil cedar notes and
what could be a touch of lemon. They work almost as makeup to hollow
out the cheeks of perfumery vetiver and give it back some of the striking
bone structure of the starting material. Beautiful work. LT

Vetiver Extrême (Guerlain) ★ *vetiver disaster* $$
This egregious screwup manages to almost obliterate the central vetiver
note that makes the normal version so pleasant, while flanking it on one
side by a dismally dry sports-fragrance accord that has no business being there and on the other by a hopelessly cheap, sweet English Leather
drydown that would be ideal in furniture polish. Awful. LT

Vetiver Oriental (Serge Lutens) ★ ★ ★ *vetiver amber* $$$
It's called an oriental but feels like an alternate universe chypre, in which
the forest smell of oakmoss has been replaced by an unusually vivid
vetiver. Just about everyone loves vetiver, but it's hard to make it bend.

Setting it in an oriental structure is at first off-puttingly sweet but surprisingly effective: curiously the vetiver feels crisper than ever against its iris-and-amber background. On skin, it loses its balance quickly, however, so you might want to spray on fabric. TS

Vetiver pour Elle (Guerlain) ★ ★ ★ ★ *floral vetiver* $ $
Guerlain's original Vetiver was in its day (circa 1965) the best of the breed: fresh, subtle, endearingly true to the raw material, and yet a proper fragrance. Time has somewhat eroded it, and the competition (Lutens, Frédéric Malle) has caught up. But this "feminine" version puts it once again ahead of the pack. Vetiver pour Elle feels like a lash-up, a jury-rigged fragrance done in a hurry, but is none the worse for it. Take the original for men, add a touch of jasmine to make it girly up top, then put in some of the powdery luminescent musk of Lauder's Pleasures to make it smell modern, and finish the whole thing off with a chypre base reminiscent of a stripped-down Mitsouko. The result is a wonderfully balanced, durable, friendly vetiver to wear every day. I wager that, were it widely available, it would be a best seller. Inexplicably, Guerlain sells it only in the duty-free stores of Paris airports and railway stations. One more reason to fly to Paris. LT

Vetiver Tonka (Hermès) ★ ★ ★ *rum vetiver* $ $ $
VT smelled familiar, and it took me a while to figure out where I'd come across this vetiver-coffee-rum accord before. The answer is the spectacular, far more intense, and irresistibly attractive Yohji Homme, Duriez's first masterpiece at Patou while he was still assistant to Jean Kerléo, and which you should get while stocks last. LT

Vetyver (Givenchy) ★ ★ ★ ★ *quality vetiver* $
This, for the tiny but growing band of vetiver fanatics, is probably the longest-awaited reissue of all time. Hubert de Givenchy's nephew once explained to me that this fragrance was his uncle's favorite, and had been kept in the line for decades despite being a slow seller. When Hu-

bert left the firm, it was discontinued. The consensus then was that, given the downward drift in quality in Guerlain's and Carven's vetivers over the years, the greatest vetiver of all had been lost. No doubt nostalgia played a part in this assessment. The reissue has a wonderfully straighforward, fresh, aldehydic, almost waxy vetiver top note, then settles down to an excellent dry-earthy heart. No surprises, just excellent quality all around. LT

Vetyver (Parfums de Nicolaï) ★ ★ ★ *complex vetiver* $
A good vetiver, perhaps a touch overly elaborate to my taste, and with the slightly rubbery aspect of that multifaceted root dominant. LT

Vetyver Cologne (Jo Malone) ★ ★ *citrus cologne* $$$
Reminds me of British sausages, which should carry the warning "May contain traces of meat." A cologne with a vetiver-shaped hole. LT

Via Camarelle (Carthusia) ★ ★ ★ *floral cologne* $$
Fleeting citrus floral with a pleasant bitter-orange top note. TS

Vicolo Fiori (Etro) ★ ★ ★ *sweet floral* $$
Pleasant, very girly, sweet-fresh millefleurs accord with a green, almost vegetable fresh-peas drydown. Slightly screechy in parts, but very good indeed. LT

Vie de Château (Parfums de Nicolaï) ★ ★ ★ ★ *citrus chypre* $$
Formerly called Cheverny, this fragrance feels like de Nicolaï's spruce-but-sexy tribute to Edmond Roudnitska: it has the woody structure of Diorella and the citrus of Eau Sauvage together with a wonderful minor chord of tarragon and costus that reminds me of the late and lamented Ocean Rain. An odd feature of this fragrance is that most days I find it perfectly sized, and then some days way too loud, for no obvious reason. LT

Vierges et Toreros (Etat Libre d'Orange) ★ ★ ★ *peppery leather* $ $
The ingredient lists on ELdO's Web site are unusually honest, at any rate
by comparison with the Dakota orchids that flourish elsewhere in the
fevered dreams of PR interns. V&T's composition lists the wonderful
base Animalis, a material I always felt Synarome should have sold directly to the public, but it fails to list a terebrant woody-amber that feels
like an ultrasonic whistle. This woody-leather was composed by the two
Antoines (Lie and Maisondieu) who have done most of ELdO's fragrances, and is wonderfully striking until you realize that it is none
other than Bulgari Black shorn of the green velvet that made the original so plush. LT

Vintage Gardenia Cologne (Jo Malone) ★ ★ *peculiar floral* $ $
Conjuring up gardenia mostly in the far drydown, VGC spends a lot of
time in a syrupy nutmeg-and-tuberose phase, with a funny bubblegum
effect probably related to Poême. Feels heavy despite being not very
strong. Not unpleasant, but not much of a gardenia. TS

Violetta (Penhaligon's) ★ ★ ★ ★ *honest violet* $ $
Violet fragrances, though usually illustrated by lovely shots of purple
flowers nestled among deep-green leaves, are actually shrines to organic
chemistry. The discovery of ionones in the 1880s lowered the price of
violet-flower smell almost a millionfold in a few years and made violets
the most popular cheap scent at the turn of the twentieth century. The
later discovery of synthetic violet-leaf materials, chiefly octin (acetylenic) esters, filled in the green in the picture. After enjoying a huge
fashion that stretched all the way to delicious sweets (try French Flavi-
gny pastilles or Choward's Violet Flavored Mints!), ionones faded into
the background as mainstays of florals, seldom getting solo roles except
in eccentric compositions like Balenciaga's sadly discontinued Le Dix
and Serge Lutens's Bois de Violette. Related molecules like damascones
and irones, respectively fruitier and classier, took over. Today few firms
do a no-holds-barred violet, and it is fitting that Penhaligon's should,

given its origins in the heyday of ionones. Violetta is exactly what it says, a lovely three-pointed accord of powdery woods, purple sugar, and mean green. Everyone should have this, not least to whip it out when, in discussions about wine or fragrance, someone says, "I'm getting violets." Leaf or flower? LT

La Violette (Annick Goutal) ★ ★ ★ ★ *fresh violet* $$$
This is a vivacious, fresh, and pink-cheeked fragrance, with all the fruity and green-leaf aspects of violet emphasized and the woody-powdery part downplayed. It has a slight smell of glue or paint thinner, which doesn't detract from the fun. Think of it as an eccentric sister to the even more exuberant Drôle de Rose. TS

Violette Précieuse (Caron) ★ ★ ★ *violet leaf* $$$
VP has gone through three known stages: first, a gorgeous, big composition of confectionary violet, holding sweetness and tartness in delicious balance, and then somewhat later a good but simple woody iris-violet, with a quiet, rainy-day feel. It was discontinued and is back utterly different again, a combination of green violet leaf and sweet violet, closer to Annick Goutal's La Violette. Would make a good masculine. TS

Virgilio (Diptyque) ★ ★ ★ ★ *thyme floral* $$
Cooking herbs tend to play a low-key but essential role in fragrances, invisibly bending everything in the direction of the edible, casting warm Provençal sunshine on all. Smelling the beautifully simple accord of Virgilio is an enlightening surprise, like getting one of the hidden mysteries of L'Heure Bleue isolated and magnified for study: how a pinch of thyme scatters earth and salt on what would otherwise have been a naively sweet floral (it's not bad on leg of lamb either). TS

Virgin Island Water (Creed) ★ ★ *piña colada* $$$
Olivier Creed has traveled the world collecting rare coconuts, limes, and bottles of rum to compose the bathtub-sized cocktail he drank before

he decided to release something this close to Bath & Body Works Coconut Lime Verbena at eleven times the price. TS

Visa (Robert Piguet) ★ ★ ★ ★ *fruity leather* $$$
I was lucky enough to smell a bit of the original Visa when a friend of mine bought a bottle on eBay from a seller who had inherited the intact inventory of a perfume shop closed for decades. Composed by the idiosyncratic Germaine Cellier in 1945, the first Visa was an intense, sweet animalic oriental, powdery with amber and civet and a dose of herbs: in other words, pretty much Tabu (1932, by Jean Carles). That kind of thing has gone seriously out of style, so when young perfumer Aurélien Guichard was called upon to reorchestrate it for modern fragrance lovers, they kept nothing but the name and started from scratch. The new Visa, which could never be mistaken for a classic fragrance, has more in common with Guichard's Chinatown for Bond No. 9 than it does with its old namesake. It is essentially a fruity chypre, a sugared peach played dry, in an austere leather-and-wood style reminiscent of Serge Lutens's recent apricot-suede Daim Blond, and given a lovely strangeness in the drydown by the burnt-sugar-and-curry note of immortelle. It's the Piguet reorchestration least respectful of the original, but ignoring that, there's no denying it's good. Like a flashlight seen through your hands, it turns out that a straightforward fruity floral glows more brightly when given something to shine through. TS

Vista sul Mare (Linari) ★ ★ *metallic citrus* $$$
"Sea View"? Let me look on the database. Marine notes . . . there! Calone. And you're lucky, the price just went down. This would be a barely passable fragrance in a Best Western squeezy-bottle shampoo called Fresh Experience but is a total, shameless rip-off in an upmarket fragrance line. LT

Viva la Juicy (Juicy Couture) ★ ★ *sugary musk* $$
I suspect that Firmenich keeps a swimming-pool-sized vat filled with a

diabolically saccharine standard mixture of fruit flavor, vanilla, and musk, fixed with a tap, for perfumers to decant for clients who use pink in the packaging. A competently crafted piece of idiocy. TS

Vivara (Pucci) ★ ★ *melon woody* $ $
The original Vivara was a spicy chypre, but this is completely different: an almost interesting melon-aquatic smell paired with a metallic amber. Faceless, chilly, alien. Makes me think of hospital instruments. TS

Vocalise (Maître Parfumeur et Gantier) ★ ★ *sweet floral* $ $
Vocalise used to be a great green floral, but no longer. It is now a cloying thing that smells of boiled sweets. LT

Voile d'Ambre (Yves Rocher) ★ ★ ★ *amber tonka* $
With Iris Noir and Rose Absolue, this is one of three upmarket fragrances courageously released by Yves Rocher. Voile d'Ambre is a perfectly respectable coumarinic amber, warm, clean and long-lasting, a bargain at the price. LT

Voile de Jasmin (Bulgari) ★ *floral wreck* $ $
Voile, meaning "veil"? More like tarp. This is one of those nauseating white florals that manage to wreck a core of perfectly respectable natural materials by making them shout into a distorting megaphone of high-impact synthetics. LT

Vol de Nuit (Guerlain) ★ ★ ★ ★ ★ *woody oriental* $ $ $
During the writing of this guide, both authors felt at regular intervals a need to recalibrate their olfactory apparatus to obtain both a reliable zero (Creed's Love in White will do fine) and a full-scale quality reading. The latter can be achieved using almost any one of the old Guerlains, but I find Vol de Nuit is best for calibration purposes because it embodies pure excellence in raw materials and, to me, little else, thereby ensuring that my judgment is not clouded by emotional associations. In

truth, VdN (Night Flight), released two years after its namesake—Saint-Exupéry's superb 1931 novel about mail flights to South America—is by Guerlain standards a somewhat shapeless perfume, lacking a legible structure. But it gives me the pleasure, the tickle of anticipation, the feeling of unobstructed space and pinpoint clarity I get when I settle into my seat at an orchestral concert and hear the players practicing. Almost all other fragrances, when compared with VdN, sound like they're being played through the sort of radio people hold up to their ear not to miss the ballgame. God bless Guerlain for still doing this stuff. LT

Voleur de Roses (L'Artisan Parfumeur) ★ ★ *rose patchouli* $ $
I've always had a soft spot for guys wearing roses—it's that English-dandy flair. Voleur de Roses is mostly a rich, grassy patchouli with a wine-like angle, colored with an equally wine-like dark fruity rose. (Curiously, it reminds me of the smell of my Strawberry Shortcake doll from second grade.) Sadly, it thins out to a merely camphoraceous patchouli after the fun boozy start. TS

Vraie Blonde (Etat Libre d'Orange) ★ ★ ★ ★ *milky floral* $ $
It is remarkable to see an apparently gimmicky firm like ELdO come up time and again with perfumes of genuine substance, complexity, and interest. To paraphrase Lady Bracknell, two is good fortune, but three looks like intelligence. This perfumer, young Antoine Maisondieu, is clearly a talent to watch. His Vraie Blonde (Real Blonde) is deeply strange, a deliberately odd structure with a bruised-fruit smell reminiscent of the decadence of Champagne (now called Yvresse), but taken even further with an almost buttermilk note in the drydown. If this is the future, I like it very much. LT

Wall Street (Bond No. 9) ★ ★ ★ *melon green* $ $ $
I used to dislike this fragrance intensely—its loud top note of violet leaf

and citrus gave the impression of a slick young dude trying to gel his hair higher than the one in the next Miata. ("Fahrenheit," said LT.) But as Wall Street mellows, it becomes almost girly, finding a pretty, fresh resting place between fruity and green. You could be fooled into trying to get to know this guy. TS

West Broadway (Bond No. 9) ★ ★ *fresh woody* $$$
The delightful top note of West Broadway hits you right in the yoga mat: a pleasingly medicinal accord of cedar and spicy notes with a fresh, green lily-of-the-valley lift—an oriental in the modern hold-the-vanilla style. Sadly, a big, blunt, synthetic woody amber overwhelms the drydown. Otherwise ayurvedic and copacetic, although one unimpressed male friend declared it Old Spice. TS

West Side (Bond No. 9) ★ ★ *heavy rose* $$$
Something is not quite right with this dense rose-vanilla from Bond No. 9, which has a very eighties heft to it. I had a chance to smell it before its release, when I seem to recall a fresh peony note gave it a much-needed breath of air. As it is now, it seems a confused muddle, reminding me of those liqueur-filled chocolates in gold foil you sometimes buy on impulse at the cash register and regret. If you still want a rose-vanilla, seek out the beautiful and clear Tocade (Rochas) instead. TS

What About Adam (Joop!) ★ ★ ★ *grapefruit lavender* $
My fondness for Calice Becker's creations is no secret, and WAA is a fine illustration of her talent. The drydown is not particularly successful, a hybrid between Caron's Pour un Homme and Lutens' Encens et Lavande without the coherence of either. But the top notes! Seldom has a masculine fragrance opened with a more incongruously interesting chord: a shimmering arpeggiato of tomato stems, grapefruit, and blackcurrant buds (all sulfur notes) that dances like a brightly colored butterfly in front of your nose and flies off before you can focus on it. LT

White Aoud (Montale) ★ ★ ★ *saffron oud* $$$
Rich, pleasant woody-spicy (saffron and oud) composition in the Arabic style; very comfortable. LT

White Diamonds (Elizabeth Taylor) ★ ★ ★ *soft bouquet* $
Jennifer Lopez was still just a Fly Girl when ur-celebrity-fragrance-queen Elizabeth Taylor came out with White Diamonds (1991), her second feminine fragrance after Passion and her best. This is a soft woody floral in the classic mold, slightly low-budget but pretty good—lush, creamy, and sweet, with a tropical white-flowers accord smelling slightly like ripe bananas, all bolstered by some of those big, powdery musks you'll recognize from your laundry soap. Seems designed to waft up from cleavage. TS

White Flowers (YOSH) ★ ★ *strident muguet* $$$
It can be difficult to do a fresh, lily-of-the-valley white floral without risking a functional feel; even some of the vintage, classic muguets I've smelled were far too close to household cleaner. YOSH's variation is more scrub powder than Diorissimo, sadly. TS

White Jasmine and Mint (Jo Malone) ★ ★ ★ *herbal cologne* $$$
An optimistic but crude cologne, which smells like a rough white floral paired with basil, and tries to make everything last longer by throwing in a tenacious musk. Vigorous but unnecessary—eau de cologne had already achieved better than this in the 1700s, and several years back Artisan Parfumeur did a lovely crisp jasmine tea with mint in its Thé pour un Eté. TS

White Linen (Estée Lauder) ★ ★ ★ ★ *aldehydic floral* $
Say "aldehydes" in a conversation about fragrance and everyone thinks of Chanel: the groundbreaking No. 5 and the even more aldehydic No. 22. If the aldehydic floral of aldehydic florals, White Linen, done in 1978 by the great Sophia Grojsman, doesn't spring to mind, that is an injus-

tice, but perhaps understandable given that White Linen is neither French nor prohibitively expensive. You simply might not see it, the way you might not see your glasses sitting on top of your head. Lauder's personal favorite (according to the company) is a canonical expression of the American ideal of sex appeal: squeaky clean, healthy, depilated and exfoliated, well rested and ready for the day. Its sharp, biting aldehydes are bright and soapy; the soft musks and woods are a richer version of your favorite fabric softener; the roses are complex, green, and a touch peppery; the whole thing is comfortable and well lit, like a warm spot on the floor where the cat sleeps. (The parfum is softer and more floral than the eau.) I think of it as having a maternal, protective aura, and it reminds me of Thomas Pynchon describing the smell of breakfast floating over World War II–era London as "a spell against falling objects." Guys and gals could both wear it when the sun shines. TS

White Patchouli (Tom Ford) ★ ★ *patchouli cleanser* $$$
There should be a hold on the use of colors in fragrance names, especially black and white, because they seem to beget little more than pretentious duds. This, like many of the Fords, is an interesting idea left unfinished: a passage-to-India patchouli set against an intensely synthetic white-flower background. The latter seems to consist mainly of so-called lily-of-the-valley aldehydes, compounds beloved of industrial cleaning firms for their ability to cover the smell of stale smoke. The cavernous interiors of Las Vegas hotels reek of the stuff. The combination with patchouli feels like sitting at breakfast at the MGM Grand next to an aging hippie on her first margarita of the day—at 6 a.m. LT

White Petals (Keiko Mecheri) ★ ★ *powdery floral* $$$
A sweet woody floral, nice but bare and quick to vanish. TS

White Red He (Armani) ★ *woody spicy* $
The name sounds like an utterance by the sort of person Oliver Sacks would be interested in. The fragrance (the work of four perfumers, usu-

ally a bad sign) is the sort of thing nobody with his brain entire would be remotely interested in. LT

White Red She (Armani) ★ *fruity floral* $
Fragrance equivalent of a Motel 6. LT

White Rose (Floris) ★ *fake rose* $$
Loud artificial rose, powdery and sweet with a dose of waxy lemon, the sort of formula they put in car air fresheners and premoistened towelettes. TS

White Shoulders (Elizabeth Arden) ★ ★ ★ *white floral* $
Irretrievably mumsy but attractive floral that has existed in some form since 1945, when it was made by Evyan. I've never smelled it before, so can't tell you how it used to be, although I suspect it would have been richer and more natural than the version on my arm right now, which is slightly hollow. It's still a pleasant, fresh muguet-tuberose with a good dose of clove, a sort of defanged Fracas, and so unbendably maternal-feminine that if Harvey Keitel sprayed it on, he would spontaneously sprout a ruffled apron and ask you if you wanted another cupcake. TS

Wild Berries (Keiko Mecheri) ★ ★ *raspberry ripple* $$
Fruity florals tend to port over scents familiar as flavors to fine fragrance, and this is the "mixed berry" of dark red hard candies everywhere, given a fresh floral air to disguise its foody origins. Yet somehow it's sad instead of cheerful, neither appetizing nor cute. TS

Wild Fig and Cassis Cologne (Jo Malone) ★ ★ ★ *fig leaf* $$$
Interesting and, by Jo Malone standards, recklessly adventurous green-leafy accord, the sort of thing that might cement your reputation of having "gone native" since Papa bought you that farmhouse in the Dordogne. LT

Wind Song (Prince Matchabelli) ★ ★ *aldehydic floral* $
I had naively assumed for years that Prince Matchabelli was the pure invention of a marketing executive with a poor grasp of Italian. I was wrong, of course: Prince George V. Matchabelli (1885–1935) was the genuine article, a Georgian aristocrat and amateur chemist who started his own perfume firm in 1924. I have no idea what the stuff smelled like at the time, but I assume it must have been pretty good (it was composed by the great Ernest Shiftan) to succeed as it did. Today's stuff is a cheap floral aldehydic, and—unless you're on the way to the prom, desperately need a smell for your cleavage, have only $5, and find Wind Song next to the beef jerky at the gas station—I see no reason to buy it. LT

Wish (Chopard) ★ ★ ★ *cherry Baileys* $ $
A well-constructed though very chemical fruity-milky oriental. One of the better exemplars of that generally dreadful genre, the Angel clones. LT

Wish Pink Diamond (Chopard) ★ *phobic floral* $ $
A 50/50 mix of Pleasures and Tommy Girl. Dire. LT

Wish Turquoise Diamond (Chopard) ★ *dire fruit* $ $
I'm always hoping against hope that one of these fruity florals will finally make it in the "so bad it's good" category. But no. LT

Wisteria (Chantecaille) ★ *Windex actually* $ $ $
Being neither botanist nor garden enthusiast, I couldn't tell you what wisteria smells like. I hope it doesn't smell like this. TS

With Love . . . (Hilary Duff) ★ ★ *pineapple cedar* $
You'd be forgiven for expecting a standard fruity floral from starlet Duff, but With Love . . . unexpectedly speeds through a pleasant milky-woody-coconut phase and ends up with a dry, butch cedar amber and a

chin in need of a razor. The TV advertising indicates that this a sophisticated, grown-up fragrance, as evidenced by Duff's evening gown and clinch in the elevator with a dopey suitor. But tell him to watch out, since the fragrance seems to say that when young women grow up, they become men. Surprise! TS

Wode (Boudicca) ★ ★ ★ *raw hide* $$$
Puckish packaging puts the scent in an aluminum spray can and tints the eau de toilette with vanishing blue dye. For several scary seconds you look like you're wearing half a bottle of Parker Quink. Could be advertised in the back of *Mad* magazine alongside the whoopee cushions: "Frighten your friends!" But how's it smell? A cruelly literal leather. Perfumery leather usually comes in a gilded-tissue idea of luxury. Despite being probably vegan-safe, Wode is closer to a crocodile vest spotted in Bangkok, with the animal's head and forelimbs dangling off the chest. Wode is not a chypre plus isoquinolines; neither is it a touch of rectified birch tar painted on iris nor a whiff of suede in vanilla. Its inky vegetal harshness smells sort of like a shoe store and is not wholly pleasant, though it's not boring either. Composed by the talented, idiosyncratic Geza Schoen. TS

Wood & Absinth (By Mark Buxton) ★ ★ *dry cheap* $$$
Cacharel pour l'Homme twenty-seven years too late. LT

Xeryus (Givenchy) ★ ★ ★ *floral fougère* $
You know you're getting old when you can't take bumper cars anymore and they start reissuing fragrances that date to when you were fully grown. Xeryus is typical of the mideighties, when masculines were following a Foghorn Leghorn strategy of crowing louder to keep up with Poison and Giorgio. Some from that period feel like a mariachi band has crept up behind you and burst into "La Paloma" without warning. Xeryus is loud but not overly so, an admirably complex composition, but like many of that transitional time it feels like a hybrid between classical

and modern, a lungfish with both legs and gills. Interesting but hard to wear. LT

Xeryus Rouge (Givenchy) ★ ★ ★ *woody oriental* $
I sometimes detect in Annick Ménardo's works (Black, Hypnotic Poison) a restless modernist urge to build structures with a classical feel but renovated from the ground up by using only modern materials. This is one of the hardest things to do in perfumery, in part because one has to replace each of the complex naturals one is trying to supersede with a completely new accord made of synthetics, and that alone is a titanic task. Xeryus Rouge comes close to an Habit Rouge–like feel but ultimately fails to convince. Is it a touch too sweet, a touch too cheap? Hard to say. Frustratingly close to greatness. LT

X for Men (Clive Christian) ★ ★ ★ *wood moss* $ $ $ $
Very reminiscent of cheerful seventies Italian masculines like Pino Silvestre, a nice spicy-woody composition that feels good and works fine. LT

X for Women (Clive Christian) ★ ★ ★ ★ *milky hefty* $ $ $ $
Halfway between the original (and far subtler) Dioressence and the daringly direct Gucci Rush, this is a big, intense, scarily tenacious fruity-milky thing. Not bad. LT

XS "Excess pour Homme" (Paco Rabanne) ★ ★ *citrus woody* $
Another green herbal fougère, but this time in a thin, sour-lemon style. If this is excess, let's trim it. TS

Y (Yves Saint Laurent) ★ ★ ★ ★ *green chypre* $ $
This is the archetypal green chypre, fresh, scrubbed, prim and proper, made of excellent raw materials, with the slightly screechy feeling of silk-clad thighs rubbing together. If this were an actress, it would be Danielle Darrieux. If it were a wine it would be a Chablis. If it were a car

it would be a vanilla-yellow convertible Citroën DS. If it were a piece of music it would be the theme of *Les Parapluies de Cherbourg*. LT

Yatagan (Caron) ★ ★ ★ ★ ★ *woody oriental* $$
Caron is home to both one of the most reassuring (Pour un Homme) and one of the most disturbing (this one) masculine fragrances of all time. In the lovely Caron corner shop on Avenue Montaigne in Paris, I witnessed more than one customer recoiling at the smell of Yatagan on his hand, while the sales assistant suavely explained that it was "big in the Middle East," as if some sort of perfume heresy had taken hold *in partibus infidelium*. The truth, of course, was that this 1976 creation and its mysterious Levantine fan club were thirty years ahead of their time. Considered as voices, many masculine orientals try very hard to be warm and husky. More Kaa the Snake than Baloo the Bear, Yatagan goes for a uniquely strange, high-pitched, hissing tone, with odd, borderline sweaty-sour notes of caraway and sage up top, and a dry, inky wood structure below. Respect, or possibly neglect, has spared Yatagan the largely disastrous recent reformulation of Caron fragrances. Rush to buy it before they screw it up. LT

Yatra (Aveda) ★ ★ ★ ★ *rose patchouli* $$
Before the Lauder purchase, Aveda used to have a full lineup of fragrances named after (what else?) the chakras, those whistle-stops of the spirit on its way up to the train shed. In my recollection, the fragrances were well put together, suffered from ills common to most all-natural perfumery, and smelled like paisley for the nose: richly colored, dark, complicated in a wallpaper sort of way, and essentially formless. Some years ago I met Aveda's distinguished Japanese perfumer, Koichi Shiozawa, and he explained to me the immense technical difficulties facing the natural perfumer: a small, expensive, and shrinking palette of variable quality. Something must have happened in the natural-materials field, because the creations are getting better, either because they use new materials or because a lost skill is being rebuilt and extended. Yatra

is remarkably similar to Aesop's Marrakech, only more floral, and is in some ways a hippie version of Aromatics Elixir. It includes a piercing earthy patchouli at the top of the heart accord, which gives it lift and brilliance and dispels what would otherwise be herbaceous murk. Yatra has some of the easy nobility of archaic fragrances but with an oddly modern touch. LT

Yerbamate (Lorenzo Villoresi) ★★ *chalky floral* $$
After a cool herbal green top note with a dark chocolate bittersweetness, there follows a combination of pipe tobacco and a cloying lilac floral reminiscent of air freshener, which then dwindles to a thin, harsh odor, the perfumery equivalent of a ringing in the ears. TS

Yohji Homme (Yohji Yamamoto) ★★★★★ *licorice fougère* $$
I shall never forget smelling Yohji Homme for the first time. I was on holidays in Corsica in 1998, and a parcel came from Patou (they used to do the Yohjis) containing a long, distinctive bottle. I sprayed it and fell in love with it so comprehensively that I sat at my computer for a couple of hours just smelling my wrist and staring at the wall. My companions berated me for not going out and enjoying the sunshine, but nothing doing: I wanted to understand this fragrance, write about it while the feeling was fresh, and find out urgently who on earth could come up with something so beautiful. Two tendencies in masculine fragrance had been converging for some time, the woody-fresh (Anthracite Homme, Mark Buxton) and the exotically spicy (Egoïste, François Demachy/Jacques Polge). But their rails could not cross until someone figured out a specially shaped piece to make them merge without derailment. The someone was Jean-Michel Duriez, and the V-shaped material belonging to both worlds at once was licorice. When I finally spoke to him, he explained that he had been carrying the structure around in his head for years and had found the keystone to his accord in Annick Ménardo's brilliant essay on Angel, Lolita Lempicka a year earlier. There are only two or three masculines out there as good as this. We include it

Youth Dew (Estée Lauder) ★ ★ ★ ★ *powdery oriental* $

Something has happened to me, or something has happened to Youth Dew. I remembered this 1953 fragrance as an old-fashioned bludgeoner of a spiced-amber oriental, better as the bath oil it originated as, hopelessly dowdy in a little ribbed brown bottle that looked dusty even when new, and with a name that sounded like a euphemism for some unspeakable bodily fluid. Then today I opened the familiar mint-and-white Lauder box of eau de parfum only to find a wildly adorable bottle in curvaceous opaque baby blue, with small, elegant brown fifties lettering: retro fabulous. On skin, it smells like a lighter Tabu, brighter up top than I remember, more floral in the middle, lively and filled out, with a sweet nutmeg charm—a bit like an animalic cola. It smells terrific, top quality, sophisticated, and easy to wear. I don't usually stoop to point out such things, but, ladies, I must add that, at this writing, the standard retail price for a 2.2-ounce bottle is $28, which means Youth Dew remains true to Estée Lauder's genius idea of making a fragrance for women to buy as an everyday luxury and not a costly occasional pleasure. It's the scent that put Lauder (and American fragrance) on the map. TS

Youth Dew Amber Nude (Estée Lauder) ★ ★ ★ ★ *rich amber* $

This was the first Lauder perfume under Tom Ford's art direction. Ford showed at Gucci that he had a great sense of fragrance, famously choosing Michel Almairac's sensational Rush in seconds, in pure "make it so" fashion. Compared to what Ford did at Gucci, which was to take on a moribund firm chiefly purveying retired pimps and their molls and turn it into a world leader, his job at Lauder is easy. Lauder is only marginally dowdy, and the otherwise terrific perfumes, solidly affordable and American, made by, so to speak, the L. L. Bean of fragrance, supposedly needed an injection of high glamour. Given all that, Ford's way with the fragrance that put Lauder on the map fifty years ago is surprisingly subtle and respectful. Most of the original Youth Dew's resinous, almost medicinal balsamic structure is still present, but without the tarpaulin note that made the original both distinctive and, at length, a little dated. Instead, Amber Nude plays on an interesting contrast between relentless warmth and unexpectedly fresh, luminous notes. The sum total, as often happens with this type of fragrance, is affable but a little spineless. The name might have been Chomsky's second choice to illustrate the idea of a meaningless string of words, his first being the famous "Colorless green ideas sleep furiously." LT

Ysatis (Givenchy) ★ ★ ★ *woody floral* $
My fond recollection of Ysatis involved an intense creamy lemon custard note it shared with Byzance and others. The present formula, though good, is much more conventionally woody-floral and less interesting. LT

Yuzu Ab Irato (Parfumerie Générale) ★ ★ ★ ★ *lemon flower* $ $ $
If the list of materials recorded in Michael Edwards's database is correct, the brilliant yuzu top note of this fragrance is achieved without actually using any citrus materials, merely by marrying mint and pepper. That in itself would be noteworthy, but the rest of the fragrance is just as interesting. After the initial fresh blast, the balance drifts gradually and seamlessly to a woody-floral heart. YAI is PG's Eau de Guerlain: more complex than a cologne, richer in the heart, and more long-lived. Very nice work. LT

Yuzu Fou (Parfum d'Empire) ★ ★ ★ ★ *polyphonic citrus* $ $ $
The vile Japanese empire (I beg PdE to skip the Third Reich in its imperial tour) is represented by this baroque fantasy of citrus played on every material at once: the bloodstone-green, unwashed, sulfurous smells of grapefruit and bitter orange peel, the rasping white-flower lift of orange blossom, the sugary punch of candied orange, and the earthy crispness

of verbena. It leans on the whole keyboard of sensations from sweet to sour to savory on the way to a drydown similar to Eau d'Orange Verte. Excellent. TS

Yuzu Rouge (Parfums 06130) ★ ★ *bottled tea* $ $ $
The first fragrance from 06130 met the demand for apologetic fragrances with a bloodless citrus-rose plus hedione, crisp but wan. TS

Zafferano (Profumo di Firenze) ★ ★ *brief saffron* $ $ $ $
A sudden flurry of saffron fragrances a couple of years ago made the note fashionable again, and several major aromachemical outfits dusted off near-forgotten saffron materials. In this one the saffron lasts for five minutes, and the remainder is a sad drydown of cloying geraniol "rose." LT

Zegna Intenso (Ermenegildo Zegna) ★ ★ *fresh woody* $ $
Cloned masculine sport fragrance, of slightly better than average quality but still achingly dull. LT

Zen (Shiseido) ★ ★ ★ *fruity woody* $ $
The original Zen, in the black bottle with gold flowers, was a perfect woody rose; the second Zen, in an elliptical white plastic bottle, was a sharp green floral; the third and most recent, in a sheer golden cube, is a lactonic fruity floral in the bright modern style of Badgley Mischka, done on a fuzzed-out woody amber, a milder variant of Gucci Rush. TS

Un Zest de Rose (Parfums de Rosine) ★ ★ ★ *citrus rose* $ $
A simple fresh citrus rose, very natural smelling, with a touch of tea. TS

Zinnia (Floris) ★ ★ *green floral* $ $
Smelling the Floris florals is like staring at a catalog of wall paints open at the magnolia page: a slew of dull, tasteful shades, each abstract and

christened with a realist name seemingly at random. In the end, you snap and decide to go for Addams Black. LT

Zizan (Ormonde Jayne) ★ ★ *chemical woody* $ $
OJ always had an unnatural fondness for the "velvety" woody synthetic Iso E Super, forgivable when in the service, as with Ormonde, of a sort of muted radiance otherwise inaccessible. But in Zizan, mixed with a loud woody amber and amidst less texture than usual, it comes across as blokeish rather than manly. Zizan adds nothing to an otherwise great lineup. LT

Zoe (Fresh Scents by Terri) ★ *floral musk* $
A simple jasmine-based white floral with a strong, sweet soapy musk. Honestly, just wear Joy. TS

Z Zegna (Ermenegildo Zegna) ★ ★ ★ ★ *citrus herbal* $ $
My heart beat faster opening this, a very handsome bottle allegedly "Designed by Ducati," the motorcycle manufacturer from Borgo Pani-gale near Bologna, dear to every sentient man for their invention of a workable desmodromic valve cam in 1956. This being a book about fragrance, I cannot go into as much detail about this as I would like. The fragrance is a very presentable modern masculine, easily in the top five of a genre distinguished by asteroidal bleakness. Amazingly, it smells as though it contains natural ingredients, and as if some effort went into its composition. Give it to the man of your dreams, and rescue him from Clone Sport Fresh Turbo Blue. LT

GLOSSARY OF MATERIALS AND TERMS

absolute A solvent-extracted fragrance material, traditionally from more delicate natural substances, such as jasmine, which would be damaged by the high temperatures of steam distillation. When both an absolute and a steam-distilled essential oil are made from the same material, as is the case with rose, they tend to differ greatly due to the lower temperature of the solvent versus the steam. Traditional absolutes are derived by using alcohol to extract the fragrance from what is known as a *concrete*, a semisolid extraction of waxes and other substances as well as fragrance, though modern solvents may allow direct extraction of the absolute.

accord Several notes combined to create an effect; related to the idea of a musical chord.

aldehyde An organic compound that ends in a C=O(H) group. Perfumers use many different aldehydes in their palettes.

aldehydic Characterized by the smell of the straight-chain aliphatic aldehydes C10, C11, and C12, first used prominently in Chanel No. 5.

amber A blend of fragrant resins, such as styrax, benzoin, and cistus labdanum, traditional to the Middle East.

ambergris A substance produced in the stomach of the sperm whale, which coughs the material up into the ocean. Its characteristic odor, rich and marine, is attained only after years of floating in the sun. Synthetic ambergris substitutes are more often used, being cheaper and more reliable, but they smell little like the natural material.

animalic Characterized by bodily smells, or smells most associated with traditional animal materials, such as musk, castoreum, or civet.

balsamic Characterized by sweet-smelling fragrant plant resins, typically balsam of Peru, or tolu balsam.

base A prefabricated building block of fragrance composed of various materials and used as a single material by perfumers, such as the famous peach base Persicol.

butyric From the Greek for butter, a molecule (or, in the case of esters, part of a molecule) with a distinctive cheesy smell, encountered in rancid butter.

Calone A synthetic aromachemical with a distinctive fresh melon-aquatic character, used heavily in the nineties.

chypre A genre of perfume built on a structure made famous by Coty's Chypre from 1917, based on oakmoss, cistus labdanum, and bergamot. Chypres can be further divided into floral chypres, fruity chypres, leather chypres, and so on.

cistus labdanum A resin extracted from the leaves and branches of a flowering shrub known as a rockrose. Sometimes called simply cistus or labdanum, it has a sweet woody smell with smoky or leathery aspects, and is a traditional amber material.

civet Traditional perfumery material obtained from glands of the civet cat, usually cultivated in Ethiopia. It has a powerfully fecal character when pure. Civet has been largely replaced in perfumery by synthetic substitutes.

cologne The oldest extant fragrance genre, dating at least from the 1700s. Traditional eau de cologne is a blend of citrus, florals, herbs, and woods.

concrete A waxy, semisolid solvent-extraction from natural materials, which when further refined gives the *absolute.*

damascone Powerful materials with rosy-apple smells, related to the ionones of violets.

dihydromyrcenol Woody-citrus material much used in recent masculines.

drydown The late stage of a fragrance that develops after the top and heart notes subside and before the smell completely fades.

enfleurage A labor-intensive, low-yield traditional method of extraction, little used today, which collects the fragrance from more delicate materials like jasmine by surrounding the flowers with a fat that absorbs the odor over time.

essential oil A natural aromamaterial extracted by steam distillation, by which steam droplets capture and carry away the fragrant molecules, which when collected separate naturally into water- and oil-soluble parts, known as the hydrosol (e.g., rosewater) and the essential oil (e.g., rose oil).

ester Combination of an acid and an alcohol, that typically but not always gives a fruity smell.

fixative A material of higher molecular weight that, when added to a perfumery mixture, slows down the evaporation time of a fragrance, which means it lasts longer.

fougère A mostly masculine genre based on the original Fougère Royale, an abstract composition of lavender, oakmoss, and the tobacco-and-hay note of coumarin.

fine fragrance Fragrance sold as fragrance, and not as the scent of another product.

functional fragrance Scent for functional products, such as soaps and cosmetics.

galbanum A plant resin used since ancient times in medicines, incenses, and perfumes, notable for its distinctive bitter green smell.

gourmand A subset of orientals that has become more popular in recent years, designed to smell distinctly dessert-like with emphasis on vanilla.

green Smelling of cut grass or leaves.

heart note The middle portion of a fragrance, after the top note subsides but before the drydown, often considered to be the fragrance's true personality.

hedione An aromachemical used to impart a feel of dewy freshness to florals, first used significantly in Eau Sauvage.

helional A synthetic aromachemical with a milky-metallic character.

IFF International Flavors and Fragrances, a U.S.-based fragrance firm.

indole A molecule with an inky, bitter, fecal odor, occurring naturally both in human feces and white flowers, such as jasmine and orange blossom.

ionone Type of aromachemical that gives the main smell of violet flowers.

iris An extract of the rhizome of the iris plant. Among the most expensive natural materials in perfumery. Also known as iris butter, orris, or orris butter.

irone Type of aromachemical that gives the main smell character of iris.

ISIPCA Institut Supérieur International du Parfum, de la Cosmetique et de l'Aromatique Alimentaire, the only professional perfumery school outside of private firms.

lactonic Characterized by perfumery materials containing cyclic ester structures known as lactones, such as peach lactone and milk lactone, which can give a creamy-fruity smell to fragrances.

leather In perfumery, characterized by bitter-smelling isoquinolines or smoky-smelling rectified birch tar, to replicate the smell of the tanning chemicals used to prepare leather.

musk Traditionally an extract of the pods of the Himalayan musk deer, used both for its smell and for its fixative qualities in perfume, now largely replaced by various cheaper, more reliable synthetics.

niche Type of fragrance firm that produces in limited quantity and sells in few shops.

note An isolated smell in a fragrance (e.g., a note of jasmine).

oakmoss [also tree moss] Different species of mosses from which are extracted dry, bitter-smelling materials essential to chypre fragrances.

oriental A fragrance genre typified by an emphasis on amber, with the oldest surviving member being Shalimar. The genre may be subdivided into floral orientals, spicy orientals, woody orientals, and gourmand orientals.

phenolic Smelling of phenols, i.e., like tar.

resin Thick, brown, sticky plant extracts such as labdanum or styrax that resemble molasses, used frequently in amber orientals or in chypres for their sweet smells and fixative qualities.

sillage French for the wake left in the water by passing ships; fragrance industry jargon for the scent trail left by a perfume at a distance from the wearer.

soliflore A fragrance meant to represent a single flower. For example, a rose soliflore is designed to smell solely of rose.

top note The first few minutes of a fragrance, when the materials with the lowest molecular weights and highest volatilities evaporate first.

woody amber A type of synthetic aromachemical now widely used to replace more expensive natural woods and ambergris. Woody ambers smell like very strong versions of rubbing alcohol.

Best feminines
- Angel
- Après l'Ondée
- Black
- Bois de Violette
- Boucheron
- L'Heure Bleue
- Homage
- Mitsouko
- Rive Gauche
- Shalimar

Best masculines
- Azzaro pour Homme
- Derby
- Eau de Guerlain
- Habit Rouge
- Knize Ten
- New York
- Ormonde Men
- Pour Monsieur
- Sycomore
- Timbuktu

Best feminines for men
- 1000
- Après l'Ondée
- Arpège
- Bandit
- Calèche
- Diorella
- Dzing!
- Jicky
- Mitsouko
- Tommy Girl

Best masculines for women
- Beyond Paradise Men
- Cool Water
- Dior Homme
- Eau Sauvage
- Jules
- New York
- Pour un Homme
- Timbuktu
- Yatagan
- Yohji Homme

Best florals

Amouage Gold
Beyond Paradise
Chamade
Joy
No. 5 parfum
Odalisque
Osmanthe Yunnan
Private Collection Tuberose
  Gardenia
Promesse de l'Aube
Rive Gauche

Best citrus

Aqua Allegoria Pamplelune
Cologne (Thierry Mugler)
Cologne à la Française
Cologne à l'Italienne
Cristalle
Eau de Cologne (Chanel)
Eau de Guerlain
Eau Sauvage
Lime Basil & Mandarin
Pour Monsieur

Best chypres

31 Rue Cambon
Aromatics Elixir
Bandit
Chinatown
Diorella
Givenchy III
Jubilation 25

Knowing
Mitsouko
Pour Monsieur

Best fougères

Azzaro pour Homme
Ça Sent Beau
Cool Water
Grey Flannel
Jicky
Kouros
Le Troisième Homme
Or Black
Rive Gauche pour Homme
Yohji Homme

Best orientals

Ambre Sultan
Angel
Attrape-Coeurs
Black
L'Heure Bleue
La Myrrhe
Patchouli 24
Shalimar
Vanilia
Vol de Nuit

Best leathers

1740
Azurée
Bandit
Bel-Ami

Cuir de Russie
Knize Ten
Oud Cuir d'Arabie
Patchouli 24
Sarrasins
S-eX

Best quiet fragrances
Après l'Ondée
Bois d'Encens
Comme des Garçons 3
Exhale
Lavender (Caldey Island)
Lime Basil & Mandarin
Osmanthe Yunnan
Pleasures
S-eX
Timbuktu

Best loud fragrances
Amarige
Angel
Badgley Mischka
Carnal Flower
Fracas
Insolence
Lolita Lempicka
Poison
Rush
Samsara

Best bang for the buck
Azurée

Breath of God
Cool Water
Lavender (Caldey Island)
Knowing
New York
Pour Monsieur
Tocade
Tommy Girl
White Linen

Best big ticket splurges
Amouage Gold
Cuir de Russie parfum
Derby
Homage
Invasion Barbare
Joy parfum
La Myrrhe
No. 5 parfum
Sycomore
Ubar

Best strange fragrances
L'Air de Rien
Black
Breath of God
Comme des Garçons 2 Man
Jasmin et Cigarette
Lonestar Memories
Muscs Koublai Khan
Sécrétions Magnifiques
S-eX
Stephen Jones

INDEX OF STAR RATINGS

★ ★ ★ ★ ★

31 Rue Cambon*; 100% Love;
1740; L'Air du Désert Marocain;
Amouage Gold; Angel; Après
l'Ondée; Aromatics Elixir;
Azurée; Azzaro pour Homme;
Badgley Mischka; Bandit; Beyond
Paradise; Beyond Paradise Men;
Black; Bois des Iles; Bois de
Violette; Bouchcron; Breath of
God; Calandre; Calyx; Ça Sent
Beau; Chamade; Chinatown;
Cool Water; Cristalle; Cuir
de Russie; Derby; Diorella*;
Dior Homme; Dune; Dzing!;
Eau de Guerlain; Eau Sauvage;
Enlèvement au Sérail; Envy; Le
Feu d'Issey; Fracas; Givenchy
III; Grey Flannel; Habit Rouge;
L'Heure Bleue; Homage;
Insensé; Insolence eau de
parfum; Invasion Barbare; Iris
Silver Mist; Jicky; Joy parfum;
Knize Ten; Knowing; Kouros;
Lavender; Lolita Lempicka;
Loulou; Missoni; Mitsouko;
MoslBuddJewChristHinDao;
La Myrrhe; Nahéma; New York;
No. 5 eau de toilette; No. 5
parfum"; Odalisque; Opium; Or
Black; Ormonde Man; Ormonde
Woman; Osmanthe Yunnan;
Oud Cuir d'Arabie; Patchouli 24;
Pleasures; Poison; Pour Monsieur;
Pour un Homme; Private
Collection; Promesse de l'Aube;
Rive Gauche; Rush; Sarrasins;
Scent (Theo Fennell); Sécrétions
Magnifiques; S-eX; Shalimar;
Sycomore; Le Temps d'une Fête;
Timbuktu; Tocade; Tommy Girl;
Le Troisième Homme; Ubar;
Vanilia; Vol de Nuit; White Linen;
Yatagan; Yohji Homme

★ ★ ★ ★

24, Faubourg; 28 La Pausa; 31
Rue Cambon*; 1000; 1725; 1804;

---

* Two different ratings given.

1826; 1828; 1873; 1876; 1969; Acqua di Giò; Acqua di Parma Colonia Assoluta; Acqua di Parma Profumo; Aedes de Venustas; Agent Provocateur DD "Diamond Dust"; Agent Provocateur Strip; Aimez Moi; L'Air de Rien; Alliage; Amanda; Ambra di Venezia; Ambre 411; Ambre Précieux; Ambre Russe; Ambre Soie; Ambre Sultan; A*Men; Amouage Gold for Men; Amoureuse; Anaïs Anaïs; Angel Innocent; Angel La Rose; Anice; Anné Pliska; Antaeus; Antihéros; Anvers 2; Aomassaï; Aqua Allegoria Pamplelune; Arabie; Aramis; Aramis 900; Aria di Capri; Arpège; A Travers le Miroir; Attrape-Coeurs; L'Autre; Aveda Men Pure-Formance; Azzaro Couture; Azzaro Men Now; Azzaro Women Now; Baghari; Baldessarini; Beach; Beautiful; Bel-Ami; Belle en Rykiel; Bel Respiro; Bendelirious; Beyond Love; Beyond Paradise Blue; Black Aoud; Black Orchid Voile de Fleur; Black Tourmaline; Blue Stratos; Body Kouros; Bois d'Encens; Bois et Fruits; Bois et Musc; Bois Oriental; Un Bois Vanille; Borneo 1834; Boucheron Eau Légère 2006; Broadway Nite; Brûlure de Rose; B Scent; Bulgari pour Femme; Byzance; Cabaret; Canali Style; Candide Effluve; Caravelle Epicée; Cardinal; Carnal Flower; Carolina Herrera; Cašmir; Cèdre Blanc; Cerruti 1881; Chant d'Arômes; Chaos; Chergui; Ciel pour Homme; Cinéma; Cinnabar; cK One; Climat; Cocktail; Coco; Coco Mademoiselle; Cologne; Cologne à la Française; Cologne à la Russe; Cologne à l'Italienne; Cologne Blanche; Cologne Grand Luxe; Comme des Garçons 2 Man; Comme des Garçons 2 Woman; Comme des Garçons 3; Comme des Garçons White; Concentré d'Orange Verte; Contradiction for Men; Coromandel; Cosmic; Cozé; Cuir; Cuir Pleine Fleur; Cuir Venenum; Dalí; Dazzling Silver; Début; Déclaration; Déclaration Essence; Dia pour Femme; Dia pour Homme; Diorella*; Dioressence*; Diorissimo*; Dior Homme Intense; Dior Homme Sport; Dirty; Divine; Divine Bergamote; DKNY Women; Donna Karan Gold; Donna Karan

---

* Two different ratings given.

Signature; Douce Amère; Drôle de Rose; Duel; Dune pour Homme; Dzongkha; L'Eau (Diptyque); Eau de Cartier; Eau de Cologne; Eau de Cologne du Coq; Eau de Cologne Impériale; Eau de Fleurs de Cédrat; L'Eau de Jatamansi; Eau de Monsieur; Eau de Rochas; Eau de Rochas Homme; Eau de Star; Eau d'Hermès; Eau d'Hiver; Eau d'Orange Verte; Eau du Fier; Eau Fraîche; Eau Lente; L'Eau Neuve; Eau Noire; Eau Parfumée au Thé Vert; Eau Turquoise; Eden; Egoïste; El Attarine; Elixir Charnel Oriental Brûlant; Eloge du Traître; Encens et Bubblegum; Encens Flamboyant; Encre Noire; Equipage; Escale à Portofino; Esprit du Tigre; Essenza di Zegna; Exhale; Fahrenheit 32; Felanilla; Féminité du Bois; Ferré; Figuier; Fire Island; First; Une Fleur de Cassie; Fleur d'Oranger 2007; Fleurs de Nuit; Fleurs des Comores; Fleurs de Sel; Flora Bella; Flower (Kenzo); Flower by Kenzo Fleurs d'Hiver/Winter Flower; Fougère Bengale; Frangipani Absolute; French Lover*; Fuel for Life; Fuel for Life Men; Fuel for Men; Funny!; Giorgio; Great Jones; Green Irish Tweed; Grezzo; Gucci Eau de Parfum II; Gucci pour Homme; Guerlain Homme; Habanita; Halston Z-14; Hanae Mori "Butterfly"; Héritage; Heure Exquise; Hindu Grass; Hindu Kush; L'Homme de Coeur; H.O.T. Always; Hypnotic Poison; Idole; Impact; Les Impératrices Japonaises; Incense Extrême; Incense Rosé; L'Infante; Inhale; Insolence; L'Instant; L'Instant pour Homme; L'Interdit; Intrigant Patchouli; Iris 39; Iris de Nuit; Iris Nobile; Iris Pallida 2007; Iris Taïzo; Ivoire; J'Adore l'Absolu; Jaïpur; Un Jardin Après la Mousson; Jasmin et Cigarette; Jasper Conran Woman; Jazz; Je Reviens Couture; Je Suis un Homme; Joy eau de parfum; Jubilation 25; Jubilation XXV; Juicy Couture; Jules; Karma solid perfume; Kenzo Air; Kenzo Amour; Kenzo Jungle "L'Eléphant"; Kenzo Jungle pour Homme; Kiki; Krizia Uomo; Ladyboy; Lady Stetson; Laguna; Lauder for Men; Le De; Let It

---

* Two different ratings given.

Rock; Liaisons Dangereuses; Lime Basil & Mandarin Cologne; Lolita Lempicka au Masculin; Lolita Lempicka Midnight; Lonestar Memories; Love (By Kilian); Love in Paris; Lovely; Luca; Lyric Man; Lyric Woman; Lys Méditerranée; M7; M7 Fresh; Ma Dame; Magie Noire; Maharanih; Les Maîtresses de Louis XIV; Manoumalia; Marrakech; Mauboussin; Messe de Minuit; Métal; Miracle Forever; Miroir des Envies; Miroir des Vanités; Miss Balmain; Miss Dior Cherie; Missoni Acqua; Mogador; Monsieur Balmain; Monsieur de Givenchy; Moschino; Mouchoir de Monsieur; Musc for Him perfume oil; Musc Samarkand; Muscs Koublai Khan; Must de Cartier pour Homme; Mystère; Mystra; Narciso Rodriguez for Her; Nautica Voyage; Neroli 36; Nicolaï pour Homme; Nina; No. 5 eau de parfum; No. 5 Eau Première; No. 5 parfum*; No. 18; No. 19; No. 22; No. 89; Noa; Noir de Noir; Noir Epices; Noir Patchouli; Notorious; Nuit de Noël; Odeur 71; Olène; Om; L'Ombre Fauve; Ombre Rose (L'Original); Omnia; Onda; Oranger Alhambra; Organza; Organza Indécence; Or Noir; Osmanthus (The Different Company); Oud 27; Outrageous; Oyédo; Paco Rabanne pour Homme; Paestum Rose; Palais Jamais; Palazzo; Paloma Picasso; Par Amour; Par Amour Toujours; Parfum de Peau; Parfum d'Été; Le Parfum de Thérèse; Parfum Sacré; Paris; Passion (Annick Goutal); Patchouli Antique; Patchouli Patch; Peau de Pêche; La Petite Robe Noire; Philosykos; Plus Que Jamais; Polo; Polo Sport; Premier Figuier Extrême; Private Collection Tuberose Gardenia; Pure Poison; Pure Turquoise; Pure White Linen; Quand Vient la Pluie; Quel Amour!; Racine; Rien; Rive Gauche pour Homme; Rosa Flamenca; Une Rose; Rose Alexandrie; Rose d'Amour; Rose de Nuit; Rose d'Homme; Rossy de Palma; Rubj; Sables; Sacrebleu; Safran Troublant; Samsara; Scent 79 Man; Scent 79 Woman; Sel de Vetiver; Sel Marin; Sex Appeal for Men; Shaal Nur; Shalini; Shiloh; Sira des

---

* Two different ratings given.

Indes; Six Scents No. 3; Songes; So Pretty; Sottile; Sous le Vent; Spigo; Stephen Jones; Stetson; Stoned; Superworldunknown; Tabac; Tabacco; Ta'if; A Taste of Heaven; Tea Rose; Thé pour un Eté; Tolu; Tom of Finland; Trésor; Très Russe; Truth; Tubéreuse Criminelle; Tuscany per Donna; Tuscany per Uomo; Twill Rose; The Unicorn Spell; Vanille Galante; Velvet Gardenia; Versace L'Homme; Verveine; Vetiver (Annick Goutal); Vetiver (Etro); Vetiver (Guerlain); Le Vetiver (Lubin); Vetiver Extraordinaire; Vetiver pour Elle; Vetyver (Givenchy); Vie de Château; Violetta; La Violette; Virgilio; Visa; Vraie Blonde; X for Women; Y; Yatra; Youth Dew; Youth Dew Amber Nude; Yuzu Ab Irato; Yuzu Fou; Z Zegna

★ ★ ★

10 Corso Como; 21 Costume National; 888; 1270; 1872 for Men; Absolutely Irrésistible; Acier Aluminium; Acqua di Giò pour Homme; Acqua di Parma; Affection; Agent Provocateur;

Agua Verde; L'Air du Temps parfum Anniversary Edition; A La Nuit; Aldehyde 44; Alessandro Dell'Acqua Man; Alessandro Dell'Acqua Woman; Alien; Allure Homme Edition Blanche; Allure Sensuelle; Alpona; Always Belong; A*Maze; Amazone; Amber; Amber Absolute; Amber and Lavender Cologne; Ambre Narguilé; Ambre Topkapi; L'Ame d'un Héros; L'Ame Soeur; Amethyst (Lalique); Ananas Fizz; L'Anarchiste; Andy Warhol's Silver Factory; Angélique Encens; Angéliques sous la Pluie; Angel Lys; Angel Pivoine; Angel Violet; Antonia's Flowers; Anvers; Après Tout; Aqua Allegoria Herba Fresca; Aqua Allegoria Lilia Bella; Armani Attitude; Armani Code pour Homme; Armani pour Homme; Around Midnight; Arpège pour Homme; Artemisia; Aspen; Aziyadé; Balkis; Balle de Match; Balmain; Beautiful Love; Beautiful Sheer; Be Delicious; Be Delicious Men; Believe; Belle de Nuit parfum; Bigarade Concentrée; Bill Blass Couture 7; Billet Doux; Black Cashmere;

* Two different ratings given.

Black Orchid; Black Vetyver Café Cologne; Black Violet; Black XS for Her; Blanc Violette; Blenheim Bouquet; Bois Blond; Bois d'Argent; Bois d'Arménie; Bois de Copaiba; Bois de Paradis; Bois d'Iris; Bois d'Ombrie; Bois du Portugal; Bois Farine; Boucheron Eau Légère 2007; Boucheron pour Homme; Boucheron pour Homme Eau de Parfum; Boucheron pour Homme Eau de Toilette Fraîcheur; Brandy; Brin de Réglisse; Brooks Brothers New York Gentlemen; Bryant Park; Bulgari BLV "Blù"; Bulgari pour Homme Extrême; Bulgari pour Homme Soir; B•United Woman; Cadjméré; Calèche; Calèche Eau Délicate; Caline; Canali Black Diamond; Carré d'As; Cédrat Intense; Cèdre (Serge Lutens); Cèdre Sandaraque; Cefiro; Celine Dion; Celine Dion Parfum Notes; Chakra 1–7; Chamade pour Homme; Champaca; Chance; La Chasse aux Papillons; Cheap and Chic; Chembur; Le Chèvrefeuille; Chic for Men; Chocolate Greedy; Chrome Legend; Cinéma Festival d'Eté; City Glam for Her; cK Be;

Cococabana; Un Coeur en Mai; Cologne du 68; Cologne Grand Siècle; Cool Water Wave; Courtesan; Crystal d'Ambre; Cuba; Cuir Beluga; Cuir d'Oranger; Cuir Mauresque; Cuir Ottoman; Cuoio; Curve; Curve for Men; Cyprès Musc; Daim Blond; Daisy; Dalimania; Dalimix; Dalissime; Le Dandy; Dans Tes Bras; Dark Amber & Ginger Lily; Datura Noir; Dazzling Gold; Dear John; Deseo; Diabolo Rose; Diamonds for Men; Dilmun; Dis Moi, Miroir; Divin'Enfant; DKNY Delicious Night; DKNY for Men; DKNY Men; DKNY Men Summer 2009; DKNY Women Summer 2009; Dolce & Gabbana pour Homme; Donna Karan Essence Jasmine; Donna Karan Essence Labdanum; Donna Karan Essence Lavender; Donna Karan Essence Wenge; Drama Nuuï; Dream Angels Divine; Dream Angels Heavenly; Dreaming*; Dunhill Black; L'Eau Bleue d'Issey Eau Fraîche; L'Eau Cheap and Chic; L'Eau d'Ambre; Eau de Bonpoint; Eau de Camille; Eau de Cartier Concentrée; Eau de Charlotte; Eau

---

* Two different ratings given.

de Dalí; Eau de Lavande; L'Eau de l'Eau; Eau d'Élide; L'Eau de Néroli; Eau de New York; Eau de Pamplemousse Rose; Eau de Réglisse; Eau des Merveilles; Eau d'Hadrien eau de toilette; L'Eau d'Issey; L'Eau d'Issey pour Homme; Eau d'Italie; L'Eau du Sud; Eau Egyptienne; L'Eau Guerrière; Eau Parfumée au Thé Blanc; Eau Suave; Eau Trois; Ecume de Rose; Elixir des Merveilles; Elle; Ellie; Ellie Nuit; Emporio Armani He; Emporio Armani She; Encens et Lavande; Enchanting; En Passant; En Sens de Bois; Enslaved; Envy for Men; Equistrius; Escada; Escentric 01; Esprit de Fleurs; Essence; The Essence; Eternity; Eternity for Men; Etra; L'Etre Aimé Femme; Euphoria; Exclamation; Explorer; Extravagance d'Amarige; Fairytales; Falling in Love; Fancy; F by Ferragamo pour Homme; Féerie; Femme; Feuilles de Tabac; Fever; Fiori di Capri; First Love; Five O'Clock au Gingembre; Fleur de Narcisse 2006; A Fleur de Peau; Fleur de Thé Rose Bulgare; Fleur du Mâle; Fleur du Matin;

Fleurissimo; Fleur Oriental; Fleurs de Bulgarie; Fleurs de Rocaille*; Fleurs d'Oranger; Florissa; Flower (Cynthia Rowley); Flower Le Parfum; Flower Oriental; Folavril; Une Folie de Rose; (For you)/ parfum trouvé; Fraîche Passiflore; Fraîcheur Muskissime; Frangipane; Frankincense and Myrrh; French Lime Blossom Cologne; Fresh Patchouli; Friends Men; Frolic; Fumerie Turque; Fumidus; Gardenia Passion; Génie des Bois; Giorgio Red; Givenchy pour Homme Blue Label; Gloria; Glow; Gomma; Gourmandises; Grand Amour; Les Grandes Amours du Taj-Mahal; Les Grandes Prêtresses Incas; Grapefruit Cologne; Green, green, and . . . green; Gucci; Gucci Eau de Parfum; Guerlinade; Gypsy Water; Habit Rouge Sport; Hadrien Absolu; La Haie Fleurie; Halston Z; Hammam Bouquet; Hanae Mori "Butterfly" Eau Fraîche; Happy; Happy for Men; Happy Heart; Harmatan Noir; Haute Couture; Heliotrope; Herrera for Men; He Wood; Une Histoire de Chypre*; HM; L'Homme Sage;

---

* Two different ratings given.

Honeysuckle and Jasmine; Hot
Couture; Hummer; Hyperessence
Matale; Hypnôse Homme Eau
Fraîche; I Am King; Ilang Ivohibe;
Imperial Opopanax; Infini; Inner
Grace; L'Inspiratrice; L'Instant
Fleur de Mandarine; L'Instant
Magic; L'Instant Magic 2008;
L'Instant Magic Elixir; Instinct;
Intense Euphoria Men; Intimately
Beckham for Men; Intimately
Beckham for Women; Intuition
for Men; Io Capri; Iris Ganache;
Iris Noir; Iris Poudre; Isfarkand;
Iskander; Island; J'Adore; Jaïpur
Homme; Jaïpur Homme
Fraicheur; Japon Noir; Jardin du
Néroli; Un Jardin en
Méditerranée; Jardins de
Bagatelle; Un Jardin sur le Nil;
Jasmal; Jasmin de Nuit; Jasmine
(Keiko Mecheri); Jasmin Vert;
Jewel; Jolie Madame; Jovan Musk
for Women; Joy Comes from
Within; Kelly Calèche; Kenzo
Amour le Parfum; Kenzo pour
Homme; Kisu; Kiton Black; L
(Lolita Lempicka); Labdanum 18;
Lady Vengeance; Lalique White;
Let Me Play the Lion; Lierre Rose;
Light My Heart; Lily and Spice;
Lipstick Rose; Liu; Louanges
Profanes; Loukhoum Eau

Poudrée; Love (B Never Too Busy
to Be Beautiful); Love de Toi; Love
Spell; Luctor et Emergo; Luxe
Champaca; Luxe Patchouli; Un
Lys; M; Madame Rochas; Madison
Soirée; Magical Moon; Magie; Ma
Griffe; Le Mâle; Mandragore;
Marc Jacobs; Le Maroc; Matthew
Williamson Collection: Incense;
Matthew Williamson Collection:
Jasmine Sambac; Matthew
Williamson Collection: Warm
Sands; Maybe Baby;
Mediterranean Lily; Mediterraneo;
Me Myself and I; Menthe Fraîche;
Mille et Une Roses; Mimosa pour
Moi; Miss Charming; M Moi;
Molecule 01; Monyette Paris;
Musc Nomade; Musc Ravageur;
Musk (Etro); Musk (Keiko
Mecheri); Myrrhe et Merveilles;
Narciso Rodriguez for Him;
Narcisse Blanc; Navegar; Néroli;
Néroli Sauvage; New Haarlem;
New Tradition; No. 1 for Men; No.
1 for Women; No. 4; No. 88; Noa
Perle; Noël au Balcon; Nombril
Immense; Nouveau Bowery; Nuit
d'Amour; Nuit de Cellophane; Les
Nuits d'Hadrien; Number One;
Numero Uno; Nutmeg and Ginger
Cologne; Obsession; Obsession
for Men; Obsession Night; O de

Lancôme; Odeur 53; Ofrésia; L'Oiseau de Nuit; Old Spice; Oliban; L'Ombre dans l'Eau; Omniscent; Onde Vertige; The One; Onyx; Opôné; Orange Blossom Cologne; Or des Indes; L'Or de Torrente; Oscar Red Satin; Osmanthus (Keiko Mecheri); Osmanthus (Ormonde Jayne); Osmanthus Interdite; Oud Wood; Oxford & Cambridge Traditional Lavender; Paco Rabanne pour Elle; Palisander; Paname; Un Parfum d'Ailleurs et Fleurs; Un Parfum de Charmes et Feuilles; Un Parfum des Sens et Bois; Passage d'Enfer; Passiflora; Passion Boisée; Passion for Men; Patchouli; Patchoulissime; Patchouly; Paul Smith London for Men; Paul Smith London Woman; Paul Smith Man; Paul Smith Rose; Paul Smith Woman; Péché Cardinal; Perfect Man Alternative; Perles de Lalique; Peut-Etre; Philtre d'Amour; Piment Brûlant; Piment des Baies; Pleasures Exotic; Pleasures for Men; Pleasures Intense; Pluie d'Aromes; Poivre 23; Poivre Piquant; Poopoo Pidou; Potion solid perfume; Poussière de Rose; Prada; Prelude to Love; Prends Garde à Toi; Les

Princesses de Venise; Promesse; Pulp; Pure (Jil Sander); Pure Grace; Pure Intense; Putain des Palaces; Quand Vient l'Eté; Quelques Fleurs L'Original; Rahat Loukhoum; Ralph; Ralph Hot; Ralph Rocks; Realm Men; Red Delicious Men; Red Delicious Woman; Red Door; Red Roses Cologne; Red Vetyver; Reverie au Jardin; Le Rivage des Syrtes; Riverside Drive; Roadster; Roberto Cavalli Oro; Rochas Man; Roma for Women; Rose; Rose Absolue (Annick Goutal); Rose Absolue (Yves Rocher); Rose Barbare; Roseberry; Rose de Feu; La Rose de Rosine; Rose de Siwa; Rose d'Eté; Rose Ikebana; Rose Opulente; Rose-Pivoine; Rose Poivrée; Royal Scottish Lavender; Rubylips; Saks Fifth Avenue for Her; Sa Majesté la Rose; Sampaquita; Sandalwood; Sand and Sable; Sander for Men; Santal Blanc; Santal de Mysore; Santal Noble; Scandal; Scarlett; Scent (Costume National); Sélection Verte; Sensi; Sensuous; Séxual; Séxual pour Homme; Shedonism; She Wood; Sienne l'Hiver; Silk Touch; Silver Cologne; Six Scents No. 1; Skin Musk; Solo Loewe Eau de Cologne Intense; So New York; Soudain; S-Perfume; Spiritus/land; Spring Flower; Spring in Paris; Stargazer; Stella; Stella in Two Amber; Stella in Two Peony; Stella Rose Absolute; Stephanotis; Stetson Black; Stetson Untamed; Sublime; Summer; Tabu; Tam Dao; Tea for Two; Terre de Bois; Terre de Sarment; Terre d'Hermès; Thé Vert au Jasmin; Tiare; Tobacco Vanille; Tom Ford for Men; Tom Ford for Men Extreme; Tommy; True Star; Tubéreuse (Annick Goutal); Tubéreuse (L'Artisan Parfumeur); Tubéreuse (Caron); Tubéreuse Indiana; Tuberose Cologne; Two Hearts Beating as One; U4EAHH!; U by Ungaro for Him; Umé; Unforgivable Woman Black; Unforgivable Woman Eau Fraîche; United Colors of Benetton Unisex; United Colors of Benetton Woman; Unspoken; Uomo; Usiku; Van Cleef; Vanilla Fields; Vanille Tonka; Velocity for Him; Vêpres Siciliennes; Vera Wang Bouquet; Verbenas of Provence Cologne; Versace; Vert Pivoine; Vétiver Babylone; Vetiver Oriental; Vetiver Tonka; Vetyver (Parfums de Nicolaï); Via Camarelle; Vicolo

Fiori; Vierges et Toreros; Violette Précieuse; Voile d'Ambre; Wall Street; What About Adam; White Aoud; White Diamonds; White Jasmine and Mint; White Shoulders; Wild Fig and Cassis Cologne; Wish; Wode; Xeryus; Xeryus Rouge; X for Men; Ysatis; Zen; Un Zest de Rose

★ ★

5th Avenue; 154 Cologne; 212 Men; 1 Million; Absinth; Adidas Moves; Adidas Moves for Her; Ageless Fantasy; L'Air du Temps; All That Matters; Allure; Amber pour Homme; Ambra; Ambra del Nepal; Ambre Cannelle; Ambre Extrême; Ambre Fétiche; Ambre Gris; Amor Amor; Andy Warhol Lexington Avenue; Angélique Noire; Angelo di Fiume; Antico Caruso; Antidote; L'Antimatière; Aoud Damascus; Aqua Allegoria Angélique-Lilas; Aqua Allegoria Figue Iris; Aqua Allegoria Laurier Réglisse; Aqua Allegoria Mandarine-Basilic; Aqua pour Homme; Aqua pour Homme Marine; Aqua Velva Classic Ice Blue; Arcus; Armani Mania pour Homme; Art of Perfumery 4; Art of Perfumery 6; Astor Place; Baby

Doll Paris; Bahiana; Le Baiser du Dragon; Baume du Doge; Beauty Comes from Within; Be Delicious Fresh Blossom; Beige; Bella Belara; Bellodgia; Benetton Sport Woman; Bill Blass Couture 3; Black Angel; Black Sun; BLV "Blù" pour Homme; Blue Agava & Cacao Cologne; Blush; Bois de Santal; Bois Rouge; Un Bois Sépia; Brooklyn; Brut; B Spot; Bulgari Rose Essentielle; Burberry London for Men; Cabochard; Caresse; Carolina; Cashmere Mist; Casual; Cèdre (Parfums 06130); Ce Soir ou Jamais; Champaca Absolute; Charogne; Chelsea Flowers; Chêne; Cherry Blossom; Cherry Blossom Fruity; Chez Bond; Chic; Chloé; Chopard pour Homme; Chypre Rouge; Citron Citron; City Glam for Him; cK One Summer; Clair de Musc; Coeur de Fleur; Coeur d'Eté; Coney Island; Cool Water Woman; Corps et Ames; Coup de Fouet; Covet; Cravache; Un Crime Exotique; Cruel Gardenia; Cruel Intentions; Damascena; Danielle; David Yurman; Daytona 500; Delicious Closet Queen; Dianthus; Dior

Addict; Dior Addict 2; Diorama; Dioressence*; Diorissimo*; Dolce & Gabbana; Dolce Vita; Donna; Don't Get Me Wrong Baby, I Don't Swallow; Douceur de Vanille; Dreaming*; Dunhill; L'Eau (Renée); L'Eau Bleue d'Issey pour Homme; L'Eau de Circé; Eau de FCUK; Eau de Gentiane Blanche; Eau de Givenchy; Eau de Grey Flannel; Eau de Jade; L'Eau de l'Artisan; Eau de Vert; Eau d'Hadrien eau de parfum; L'Eau d'Issey pour Homme Intense; Eau du Navigateur; Eau Emotionelle; Eau Illuminée; Eau Parfumée au Thé Rouge; L'Eau par Kenzo pour Femme; L'Eau par Kenzo pour Homme; L'Eau Rare Matale; Eclat d'Arpège; Eclat de Jasmin; Edwardian Bouquet; Effusion Woman; Egoïste Platinum; Eleganza Luminosa; Elixir; Elixir Charnel Chypre Fatal; Elixir Charnel Gourmand Coquin; En Avion; Endymion; Energy Man; English Breakfast; English Fern; English Leather; Escape; Escape for Men; Les Espionnes du Tsar; Estée; L'Eté en Douce; L'Etre Aimé Homme; Euphoria

---

* Two different ratings given.

Blossom; Fahrenheit; Fantasy; Fashion Avenue; Feuille de Réglisse; F for Fascinating; Figue Amère; Fleur; Fleur de Cabotine; Fleur de Liane; Fleur de Rocaille; Fleurs de Citronnier; Fleurs de Rocaille*; Fleurs d'Ombre Ombre Bleue; Fleurs d'Ombre Rose; Fleurs d'Ombre Violette-Menthe; Floret; Fou d'Absinthe; French Connection Fragrance; French Lover*; Fresh; Fruit de Bois; Fuel for Life Unlimited; Gardenia (Floris); Garden Sensuel; Garrigue; Ginger Ciao; Ginger Essence; Ginger with a Twist; Ginseng NRG "Energy"; Givenchy Gentleman; Glamour; Glow After Dark; Goddess; Go Green; Golden Amber; Green Tea; Gregory; Grenats; Gucci by Gucci Pour Homme; Gucci pour Homme II; Guess by Marciano; Hanae; Hei; Herrera Aqua; Higher; High Intensity; Hilfiger; Himalaya; Hippy Fizz; Une Histoire de Chypre*; L'Homme; Hot Leather; Hugo; Hugo XY; Hypnôse; Hypnôse Homme; Iceberg Twice; IF; Incensi; Infusion d'Homme; Infusion d'Iris; Insolence Eau Glacée; Instinct After Dark; Intuition; Iris; Island Gardenia; Itislove; Le Jasmin (Annick Goutal); Jasmine (Renée); Jasmin Noir; Jean Paul Gaultier Monsieur; JF; Jil Sander Pure for Men; John Galliano; John Varvatos; Joop! Homme; Joop! Jump; Jour de Fête; Jovan White Musk; Juozas Statkevicius; Just Cavalli Him; Kate Moss; Kenzo Amour Indian Holi; Kenzo pour Homme Fresh; Kiton Man; L (L.A.M.B.); Lady Caron; Lalique Eau de Parfum; Lanvin L'Homme; Lauren; Lavandula; L de Lubin; Lemon Sorbet; Lentisque; Liberté; Ligea "La Sirena"; Lily of the Valley (Floris); Lily of the Valley (Penhaligon's); Look; Loukhoum Parfum de Soir; Louve; Love (Ralph Lauren); Madagascar Orchid; Magnifique; Magnolia Romana; Magot; Maîtresse; Malabah; Le Mâle Eau d'Eté; Mandarine Mandarin; Mandarine Tout Simplement; Mary-Kate and Ashley One; Mary-Kate and Ashley Two; Un Matin d'Orage; Matthew Williamson Collection: Pink Lotus; Max Mara; Mensonge;

---

* Two different ratings given.

Metalys; Midnight Rain; Mihimé; Millésime Impérial; Miracle; Miroir des Secrets; Miss Dior; Le Monde Est Beau; Montaigne; Montana Homme; Montana Mood Sensual; Moss Breches; Muguet du Bonheur; Mûre et Musc; Mûre et Musc extrait de parfum; Mûre et Musc Extrême; Musc Maori; Musk (Renée); My Insolence; My Life; My Man; My Passion; MyQueen; Myrrhe Ardente; N'Aimez que Moi; Nameless; Narcisse Noir eau de toilette; Narcotic Venus; Nectarine Blossom and Honey Cologne; Neroli Portofino; Night-Scented Jasmine; Noa Fleur; Nocturnes; Noir; Noix de Tubéreuse; Notte Bianca; Nuit de Longchamp; Nuits de Noho; Onde Extase; Onde Mystère; Opium pour Homme; Or et Noir; Oriental Lumpur; Orris Noir; Oscar; Oscar Citrus; Oscar Red Orchid; Oud Sensuel; Paprika Brasil; Park Avenue; Perfect Kiss; Petite Cherie; Pierre de Lune; Play (Comme des Garçons); Play (Givenchy); Pois de Senteur; Poivre; Poivre Samarcande; Polo Double Black; Pomegranate Noir Cologne; Possibilities; Pour une Femme; Prada Tendre; Premier Jour; Pure (Alfred Sung); Pure (Dunhill); Pure White Linen Light Breeze; Purple Label; Purplelight; Purple Lips; Purple Patchouli; Quelques Fleurs Royale; Quercus; Querelle; Ralph Cool; Rêve en Cuir; Roberto Cavalli; Rock Crystal; Romance; Romance Men Silver; Rose 31; Rose Intense; Rouge (Christian Lacroix); Rousse; Royal Pavillon; Le Roy Soleil Homme; Rush II; Safari for Men; Sanguine, Santal; Santal Impérial; Santos; Scent of Peace; Sensations; Sentiment; Seringa; Séxual pour Femme; Sexy Little Things; Shania; Shania Starlight; Sheer; Sheer Halston; Sheer Obsession; Sicily; Silky Underwear solid perfume; Silver Musk; Silver Shadow; Snowpeach; Sogni di Mare; Soleil de Rochas; Sounds & Visions; Les Souveraines d'Egypte; Spiritueuse Double Vanille; Story; Straight to Heaven; Sun; Sunset Heat; Sunset Heat for Men; Sweet Lime & Cedar; Tabarôme; Tangerine Vert; Thé Blanc; Thé Brun; Tiempe Passate; Tilleul; Tokyo; Truly Pink; Tubéreuse 40; Tuberose; Tuscan Leather; U by Ungaro for Her; Unbound; Unbound for

Men; Unforgivable; Unforgivable Black; Unforgivable Eau Fraîche; Unforgivable Woman; Uomo?; Valentino pour Homme; Vanille Exquise; Velvet Hour; Versace Man; Vert d'Eau; Verte Violette; Very Pretty; Very Sexy for Him; Vetiver (Floris); Vetiver (Lorenzo Villoresi); Vetiver 46; Vetiver Dance; Vetyver Cologne; Vintage Gardenia Cologne; Virgin Island Water; Vista sul Mare; Viva la Juicy; Vivara; Vocalise; Voleur de Roses; West Broadway; West Side; White Flowers; White Patchouli; White Petals; Wild Berries; Wind Song; With Love . . .; Wood & Absinth; XS "Excess pour Homme"; Yerbamate; Yuzu Rouge; Zafferano; Zegna Intenso; Zinnia; Zizan

★

212; 212 Sexy Men; 1872 for Women; Acaciosa; Acqua di Sale; Adidas Moves 0:01; Adventure; Aki; Alamut; Alba; Allure Homme; Allure Homme Sport; Allure Homme Sport Cologne; Almost Bare; Amarige; Amarige Mariage; Amazing Grace; Ambre de Cabochard; Ambrette 9; Amethyst (Olivier Durbano); Amor pour

Homme; Andy Warhol Union Square; Ange ou Démon; Anglomania; Aqua Allegoria Cherry Blossom; Aqua Allegoria Grosellina; Aqua Allegoria Lemon Fresca; Aqua Allegoria Pivoine Magnifica; Aqua Allegoria Tiaré Mimosa; Aqua Allegoria Tutti Kiwi; Aquawoman; Armani Code Elixir de Parfum; Armani Code for Women; Art of Perfumery 1; Art of Perfumery 2; Art of Perfumery 3; Art of Perfumery 5; Art of Perfumery 7; Atlas Cedar; Atman; Avatar; Baby Grace; Baldessarini Ambré; Balmya; B de Boucheron; b.e.; Beat; Beauty Rush Appletini; Beckham Signature Women; Belong; Bergamote 22; Bill Blass Couture 8; Black XS; Bleecker Street; Bluebell; Bobbi; Bond Girl 007; Boudoir; Boudoir Sin Garden; Breathe; Bright Crystal; Brooks Brothers Classic; Brooks Brothers New York Ladies; B•United Jeans Man; Burberry London; Burberry London for Men Special Edition 2008; Burberry London for Women Special Edition 2008; Cabotine; Cacharel pour l'Homme; Can Can; Carnation; Carthusia Uomo; Cast a Spell;

Central Park; C'est la Fête; CH; Champs-Elysées; Chance Eau Fraiche; Charlie!; China Rose; Chrome; Ciel; Cirrus; cK IN2U Her; cK IN2U His; Clean; Clean Fresh Laundry; Clean Lather; Clean Men; Clean Provence; Clean Shower Fresh; Clean Ultimate; Clean Warm Cotton; Confetto; Coriandre; Crystal Noir; Cuir Améthyste; Cumbia Colors Man; Cumbia Colors Woman; Curious; Daliflor; Délices eau de toilette; Délices parfum; Design; Désir de Rochas Femme; Désir de Rochas Homme; Desire Blue; Diamonds; Domain; Do Son; Dream; Duro; Eau de Lierre; Eau de Noho; Eau de Rubylips; Eau de Shalimar; Eau du Soir; Echo; Echo Woman; Effusion Man; Elige; Emeraude; Energy Woman; Erolfa; Essence of Man; Essence of Woman; Essential; Euphoria Men; Fairy Dust; Farnesiana; Fig Tea; Fiore d'Ambra; Fleur d'Oranger 27; Fleurs d'Ombre Jasmin Lilas; Flowerbomb; Fool for Love; Forever Elizabeth; French Cancan; Gardenia (Chanel); Gardenia (Elizabeth Taylor); Garofano; Gaultier2; Ghost Cherish; Golden Goddess; Gold Man; Gold Woman; Gramercy Park; Guess Man; Guess Woman; Hamptons; Heiress; Higher Energy; Hiris; Honey I Washed the Kids; Hugo XX; Iceberg Homme; Iceberg Twice Men; Ichnusa; Individuel; Inspiration; Irisia; Island Bermuda; Jade; Jaïpur Saphir; Jamais le Dimanche; Le Jasmin (Chantecaille); Jasmin 17; Jean Paul Gaultier "Classique" Eau d'Eté; Jean Paul Gaultier "Classique" Eau de Toilette; Jil Sander Style; Joop! Go; Just Cavalli Her; Just Me; Just Me for Men; Keep It Fluffy; Kingdom; L (Apothia); Laguna Homme; L.A. Style; Lauren Style; Light Blue; Light Blue pour Homme; Light Comes from Within; Little Italy; Lotus Blossom & Water Lily; Loukhoum; Love in Black; Love in White; Lulu; Lulu Guinness; Lux; Lys; Marc Jacobs Men; Mauboussin Homme; Mayotte; Méchant Loup; Mediterranean; Michael; Midnight Poison; Miel de Bois; Miss Boucheron; Miss Rocaille; Miss Sixty; Montana Mood Sexy; Montana Mood Soft; Morgan de Toi; Must de Cartier; My Dream; Nanette Lepore; New York Fling; Nuit Noire; N.Y. Chic;

Oh Baby; Oiro; Omnia Green Jade; O Oui!; Original Santal; Original Vetiver; Le Parfum; Paris Hilton; Pasha; Passion (Elizabeth Taylor); Pi; Piège à Filles; Pink Beach; Poême; Polo Black; Polo Blue; Pour Monsieur Concentré; Princess; Private Collection Amber Ylang Ylang; Provocative Woman; Pure Purple; Pure Sport for Men; Pure Sport for Women; Purple Fantasy; Pursuit; Reflection; Reflection Man; Remix for Her; Rock'n Rose; Romance Eau Fraîche 2008; Romance Men; Roots Spirit; Roots Spirit Man; Rouge (Hermès); Royal Bain de Caron; RSVP; Rumeur; Sacré Coeur; Saks Fifth Avenue for Him; Sea and Sun in Cadaquès; Secret Obsession; Secret Wish; Selection; Sentiment pour Homme; Serge Noire; Serpentine; Sexy Darling; Shanghai Butterfly; Sheer Stella 2007; Silver Mountain Water; Silver Rain; Six Scents No. 2; Six Scents No. 4; Six Scents No. 5; Six Scents No. 6; Soir de Lune; Spellbound; Sport; Starwalker; Sung; Sweet Paradise; Tabac Blond; Thundra; Tribute; Trouble; Trouble Eau Légère; Ultraviolet; Ultraviolet Man; United Colors of Benetton Man; Valentino; Velocity; Velvet Rope; Vent Vert; Vera Wang for Men; Versace Jeans Couture Man; Versace Man Eau Fraîche; Versace pour Homme; Very Irrésistible; Very Irrésistible for Men; Very Irrésistible Fresh Attitude; Very Irrésistible Sensual eau de parfum; Very Sexy for Her; Very Sexy Hot; Vetiver (Creed); Vetiver Extrême; Voile de Jasmin; White Red He; White Red She; White Rose; Wish Pink Diamond; Wish Turquoise Diamond; Wisteria; Zoe

INDEX OF BRANDS

Anna Sui
Secret Wish

Anné Pliska
Anné Pliska

Annick Goutal
Ambre Fétiche; Ce Soir ou
Jamais; Le Chèvrefeuille; Duel;
Eau de Bonpoint; Eau de
Camille; Eau de Charlotte; Eau de
Lavande; Eau de Monsieur; Eau
d'Hadrien eau de parfum; Eau
d'Hadrien eau de toilette; Eau
du Fier; L'Eau du Sud; Encens
Flamboyant; Folavril; Gardenia
Passion; Grand Amour; Hadrien
Absolu; Heure Exquise; Le
Jasmin; Mandragore; Un Matin
d'Orage; Musc Nomade; Myrrhe
Ardente; Néroli; Les Nuits
d'Hadrien; Passion; Petite Cherie;
Quel Amour!; Rose Absolue;
Sables; Songes; Tubéreuse; Vanille
Exquise; Vetiver; La Violette

Ann Taylor
Possibilities

Antonia's Flowers
Antonia's Flowers; Floret; Sogni
di Mare; Tiempe Passate

Apothia
IF; L; Velvet Rope

Aramis
Aramis; Aramis 900; Tuscany per
Donna; Tuscany per Uomo

Armani
Acqua di Giò; Acqua di Giò
pour Homme; Armani Attitude;
Armani Code Elixir de Parfum;
Armani Code for Women; Armani
Code pour Homme; Armani
Mania pour Homme; Armani
pour Homme; City Glam for Her;
City Glam for Him; Diamonds;
Diamonds for Men; Emporio
Armani He; Emporio Armani She;
Onde Extase; Onde Mystère; Onde
Vertige; Remix for Her; Sensi;
White Red He; White Red She

Armani Privé
Ambre Soie; Bois d'Encens; Cuir
Améthyste; Eau de Jade; Eclat de
Jasmin; Oranger Alhambra; Pierre
de Lune; Rose Alexandrie; Vétiver
Babylone

L'Artisan Parfumeur
Aedes de Venustas; Ambre
Extrême; Ananas Fizz; Bois
Farine; La Chasse aux Papillons;

Drôle de Rose; Dzing!;
Dzongkha; L'Eau d'Ambre; L'Eau
de Jatamansi; L'Eau de l'Artisan;
Eau du Navigateur; L'Eté en
Douce; Fleur de Liane; Fleur de
Narcisse 2006; Fleur d'Oranger
2007; Fou d'Absinthe; La Haie
Fleurie; Iris Pallida
2007; Jour de Fête; Mandarine
Tout Simplement; Méchant Loup;
Mimosa pour Moi;
Mûre et Musc; Mûre et Musc
extrait de parfum; Mûre et
Musc Extrême; Navegar; Passage
d'Enfer; Patchouli Patch;
Piment Brûlant; Poivre Piquant;
Premier Figuier Extrême; Safran
Troublant; Tea for Two; Thé pour
un Eté; Timbuktu; Tubéreuse;
Vanilia; Verte Violette; Voleur
de Roses

Art of Perfumery
Art of Perfumery 1; Art of
Perfumery 2; Art of Perfumery
3; Art of Perfumery 4; Art of
Perfumery 5; Art of Perfumery 6;
Art of Perfumery 7

Aveda
Aveda Men Pure-Formance;
Chakra 1–7; Yatra

Avon
Bond Girl 007

Azzaro
Azzaro Couture; Azzaro Men
Now; Azzaro pour Homme;
Azzaro Women Now; Chrome;
Chrome Legend; Onyx

Baby Phat
Goddess; Golden Goddess

Badgley Mischka
Badgley Mischka; Fleurs de Nuit

Balmain
Ambre Gris; Balmain; Balmya;
Ivoire; Jolie Madame; Miss
Balmain; Monsieur Balmain; Vent
Vert

Becker Eshaya
b.e.; Golden Amber

Beckham
Instinct; Instinct After Dark;
Intimately Beckham for Women

Bella Bellissima
Perfect Man Alternative

Benefit
B Spot; Maybe Baby

Benetton

Benetton Sport Woman; B•United Jeans Man; B•United Woman; Cumbia Colors Man; Cumbia Colors Woman; Pure Sport for Men; Pure Sport for Women; Sport; United Colors of Benetton Man; United Colors of Benetton Unisex; United Colors of Benetton Woman

Bill Blass

Bill Blass Couture 3; Bill Blass Couture 7; Bill Blass Couture 8

B Never Too Busy to Be Beautiful

Breath of God; B Scent; Cocktail; Dear John; Dirty; Exhale; Inhale; Keep It Fluffy; Ladyboy; Love; Om; Superworldunknown; Two Hearts Beating as One

Bobbi Brown

Almost Bare; Beach; Bobbi

Bond No. 9

Andy Warhol Lexington Avenue; Andy Warhol's Silver Factory; Andy Warhol Union Square; Astor Place; Bleecker Street; Broadway Nite; Brooklyn; Bryant Park; Central Park; Chelsea Flowers; Chez Bond; Chinatown; Coney Island; Eau de New York; Eau de Noho; Fashion Avenue; Fire Island; Gramercy Park; Great Jones; Hamptons; H.O.T. Always; Little Italy; Madison Soirée; New Haarlem; New York Fling; Nouveau Bowery; Nuits de Noho; Park Avenue; Riverside Drive; Saks Fifth Avenue for Her; Saks Fifth Avenue for Him; Scent of Peace; So New York; Wall Street; West Broadway; West Side

Boucheron

B de Boucheron; Boucheron; Boucheron Eau Légère 2006; Boucheron Eau Légère 2007; Boucheron pour Homme; Boucheron pour Homme Eau de Parfum; Boucheron pour Homme Eau de Toilette Fraîcheur; Jaïpur; Jaïpur Homme; Jaïpur Homme Fraicheur; Jaïpur Saphir; Miss Boucheron; Trouble; Trouble Eau Légère

Boudicca

Wode

Brandy

Brandy

Britney Spears

Believe; Curious; Fantasy

Brooks Brothers
Brooks Brothers Classic; Brooks
Brothers New York Gentlemen;
Brooks Brothers New York Ladies

Bulgari
Aqua pour Homme; Aqua pour
Homme Marine; Black; BLV "Blù"
pour Homme; Bulgari BLV "Blù";
Bulgari pour Femme; Bulgari
pour Homme Extrême; Bulgari
pour Homme Soir; Bulgari Rose
Essentielle; Eau Parfumée au
Thé Blanc; Eau Parfumée au Thé
Rouge; Eau Parfumée au Thé
Vert; Jasmin Noir; Omnia; Omnia
Green Jade; Voile de Jasmin

Burberry
Burberry London; Burberry
London for Men; Burberry
London for Men Special Edition
2008; Burberry London for
Women Special Edition 2008

By Kilian
Beyond Love; Cruel Intentions;
Liaisons Dangereuses; Love;
Prelude to Love; Straight to
Heaven; A Taste of Heaven

By Mark Buxton
Around Midnight; Black Angel;
English Breakfast; Hot Leather;
Nameless; Sounds & Visions;
Wood & Absinth

Byredo
Chembur; Gypsy Water; Pulp

Cacharel
Amor Amor; Amor pour Homme;
Anaïs Anaïs; Cacharel pour
l'Homme; Eden; Gloria; Liberté;
Loulou; Nuu; Noa Fleur; Noa
Perle; Promesse

Caldey Island
Lavender

Calvin Klein
cK Be; cK IN2U Her; cK IN2U
His; cK One; cK One Summer;
Contradiction for Men; Escape;
Escape for Men; Eternity; Eternity
for Men; Euphoria; Euphoria
Blossom; Euphoria Men; Intense
Euphoria Men; Obsession;
Obsession for Men; Obsession
Night; Secret Obsession; Sheer
Obsession; Truth

Canali
Canali Black Diamond; Canali
Style

Carolina Herrera
212; 212 Men; 212 Sexy Men;
Carolina; Carolina Herrera; CH;
Chic; Chic for Men; Herrera Aqua;
Herrera for Men

Caron
Acaciosa; Aimez Moi; Alpona;
L'Anarchiste; Bellodgia; Coup de
Fouet; Eau de Réglisse; En Avion;
Farnesiana; Fleur de Rocaille;
Fleurs de Rocaille; French Cancan;
Impact; Infini; Lady Caron; Miss
Rocaille; Montaigne; Muguet
du Bonheur; N'Aimez que Moi;
Narcisse Blanc; Narcisse Noir eau
de toilette; Nocturnes; Nuit de
Noël; Or et Noir; Parfum Sacré;
Pois de Senteur; Poivre; Pour une
Femme; Pour un Homme; Rose;
Royal Bain de Caron; Tabac Blond;
Le Troisième Homme; Tubéreuse;
Violette Précieuse; Yatagan

Carthusia
Aria di Capri; Carthusia Uomo;
Fiori di Capri; Io Capri; Ligea "La
Sirena"; Mediterraneo; Numero
Uno; Via Camarelle

Cartier
Le Baiser du Dragon; Déclaration;
Déclaration Essence; Délices
eau de toilette; Délices parfum;
Eau de Cartier; Eau de Cartier
Concentrée; Must de Cartier;
Must de Cartier pour Homme;
Pasha; Roadster; Santos; So Pretty

Carven
Ma Griffe

Cavalli
Serpentine

Celine Dion
Always Belong; Belong; Celine
Dion; Celine Dion Parfum Notes;
Enchanting; Spring in Paris

Cerruti
Cerruti 1881

Chanel
28 La Pausa; 31 Rue Cambon;
Allure; Allure Homme; Allure
Homme Edition Blanche;
Allure Homme Sport; Allure
Homme Sport Cologne; Allure
Sensuelle; Antaeus; Beige; Bel
Respiro; Bois des Iles; Chance;
Chance Eau Fraiche; Coco; Coco
Mademoiselle; Coromandel;
Cristalle; Cuir de Russie; Eau
de Cologne; Egoïste; Egoïste
Platinum; Gardenia; No. 5 eau

de parfum; No. 5 eau de toilette;
No. 5 Eau Première; No. 5
parfum; No. 18; No. 19; No. 22;
Pour Monsieur; Pour Monsieur
Concentré; Sycomore

Chantecaille
Frangipane; Le Jasmin; Tiare;
Wisteria

Chloé
Chloé

Chopard
Cašmir; Chopard pour Homme;
Wish; Wish Pink Diamond; Wish
Turquoise Diamond

Christian Lacroix
C'est la Fête; Noir; Rouge

Cinq Mondes
Eau Egyptienne; Pluie d'Aromes

Clarins
Par Amour; Par Amour Toujours

Clean
Clean; Clean Fresh Laundry;
Clean Lather; Clean Men; Clean
Provence; Clean Shower Fresh;
Clean Ultimate; Clean Warm
Cotton

Clinique
Aromatics Elixir; Happy; Happy
for Men; Happy Heart

Clive Christian
1872 for Men; 1872 for Women;
No. 1 for Men; No. 1 for Women;
X for Men; X for Women

Combe, Inc.
Aqua Velva Classic Ice Blue

Comme des Garçons
888; Comme des Garçons 2
Man; Comme des Garçons 2
Woman; Comme des Garçons
3; Comme des Garçons White;
Luxe Champaca; Luxe Patchouli;
Odeur 53; Odeur 71; Palisander;
Patchouli; Play; Stephen Jones

Costume National
21 Costume National; Scent

Coty
Aspen; Avatar; Beckham Signature
Women; Emeraude; Exclamation;
Intimately Beckham for Men;
Miss Sixty; Sand and Sable; Vanilla
Fields

Creative Scentualization
Beauty Comes from Within; Joy

Comes from Within; Light Comes from Within; Perfect Kiss

Creed
Acier Aluminium; Ambre Cannelle; Angélique Encens; Bois du Portugal; Cyprès Musc; Erolfa; Fleur de Thé Rose Bulgare; Fleurissimo; Fleurs de Bulgarie; Green Irish Tweed; Himalaya; Irisia; Jasmal; Love in Black; Love in White; Millésime Impérial; Néroli Sauvage; Original Santal; Original Vetiver; Royal Scottish Lavender; Santal Impérial; Sélection Verte; Silver Mountain Water; Spring Flower; Tabarôme; Tubéreuse Indiana; Vetiver; Virgin Island Water

Cynthia Rowley
Flower

Czech & Speake
Cuba; Frankincense and Myrrh; No. 88; Oxford & Cambridge Traditional Lavender

Dana
English Leather; Tabu

Danielle Steel
Danielle

Davidoff
Cool Water; Cool Water Wave; Cool Water Woman; Echo; Echo Woman; Silver Shadow

David Yurman
David Yurman

Diesel
Fuel for Life; Fuel for Life Men; Fuel for Life Unlimited

The Different Company
Bois d'Iris; Divine; Divine Bergamote; Jasmin de Nuit; Osmanthus; Un Parfum d'Ailleurs et Fleurs; Un Parfum de Charmes et Feuilles; Un Parfum des Sens et Bois; Rose Poivrée; Sel de Vetiver

Dior
Bois d'Argent; Cologne Blanche; Dior Addict; Dior Addict 2; Diorama; Diorella; Dioressence; Dior Homme; Dior Homme Intense; Dior Homme Sport; Diorissimo; Dolce Vita; Dune; Dune pour Homme; Eau Fraîche; Eau Noire; Eau Sauvage; Escale à Portofino; Fahrenheit; Fahrenheit 32; Higher; Higher Energy; Hypnotic Poison; J'Adore; J'Adore l'Absolu; Jules;

Midnight Poison; Miss Dior;
Miss Dior Cherie; Poison; Pure
Poison

Diptyque
L'Autre; Do Son; L'Eau; L'Eau
de l'Eau; Eau d'Élide; Eau de
Lierre; L'Eau de Néroli; Eau
Lente; Eau Trois; Ofrésia; Olene;
L'Ombre dans l'Eau; Opôné;
Oyédo; Philosykos; Tam Dao;
Virgilio

Divine
L'Ame Soeur; Divine; L'Etre Aimé
Femme; L'Etre Aimé Homme;
L'Homme de Coeur; L'Homme
Sage; L'Infante; L'Inspiratrice

Dolce & Gabbana
Dolce & Gabbana; Dolce &
Gabbana pour Homme; Light
Blue; Light Blue pour Homme;
The One; Sicily

Donna Karan
Be Delicious; Be Delicious Fresh
Blossom; Be Delicious Men; Black
Cashmere; Cashmere Mist; Chaos;
DKNY Delicious Night; DKNY
for Men; DKNY Men; DKNY Men
Summer 2009; DKNY Women;
DKNY Women Summer 2009;

Donna Karan Essence Jasmine;
Donna Karan Essence Labdanum;
Donna Karan Essence Lavender;
Donna Karan Essence Wenge;
Donna Karan Gold; Donna Karan
Signature; Fuel for Men; Red
Delicious Men; Red Delicious
Woman

Dsquared2
He Wood; She Wood

Dunhill
Desire Blue; Dunhill; Dunhill
Black; Fresh; Pure; Pursuit

Eau d'Italie
Baume du Doge; Bois d'Ombrie;
Eau d'Italie; Magnolia Romana;
Paestum Rose; Sienne l'Hiver

Ego Facto
Fool for Love; Jamais le
Dimanche; Me Myself and I; Piège
à Filles; Poopoo Pidou; Prends
Garde à Toi; Sacré Coeur

Elizabeth Arden
5th Avenue; Daytona 500; Green
Tea; Mediterranean; Provocative
Woman; Red Door; White
Shoulders

Elizabeth Taylor
Forever Elizabeth; Gardenia;
Passion; Passion for Men; White
Diamonds

Ellie D
Ellie; Ellie Nuit

Elternhaus
MoslBuddJewChristHinDao

Ermenegildo Zegna
Essenza di Zegna; Zegna Intenso;
Z Zegna

Erox
Realm Men

Escada
Escada; Sentiment; Sentiment
pour Homme; Sunset Heat;
Sunset Heat for Men

Escentric Molecules
Escentric 01; Molecule 01

Estée Lauder
Alliage; Azurée; Beautiful;
Beautiful Love; Beautiful Sheer;
Beyond Paradise; Beyond
Paradise Blue; Beyond Paradise
Men; Cinnabar; Dazzling Gold;
Dazzling Silver; Estée; Intuition;
Intuition for Men; Knowing;
Lauder for Men; Pleasures;
Pleasures Exotic; Pleasures for
Men; Pleasures Intense; Private
Collection; Private Collection
Amber Ylang Ylang; Private
Collection Tuberose Gardenia;
Pure White Linen; Pure White
Linen Light Breeze; Sensuous;
Spellbound; White Linen; Youth
Dew; Youth Dew Amber Nude

Etat Libre d'Orange
Antihéros; Bendelirious;
Charogne; Delicious Closet
Queen; Divin'Enfant; Don't Get
Me Wrong Baby, I Don't Swallow;
Eloge du Traître; Encens et
Bubblegum; Jasmin et Cigarette;
Je Suis un Homme; Noël au
Balcon; Nombril Immense;
Putain des Palaces; Rien; Rossy de
Palma; Sécrétions Magnifiques;
Tom of Finland; Vierges et
Toreros; Vraie Blonde

Etro
Ambra; Anice; Dianthus; Etra;
Gomma; Heliotrope; Lemon
Sorbet; Magot; Messe de Minuit;
Musk; New Tradition; Palais
Jamais; Patchouly; Royal Pavillon;
Shaal Nur; Vetiver; Vicolo Fiori

FCUK
Eau de FCUK; French Connection
Fragrance

Fendi
Palazzo

Floris
Cefiro; China Rose; Edwardian
Bouquet; Fleur; Florissa;
Gardenia; JF; Lily of the Valley;
Night-Scented Jasmine; No. 89;
Sandalwood; Santal; Seringa;
Stephanotis; Vetiver; White Rose;
Zinnia

Fragonard
Après Tout; Belle de Nuit parfum;
Billet Doux; Caresse; Cologne
Grand Luxe; Mensonge; Soudain

Frapin
1270; Caravelle Epicée; Esprit de
Fleurs; Passion Boisée; Terre de
Sarment

Frédéric Malle
Angéliques sous la Pluie; Bigarade
Concentrée; Carnal Flower; Dans
Tes Bras; Eau d'Hiver; En Passant;
Une Fleur de Cassie; French
Lover; Iris Poudre; Lipstick Rose;
Lys Méditerranée; Musc Ravageur;

Noir Epices; Outrageous; Le
Parfum de Thérèse; Une Rose;
Vetiver Extraordinaire

Fresh Scents by Terri
Breathe; Dream; Gregory; Lulu;
My Man; Oh Baby; Zoe

Gant
Adventure

Geoffrey Beene
Eau de Grey Flannel, Grey Flannel

Ghost
Ghost Cherish

Gianfranco Ferré
Ferré

Giorgio Beverly Hills
Giorgio; Giorgio Red

Givenchy
Absolutely Irrésistible; Amarige;
Amarige Mariage; Ange ou
Démon; Eau de Givenchy;
Extravagance d'Amarige;
Givenchy III; Givenchy
Gentleman; Givenchy pour
Homme Blue Label; Hot Couture;
Insensé; L'Interdit; Le De;
Monsieur de Givenchy; Organza;

Organza Indécence; Pi; Play; Very Irrésistible; Very Irrésistible for Men; Very Irrésistible Fresh Attitude; Very Irrésistible Sensual eau de parfum; Vetyver; Xeryus; Xeryus Rouge; Ysatis

Grès
Ambre de Cabochard; Cabaret; Cabochard; Cabotine; Caline; Fleur de Cabotine; My Dream; My Life; My Passion

Gucci
Envy; Envy for Men; Gucci; Gucci by Gucci Pour Homme; Gucci Eau de Parfum; Gucci Eau de Parfum II; Gucci pour Homme; Gucci pour Homme II; Rush; Rush II

Guerlain
L'Ame d'un Héros; Angélique Noire; Après l'Ondée; Aqua Allegoria Angélique-Lilas; Aqua Allegoria Cherry Blossom; Aqua Allegoria Figue Iris; Aqua Allegoria Grosellina; Aqua Allegoria Herba Fresca; Aqua Allegoria Laurier Réglisse; Aqua Allegoria Lemon Fresca; Aqua Allegoria Lilia Bella; Aqua Allegoria Mandarine-Basilic; Aqua Allegoria Pamplelune;

Aqua Allegoria Pivoine Magnifica; Aqua Allegoria Tiaré Mimosa; Aqua Allegoria Tutti Kiwi; Attrape-Coeurs; Bois d'Arménie; Candide Effluve; Chamade; Chamade pour Homme; Champs-Elysées; Chant d'Arômes; Cherry Blossom Fruity; Cologne du 68; Cruel Gardenia; Cuir Beluga; Derby; Eau de Cologne du Coq; Eau de Cologne Impériale; Eau de Fleurs de Cédrat; Eau de Guerlain; Eau de Shalimar; Elixir Charnel Chypre Fatal; Elixir Charnel Gourmand Coquin; Elixir Charnel Oriental Brûlant; Garden Sensuel; Guerlain Homme; Guerlinade; Habit Rouge; Habit Rouge Sport; Héritage; L'Heure Bleue; Insolence; Insolence eau de parfum; Insolence Eau Glacée; L'Instant; L'Instant Fleur de Mandarine; L'Instant Magic; L'Instant Magic 2008; L'Instant Magic Elixir; L'Instant pour Homme; Iris Ganache; Jardins de Bagatelle; Jicky; Liu; Mayotte; Metalys; Mitsouko; Mouchoir de Monsieur; My Insolence; Nahéma; Nuit d'Amour; Oud Sensuel; La Petite Robe Noire; Philtre d'Amour; Plus Que

Jamais; Purple Fantasy; Quand
Vient la Pluie; Quand Vient l'Été;
Rose Barbare; Samsara; Shalimar;
Sous le Vent; Spiritueuse Double
Vanille; Vetiver; Vetiver Extrême;
Vetiver pour Elle; Vol de Nuit

Guess
Guess by Marciano; Guess Man;
Guess Woman

Halston
Halston Z; Halston Z-14; Sheer
Halston; Unbound; Unbound for
Men

Hanae Mori
Hanae Mori "Butterfly"; Hanae
Mori "Butterfly" Eau Fraîche;
Haute Couture; HM; Magical
Moon

Harvey Prince
Ageless Fantasy

Heeley
Cardinal; Cèdre Blanc; Cuir Pleine
Fleur; Esprit du Tigre; Figuier;
Iris de Nuit; Menthe Fraîche; Sel
Marin; Verveine

Helen of Troy Ltd.
Brut

Hermès
24, Faubourg; Amazone; Ambre
Narguilé; Bel-Ami; Brin de
Réglisse; Calèche; Calèche Eau
Délicate; Concentré d'Orange
Verte; Eau de Gentiane Blanche;
Eau de Pamplemousse Rose; Eau
des Merveilles; Eau d'Hermès;
Eau d'Orange Verte; Elixir des
Merveilles; Equipage; Hiris;
Un Jardin Après la Mousson;
Un Jardin en Méditerranée; Un
Jardin sur le Nil; Kelly Calèche;
Osmanthe Yunnan; Paprika Brasil;
Poivre Samarcande; Rose Ikebana;
Rouge; Terre d'Hermès; Vanille
Galante; Vetiver Tonka

Hilary Duff
With Love . . .

Histoires de Parfums
1725; 1740; 1804; 1826; 1828;
1873; 1876; 1969; Ambre 411;
Blanc Violette; Noir Patchouli;
Vert Pivoine

Hors là Monde
Shiloh

Houbigant
Quelques Fleurs L'Original;
Quelques Fleurs Royale

Hugo Boss
Baldessarini; Baldessarini Ambré; Hugo; Hugo XX; Hugo XY; Pure Purple; Selection

Iceberg
Effusion Man; Effusion Woman; Iceberg Homme; Iceberg Twice; Iceberg Twice Men

Indult
Rêve en Cuir

Institut Très Bien
Cologne à la Française; Cologne à la Russe; Cologne à l'Italienne; Très Russe

I Profumi di Firenze
Ambra del Nepal

Issey Miyake
L'Eau Bleue d'Issey Eau Fraîche; L'Eau Bleue d'Issey pour Homme; L'Eau d'Issey; L'Eau d'Issey pour Homme; L'Eau d'Issey pour Homme Intense; Le Feu d'Issey

Jasper Conran
Jasper Conran Woman

Jean-Charles Brosseau
Atlas Cedar; Fleurs d'Ombre Jasmin Lilas; Fleurs d'Ombre Ombre Bleue; Fleurs d'Ombre Rose; Fleurs d'Ombre Violette-Menthe; Fruit de Bois; Ombre Rose (L'Original); Thé Brun

Jean Couturier
Coriandre

Jean Patou
1000; Joy eau de parfum; Joy parfum; Sublime

Jean Paul Gaultier
Fleur du Mâle; Gaultier2; Jean Paul Gaultier "Classique" Eau d'Eté; Jean Paul Gaultier "Classique" Eau de Toilette; Jean Paul Gaultier Monsieur; Ma Dame; Le Mâle; Le Mâle Eau d'Eté

Jennifer Lopez
Deseo

Jessica Simpson
Fancy

Jil Sander
Jil Sander Pure for Men; Jil Sander Style; No. 4; Pure; Pure Intense; Sander for Men; Scent 79 Man; Scent 79 Woman; Sensations; Sun

J-Lo
Glow; Glow After Dark

John Galliano
John Galliano

John Varvatos
John Varvatos

Jo Malone
154 Cologne; Amber and Lavender
Cologne; Black Vétyver Café
Cologne; Blue Agava & Cacao
Cologne; Dark Amber & Ginger
Lily; French Lime Blossom
Cologne; Grapefruit Cologne;
Honeysuckle and Jasmine; Lime
Basil & Mandarin Cologne; Lotus
Blossom & Water Lily; Nectarine
Blossom and Honey Cologne;
Nutmeg and Ginger Cologne;
Orange Blossom Cologne;
Pomegranate Noir Cologne;
Red Roses Cologne; Sweet Lime
& Cedar; Tuberose Cologne;
Verbenas of Provence Cologne;
Vetyver Cologne; Vintage Gardenia
Cologne; White Jasmine and Mint;
Wild Fig and Cassis Cologne

Joop!
Joop! Go; Joop! Homme; Joop!
Jump; What About Adam

Jovan
Fresh Patchouli; Ginseng NRG
"Energy"; Island Gardenia; Jovan
Musk for Women; Jovan White
Musk; Sex Appeal for Men

Jo Wood Organics
Usiku

Juicy Couture
Juicy Couture; Viva la Juicy

Juliette Has a Gun
Lady Vengeance; Miss Charming

Juozas Statkevicius
Juozas Statkevicius

Kate Moss
Kate Moss; Velvet Hour

Keiko Mecheri
Bois de Santal; Crystal d'Ambre;
Damascena; A Fleur de Peau;
Génie des Bois; Gourmandises;
Grenats; Hanae; Jasmine;
Loukhoum; Loukhoum Eau
Poudrée; Loukhoum Parfum
de Soir; Mihimé; Mogador;
Musk; Myrrhe et Merveilles;
Oliban; Osmanthus; Paname;
Passiflora; Patchoulissime;
Peau de Pêche; Sanguine;

Scarlett; Umé; White Petals; Wild
Berries

Kenneth Cole
RSVP

Kenzo
Ça Sent Beau; L'Eau par Kenzo
pour Femme; L'Eau par Kenzo
pour Homme; Flower; Flower
by Kenzo Fleurs d'Hiver/Winter
Flower; Flower Le Parfum;
Flower Oriental; Kenzo Air;
Kenzo Amour; Kenzo Amour
Indian Holi; Kenzo Amour
le Parfum; Kenzo Jungle
"L'Eléphant"; Kenzo Jungle pour
Homme; Kenzo pour Homme;
Kenzo pour Homme Fresh; Le
Monde Est Beau; Parfum d'Été;
Summer; Tokyo

Kiton
Kiton Black; Kiton Man

Knize
Knize Ten

Krizia
Krizia Uomo

Kylie Minogue
Sexy Darling

Lacoste
Essential; Inspiration

Lalique
Amethyst; Encre Noire; Flora
Bella; Lalique Eau de Parfum;
Lalique White; Le Parfum; Perles
de Lalique

L.A.M.B.
L

Lancôme
Climat; Cuir; Hypnôse; Hypnôse
Homme; Hypnôse Homme Eau
Fraîche; Magie; Magie Noire;
Magnifique; Mille et Une Roses;
Miracle; Miracle Forever; O de
Lancôme; O Oui!; Peut-Etre;
Poême; Trésor

Lanvin
Arpège; Arpège pour Homme;
Eclat d'Arpège; Lanvin L'Homme;
Rumeur

La Prairie
Midnight Rain; Silver Rain

Laura Biagiotti
Roma for Women

Le Labo
Aldehyde 44; Ambrette 9;
Bergamote 22; Fleur d'Oranger
27; Iris 39; Jasmin 17; Labdanum
18; Neroli 36; Oud 27; Patchouli
24; Poivre 23; Rose 31; Tubéreuse
40; Vetiver 46

LesNez
L'Antimatière; Let Me Play the Lion;
Manoumalia; The Unicorn Spell

Linari
Angelo di Fiume; Eleganza
Luminosa; Notte Bianca; Vista sul
Marc

Lisa Hoffman
Madagascar Orchid

Liz Claiborne
Curve; Curve for Men

L'Occitane
Cherry Blossom; Thé Blanc; Thé
Vert au Jasmin

Loewe
Solo Loewe Eau de Cologne
Intense

Lolita Lempicka
L; Lolita Lempicka; Lolita

Lempicka au Masculin; Lolita
Lempicka Midnight

Lorenzo Villoresi
Alamut; Dilmun; Donna;
Garofano; Incensi; Uomo; Vetiver;
Yerbamate

Lubin
L'Eau Neuve; Idole; L de Lubin;
Nuit de Longchamp; Le Vetiver

Lulu Guinness
Cast a Spell; Fairytales; Lulu
Guinness

LUSH
Fever; Go Green; Honey I Washed
the Kids; Karma solid perfume;
Potion solid perfume; Silky
Underwear solid perfume

Maître Parfumeur et Gantier
Ambre Précieux; Bahiana; Fleurs
des Comores; Fraîche Passiflore;
Fraîcheur Muskissime; Garrigue;
Jardin du Néroli; Or des Indes;
Racine; Rose Opulente; Santal
Noble; Vocalise

Marc Jacobs
Blush; Daisy; Essence; Marc
Jacobs; Marc Jacobs Men

Mariah Carey
M

Mary-Kate and Ashley
L.A. Style; Mary-Kate and Ashley
One; Mary-Kate and Ashley Two;
N.Y. Chic

Mary Kay
Affection; Bella Belara; Domain;
Elige; High Intensity; Tribute;
Velocity; Velocity for Him

Matthew Williamson
Matthew Williamson Collection:
Incense; Matthew Williamson
Collection: Jasmine Sambac;
Matthew Williamson
Collection: Pink Lotus; Matthew
Williamson Collection: Warm
Sands; Sheer

Mauboussin
Mauboussin; Mauboussin
Homme; M Moi

Max Mara
Max Mara; Silk Touch

Michael Kors
Island; Island Bermuda; Michael;
Very Pretty

Michel Germain
Séxual; Séxual pour Femme;
Séxual pour Homme

Miller et Bertaux
(For you)/parfum trouvé; Green,
green, and . . . green; Spiritus/land

Miller Harris
L'Air de Rien; Citron Citron;
Coeur de Fleur; Coeur d'Eté; Cuir
d'Oranger; Eau de Vert; En Sens
de Bois; Feuilles de Tabac; Figue
Amère; Fleur du Matin; Fleur
Oriental; Fleurs de Sel; Jasmin Vert;
Noix de Tubéreuse; Piment des
Baies; Tangerine Vert; Terre de Bois

Missoni
Missoni; Missoni Acqua

Molinard
Habanita

Molinard for Aedes de Venustas
Une Histoire de Chypre

Mona di Orio
Carnation; Lux; Nuit Noire; Oiro

Montale
Aoud Damascus; Black Aoud;
Chocolate Greedy; Oud Cuir

d'Arabie; Red Vetyver; White
Aoud

Montana
Montana Homme; Montana
Mood Sensual; Montana Mood
Sexy; Montana Mood Soft;
Parfum de Peau

Mont Blanc
Individuel; Starwalker

Monyette Paris
Monyette Paris

Morgan
Morgan de Toi; Sweet Paradise

Morgan de Toi
Light My Heart; Love de Toi

Moschino
Cheap and Chic; L'Eau Cheap
and Chic; Friends Men; Funny!;
Glamour; Hippy Fizz; Moschino;
Uomo?

Mugler
Alien

Nanette Lepore
Nanette Lepore; Shanghai
Butterfly

Narciso Rodriguez
Musc for Him perfume oil;
Narciso Rodriguez for Her;
Narciso Rodriguez for Him

Nasomatto
Absinth; Duro; Hindu Grass;
Narcotic Venus; Silver Musk

Nautica
Nautica Voyage

Les Néréides
Douceur de Vanille; Imperial
Opopanax; Musc Samarkand;
Oriental Lumpur; Patchouli
Antique; Vert d'Eau

Nina Ricci
L'Air du Temps; L'Air du Temps
parfum Anniversary Edition; Love
in Paris; Nina; Premier Jour

Olivier Durbano
Amethyst; Black Tourmaline; Jade;
Rock Crystal

Origins
Frolic; Ginger Essence; Ginger
with a Twist; Shedonism

Ormonde Jayne
Champaca; Frangipani Absolute;

Isfarkand; Ormonde Man;
Ormonde Woman; Orris Noir;
Osmanthus; Sampaquita; Ta'if;
Tolu; Zizan

Oscar de la Renta
Oscar; Oscar Citrus; Oscar Red
Orchid; Oscar Red Satin

Paco Rabanne
1 Million; Black XS; Black XS
for Her; Calandre; Métal; Paco
Rabanne pour Elle; Paco Rabanne
pour Homme; Ultraviolet;
Ultraviolet Man; XS "Excess pour
Homme"

Paloma Picasso
Paloma Picasso

Parfum d'Empire
Ambre Russe; Aziyadé; Cuir
Ottoman; Eau Suave; Equistrius;
Fougère Bengale; Iskander;
Osmanthus Interdite; Yuzu Fou

Parfumerie Générale
Aomassaï; Bois Blond; Bois
de Copaiba; Brûlure de Rose;
Cadjméré; Cèdre Sandaraque;
Cologne Grand Siècle; Corps et
Ames; Cozé; Un Crime Exotique;
Cuir Venenum; Drama Nuuï;

L'Eau de Circé; L'Eau Guerrière;
L'Eau Rare Matale; Felanilla;
Harmatan Noir; Hyperessence
Matale; Ilang Ivohibe; Intrigant
Patchouli; Iris Taïzo; Louanges
Profanes; Musc Maori; L'Oiseau
de Nuit; L'Ombre Fauve; Querelle;
Yuzu Ab Irato

Parfums 06130
Cèdre; Feuille de Réglisse;
Lentisque; Lierre Rose; Lys; Yuzu
Rouge

Parfums Bleu
Blue Stratos

Parfums de Coeur
Skin Musk

Parfums DelRae
Amoureuse; Bois de Paradis;
Début; Eau Illuminée

Parfums de Nicolaï
Balkis; Balle de Match; Carré d'As;
Cédrat Intense; Cococabana; Eau
Turquoise; Fig Tea; Maharanih;
New York; Nicolaï pour Homme;
Number One; Odalisque; Rose
Intense; Rose-Pivoine; Sacrebleu;
Le Temps d'une Fête; Vanille
Tonka; Vetyver; Vie de Château

Parfums de Rosine
Diabolo Rose; Ecume de Rose;
Une Folie de Rose; Poussière de
Rose; Rosa Flamenca; Roseberry;
Rose d'Amour; Rose de Feu; La
Rose de Rosine; Rose d'Été; Rose
d'Homme; Twill Rose; Un Zest de
Rose

Parfums d'Orsay
Le Dandy; Tilleul

Parfums MDCI
Ambre Topkapi; Un Coeur en
Mai; Enlèvement au Sérail;
Invasion Barbare; Péché Cardinal;
Promesse de l'Aube; Le Rivage
des Syrtes; Rose de Siwa; Vêpres
Siciliennes

Paris Hilton
Can Can; Fairy Dust; Heiress;
Just Me; Just Me for Men; Paris
Hilton

Pascal Morabito
Or Black; Or Noir

Patou
Sira des Indes

Paul Sebastian
Casual; Design

Paul Smith
Paul Smith London for Men;
Paul Smith London Woman; Paul
Smith Man; Paul Smith Rose; Paul
Smith Woman; Story

Penhaligon's
Artemisia; Blenheim Bouquet;
Bluebell; Elixir; Endymion;
English Fern; Hammam Bouquet;
Lavandula; Lily and Spice; Lily
of the Valley; Malabah; Quercus;
Violetta

People of the Labyrinths
A*Maze; Luctor et Emergo

Perfumer's Workshop
Tea Rose

Phat Farm
Atman

Philosophy
Amazing Grace; Baby Grace;
Falling in Love; Inner Grace; Pure
Grace

Porsche Design
The Essence

Prada
Amber pour Homme; Infusion

d'Homme; Infusion d'Iris; Prada;
Prada Tendre

Prescriptives
Calyx

Prince Matchabelli
Wind Song

Procter & Gamble
Old Spice

Profumo di Firenze
Cuoio; Iris; Spigo; Tabacco;
Zafferano

Profumum
Acqua di Sale; Alba; Antico
Caruso; Confetto; Fiore d'Ambra;
Fumidus; Ichnusa; Thundra

Pucci
Vivara

Ralph Lauren
Explorer; Lauren; Lauren
Style; Love; Notorious; Polo;
Polo Black; Polo Blue; Polo
Double Black; Polo Sport; Pure
Turquoise; Purple Label; Ralph;
Ralph Cool; Ralph Hot; Ralph
Rocks; Romance; Romance Eau
Fraîche 2008; Romance Men;

Romance Men Silver; Safari for
Men

Renée
Amber; L'Eau; Jasmine;
Mediterranean Lily; Musk;
Snowpeach; Tuberose

Revlon
Charlie!

Rimmel
Beat

Riviera Concepts
Hummer

Roberto Cavalli
Just Cavalli Her; Just Cavalli Him;
Roberto Cavalli; Roberto Cavalli
Oro

Robert Piguet
Baghari; Bandit; Cravache; Fracas;
Visa

Rochas
Aquawoman; Byzance; Désir de
Rochas Femme; Désir de Rochas
Homme; Eau de Rochas; Eau
de Rochas Homme; Femme;
Madame Rochas; Mystère; Rochas
Man; Soleil de Rochas; Tocade

Roja Dove
Enslaved; Scandal; Unspoken

Roméa d'Améor
Les Espionnes du Tsar; Les
Grandes Amours du Taj-Mahal;
Les Grandes Prêtresses Incas;
Les Impératrices Japonaises;
Les Maîtresses de Louis XIV;
Les Princesses de Venise; Les
Souveraines d'Egypte

Roots
Roots Spirit; Roots Spirit Man

Salvador Dalí
Agua Verde; Black Sun; Dalí;
Daliflor; Dalimania; Dalimix;
Dalissime; Eau de Dalí; Eau de
Rubylips; Itislove; Laguna; Laguna
Homme; Purplelight; Purple Lips;
Le Roy Soleil Homme; Rubylips;
Sea and Sun in Cadaquès

Salvatore Ferragamo
F by Ferragamo pour Homme; F
for Fascinating

Sarah Jessica Parker
Covet; Lovely

Sean John
I Am King; Unforgivable;
Unforgivable Black; Unforgivable

Eau Fraîche; Unforgivable
Woman; Unforgivable Woman
Black; Unforgivable Woman Eau
Fraîche

Serge Lutens
A La Nuit; Ambre Sultan; Arabie;
Bois de Violette; Bois et Fruits;
Bois et Musc; Bois Oriental;
Un Bois Sépia; Un Bois Vanille;
Borneo 1834; Cèdre; Chêne;
Chergui; Chypre Rouge; Clair de
Musc; Cuir Mauresque;
Daim Blond; Datura Noir;
Douce Amère; El Attarine;
Encens et Lavande; Féminité
du Bois; Five O'Clock au
Gingembre; Fleurs de Citronnier;
Fleurs d'Oranger; Fumerie
Turque; Iris Silver Mist; Louve;
Un Lys; Mandarine Mandarin;
Miel de Bois; Muscs Koublai
Khan; La Myrrhe; Nuit de
Cellophane; Rahat Loukhoum;
Rose de Nuit; Rousse; Sa Majesté
la Rose; Santal Blanc; Santal de
Mysore; Sarrasins; Serge Noire;
Tubéreuse Criminelle; Vetiver
Oriental

Shalini
Shalini

Torrente
L'Or de Torrente

Ulrich Lang
Anvers; Anvers 2

Ungaro
U by Ungaro for Her; U by Ungaro for Him

United Colors of Benetton
Energy Man; Energy Woman; Essence of Man; Essence of Woman; Gold Man; Gold Woman

Valentino
Rock'n Rose; Valentino; Valentino pour Homme

Van Cleef & Arpels
Féerie; First; First Love; Van Cleef

Vera Wang
Look; Princess; Truly Pink; Vera Wang Bouquet; Vera Wang for Men

Vero Profumo
Kiki; Onda; Rubj

Versace
Bright Crystal; Crystal Noir; Versace; Versace Jeans Couture Man; Versace L'Homme; Versace Man; Versace Man Eau Fraîche; Versace pour Homme

La Via del Profumo
Grezzo; Hindu Kush; Luca; Tabac

Victoria's Secret
Beauty Rush Appletini; Dream Angels Divine; Dream Angels Heavenly; Love Spell; Pink Beach; Sexy Little Things; Very Sexy for Her; Very Sexy for Him; Very Sexy Hot

Viktor and Rolf
Antidote; Flowerbomb

Vivienne Westwood
Anglomania; Boudoir; Boudoir Sin Garden; Let It Rock

Worth
Courtesan; Je Reviens Couture

Yohji Yamamoto
Yohji Homme

YOSH
Ginger Ciao; Omniscent; Sottile; Stargazer; U4EAHH!; White Flowers

Yves Rocher
Iris Noir; Rose Absolue; Voile
d'Ambre

Yves Saint Laurent
Baby Doll Paris; Body Kouros;
Cinéma; Cinéma Festival d'Eté;
Elle; L'Homme; Jazz; Kouros; M7;
M7 Fresh; Opium; Opium pour
Homme; Paris; Rive Gauche; Rive
Gauche pour Homme; Y